Bible

New Testament with Psalms and Proverbs

Tyndale House Publishers, Inc.
WHEATON, ILLINOIS

CONTENTS

Alphabetical List of the Books of the Bible

TYNDALE
Bible Verse Finder

ACCOUNTABILITY
We are accountable for every word that we speak (Matthew 12:36)
Confronting others with their sins should be done in private
   (Matthew 18:15)
We should hold each other accountable (Luke 17:3)
We are accountable for what we believe (John 3:18)
God holds Christians accountable (Romans 14:11-12)
God will reward Christians for their good deeds (1 Corinthians 3:8)
God will examine our actions (2 Corinthians 5:10)

ADOPTION, SPIRITUAL
Do not despise God's discipline (Proverbs 3:11-12)
God is our Father (Matthew 6:9)
Christians are God's children (John 1:12)
God's Spirit leads his children (Romans 8:14-17)
Christians should be separate from the world (2 Corinthians 6:17-18)
All of God's children are equal in God's eyes (Galatians 3:28)
God's children will receive a spiritual inheritance (Galatians 4:4-7)
God chose us to be his children (Ephesians 1:4-5)
Jesus is our spiritual brother (Hebrews 2:11)

ADULTERY
Adultery has consequences (Proverbs 6:26)
Adultery is foolish (Proverbs 6:32)
God considers lust as sinful as adultery (Matthew 5:27-28)
Divorce often leads to adultery (Mark 10:11-12)
God can forgive the adulterer (John 8:1-11)

ANGELS
Angels serve God (Psalm 103:21)
Angels praise God (Psalm 148:2)
Angels do not marry (Matthew 22:30)
Angels do not die (Luke 20:36)
Angels will be judged by people (1 Corinthians 6:3)
Satan disguises himself as an angel of light (2 Corinthians 11:14)
Angels encourage Christians (Hebrews 1:14)
Angels who sinned were thrown into hell (2 Peter 2:4)
Angels are holy (Jude 1:14)
Angels are in the presence of God (Revelation 4:8)
Angels should not be worshiped (Revelation 22:8-9)

ANGER
Anger leads to evil actions (Psalm 37:8)

Showing anger is foolish (Proverbs 12:16)
Gentle words can soothe anger (Proverbs 15:1)
Anger is like murdering someone (Matthew 5:21-22)
Jesus grew angry at sin (John 2:13-17)
Anger can give Satan a place in your life (Ephesians 4:26-27)
Christians should get rid of anger (Colossians 3:8)
Leaders in the church should not be quick-tempered (Titus 1:7)
Be slow to become angry (James 1:19)

ANTICHRIST
Many will claim to be God's messenger (Matthew 24:5)
Many will have miraculous powers (Matthew 24:24)
Many will claim to be Christ (Luke 21:8)
The Antichrist will be lawless and deceitful (2 Thessalonians 2:1-10)
There are many antichrists (1 John 2:18)
The Antichrist will oppose God (1 John 4:3)
The Antichrist will curse God (Revelation 13:1-8)
The Antichrist will be punished by God (Revelation 20:10)

APPEARANCE
Physical beauty fades (Proverbs 31:30)
Do not worry about clothes (Matthew 6:25-34)
Appearances can be deceiving (Matthew 23:27)
Christians should care more about their spiritual welfare than
    their physical appearance (1 Timothy 2:9-10)
Do not judge others by their appearance (James 2:2-4)
Inner beauty is more important than physical beauty (1 Peter 3:1-6)

ARGUMENTS
Arguments can be avoided by using gentle words (Proverbs 15:1)
Loving arguments is a sin (Proverbs 17:19)
A fool is quick to argue (Proverbs 20:3)
Avoid becoming entangled in others' arguments (Proverbs
    26:17)
Avoid arguing with a weak Christian (Romans 14:1)
We should avoid arguments (Philippians 2:14)
Arguments between Christians are useless (Titus 3:9)

ARMOR
Spiritual armor prepares us for life (Romans 13:12)
Righteousness is a spiritual weapon (2 Corinthians 6:7)
God's weapons conquer Satan's strongholds (2 Corinthians 10:4)
Put on the armor of God (Ephesians 6:11-18)

ASSURANCE
God always holds his children (Psalm 37:23-24)
God will never abandon his people (Psalm 138:8)
False assurance is dangerous (Luke 18:18-30)
We can be assured of eternal life (John 5:24)
God will not refuse any who come to him (John 6:37-40)
Our place in God's family is secure (John 10:27-28)
Christians have peace with God (Romans 5:1-5)
Nothing can separate us from God's love (Romans 8:35-39)
Salvation cannot be canceled (Romans 11:29)
Accountability should help others (Galatians 6:1)
Our salvation was guaranteed before Creation (Ephesians 1:4-5)

Assurance comes from faith (Ephesians 3:12)
God will guard what has been entrusted to him (2 Timothy 1:12)

ATONEMENT

Atonement is good news (Luke 4:18-19)
Jesus willingly died for our sins (John 10:17)
Christ secured salvation through his blood (Acts 20:28)
Jesus provided the atonement for sins (Romans 3:23-25)
Jesus' death purchased forgiveness (1 Corinthians 7:23)
Jesus died for sins (1 Corinthians 15:3)
Our atonement allows us to know God (Ephesians 2:13)
Jesus' death rescues us from eternal punishment (Colossians 1:13)
Christ's death purifies God's people (Titus 2:14)
Sin requires that a sacrifice be made (Hebrews 9:22)
Jesus' sacrifice was perfect (1 Peter 1:18-19)
Jesus took our punishment (1 Peter 2:21-24)
We cannot improve Jesus' sacrifice (1 Peter 3:18)

ATTITUDE

Always trust God for your life (Proverbs 29:25)
God will reward the meek (Matthew 5:5)
God gives Christians a new attitude (Philippians 1:20-25)
We should imitate Jesus' attitude (Philippians 2:5)
Christians should always rejoice (Philippians 4:4)
Never be anxious (Philippians 4:6-7)

AUTHORITY *(see also Respect)*

Jesus is the highest authority (Matthew 28:18)
God gave government its authority (John 19:11)
Christians should obey the government (Romans 13:1-2)
Parents are authorities to their children (Ephesians 6:1)
The Bible is our authority (2 Timothy 3:16)
Church leaders are authoritative (Hebrews 13:17)

BAPTISM

Baptism signifies repentance (Matthew 3:11)
All followers of Jesus should be baptized (Matthew 28:19)
Jesus was baptized (Mark 1:9)
Jesus baptizes with the Holy Spirit (John 1:32-33)
Baptism is closely linked with a changed life (Acts 2:38)
New Christians should be baptized (Acts 8:12-17)
Entire families of the early church were baptized (Acts 16:33-34)
Baptism initiates us into Christ (Romans 6:3-8)
Salvation is identified with baptism (1 Peter 3:21)

BIBLE

The Bible is perfect (Psalm 18:30)
The Bible is true (Psalm 33:4)
The Bible will last forever (Psalm 119:89)
The Bible gives us wisdom (Psalm 119:99)
The Bible can be trusted (Psalm 119:138)
The Bible reveals the truth (Acts 18:28)
The Bible is holy (Romans 1:2)
God's Holy Spirit helps us understand the Bible (1 Corinthians 2:12-16)
The Bible is authoritative (Galatians 3:10)
The Bible is a Christian's spiritual weapon (Ephesians 6:17)

The Bible is inspired by God (2 Timothy 3:16)
The Bible judges our life (Hebrews 4:12)
The Bible helps us grow spiritually (1 Peter 2:2)

BLESSING
God blesses godly people (Psalm 5:12)
We are blessed when we worship God (Psalm 24:3-6)
Christians bless God through praise (Psalm 103:1)
God will bless those who fear him (Psalm 112:1-3)
God blesses us when we seek to please him (Matthew 6:33)
Christians should bless their enemies (Luke 6:28)
Salvation is our greatest blessing (Ephesians 1:3)
The Bible brings us blessing (James 1:25)

BLOOD
Jesus' blood seals God's relationship with his people (Matthew 26:28)
Jesus' blood allows us to have access to God (Romans 5:8-9)
Christians are redeemed by Jesus' blood (Ephesians 1:5-7)
Blood is required for forgiveness (Hebrews 9:22)

BODY OF CHRIST
The body of Christ has been given many gifts (Romans 12:3-6)
There are many parts, but one body (1 Corinthians 12:12-13)
Christians make up the body of Christ (1 Corinthians 12:27)
Christians of different nationalities form one body (Ephesians 3:6)
There must be unity in the body of Christ (Ephesians 4:3)
Different members of the body help each other grow (Ephesians 4:11-12)
Jesus is the head of the body (Colossians 1:18)

CHILDREN
Christians are children of God (John 1:12)
Children of God should imitate God (Ephesians 5:1)
Parents should nurture their children (Ephesians 6:4)
Children must obey their parents (Colossians 3:20)

CHURCH *(see also Worship)*
Jesus is the cornerstone of the church (Psalm 118:22)
We should have joy going to God's house (Psalm 122:1)
Satan works against the church (Matthew 16:18)
Members of the church should take care of each other (Acts 2:44)
The church sends out missionaries (Acts 13:2)
The church is like a body (1 Corinthians 12:12-13)
The church is a family of Christians (Galatians 6:10)
God's children form the church (Ephesians 2:19-22)
The church should not allow immoral behavior by its members (Ephesians 5:3-4)
Christ is the head of the church (Colossians 1:18)
Many people groups form one universal church (Colossians 3:11)
Church leaders are qualified to lead by their character (Titus 1:6-9)
The church is made up of God's children (1 John 3:1)
The church is the bride of Christ (Revelation 19:7-8)

COMFORT
God promises to comfort those who mourn (Matthew 5:4)
God's Holy Spirit is our Comforter (John 14:16)

Jesus has overcome the world's troubles (John 16:33)
God comforts those who are hurting (2 Corinthians 1:3-11)
Christians should comfort each other (1 Thessalonians 4:18)
All pain will end (Revelation 21:3-4)

COMPLAIN
Bring your complaints to God (Psalm 142:1-2)
Christians should not complain to each other (Philippians 2:14)
People complain because they want their own way (Jude 1:16)

CONFESSION OF SIN *(see also Repentance)*
God forgives confessed sins (Psalm 32:5)
Do not try to hide sin (Proverbs 28:13)
Confession of sin accompanies a changed lifestyle (2 Timothy 2:19)
God purifies those who confess their sin (1 John 1:9)

COURAGE
God gives us victory (Psalm 112:8)
Jesus' strength gives us courage (John 16:33)
Courage helps us boldly represent Christ (Acts 4:31)
Christians should be courageous (1 Corinthians 16:13)
Pray for courage (Ephesians 6:19-20)
Christians can pray to God with confidence (Hebrews 4:16)

CREATION
God the Father was involved in Creation (Psalm 33:6)
God rules over his creation (Psalm 89:11)
God created every angel (Psalm 148:2-5)
Jesus was involved in Creation (Colossians 1:16)
God the Creator is worthy of worship (Revelation 4:11)
God will make a new heaven and new earth (Revelation 21:1-4)

CRITICISM
Take care of your own problems before criticizing others
    (Matthew 7:3-5)
Criticism should help people deepen their relationship with God
    (Luke 17:3-5)
Criticism should be given with a loving attitude (1 Corinthians
    13:4-5)
Harsh criticism can destroy rather than help (Galatians 5:15)

CROSS
Jesus was crucified (Matthew 27:31-35)
Christians should pick up their own crosses (Mark 8:34-38)
Jesus' death was powerful (1 Corinthians 1:17-18)
Jesus' death unified all Christians (Ephesians 2:16)
Jesus' death was a sacrifice (Colossians 1:20-22)
Jesus' death defeated Satan (Colossians 2:14-15)
Jesus' cross is an example for us (Hebrews 12:2)

CULT
False teachers will come (Matthew 7:15)
Only Jesus brings salvation (John 14:6)
Members of the occult will never enter God's Kingdom
    (Galatians 5:19-21)
Be careful in your spiritual life (1 Thessalonians 5:21)

DEATH

Every person will face death (Psalm 89:48)
Death of Christians is precious (Psalm 116:15)
God has power over death (John 14:19)
The death of Christians brings fellowship with Jesus (Acts 7:59)
God provides eternal life (Romans 6:23)
Jesus will raise everyone who has died (1 Corinthians 15:20-23)
Living in heaven is better than living on earth (2 Corinthians 5:6-7)
Death is not the end of a person (1 Thessalonians 4:13-14)
Prepare your spiritual life for death (Hebrews 9:27-28)
We don't know how long we'll live (James 4:13-14)
God will destroy death (Revelation 21:4)

DECISIONS

God's Word helps us make decisions (Psalm 119:105)
Get good advice before making decisions (Proverbs 18:15)
Ask God for wisdom before making decisions (James 1:2-8)

DEMONS *(see also Satan)*

Worship in false religions honors demons (Psalm 106:37)
Demons are no match for Jesus (Mark 1:34)
Demons want to destroy people (Mark 5:5)
Demons submit to the name of Jesus (Luke 10:17)
Demons can be driven out by Jesus' followers (Acts 16:16-18)
Demons are powerful (Acts 19:16)
Demons cannot separate people from God's love (Romans 8:38-39)
Demons deceive people (2 Corinthians 11:13-15)
Christians fight against the plans of demons (Ephesians 6:12)
Demons want to mislead people (1 Timothy 4:1-2)
Demons believe in God (James 2:19)
Demons are angels that have sinned (2 Peter 2:4)
God will judge demons (Jude 1:6)
Do not take demons lightly (Jude 1:8-9)
Demons can work miracles (Revelation 16:13-14)
In the last days, demons will be bound by God (Revelation 20:1-3)

DEPRESSION

God helps those who feel crushed (Psalm 34:18)
Abraham had hope when there was no reason to hope (Romans 4:18-22)
God will wipe away depression (Revelation 21:4)

DESIRES

You should not desire something that belongs to someone else (Exodus 20:17)
Wicked people desire evil (Psalm 36:1-4)
God gives those who fellowship with him what they desire (Psalm 37:4)
Desire to know God (Psalm 42:1)
Desire to worship God (Psalm 84:1-2)
Desire to honor God (Psalm 86:12)
Do not desire self-promotion (Psalm 119:36)
Christians should not give in to sinful desires (Ephesians 4:22)
Sinful desires should not have a home with God's children (1 Peter 1:14)

Desire to do God's will (1 Peter 4:2)
God's children desire to obey God (1 John 2:3-6)

DISCERNMENT
The Bible will help you discern bad teaching (Acts 17:11)
God grants discernment (1 Corinthians 12:10)
Discern between right and wrong behavior (Hebrews 5:14)
Ask God for help in discerning his will (James 1:5)

DISCIPLINE
God's punishment does not change his love for us (Psalm 89:32-33)
The Lord disciplines those he loves (Proverbs 3:11-12)
Parents are responsible to discipline their children (Proverbs 13:24)
Punishment for sin may be swift and severe (Acts 5:1-11)
Paul commanded punishment for blatant sin in the church (1 Corinthians 5:1-5)
Punishment should lead to repentance (2 Corinthians 7:8-9)
Sometimes God punishes us to bring us back to himself (Hebrews 12:5-11)

DISCRIMINATION
God does not discriminate among his people (Acts 10:34)
All Christians are equal in God's eyes (Galatians 3:28)
God will judge those who discriminate (Colossians 3:25)
Do not discriminate against the poor (James 2:1-9)

DISHONESTY
Dishonest people cannot know God (Psalm 101:7)
God hates deception (Proverbs 12:22)
God will punish those who take advantage of others (1 Thessalonians 4:6)

DOUBT
God will help us overcome doubts (Psalm 42:5-6)
Help those who have spiritual doubts (Hebrews 3:12)
Doubt inhibits our prayers (James 1:5-7)

DRINKING
People controlled by alcohol are fools (Proverbs 20:1)
Alcohol can cause you to become poor (Proverbs 21:17)
Alcohol can destroy you (Proverbs 23:29-35)
Becoming drunk is dangerous (Luke 21:34)
Drunkenness is not fitting for a Christian (Romans 13:11-14)
Drunkenness can cause immoral behavior (Ephesians 5:18)

EDUCATION
Train children to follow God (Proverbs 22:6)
Christians should always learn more about God (Ephesians 4:14-15)

EMOTIONS
God heals those with broken hearts (Psalm 34:18)
Carefully guard your emotions (Proverbs 4:23)
Emotions can crush us (Proverbs 15:13)
Do not be led by emotions (Proverbs 19:2)
Jesus experienced emotions (John 11:35)

Emotions are not reliable guides (Galatians 5:1-17)
Some emotions can be sinful (Ephesians 4:31)

ENCOURAGEMENT

The Holy Spirit encourages us (Acts 9:31)
Encourage your neighbor (Romans 15:2)
The Bible encourages us (Romans 15:4)
Our position in Christ encourages us (Philippians 2:1)
We should encourage each other (1 Thessalonians 4:18)
Encourage those who are weak and afraid (1 Thessalonians 5:14)
Encourage elderly people (1 Timothy 5:1-4)
Encourage others not to sin (Hebrews 3:13)
Encourage others to love (Hebrews 10:24)

ENVY

Do not envy those who do wrong (Psalm 37:1)
Do not envy the prosperity of wicked people (Psalm 73:2-3)
Envy steals your peace (Proverbs 14:30)
Envy is a powerful enemy (Proverbs 27:4)
Envy can cause you to act rashly (Acts 7:9)
Envy characterizes sinful people (Romans 1:29)
We should not envy other Christians (Galatians 5:26)
Envy has no place in a Christian's life (Titus 3:3)
Do not harbor envy (James 3:14-15)
Get rid of envy (1 Peter 2:1)

ETERNAL LIFE

Eternal life is only for those who do God's will (Matthew 7:21)
The righteous will receive eternal life (Matthew 25:46)
Belief in Jesus is required for eternal life (John 3:15-16)
Evil people will receive eternal punishment (John 5:28-29)
Jesus came to give life (John 10:10)
Jesus gives eternal life (John 11:25)
Jesus is eternal life (John 14:6)
Eternal life cannot be earned (Ephesians 2:8-9)
Eternal life comes from God (Titus 1:2)
Eternal life gives us hope (Titus 3:7)

EVANGELISM *(see also Witnessing)*

Christians bring light to a spiritually dark world (Matthew 5:14-16)
Jesus made salvation available to all people (Matthew 9:9-13)
Be bold in your evangelism (Matthew 10:33)
Jesus sent his followers to make disciples (Matthew 28:18-20)
The Holy Spirit gives us power to evangelize (Acts 1:8)

EVIL

God helps keep his people from sin (Psalm 19:13)
God hates people who do evil (Psalm 26:5)
God permits evil (Romans 1:24-28)
God cannot coexist with evil (Galatians 5:16-17)
Christians should put away evil from their lives (Ephesians 4:22)
There are spiritual forces behind evil (Ephesians 6:12)

FAITH

Only a small amount of faith is needed (Luke 17:6)
Faith is needed for salvation (Romans 3:28)

Faith puts us in a right relationship with God (Romans 5:1)
Faith comes from hearing the Word of God (Romans 10:17)
Accept the person who has weak faith (Romans 14:1)
Christianity is the only true faith (Ephesians 4:5)
Faith is hoping in what is not seen (Hebrews 11:1)
Faith accompanies obedience to God (Hebrews 11:7-12)

FAMILY
Do not let sin affect your family life (Psalm 101:2)
Do not bring trouble to a family (Proverbs 11:29)
Christian faith is of greater importance than family (Luke 12:51-53)
Christians are members of God's family (Ephesians 2:19)
Husbands and wives should love each other (Ephesians 5:21-33)
Children should obey their parents (Ephesians 6:1)
Church leaders must have a good family life (1 Timothy 3:4-5)
Families should take care of each other (1 Timothy 5:3-5)

FEAR
We should fear God (Psalm 25:12)
Christians do not need to fear anyone (Psalm 27:1)
God strengthens us (Psalm 46:1-3)
We do not need to fear darkness or violence (Psalm 91:5)
We do not need to fear bad news (Psalm 112:7)
Love drives fear away (1 John 4:18)

FORGIVENESS
God forgives our many sins (Psalm 65:3)
God forgives us because he loves us (Psalm 86:5)
We must forgive others (Matthew 6:14-15)
Don't keep track of how many times you forgive (Matthew 18:21-35)
Freely forgive others as God has forgiven you (Colossians 3:13)
God will forgive our sins if we confess them (1 John 1:8-9)

FOUL LANGUAGE
Foul language is not fitting for a Christian (Ephesians 5:4)
Our speech reflects our relationship with God (Colossians 4:6)
Our speech should be an example to others (1 Timothy 4:12)

FRIENDSHIP *(see also Relationships)*
Friends can cause great pain (Psalm 55:12-14)
Friends love during difficult times (Proverbs 17:17)
Faithful friends are not common (Proverbs 18:24)
Friends influence you (Proverbs 22:24-25)
Friendship is marked by sacrifice (John 15:13-15)
We can be friends with God (James 2:23)

FUTURE
God prepares a future for us (1 Corinthians 2:9)

GIVING
God will reward us for giving to others (Mark 9:41)
Giving helps others live (Acts 2:44-45)
We should support Christian workers (Acts 28:10)
Wealthy people should give generously (1 Timothy 6:17-19)
God is pleased with our gifts (Hebrews 13:16)
Giving reflects God's love (1 John 3:17)

GOD

God is good (Psalm 34:8)
God helps his people when they are in trouble (Psalm 46:1)
God is mighty (Psalm 50:1)
God is our rock (Psalm 62:6)
God is our hope (Psalm 71:5)
God is near everyone (Psalm 75:1)
God is our father (Matthew 6:9)
God is all-powerful (Luke 1:37)
God is spirit (John 4:24)
God is all-knowing (Romans 11:33)
God is knowable (Ephesians 1:17)
God is living (1 Timothy 4:10)
God is King of kings (1 Timothy 6:15)
God is approachable (James 4:8)
God is judge (James 4:12)
God is love (1 John 4:16)
God is almighty (Revelation 1:8)

GOD'S WILL

God guides us (Psalm 16:7)
Ask God for guidance (Psalm 25:4-7)
God will direct you (Psalm 48:14)
God works everything out for his plan (Proverbs 16:4)
God directs events in our life (Acts 16:6-7)
God gives wisdom for making decisions (James 1:2-5)

GOSPEL

Christians should tell others about the gospel (Matthew 28:18-19)
The gospel's message is for everyone (Luke 24:46-47)
People should respond to the gospel with faith (John 1:12)
The gospel is powerful (Romans 1:16)
The gospel of Jesus (1 Corinthians 15:1-5)
Believing the gospel brings a change to life (1 Thessalonians 1:4-5)

GOSSIP

Gossiping betrays confidence (Proverbs 11:13)
Gossip separates friends (Proverbs 16:28)
Gossip prolongs tension between people (Proverbs 26:20)
Gossip is attractive (Proverbs 26:22)
People who gossip are wicked (Romans 1:29)
Gossip should have no place among Christians (1 Timothy 5:13)

GOVERNMENT

God gives authority to those in government (Romans 13:1)
Christians should obey the government (Titus 3:1)

GRACE

God is slow to become angry (Psalm 86:15)
God's grace makes salvation possible (Ephesians 1:7-8)
God accepts us by his grace (Ephesians 2:8-9)
God's grace gives us hope (1 Peter 1:13)

GREED

Greed creates disagreement (Proverbs 28:25)
The Pharisees had greedy hearts (Matthew 23:25)

Christians should avoid being greedy (Ephesians 5:3)
People full of greed will not enter heaven (Ephesians 5:5)
Leaders of the church must not be greedy (Titus 1:7)

GRIEF *(see also Sorrow)*
God promises to comfort those who grieve (Matthew 5:4)
God's Holy Spirit is our Comforter (John 14:16)
Jesus has overcome the world's troubles (John 16:33)
The Holy Spirit comforts us (Acts 9:31)
The Bible comforts us (Romans 15:4)
God comforts those who grieve (2 Corinthians 1:3-11)
All grief will end (Revelation 21:3-4)

GUILT
Ask God to forgive hidden sins (Psalm 19:12-13)
God forgives sins and removes guilt (Psalm 32:5)
God can cleanse us from all sin (Psalm 51:2)
All people are guilty of sin (Romans 3:9-12)
Jesus Christ takes away all guilt (Romans 3:23-24)

HATRED
Hatred causes trouble (Proverbs 10:12)
Followers of Jesus will be hated (Matthew 10:22)
Many in the world hate Jesus (John 15:18)
Christians should hate evil (Romans 12:9)
All people are equal in Christ (Galatians 3:28-29)
Christians need to get rid of their own hatred (Colossians 3:8)

HEAVEN
Only righteous people will enter heaven (Matthew 5:17-20)
Few people will enter heaven (Matthew 7:13-14)
Jesus is preparing heaven for his followers (John 14:2-3)
Our lives will not be complete until we enter heaven
    (2 Corinthians 5:2)
Heaven is much better than earth (Philippians 1:23)
Christians should look forward to heaven (Colossians 3:1-5)
Heaven is the home of righteousness (2 Peter 3:13)
God is the focus of attention in heaven (Revelation 7:17)
There will not be any sadness in heaven (Revelation 21:4)
People in heaven will walk with God (Revelation 22:5)

HELL
God will deliver his children from hell (Psalm 86:13)
Hell is a place of weeping (Matthew 8:12)
Hell was prepared for Satan and demons (Matthew 25:41)
Wicked people will receive punishment (Romans 1:18-20)
God will punish those who do not turn from their sin (2 Peter 2:4-9)
Hell is a place of eternal fire (Jude 1:7)
God will send to hell those who do not believe in him
    (Revelation 21:8)

HOLY
God is known for his holiness (Psalm 93:5)
God uses his Word to make us holy (John 17:17)
Christians should try to be holy (1 Peter 1:15)
God is worthy of praise because he is holy (Revelation 4:8)

HOLY SPIRIT

The Holy Spirit teaches us (John 14:26)
The Holy Spirit guides us (John 16:13)
The Holy Spirit empowers us to be witnesses (Acts 1:8)
The Holy Spirit lives within us (Romans 8:11)
The Holy Spirit sanctifies us (Romans 15:16)
The Holy Spirit opens our spiritual eyes (1 Corinthians 2:10)
The Holy Spirit is involved in salvation (Titus 3:5)

HOMOSEXUALITY

God will judge those who practice homosexual behavior
    (Romans 1:18-32)
Homosexual behavior has no place among Christians
    (1 Corinthians 6:9-10)

HONESTY

Only honest people can worship God (Psalm 24:3-4)
God is truth and desires truth (Psalm 51:6)
God hates lies (Proverbs 6:16-17)
Be honest (Proverbs 19:1)
Christians should be known by their honesty (Matthew 5:37)
Lies make someone unclean before God (Matthew 15:18-20)
Christians should put away dishonesty from their lives
    (Ephesians 4:25)

HOPE

God gives hope to the needy (Psalm 9:18)
Hope gives us confidence (Psalm 25:3)
The Bible gives us hope (Psalm 119:43)
Christians always have hope (Romans 8:28)
Hope comes from the Holy Spirit (Romans 15:13)
Jesus' resurrection gives us hope (1 Corinthians 6:14)
We have hope in Jesus (1 Corinthians 15:19)
We have confidence of eternal life (Titus 1:1-2)

HOSPITALITY

Christians should take care of those in need (Matthew 25:34-40)
Hospitality brings heavenly reward (Mark 9:41)
Christians should be hospitable (Romans 12:13)
Christians should be hospitable to people they do not know
    well (Hebrews 13:2)
Be cheerful about being hospitable (1 Peter 4:9-11)
Hospitality reflects God's love (3 John 1:5-8)

HUMILITY

God saves those who are humble (Psalm 18:27)
God preserves the lives of humble people (Psalm 147:6)
Those who are humble become wise (Proverbs 11:2)
God will exalt the humble (Luke 18:14)
Be humble in dealing with others (Philippians 2:1-11)
Humble yourself before God (James 4:10)

IDOLATRY

We give in to idolatry when we forget God (Psalm 106:19-22)
Christians cannot serve both God and the things of this world
    (Luke 16:13)

IMMORALITY
Stay away from immoral Christians (1 Corinthians 5:9-11)
Practicing immorality treats God lightly (1 Corinthians 6:19-20)
Immorality should have no place among Christians (Ephesians 4:17-19)

JEALOUSY
Do not envy those who do wrong (Psalm 37:1)
Do not be jealous of wicked people (Psalm 73:2-3)
Jealousy steals away peace (Proverbs 14:30)
Jealousy is a powerful enemy (Proverbs 27:4)
Jealousy can cause rash behavior (Acts 7:9)
We should not be jealous of other Christians (Galatians 5:26)
Jealousy has no place in a Christian's life (Titus 3:3-5)

JESUS CHRIST
Jesus has authority over demons (Mark 1:27)
Jesus is the Son of God (Luke 1:35)
Jesus is God (John 1:1-5)
Jesus is the Messiah (John 4:25-26)
Jesus is the Judge (John 5:22)
Jesus gives life (John 10:10)
Jesus is the Good Shepherd (John 10:11)
Jesus is the only way to God (John 14:6)
Jesus is the author of life (Acts 3:15)
Jesus is the wisdom of God (1 Corinthians 1:21-24)
Jesus is the head of the church (Ephesians 5:23)
Jesus is the highest authority (Philippians 2:9-10)
Jesus is the Creator (Colossians 1:15-16)
Jesus is faithful (2 Timothy 2:13)
Jesus is coming again (Titus 2:13)
Jesus is sinless (Hebrews 4:15)
Jesus is holy (Hebrews 7:26)
Jesus is the King of the ages (Revelation 15:3)
Jesus is the Lamb of God (Revelation 21:22)

JUSTICE
God loves justice (Psalm 11:7)
Jesus' death was justice for sin (Romans 3:25-26)

KINDNESS
Christians should be kind to each other (Ephesians 4:32)
Be kind to people who treat you wrongly (1 Thessalonians 5:15)
Choose to be kind rather than to argue (2 Timothy 2:24)
Being kind takes effort (2 Peter 1:5-7)

KINGDOM OF GOD/HEAVEN
You must turn from sin before you can enter God's Kingdom (Matthew 3:1-2)
Jesus describes members of God's Kingdom (Matthew 5:1-19)
Obeying God's commands yields great rewards in his Kingdom (Matthew 5:19)
Only righteous people will enter God's Kingdom (Matthew 5:20)
God's Kingdom is open to those who do his will (Matthew 7:21)
Healed lives are associated with God's Kingdom (Matthew 9:35-36)

Entering God's Kingdom costs someone everything (Matthew 13:44-45)
God's Kingdom is reserved for the humble (Matthew 18:2-3)
No one deserves God's Kingdom (Matthew 18:23-35)
God's Kingdom is within our hearts (Luke 17:20-21)
God's Kingdom will fully arrive in the future (Luke 21:25-31)
Only those who are spiritually reborn can enter God's Kingdom (John 3:3)
Entering God's Kingdom is not easy (Acts 14:22)
Christians should tell others about the Kingdom of God (Acts 28:31)
God's Kingdom affects our lives (Romans 14:17)
God's Kingdom is powerful (1 Corinthians 4:20)
No immoral person will be allowed into God's Kingdom (Ephesians 5:5)
Christians are members of God's Kingdom (Colossians 1:13)
Christians' lives should reflect their membership in God's Kingdom (1 Thessalonians 2:12)
God calls people into his Kingdom (1 Thessalonians 2:12)
God's Kingdom cannot be shaken (Hebrews 12:28)
God's Kingdom will one day be fully consummated (Revelation 11:15)

LEADERSHIP
Leaders should receive advice (Proverbs 11:14)
Leaders must serve others (Matthew 20:26-28)
Leaders should sacrifice for others (John 10:11)
Leaders should be obeyed (Romans 13:1-4)
Leaders give an account to God for their actions (Hebrews 13:17)

LIFE
God carefully creates each person (Psalm 139:13-14)
People must be reborn spiritually to enter heaven (John 3:3)
Jesus came to give abundant life (John 10:10)
We should live lives worthy of our Christian calling (Ephesians 4:1)
Christ is the reason for life (Philippians 1:21)
Our lives should honor God (Colossians 3:17)

LONELINESS
God takes care of lonely people (Psalm 68:6)
God remains with us (Matthew 28:20)

LORD'S SUPPER
Jesus celebrated the Lord's Supper with his disciples (Matthew 26:26-29)
Christians should be thankful for the Lord's Supper (1 Corinthians 10:16)
Christians who celebrate the Lord's Supper together should be unified (1 Corinthians 11:20-34)

LOVE
Love your enemies (Matthew 5:43-44)
Loving God is the most important command (Mark 12:29-30)
Christians must love each other (John 13:34)
We cannot be separated from Jesus' love (Romans 8:35-39)
Love must be genuine (Romans 12:9)
Love never quits (1 Corinthians 13:4-8)

God's love for us is beyond our understanding (Ephesians 3:18)
Love helps you look past offenses (1 Peter 4:8)
God is love (1 John 4:16)
We must be known for our love (2 John 1:5)

LOYALTY
Friends are loyal (Proverbs 17:17)
We cannot divide our loyalty (Matthew 6:24)
There must be loyalty in marriage (Hebrews 13:4)

LUST
Lustful thoughts are sinful (Matthew 5:28)
Christians should not give in to lust (Colossians 3:5)
Christians should avoid lust (1 Thessalonians 4:3-5)
Godless people enjoy immorality (1 Peter 4:3)

LYING *(see Dishonesty)*

MARRIAGE
Two people become one through marriage (Mark 10:2-12)
Angels do not get married (Mark 12:25)
Married partners should meet each other's needs (1 Corinthians 7:2-5)
Married partners are united to each other for life (1 Corinthians 7:39)
A Christian wife can witness to her non-Christian husband (1 Peter 3:1-6)

MESSIAH
Jesus' disciples knew he was the Messiah (Mark 8:27-29)
The Messiah will come again (Mark 14:61-62)
Jesus claimed to be the Messiah (John 4:25-42)
The Messiah brings salvation (Hebrews 2:10)

MONEY
Greed brings trouble (Proverbs 15:27)
Do not make money the most important part of your life (Matthew 6:19)
Money can distract people from God (Mark 10:17-24)
You cannot serve both God and money (Luke 16:13)
Christians should share their resources with those in need (Acts 2:42-45)
Christians should not be lovers of money (1 Timothy 3:3)
We should look to God for security, not money (1 Timothy 6:17-19)
Do not love money (Hebrews 13:5)
Be careful to treat rich and poor equally (James 2:1-9)

MURDER
Hateful anger is the same in God's eyes as murder (Matthew 5:21-22)

OBEDIENCE
People who obey God's Word will be blessed (Luke 11:28)
Christians should obey the government (Romans 13:1-4)
Children should obey their parents (Ephesians 6:1)
Christians obey God (1 John 2:3)

PAIN
God watches over the weak (Psalm 12:5)
God comforts us (Isaiah 40:9-11)

God promises to comfort those who mourn (Matthew 5:4)
God's Holy Spirit is our Comforter (John 14:16)
Christians should comfort each other (1 Thessalonians 4:18)
All pain will end (Revelation 21:3-4)

PATIENCE
Be patient with God (Psalm 75:2)
Patience is valuable (Proverbs 25:15)
Patience demonstrates love (1 Corinthians 13:4)
Patience is evidence of the Holy Spirit working in our lives
  (Galatians 5:22)
Be patient with each other (Ephesians 4:2)

PEACE
Be full of peace (Psalm 34:14)
Make peace with others quickly (Matthew 5:23-26)
The peace Jesus gives is different than the world's peace (John 14:27)
Jesus gives us peace (Romans 5:1)
Peace is evidence of the Holy Spirit working in our lives
  (Galatians 5:22)
We can have peace through prayer (Philippians 4:4-7)

POWER
Christians receive power from the Holy Spirit (Acts 1:8)
The Bible is a powerful weapon (Ephesians 6:17)
Jesus is the greatest power (Hebrews 1:1-4)
Prayer can be powerful (James 5:16)
Christians have power to overcome the world (1 John 5:4-5)

PRAISE *(see Worship)*

PRAYER
Ask God for help (Psalm 40:13)
Prayer should not be a show (Matthew 6:6)
Jesus taught his disciples how to pray (Matthew 6:9-13)
Pray with an attitude of humility (Luke 18:9-14)
Pray in Jesus' name (John 16:23-24)
Pray all the time (Ephesians 6:18)
Pray without doubting (James 1:6)
Pray with the right motives (James 4:3)
Pray according to God's will (1 John 5:14-15)

PRIDE *(see also Self-Esteem)*
Pride leads to shame (Proverbs 11:2)
Pride leads to arguments (Proverbs 13:10)
Pride will be punished (Proverbs 16:5)
Pride ends in destruction (Proverbs 16:18)
Pride cuts us off from God and others (Luke 18:9-14)
There is no place for proud boasting in the Christian life
  (Romans 3:27)
God chose to reveal himself to the humble, not the proud
  (1 Corinthians 1:26-31)
Pride is not compatible with the fruit of the Spirit (Galatians 5:22-26)
God opposes the proud (James 4:6)

PROBLEMS *(see Stress, Suffering, Trials)*

PROPHECY *(see also Teaching)*
Claiming to prophesy does not indicate salvation (Matthew 7:21-23)
The Holy Spirit allows believers to prophesy (Acts 2:17-18)
Prophecy is a spiritual gift (1 Corinthians 14:1-5)
We should listen to God's message (1 Thessalonians 5:20)
True prophets speak God's words (2 Peter 1:20-21)

PURITY
Only God can make us pure (Psalm 51:1-10)
We can remain pure by following God's Word (Psalm 119:1-20)
We cannot claim purity apart from God (Proverbs 20:9)
The pure in heart will see God (Matthew 5:8)
Purity begins in the heart (Matthew 5:27-30)
Outward purity cannot substitute for inner purity (Matthew 23:25-28)
Purity comes from God (John 17:17)
Purity ought to mark believers' lives (Ephesians 5:1-4)
Our minds should think about things that are pure (Philippians 4:8)
One day our purity will be like Christ's (1 John 3:1-3)

RAPTURE *(see Second Coming of Christ)*

RELATIONSHIPS *(see also Friendship, Marriage)*
Our relationship with God is made possible through Jesus Christ
    (John 14:19-21)
Our relationships should not compromise our faith
    (2 Corinthians 6:14-18)
We are unified with all believers in God's family (Ephesians 2:21-22)
Our relationship with Christ is deep and abiding (2 Timothy 2:11-13)
Our relationship with Christ makes us children of God (1 John 3:1-3)

REPENTANCE *(see also Confession of Sin)*
Repentance of sin opens the way for a relationship with God
    (Luke 3:7-8)
Unless we repent of our sins, we will perish (Luke 13:3-5)
Angels rejoice when a sinner repents (Luke 15:7)
Forgive those who repent of wrongs done to you (Luke 17:4)
Repentance is essential for the Holy Spirit to work (Acts 2:38)
God can use difficulties to encourage us to repent (2 Corinthians
    7:9-10)
God would like everyone to repent and believe (2 Peter 3:9)

REPUTATION
A bad reputation will follow you (Proverbs 25:9-10)
The Christians in Rome had a reputation for obedience (Romans
    16:19)
Guard your reputation (2 Corinthians 8:18-24)
Maintain a good reputation among non-Christians (Colossians 4:5)

RESPECT *(see also Authority)*
Husbands and wives should respect each other (Ephesians 5:33)
Those in leadership should have respectful children (1 Timothy 3:4)
Show respect to all people (1 Peter 2:17)

REST
Jesus promises to give us rest from our burdens (Matthew 11:28-30)
Rest is a gift of God (Hebrews 4:9-11)
Heaven will be a place of rest (Revelation 14:13)

RESURRECTION

Christ's resurrection is a historical fact (Matthew 28:5-10)
All people will be resurrected (John 5:24-30)
Jesus promised to raise his followers (John 6:38-40)
We know we will be resurrected (John 11:24-26)
We will experience resurrection (Romans 6:3-11)
Jesus' resurrection is the foundation of Christianity
    (1 Corinthians 15:12-21)
Our resurrected bodies will be eternal bodies (1 Corinthians
    15:51-53)

REVENGE

Do not pay back evil for evil (Proverbs 24:29)
Believers ought to resist revenge (Matthew 5:38-42)
Leave revenge in God's hands (Romans 12:19)
Desire for revenge is not compatible with the Christian life
    (1 Thessalonians 5:15)
Jesus is our example (1 Peter 2:21-23)

RIGHTEOUS/RIGHTEOUSNESS

Human nature is the opposite of righteousness (Romans 3:10-18)
Righteousness is not attained by works (Romans 4:18-25)
Strict legalism cannot make us righteous (Galatians 3:11-21)
Our God-given righteousness is armor against Satan's attacks
    (Ephesians 6:14)
We become righteous through faith in Christ (Philippians 3:9)
Studying God's Word helps us grow in righteousness (2 Timothy
    3:16)
Righteousness ought to characterize each believer's life (1 Peter 2:24)

SADNESS *(see Grief, Sorrow)*

SALVATION

Those who receive salvation become God's children (John 1:12-13)
Salvation is a work of the Holy Spirit in a person's life (John 3:1-16)
Belief and trust in Jesus Christ are the only way to be saved
    (John 14:6)
Salvation includes gaining a relationship with God (John 17:1-5)
Receiving salvation means we must turn from our sins (Acts 2:37-38)
Salvation cannot be earned; it is a gift of God (Romans 6:23)
Receiving salvation is simple and personal (Romans 10:8-10)
Salvation is by God's grace alone (Ephesians 2:1-9)
Salvation rescues us from Satan's dominion (Colossians 1:13-14)
Our salvation was obtained by Jesus' blood (1 Peter 1:18-19)

SATAN *(see also Demons)*

Satan will tempt Jesus' followers (Matthew 4:1-11)
Satan is completely evil (John 8:44)
Satan is the temporary ruler over this world (Ephesians 2:1-2)
Satan and his demons are spiritual (Ephesians 6:12)
Satan works through an army of demons (1 Timothy 4:1)
Believers have the authority to resist Satan (James 4:1-10)
Satan is an enemy to Christians (1 Peter 5:8)
Jesus destroyed Satan's work with his death on the cross (1 John
    3:7-8)
Satan is a defeated enemy (Revelation 20:10)

SECOND COMING OF CHRIST
We do not know when Jesus will return (Matthew 24:36)
Christ's return will be unmistakable (Mark 13:26-27)
Christ's return will be joyous for those who are ready (Luke 12:35-40)
The Second Coming will be a time of judgment on unbelievers
(John 12:37-50)
At Christ's second coming we will be with him forever (John 14:1-3)
The promise of Christ's return (Acts 1:10-11)
Believers will be resurrected and given glorious bodies
(1 Corinthians 15:51-57)
Christ's return will be visible and glorious (1 Thessalonians 4:16)
At Christ's return, Christians who are dead and alive will rise to
meet him (1 Thessalonians 4:16-17)
Continue to serve God as you await the Second Coming (1 Peter
4:7-8)
Patiently await Christ's return (2 Peter 3:8-13)
Jesus is coming soon (Revelation 22:20-21)

SELF-ESTEEM *(see also Pride)*
We are a little lower than the angels (Psalm 8:3-5)
God took special care to create us (Psalm 139:1-18)
We are of great value to God (Luke 12:4-12)
God gave his Son for us (John 3:16)
Our self-esteem is affected by our relationship with Christ
(Romans 12:1-8)
Our self-esteem is based on God's approval (2 Corinthians 10:12-18)
We should not overestimate ourselves (Galatians 6:3-5)

SEX
Sex is God's gift to married people (Proverbs 5:15-21)
Sex outside of marriage is foolish (Proverbs 6:23-35)
Sexual sin begins in the mind (Matthew 5:27-30)
Sex is a powerful bond not meant to be taken lightly
(1 Corinthians 6:13-20)
Sexual immorality has no place among Christians (Ephesians 5:1-3)
We are to have nothing to do with sexual immorality
(Colossians 3:5)
God wants us to live in holiness, not lustful passion
(1 Thessalonians 4:1-8)
Sex in marriage is honorable and pure (Hebrews 13:4)

SICKNESS
God cares for the sick (Psalm 41:1-13)
A cheerful spirit can act as good medicine against sickness
(Proverbs 17:22)
Jesus can heal sickness (Matthew 4:23-25)
Believers ought to have compassion on the sick (Matthew 25:34-40)
It is better to be physically crippled than spiritually crippled
(Mark 9:43-48)
Paul had an infirmity that God would not remove
(2 Corinthians 12:7-10)

SIN
We should ask God to forgive our sins (Psalm 51:1-10)
Stay away from people who lead you to sin (Proverbs 1:10-19)

Sin begins in the mind (Matthew 5:27-28)
All people have sinned (Romans 3:23)
Sin leads to eternal death (Romans 6:23)
Jesus takes the penalty of our sin on himself (Romans 8:1-2)
Sin begins with temptation (James 1:15)
We can sin by avoiding something we should do (James 4:17)
God is willing to forgive our sins (1 John 1:8-9)

SINGLENESS
Some people remain single to work for God's Kingdom
 (Matthew 19:12)
Singleness is a gift from God (1 Corinthians 7:7-8)
Single people can serve God (1 Corinthians 7:25-31)
Single people have more time to focus on service for God
 (1 Corinthians 7:32-35)

SORROW *(see also Grief)*
Weeping will be followed by joy (Psalm 30:5)
God promises comfort to those who experience sorrow
 (Matthew 5:4)
God may use sorrow to point out sin and draw us back to him
 (2 Corinthians 7:10-11)
We sorrow over believers who die, but one day we will meet
 again (1 Thessalonians 4:13-18)
Sorrow will not exist in God's Kingdom (Revelation 21:3-4)

SOUL
People cannot destroy your soul (Matthew 10:28)
We are to love God with our whole being—heart, soul, and
 mind (Matthew 22:36-40)
It is of no value to gain the world but lose your soul (Mark 8:34-38)
We can place our soul under Christ's protection (John 10:27-29)
Believers are assured of immortality (1 Corinthians 15:46-53)

STRESS
God is a refuge in times of stress (Psalm 62:1-8)
Pray to God in times of stress (Psalm 69:1-36)
God is always with us (Romans 8:31-39)
God cares about our stress (2 Corinthians 4:8-12)
Don't let stress cause you to worry (Philippians 4:4-9)

SUBMISSION *(see also Obedience)*
Christ is our example of submission to the Father's will
 (Matthew 26:39, 42)
Following Christ requires submission to him (Luke 14:27)
God created lines of authority for harmonious relationships
 (1 Corinthians 11:2-16)
Marriage calls for mutual submission (Ephesians 5:21-33)
Submit to God (James 4:7-10)

SUFFERING *(see also Trials)*
Christ's followers will face suffering (Matthew 16:21-26)
Our suffering helps us comfort others who are suffering
 (2 Corinthians 1:3-7)
Our suffering will end in glory (2 Corinthians 4:17-18)
Jesus can help us through suffering (Hebrews 2:11-18)

Christ showed how to handle suffering (1 Peter 2:21-24)
There will be no suffering in Christ's Kingdom (Revelation 21:4)

TEMPTATION
How to avoid temptation (Proverbs 7:1-5)
How to respond when tempted (Matthew 4:1-11)
God will provide a way of escape from every temptation
   (1 Corinthians 10:13)
Run from temptation (2 Timothy 2:22)
Christ can help us, for he, too, has faced temptation (Hebrews
   4:15-16)
God never tempts people to sin (James 1:13-15)

THANKFULNESS
Thank the Lord because he is good (Psalm 107:1-3)
Be thankful for answers to prayer (Psalm 138:1-5)
Be thankful for salvation (Ephesians 2:4-10)
Our prayers should include words of thankfulness (Philippians 4:6)
Our life should be characterized by thankfulness to God
   (Colossians 3:15-17)
We are called to give thanks in all circumstances
   (1 Thessalonians 5:16-18)

TRIALS *(see also Suffering)*
Christ promises us rest from our trials (Matthew 11:28-30)
Jesus understands our struggles (John 15:18)
Have peace in trials (John 16:33)
Trials help us develop patience (Romans 5:1-5)
God knows what he is doing with our life (Romans 8:28)
Believers can expect to suffer for their faith (2 Corinthians 6:3-13)
Present trials fade in comparison to the joy of our relationship
   with Christ (Philippians 3:7-11)
God expects us to grow through our trials (James 1:2-4)

TRUST *(see Faith)*

TRUTH
God wants us to be true and righteous (Psalm 51:1-6)
Truth never changes (Proverbs 12:19)
Truth sets us free (John 8:31-32)
Truth is found in Jesus Christ (John 14:6)
God's Word is truth (John 17:17)
We must not only believe the truth but also live by it (1 John 1:5-7)

WISDOM
The fear of God is the beginning of wisdom (Proverbs 1:7)
To find wisdom, first find God (Proverbs 2:6-12)
Wise people accept advice (Proverbs 13:10)
Wise people build on the solid foundation of God and his Word
   (Matthew 7:24-27)
God's wisdom is different from the world's wisdom
   (1 Corinthians 2:1-16)
God will give us wisdom if we ask for it (James 1:5)

WITNESSING *(see also Evangelism, Teaching)*
Let your light shine (Matthew 5:14-16)
Jesus commanded all believers to witness (Matthew 28:16-20)

If we acknowledge our faith before people, Jesus will
    acknowledge us (Luke 12:8-9)
Christians are called to spread the gospel across the world (Acts 1:8)
We plant or water the seed of faith, but only God makes it grow
    (1 Corinthians 3:5-9)
God has entrusted us with the message we need to share with
    others (2 Corinthians 5:18-21)
Always be ready to tell what God has done for you (1 Peter 3:15)

WOMEN
Women should fulfill their responsibilities well (Proverbs 31:10-31)
Women and men are equal before God (Galatians 3:28)
The church should care for widows who have no relatives
    (1 Timothy 5:3-16)

WORK
Hard work brings rewards (Proverbs 12:14)
Hard work helps supply basic needs (Proverbs 28:19)
Our work for God is never wasted (1 Corinthians 15:58)
All work should be done as though we are working for God
    (Ephesians 6:5-9)

WORRY *(see Stress)*

WORSHIP *(see also Church)*
In worship, we ascribe to the Lord the glory due him (Psalm
    29:1-2)
We can worship because of Christ's sacrifice on our behalf
    (Hebrews 10:1-10)
We should worship with reverence for God (Hebrews 12:28)
When we draw near to God, he draws near to us (James 4:8)

A Note to Readers

With 40 million copies in print, *The Living Bible* has been meeting a great need in people's hearts for more than thirty years. But even good things can be improved, so ninety evangelical scholars from various theological backgrounds and denominations were commissioned in 1989 to begin revising *The Living Bible*. The end result of this seven-year process is the *Holy Bible,* New Living Translation—a general-purpose translation that is accurate, easy to read, and excellent for study.

The goal of any Bible translation is to convey the meaning of the ancient Hebrew and Greek texts as accurately as possible to the modern reader. The New Living Translation is based on the most recent scholarship in the theory of translation. The challenge for the translators was to create a text that would make the same impact in the life of modern readers that the original text had for the original readers. In the New Living Translation, this is accomplished by translating entire thoughts (rather than just words) into natural, everyday English. The end result is a translation that is easy to read and understand and that accurately communicates the meaning of the original text.

We believe that this new translation, which combines the latest in scholarship with the best in translation style, will speak to your heart. We present the New Living Translation with the prayer that God will use it to speak his timeless truth to the church and to the world in a fresh, new way.

The Publishers
JULY 1996

MATTHEW

CHAPTER 1

The Record of Jesus' Ancestors

This is a record of the ancestors of Jesus the Messiah, a descendant of King David and of Abraham:

2 Abraham was the father of Isaac.
   Isaac was the father of Jacob.
   Jacob was the father of Judah and his brothers.
3 Judah was the father of Perez and Zerah (their mother was Tamar).
   Perez was the father of Hezron.
   Hezron was the father of Ram.*
4 Ram was the father of Amminadab.
   Amminadab was the father of Nahshon.
   Nahshon was the father of Salmon.
5 Salmon was the father of Boaz (his mother was Rahab).
   Boaz was the father of Obed (his mother was Ruth).
   Obed was the father of Jesse.
6 Jesse was the father of King David.
   David was the father of Solomon (his mother was Bathsheba, the widow of Uriah).
7 Solomon was the father of Rehoboam.
   Rehoboam was the father of Abijah.
   Abijah was the father of Asaph.*
8 Asaph was the father of Jehoshaphat.
   Jehoshaphat was the father of Jehoram.*
   Jehoram was the father* of Uzziah.
9 Uzziah was the father of Jotham.
   Jotham was the father of Ahaz.
   Ahaz was the father of Hezekiah.
10 Hezekiah was the father of Manasseh.
   Manasseh was the father of Amos.*
   Amos was the father of Josiah.
11 Josiah was the father of Jehoiachin* and his brothers (born at the time of the exile to Babylon).
12 After the Babylonian exile:
   Jehoiachin was the father of Shealtiel.
   Shealtiel was the father of Zerubbabel.
13 Zerubbabel was the father of Abiud.
   Abiud was the father of Eliakim.
   Eliakim was the father of Azor.
14 Azor was the father of Zadok.
   Zadok was the father of Akim.

1:3 Greek *Aram;* also in 1:4. See 1 Chr 2:9-10.   1:7 *Asaph* is the same person as Asa; also in 1:8. See 1 Chr 3:10.   1:8a Greek *Joram.* See 1 Kgs 22:50 and note at 1 Chr 3:11.   1:8b Or *ancestor;* also in 1:11.   1:10 *Amos* is the same person as Amon. See 1 Chr 3:14.   1:11 Greek *Jeconiah;* also in 1:12. See 2 Kgs 24:6 and note at 1 Chr 3:16.

Akim was the father of Eliud.
15 Eliud was the father of Eleazar.
Eleazar was the father of Matthan.
Matthan was the father of Jacob.
16 Jacob was the father of Joseph, the husband of Mary.
Mary was the mother of Jesus, who is called the Messiah.

17All those listed above include fourteen generations from Abraham to King David, and fourteen from David's time to the Babylonian exile, and fourteen from the Babylonian exile to the Messiah.

The Birth of Jesus the Messiah

18Now this is how Jesus the Messiah was born. His mother, Mary, was engaged to be married to Joseph. But while she was still a virgin, she became pregnant by the Holy Spirit. 19Joseph, her fiancé, being a just man, decided to break the engagement quietly, so as not to disgrace her publicly.

20As he considered this, he fell asleep, and an angel of the Lord appeared to him in a dream. "Joseph, son of David," the angel said, "do not be afraid to go ahead with your marriage to Mary. For the child within her has been conceived by the Holy Spirit. 21And she will have a son, and you are to name him Jesus,* for he will save his people from their sins." 22All of this happened to fulfill the Lord's message through his prophet:

23 "Look! The virgin will conceive a child!
      She will give birth to a son,
   and he will be called Immanuel*
      (meaning, God is with us)."

24When Joseph woke up, he did what the angel of the Lord commanded. He brought Mary home to be his wife, 25but she remained a virgin until her son was born. And Joseph named him Jesus.

CHAPTER 2

The Visit of the Wise Men

Jesus was born in the town of Bethlehem in Judea, during the reign of King Herod. About that time some wise men* from eastern lands arrived in Jerusalem, asking, 2"Where is the newborn king of the Jews? We have seen his star as it arose,* and we have come to worship him."

3Herod was deeply disturbed by their question, as was all of Jerusalem. 4He called a meeting of the leading priests and teachers of religious law. "Where did the prophets say the Messiah would be born?" he asked them.

5"In Bethlehem," they said, "for this is what the prophet wrote:

6 'O Bethlehem of Judah,
      you are not just a lowly village in Judah,
   for a ruler will come from you
      who will be the shepherd for my people Israel.'*"

7Then Herod sent a private message to the wise men, asking them to come see him. At this meeting he learned the exact time

1:21 *Jesus* means "The LORD saves."   1:23 Isa 7:14; 8:8, 10.   2:1 Or *royal astrologers;*
Greek reads *magi;* also in 2:7, 16.   2:2 Or *in the east.*   2:6 Mic 5:2; 2 Sam 5:2.

when they first saw the star. [8] Then he told them, "Go to Bethlehem and search carefully for the child. And when you find him, come back and tell me so that I can go and worship him, too!"

[9] After this interview the wise men went their way. Once again the star appeared to them, guiding them to Bethlehem. It went ahead of them and stopped over the place where the child was. [10] When they saw the star, they were filled with joy! [11] They entered the house where the child and his mother, Mary, were, and they fell down before him and worshiped him. Then they opened their treasure chests and gave him gifts of gold, frankincense, and myrrh. [12] But when it was time to leave, they went home another way, because God had warned them in a dream not to return to Herod.

The Escape to Egypt

[13] After the wise men were gone, an angel of the Lord appeared to Joseph in a dream. "Get up and flee to Egypt with the child and his mother," the angel said. "Stay there until I tell you to return, because Herod is going to try to kill the child." [14] That night Joseph left for Egypt with the child and Mary, his mother, [15] and they stayed there until Herod's death. This fulfilled what the Lord had spoken through the prophet: "I called my Son out of Egypt."*

[16] Herod was furious when he learned that the wise men had outwitted him. He sent soldiers to kill all the boys in and around Bethlehem who were two years old and under, because the wise men had told him the star first appeared to them about two years earlier.* [17] Herod's brutal action fulfilled the prophecy of Jeremiah:

[18] "A cry of anguish is heard in Ramah—
weeping and mourning unrestrained.
Rachel weeps for her children,
refusing to be comforted—for they are dead."*

The Return to Nazareth

[19] When Herod died, an angel of the Lord appeared in a dream to Joseph in Egypt and told him, [20] "Get up and take the child and his mother back to the land of Israel, because those who were trying to kill the child are dead." [21] So Joseph returned immediately to Israel with Jesus and his mother. [22] But when he learned that the new ruler was Herod's son Archelaus, he was afraid. Then, in another dream, he was warned to go to Galilee. [23] So they went and lived in a town called Nazareth. This fulfilled what was spoken by the prophets concerning the Messiah: "He will be called a Nazarene."

CHAPTER 3

John the Baptist Prepares the Way

In those days John the Baptist began preaching in the Judean wilderness. His message was, [2] "Turn from your sins and turn to God, because the Kingdom of Heaven is near.*" [3] Isaiah had spoken of John when he said,

"He is a voice shouting in the wilderness:
'Prepare a pathway for the Lord's coming!
Make a straight road for him!'"*

2:15 Hos 11:1. 2:16 Or *according to the time he calculated from the wise men.* 2:18 Jer 31:15. 3:2 Or *has come* or *is coming soon.* 3:3 Isa 40:3.

4John's clothes were woven from camel hair, and he wore a leather belt; his food was locusts and wild honey. 5People from Jerusalem and from every section of Judea and from all over the Jordan Valley went out to the wilderness to hear him preach. 6And when they confessed their sins, he baptized them in the Jordan River.

7But when he saw many Pharisees and Sadducees coming to be baptized, he denounced them. "You brood of snakes!" he exclaimed. "Who warned you to flee God's coming judgment? 8Prove by the way you live that you have really turned from your sins and turned to God. 9Don't just say, 'We're the descendants of Abraham.' That proves nothing. God can change these stones here into children of Abraham. 10Even now the ax of God's judgment is poised, ready to sever your roots. Yes, every tree that does not produce good fruit will be chopped down and thrown into the fire.

11"I baptize with* water those who turn from their sins and turn to God. But someone is coming soon who is far greater than I am—so much greater that I am not even worthy to be his slave.* He will baptize you with the Holy Spirit and with fire.* 12He is ready to separate the chaff from the grain with his winnowing fork. Then he will clean up the threshing area, storing the grain in his barn but burning the chaff with never-ending fire."

The Baptism of Jesus

13Then Jesus went from Galilee to the Jordan River to be baptized by John. 14But John didn't want to baptize him. "I am the one who needs to be baptized by you," he said, "so why are you coming to me?"

15But Jesus said, "It must be done, because we must do everything that is right.*" So then John baptized him.

16After his baptism, as Jesus came up out of the water, the heavens were opened and he saw the Spirit of God descending like a dove and settling on him. 17And a voice from heaven said, "This is my beloved Son, and I am fully pleased with him."

CHAPTER 4

The Temptation of Jesus

Then Jesus was led out into the wilderness by the Holy Spirit to be tempted there by the Devil. 2For forty days and forty nights he ate nothing and became very hungry. 3Then the Devil* came and said to him, "If you are the Son of God, change these stones into loaves of bread."

4But Jesus told him, "No! The Scriptures say,

'People need more than bread for their life;
    they must feed on every word of God.'*"

5Then the Devil took him to Jerusalem, to the highest point of the Temple, 6and said, "If you are the Son of God, jump off! For the Scriptures say,

'He orders his angels to protect you.
And they will hold you with their hands
    to keep you from striking your foot on a stone.'*"

3:11a Or in.   3:11b Greek *to carry his sandals.*   3:11c Or *in the Holy Spirit and in fire.*
3:15 Or *we must fulfill all righteousness.*   4:3 Greek *the tempter.*   4:4 Deut 8:3.
4:6 Ps 91:11-12.

⁷Jesus responded, "The Scriptures also say, 'Do not test the Lord your God.'*"

⁸Next the Devil took him to the peak of a very high mountain and showed him the nations of the world and all their glory. ⁹"I will give it all to you," he said, "if you will only kneel down and worship me."

¹⁰"Get out of here, Satan," Jesus told him. "For the Scriptures say,

'You must worship the Lord your God;
    serve only him.'*"

¹¹Then the Devil went away, and angels came and cared for Jesus.

The Ministry of Jesus Begins

¹²When Jesus heard that John had been arrested, he left Judea and returned to Galilee. ¹³But instead of going to Nazareth, he went to Capernaum, beside the Sea of Galilee, in the region of Zebulun and Naphtali. ¹⁴This fulfilled Isaiah's prophecy:

¹⁵ "In the land of Zebulun and of Naphtali,
    beside the sea, beyond the Jordan River—
    in Galilee where so many Gentiles live—
¹⁶ the people who sat in darkness
    have seen a great light.
And for those who lived in the land where death casts its
        shadow,
    a light has shined."*

¹⁷From then on, Jesus began to preach, "Turn from your sins and turn to God, because the Kingdom of Heaven is near.*"

The First Disciples

¹⁸One day as Jesus was walking along the shore beside the Sea of Galilee, he saw two brothers—Simon, also called Peter, and Andrew—fishing with a net, for they were commercial fishermen. ¹⁹Jesus called out to them, "Come, be my disciples, and I will show you how to fish for people!" ²⁰And they left their nets at once and went with him.

²¹A little farther up the shore he saw two other brothers, James and John, sitting in a boat with their father, Zebedee, mending their nets. And he called them to come, too. ²²They immediately followed him, leaving the boat and their father behind.

The Ministry of Jesus in Galilee

²³Jesus traveled throughout Galilee teaching in the synagogues, preaching everywhere the Good News about the Kingdom. And he healed people who had every kind of sickness and disease. ²⁴News about him spread far beyond the borders of Galilee so that the sick were soon coming to be healed from as far away as Syria. And whatever their illness and pain, or if they were possessed by demons, or were epileptics, or were paralyzed—he healed them all. ²⁵Large crowds followed him wherever he went—people from Galilee, the Ten Towns,* Jerusalem, from all over Judea, and from east of the Jordan River.

4:7 Deut 6:16.   4:10 Deut 6:13.   4:15-16 Isa 9:1-2.   4:17 Or *has come* or *is coming soon.*   4:25 Greek *Decapolis.*

CHAPTER 5

The Sermon on the Mount
One day as the crowds were gathering, Jesus went up the mountainside with his disciples and sat down to teach them.

The Beatitudes
²This is what he taught them:

3 "God blesses those who realize their need for him,*
   for the Kingdom of Heaven is given to them.
4 God blesses those who mourn,
   for they will be comforted.
5 God blesses those who are gentle and lowly,
   for the whole earth will belong to them.
6 God blesses those who are hungry and thirsty for justice,
   for they will receive it in full.
7 God blesses those who are merciful,
   for they will be shown mercy.
8 God blesses those whose hearts are pure,
   for they will see God.
9 God blesses those who work for peace,
   for they will be called the children of God.
10 God blesses those who are persecuted because they live for God,
   for the Kingdom of Heaven is theirs.

¹¹"God blesses you when you are mocked and persecuted and lied about because you are my followers. ¹²Be happy about it! Be very glad! For a great reward awaits you in heaven. And remember, the ancient prophets were persecuted, too.

Teaching about Salt and Light
¹³"You are the salt of the earth. But what good is salt if it has lost its flavor? Can you make it useful again? It will be thrown out and trampled underfoot as worthless. ¹⁴You are the light of the world—like a city on a mountain, glowing in the night for all to see. ¹⁵Don't hide your light under a basket! Instead, put it on a stand and let it shine for all. ¹⁶In the same way, let your good deeds shine out for all to see, so that everyone will praise your heavenly Father.

Teaching about the Law
¹⁷"Don't misunderstand why I have come. I did not come to abolish the law of Moses or the writings of the prophets. No, I came to fulfill them. ¹⁸I assure you, until heaven and earth disappear, even the smallest detail of God's law will remain until its purpose is achieved. ¹⁹So if you break the smallest commandment and teach others to do the same, you will be the least in the Kingdom of Heaven. But anyone who obeys God's laws and teaches them will be great in the Kingdom of Heaven.

²⁰"But I warn you—unless you obey God better than the teachers of religious law and the Pharisees do, you can't enter the Kingdom of Heaven at all!

Teaching about Anger
²¹"You have heard that the law of Moses says, 'Do not murder. If you commit murder, you are subject to judgment.'* ²²But I say, if

5:3 Greek *the poor in spirit.*   **5:21** Exod 20:13; Deut 5:17.

you are angry with someone,* you are subject to judgment! If you call someone an idiot,* you are in danger of being brought before the high council. And if you curse someone,* you are in danger of the fires of hell.

23 "So if you are standing before the altar in the Temple, offering a sacrifice to God, and you suddenly remember that someone has something against you, 24leave your sacrifice there beside the altar. Go and be reconciled to that person. Then come and offer your sacrifice to God. 25Come to terms quickly with your enemy before it is too late and you are dragged into court, handed over to an officer, and thrown in jail. 26I assure you that you won't be free again until you have paid the last penny.

Teaching about Adultery

27 "You have heard that the law of Moses says, 'Do not commit adultery.'* 28But I say, anyone who even looks at a woman with lust in his eye has already committed adultery with her in his heart. 29So if your eye—even if it is your good eye*—causes you to lust, gouge it out and throw it away. It is better for you to lose one part of your body than for your whole body to be thrown into hell. 30And if your hand—even if it is your stronger hand*—causes you to sin, cut it off and throw it away. It is better for you to lose one part of your body than for your whole body to be thrown into hell.

Teaching about Divorce

31 "You have heard that the law of Moses says, 'A man can divorce his wife by merely giving her a letter of divorce.'* 32But I say that a man who divorces his wife, unless she has been unfaithful, causes her to commit adultery. And anyone who marries a divorced woman commits adultery.

Teaching about Vows

33 "Again, you have heard that the law of Moses says, 'Do not break your vows; you must carry out the vows you have made to the Lord.'* 34But I say, don't make any vows! If you say, 'By heaven!' it is a sacred vow because heaven is God's throne. 35And if you say, 'By the earth!' it is a sacred vow because the earth is his footstool. And don't swear, 'By Jerusalem!' for Jerusalem is the city of the great King. 36Don't even swear, 'By my head!' for you can't turn one hair white or black. 37Just say a simple, 'Yes, I will,' or 'No, I won't.' Your word is enough. To strengthen your promise with a vow shows that something is wrong.*

Teaching about Revenge

38 "You have heard that the law of Moses says, 'If an eye is injured, injure the eye of the person who did it. If a tooth gets knocked out, knock out the tooth of the person who did it.'* 39But I say, don't resist an evil person! If you are slapped on the right cheek, turn the other, too. 40If you are ordered to court and your shirt is taken from you, give your coat, too. 41If a soldier demands that you carry his gear for a mile,* carry it two miles. 42Give to those who ask, and don't turn away from those who want to borrow.

5:22a Greek *your brother;* also in 5:23. Some manuscripts add *without cause.*
5:22b Greek uses an Aramaic term of contempt; *If you say to your brother, 'Raca.'*
5:22c Greek *if you say, 'You fool.'*   5:27 Exod 20:14; Deut 5:18.   5:29 Greek *your right eye.*
5:30 Greek *your right hand.*   5:31 Deut 24:1.   5:33 Num 30:2.   5:37 Or *Anything beyond this is from the evil one.*   5:38 Greek *'An eye for an eye and a tooth for a tooth.'* Exod 21:24; Lev 24:20; Deut 19:21.   5:41 Greek *milion* [4,854 feet or 1,478 meters].

Teaching about Love for Enemies

43"You have heard that the law of Moses says, 'Love your neighbor'* and hate your enemy. 44But I say, love your enemies!* Pray for those who persecute you! 45In that way, you will be acting as true children of your Father in heaven. For he gives his sunlight to both the evil and the good, and he sends rain on the just and on the unjust, too. 46If you love only those who love you, what good is that? Even corrupt tax collectors do that much. 47If you are kind only to your friends,* how are you different from anyone else? Even pagans do that. 48But you are to be perfect, even as your Father in heaven is perfect.

CHAPTER 6

Teaching about Giving to the Needy

"Take care! Don't do your good deeds publicly, to be admired, because then you will lose the reward from your Father in heaven. 2When you give a gift to someone in need, don't announce it as the hypocrites do—blowing trumpets in the synagogues and streets to call attention to their acts of charity! I assure you, they have received all the reward they will ever get. 3But when you give to someone in need, don't tell your left hand what your right hand is doing. 4Give your gifts in secret, and your Father, who knows all secrets, will reward you.

Teaching about Prayer and Fasting

5"And now about prayer. When you pray, don't be like the hypocrites who love to pray publicly on street corners and in the synagogues where everyone can see them. I assure you, that is all the reward they will ever get. 6But when you pray, go away by yourself, shut the door behind you, and pray to your Father secretly. Then your Father, who knows all secrets, will reward you.

7"When you pray, don't babble on and on as people of other religions do. They think their prayers are answered only by repeating their words again and again. 8Don't be like them, because your Father knows exactly what you need even before you ask him! 9Pray like this:

Our Father in heaven,
    may your name be honored.
10 May your Kingdom come soon.
    May your will be done here on earth,
        just as it is in heaven.
11 Give us our food for today,*
12 and forgive us our sins,
    just as we have forgiven those who have sinned against us.
13 And don't let us yield to temptation,
        but deliver us from the evil one.*

14"If you forgive those who sin against you, your heavenly Father will forgive you. 15But if you refuse to forgive others, your Father will not forgive your sins.

5:43 Lev 19:18.   5:44 Some manuscripts add *Bless those who curse you, do good to those who hate you.*   5:47 Greek *your brothers.*   6:11 Or *for tomorrow.*   6:13 Or *from evil.* Some manuscripts add *For yours is the kingdom and the power and the glory forever. Amen.*

¹⁶"And when you fast, don't make it obvious, as the hypocrites do, who try to look pale and disheveled so people will admire them for their fasting. I assure you, that is the only reward they will ever get. ¹⁷But when you fast, comb your hair and wash your face. ¹⁸Then no one will suspect you are fasting, except your Father, who knows what you do in secret. And your Father, who knows all secrets, will reward you.

Teaching about Money and Possessions

¹⁹"Don't store up treasures here on earth, where they can be eaten by moths and get rusty, and where thieves break in and steal. ²⁰Store your treasures in heaven, where they will never become moth-eaten or rusty and where they will be safe from thieves. ²¹Wherever your treasure is, there your heart and thoughts will also be.

²²"Your eye is a lamp for your body. A pure eye lets sunshine into your soul. ²³But an evil eye shuts out the light and plunges you into darkness. If the light you think you have is really darkness, how deep that darkness will be!

²⁴"No one can serve two masters. For you will hate one and love the other, or be devoted to one and despise the other. You cannot serve both God and money.

²⁵"So I tell you, don't worry about everyday life—whether you have enough food, drink, and clothes. Doesn't life consist of more than food and clothing? ²⁶Look at the birds. They don't need to plant or harvest or put food in barns because your heavenly Father feeds them. And you are far more valuable to him than they are. ²⁷Can all your worries add a single moment to your life? Of course not.

²⁸"And why worry about your clothes? Look at the lilies and how they grow. They don't work or make their clothing, ²⁹yet Solomon in all his glory was not dressed as beautifully as they are. ³⁰And if God cares so wonderfully for flowers that are here today and gone tomorrow, won't he more surely care for you? You have so little faith!

³¹"So don't worry about having enough food or drink or clothing. ³²Why be like the pagans who are so deeply concerned about these things? Your heavenly Father already knows all your needs, ³³and he will give you all you need from day to day if you live for him and make the Kingdom of God your primary concern.

³⁴"So don't worry about tomorrow, for tomorrow will bring its own worries. Today's trouble is enough for today.

CHAPTER 7

Don't Condemn Others

"Stop judging others, and you will not be judged. ²For others will treat you as you treat them.* Whatever measure you use in judging others, it will be used to measure how you are judged. ³And why worry about a speck in your friend's eye* when you have a log in your own? ⁴How can you think of saying, 'Let me help you get rid of that speck in your eye,' when you can't see past the log in your own eye? ⁵Hypocrite! First get rid of the log from your own

7:2 Or *For God will treat you as you treat others;* Greek reads *For with the judgment you judge you will be judged.* 7:3 Greek *your brother's eye;* also in 7:5.

eye; then perhaps you will see well enough to deal with the speck in your friend's eye.

⁶"Don't give what is holy to unholy people.* Don't give pearls to swine! They will trample the pearls, then turn and attack you.

Effective Prayer

⁷"Keep on asking, and you will be given what you ask for. Keep on looking, and you will find. Keep on knocking, and the door will be opened. ⁸For everyone who asks, receives. Everyone who seeks, finds. And the door is opened to everyone who knocks. ⁹You parents—if your children ask for a loaf of bread, do you give them a stone instead? ¹⁰Or if they ask for a fish, do you give them a snake? Of course not! ¹¹If you sinful people know how to give good gifts to your children, how much more will your heavenly Father give good gifts to those who ask him.

The Golden Rule

¹²"Do for others what you would like them to do for you. This is a summary of all that is taught in the law and the prophets.

The Narrow Gate

¹³"You can enter God's Kingdom only through the narrow gate. The highway to hell* is broad, and its gate is wide for the many who choose the easy way. ¹⁴But the gateway to life is small, and the road is narrow, and only a few ever find it.

The Tree and Its Fruit

¹⁵"Beware of false prophets who come disguised as harmless sheep, but are really wolves that will tear you apart. ¹⁶You can detect them by the way they act, just as you can identify a tree by its fruit. You don't pick grapes from thornbushes, or figs from thistles. ¹⁷A healthy tree produces good fruit, and an unhealthy tree produces bad fruit. ¹⁸A good tree can't produce bad fruit, and a bad tree can't produce good fruit. ¹⁹So every tree that does not produce good fruit is chopped down and thrown into the fire. ²⁰Yes, the way to identify a tree or a person is by the kind of fruit that is produced.

True Disciples

²¹"Not all people who sound religious are really godly. They may refer to me as 'Lord,' but they still won't enter the Kingdom of Heaven. The decisive issue is whether they obey my Father in heaven. ²²On judgment day many will tell me, 'Lord, Lord, we prophesied in your name and cast out demons in your name and performed many miracles in your name.' ²³But I will reply, 'I never knew you. Go away; the things you did were unauthorized.*'

Building on a Solid Foundation

²⁴"Anyone who listens to my teaching and obeys me is wise, like a person who builds a house on solid rock. ²⁵Though the rain comes in torrents and the floodwaters rise and the winds beat against that house, it won't collapse, because it is built on rock. ²⁶But anyone who hears my teaching and ignores it is foolish, like a person who builds a house on sand. ²⁷When the rains and floods come and the winds beat against that house, it will fall with a mighty crash."

7:6 Greek *Don't give the sacred to dogs.*   7:13 Greek *The way that leads to destruction.*
7:23 Or *unlawful.*

28After Jesus finished speaking, the crowds were amazed at his teaching, 29for he taught as one who had real authority—quite unlike the teachers of religious law.

CHAPTER 8

Jesus Heals a Man with Leprosy

Large crowds followed Jesus as he came down the mountainside. 2Suddenly, a man with leprosy approached Jesus. He knelt before him, worshiping. "Lord," the man said, "if you want to, you can make me well again."

3Jesus touched him. "I want to," he said. "Be healed!" And instantly the leprosy disappeared. 4Then Jesus said to him, "Go right over to the priest and let him examine you. Don't talk to anyone along the way. Take along the offering required in the law of Moses for those who have been healed of leprosy, so everyone will have proof of your healing."

Faith of the Roman Officer

5When Jesus arrived in Capernaum, a Roman officer came and pleaded with him, 6"Lord, my young servant lies in bed, paralyzed and racked with pain."

7Jesus said, "I will come and heal him."

8Then the officer said, "Lord, I am not worthy to have you come into my home. Just say the word from where you are, and my servant will be healed! 9I know, because I am under the authority of my superior officers and I have authority over my soldiers. I only need to say, 'Go,' and they go, or 'Come,' and they come. And if I say to my slaves, 'Do this or that,' they do it."

10When Jesus heard this, he was amazed. Turning to the crowd, he said, "I tell you the truth, I haven't seen faith like this in all the land of Israel! 11And I tell you this, that many Gentiles will come from all over the world and sit down with Abraham, Isaac, and Jacob at the feast in the Kingdom of Heaven. 12But many Israelites—those for whom the Kingdom was prepared—will be cast into outer darkness, where there will be weeping and gnashing of teeth."

13Then Jesus said to the Roman officer, "Go on home. What you have believed has happened." And the young servant was healed that same hour.

Jesus Heals Many People

14When Jesus arrived at Peter's house, Peter's mother-in-law was in bed with a high fever. 15But when Jesus touched her hand, the fever left her. Then she got up and prepared a meal for him.

16That evening many demon-possessed people were brought to Jesus. All the spirits fled when he commanded them to leave; and he healed all the sick. 17This fulfilled the word of the Lord through Isaiah, who said, "He took our sicknesses and removed our diseases."*

The Cost of Following Jesus

18When Jesus noticed how large the crowd was growing, he instructed his disciples to cross to the other side of the lake.

8:17 Isa 53:4.

¹⁹Then one of the teachers of religious law said to him, "Teacher, I will follow you no matter where you go!"

²⁰But Jesus said, "Foxes have dens to live in, and birds have nests, but I, the Son of Man, have no home of my own, not even a place to lay my head."

²¹Another of his disciples said, "Lord, first let me return home and bury my father."

²²But Jesus told him, "Follow me now! Let those who are spiritually dead care for their own dead."*

Jesus Calms the Storm

²³Then Jesus got into the boat and started across the lake with his disciples. ²⁴Suddenly, a terrible storm came up, with waves breaking into the boat. But Jesus was sleeping. ²⁵The disciples went to him and woke him up, shouting, "Lord, save us! We're going to drown!"

²⁶And Jesus answered, "Why are you afraid? You have so little faith!" Then he stood up and rebuked the wind and waves, and suddenly all was calm. ²⁷The disciples just sat there in awe. "Who is this?" they asked themselves. "Even the wind and waves obey him!"

Jesus Heals Two Demon-Possessed Men

²⁸When Jesus arrived on the other side of the lake in the land of the Gadarenes,* two men who were possessed by demons met him. They lived in a cemetery and were so dangerous that no one could go through that area. ²⁹They began screaming at him, "Why are you bothering us, Son of God? You have no right to torture us before God's appointed time!" ³⁰A large herd of pigs was feeding in the distance. ³¹so the demons begged, "If you cast us out, send us into that herd of pigs."

³²"All right, go!" Jesus commanded them. So the demons came out of the men and entered the pigs, and the whole herd plunged down the steep hillside into the lake and drowned in the water. ³³The herdsmen fled to the nearby city, telling everyone what happened to the demon-possessed men. ³⁴The entire town came out to meet Jesus, but they begged him to go away and leave them alone.

CHAPTER 9

Jesus Heals a Paralyzed Man

Jesus climbed into a boat and went back across the lake to his own town. ²Some people brought to him a paralyzed man on a mat. Seeing their faith, Jesus said to the paralyzed man, "Take heart, son! Your sins are forgiven."

³"Blasphemy! This man talks like he is God!" some of the teachers of religious law said among themselves.

⁴Jesus knew what they were thinking, so he asked them, "Why are you thinking such evil thoughts? ⁵Is it easier to say, 'Your sins are forgiven' or 'Get up and walk'? ⁶I will prove that I, the Son of Man, have the authority on earth to forgive sins." Then Jesus turned to the paralyzed man and said, "Stand up, take your mat, and go on home, because you are healed!"

8:22 Greek *Let the dead bury their own dead.* **8:28** Some manuscripts read *Gerasenes*; other manuscripts read *Gergesenes.* See Mark 5:1; Luke 8:26.

7And the man jumped up and went home! 8Fear swept through the crowd as they saw this happen right before their eyes. They praised God for sending a man with such great authority.

Jesus Calls Matthew

9As Jesus was going down the road, he saw Matthew sitting at his tax-collection booth. "Come, be my disciple," Jesus said to him. So Matthew got up and followed him.

10That night Matthew invited Jesus and his disciples to be his dinner guests, along with his fellow tax collectors and many other notorious sinners. 11The Pharisees were indignant. "Why does your teacher eat with such scum*?" they asked his disciples.

12When he heard this, Jesus replied, "Healthy people don't need a doctor—sick people do." 13Then he added, "Now go and learn the meaning of this Scripture: 'I want you to be merciful; I don't want your sacrifices.'* For I have come to call sinners, not those who think they are already good enough."

A Discussion about Fasting

14One day the disciples of John the Baptist came to Jesus and asked him, "Why do we and the Pharisees fast, but your disciples don't fast?"

15Jesus responded, "Should the wedding guests mourn while celebrating with the groom? Someday he will be taken from them, and then they will fast. 16And who would patch an old garment with unshrunk cloth? For the patch shrinks and pulls away from the old cloth, leaving an even bigger hole than before. 17And no one puts new wine into old wineskins. The old skins would burst from the pressure, spilling the wine and ruining the skins. New wine must be stored in new wineskins. That way both the wine and the wineskins are preserved."

Jesus Heals in Response to Faith

18As Jesus was saying this, the leader of a synagogue came and knelt down before him. "My daughter has just died," he said, "but you can bring her back to life again if you just come and lay your hand upon her."

19As Jesus and the disciples were going to the official's home, 20a woman who had had a hemorrhage for twelve years came up behind him. She touched the fringe of his robe, 21for she thought, "If I can just touch his robe, I will be healed."

22Jesus turned around and said to her, "Daughter, be encouraged! Your faith has made you well." And the woman was healed at that moment.

23When Jesus arrived at the official's home, he noticed the noisy crowds and heard the funeral music. 24He said, "Go away, for the girl isn't dead; she's only asleep." But the crowd laughed at him. 25When the crowd was finally outside, Jesus went in and took the girl by the hand, and she stood up! 26The report of this miracle swept through the entire countryside.

Jesus Heals the Blind and Mute

27After Jesus left the girl's home, two blind men followed along behind him, shouting, "Son of David, have mercy on us!"

9:11 Greek *with tax collectors and sinners.*   **9:13** Hos 6:6.

²⁸They went right into the house where he was staying, and Jesus asked them, "Do you believe I can make you see?"

"Yes, Lord," they told him, "we do."

²⁹Then he touched their eyes and said, "Because of your faith, it will happen." ³⁰And suddenly they could see! Jesus sternly warned them, "Don't tell anyone about this." ³¹But instead, they spread his fame all over the region.

³²When they left, some people brought to him a man who couldn't speak because he was possessed by a demon. ³³So Jesus cast out the demon, and instantly the man could talk. The crowds marveled. "Nothing like this has ever happened in Israel!" they exclaimed.

³⁴But the Pharisees said, "He can cast out demons because he is empowered by the prince of demons."

The Need for Workers

³⁵Jesus traveled through all the cities and villages of that area, teaching in the synagogues and announcing the Good News about the Kingdom. And wherever he went, he healed people of every sort of disease and illness. ³⁶He felt great pity for the crowds that came, because their problems were so great and they didn't know where to go for help. They were like sheep without a shepherd. ³⁷He said to his disciples, "The harvest is so great, but the workers are so few. ³⁸So pray to the Lord who is in charge of the harvest; ask him to send out more workers for his fields."

CHAPTER 10

Jesus Sends Out the Twelve Apostles

Jesus called his twelve disciples to him and gave them authority to cast out evil spirits and to heal every kind of disease and illness. ²Here are the names of the twelve apostles:

first Simon (also called Peter),
then Andrew (Peter's brother),
James (son of Zebedee),
John (James's brother),
³ Philip,
Bartholomew,
Thomas,
Matthew (the tax collector),
James (son of Alphaeus),
Thaddaeus,
⁴ Simon (the Zealot*),
Judas Iscariot (who later betrayed him).

⁵Jesus sent the twelve disciples out with these instructions: "Don't go to the Gentiles or the Samaritans, ⁶but only to the people of Israel—God's lost sheep. ⁷Go and announce to them that the Kingdom of Heaven is near.* ⁸Heal the sick, raise the dead, cure those with leprosy, and cast out demons. Give as freely as you have received!

⁹"Don't take any money with you. ¹⁰Don't carry a traveler's bag with an extra coat and sandals or even a walking stick. Don't hesitate to accept hospitality, because those who work deserve to be fed.*

10:4 Greek *the Cananean.*   **10:7** Or *has come* or *is coming soon.*   **10:10** Or *the worker is worthy of support.*

¹¹Whenever you enter a city or village, search for a worthy man and stay in his home until you leave for the next town. ¹²When you are invited into someone's home, give it your blessing. ¹³If it turns out to be a worthy home, let your blessing stand; if it is not, take back the blessing. ¹⁴If a village doesn't welcome you or listen to you, shake off the dust of that place from your feet as you leave. ¹⁵I assure you, the wicked cities of Sodom and Gomorrah will be better off on the judgment day than that place will be.

¹⁶"Look, I am sending you out as sheep among wolves. Be as wary as snakes and harmless as doves. ¹⁷But beware! For you will be handed over to the courts and beaten in the synagogues. ¹⁸And you must stand trial before governors and kings because you are my followers. This will be your opportunity to tell them about me—yes, to witness to the world. ¹⁹When you are arrested, don't worry about what to say in your defense, because you will be given the right words at the right time. ²⁰For it won't be you doing the talking—it will be the Spirit of your Father speaking through you.

²¹"Brother will betray brother to death, fathers will betray their own children, and children will rise against their parents and cause them to be killed. ²²And everyone will hate you because of your allegiance to me. But those who endure to the end will be saved. ²³When you are persecuted in one town, flee to the next. I assure you that I, the Son of Man, will return before you have reached all the towns of Israel.

²⁴"A student is not greater than the teacher. A servant is not greater than the master. ²⁵The student shares the teacher's fate. The servant shares the master's fate. And since I, the master of the household, have been called the prince of demons,* how much more will it happen to you, the members of the household! ²⁶But don't be afraid of those who threaten you. For the time is coming when everything will be revealed; all that is secret will be made public. ²⁷What I tell you now in the darkness, shout abroad when daybreak comes. What I whisper in your ears, shout from the housetops for all to hear!

²⁸"Don't be afraid of those who want to kill you. They can only kill your body; they cannot touch your soul. Fear only God, who can destroy both soul and body in hell. ²⁹Not even a sparrow, worth only half a penny, can fall to the ground without your Father knowing it. ³⁰And the very hairs on your head are all numbered. ³¹So don't be afraid; you are more valuable to him than a whole flock of sparrows.

³²"If anyone acknowledges me publicly here on earth, I will openly acknowledge that person before my Father in heaven. ³³But if anyone denies me here on earth, I will deny that person before my Father in heaven.

³⁴"Don't imagine that I came to bring peace to the earth! No, I came to bring a sword. ³⁵I have come to set a man against his father, and a daughter against her mother, and a daughter-in-law against her mother-in-law. ³⁶Your enemies will be right in your own household! ³⁷If you love your father or mother more than you love me, you are not worthy of being mine; or if you love your son or daughter more than me, you are not worthy of being mine. ³⁸If

10:25 Greek *Beelzeboul.*

you refuse to take up your cross and follow me, you are not worthy of being mine. ³⁹If you cling to your life, you will lose it; but if you give it up for me, you will find it.

⁴⁰"Anyone who welcomes you is welcoming me, and anyone who welcomes me is welcoming the Father who sent me. ⁴¹If you welcome a prophet as one who speaks for God,* you will receive the same reward a prophet gets. And if you welcome good and godly people because of their godliness, you will be given a reward like theirs. ⁴²And if you give even a cup of cold water to one of the least of my followers, you will surely be rewarded."

CHAPTER 11
Jesus and John the Baptist
When Jesus had finished giving these instructions to his twelve disciples, he went off teaching and preaching in towns throughout the country.

²John the Baptist, who was now in prison, heard about all the things the Messiah was doing. So he sent his disciples to ask Jesus, ³"Are you really the Messiah we've been waiting for, or should we keep looking for someone else?"

⁴Jesus told them, "Go back to John and tell him about what you have heard and seen—⁵the blind see, the lame walk, the lepers are cured, the deaf hear, the dead are raised to life, and the Good News is being preached to the poor. ⁶And tell him: 'God blesses those who are not offended by me.*'"

⁷When John's disciples had gone, Jesus began talking about him to the crowds. "Who is this man in the wilderness that you went out to see? Did you find him weak as a reed, moved by every breath of wind? ⁸Or were you expecting to see a man dressed in expensive clothes? Those who dress like that live in palaces, not out in the wilderness. ⁹Were you looking for a prophet? Yes, and he is more than a prophet. ¹⁰John is the man to whom the Scriptures refer when they say,

'Look, I am sending my messenger before you,
    and he will prepare your way before you.'*

¹¹"I assure you, of all who have ever lived, none is greater than John the Baptist. Yet even the most insignificant person in the Kingdom of Heaven is greater than he is! ¹²And from the time John the Baptist began preaching and baptizing until now, the Kingdom of Heaven has been forcefully advancing, and violent people attack it.* ¹³For before John came, all the teachings of the Scriptures looked forward to this present time. ¹⁴And if you are willing to accept what I say, he is Elijah, the one the prophets said would come.* ¹⁵Anyone who is willing to hear should listen and understand!

¹⁶"How shall I describe this generation? These people are like a group of children playing a game in the public square. They complain to their friends, ¹⁷'We played wedding songs, and you weren't happy, so we played funeral songs, but you weren't sad.' ¹⁸For John the Baptist didn't drink wine and he often fasted, and

10:41 Greek *welcome a prophet in the name of a prophet.* **11:6** Or *who don't fall away because of me.* **11:10** Mal 3:1. **11:12** Or *until now, eager multitudes have been pressing into the Kingdom of Heaven.* **11:14** See Mal 4:5.

you say, 'He's demon possessed.' [19]And I, the Son of Man, feast and drink, and you say, 'He's a glutton and a drunkard, and a friend of the worst sort of sinners!' But wisdom is shown to be right by what results from it."

Judgment for the Unbelievers

[20]Then Jesus began to denounce the cities where he had done most of his miracles, because they hadn't turned from their sins and turned to God. [21]"What horrors await you, Korazin and Bethsaida! For if the miracles I did in you had been done in wicked Tyre and Sidon, their people would have sat in deep repentance long ago, clothed in sackcloth and throwing ashes on their heads to show their remorse. [22]I assure you, Tyre and Sidon will be better off on the judgment day than you! [23]And you people of Capernaum, will you be exalted to heaven? No, you will be brought down to the place of the dead.* For if the miracles I did for you had been done in Sodom, it would still be here today. [24]I assure you, Sodom will be better off on the judgment day than you."

Jesus' Prayer of Thanksgiving

[25]Then Jesus prayed this prayer: "O Father, Lord of heaven and earth, thank you for hiding the truth from those who think themselves so wise and clever, and for revealing it to the childlike. [26]Yes, Father, it pleased you to do it this way!

[27]"My Father has given me authority over everything. No one really knows the Son except the Father, and no one really knows the Father except the Son and those to whom the Son chooses to reveal him."

[28]Then Jesus said, "Come to me, all of you who are weary and carry heavy burdens, and I will give you rest. [29]Take my yoke upon you. Let me teach you, because I am humble and gentle, and you will find rest for your souls. [30]For my yoke fits perfectly, and the burden I give you is light."

CHAPTER 12

Controversy about the Sabbath

At about that time Jesus was walking through some grainfields on the Sabbath. His disciples were hungry, so they began breaking off heads of wheat and eating the grain. [2]Some Pharisees saw them do it and protested, "Your disciples shouldn't be doing that! It's against the law to work by harvesting grain on the Sabbath."

[3]But Jesus said to them, "Haven't you ever read in the Scriptures what King David did when he and his companions were hungry? [4]He went into the house of God, and they ate the special bread reserved for the priests alone. That was breaking the law, too. [5]And haven't you ever read in the law of Moses that the priests on duty in the Temple may work on the Sabbath? [6]I tell you, there is one here who is even greater than the Temple! [7]But you would not have condemned those who aren't guilty if you knew the meaning of this Scripture: 'I want you to be merciful; I don't want your sacrifices.'* [8]For I, the Son of Man, am master even of the Sabbath."

[9]Then he went over to the synagogue, [10]where he noticed a man with a deformed hand. The Pharisees asked Jesus, "Is it legal to

11:23 Greek *to Hades.* **12:7** Hos 6:6.

work by healing on the Sabbath day?" (They were, of course, hoping he would say yes, so they could bring charges against him.)

11And he answered, "If you had one sheep, and it fell into a well on the Sabbath, wouldn't you get to work and pull it out? Of course you would. 12And how much more valuable is a person than a sheep! Yes, it is right to do good on the Sabbath." 13Then he said to the man, "Reach out your hand." The man reached out his hand, and it became normal, just like the other one. 14Then the Pharisees called a meeting and discussed plans for killing Jesus.

Jesus, God's Chosen Servant

15But Jesus knew what they were planning. He left that area, and many people followed him. He healed all the sick among them, 16but he warned them not to say who he was. 17This fulfilled the prophecy of Isaiah concerning him:

18 "Look at my Servant,
    whom I have chosen.
  He is my Beloved,
    and I am very pleased with him.
  I will put my Spirit upon him,
    and he will proclaim justice to the nations.
19 He will not fight or shout;
    he will not raise his voice in public.
20 He will not crush those who are weak,
    or quench the smallest hope,
    until he brings full justice with his final victory.
21 And his name will be the hope
    of all the world."*

Jesus and the Prince of Demons

22Then a demon-possessed man, who was both blind and unable to talk, was brought to Jesus. He healed the man so that he could both speak and see. 23The crowd was amazed. "Could it be that Jesus is the Son of David, the Messiah?" they wondered out loud.

24But when the Pharisees heard about the miracle, they said, "No wonder he can cast out demons. He gets his power from Satan,* the prince of demons."

25Jesus knew their thoughts and replied, "Any kingdom at war with itself is doomed. A city or home divided against itself is doomed. 26And if Satan is casting out Satan, he is fighting against himself. His own kingdom will not survive. 27And if I am empowered by the prince of demons,* what about your own followers? They cast out demons, too, so they will judge you for what you have said. 28But if I am casting out demons by the Spirit of God, then the Kingdom of God has arrived among you. 29Let me illustrate this. You can't enter a strong man's house and rob him without first tying him up. Only then can his house be robbed!* 30Anyone who isn't helping me opposes me, and anyone who isn't working with me is actually working against me.

31"Every sin or blasphemy can be forgiven—except blasphemy against the Holy Spirit, which can never be forgiven. 32Anyone

12:18-21 Isa 42:1-4.   12:24 Greek *Beelzeboul.*   12:27 Greek *by Beelzeboul.*   12:29 Or *One cannot rob Satan's kingdom without first tying him up. Only then can his demons be cast out.*

who blasphemes against me, the Son of Man, can be forgiven, but blasphemy against the Holy Spirit will never be forgiven, either in this world or in the world to come.

³³"A tree is identified by its fruit. Make a tree good, and its fruit will be good. Make a tree bad, and its fruit will be bad. ³⁴You brood of snakes! How could evil men like you speak what is good and right? For whatever is in your heart determines what you say. ³⁵A good person produces good words from a good heart, and an evil person produces evil words from an evil heart. ³⁶And I tell you this, that you must give an account on judgment day of every idle word you speak. ³⁷The words you say now reflect your fate then; either you will be justified by them or you will be condemned."

The Sign of Jonah

³⁸One day some teachers of religious law and Pharisees came to Jesus and said, "Teacher, we want you to show us a miraculous sign to prove that you are from God."

³⁹But Jesus replied, "Only an evil, faithless generation would ask for a miraculous sign; but the only sign I will give them is the sign of the prophet Jonah. ⁴⁰For as Jonah was in the belly of the great fish for three days and three nights, so I, the Son of Man, will be in the heart of the earth for three days and three nights. ⁴¹The people of Nineveh will rise up against this generation on judgment day and condemn it, because they repented at the preaching of Jonah. And now someone greater than Jonah is here—and you refuse to repent. ⁴²The queen of Sheba* will also rise up against this generation on judgment day and condemn it, because she came from a distant land to hear the wisdom of Solomon. And now someone greater than Solomon is here—and you refuse to listen to him.

⁴³"When an evil spirit leaves a person, it goes into the desert, seeking rest but finding none. ⁴⁴Then it says, 'I will return to the person I came from.' So it returns and finds its former home empty, swept, and clean. ⁴⁵Then the spirit finds seven other spirits more evil than itself, and they all enter the person and live there. And so that person is worse off than before. That will be the experience of this evil generation."

The True Family of Jesus

⁴⁶As Jesus was speaking to the crowd, his mother and brothers were outside, wanting to talk with him. ⁴⁷Someone told Jesus, "Your mother and your brothers are outside, and they want to speak to you."

⁴⁸Jesus asked, "Who is my mother? Who are my brothers?" ⁴⁹Then he pointed to his disciples and said, "These are my mother and brothers. ⁵⁰Anyone who does the will of my Father in heaven is my brother and sister and mother!"

CHAPTER 13

Story of the Farmer Scattering Seed

Later that same day, Jesus left the house and went down to the shore, ²where an immense crowd soon gathered. He got into a boat, where he sat and taught as the people listened on the shore. ³He told many stories such as this one:

12:42 Greek *The queen of the south.*

"A farmer went out to plant some seed. [4]As he scattered it across his field, some seeds fell on a footpath, and the birds came and ate them. [5]Other seeds fell on shallow soil with underlying rock. The plants sprang up quickly, [6]but they soon wilted beneath the hot sun and died because the roots had no nourishment in the shallow soil. [7]Other seeds fell among thorns that shot up and choked out the tender blades. [8]But some seeds fell on fertile soil and produced a crop that was thirty, sixty, and even a hundred times as much as had been planted. [9]Anyone who is willing to hear should listen and understand!"

[10]His disciples came and asked him, "Why do you always tell stories when you talk to the people?"

[11]Then he explained to them, "You have been permitted to understand the secrets of the Kingdom of Heaven, but others have not. [12]To those who are open to my teaching, more understanding will be given, and they will have an abundance of knowledge. But to those who are not listening, even what they have will be taken away from them. [13]That is why I tell these stories, because people see what I do, but they don't really see. They hear what I say, but they don't really hear, and they don't understand. [14]This fulfills the prophecy of Isaiah, which says:

'You will hear my words,
  but you will not understand;
you will see what I do,
  but you will not perceive its meaning.
[15] For the hearts of these people are hardened,
  and their ears cannot hear,
  and they have closed their eyes—
so their eyes cannot see,
  and their ears cannot hear,
  and their hearts cannot understand,
and they cannot turn to me
  and let me heal them.'*

[16]"But blessed are your eyes, because they see; and your ears, because they hear. [17]I assure you, many prophets and godly people have longed to see and hear what you have seen and heard, but they could not.

[18]"Now here is the explanation of the story I told about the farmer sowing grain: [19]The seed that fell on the hard path represents those who hear the Good News about the Kingdom and don't understand it. Then the evil one comes and snatches the seed away from their hearts. [20]The rocky soil represents those who hear the message and receive it with joy. [21]But like young plants in such soil, their roots don't go very deep. At first they get along fine, but they wilt as soon as they have problems or are persecuted because they believe the word. [22]The thorny ground represents those who hear and accept the Good News, but all too quickly the message is crowded out by the cares of this life and the lure of wealth, so no crop is produced. [23]The good soil represents the hearts of those who truly accept God's message and produce a huge harvest— thirty, sixty, or even a hundred times as much as had been planted."

13:14-15 Isa 6:9-10.

Story of the Wheat and Weeds

24Here is another story Jesus told: "The Kingdom of Heaven is like a farmer who planted good seed in his field. 25But that night as everyone slept, his enemy came and planted weeds among the wheat. 26When the crop began to grow and produce grain, the weeds also grew. 27The farmer's servants came and told him, 'Sir, the field where you planted that good seed is full of weeds!'

28"'An enemy has done it!' the farmer exclaimed.

"'Shall we pull out the weeds?' they asked.

29"He replied, 'No, you'll hurt the wheat if you do. 30Let both grow together until the harvest. Then I will tell the harvesters to sort out the weeds and burn them and to put the wheat in the barn.'"

Illustration of the Mustard Seed

31Here is another illustration Jesus used: "The Kingdom of Heaven is like a mustard seed planted in a field. 32It is the smallest of all seeds, but it becomes the largest of garden plants and grows into a tree where birds can come and find shelter in its branches."

Illustration of the Yeast

33Jesus also used this illustration: "The Kingdom of Heaven is like yeast used by a woman making bread. Even though she used a large amount* of flour, the yeast permeated every part of the dough."

34Jesus always used stories and illustrations like these when speaking to the crowds. In fact, he never spoke to them without using such parables. 35This fulfilled the prophecy that said,

"I will speak to you in parables.
 I will explain mysteries hidden since the creation of the
  world."*

The Wheat and Weeds Explained

36Then, leaving the crowds outside, Jesus went into the house. His disciples said, "Please explain the story of the weeds in the field."

37"All right," he said. "I, the Son of Man, am the farmer who plants the good seed. 38The field is the world, and the good seed represents the people of the Kingdom. The weeds are the people who belong to the evil one. 39The enemy who planted the weeds among the wheat is the Devil. The harvest is the end of the world, and the harvesters are the angels.

40"Just as the weeds are separated out and burned, so it will be at the end of the world. 41I, the Son of Man, will send my angels, and they will remove from my Kingdom everything that causes sin and all who do evil, 42and they will throw them into the furnace and burn them. There will be weeping and gnashing of teeth. 43Then the godly will shine like the sun in their Father's Kingdom. Anyone who is willing to hear should listen and understand!

Illustration of the Hidden Treasure

44"The Kingdom of Heaven is like a treasure that a man discovered hidden in a field. In his excitement, he hid it again and sold everything he owned to get enough money to buy the field—and to get the treasure, too!

13:33 Greek *3 measures.*   **13:35** Ps 78:2.

Illustration of the Pearl Merchant

45"Again, the Kingdom of Heaven is like a pearl merchant on the lookout for choice pearls. 46When he discovered a pearl of great value, he sold everything he owned and bought it!

Illustration of the Fishing Net

47"Again, the Kingdom of Heaven is like a fishing net that is thrown into the water and gathers fish of every kind. 48When the net is full, they drag it up onto the shore, sit down, sort the good fish into crates, and throw the bad ones away. 49That is the way it will be at the end of the world. The angels will come and separate the wicked people from the godly, 50throwing the wicked into the fire. There will be weeping and gnashing of teeth. 51Do you understand?"

"Yes," they said, "we do."

52Then he added, "Every teacher of religious law who has become a discile in the Kingdom of Heaven is like a person who brings out of the storehouse the new teachings as well as the old."

Jesus Rejected at Nazareth

53When Jesus had finished telling these stories, he left that part of the country. 54He returned to Nazareth, his hometown. When he taught there in the synagogue, everyone was astonished and said, "Where does he get his wisdom and his miracles? 55He's just a carpenter's son, and we know Mary, his mother, and his brothers—James, Joseph, Simon, and Judas. 56All his sisters live right here among us. What makes him so great?" 57And they were deeply offended and refused to believe in him.

Then Jesus told them, "A prophet is honored everywhere except in his own hometown and among his own family." 58And so he did only a few miracles there because of their unbelief.

CHAPTER 14

The Death of John the Baptist

When Herod Antipas* heard about Jesus, 2he said to his advisers, "This must be John the Baptist come back to life again! That is why he can do such miracles." 3For Herod had arrested and imprisoned John as a favor to his wife Herodias (the former wife of Herod's brother Philip). 4John kept telling Herod, "It is illegal for you to marry her." 5Herod would have executed John, but he was afraid of a riot, because all the people believed John was a prophet.

6But at a birthday party for Herod, Herodias's daughter performed a dance that greatly pleased him, 7so he promised with an oath to give her anything she wanted. 8At her mother's urging, the girl asked, "I want the head of John the Baptist on a tray!" 9The king was sorry, but because of his oath and because he didn't want to back down in front of his guests, he issued the necessary orders. 10So John was beheaded in the prison, 11and his head was brought on a tray and given to the girl, who took it to her mother. 12John's disciples came for his body and buried it. Then they told Jesus what had happened.

Jesus Feeds Five Thousand

13As soon as Jesus heard the news, he went off by himself in a boat to a remote area to be alone. But the crowds heard where he was

14:1 Greek *Herod the tetrarch.* He was a son of King Herod and was ruler over one of the four districts in Palestine.

headed and followed by land from many villages. ¹⁴A vast crowd was there as he stepped from the boat, and he had compassion on them and healed their sick.

¹⁵That evening the disciples came to him and said, "This is a desolate place, and it is getting late. Send the crowds away so they can go to the villages and buy food for themselves."

¹⁶But Jesus replied, "That isn't necessary—you feed them."

¹⁷"Impossible!" they exclaimed. "We have only five loaves of bread and two fish!"

¹⁸"Bring them here," he said. ¹⁹Then he told the people to sit down on the grass. And he took the five loaves and two fish, looked up toward heaven, and asked God's blessing on the food. Breaking the loaves into pieces, he gave some of the bread and fish to each disciple, and the disciples gave them to the people. ²⁰They all ate as much as they wanted, and they picked up twelve baskets of leftovers. ²¹About five thousand men had eaten from those five loaves, in addition to all the women and children!

Jesus Walks on Water

²²Immediately after this, Jesus made his disciples get back into the boat and cross to the other side of the lake while he sent the people home. ²³Afterward he went up into the hills by himself to pray. Night fell while he was there alone. ²⁴Meanwhile, the disciples were in trouble far away from land, for a strong wind had risen, and they were fighting heavy waves.

²⁵About three o'clock in the morning* Jesus came to them, walking on the water. ²⁶When the disciples saw him, they screamed in terror, thinking he was a ghost. ²⁷But Jesus spoke to them at once. "It's all right," he said. "I am here! Don't be afraid."

²⁸Then Peter called to him, "Lord, if it's really you, tell me to come to you by walking on water."

²⁹"All right, come," Jesus said.

So Peter went over the side of the boat and walked on the water toward Jesus. ³⁰But when he looked around at the high waves, he was terrified and began to sink. "Save me, Lord!" he shouted.

³¹Instantly Jesus reached out his hand and grabbed him. "You don't have much faith," Jesus said. "Why did you doubt me?" ³²And when they climbed back into the boat, the wind stopped.

³³Then the disciples worshiped him. "You really are the Son of God!" they exclaimed.

³⁴After they had crossed the lake, they landed at Gennesaret. ³⁵The news of their arrival spread quickly throughout the whole surrounding area, and soon people were bringing all their sick to be healed. ³⁶The sick begged him to let them touch even the fringe of his robe, and all who touched it were healed.

CHAPTER 15

Jesus Teaches about Inner Purity

Some Pharisees and teachers of religious law now arrived from Jerusalem to interview Jesus. ²"Why do your disciples disobey our age-old traditions?" they demanded. "They ignore our tradition of ceremonial hand washing before they eat."

14:25 Greek *In the fourth watch of the night.*

³Jesus replied, "And why do you, by your traditions, violate the direct commandments of God? ⁴For instance, God says, 'Honor your father and mother,' and 'Anyone who speaks evil of father or mother must be put to death.'* ⁵But you say, 'You don't need to honor your parents by caring for their needs if you give the money to God instead.' ⁶And so, by your own tradition, you nullify the direct commandment of God. ⁷You hypocrites! Isaiah was prophesying about you when he said,

⁸ 'These people honor me with their lips,
   but their hearts are far away.
⁹ Their worship is a farce,
   for they replace God's commands with their own
      man-made teachings.'* "

¹⁰Then Jesus called to the crowds and said, "Listen to what I say and try to understand. ¹¹You are not defiled by what you eat; you are defiled by what you say and do.* "

¹²Then the disciples came to him and asked, "Do you realize you offended the Pharisees by what you just said?"

¹³Jesus replied, "Every plant not planted by my heavenly Father will be rooted up, ¹⁴so ignore them. They are blind guides leading the blind, and if one blind person guides another, they will both fall into a ditch."

¹⁵Then Peter asked Jesus, "Explain what you meant when you said people aren't defiled by what they eat."

¹⁶"Don't you understand?" Jesus asked him. ¹⁷"Anything you eat passes through the stomach and then goes out of the body. ¹⁸But evil words come from an evil heart and defile the person who says them. ¹⁹For from the heart come evil thoughts, murder, adultery, all other sexual immorality, theft, lying, and slander. ²⁰These are what defile you. Eating with unwashed hands could never defile you and make you unacceptable to God!"

The Faith of a Gentile Woman

²¹Jesus then left Galilee and went north to the region of Tyre and Sidon. ²²A Gentile* woman who lived there came to him, pleading, "Have mercy on me, O Lord, Son of David! For my daughter has a demon in her, and it is severely tormenting her."

²³But Jesus gave her no reply—not even a word. Then his disciples urged him to send her away. "Tell her to leave," they said. "She is bothering us with all her begging."

²⁴Then he said to the woman, "I was sent only to help the people of Israel—God's lost sheep—not the Gentiles."

²⁵But she came and worshiped him and pleaded again, "Lord, help me!"

²⁶"It isn't right to take food from the children and throw it to the dogs," he said.

²⁷"Yes, Lord," she replied, "but even dogs are permitted to eat crumbs that fall beneath their master's table."

²⁸"Woman," Jesus said to her, "your faith is great. Your request is granted." And her daughter was instantly healed.

15:4 Exod 20:12; 21:17; Lev 20:9; Deut 5:16.   15:8-9 Isa 29:13.   15:11 Or *what comes out of the mouth defiles a person.*   15:22 Greek *Canaanite.*

Jesus Heals Many People

²⁹Jesus returned to the Sea of Galilee and climbed a hill and sat down. ³⁰A vast crowd brought him the lame, blind, crippled, mute, and many others with physical difficulties, and they laid them before Jesus. And he healed them all. ³¹The crowd was amazed! Those who hadn't been able to speak were talking, the crippled were made well, the lame were walking around, and those who had been blind could see again! And they praised the God of Israel.

Jesus Feeds Four Thousand

³²Then Jesus called his disciples to him and said, "I feel sorry for these people. They have been here with me for three days, and they have nothing left to eat. I don't want to send them away hungry, or they will faint along the road."

³³The disciples replied, "And where would we get enough food out here in the wilderness for all of them to eat?"

³⁴Jesus asked, "How many loaves of bread do you have?"

They replied, "Seven, and a few small fish." ³⁵So Jesus told all the people to sit down on the ground. ³⁶Then he took the seven loaves and the fish, thanked God for them, broke them into pieces, and gave them to the disciples, who distributed the food to the crowd.

³⁷They all ate until they were full, and when the scraps were picked up, there were seven large baskets of food left over! ³⁸There were four thousand men who were fed that day, in addition to all the women and children. ³⁹Then Jesus sent the people home, and he got into a boat and crossed over to the region of Magadan.

CHAPTER 16

Leaders Demand a Miraculous Sign

One day the Pharisees and Sadducees came to test Jesus' claims by asking him to show them a miraculous sign from heaven.

²He replied, "You know the saying, 'Red sky at night means fair weather tomorrow, ³red sky in the morning means foul weather all day.' You are good at reading the weather signs in the sky, but you can't read the obvious signs of the times!* ⁴Only an evil, faithless generation would ask for a miraculous sign, but the only sign I will give them is the sign of the prophet Jonah." Then Jesus left them and went away.

Yeast of the Pharisees and Sadducees

⁵Later, after they crossed to the other side of the lake, the disciples discovered they had forgotten to bring any food. ⁶"Watch out!" Jesus warned them. "Beware of the yeast of the Pharisees and Sadducees."

⁷They decided he was saying this because they hadn't brought any bread. ⁸Jesus knew what they were thinking, so he said, "You have so little faith! Why are you worried about having no food? ⁹Won't you ever understand? Don't you remember the five thousand I fed with five loaves, and the baskets of food that were left over? ¹⁰Don't you remember the four thousand I fed with seven loaves, with baskets of food left over? ¹¹How could you even think

---

16:2-3 Several manuscripts do not include any of the words in 16:2-3 after *He replied.*

I was talking about food? So again I say, 'Beware of the yeast of the Pharisees and Sadducees.'"

12Then at last they understood that he wasn't speaking about yeast or bread but about the false teaching of the Pharisees and Sadducees.

Peter's Declaration about Jesus

13When Jesus came to the region of Caesarea Philippi, he asked his disciples, "Who do people say that the Son of Man is?"

14"Well," they replied, "some say John the Baptist, some say Elijah, and others say Jeremiah or one of the other prophets."

15Then he asked them, "Who do you say I am?"

16Simon Peter answered, "You are the Messiah, the Son of the living God."

17Jesus replied, "You are blessed, Simon son of John,* because my Father in heaven has revealed this to you. You did not learn this from any human being. 18Now I say to you that you are Peter,* and upon this rock I will build my church, and all the powers of hell* will not conquer it. 19And I will give you the keys of the Kingdom of Heaven. Whatever you lock on earth will be locked in heaven, and whatever you open on earth will be opened in heaven."

20Then he sternly warned them not to tell anyone that he was the Messiah.

Jesus Predicts His Death

21From then on Jesus began to tell his disciples plainly that he had to go to Jerusalem, and he told them what would happen to him there. He would suffer at the hands of the leaders and the leading priests and the teachers of religious law. He would be killed, and he would be raised on the third day.

22But Peter took him aside and corrected him. "Heaven forbid, Lord," he said. "This will never happen to you!"

23Jesus turned to Peter and said, "Get away from me, Satan! You are a dangerous trap to me. You are seeing things merely from a human point of view, and not from God's."

24Then Jesus said to the disciples, "If any of you wants to be my follower, you must put aside your selfish ambition, shoulder your cross, and follow me. 25If you try to keep your life for yourself, you will lose it. But if you give up your life for me, you will find true life. 26And how do you benefit if you gain the whole world but lose your own soul* in the process? Is anything worth more than your soul? 27For I, the Son of Man, will come in the glory of my Father with his angels and will judge all people according to their deeds. 28And I assure you that some of you standing here right now will not die before you see me, the Son of Man, coming in my Kingdom."

CHAPTER 17

The Transfiguration

Six days later Jesus took Peter and the two brothers, James and John, and led them up a high mountain. 2As the men watched, Jesus' appearance changed so that his face shone like the sun, and his clothing became dazzling white. 3Suddenly, Moses and Elijah appeared and began talking with Jesus. 4Peter blurted out, "Lord,

16:17 Greek *Simon son of Jonah;* see John 1:42; 21:15-17.   16:18a *Peter* means "stone" or "rock."   16:18b Greek *and the gates of Hades.*   16:26 Or *your life.*

this is wonderful! If you want me to, I'll make three shrines,* one for you, one for Moses, and one for Elijah."

⁵But even as he said it, a bright cloud came over them, and a voice from the cloud said, "This is my beloved Son, and I am fully pleased with him. Listen to him." ⁶The disciples were terrified and fell face down on the ground.

⁷Jesus came over and touched them. "Get up," he said, "don't be afraid." ⁸And when they looked, they saw only Jesus with them. ⁹As they descended the mountain, Jesus commanded them, "Don't tell anyone what you have seen until I, the Son of Man, have been raised from the dead."

¹⁰His disciples asked, "Why do the teachers of religious law insist that Elijah must return before the Messiah comes*?"

¹¹Jesus replied, "Elijah is indeed coming first to set everything in order. ¹²But I tell you, he has already come, but he wasn't recognized, and he was badly mistreated. And soon the Son of Man will also suffer at their hands." ¹³Then the disciples realized he had been speaking of John the Baptist.

Jesus Heals a Demon-Possessed Boy

¹⁴When they arrived at the foot of the mountain, a huge crowd was waiting for them. A man came and knelt before Jesus and said, ¹⁵"Lord, have mercy on my son, because he has seizures and suffers terribly. He often falls into the fire or into the water. ¹⁶So I brought him to your disciples, but they couldn't heal him."

¹⁷Jesus replied, "You stubborn, faithless people! How long must I be with you until you believe? How long must I put up with you? Bring the boy to me." ¹⁸Then Jesus rebuked the demon in the boy, and it left him. From that moment the boy was well.

¹⁹Afterward the disciples asked Jesus privately, "Why couldn't we cast out that demon?"

²⁰"You didn't have enough faith," Jesus told them. "I assure you, even if you had faith as small as a mustard seed you could say to this mountain, 'Move from here to there,' and it would move. Nothing would be impossible."*

Jesus Again Predicts His Death

²²One day after they had returned to Galilee, Jesus told them, "The Son of Man is going to be betrayed. ²³He will be killed, but three days later he will be raised from the dead." And the disciples' hearts were filled with grief.

Payment of the Temple Tax

²⁴On their arrival in Capernaum, the tax collectors for the Temple tax came to Peter and asked him, "Doesn't your teacher pay the Temple tax?"

²⁵"Of course he does," Peter replied. Then he went into the house to talk to Jesus about it.

But before he had a chance to speak, Jesus asked him, "What do you think, Peter*? Do kings tax their own people or the foreigners they have conquered?"

17:4 Or *shelters*; Greek reads *tabernacles.*   17:10 Greek *that Elijah must come first.*
17:20 Some manuscripts add verse 21, *But this kind of demon won't leave unless you have prayed and fasted.*   17:25 Greek *Simon.*

²⁶"They tax the foreigners," Peter replied.

"Well, then," Jesus said, "the citizens are free! ²⁷However, we don't want to offend them, so go down to the lake and throw in a line. Open the mouth of the first fish you catch, and you will find a coin. Take the coin and pay the tax for both of us."

CHAPTER 18

The Greatest in the Kingdom

About that time the disciples came to Jesus and asked, "Which of us is greatest in the Kingdom of Heaven?"

²Jesus called a small child over to him and put the child among them. ³Then he said, "I assure you, unless you turn from your sins and become as little children, you will never get into the Kingdom of Heaven. ⁴Therefore, anyone who becomes as humble as this little child is the greatest in the Kingdom of Heaven. ⁵And anyone who welcomes a little child like this on my behalf is welcoming me. ⁶But if anyone causes one of these little ones who trusts in me to lose faith, it would be better for that person to be thrown into the sea with a large millstone tied around the neck.

⁷"How terrible it will be for anyone who causes others to sin. Temptation to do wrong is inevitable, but how terrible it will be for the person who does the tempting. ⁸So if your hand or foot causes you to sin, cut it off and throw it away. It is better to enter heaven* crippled or lame than to be thrown into the unquenchable fire with both of your hands and feet. ⁹And if your eye causes you to sin, gouge it out and throw it away. It is better to enter heaven half blind than to have two eyes and be thrown into hell.

¹⁰"Beware that you don't despise a single one of these little ones. For I tell you that in heaven their angels are always in the presence of my heavenly Father.*

Story of the Lost Sheep

¹²"If a shepherd has one hundred sheep, and one wanders away and is lost, what will he do? Won't he leave the ninety-nine others and go out into the hills to search for the lost one? ¹³And if he finds it, he will surely rejoice over it more than over the ninety-nine that didn't wander away! ¹⁴In the same way, it is not my heavenly Father's will that even one of these little ones should perish.

Correcting a Fellow Believer

¹⁵"If another believer* sins against you, go privately and point out the fault. If the other person listens and confesses it, you have won that person back. ¹⁶But if you are unsuccessful, take one or two others with you and go back again, so that everything you say may be confirmed by two or three witnesses. ¹⁷If that person still refuses to listen, take your case to the church. If the church decides you are right, but the other person won't accept it, treat that person as a pagan or a corrupt tax collector. ¹⁸I tell you this: Whatever you prohibit on earth is prohibited in heaven, and whatever you allow on earth is allowed in heaven.

¹⁹"I also tell you this: If two of you agree down here on earth concerning anything you ask, my Father in heaven will do it for

18:8 Greek *enter life;* also in 18:9.   **18:10** Some manuscripts add verse 11, *And I, the Son of Man, have come to save the lost.*   **18:15** Greek *your brother.*

you. ²⁰For where two or three gather together because they are mine,* I am there among them."

Story of the Unforgiving Debtor

²¹Then Peter came to him and asked, "Lord, how often should I forgive someone* who sins against me? Seven times?"

²²"No!" Jesus replied, "seventy times seven!*

²³"For this reason, the Kingdom of Heaven can be compared to a king who decided to bring his accounts up to date with servants who had borrowed money from him. ²⁴In the process, one of his debtors was brought in who owed him millions of dollars.* ²⁵He couldn't pay, so the king ordered that he, his wife, his children, and everything he had be sold to pay the debt. ²⁶But the man fell down before the king and begged him, 'Oh, sir, be patient with me, and I will pay it all.' ²⁷Then the king was filled with pity for him, and he released him and forgave his debt.

²⁸"But when the man left the king, he went to a fellow servant who owed him a few thousand dollars.* He grabbed him by the throat and demanded instant payment. ²⁹His fellow servant fell down before him and begged for a little more time. 'Be patient and I will pay it,' he pleaded. ³⁰But his creditor wouldn't wait. He had the man arrested and jailed until the debt could be paid in full.

³¹"When some of the other servants saw this, they were very upset. They went to the king and told him what had happened. ³²Then the king called in the man he had forgiven and said, 'You evil servant! I forgave you that tremendous debt because you pleaded with me. ³³Shouldn't you have mercy on your fellow servant, just as I had mercy on you?' ³⁴Then the angry king sent the man to prison until he had paid every penny.

³⁵"That's what my heavenly Father will do to you if you refuse to forgive your brothers and sisters* in your heart."

CHAPTER 19

Discussion about Divorce and Marriage

After Jesus had finished saying these things, he left Galilee and went southward to the region of Judea and into the area east of the Jordan River. ²Vast crowds followed him there, and he healed their sick.

³Some Pharisees came and tried to trap him with this question: "Should a man be allowed to divorce his wife for any reason?"

⁴"Haven't you read the Scriptures?" Jesus replied. "They record that from the beginning 'God made them male and female.'* ⁵And he said, 'This explains why a man leaves his father and mother and is joined to his wife, and the two are united into one.'* ⁶Since they are no longer two but one, let no one separate them, for God has joined them together."

⁷"Then why did Moses say a man could merely write an official letter of divorce and send her away?"* they asked.

⁸Jesus replied, "Moses permitted divorce as a concession to your hard-hearted wickedness, but it was not what God had originally intended. ⁹And I tell you this, a man who divorces his wife and

---

18:20 Greek *gather together in my name.*   **18:21** Greek *my brother.*   **18:22** Or *77 times.*
18:24 Greek *10,000 talents.*   **18:28** Greek *100 denarii.* A denarius was the equivalent of a full day's wage.   **18:35** Greek *your brother.*   **19:4** Gen 1:27; 5:2.   **19:5** Gen 2:24.
19:7 Deut 24:1.

marries another commits adultery—unless his wife has been unfaithful.*"

¹⁰Jesus' disciples then said to him, "Then it is better not to marry!"

¹¹"Not everyone can accept this statement," Jesus said. "Only those whom God helps. ¹²Some are born as eunuchs, some have been made that way by others, and some choose not to marry for the sake of the Kingdom of Heaven. Let anyone who can, accept this statement."

Jesus Blesses the Children

¹³Some children were brought to Jesus so he could lay his hands on them and pray for them. The disciples told them not to bother him. ¹⁴But Jesus said, "Let the children come to me. Don't stop them! For the Kingdom of Heaven belongs to such as these." ¹⁵And he put his hands on their heads and blessed them before he left.

The Rich Young Man

¹⁶Someone came to Jesus with this question: "Teacher,* what good things must I do to have eternal life?"

¹⁷"Why ask me about what is good?" Jesus replied. "Only God is good. But to answer your question, you can receive eternal life if you keep the commandments."

¹⁸"Which ones?" the man asked.

And Jesus replied: " 'Do not murder. Do not commit adultery. Do not steal. Do not testify falsely. ¹⁹Honor your father and mother. Love your neighbor as yourself.'*"

²⁰"I've obeyed all these commandments," the young man replied. "What else must I do?"

²¹Jesus told him, "If you want to be perfect, go and sell all you have and give the money to the poor, and you will have treasure in heaven. Then come, follow me." ²²But when the young man heard this, he went sadly away because he had many possessions.

²³Then Jesus said to his disciples, "I tell you the truth, it is very hard for a rich person to get into the Kingdom of Heaven. ²⁴I say it again—it is easier for a camel to go through the eye of a needle than for a rich person to enter the Kingdom of God!"

²⁵The disciples were astounded. "Then who in the world can be saved?" they asked.

²⁶Jesus looked at them intently and said, "Humanly speaking, it is impossible. But with God everything is possible."

²⁷Then Peter said to him, "We've given up everything to follow you. What will we get out of it?"

²⁸And Jesus replied, "I assure you that when I, the Son of Man, sit upon my glorious throne in the Kingdom,* you who have been my followers will also sit on twelve thrones, judging the twelve tribes of Israel. ²⁹And everyone who has given up houses or brothers or sisters or father or mother or children or property, for my sake, will receive a hundred times as much in return and will have eternal life. ³⁰But many who seem to be important now will

19:9 Some manuscripts add *And the man who marries a divorced woman commits adultery.*
19:16 Some manuscripts read *Good Teacher.*   19:18-19 Exod 20:12-16; Lev 19:18; Deut 5:16-20.   19:28 Greek *in the regeneration.*

be the least important then, and those who are considered least here will be the greatest then.*

CHAPTER 20

Story of the Vineyard Workers

"For the Kingdom of Heaven is like the owner of an estate who went out early one morning to hire workers for his vineyard. ²He agreed to pay the normal daily wage* and sent them out to work.

³"At nine o'clock in the morning he was passing through the marketplace and saw some people standing around doing nothing. ⁴So he hired them, telling them he would pay them whatever was right at the end of the day. ⁵At noon and again around three o'clock he did the same thing. ⁶At five o'clock that evening he was in town again and saw some more people standing around. He asked them, 'Why haven't you been working today?'

⁷"They replied, 'Because no one hired us.'

"The owner of the estate told them, 'Then go on out and join the others in my vineyard.'

⁸"That evening he told the foreman to call the workers in and pay them, beginning with the last workers first. ⁹When those hired at five o'clock were paid, each received a full day's wage. ¹⁰When those hired earlier came to get their pay, they assumed they would receive more. But they, too, were paid a day's wage. ¹¹When they received their pay, they protested, ¹²'Those people worked only one hour, and yet you've paid them just as much as you paid us who worked all day in the scorching heat.'

¹³"He answered one of them, 'Friend, I haven't been unfair! Didn't you agree to work all day for the usual wage? ¹⁴Take it and go. I wanted to pay this last worker the same as you. ¹⁵Is it against the law for me to do what I want with my money? Should you be angry because I am kind?'

¹⁶"And so it is, that many who are first now will be last then; and those who are last now will be first then."

Jesus Again Predicts His Death

¹⁷As Jesus was on the way to Jerusalem, he took the twelve disciples aside privately and told them what was going to happen to him. ¹⁸"When we get to Jerusalem," he said, "the Son of Man will be betrayed to the leading priests and the teachers of religious law. They will sentence him to die. ¹⁹Then they will hand him over to the Romans to be mocked, whipped, and crucified. But on the third day he will be raised from the dead."

Jesus Teaches about Serving Others

²⁰Then the mother of James and John, the sons of Zebedee, came to Jesus with her sons. She knelt respectfully to ask a favor. ²¹"What is your request?" he asked.

She replied, "In your Kingdom, will you let my two sons sit in places of honor next to you, one at your right and the other at your left?"

²²But Jesus told them, "You don't know what you are asking! Are you able to drink from the bitter cup of sorrow I am about to drink?"

19:30 Greek *But many who are first will be last; and the last, first.*   **20:2** Greek *a denarius,* the payment for a full day's labor; also in 20:9, 10, 13.

"Oh yes," they replied, "we are able!"

²³"You will indeed drink from it," he told them. "But I have no right to say who will sit on the thrones next to mine. My Father has prepared those places for the ones he has chosen."

²⁴When the ten other disciples heard what James and John had asked, they were indignant. ²⁵But Jesus called them together and said, "You know that in this world kings are tyrants, and officials lord it over the people beneath them. ²⁶But among you it should be quite different. Whoever wants to be a leader among you must be your servant, ²⁷and whoever wants to be first must become your slave. ²⁸For even I, the Son of Man, came here not to be served but to serve others, and to give my life as a ransom for many."

Jesus Heals Two Blind Men

²⁹As Jesus and the disciples left the city of Jericho, a huge crowd followed behind. ³⁰Two blind men were sitting beside the road. When they heard that Jesus was coming that way, they began shouting, "Lord, Son of David, have mercy on us!" ³¹The crowd told them to be quiet, but they only shouted louder, "Lord, Son of David, have mercy on us!"

³²Jesus stopped in the road and called, "What do you want me to do for you?"

³³"Lord," they said, "we want to see!" ³⁴Jesus felt sorry for them and touched their eyes. Instantly they could see! Then they followed him.

CHAPTER 21
The Triumphal Entry

As Jesus and the disciples approached Jerusalem, they came to the town of Bethphage on the Mount of Olives. Jesus sent two of them on ahead. ²"Go into the village over there," he said, "and you will see a donkey tied there, with its colt beside it. Untie them and bring them here. ³If anyone asks what you are doing, just say, 'The Lord needs them,' and he will immediately send them." ⁴This was done to fulfill the prophecy,

5 "Tell the people of Israel,*
    'Look, your King is coming to you.
   He is humble, riding on a donkey—
       even on a donkey's colt.' "*

⁶The two disciples did as Jesus said. ⁷They brought the animals to him and threw their garments over the colt, and he sat on it.*

⁸Most of the crowd spread their coats on the road ahead of Jesus, and others cut branches from the trees and spread them on the road. ⁹He was in the center of the procession, and the crowds all around him were shouting,

   "Praise God* for the Son of David!
   Bless the one who comes in the name of the Lord!
   Praise God in highest heaven!"*

21:5a Greek *Tell the daughter of Zion.* Isa 62:11.   21:5b Zech 9:9.   21:7 Greek *over them, and he sat on them.*   21:9a Greek *Hosanna,* an exclamation of praise that literally means "save now"; also in 21:9b, 15.   21:9b Pss 118:25-26; 148:1.

¹⁰The entire city of Jerusalem was stirred as he entered. "Who is this?" they asked.

¹¹And the crowds replied, "It's Jesus, the prophet from Nazareth in Galilee."

Jesus Clears the Temple

¹²Jesus entered the Temple and began to drive out the merchants and their customers. He knocked over the tables of the money changers and the stalls of those selling doves. ¹³He said, "The Scriptures declare, 'My Temple will be called a place of prayer,' but you have turned it into a den of thieves!"*

¹⁴The blind and the lame came to him, and he healed them there in the Temple. ¹⁵The leading priests and the teachers of religious law saw these wonderful miracles and heard even the little children in the Temple shouting, "Praise God for the Son of David." But they were indignant ¹⁶and asked Jesus, "Do you hear what these children are saying?"

"Yes," Jesus replied. "Haven't you ever read the Scriptures? For they say, 'You have taught children and infants to give you praise.'*" ¹⁷Then he returned to Bethany, where he stayed overnight.

Jesus Curses the Fig Tree

¹⁸In the morning, as Jesus was returning to Jerusalem, he was hungry, ¹⁹and he noticed a fig tree beside the road. He went over to see if there were any figs on it, but there were only leaves. Then he said to it, "May you never bear fruit again!" And immediately the fig tree withered up.

²⁰The disciples were amazed when they saw this and asked, "How did the fig tree wither so quickly?"

²¹Then Jesus told them, "I assure you, if you have faith and don't doubt, you can do things like this and much more. You can even say to this mountain, 'May God lift you up and throw you into the sea,' and it will happen. ²²If you believe, you will receive whatever you ask for in prayer."

The Authority of Jesus Challenged

²³When Jesus returned to the Temple and began teaching, the leading priests and other leaders came up to him. They demanded, "By whose authority did you drive out the merchants from the Temple?* Who gave you such authority?"

²⁴"I'll tell you who gave me the authority to do these things if you answer one question," Jesus replied. ²⁵"Did John's baptism come from heaven or was it merely human?"

They talked it over among themselves. "If we say it was from heaven, he will ask why we didn't believe him. ²⁶But if we say it was merely human, we'll be mobbed, because the people think he was a prophet." ²⁷So they finally replied, "We don't know."

And Jesus responded, "Then I won't answer your question either.

Story of the Two Sons

²⁸"But what do you think about this? A man with two sons told the older boy, 'Son, go out and work in the vineyard today.' ²⁹The son answered, 'No, I won't go,' but later he changed his mind and

21:13 Isa 56:7; Jer 7:11.   **21:16** Ps 8:2.   **21:23** Or *By whose authority do you do these things?*

went anyway. ³⁰Then the father told the other son, 'You go,' and he said, 'Yes, sir, I will.' But he didn't go. ³¹Which of the two was obeying his father?"

They replied, "The first, of course."

Then Jesus explained his meaning: "I assure you, corrupt tax collectors and prostitutes will get into the Kingdom of God before you do. ³²For John the Baptist came and showed you the way to life, and you didn't believe him, while tax collectors and prostitutes did. And even when you saw this happening, you refused to turn from your sins and believe him.

Story of the Evil Farmers

³³"Now listen to this story. A certain landowner planted a vineyard, built a wall around it, dug a pit for pressing out the grape juice, and built a lookout tower. Then he leased the vineyard to tenant farmers and moved to another country. ³⁴At the time of the grape harvest he sent his servants to collect his share of the crop. ³⁵But the farmers grabbed his servants, beat one, killed one, and stoned another. ³⁶So the landowner sent a larger group of his servants to collect for him, but the results were the same.

³⁷"Finally, the owner sent his son, thinking, 'Surely they will respect my son.'

³⁸"But when the farmers saw his son coming, they said to one another, 'Here comes the heir to this estate. Come on, let's kill him and get the estate for ourselves!' ³⁹So they grabbed him, took him out of the vineyard, and murdered him.

⁴⁰"When the owner of the vineyard returns," Jesus asked, "what do you think he will do to those farmers?"

⁴¹The religious leaders replied, "He will put the wicked men to a horrible death and lease the vineyard to others who will give him his share of the crop after each harvest."

⁴²Then Jesus asked them, "Didn't you ever read this in the Scriptures?

'The stone rejected by the builders
   has now become the cornerstone.
This is the Lord's doing,
   and it is marvelous to see.'*

⁴³What I mean is that the Kingdom of God will be taken away from you and given to a nation that will produce the proper fruit. ⁴⁴Anyone who stumbles over that stone will be broken to pieces, and it will crush anyone on whom it falls.*"

⁴⁵When the leading priests and Pharisees heard Jesus, they realized he was pointing at them—that they were the farmers in his story. ⁴⁶They wanted to arrest him, but they were afraid to try because the crowds considered Jesus to be a prophet.

CHAPTER 22

Story of the Great Feast

Jesus told them several other stories to illustrate the Kingdom. He said, ²"The Kingdom of Heaven can be illustrated by the story of a king who prepared a great wedding feast for his son. ³Many guests were invited, and when the banquet was ready, he sent his

21:42 Ps 118:22-23.   21:44 This verse is omitted in some early manuscripts.

servants to notify everyone that it was time to come. But they all refused! 4So he sent other servants to tell them, 'The feast has been prepared, and choice meats have been cooked. Everything is ready. Hurry!' 5But the guests he had invited ignored them and went about their business, one to his farm, another to his store. 6Others seized his messengers and treated them shamefully, even killing some of them.

7"Then the king became furious. He sent out his army to destroy the murderers and burn their city. 8And he said to his servants, 'The wedding feast is ready, and the guests I invited aren't worthy of the honor. 9Now go out to the street corners and invite everyone you see.'

10"So the servants brought in everyone they could find, good and bad alike, and the banquet hall was filled with guests. 11But when the king came in to meet the guests, he noticed a man who wasn't wearing the proper clothes for a wedding. 12'Friend,' he asked, 'how is it that you are here without wedding clothes?' And the man had no reply. 13Then the king said to his aides, 'Bind him hand and foot and throw him out into the outer darkness, where there is weeping and gnashing of teeth.' 14For many are called, but few are chosen."

Taxes for Caesar

15Then the Pharisees met together to think of a way to trap Jesus into saying something for which they could accuse him. 16They decided to send some of their disciples, along with the supporters of Herod, to ask him this question: "Teacher, we know how honest you are. You teach about the way of God regardless of the consequences. You are impartial and don't play favorites. 17Now tell us what you think about this: Is it right to pay taxes to the Roman government or not?"

18But Jesus knew their evil motives. "You hypocrites!" he said. "Whom are you trying to fool with your trick questions? 19Here, show me the Roman coin used for the tax." When they handed him the coin,* 20he asked, "Whose picture and title are stamped on it?"

21"Caesar's," they replied.

"Well, then," he said, "give to Caesar what belongs to him. But everything that belongs to God must be given to God." 22His reply amazed them, and they went away.

Discussion about Resurrection

23That same day some Sadducees stepped forward—a group of Jews who say there is no resurrection after death. They posed this question: 24"Teacher, Moses said, 'If a man dies without children, his brother should marry the widow and have a child who will be the brother's heir.'* 25Well, there were seven brothers. The oldest married and then died without children, so the second brother married the widow. 26This brother also died without children, and the wife was married to the next brother, and so on until she had been the wife of each of them. 27And then she also died. 28So tell us, whose wife will she be in the resurrection? For she was the wife of all seven of them!"

29Jesus replied, "Your problem is that you don't know the Scriptures, and you don't know the power of God. 30For when the

22:19 Greek *a denarius.*   22:24 Deut 25:5-6.

dead rise, they won't be married. They will be like the angels in heaven. ³¹But now, as to whether there will be a resurrection of the dead—haven't you ever read about this in the Scriptures? Long after Abraham, Isaac, and Jacob had died, God said,* ³²'I am the God of Abraham, the God of Isaac, and the God of Jacob.'* So he is the God of the living, not the dead."

³³When the crowds heard him, they were impressed with his teaching.

The Most Important Commandment

³⁴But when the Pharisees heard that he had silenced the Sadducees with his reply, they thought up a fresh question of their own to ask him. ³⁵One of them, an expert in religious law, tried to trap him with this question: ³⁶"Teacher, which is the most important commandment in the law of Moses?"

³⁷Jesus replied, " 'You must love the Lord your God with all your heart, all your soul, and all your mind.'* ³⁸This is the first and greatest commandment. ³⁹A second is equally important: 'Love your neighbor as yourself.'* ⁴⁰All the other commandments and all the demands of the prophets are based on these two commandments."

Whose Son Is the Messiah?

⁴¹Then, surrounded by the Pharisees, Jesus asked them a question: ⁴²"What do you think about the Messiah? Whose son is he?"

They replied, "He is the son of David."

⁴³Jesus responded, "Then why does David, speaking under the inspiration of the Holy Spirit, call him Lord? For David said,

⁴⁴ 'The LORD said to my Lord,

Sit in honor at my right hand

until I humble your enemies beneath your feet.'*

⁴⁵Since David called him Lord, how can he be his son at the same time?"

⁴⁶No one could answer him. And after that, no one dared to ask him any more questions.

CHAPTER 23

Jesus Warns the Religious Leaders

Then Jesus said to the crowds and to his disciples, ²"The teachers of religious law and the Pharisees are the official interpreters of the Scriptures. ³So practice and obey whatever they say to you, but don't follow their example. For they don't practice what they teach. ⁴They crush you with impossible religious demands and never lift a finger to help ease the burden.

⁵ "Everything they do is for show. On their arms they wear extra wide prayer boxes with Scripture verses inside,* and they wear extra long tassels on their robes. ⁶And how they love to sit at the head table at banquets and in the most prominent seats in the synagogue! ⁷They enjoy the attention they get on the streets, and they enjoy being called 'Rabbi.'* ⁸Don't ever let anyone call you 'Rabbi,' for you have only one teacher, and all of you are on the same level as brothers and sisters.* ⁹And don't address anyone here

---

22:31 Greek *in the Scriptures? God said.* 22:32 Exod 3:6. 22:37 Deut 6:5. 22:39 Lev 19:18. 22:44 Ps 110:1. 23:5 Greek *They enlarge their phylacteries.* 23:7 *Rabbi,* from Aramaic, means "master" or "teacher." 23:8 Greek *brothers.*

on earth as 'Father,' for only God in heaven is your spiritual Father. [10]And don't let anyone call you 'Master,' for there is only one master, the Messiah. [11]The greatest among you must be a servant. [12]But those who exalt themselves will be humbled, and those who humble themselves will be exalted.

[13]"How terrible it will be for you teachers of religious law and you Pharisees. Hypocrites! For you won't let others enter the Kingdom of Heaven, and you won't go in yourselves.* [15]Yes, how terrible it will be for you teachers of religious law and you Pharisees. For you cross land and sea to make one convert, and then you turn him into twice the son of hell as you yourselves are.

[16]"Blind guides! How terrible it will be for you! For you say that it means nothing to swear 'by God's Temple'—you can break that oath. But then you say that it is binding to swear 'by the gold in the Temple.' [17]Blind fools! Which is greater, the gold, or the Temple that makes the gold sacred? [18]And you say that to take an oath 'by the altar' can be broken, but to swear 'by the gifts on the altar' is binding? [19]How blind! For which is greater, the gift on the altar, or the altar that makes the gift sacred? [20]When you swear 'by the altar,' you are swearing by it and by everything on it. [21]And when you swear 'by the Temple,' you are swearing by it and by God, who lives in it. [22]And when you swear 'by heaven,' you are swearing by the throne of God and by God, who sits on the throne.

[23]"How terrible it will be for you teachers of religious law and you Pharisees. Hypocrites! For you are careful to tithe even the tiniest part of your income,* but you ignore the important things of the law—justice, mercy, and faith. You should tithe, yes, but you should not leave undone the more important things. [24]Blind guides! You strain your water so you won't accidentally swallow a gnat; then you swallow a camel!

[25]"How terrible it will be for you teachers of religious law and you Pharisees. Hypocrites! You are so careful to clean the outside of the cup and the dish, but inside you are filthy—full of greed and self-indulgence! [26]Blind Pharisees! First wash the inside of the cup, and then the outside will become clean, too.

[27]"How terrible it will be for you teachers of religious law and you Pharisees. Hypocrites! You are like whitewashed tombs—beautiful on the outside but filled on the inside with dead people's bones and all sorts of impurity. [28]You try to look like upright people outwardly, but inside your hearts are filled with hypocrisy and lawlessness.

[29]"How terrible it will be for you teachers of religious law and you Pharisees. Hypocrites! For you build tombs for the prophets your ancestors killed and decorate the graves of the godly people your ancestors destroyed. [30]Then you say, 'We never would have joined them in killing the prophets.'

[31]"In saying that, you are accusing yourselves of being the descendants of those who murdered the prophets. [32]Go ahead. Finish what they started. [33]Snakes! Sons of vipers! How will you escape the judgment of hell? [34]I will send you prophets and wise

23:13 Some manuscripts add verse 14, *How terrible it will be for you teachers of religious law and you Pharisees. Hypocrites! You shamelessly cheat widows out of their property, and then, to cover up the kind of people you really are, you make long prayers in public. Because of this, your punishment will be the greater.*   23:23 Greek *to tithe the mint, the dill, and the cumin.*

men and teachers of religious law. You will kill some by crucifixion and whip others in your synagogues, chasing them from city to city. ³⁵As a result, you will become guilty of murdering all the godly people from righteous Abel to Zechariah son of Barachiah, whom you murdered in the Temple between the altar and the sanctuary. ³⁶I assure you, all the accumulated judgment of the centuries will break upon the heads of this very generation.

Jesus Grieves over Jerusalem

³⁷"O Jerusalem, Jerusalem, the city that kills the prophets and stones God's messengers! How often I have wanted to gather your children together as a hen protects her chicks beneath her wings, but you wouldn't let me. ³⁸And now look, your house is left to you, empty and desolate. ³⁹For I tell you this, you will never see me again until you say, 'Bless the one who comes in the name of the Lord!'*"

CHAPTER 24

Jesus Foretells the Future

As Jesus was leaving the Temple grounds, his disciples pointed out to him the various Temple buildings. ²But he told them, "Do you see all these buildings? I assure you, they will be so completely demolished that not one stone will be left on top of another!"

³Later, Jesus sat on the slopes of the Mount of Olives. His disciples came to him privately and asked, "When will all this take place? And will there be any sign ahead of time to signal your return and the end of the world*?"

⁴Jesus told them, "Don't let anyone mislead you. ⁵For many will come in my name, saying, 'I am the Messiah.' They will lead many astray. ⁶And wars will break out near and far, but don't panic. Yes, these things must come, but the end won't follow immediately. ⁷The nations and kingdoms will proclaim war against each other, and there will be famines and earthquakes in many parts of the world. ⁸But all this will be only the beginning of the horrors to come.

⁹"Then you will be arrested, persecuted, and killed. You will be hated all over the world because of your allegiance to me. ¹⁰And many will turn away from me and betray and hate each other. ¹¹And many false prophets will appear and will lead many people astray. ¹²Sin will be rampant everywhere, and the love of many will grow cold. ¹³But those who endure to the end will be saved. ¹⁴And the Good News about the Kingdom will be preached throughout the whole world, so that all nations will hear it; and then, finally, the end will come.

¹⁵"The time will come when you will see what Daniel the prophet spoke about: the sacrilegious object that causes desecration* standing in the Holy Place"—reader, pay attention! ¹⁶"Then those in Judea must flee to the hills. ¹⁷A person outside the house* must not go inside to pack. ¹⁸A person in the field must not return even to get a coat. ¹⁹How terrible it will be for pregnant women and for mothers nursing their babies in those days. ²⁰And pray that your flight will not be in winter or on the Sabbath. ²¹For that will

23:39 Ps 118:26.   24:3 Or *the age.*   24:15 Greek *the abomination of desolation.* See Dan 9:27; 11:31; 12:11.   24:17 Greek *on the roof.*

be a time of greater horror than anything the world has ever seen or will ever see again. ²²In fact, unless that time of calamity is shortened, the entire human race will be destroyed. But it will be shortened for the sake of God's chosen ones.

²³"Then if anyone tells you, 'Look, here is the Messiah,' or 'There he is,' don't pay any attention. ²⁴For false messiahs and false prophets will rise up and perform great miraculous signs and wonders so as to deceive, if possible, even God's chosen ones. ²⁵See, I have warned you.

²⁶"So if someone tells you, 'Look, the Messiah is out in the desert,' don't bother to go and look. Or, 'Look, he is hiding here,' don't believe it! ²⁷For as the lightning lights up the entire sky, so it will be when the Son of Man comes. ²⁸Just as the gathering of vultures shows there is a carcass nearby, so these signs indicate that the end is near.*

²⁹"Immediately after those horrible days end,

the sun will be darkened,
    the moon will not give light,
the stars will fall from the sky,
    and the powers of heaven will be shaken.*

³⁰And then at last, the sign of the coming of the Son of Man will appear in the heavens, and there will be deep mourning among all the nations of the earth. And they will see the Son of Man arrive on the clouds of heaven with power and great glory.* ³¹And he will send forth his angels with the sound of a mighty trumpet blast, and they will gather together his chosen ones from the farthest ends of the earth and heaven.

³²"Now learn a lesson from the fig tree. When its buds become tender and its leaves begin to sprout, you know without being told that summer is near. ³³Just so, when you see the events I've described beginning to happen, you can know his return is very near, right at the door. ³⁴I assure you, this generation* will not pass from the scene before all these things take place. ³⁵Heaven and earth will disappear, but my words will remain forever.

³⁶"However, no one knows the day or the hour when these things will happen, not even the angels in heaven or the Son himself.* Only the Father knows.

³⁷"When the Son of Man returns, it will be like it was in Noah's day. ³⁸In those days before the Flood, the people were enjoying banquets and parties and weddings right up to the time Noah entered his boat. ³⁹People didn't realize what was going to happen until the Flood came and swept them all away. That is the way it will be when the Son of Man comes.

⁴⁰"Two men will be working together in the field; one will be taken, the other left. ⁴¹Two women will be grinding flour at the mill; one will be taken, the other left. ⁴²So be prepared, because you don't know what day your Lord is coming.

⁴³"Know this: A homeowner who knew exactly when a burglar was coming would stay alert and not permit the house to be

24:28 Greek *Wherever the carcass is, the vultures gather.*   **24:29** See Isa 13:10; 34:4; Joel 2:10.   **24:30** See Dan 7:13.   **24:34** Or *this age,* or *this nation.*   **24:36** Some manuscripts omit the phrase *or the Son himself.*

broken into. 44You also must be ready all the time. For the Son of Man will come when least expected.

45"Who is a faithful, sensible servant, to whom the master can give the responsibility of managing his household and feeding his family? 46If the master returns and finds that the servant has done a good job, there will be a reward. 47I assure you, the master will put that servant in charge of all he owns. 48But if the servant is evil and thinks, 'My master won't be back for a while,' 49and begins oppressing the other servants, partying, and getting drunk—50well, the master will return unannounced and unexpected. 51He will tear the servant apart and banish him with the hypocrites. In that place there will be weeping and gnashing of teeth.

CHAPTER 25

Story of the Ten Bridesmaids

"The Kingdom of Heaven can be illustrated by the story of ten bridesmaids* who took their lamps and went to meet the bridegroom. 2Five of them were foolish, and five were wise. 3The five who were foolish took no oil for their lamps, 4but the other five were wise enough to take along extra oil. 5When the bridegroom was delayed, they all lay down and slept. 6At midnight they were roused by the shout, 'Look, the bridegroom is coming! Come out and welcome him!'

7"All the bridesmaids got up and prepared their lamps. 8Then the five foolish ones asked the others, 'Please give us some of your oil because our lamps are going out.' 9But the others replied, 'We don't have enough for all of us. Go to a shop and buy some for yourselves.'

10"But while they were gone to buy oil, the bridegroom came, and those who were ready went in with him to the marriage feast, and the door was locked. 11Later, when the other five bridesmaids returned, they stood outside, calling, 'Sir, open the door for us!' 12But he called back, 'I don't know you!'

13"So stay awake and be prepared, because you do not know the day or hour of my return.

Story of the Three Servants

14"Again, the Kingdom of Heaven can be illustrated by the story of a man going on a trip. He called together his servants and gave them money to invest for him while he was gone. 15He gave five bags of gold* to one, two bags of gold to another, and one bag of gold to the last—dividing it in proportion to their abilities—and then left on his trip. 16The servant who received the five bags of gold began immediately to invest the money and soon doubled it. 17The servant with two bags of gold also went right to work and doubled the money. 18But the servant who received the one bag of gold dug a hole in the ground and hid the master's money for safekeeping.

19"After a long time their master returned from his trip and called them to give an account of how they had used his money. 20The servant to whom he had entrusted the five bags of gold said, 'Sir, you gave me five bags of gold to invest, and I have doubled the

25:1 Or *virgins;* also in 25:7, 11.   25:15 Greek *talents;* also throughout the story. A talent is equal to 75 pounds or 34 kilograms.

amount.' [21]The master was full of praise. 'Well done, my good and faithful servant. You have been faithful in handling this small amount, so now I will give you many more responsibilities. Let's celebrate together!'

[22]"Next came the servant who had received the two bags of gold, with the report, 'Sir, you gave me two bags of gold to invest, and I have doubled the amount.' [23]The master said, 'Well done, my good and faithful servant. You have been faithful in handling this small amount, so now I will give you many more responsibilities. Let's celebrate together!'

[24]"Then the servant with the one bag of gold came and said, 'Sir, I know you are a hard man, harvesting crops you didn't plant and gathering crops you didn't cultivate. [25]I was afraid I would lose your money, so I hid it in the earth and here it is.'

[26]"But the master replied, 'You wicked and lazy servant! You think I'm a hard man, do you, harvesting crops I didn't plant and gathering crops I didn't cultivate? [27]Well, you should at least have put my money into the bank so I could have some interest. [28]Take the money from this servant and give it to the one with the ten bags of gold. [29]To those who use well what they are given, even more will be given, and they will have an abundance. But from those who are unfaithful,* even what little they have will be taken away. [30]Now throw this useless servant into outer darkness, where there will be weeping and gnashing of teeth.'

The Final Judgment

[31]"But when the Son of Man comes in his glory, and all the angels with him, then he will sit upon his glorious throne. [32]All the nations will be gathered in his presence, and he will separate them as a shepherd separates the sheep from the goats. [33]He will place the sheep at his right hand and the goats at his left. [34]Then the King will say to those on the right, 'Come, you who are blessed by my Father, inherit the Kingdom prepared for you from the foundation of the world. [35]For I was hungry, and you fed me. I was thirsty, and you gave me a drink. I was a stranger, and you invited me into your home. [36]I was naked, and you gave me clothing. I was sick, and you cared for me. I was in prison, and you visited me.'

[37]"Then these righteous ones will reply, 'Lord, when did we ever see you hungry and feed you? Or thirsty and give you something to drink? [38]Or a stranger and show you hospitality? Or naked and give you clothing? [39]When did we ever see you sick or in prison, and visit you?' [40]And the King will tell them, 'I assure you, when you did it to one of the least of these my brothers and sisters,* you were doing it to me!'

[41]"Then the King will turn to those on the left and say, 'Away with you, you cursed ones, into the eternal fire prepared for the Devil and his demons! [42]For I was hungry, and you didn't feed me. I was thirsty, and you didn't give me anything to drink. [43]I was a stranger, and you didn't invite me into your home. I was naked, and you gave me no clothing. I was sick and in prison, and you didn't visit me.'

[44]"Then they will reply, 'Lord, when did we ever see you

25:29 Or *who have nothing.*   **25:40** Greek *my brothers.*

hungry or thirsty or a stranger or naked or sick or in prison, and not help you?' ⁴⁵And he will answer, 'I assure you, when you refused to help the least of these my brothers and sisters, you were refusing to help me.' ⁴⁶And they will go away into eternal punishment, but the righteous will go into eternal life."

CHAPTER 26

The Plot to Kill Jesus

When Jesus had finished saying these things, he said to his disciples, ²"As you know, the Passover celebration begins in two days, and I, the Son of Man, will be betrayed and crucified."

³At that same time the leading priests and other leaders were meeting at the residence of Caiaphas, the high priest, ⁴to discuss how to capture Jesus secretly and put him to death. ⁵"But not during the Passover," they agreed, "or there will be a riot."

Jesus Anointed at Bethany

⁶Meanwhile, Jesus was in Bethany at the home of Simon, a man who had leprosy. ⁷During supper, a woman came in with a beautiful jar* of expensive perfume and poured it over his head. ⁸The disciples were indignant when they saw this. "What a waste of money," they said. ⁹"She could have sold it for a fortune and given the money to the poor."

¹⁰But Jesus replied, "Why berate her for doing such a good thing to me? ¹¹You will always have the poor among you, but I will not be here with you much longer. ¹²She has poured this perfume on me to prepare my body for burial. ¹³I assure you, wherever the Good News is preached throughout the world, this woman's deed will be talked about in her memory."

Judas Agrees to Betray Jesus

¹⁴Then Judas Iscariot, one of the twelve disciples, went to the leading priests ¹⁵and asked, "How much will you pay me to betray Jesus to you?" And they gave him thirty pieces of silver. ¹⁶From that time on, Judas began looking for the right time and place to betray Jesus.

The Last Supper

¹⁷On the first day of the Festival of Unleavened Bread, the disciples came to Jesus and asked, "Where do you want us to prepare the Passover supper?"

¹⁸"As you go into the city," he told them, "you will see a certain man. Tell him, 'The Teacher says, My time has come, and I will eat the Passover meal with my disciples at your house.'" ¹⁹So the disciples did as Jesus told them and prepared the Passover supper there.

²⁰When it was evening, Jesus sat down at the table with the twelve disciples. ²¹While they were eating, he said, "The truth is, one of you will betray me."

²²Greatly distressed, one by one they began to ask him, "I'm not the one, am I, Lord?"

²³He replied, "One of you who is eating with me now* will betray me. ²⁴For I, the Son of Man, must die, as the Scriptures

26:7 Greek *an alabaster jar.*   26:23 Or *The one who has dipped his hand in the bowl with me.*

declared long ago. But how terrible it will be for my betrayer. Far better for him if he had never been born!"

²⁵Judas, the one who would betray him, also asked, "Teacher, I'm not the one, am I?"

And Jesus told him, "You have said it yourself."

²⁶As they were eating, Jesus took a loaf of bread and asked God's blessing on it. Then he broke it in pieces and gave it to the disciples, saying, "Take it and eat it, for this is my body." ²⁷And he took a cup of wine and gave thanks to God for it. He gave it to them and said, "Each of you drink from it, ²⁸for this is my blood, which seals the covenant* between God and his people. It is poured out to forgive the sins of many. ²⁹Mark my words—I will not drink wine again until the day I drink it new with you in my Father's Kingdom." ³⁰Then they sang a hymn and went out to the Mount of Olives.

Jesus Predicts Peter's Denial

³¹"Tonight all of you will desert me," Jesus told them. "For the Scriptures say,

'God* will strike the Shepherd,
    and the sheep of the flock will be scattered.'*

³²But after I have been raised from the dead, I will go ahead of you to Galilee and meet you there."

³³Peter declared, "Even if everyone else deserts you, I never will."

³⁴"Peter," Jesus replied, "the truth is, this very night, before the rooster crows, you will deny me three times."

³⁵"No!" Peter insisted. "Not even if I have to die with you! I will never deny you!" And all the other disciples vowed the same.

Jesus Prays in Gethsemane

³⁶Then Jesus brought them to an olive grove called Gethsemane, and he said, "Sit here while I go on ahead to pray." ³⁷He took Peter and Zebedee's two sons, James and John, and he began to be filled with anguish and deep distress. ³⁸He told them, "My soul is crushed with grief to the point of death. Stay here and watch with me."

³⁹He went on a little farther and fell face down on the ground, praying, "My Father! If it is possible, let this cup of suffering be taken away from me. Yet I want your will, not mine." ⁴⁰Then he returned to the disciples and found them asleep. He said to Peter, "Couldn't you stay awake and watch with me even one hour? ⁴¹Keep alert and pray. Otherwise temptation will overpower you. For though the spirit is willing enough, the body is weak!"

⁴²Again he left them and prayed, "My Father! If this cup cannot be taken away until I drink it, your will be done." ⁴³He returned to them again and found them sleeping, for they just couldn't keep their eyes open.

⁴⁴So he went back to pray a third time, saying the same things again. ⁴⁵Then he came to the disciples and said, "Still sleeping? Still resting?* Look, the time has come. I, the Son of Man, am

26:28 Some manuscripts read *the new covenant.*   26:31a Greek *I.*   26:31b Zech 13:7.
26:45 Or *Sleep on, take your rest.*

betrayed into the hands of sinners. ⁴⁶Up, let's be going. See, my betrayer is here!"

Jesus Is Arrested

⁴⁷And even as he said this, Judas, one of the twelve disciples, arrived with a mob that was armed with swords and clubs. They had been sent out by the leading priests and other leaders of the people. ⁴⁸Judas had given them a prearranged signal: "You will know which one to arrest when I go over and give him the kiss of greeting." ⁴⁹So Judas came straight to Jesus. "Greetings, Teacher!" he exclaimed and gave him the kiss.

⁵⁰Jesus said, "My friend, go ahead and do what you have come for." Then the others grabbed Jesus and arrested him. ⁵¹One of the men with Jesus pulled out a sword and slashed off an ear of the high priest's servant.

⁵²"Put away your sword," Jesus told him. "Those who use the sword will be killed by the sword. ⁵³Don't you realize that I could ask my Father for thousands* of angels to protect us, and he would send them instantly? ⁵⁴But if I did, how would the Scriptures be fulfilled that describe what must happen now?"

⁵⁵Then Jesus said to the crowd, "Am I some dangerous criminal, that you have come armed with swords and clubs to arrest me? Why didn't you arrest me in the Temple? I was there teaching every day. ⁵⁶But this is all happening to fulfill the words of the prophets as recorded in the Scriptures." At that point, all the disciples deserted him and fled.

Jesus before the Council

⁵⁷Then the people who had arrested Jesus led him to the home of Caiaphas, the high priest, where the teachers of religious law and other leaders had gathered. ⁵⁸Meanwhile, Peter was following far behind and eventually came to the courtyard of the high priest's house. He went in, sat with the guards, and waited to see what was going to happen to Jesus.

⁵⁹Inside, the leading priests and the entire high council* were trying to find witnesses who would lie about Jesus, so they could put him to death. ⁶⁰But even though they found many who agreed to give false witness, there was no testimony they could use. Finally, two men were found ⁶¹who declared, "This man said, 'I am able to destroy the Temple of God and rebuild it in three days.'"

⁶²Then the high priest stood up and said to Jesus, "Well, aren't you going to answer these charges? What do you have to say for yourself?" ⁶³But Jesus remained silent. Then the high priest said to him, "I demand in the name of the living God that you tell us whether you are the Messiah, the Son of God."

⁶⁴Jesus replied, "Yes, it is as you say. And in the future you will see me, the Son of Man, sitting at God's right hand in the place of power and coming back on the clouds of heaven."*

⁶⁵Then the high priest tore his clothing to show his horror, shouting, "Blasphemy! Why do we need other witnesses? You have all heard his blasphemy. ⁶⁶What is your verdict?"

"Guilty!" they shouted. "He must die!"

⁶⁷Then they spit in Jesus' face and hit him with their fists. And

26:53 Greek *12 legions.*   26:59 Greek *the Sanhedrin.*   26:64 See Ps 110:1; Dan 7:13.

some slapped him, 68saying, "Prophesy to us, you Messiah! Who hit you that time?"

Peter Denies Jesus

69Meanwhile, as Peter was sitting outside in the courtyard, a servant girl came over and said to him, "You were one of those with Jesus the Galilean."

70But Peter denied it in front of everyone. "I don't know what you are talking about," he said.

71Later, out by the gate, another servant girl noticed him and said to those standing around, "This man was with Jesus of Nazareth."

72Again Peter denied it, this time with an oath. "I don't even know the man," he said.

73A little later some other bystanders came over to him and said, "You must be one of them; we can tell by your Galilean accent."

74Peter said, "I swear by God, I don't know the man." And immediately the rooster crowed. 75Suddenly, Jesus' words flashed through Peter's mind: "Before the rooster crows, you will deny me three times." And he went away, crying bitterly.

CHAPTER 27

Judas Hangs Himself

Very early in the morning, the leading priests and other leaders met again to discuss how to persuade the Roman government to sentence Jesus to death. 2Then they bound him and took him to Pilate, the Roman governor.

3When Judas, who had betrayed him, realized that Jesus had been condemned to die, he was filled with remorse. So he took the thirty pieces of silver back to the leading priests and other leaders. 4"I have sinned," he declared, "for I have betrayed an innocent man."

"What do we care?" they retorted. "That's your problem."

5Then Judas threw the money onto the floor of the Temple and went out and hanged himself. 6The leading priests picked up the money. "We can't put it in the Temple treasury," they said, "since it's against the law to accept money paid for murder." 7After some discussion they finally decided to buy the potter's field, and they made it into a cemetery for foreigners. 8That is why the field is still called the Field of Blood. 9This fulfilled the prophecy of Jeremiah that says,

"They took* the thirty pieces of silver—
  the price at which he was valued by the people of Israel—
10 and purchased the potter's field,
  as the Lord directed.*"

Jesus' Trial before Pilate

11Now Jesus was standing before Pilate, the Roman governor. "Are you the King of the Jews?" the governor asked him.

Jesus replied, "Yes, it is as you say."

12But when the leading priests and other leaders made their accusations against him, Jesus remained silent. 13"Don't you hear their many charges against you?" Pilate demanded. 14But Jesus said nothing, much to the governor's great surprise.

27:9 Or I took.   27:9-10 Greek as the Lord directed. me Zech 11:12-13; Jer 32:6-9.

¹⁵Now it was the governor's custom to release one prisoner to the crowd each year during the Passover celebration—anyone they wanted. ¹⁶This year there was a notorious criminal in prison, a man named Barabbas.* ¹⁷As the crowds gathered before Pilate's house that morning, he asked them, "Which one do you want me to release to you—Barabbas, or Jesus who is called the Messiah?" ¹⁸(He knew very well that the Jewish leaders had arrested Jesus out of envy.)

¹⁹Just then, as Pilate was sitting on the judgment seat, his wife sent him this message: "Leave that innocent man alone, because I had a terrible nightmare about him last night."

²⁰Meanwhile, the leading priests and other leaders persuaded the crowds to ask for Barabbas to be released and for Jesus to be put to death. ²¹So when the governor asked again, "Which of these two do you want me to release to you?" the crowd shouted back their reply: "Barabbas!"

²²"But if I release Barabbas," Pilate asked them, "what should I do with Jesus who is called the Messiah?"

And they all shouted, "Crucify him!"

²³"Why?" Pilate demanded. "What crime has he committed?"

But the crowd only roared the louder, "Crucify him!"

²⁴Pilate saw that he wasn't getting anywhere and that a riot was developing. So he sent for a bowl of water and washed his hands before the crowd, saying, "I am innocent of the blood of this man. The responsibility is yours!"

²⁵And all the people yelled back, "We will take responsibility for his death—we and our children!"*

²⁶So Pilate released Barabbas to them. He ordered Jesus flogged with a lead-tipped whip, then turned him over to the Roman soldiers to crucify him.

The Soldiers Mock Jesus

²⁷Some of the governor's soldiers took Jesus into their headquarters and called out the entire battalion. ²⁸They stripped him and put a scarlet robe on him. ²⁹They made a crown of long, sharp thorns and put it on his head, and they placed a stick in his right hand as a scepter. Then they knelt before him in mockery, yelling, "Hail! King of the Jews!" ³⁰And they spit on him and grabbed the stick and beat him on the head with it. ³¹When they were finally tired of mocking him, they took off the robe and put his own clothes on him again. Then they led him away to be crucified.

The Crucifixion

³²As they were on the way, they came across a man named Simon, who was from Cyrene,* and they forced him to carry Jesus' cross. ³³Then they went out to a place called Golgotha (which means Skull Hill). ³⁴The soldiers gave Jesus wine mixed with bitter gall, but when he had tasted it, he refused to drink it.

³⁵After they had nailed him to the cross, the soldiers gambled for his clothes by throwing dice.* ³⁶Then they sat around and kept

27:16 Some manuscripts read *Jesus Barabbas*; also in 27:17. 27:25 Greek *"His blood be on us and on our children."* 27:32 *Cyrene* was a city in northern Africa. 27:35 Greek *by casting lots.* A few late manuscripts add *This fulfilled the word of the prophet: "They divided my clothes among themselves and cast lots for my robe."* See Ps 22:18.

guard as he hung there. [37]A signboard was fastened to the cross above Jesus' head, announcing the charge against him. It read: "This is Jesus, the King of the Jews."

[38]Two criminals were crucified with him, their crosses on either side of his. [39]And the people passing by shouted abuse, shaking their heads in mockery. [40]"So! You can destroy the Temple and build it again in three days, can you? Well then, if you are the Son of God, save yourself and come down from the cross!"

[41]The leading priests, the teachers of religious law, and the other leaders also mocked Jesus. [42]"He saved others," they scoffed, "but he can't save himself! So he is the king of Israel, is he? Let him come down from the cross, and we will believe in him! [43]He trusted God—let God show his approval by delivering him! For he said, 'I am the Son of God.'" [44]And the criminals who were crucified with him also shouted the same insults at him.

The Death of Jesus

[45]At noon, darkness fell across the whole land until three o'clock. [46]At about three o'clock, Jesus called out with a loud voice, *"Eli, Eli, lema sabachthani?"* which means, "My God, my God, why have you forsaken me?"*

[47]Some of the bystanders misunderstood and thought he was calling for the prophet Elijah. [48]One of them ran and filled a sponge with sour wine, holding it up to him on a stick so he could drink. [49]But the rest said, "Leave him alone. Let's see whether Elijah will come and save him."*

[50]Then Jesus shouted out again, and he gave up his spirit. [51]At that moment the curtain in the Temple was torn in two, from top to bottom. The earth shook, rocks split apart, [52]and tombs opened. The bodies of many godly men and women who had died were raised from the dead [53]after Jesus' resurrection. They left the cemetery, went into the holy city of Jerusalem, and appeared to many people.*

[54]The Roman officer and the other soldiers at the crucifixion were terrified by the earthquake and all that had happened. They said, "Truly, this was the Son of God!"

[55]And many women who had come from Galilee with Jesus to care for him were watching from a distance. [56]Among them were Mary Magdalene, Mary (the mother of James and Joseph), and Zebedee's wife, the mother of James and John.

The Burial of Jesus

[57]As evening approached, Joseph, a rich man from Arimathea who was one of Jesus' followers, [58]went to Pilate and asked for Jesus' body. And Pilate issued an order to release it to him. [59]Joseph took the body and wrapped it in a long linen cloth. [60]He placed it in his own new tomb, which had been carved out of the rock. Then he rolled a great stone across the entrance as he left. [61]Both Mary Magdalene and the other Mary were sitting nearby watching.

27:46 Ps 22:1.   27:49 Some manuscripts add *And another took a spear and pierced his side, and out came water and blood.*   27:51-53 Or *The earth shook, rocks split apart, tombs opened, and the bodies of many godly men and women who had died were raised. After Jesus' resurrection, they left the cemetery, went into the holy city of Jerusalem, and appeared to many people.*

The Guard at the Tomb

62The next day—on the first day of the Passover ceremonies*—the leading priests and Pharisees went to see Pilate. 63They told him, "Sir, we remember what that deceiver once said while he was still alive: 'After three days I will be raised from the dead.' 64So we request that you seal the tomb until the third day. This will prevent his disciples from coming and stealing his body and then telling everyone he came back to life! If that happens, we'll be worse off than we were at first."

65Pilate replied, "Take guards and secure it the best you can." 66So they sealed the tomb and posted guards to protect it.

CHAPTER 28

The Resurrection

Early on Sunday morning,* as the new day was dawning, Mary Magdalene and the other Mary went out to see the tomb. 2Suddenly there was a great earthquake, because an angel of the Lord came down from heaven and rolled aside the stone and sat on it. 3His face shone like lightning, and his clothing was as white as snow. 4The guards shook with fear when they saw him, and they fell into a dead faint.

5Then the angel spoke to the women. "Don't be afraid!" he said. "I know you are looking for Jesus, who was crucified. 6He isn't here! He has been raised from the dead, just as he said would happen. Come, see where his body was lying. 7And now, go quickly and tell his disciples he has been raised from the dead, and he is going ahead of you to Galilee. You will see him there. Remember, I have told you."

8The women ran quickly from the tomb. They were very frightened but also filled with great joy, and they rushed to find the disciples to give them the angel's message. 9And as they went, Jesus met them. "Greetings!" he said. And they ran to him, held his feet, and worshiped him. 10Then Jesus said to them, "Don't be afraid! Go tell my brothers to leave for Galilee, and they will see me there."

The Report of the Guard

11As the women were on their way into the city, some of the men who had been guarding the tomb went to the leading priests and told them what had happened. 12A meeting of all the religious leaders was called, and they decided to bribe the soldiers. 13They told the soldiers, "You must say, 'Jesus' disciples came during the night while we were sleeping, and they stole his body.' 14If the governor hears about it, we'll stand up for you and everything will be all right." 15So the guards accepted the bribe and said what they were told to say. Their story spread widely among the Jews, and they still tell it today.

The Great Commission

16Then the eleven disciples left for Galilee, going to the mountain where Jesus had told them to go. 17When they saw him, they worshiped him—but some of them still doubted!

18Jesus came and told his disciples, "I have been given complete authority in heaven and on earth. 19Therefore, go and make disci-

27:62 Or *On the next day, which is after the Preparation.*   28:1 Greek *After the Sabbath, on the first day of the week.*

ples of all the nations, baptizing them in the name of the Father and the Son and the Holy Spirit. ²⁰Teach these new disciples to obey all the commands I have given you. And be sure of this: I am with you always, even to the end of the age."

MARK

CHAPTER 1

John the Baptist Prepares the Way

Here begins the Good News about Jesus the Messiah, the Son of God.*

²In the book of the prophet Isaiah, God said,

"Look, I am sending my messenger before you,
    and he will prepare your way.*
³ He is a voice shouting in the wilderness:
    'Prepare a pathway for the Lord's coming!
    Make a straight road for him!'*"

⁴This messenger was John the Baptist. He lived in the wilderness and was preaching that people should be baptized to show that they had turned from their sins and turned to God to be forgiven.* ⁵People from Jerusalem and from all over Judea traveled out into the wilderness to see and hear John. And when they confessed their sins, he baptized them in the Jordan River. ⁶His clothes were woven from camel hair, and he wore a leather belt; his food was locusts and wild honey. ⁷He announced: "Someone is coming soon who is far greater than I am—so much greater that I am not even worthy to be his slave.* ⁸I baptize you with* water, but he will baptize you with the Holy Spirit!"

The Baptism of Jesus

⁹One day Jesus came from Nazareth in Galilee, and he was baptized by John in the Jordan River. ¹⁰And when Jesus came up out of the water, he saw the heavens split open and the Holy Spirit descending like a dove on him. ¹¹And a voice came from heaven saying, "You are my beloved Son, and I am fully pleased with you."

The Temptation of Jesus

¹²Immediately the Holy Spirit compelled Jesus to go into the wilderness. ¹³He was there for forty days, being tempted by Satan. He was out among the wild animals, and angels took care of him.

The First Disciples

¹⁴Later on, after John was arrested by Herod Antipas, Jesus went to Galilee to preach God's Good News. ¹⁵"At last the time has come!" he announced. "The Kingdom of God is near! Turn from your sins and believe this Good News!"

1:1 Some manuscripts do not include *the Son of God.* 1:2 Mal 3:1. 1:3 Isa 40:3. 1:4 Greek *preaching a baptism of repentance for the forgiveness of sins.* 1:7 Greek *to stoop down and untie his sandals.* 1:8 Or *in.*

¹⁶One day as Jesus was walking along the shores of the Sea of Galilee, he saw Simon* and his brother, Andrew, fishing with a net, for they were commercial fishermen. ¹⁷Jesus called out to them, "Come, be my disciples, and I will show you how to fish for people!" ¹⁸And they left their nets at once and went with him.

¹⁹A little farther up the shore Jesus saw Zebedee's sons, James and John, in a boat mending their nets. ²⁰He called them, too, and immediately they left their father, Zebedee, in the boat with the hired men and went with him.

Jesus Casts Out an Evil Spirit

²¹Jesus and his companions went to the town of Capernaum, and every Sabbath day he went into the synagogue and taught the people. ²²They were amazed at his teaching, for he taught as one who had real authority—quite unlike the teachers of religious law.

²³A man possessed by an evil spirit was in the synagogue, ²⁴and he began shouting, "Why are you bothering us, Jesus of Nazareth? Have you come to destroy us? I know who you are—the Holy One sent from God!"

²⁵Jesus cut him short. "Be silent! Come out of the man." ²⁶At that, the evil spirit screamed and threw the man into a convulsion, but then he left him.

²⁷Amazement gripped the audience, and they began to discuss what had happened. "What sort of new teaching is this?" they asked excitedly. "It has such authority! Even evil spirits obey his orders!" ²⁸The news of what he had done spread quickly through that entire area of Galilee.

Jesus Heals Many People

²⁹After Jesus and his disciples left the synagogue, they went over to Simon and Andrew's home, and James and John were with them. ³⁰Simon's mother-in-law was sick in bed with a high fever. They told Jesus about her right away. ³¹He went to her bedside, and as he took her by the hand and helped her to sit up, the fever suddenly left, and she got up and prepared a meal for them.

³²That evening at sunset, many sick and demon-possessed people were brought to Jesus. ³³And a huge crowd of people from all over Capernaum gathered outside the door to watch. ³⁴So Jesus healed great numbers of sick people who had many different kinds of diseases, and he ordered many demons to come out of their victims. But because they knew who he was, he refused to allow the demons to speak.

Jesus Preaches in Galilee

³⁵The next morning Jesus awoke long before daybreak and went out alone into the wilderness to pray. ³⁶Later Simon and the others went out to find him. ³⁷They said, "Everyone is asking for you."

³⁸But he replied, "We must go on to other towns as well, and I will preach to them, too, because that is why I came." ³⁹So he traveled throughout the region of Galilee, preaching in the synagogues and expelling demons from many people.

1:16 *Simon* is called *Peter* in 3:16 and thereafter.

Jesus Heals a Man with Leprosy

⁴⁰A man with leprosy came and knelt in front of Jesus, begging to be healed. "If you want to, you can make me well again," he said.

⁴¹Moved with pity,* Jesus touched him. "I want to," he said. "Be healed!" ⁴²Instantly the leprosy disappeared—the man was healed. ⁴³Then Jesus sent him on his way and told him sternly, ⁴⁴"Go right over to the priest and let him examine you. Don't talk to anyone along the way. Take along the offering required in the law of Moses for those who have been healed of leprosy, so everyone will have proof of your healing."

⁴⁵But as the man went on his way, he spread the news, telling everyone what had happened to him. As a result, such crowds soon surrounded Jesus that he couldn't enter a town anywhere publicly. He had to stay out in the secluded places, and people from everywhere came to him there.

CHAPTER 2

Jesus Heals a Paralyzed Man

Several days later Jesus returned to Capernaum, and the news of his arrival spread quickly through the town. ²Soon the house where he was staying was so packed with visitors that there wasn't room for one more person, not even outside the door. And he preached the word to them. ³Four men arrived carrying a paralyzed man on a mat. ⁴They couldn't get to Jesus through the crowd, so they dug through the clay roof above his head. Then they lowered the sick man on his mat, right down in front of Jesus. ⁵Seeing their faith, Jesus said to the paralyzed man, "My son, your sins are forgiven."

⁶But some of the teachers of religious law who were sitting there said to themselves, ⁷"What? This is blasphemy! Who but God can forgive sins!"

⁸Jesus knew what they were discussing among themselves, so he said to them, "Why do you think this is blasphemy? ⁹Is it easier to say to the paralyzed man, 'Your sins are forgiven' or 'Get up, pick up your mat, and walk'? ¹⁰I will prove that I, the Son of Man, have the authority on earth to forgive sins." Then Jesus turned to the paralyzed man and said, ¹¹"Stand up, take your mat, and go on home, because you are healed!"

¹²The man jumped up, took the mat, and pushed his way through the stunned onlookers. Then they all praised God. "We've never seen anything like this before!" they exclaimed.

Jesus Calls Levi (Matthew)

¹³Then Jesus went out to the lakeshore again and taught the crowds that gathered around him. ¹⁴As he walked along, he saw Levi son of Alphaeus sitting at his tax-collection booth. "Come, be my disciple," Jesus said to him. So Levi got up and followed him.

¹⁵That night Levi invited Jesus and his disciples to be his dinner guests, along with his fellow tax collectors and many other notorious sinners. (There were many people of this kind among the crowds that followed Jesus.) ¹⁶But when some of the teachers of religious law who were Pharisees* saw him eating with people like

1:41 Some manuscripts read *Moved with anger.*   **2:16a** Greek *the scribes of the Pharisees.*

that, they said to his disciples, "Why does he eat with such scum*?"

[17]When Jesus heard this, he told them, "Healthy people don't need a doctor—sick people do. I have come to call sinners, not those who think they are already good enough."

A Discussion about Fasting

[18]John's disciples and the Pharisees sometimes fasted. One day some people came to Jesus and asked, "Why do John's disciples and the Pharisees fast, but your disciples don't fast?"

[19]Jesus replied, "Do wedding guests fast while celebrating with the groom? Of course not. They can't fast while they are with the groom. [20]But someday he will be taken away from them, and then they will fast. [21]And who would patch an old garment with unshrunk cloth? For the new patch shrinks and pulls away from the old cloth, leaving an even bigger hole than before. [22]And no one puts new wine into old wineskins. The wine would burst the wineskins, spilling the wine and ruining the skins. New wine needs new wineskins."

A Discussion about the Sabbath

[23]One Sabbath day as Jesus was walking through some grainfields, his disciples began breaking off heads of wheat. [24]But the Pharisees said to Jesus, "They shouldn't be doing that! It's against the law to work by harvesting grain on the Sabbath."

[25]But Jesus replied, "Haven't you ever read in the Scriptures what King David did when he and his companions were hungry? [26]He went into the house of God (during the days when Abiathar was high priest), ate the special bread reserved for the priests alone, and then gave some to his companions. That was breaking the law, too." [27]Then he said to them, "The Sabbath was made to benefit people, and not people to benefit the Sabbath. [28]And I, the Son of Man, am master even of the Sabbath!"

CHAPTER 3

Jesus Heals on the Sabbath

Jesus went into the synagogue again and noticed a man with a deformed hand. [2]Since it was the Sabbath, Jesus' enemies watched him closely. Would he heal the man's hand on the Sabbath? If he did, they planned to condemn him. [3]Jesus said to the man, "Come and stand in front of everyone." [4]Then he turned to his critics and asked, "Is it legal to do good deeds on the Sabbath, or is it a day for doing harm? Is this a day to save life or to destroy it?" But they wouldn't answer him. [5]He looked around at them angrily, because he was deeply disturbed by their hard hearts. Then he said to the man, "Reach out your hand." The man reached out his hand, and it became normal again! [6]At once the Pharisees went away and met with the supporters of Herod to discuss plans for killing Jesus.

Crowds Follow Jesus

[7]Jesus and his disciples went out to the lake, followed by a huge crowd from all over Galilee, Judea, [8]Jerusalem, Idumea, from east of the Jordan River, and even from as far away as Tyre and Sidon. The news about his miracles had spread far and wide, and vast numbers of people came to see him for themselves.

2:16b Greek *with tax collectors and sinners.*

⁹Jesus instructed his disciples to bring around a boat and to have it ready in case he was crowded off the beach. ¹⁰There had been many healings that day. As a result, many sick people were crowding around him, trying to touch him. ¹¹And whenever those possessed by evil spirits caught sight of him, they would fall down in front of him shrieking, "You are the Son of God!" ¹²But Jesus strictly warned them not to say who he was.

Jesus Chooses the Twelve Apostles

¹³Afterward Jesus went up on a mountain and called the ones he wanted to go with him. And they came to him. ¹⁴Then he selected twelve of them to be his regular companions, calling them apostles.* He sent them out to preach, ¹⁵and he gave them authority to cast out demons. ¹⁶These are the names of the twelve he chose:

Simon (he renamed him Peter),

¹⁷ James and John (the sons of Zebedee, but Jesus nicknamed them "Sons of Thunder"*),

¹⁸ Andrew,
Philip,
Bartholomew,
Matthew,
Thomas,
James (son of Alphaeus),
Thaddaeus,
Simon (the Zealot*),

¹⁹ Judas Iscariot (who later betrayed him).

Jesus and the Prince of Demons

²⁰When Jesus returned to the house where he was staying, the crowds began to gather again, and soon he and his disciples couldn't even find time to eat. ²¹When his family heard what was happening, they tried to take him home with them. "He's out of his mind," they said.

²²But the teachers of religious law who had arrived from Jerusalem said, "He's possessed by Satan,* the prince of demons. That's where he gets the power to cast out demons."

²³Jesus called them over and said to them by way of illustration, "How can Satan cast out Satan? ²⁴A kingdom at war with itself will collapse. ²⁵A home divided against itself is doomed. ²⁶And if Satan is fighting against himself, how can he stand? He would never survive. ²⁷Let me illustrate this. You can't enter a strong man's house and rob him without first tying him up. Only then can his house be robbed!*

²⁸"I assure you that any sin can be forgiven, including blasphemy; ²⁹but anyone who blasphemes against the Holy Spirit will never be forgiven. It is an eternal sin." ³⁰He told them this because they were saying he had an evil spirit.

The True Family of Jesus

³¹Jesus' mother and brothers arrived at the house where he was teaching. They stood outside and sent word for him to come out

3:14 Some manuscripts do not include *calling them apostles.* **3:17** Greek *whom he named Boanerges, which means Sons of Thunder.* **3:18** Greek *the Cananean.* **3:22** Greek *Beelzeboul.* **3:27** Or *One cannot rob Satan's kingdom without first tying him up. Only then can his demons be cast out.*

and talk with them. 32There was a crowd around Jesus, and someone said, "Your mother and your brothers and sisters* are outside, asking for you."

33Jesus replied, "Who is my mother? Who are my brothers?" 34Then he looked at those around him and said, "These are my mother and brothers. 35Anyone who does God's will is my brother and sister and mother."

CHAPTER 4

Story of the Farmer Scattering Seed

Once again Jesus began teaching by the lakeshore. There was such a large crowd along the shore that he got into a boat and sat down and spoke from there. 2He began to teach the people by telling many stories such as this one:

3"Listen! A farmer went out to plant some seed. 4As he scattered it across his field, some seed fell on a footpath, and the birds came and ate it. 5Other seed fell on shallow soil with underlying rock. The plant sprang up quickly, 6but it soon wilted beneath the hot sun and died because the roots had no nourishment in the shallow soil. 7Other seed fell among thorns that shot up and choked out the tender blades so that it produced no grain. 8Still other seed fell on fertile soil and produced a crop that was thirty, sixty, and even a hundred times as much as had been planted." Then he said, 9"Anyone who is willing to hear should listen and understand!"

10Later, when Jesus was alone with the twelve disciples and with the others who were gathered around, they asked him, "What do your stories mean?"

11He replied, "You are permitted to understand the secret about the Kingdom of God. But I am using these stories to conceal everything about it from outsiders, 12so that the Scriptures might be fulfilled:

'They see what I do,
    but they don't perceive its meaning.
They hear my words,
    but they don't understand.
So they will not turn from their sins
    and be forgiven.'*

13"But if you can't understand this story, how will you understand all the others I am going to tell? 14The farmer I talked about is the one who brings God's message to others. 15The seed that fell on the hard path represents those who hear the message, but then Satan comes at once and takes it away from them. 16The rocky soil represents those who hear the message and receive it with joy. 17But like young plants in such soil, their roots don't go very deep. At first they get along fine, but they wilt as soon as they have problems or are persecuted because they believe the word. 18The thorny ground represents those who hear and accept the Good News, 19but all too quickly the message is crowded out by the cares of this life, the lure of wealth, and the desire for nice things, so no crop is produced. 20But the good soil represents

3:32 Some manuscripts do not include *and sisters.*   4:12 Isa 6:9-10.

those who hear and accept God's message and produce a huge harvest—thirty, sixty, or even a hundred times as much as had been planted."

Illustration of the Lamp

21Then Jesus asked them, "Would anyone light a lamp and then put it under a basket or under a bed to shut out the light? Of course not! A lamp is placed on a stand, where its light will shine.

22"Everything that is now hidden or secret will eventually be brought to light. 23Anyone who is willing to hear should listen and understand! 24And be sure to pay attention to what you hear. The more you do this, the more you will understand—and even more, besides. 25To those who are open to my teaching, more understanding will be given. But to those who are not listening, even what they have will be taken away from them."

Illustration of the Growing Seed

26Jesus also said, "Here is another illustration of what the Kingdom of God is like: A farmer planted seeds in a field, 27and then he went on with his other activities. As the days went by, the seeds sprouted and grew without the farmer's help, 28because the earth produces crops on its own. First a leaf blade pushes through, then the heads of wheat are formed, and finally the grain ripens. 29And as soon as the grain is ready, the farmer comes and harvests it with a sickle."

Illustration of the Mustard Seed

30Jesus asked, "How can I describe the Kingdom of God? What story should I use to illustrate it? 31It is like a tiny mustard seed. Though this is one of the smallest of seeds, 32it grows to become one of the largest of plants, with long branches where birds can come and find shelter."

33He used many such stories and illustrations to teach the people as much as they were able to understand. 34In fact, in his public teaching he taught only with parables, but afterward when he was alone with his disciples, he explained the meaning to them.

Jesus Calms the Storm

35As evening came, Jesus said to his disciples, "Let's cross to the other side of the lake." 36He was already in the boat, so they started out, leaving the crowds behind (although other boats followed). 37But soon a fierce storm arose. High waves began to break into the boat until it was nearly full of water.

38Jesus was sleeping at the back of the boat with his head on a cushion. Frantically they woke him up, shouting, "Teacher, don't you even care that we are going to drown?"

39When he woke up, he rebuked the wind and said to the water, "Quiet down!" Suddenly the wind stopped, and there was a great calm. 40And he asked them, "Why are you so afraid? Do you still not have faith in me?"

41And they were filled with awe and said among themselves, "Who is this man, that even the wind and waves obey him?"

CHAPTER 5

Jesus Heals a Demon-Possessed Man

So they arrived at the other side of the lake, in the land of the Gerasenes.* ²Just as Jesus was climbing from the boat, a man possessed by an evil spirit ran out from a cemetery to meet him. ³This man lived among the tombs and could not be restrained, even with a chain. ⁴Whenever he was put into chains and shackles—as he often was—he snapped the chains from his wrists and smashed the shackles. No one was strong enough to control him. ⁵All day long and throughout the night, he would wander among the tombs and in the hills, screaming and hitting himself with stones.

⁶When Jesus was still some distance away, the man saw him. He ran to meet Jesus and fell down before him. ⁷He gave a terrible scream, shrieking, "Why are you bothering me, Jesus, Son of the Most High God? For God's sake, don't torture me!" ⁸For Jesus had already said to the spirit, "Come out of the man, you evil spirit."

⁹Then Jesus asked, "What is your name?"

And the spirit replied, "Legion, because there are many of us here inside this man." ¹⁰Then the spirits begged him again and again not to send them to some distant place. ¹¹There happened to be a large herd of pigs feeding on the hillside nearby. ¹²"Send us into those pigs," the evil spirits begged. ¹³Jesus gave them permission. So the evil spirits came out of the man and entered the pigs, and the entire herd of two thousand pigs plunged down the steep hillside into the lake, where they drowned.

¹⁴The herdsmen fled to the nearby city and the surrounding countryside, spreading the news as they ran. Everyone rushed out to see for themselves. ¹⁵A crowd soon gathered around Jesus, but they were frightened when they saw the man who had been demon possessed, for he was sitting there fully clothed and perfectly sane. ¹⁶Those who had seen what happened to the man and to the pigs told everyone about it, ¹⁷and the crowd began pleading with Jesus to go away and leave them alone.

¹⁸When Jesus got back into the boat, the man who had been demon possessed begged to go, too. ¹⁹But Jesus said, "No, go home to your friends, and tell them what wonderful things the Lord has done for you and how merciful he has been." ²⁰So the man started off to visit the Ten Towns* of that region and began to tell everyone about the great things Jesus had done for him; and everyone was amazed at what he told them.

Jesus Heals in Response to Faith

²¹When Jesus went back across to the other side of the lake, a large crowd gathered around him on the shore. ²²A leader of the local synagogue, whose name was Jairus, came and fell down before him, ²³pleading with him to heal his little daughter. "She is about to die," he said in desperation. "Please come and place your hands on her; heal her so she can live."

²⁴Jesus went with him, and the crowd thronged behind. ²⁵And there was a woman in the crowd who had had a hemorrhage for twelve years. ²⁶She had suffered a great deal from many doctors

5:1 Some manuscripts read *Gadarenes*; others read *Gergesenes*. See Matt 8:28; Luke 8:26.
5:20 Greek *Decapolis*.

through the years and had spent everything she had to pay them, but she had gotten no better. In fact, she was worse. 27She had heard about Jesus, so she came up behind him through the crowd and touched the fringe of his robe. 28For she thought to herself, "If I can just touch his clothing, I will be healed." 29Immediately the bleeding stopped, and she could feel that she had been healed!

30Jesus realized at once that healing power had gone out from him, so he turned around in the crowd and asked, "Who touched my clothes?"

31His disciples said to him, "All this crowd is pressing around you. How can you ask, 'Who touched me?'"

32But he kept on looking around to see who had done it. 33Then the frightened woman, trembling at the realization of what had happened to her, came and fell at his feet and told him what she had done. 34And he said to her, "Daughter, your faith has made you well. Go in peace. You have been healed."

35While he was still speaking to her, messengers arrived from Jairus's home with the message, "Your daughter is dead. There's no use troubling the Teacher now."

36But Jesus ignored their comments and said to Jairus, "Don't be afraid. Just trust me." 37Then Jesus stopped the crowd and wouldn't let anyone go with him except Peter and James and John. 38When they came to the home of the synagogue leader, Jesus saw the commotion and the weeping and wailing. 39He went inside and spoke to the people. "Why all this weeping and commotion?" he asked. "The child isn't dead; she is only asleep."

40The crowd laughed at him, but he told them all to go outside. Then he took the girl's father and mother and his three disciples into the room where the girl was lying. 41Holding her hand, he said to her, "Get up, little girl!"* 42And the girl, who was twelve years old, immediately stood up and walked around! Her parents were absolutely overwhelmed. 43Jesus commanded them not to tell anyone what had happened, and he told them to give her something to eat.

CHAPTER 6

Jesus Rejected at Nazareth

Jesus left that part of the country and returned with his disciples to Nazareth, his hometown. 2The next Sabbath he began teaching in the synagogue, and many who heard him were astonished. They asked, "Where did he get all his wisdom and the power to perform such miracles? 3He's just the carpenter, the son of Mary and brother of James, Joseph,* Judas, and Simon. And his sisters live right here among us." They were deeply offended and refused to believe in him.

4Then Jesus told them, "A prophet is honored everywhere except in his own hometown and among his relatives and his own family." 5And because of their unbelief, he couldn't do any mighty miracles among them except to place his hands on a few sick people and heal them. 6And he was amazed at their unbelief.

Jesus Sends Out the Twelve Apostles

Then Jesus went out from village to village, teaching. 7And he called his twelve disciples together and sent them out two by two,

5:41 Greek text uses Aramaic *"Talitha cumi"* and then translates it as "Get up, little girl."
6:3 Greek *Joses*; see Matt 13:55.

with authority to cast out evil spirits. [8]He told them to take nothing with them except a walking stick—no food, no traveler's bag, no money. [9]He told them to wear sandals but not to take even an extra coat. [10]"When you enter each village, be a guest in only one home," he said. [11]"And if a village won't welcome you or listen to you, shake off its dust from your feet as you leave. It is a sign that you have abandoned that village to its fate."

[12]So the disciples went out, telling all they met to turn from their sins. [13]And they cast out many demons and healed many sick people, anointing them with olive oil.

The Death of John the Baptist

[14]Herod Antipas, the king, soon heard about Jesus, because people everywhere were talking about him. Some were saying,* "This must be John the Baptist come back to life again. That is why he can do such miracles." [15]Others thought Jesus was the ancient prophet Elijah. Still others thought he was a prophet like the other great prophets of the past. [16]When Herod heard about Jesus, he said, "John, the man I beheaded, has come back from the dead."

[17]For Herod had sent soldiers to arrest and imprison John as a favor to Herodias. She had been his brother Philip's wife, but Herod had married her. [18]John kept telling Herod, "It is illegal for you to marry your brother's wife." [19]Herodias was enraged and wanted John killed in revenge, but without Herod's approval she was powerless. [20]And Herod respected John, knowing that he was a good and holy man, so he kept him under his protection. Herod was disturbed whenever he talked with John, but even so, he liked to listen to him.

[21]Herodias's chance finally came. It was Herod's birthday, and he gave a party for his palace aides, army officers, and the leading citizens of Galilee. [22]Then his daughter, also named Herodias,* came in and performed a dance that greatly pleased them all. "Ask me for anything you like," the king said to the girl, "and I will give it to you." [23]Then he promised, "I will give you whatever you ask, up to half of my kingdom!"

[24]She went out and asked her mother, "What should I ask for?" Her mother told her, "Ask for John the Baptist's head!"

[25]So the girl hurried back to the king and told him, "I want the head of John the Baptist, right now, on a tray!"

[26]Then the king was very sorry, but he was embarrassed to break his oath in front of his guests. [27]So he sent an executioner to the prison to cut off John's head and bring it to him. The soldier beheaded John in the prison, [28]brought his head on a tray, and gave it to the girl, who took it to her mother. [29]When John's disciples heard what had happened, they came for his body and buried it in a tomb.

Jesus Feeds Five Thousand

[30]The apostles returned to Jesus from their ministry tour and told him all they had done and what they had taught. [31]Then Jesus said, "Let's get away from the crowds for a while and rest." There were so many people coming and going that Jesus and his apostles

6:14 Some manuscripts read *He was saying.*   6:22 Some manuscripts read *the daughter of Herodias herself.*

didn't even have time to eat. [32]They left by boat for a quieter spot. [33]But many people saw them leaving, and people from many towns ran ahead along the shore and met them as they landed. [34]A vast crowd was there as he stepped from the boat, and he had compassion on them because they were like sheep without a shepherd. So he taught them many things.

[35]Late in the afternoon his disciples came to him and said, "This is a desolate place, and it is getting late. [36]Send the crowds away so they can go to the nearby farms and villages and buy themselves some food."

[37]But Jesus said, "You feed them."

"With what?" they asked. "It would take a small fortune* to buy food for all this crowd!"

[38]"How much food do you have?" he asked. "Go and find out."

They came back and reported, "We have five loaves of bread and two fish." [39]Then Jesus told the crowd to sit down in groups on the green grass. [40]So they sat in groups of fifty or a hundred.

[41]Jesus took the five loaves and two fish, looked up toward heaven, and asked God's blessing on the food. Breaking the loaves into pieces, he kept giving the bread and fish to the disciples to give to the people. [42]They all ate as much as they wanted, [43]and they picked up twelve baskets of leftover bread and fish. [44]Five thousand men had eaten from those five loaves!

Jesus Walks on Water

[45]Immediately after this, Jesus made his disciples get back into the boat and head out across the lake to Bethsaida, while he sent the people home. [46]Afterward he went up into the hills by himself to pray.

[47]During the night, the disciples were in their boat out in the middle of the lake, and Jesus was alone on land. [48]He saw that they were in serious trouble, rowing hard and struggling against the wind and waves. About three o'clock in the morning* he came to them, walking on the water. He started to go past them, [49]but when they saw him walking on the water, they screamed in terror, thinking he was a ghost. [50]They were all terrified when they saw him. But Jesus spoke to them at once. "It's all right," he said. "I am here! Don't be afraid." [51]Then he climbed into the boat, and the wind stopped. They were astonished at what they saw. [52]They still didn't understand the significance of the miracle of the multiplied loaves, for their hearts were hard and they did not believe.

[53]When they arrived at Gennesaret on the other side of the lake, they anchored the boat [54]and climbed out. The people standing there recognized him at once, [55]and they ran throughout the whole area and began carrying sick people to him on mats. [56]Wherever he went—in villages and cities and out on the farms—they laid the sick in the market plazas and streets. The sick begged him to let them at least touch the fringe of his robe, and all who touched it were healed.

CHAPTER 7

Jesus Teaches about Inner Purity

One day some Pharisees and teachers of religious law arrived from Jerusalem to confront Jesus. [2]They noticed that some of Jesus'

6:37 Greek *200 denarii*. A denarius was the equivalent of a full day's wage.   6:48 Greek *About the fourth watch of the night.*

disciples failed to follow the usual Jewish ritual of hand washing before eating. ³(The Jews, especially the Pharisees, do not eat until they have poured water over their cupped hands,* as required by their ancient traditions. ⁴Similarly, they eat nothing bought from the market unless they have immersed their hands in water. This is but one of many traditions they have clung to—such as their ceremony of washing cups, pitchers, and kettles.*) ⁵So the Pharisees and teachers of religious law asked him, "Why don't your disciples follow our age-old customs? For they eat without first performing the hand-washing ceremony."

⁶Jesus replied, "You hypocrites! Isaiah was prophesying about you when he said,

⁷ 'These people honor me with their lips,
　　but their hearts are far away.
　Their worship is a farce,
　　for they replace God's commands with their own
　　　man-made teachings.'*

⁸For you ignore God's specific laws and substitute your own traditions."

⁹Then he said, "You reject God's laws in order to hold on to your own traditions. ¹⁰For instance, Moses gave you this law from God: 'Honor your father and mother,' and 'Anyone who speaks evil of father or mother must be put to death.'* ¹¹But you say it is all right for people to say to their parents, 'Sorry, I can't help you. For I have vowed to give to God what I could have given to you.'* ¹²You let them disregard their needy parents. ¹³As such, you break the law of God in order to protect your own tradition. And this is only one example. There are many, many others."

¹⁴Then Jesus called to the crowd to come and hear. "All of you listen," he said, "and try to understand. ¹⁵You are not defiled by what you eat; you are defiled by what you say and do!*"

¹⁷Then Jesus went into a house to get away from the crowds, and his disciples asked him what he meant by the statement he had made. ¹⁸"Don't you understand either?" he asked. "Can't you see that what you eat won't defile you? ¹⁹Food doesn't come in contact with your heart, but only passes through the stomach and then comes out again." (By saying this, he showed that every kind of food is acceptable.)

²⁰And then he added, "It is the thought-life that defiles you. ²¹For from within, out of a person's heart, come evil thoughts, sexual immorality, theft, murder, ²²adultery, greed, wickedness, deceit, eagerness for lustful pleasure, envy, slander, pride, and foolishness. ²³All these vile things come from within; they are what defile you and make you unacceptable to God."

The Faith of a Gentile Woman

²⁴Then Jesus left Galilee and went north to the region of Tyre.* He tried to keep it secret that he was there, but he couldn't. As usual,

---

7:3 Greek *washed with the fist.*　7:4 Some Greek manuscripts add *and dining couches.*
7:7 Isa 29:13.　7:10 Exod 20:12; 21:17; Lev 20:9; Deut 5:16.　7:11 Greek *'What I could have given to you is Corban' (that is, a gift).*　7:15 Some manuscripts add verse 16, *Anyone who is willing to hear should listen and understand.*　7:24 Some Greek manuscripts add *and Sidon.*

the news of his arrival spread fast. ²⁵Right away a woman came to him whose little girl was possessed by an evil spirit. She had heard about Jesus, and now she came and fell at his feet. ²⁶She begged him to release her child from the demon's control.

Since she was a Gentile, born in Syrian Phoenicia, ²⁷Jesus told her, "First I should help my own family, the Jews.* It isn't right to take food from the children and throw it to the dogs."

²⁸She replied, "That's true, Lord, but even the dogs under the table are given some crumbs from the children's plates."

²⁹"Good answer!" he said. "And because you have answered so well, I have healed your daughter." ³⁰And when she arrived home, her little girl was lying quietly in bed, and the demon was gone.

Jesus Heals a Deaf and Mute Man

³¹Jesus left Tyre and went to Sidon, then back to the Sea of Galilee and the region of the Ten Towns.* ³²A deaf man with a speech impediment was brought to him, and the people begged Jesus to lay his hands on the man to heal him. ³³Jesus led him to a private place away from the crowd. He put his fingers into the man's ears. Then, spitting onto his own fingers, he touched the man's tongue with the spittle. ³⁴And looking up to heaven, he sighed and commanded, "Be opened!"* ³⁵Instantly the man could hear perfectly and speak plainly!

³⁶Jesus told the crowd not to tell anyone, but the more he told them not to, the more they spread the news, ³⁷for they were completely amazed. Again and again they said, "Everything he does is wonderful. He even heals those who are deaf and mute."

CHAPTER 8

Jesus Feeds Four Thousand

About this time another great crowd had gathered, and the people ran out of food again. Jesus called his disciples and told them, ²"I feel sorry for these people. They have been here with me for three days, and they have nothing left to eat. ³And if I send them home without feeding them, they will faint along the road. For some of them have come a long distance."

⁴"How are we supposed to find enough food for them here in the wilderness?" his disciples asked.

⁵"How many loaves of bread do you have?" he asked.

"Seven," they replied. ⁶So Jesus told all the people to sit down on the ground. Then he took the seven loaves, thanked God for them, broke them into pieces, and gave them to his disciples, who distributed the bread to the crowd. ⁷A few small fish were found, too, so Jesus also blessed these and told the disciples to pass them out.

⁸They ate until they were full, and when the scraps were picked up, there were seven large baskets of food left over! ⁹There were about four thousand people in the crowd that day, and he sent them home after they had eaten. ¹⁰Immediately after this, he got into a boat with his disciples and crossed over to the region of Dalmanutha.

Pharisees Demand a Miraculous Sign

¹¹When the Pharisees heard that Jesus had arrived, they came to argue with him. Testing him to see if he was from God, they

---

7:27 Greek *Let the children eat first.*   7:31 Greek *Decapolis.*   7:34 Greek text uses Aramaic *"Ephphatha"* and then translates it as "Be opened."

demanded, "Give us a miraculous sign from heaven to prove yourself."

[12]When he heard this, he sighed deeply and said, "Why do you people keep demanding a miraculous sign? I assure you, I will not give this generation any such sign." [13]So he got back into the boat and left them, and he crossed to the other side of the lake.

Yeast of the Pharisees and Herod

[14]But the disciples discovered they had forgotten to bring any food, so there was only one loaf of bread with them in the boat. [15]As they were crossing the lake, Jesus warned them, "Beware of the yeast of the Pharisees and of Herod."

[16]They decided he was saying this because they hadn't brought any bread. [17]Jesus knew what they were thinking, so he said, "Why are you so worried about having no food? Won't you ever learn or understand? Are your hearts too hard to take it in? [18]'You have eyes—can't you see? You have ears—can't you hear?'* Don't you remember anything at all? [19]What about the five thousand men I fed with five loaves of bread? How many baskets of leftovers did you pick up afterward?"

"Twelve," they said.

[20]"And when I fed the four thousand with seven loaves, how many large baskets of leftovers did you pick up?"

"Seven," they said.

[21]"Don't you understand even yet?" he asked them.

Jesus Heals a Blind Man

[22]When they arrived at Bethsaida, some people brought a blind man to Jesus, and they begged him to touch and heal the man. [23]Jesus took the blind man by the hand and led him out of the village. Then, spitting on the man's eyes, he laid his hands on him and asked, "Can you see anything now?"

[24]The man looked around. "Yes," he said, "I see people, but I can't see them very clearly. They look like trees walking around."

[25]Then Jesus placed his hands over the man's eyes again. As the man stared intently, his sight was completely restored, and he could see everything clearly. [26]Jesus sent him home, saying, "Don't go back into the village on your way home."

Peter's Declaration about Jesus

[27]Jesus and his disciples left Galilee and went up to the villages of Caesarea Philippi. As they were walking along, he asked them, "Who do people say I am?"

[28]"Well," they replied, "some say John the Baptist, some say Elijah, and others say you are one of the other prophets."

[29]Then Jesus asked, "Who do you say I am?"

Peter replied, "You are the Messiah." [30]But Jesus warned them not to tell anyone about him.

Jesus Predicts His Death

[31]Then Jesus began to tell them that he, the Son of Man, would suffer many terrible things and be rejected by the leaders, the leading priests, and the teachers of religious law. He would be killed, and three days later he would rise again. [32]As he talked

8:18 Jer 5:21.

about this openly with his disciples, Peter took him aside and told him he shouldn't say things like that.*

³³Jesus turned and looked at his disciples and then said to Peter very sternly, "Get away from me, Satan! You are seeing things merely from a human point of view, not from God's."

³⁴Then he called his disciples and the crowds to come over and listen. "If any of you wants to be my follower," he told them, "you must put aside your selfish ambition, shoulder your cross, and follow me. ³⁵If you try to keep your life for yourself, you will lose it. But if you give up your life for my sake and for the sake of the Good News, you will find true life. ³⁶And how do you benefit if you gain the whole world but lose your own soul* in the process? ³⁷Is anything worth more than your soul? ³⁸If a person is ashamed of me and my message in these adulterous and sinful days, I, the Son of Man, will be ashamed of that person when I return in the glory of my Father with the holy angels."

C H A P T E R 9

Jesus went on to say, "I assure you that some of you standing here right now will not die before you see the Kingdom of God arrive in great power!"

The Transfiguration

²Six days later Jesus took Peter, James, and John to the top of a mountain. No one else was there. As the men watched, Jesus' appearance changed, ³and his clothing became dazzling white, far whiter than any earthly process could ever make it. ⁴Then Elijah and Moses appeared and began talking with Jesus.

⁵"Teacher, this is wonderful!" Peter exclaimed. "We will make three shrines*—one for you, one for Moses, and one for Elijah." ⁶He didn't really know what to say, for they were all terribly afraid.

⁷Then a cloud came over them, and a voice from the cloud said, "This is my beloved Son. Listen to him." ⁸Suddenly they looked around, and Moses and Elijah were gone, and only Jesus was with them. ⁹As they descended the mountainside, he told them not to tell anyone what they had seen until he, the Son of Man, had risen from the dead. ¹⁰So they kept it to themselves, but they often asked each other what he meant by "rising from the dead."

¹¹Now they began asking him, "Why do the teachers of religious law insist that Elijah must return before the Messiah comes?"

¹²Jesus responded, "Elijah is indeed coming first to set everything in order. Why then is it written in the Scriptures that the Son of Man must suffer and be treated with utter contempt? ¹³But I tell you, Elijah has already come, and he was badly mistreated, just as the Scriptures predicted."

Jesus Heals a Boy Possessed by an Evil Spirit

¹⁴At the foot of the mountain they found a great crowd surrounding the other disciples, as some teachers of religious law were arguing with them. ¹⁵The crowd watched Jesus in awe as he came toward them, and then they ran to greet him. ¹⁶"What is all this arguing about?" he asked.

¹⁷One of the men in the crowd spoke up and said, "Teacher, I

8:32 Or *and began to correct him.* 8:36 Or *your life;* also in 8:37. 9:5 Or *shelters;* Greek reads *tabernacles.*

brought my son for you to heal him. He can't speak because he is possessed by an evil spirit that won't let him talk. 18And whenever this evil spirit seizes him, it throws him violently to the ground and makes him foam at the mouth and grind his teeth and become rigid.* So I asked your disciples to cast out the evil spirit, but they couldn't do it."

19Jesus said to them, "You faithless people! How long must I be with you until you believe? How long must I put up with you? Bring the boy to me." 20So they brought the boy. But when the evil spirit saw Jesus, it threw the child into a violent convulsion, and he fell to the ground, writhing and foaming at the mouth. 21"How long has this been happening?" Jesus asked the boy's father.

He replied, "Since he was very small. 22The evil spirit often makes him fall into the fire or into water, trying to kill him. Have mercy on us and help us. Do something if you can."

23"What do you mean, 'If I can'?" Jesus asked. "Anything is possible if a person believes."

24The father instantly replied, "I do believe, but help me not to doubt!"

25When Jesus saw that the crowd of onlookers was growing, he rebuked the evil spirit. "Spirit of deafness and muteness," he said, "I command you to come out of this child and never enter him again!" 26Then the spirit screamed and threw the boy into another violent convulsion and left him. The boy lay there motionless, and he appeared to be dead. A murmur ran through the crowd, "He's dead." 27But Jesus took him by the hand and helped him to his feet, and he stood up.

28Afterward, when Jesus was alone in the house with his disciples, they asked him, "Why couldn't we cast out that evil spirit?"

29Jesus replied, "This kind can be cast out only by prayer.*"

Jesus Again Predicts His Death

30Leaving that region, they traveled through Galilee. Jesus tried to avoid all publicity 31in order to spend more time with his disciples and teach them. He said to them, "The Son of Man is going to be betrayed. He will be killed, but three days later he will rise from the dead." 32But they didn't understand what he was saying, and they were afraid to ask him what he meant.

The Greatest in the Kingdom

33After they arrived at Capernaum, Jesus and his disciples settled in the house where they would be staying. Jesus asked them, "What were you discussing out on the road?" 34But they didn't answer, because they had been arguing about which of them was the greatest. 35He sat down and called the twelve disciples over to him. Then he said, "Anyone who wants to be the first must take last place and be the servant of everyone else."

36Then he put a little child among them. Taking the child in his arms, he said to them, 37"Anyone who welcomes a little child like this on my behalf welcomes me, and anyone who welcomes me welcomes my Father who sent me."

9:18 Or *become weak.*   9:29 Some manuscripts add *and fasting.*

Using the Name of Jesus

38John said to Jesus, "Teacher, we saw a man using your name to cast out demons, but we told him to stop because he isn't one of our group."

39"Don't stop him!" Jesus said. "No one who performs miracles in my name will soon be able to speak evil of me. 40Anyone who is not against us is for us. 41If anyone gives you even a cup of water because you belong to the Messiah, I assure you, that person will be rewarded.

42"But if anyone causes one of these little ones who trusts in me to lose faith, it would be better for that person to be thrown into the sea with a large millstone tied around the neck. 43If your hand causes you to sin, cut it off. It is better to enter heaven* with only one hand than to go into the unquenchable fires of hell with two hands.* 45If your foot causes you to sin, cut it off. It is better to enter heaven with only one foot than to be thrown into hell with two feet.* 47And if your eye causes you to sin, gouge it out. It is better to enter the Kingdom of God half blind than to have two eyes and be thrown into hell, 48'where the worm never dies and the fire never goes out.'*

49"For everyone will be purified with fire.* 50Salt is good for seasoning. But if it loses its flavor, how do you make it salty again? You must have the qualities of salt among yourselves and live in peace with each other."

CHAPTER 10

Discussion about Divorce and Marriage

Then Jesus left Capernaum and went southward to the region of Judea and into the area east of the Jordan River. As always there were the crowds, and as usual he taught them.

2Some Pharisees came and tried to trap him with this question: "Should a man be allowed to divorce his wife?"

3"What did Moses say about divorce?" Jesus asked them.

4"Well, he permitted it," they replied. "He said a man merely has to write his wife an official letter of divorce and send her away."

5But Jesus responded, "He wrote those instructions only as a concession to your hard-hearted wickedness. 6But God's plan was seen from the beginning of creation, for 'He made them male and female.'* 7'This explains why a man leaves his father and mother and is joined to his wife,* 8and the two are united into one.'* Since they are no longer two but one, 9let no one separate them, for God has joined them together."

10Later, when he was alone with his disciples in the house, they brought up the subject again. 11He told them, "Whoever divorces his wife and marries someone else commits adultery against her. 12And if a woman divorces her husband and remarries, she commits adultery."

Jesus Blesses the Children

13One day some parents brought their children to Jesus so he could touch them and bless them, but the disciples told them not to

---

9:43a Greek *enter life*; also in 9:45. 9:43b Some manuscripts add verse 44 (which is identical with 9:48). 9:45 Some manuscripts add verse 46 (which is identical with 9:48). 9:48 Isa 66:24. 9:49 Greek *salted with fire*. Some manuscripts add *and every sacrifice will be salted with salt.* 10:4 Deut 24:1. 10:6 Gen 1:27; 5:2. 10:7 Some manuscripts do not include *and is joined to his wife.* 10:7-8 Gen 2:24.

bother him. 14But when Jesus saw what was happening, he was very displeased with his disciples. He said to them, "Let the children come to me. Don't stop them! For the Kingdom of God belongs to such as these. 15I assure you, anyone who doesn't have their kind of faith will never get into the Kingdom of God." 16Then he took the children into his arms and placed his hands on their heads and blessed them.

The Rich Man

17As he was starting out on a trip, a man came running up to Jesus, knelt down, and asked, "Good Teacher, what should I do to get eternal life?"

18"Why do you call me good?" Jesus asked. "Only God is truly good. 19But as for your question, you know the commandments: 'Do not murder. Do not commit adultery. Do not steal. Do not testify falsely. Do not cheat. Honor your father and mother.'* "

20"Teacher," the man replied, "I've obeyed all these commandments since I was a child."

21Jesus felt genuine love for this man as he looked at him. "You lack only one thing," he told him. "Go and sell all you have and give the money to the poor, and you will have treasure in heaven. Then come, follow me." 22At this, the man's face fell, and he went sadly away because he had many possessions.

23Jesus looked around and said to his disciples, "How hard it is for rich people to get into the Kingdom of God!" 24This amazed them. But Jesus said again, "Dear children, it is very hard* to get into the Kingdom of God. 25It is easier for a camel to go through the eye of a needle than for a rich person to enter the Kingdom of God!"

26The disciples were astounded. "Then who in the world can be saved?" they asked.

27Jesus looked at them intently and said, "Humanly speaking, it is impossible. But not with God. Everything is possible with God."

28Then Peter began to mention all that he and the other disciples had left behind. "We've given up everything to follow you," he said.

29And Jesus replied, "I assure you that everyone who has given up house or brothers or sisters or mother or father or children or property, for my sake and for the Good News, 30will receive now in return, a hundred times over, houses, brothers, sisters, mothers, children, and property—with persecutions. And in the world to come they will have eternal life. 31But many who seem to be important now will be the least important then, and those who are considered least here will be the greatest then.* "

Jesus Again Predicts His Death

32They were now on the way to Jerusalem, and Jesus was walking ahead of them. The disciples were filled with dread and the people following behind were overwhelmed with fear. Taking the twelve disciples aside, Jesus once more began to describe everything that was about to happen to him in Jerusalem. 33"When we get to Jerusalem," he told them, "the Son of Man will be betrayed to the

10:19 Exod 20:12-16; Deut 5:16-20.   **10:24** Some manuscripts add *for those who trust in riches.*   **10:31** Greek *But many who are first will be last; and the last, first.*

leading priests and the teachers of religious law. They will sentence him to die and hand him over to the Romans. ³⁴They will mock him, spit on him, beat him with their whips, and kill him, but after three days he will rise again."

Jesus Teaches about Serving Others

³⁵Then James and John, the sons of Zebedee, came over and spoke to him. "Teacher," they said, "we want you to do us a favor."

³⁶"What is it?" he asked.

³⁷"In your glorious Kingdom, we want to sit in places of honor next to you," they said, "one at your right and the other at your left."

³⁸But Jesus answered, "You don't know what you are asking! Are you able to drink from the bitter cup of sorrow I am about to drink? Are you able to be baptized with the baptism of suffering I must be baptized with?"

³⁹"Oh yes," they said, "we are able!"

And Jesus said, "You will indeed drink from my cup and be baptized with my baptism, ⁴⁰but I have no right to say who will sit on the thrones next to mine. God has prepared those places for the ones he has chosen."

⁴¹When the ten other disciples discovered what James and John had asked, they were indignant. ⁴²So Jesus called them together and said, "You know that in this world kings are tyrants, and officials lord it over the people beneath them. ⁴³But among you it should be quite different. Whoever wants to be a leader among you must be your servant, ⁴⁴and whoever wants to be first must be the slave of all. ⁴⁵For even I, the Son of Man, came here not to be served but to serve others, and to give my life as a ransom for many."

Jesus Heals Blind Bartimaeus

⁴⁶And so they reached Jericho. Later, as Jesus and his disciples left town, a great crowd was following. A blind beggar named Bartimaeus (son of Timaeus) was sitting beside the road as Jesus was going by. ⁴⁷When Bartimaeus heard that Jesus from Nazareth was nearby, he began to shout out, "Jesus, Son of David, have mercy on me!"

⁴⁸"Be quiet!" some of the people yelled at him.

But he only shouted louder, "Son of David, have mercy on me!"

⁴⁹When Jesus heard him, he stopped and said, "Tell him to come here."

So they called the blind man. "Cheer up," they said. "Come on, he's calling you!" ⁵⁰Bartimaeus threw aside his coat, jumped up, and came to Jesus.

⁵¹"What do you want me to do for you?" Jesus asked.

"Teacher," the blind man said, "I want to see!"

⁵²And Jesus said to him, "Go your way. Your faith has healed you." And instantly the blind man could see! Then he followed Jesus down the road.*

CHAPTER 11

The Triumphal Entry

As Jesus and his disciples approached Jerusalem, they came to the towns of Bethphage and Bethany, on the Mount of Olives. Jesus

10:52 Or *on the way.*

sent two of them on ahead. ²"Go into that village over there," he told them, "and as soon as you enter it, you will see a colt tied there that has never been ridden. Untie it and bring it here. ³If anyone asks what you are doing, just say, 'The Lord needs it and will return it soon.'"

⁴The two disciples left and found the colt standing in the street, tied outside a house. ⁵As they were untying it, some bystanders demanded, "What are you doing, untying that colt?" ⁶They said what Jesus had told them to say, and they were permitted to take it. ⁷Then they brought the colt to Jesus and threw their garments over it, and he sat on it.

⁸Many in the crowd spread their coats on the road ahead of Jesus, and others cut leafy branches in the fields and spread them along the way. ⁹He was in the center of the procession, and the crowds all around him were shouting,

"Praise God!*
    Bless the one who comes in the name of the Lord!
¹⁰ Bless the coming kingdom of our ancestor David!
    Praise God in highest heaven!"*

¹¹So Jesus came to Jerusalem and went into the Temple. He looked around carefully at everything, and then he left because it was late in the afternoon. Then he went out to Bethany with the twelve disciples.

Jesus Curses the Fig Tree
¹²The next morning as they were leaving Bethany, Jesus felt hungry. ¹³He noticed a fig tree a little way off that was in full leaf, so he went over to see if he could find any figs on it. But there were only leaves because it was too early in the season for fruit. ¹⁴Then Jesus said to the tree, "May no one ever eat your fruit again!" And the disciples heard him say it.

Jesus Clears the Temple
¹⁵When they arrived back in Jerusalem, Jesus entered the Temple and began to drive out the merchants and their customers. He knocked over the tables of the money changers and the stalls of those selling doves, ¹⁶and he stopped everyone from bringing in merchandise. ¹⁷He taught them, "The Scriptures declare, 'My Temple will be called a place of prayer for all nations,' but you have turned it into a den of thieves."*

¹⁸When the leading priests and teachers of religious law heard what Jesus had done, they began planning how to kill him. But they were afraid of him because the people were so enthusiastic about Jesus' teaching. ¹⁹That evening Jesus and the disciples* left the city.

²⁰The next morning as they passed by the fig tree he had cursed, the disciples noticed it was withered from the roots. ²¹Peter remembered what Jesus had said to the tree on the previous day and exclaimed, "Look, Teacher! The fig tree you cursed has withered!"

²²Then Jesus said to the disciples, "Have faith in God. ²³I assure

11:9 Greek *Hosanna,* an exclamation of praise that literally means "save now"; also in 11:10.   11:9-10 Pss 118:25-26; 148:1.   11:17 Isa 56:7; Jer 7:11.   11:19 Greek *they;* some manuscripts read *he.*

you that you can say to this mountain, 'May God lift you up and throw you into the sea,' and your command will be obeyed. All that's required is that you really believe and do not doubt in your heart. ²⁴Listen to me! You can pray for anything, and if you believe, you will have it. ²⁵But when you are praying, first forgive anyone you are holding a grudge against, so that your Father in heaven will forgive your sins, too.*"

The Authority of Jesus Challenged

²⁷By this time they had arrived in Jerusalem again. As Jesus was walking through the Temple area, the leading priests, the teachers of religious law, and the other leaders came up to him. They demanded, ²⁸"By whose authority did you drive out the merchants from the Temple?* Who gave you such authority?"

²⁹"I'll tell who gave me authority to do these things if you answer one question," Jesus replied. ³⁰"Did John's baptism come from heaven or was it merely human? Answer me!"

³¹They talked it over among themselves. "If we say it was from heaven, he will ask why we didn't believe him. ³²But do we dare say it was merely human?" For they were afraid that the people would start a riot, since everyone thought that John was a prophet. ³³So they finally replied, "We don't know."

And Jesus responded, "Then I won't answer your question either."

CHAPTER 12

Story of the Evil Farmers

Then Jesus began telling them stories: "A man planted a vineyard, built a wall around it, dug a pit for pressing out the grape juice, and built a lookout tower. Then he leased the vineyard to tenant farmers and moved to another country. ²At grape-picking time he sent one of his servants to collect his share of the crop. ³But the farmers grabbed the servant, beat him up, and sent him back empty-handed.

⁴"The owner then sent another servant, but they beat him over the head and treated him shamefully. ⁵The next servant he sent was killed. Others who were sent were either beaten or killed, ⁶until there was only one left—his son whom he loved dearly. The owner finally sent him, thinking, 'Surely they will respect my son.'

⁷"But the farmers said to one another, 'Here comes the heir to this estate. Let's kill him and get the estate for ourselves!' ⁸So they grabbed him and murdered him and threw his body out of the vineyard.

⁹"What do you suppose the owner of the vineyard will do?" Jesus asked. "I'll tell you—he will come and kill them all and lease the vineyard to others. ¹⁰Didn't you ever read this in the Scriptures?

'The stone rejected by the builders
    has now become the cornerstone.
¹¹ This is the Lord's doing,
    and it is marvelous to see.'*"

11:25 Some manuscripts add verse 26, *But if you do not forgive, neither will your Father who is in heaven forgive your sins.* 11:28 Or *By whose authority do you do these things?*
12:10-11 Ps 118:22-23.

¹²The Jewish leaders wanted to arrest him for using this illustration because they realized he was pointing at them—they were the wicked farmers in his story. But they were afraid to touch him because of the crowds. So they left him and went away.

Taxes for Caesar

¹³The leaders sent some Pharisees and supporters of Herod to try to trap Jesus into saying something for which he could be arrested. ¹⁴"Teacher," these men said, "we know how honest you are. You are impartial and don't play favorites. You sincerely teach the ways of God. Now tell us—is it right to pay taxes to the Roman government or not? ¹⁵Should we pay them, or should we not?"

Jesus saw through their hypocrisy and said, "Whom are you trying to fool with your trick questions? Show me a Roman coin,* and I'll tell you." ¹⁶When they handed it to him, he asked, "Whose picture and title are stamped on it?"

"Caesar's," they replied.

¹⁷"Well, then," Jesus said, "give to Caesar what belongs to him. But everything that belongs to God must be given to God." This reply completely amazed them.

Discussion about Resurrection

¹⁸Then the Sadducees stepped forward—a group of Jews who say there is no resurrection after death. They posed this question: ¹⁹"Teacher, Moses gave us a law that if a man dies, leaving a wife without children, his brother should marry the widow and have a child who will be the brother's heir.* ²⁰Well, there were seven brothers. The oldest of them married and then died without children. ²¹So the second brother married the widow, but soon he too died and left no children. Then the next brother married her and died without children. ²²This continued until all the brothers had married her and died, and still there were no children. Last of all, the woman died, too. ²³So tell us, whose wife will she be in the resurrection? For all seven were married to her."

²⁴Jesus replied, "Your problem is that you don't know the Scriptures, and you don't know the power of God. ²⁵For when the dead rise, they won't be married. They will be like the angels in heaven. ²⁶But now, as to whether the dead will be raised—haven't you ever read about this in the writings of Moses, in the story of the burning bush? Long after Abraham, Isaac, and Jacob had died, God said to Moses,* 'I am the God of Abraham, the God of Isaac, and the God of Jacob.'* ²⁷So he is the God of the living, not the dead. You have made a serious error."

The Most Important Commandment

²⁸One of the teachers of religious law was standing there listening to the discussion. He realized that Jesus had answered well, so he asked, "Of all the commandments, which is the most important?"

²⁹Jesus replied, "The most important commandment is this: 'Hear, O Israel! The Lord our God is the one and only Lord. ³⁰And you must love the Lord your God with all your heart, all your soul, all your mind, and all your strength.'* ³¹The second is equally

12:15 Greek *a denarius.* **12:19** Deut 25:5-6. **12:26a** Greek *in the story of the bush? God said to him.* **12:26b** Exod 3:6. **12:29-30** Deut 6:4-5.

important: 'Love your neighbor as yourself.'* No other command-ment is greater than these."

³²The teacher of religious law replied, "Well said, Teacher. You have spoken the truth by saying that there is only one God and no other. ³³And I know it is important to love him with all my heart and all my understanding and all my strength, and to love my neighbors as myself. This is more important than to offer all of the burnt offerings and sacrifices required in the law."

³⁴Realizing this man's understanding, Jesus said to him, "You are not far from the Kingdom of God." And after that, no one dared to ask him any more questions.

Whose Son Is the Messiah?

³⁵Later, as Jesus was teaching the people in the Temple, he asked, "Why do the teachers of religious law claim that the Messiah will be the son of David? ³⁶For David himself, speaking under the inspiration of the Holy Spirit, said,

'The LORD said to my Lord,
Sit in honor at my right hand
    until I humble your enemies beneath your feet.'*

³⁷Since David himself called him Lord, how can he be his son at the same time?" And the crowd listened to him with great interest.

³⁸Here are some of the other things he taught them at this time: "Beware of these teachers of religious law! For they love to parade in flowing robes and to have everyone bow to them as they walk in the marketplaces. ³⁹And how they love the seats of honor in the synagogues and at banquets. ⁴⁰But they shamelessly cheat widows out of their property, and then, to cover up the kind of people they really are, they make long prayers in public. Because of this, their punishment will be the greater."

The Widow's Offering

⁴¹Jesus went over to the collection box in the Temple and sat and watched as the crowds dropped in their money. Many rich people put in large amounts. ⁴²Then a poor widow came and dropped in two pennies.* ⁴³He called his disciples to him and said, "I assure you, this poor widow has given more than all the others have given. ⁴⁴For they gave a tiny part of their surplus, but she, poor as she is, has given everything she has."

CHAPTER 13

Jesus Foretells the Future

As Jesus was leaving the Temple that day, one of his disciples said, "Teacher, look at these tremendous buildings! Look at the massive stones in the walls!"

²Jesus replied, "These magnificent buildings will be so com-pletely demolished that not one stone will be left on top of another."

³Later, Jesus sat on the slopes of the Mount of Olives across the valley from the Temple. Peter, James, John, and Andrew came to him privately and asked him, ⁴"When will all this take place? And

12:31 Lev 19:18. **12:36** Ps 110:1. **12:42** Greek *2 lepta, which is a kodrantes.*

will there be any sign ahead of time to show us when all this will be fulfilled?"

5Jesus replied, "Don't let anyone mislead you, 6because many will come in my name, claiming to be the Messiah.* They will lead many astray. 7And wars will break out near and far, but don't panic. Yes, these things must come, but the end won't follow immediately. 8Nations and kingdoms will proclaim war against each other, and there will be earthquakes in many parts of the world, and famines. But all this will be only the beginning of the horrors to come. 9But when these things begin to happen, watch out! You will be handed over to the courts and beaten in the synagogues. You will be accused before governors and kings of being my followers. This will be your opportunity to tell them about me.* 10And the Good News must first be preached to every nation. 11But when you are arrested and stand trial, don't worry about what to say in your defense. Just say what God tells you to. Then it is not you who will be speaking, but the Holy Spirit.

12"Brother will betray brother to death, fathers will betray their own children, and children will rise against their parents and cause them to be killed. 13And everyone will hate you because of your allegiance to me. But those who endure to the end will be saved.

14"The time will come when you will see the sacrilegious object that causes desecration* standing where it should not be"— reader, pay attention! "Then those in Judea must flee to the hills. 15A person outside the house* must not go back into the house to pack. 16A person in the field must not return even to get a coat. 17How terrible it will be for pregnant women and for mothers nursing their babies in those days. 18And pray that your flight will not be in winter. 19For those will be days of greater horror than at any time since God created the world. And it will never happen again. 20In fact, unless the Lord shortens that time of calamity, the entire human race will be destroyed. But for the sake of his chosen ones he has shortened those days.

21"And then if anyone tells you, 'Look, here is the Messiah,' or, 'There he is,' don't pay any attention. 22For false messiahs and false prophets will rise up and perform miraculous signs and wonders so as to deceive, if possible, even God's chosen ones. 23Watch out! I have warned you!

24"At that time, after those horrible days end,

the sun will be darkened,
the moon will not give light,
25 the stars will fall from the sky,
and the powers of heaven will be shaken.*

26Then everyone will see the Son of Man arrive on the clouds with great power and glory.* 27And he will send forth his angels to gather together his chosen ones from all over the world—from the farthest ends of the earth and heaven.

28"Now, learn a lesson from the fig tree. When its buds become tender and its leaves begin to sprout, you know without being told that summer is near. 29Just so, when you see the events I've

---

13:6 Greek *name, saying, 'I am.'*   **13:9** Or *This will be your testimony against them.*
13:14 Greek *the abomination of desolation.* See Dan 9:27; 11:31; 12:11.   **13:15** Greek *on the roof.*   **13:24-25** See Isa 13:10; 34:4; Joel 2:10.   **13:26** See Dan 7:13.

described beginning to happen, you can be sure that his return is very near, right at the door. ³⁰I assure you, this generation* will not pass from the scene until all these events have taken place. ³¹Heaven and earth will disappear, but my words will remain forever.

³²"However, no one knows the day or hour when these things will happen, not even the angels in heaven or the Son himself. Only the Father knows. ³³And since you don't know when they will happen, stay alert and keep watch.*

³⁴"The coming of the Son of Man can be compared with that of a man who left home to go on a trip. He gave each of his employees instructions about the work they were to do, and he told the gatekeeper to watch for his return. ³⁵So keep a sharp lookout! For you do not know when the homeowner will return—at evening, midnight, early dawn, or late daybreak. ³⁶Don't let him find you sleeping when he arrives without warning. ³⁷What I say to you I say to everyone: Watch for his return!"

CHAPTER 14

Jesus Anointed at Bethany

It was now two days before the Passover celebration and the Festival of Unleavened Bread. The leading priests and the teachers of religious law were still looking for an opportunity to capture Jesus secretly and put him to death. ²"But not during the Passover," they agreed, "or there will be a riot."

³Meanwhile, Jesus was in Bethany at the home of Simon, a man who had leprosy. During supper, a woman came in with a beautiful jar of expensive perfume.* She broke the seal and poured the perfume over his head. ⁴Some of those at the table were indignant. "Why was this expensive perfume wasted?" they asked. ⁵"She could have sold it for a small fortune* and given the money to the poor!" And they scolded her harshly.

⁶But Jesus replied, "Leave her alone. Why berate her for doing such a good thing to me? ⁷You will always have the poor among you, and you can help them whenever you want to. But I will not be here with you much longer. ⁸She has done what she could and has anointed my body for burial ahead of time. ⁹I assure you, wherever the Good News is preached throughout the world, this woman's deed will be talked about in her memory."

Judas Agrees to Betray Jesus

¹⁰Then Judas Iscariot, one of the twelve disciples, went to the leading priests to arrange to betray Jesus to them. ¹¹The leading priests were delighted when they heard why he had come, and they promised him a reward. So he began looking for the right time and place to betray Jesus.

The Last Supper

¹²On the first day of the Festival of Unleavened Bread (the day the Passover lambs were sacrificed), Jesus' disciples asked him, "Where do you want us to go to prepare the Passover supper?"

¹³So Jesus sent two of them into Jerusalem to make the arrange-

13:30 Or *this age,* or *this nation.*   13:33 Some manuscripts add *and pray.*   14:3 Greek *an alabaster jar of expensive ointment, pure nard.*   14:5 Greek *300 denarii. A denarius was the equivalent of a full day's wage.*

ments. "As you go into the city," he told them, "a man carrying a pitcher of water will meet you. Follow him. [14]At the house he enters, say to the owner, 'The Teacher asks, Where is the guest room where I can eat the Passover meal with my disciples?' [15]He will take you upstairs to a large room that is already set up. That is the place; go ahead and prepare our supper there." [16]So the two disciples went on ahead into the city and found everything just as Jesus had said, and they prepared the Passover supper there.

[17]In the evening Jesus arrived with the twelve disciples. [18]As they were sitting around the table eating, Jesus said, "The truth is, one of you will betray me, one of you who is here eating with me."

[19]Greatly distressed, one by one they began to ask him, "I'm not the one, am I?"

[20]He replied, "It is one of you twelve, one who is eating with me now.* [21]For I, the Son of Man, must die, as the Scriptures declared long ago. But how terrible it will be for my betrayer. Far better for him if he had never been born!"

[22]As they were eating, Jesus took a loaf of bread and asked God's blessing on it. Then he broke it in pieces and gave it to the disciples, saying, "Take it, for this is my body."

[23]And he took a cup of wine and gave thanks to God for it. He gave it to them, and they all drank from it. [24]And he said to them, "This is my blood, poured out for many, sealing the covenant* between God and his people. [25]I solemnly declare that I will not drink wine again until that day when I drink it new in the Kingdom of God." [26]Then they sang a hymn and went out to the Mount of Olives.

Jesus Predicts Peter's Denial

[27]"All of you will desert me," Jesus told them. "For the Scriptures say,

'God* will strike the Shepherd,
    and the sheep will be scattered.'*

[28]But after I am raised from the dead, I will go ahead of you to Galilee and meet you there."

[29]Peter said to him, "Even if everyone else deserts you, I never will."

[30]"Peter," Jesus replied, "the truth is, this very night, before the rooster crows twice, you will deny me three times."

[31]"No!" Peter insisted. "Not even if I have to die with you! I will never deny you!" And all the others vowed the same.

Jesus Prays in Gethsemane

[32]And they came to an olive grove called Gethsemane, and Jesus said, "Sit here while I go and pray." [33]He took Peter, James, and John with him, and he began to be filled with horror and deep distress. [34]He told them, "My soul is crushed with grief to the point of death. Stay here and watch with me."

[35]He went on a little farther and fell face down on the ground. He prayed that, if it were possible, the awful hour awaiting him might pass him by. [36]"Abba,* Father," he said, "everything is

14:20 Or *one who is dipping bread into the bowl with me.* 14:24 Some manuscripts read *the new covenant.* 14:27a Greek *I.* 14:27b Zech 13:7. 14:36 *Abba* is an Aramaic term for "father."

possible for you. Please take this cup of suffering away from me. Yet I want your will, not mine."

37Then he returned and found the disciples asleep. "Simon!" he said to Peter. "Are you asleep? Couldn't you stay awake and watch with me even one hour? 38Keep alert and pray. Otherwise temptation will overpower you. For though the spirit is willing enough, the body is weak."

39Then Jesus left them again and prayed, repeating his pleadings. 40Again he returned to them and found them sleeping, for they just couldn't keep their eyes open. And they didn't know what to say.

41When he returned to them the third time, he said, "Still sleeping? Still resting?* Enough! The time has come. I, the Son of Man, am betrayed into the hands of sinners. 42Up, let's be going. See, my betrayer is here!"

Jesus Is Betrayed and Arrested

43And immediately, as he said this, Judas, one of the twelve disciples, arrived with a mob that was armed with swords and clubs. They had been sent out by the leading priests, the teachers of religious law, and the other leaders. 44Judas had given them a prearranged signal: "You will know which one to arrest when I go over and give him the kiss of greeting. Then you can take him away under guard."

45As soon as they arrived, Judas walked up to Jesus. "Teacher!" he exclaimed, and gave him the kiss. 46Then the others grabbed Jesus and arrested him. 47But someone pulled out a sword and slashed off an ear of the high priest's servant.

48Jesus asked them, "Am I some dangerous criminal, that you come armed with swords and clubs to arrest me? 49Why didn't you arrest me in the Temple? I was there teaching every day. But these things are happening to fulfill what the Scriptures say about me."

50Meanwhile, all his disciples deserted him and ran away. 51There was a young man following along behind, clothed only in a linen nightshirt. When the mob tried to grab him, 52they tore off his clothes, but he escaped and ran away naked.

Jesus before the Council

53Jesus was led to the high priest's home where the leading priests, other leaders, and teachers of religious law had gathered. 54Meanwhile, Peter followed far behind and then slipped inside the gates of the high priest's courtyard. For a while he sat with the guards, warming himself by the fire.

55Inside, the leading priests and the entire high council* were trying to find witnesses who would testify against Jesus, so they could put him to death. But their efforts were in vain. 56Many false witnesses spoke against him, but they contradicted each other. 57Finally, some men stood up to testify against him with this lie: 58"We heard him say, 'I will destroy this Temple made with human hands, and in three days I will build another, made without human hands.'" 59But even then they didn't get their stories straight!

60Then the high priest stood up before the others and asked Jesus, "Well, aren't you going to answer these charges? What do

14:41 Or *Sleep on, take your rest.*   14:55 Greek *the Sanhedrin.*

you have to say for yourself?" 61Jesus made no reply. Then the high priest asked him, "Are you the Messiah, the Son of the blessed God?"

62Jesus said, "I am, and you will see me, the Son of Man, sitting at God's right hand in the place of power and coming back on the clouds of heaven."*

63Then the high priest tore his clothing to show his horror and said, "Why do we need other witnesses? 64You have all heard his blasphemy. What is your verdict?" And they all condemned him to death.

65Then some of them began to spit at him, and they blindfolded him and hit his face with their fists. "Who hit you that time, you prophet?" they jeered. And even the guards were hitting him as they led him away.

Peter Denies Jesus

66Meanwhile, Peter was below in the courtyard. One of the servant girls who worked for the high priest 67noticed Peter warming himself at the fire. She looked at him closely and then said, "You were one of those with Jesus, the Nazarene."

68Peter denied it. "I don't know what you're talking about," he said, and he went out into the entryway. Just then, a rooster crowed.*

69The servant girl saw him standing there and began telling the others, "That man is definitely one of them!" 70Peter denied it again.

A little later some other bystanders began saying to Peter, "You must be one of them because you are from Galilee."

71Peter said, "I swear by God, I don't know this man you're talking about." 72And immediately the rooster crowed the second time. Suddenly, Jesus' words flashed through Peter's mind: "Before the rooster crows twice, you will deny me three times." And he broke down and cried.

CHAPTER 15

Jesus' Trial before Pilate

Very early in the morning the leading priests, other leaders, and teachers of religious law—the entire high council*—met to discuss their next step. They bound Jesus and took him to Pilate, the Roman governor.

2Pilate asked Jesus, "Are you the King of the Jews?"

Jesus replied, "Yes, it is as you say."

3Then the leading priests accused him of many crimes, 4and Pilate asked him, "Aren't you going to say something? What about all these charges against you?" 5But Jesus said nothing, much to Pilate's surprise.

6Now it was the governor's custom to release one prisoner each year at Passover time—anyone the people requested. 7One of the prisoners at that time was Barabbas, convicted along with others for murder during an insurrection. 8The mob began to crowd in toward Pilate, asking him to release a prisoner as usual. 9"Should I give you the King of the Jews?" Pilate asked. 10(For he realized by now that the leading

14:62 See Ps 110:1; Dan 7:13.   14:68 Some manuscripts do not include *Just then, a rooster crowed.*   15:1 Greek *the Sanhedrin;* also in 15:43.

priests had arrested Jesus out of envy.) 11But at this point the leading priests stirred up the mob to demand the release of Barabbas instead of Jesus. 12"But if I release Barabbas," Pilate asked them, "what should I do with this man you call the King of the Jews?"

13They shouted back, "Crucify him!"

14"Why?" Pilate demanded. "What crime has he committed?"

But the crowd only roared the louder, "Crucify him!"

15So Pilate, anxious to please the crowd, released Barabbas to them. He ordered Jesus flogged with a lead-tipped whip, then turned him over to the Roman soldiers to crucify him.

The Soldiers Mock Jesus

16The soldiers took him into their headquarters* and called out the entire battalion. 17They dressed him in a purple robe and made a crown of long, sharp thorns and put it on his head. 18Then they saluted, yelling, "Hail! King of the Jews!" 19And they beat him on the head with a stick, spit on him, and dropped to their knees in mock worship. 20When they were finally tired of mocking him, they took off the purple robe and put his own clothes on him again. Then they led him away to be crucified.

The Crucifixion

21A man named Simon, who was from Cyrene,* was coming in from the country just then, and they forced him to carry Jesus' cross. (Simon is the father of Alexander and Rufus.) 22And they brought Jesus to a place called Golgotha (which means Skull Hill). 23They offered him wine drugged with myrrh, but he refused it. 24Then they nailed him to the cross. They gambled for his clothes, throwing dice* to decide who would get them.

25It was nine o'clock in the morning when the crucifixion took place. 26A signboard was fastened to the cross above Jesus' head, announcing the charge against him. It read: "The King of the Jews." 27Two criminals were crucified with him, their crosses on either side of his.* 29And the people passing by shouted abuse, shaking their heads in mockery. "Ha! Look at you now!" they yelled at him. "You can destroy the Temple and rebuild it in three days, can you? 30Well then, save yourself and come down from the cross!"

31The leading priests and teachers of religious law also mocked Jesus. "He saved others," they scoffed, "but he can't save himself! 32Let this Messiah, this king of Israel, come down from the cross so we can see it and believe him!" Even the two criminals who were being crucified with Jesus ridiculed him.

The Death of Jesus

33At noon, darkness fell across the whole land until three o'clock. 34Then, at that time Jesus called out with a loud voice, "Eloi, Eloi, lema sabachthani?" which means, "My God, my God, why have you forsaken me?"*

35Some of the bystanders misunderstood and thought he was calling for the prophet Elijah. 36One of them ran and filled a sponge with sour wine, holding it up to him on a stick so he could

---

15:16 Greek *the courtyard, which is the praetorium.*   **15:21** *Cyrene* was a city in northern Africa.   **15:24** Greek *casting lots.* See Ps 22:18.   **15:27** Some manuscripts add verse 28, *And the Scripture was fulfilled that said, "He was counted among those who were rebels."* See Isa 53:12.   **15:34** Ps 22:1.

drink. "Leave him alone. Let's see whether Elijah will come and take him down!" he said.

37Then Jesus uttered another loud cry and breathed his last. 38And the curtain in the Temple was torn in two, from top to bottom. 39When the Roman officer who stood facing him saw how he had died, he exclaimed, "Truly, this was the Son of God!"

40Some women were there, watching from a distance, including Mary Magdalene, Mary (the mother of James the younger and of Joseph*), and Salome. 41They had been followers of Jesus and had cared for him while he was in Galilee. Then they and many other women had come with him to Jerusalem.

The Burial of Jesus

42This all happened on Friday, the day of preparation,* the day before the Sabbath. As evening approached, 43an honored member of the high council, Joseph from Arimathea (who was waiting for the Kingdom of God to come), gathered his courage and went to Pilate to ask for Jesus' body. 44Pilate couldn't believe that Jesus was already dead, so he called for the Roman military officer in charge and asked him. 45The officer confirmed the fact, and Pilate told Joseph he could have the body. 46Joseph bought a long sheet of linen cloth, and taking Jesus' body down from the cross, he wrapped it in the cloth and laid it in a tomb that had been carved out of the rock. Then he rolled a stone in front of the entrance. 47Mary Magdalene and Mary the mother of Joseph saw where Jesus' body was laid.

CHAPTER 16

The Resurrection

The next evening, when the Sabbath ended, Mary Magdalene and Salome and Mary the mother of James went out and purchased burial spices to put on Jesus' body. 2Very early on Sunday morning,* just at sunrise, they came to the tomb. 3On the way they were discussing who would roll the stone away from the entrance to the tomb. 4But when they arrived, they looked up and saw that the stone—a very large one—had already been rolled aside. 5So they entered the tomb, and there on the right sat a young man clothed in a white robe. The women were startled, 6but the angel said, "Do not be so surprised. You are looking for Jesus, the Nazarene, who was crucified. He isn't here! He has been raised from the dead! Look, this is where they laid his body. 7Now go and give this message to his disciples, including Peter: Jesus is going ahead of you to Galilee. You will see him there, just as he told you before he died!" 8The women fled from the tomb, trembling and bewildered, saying nothing to anyone because they were too frightened to talk.*

[Shorter Ending of Mark]

Then they reported all these instructions briefly to Peter and his companions. Afterward Jesus himself sent them out from east to west with the sacred and unfailing message of salvation that gives eternal life. Amen.

15:40 Greek *Joses;* also in 15:47. See Matt 27:56.   **15:42** Greek *on the day of preparation.* **16:2** Greek *on the first day of the week;* also in 16:9.   **16:8** The most reliable early manuscripts conclude the Gospel of Mark at verse 8. Other manuscripts include various endings to the Gospel. Two of the more noteworthy endings are printed here.

[Longer Ending of Mark]

9It was early on Sunday morning when Jesus rose from the dead, and the first person who saw him was Mary Magdalene, the woman from whom he had cast out seven demons. 10She went and found the disciples, who were grieving and weeping. 11But when she told them that Jesus was alive and she had seen him, they didn't believe her.

12Afterward he appeared to two who were walking from Jerusalem into the country, but they didn't recognize him at first because he had changed his appearance. 13When they realized who he was, they rushed back to tell the others, but no one believed them.

14Still later he appeared to the eleven disciples as they were eating together. He rebuked them for their unbelief—their stubborn refusal to believe those who had seen him after he had risen.

15And then he told them, "Go into all the world and preach the Good News to everyone, everywhere. 16Anyone who believes and is baptized will be saved. But anyone who refuses to believe will be condemned. 17These signs will accompany those who believe: They will cast out demons in my name, and they will speak new languages.* 18They will be able to handle snakes with safety, and if they drink anything poisonous, it won't hurt them. They will be able to place their hands on the sick and heal them."

19When the Lord Jesus had finished talking with them, he was taken up into heaven and sat down in the place of honor at God's right hand. 20And the disciples went everywhere and preached, and the Lord worked with them, confirming what they said by many miraculous signs.

16:17 Or *new tongues.* Some manuscripts omit *new.*

LUKE

CHAPTER 1

Introduction

Most honorable Theophilus:

Many people have written accounts about the events that took place* among us. 2They used as their source material the reports circulating among us from the early disciples and other eyewitnesses of what God has done in fulfillment of his promises. 3Having carefully investigated all of these accounts from the beginning, I have decided to write a careful summary for you, 4to reassure you of the truth of all you were taught.

The Birth of John the Baptist Foretold

5It all begins with a Jewish priest, Zechariah, who lived when Herod was king of Judea. Zechariah was a member of the priestly order of Abijah. His wife, Elizabeth, was also from the priestly line of Aaron. 6Zechariah and Elizabeth were righteous in God's eyes, careful to obey all of the Lord's commandments and regulations.

1:1 Or *have been fulfilled.*

⁷They had no children because Elizabeth was barren, and now they were both very old.

⁸One day Zechariah was serving God in the Temple, for his order was on duty that week. ⁹As was the custom of the priests, he was chosen by lot to enter the sanctuary and burn incense in the Lord's presence. ¹⁰While the incense was being burned, a great crowd stood outside, praying.

¹¹Zechariah was in the sanctuary when an angel of the Lord appeared, standing to the right of the incense altar. ¹²Zechariah was overwhelmed with fear. ¹³But the angel said, "Don't be afraid, Zechariah! For God has heard your prayer, and your wife, Elizabeth, will bear you a son! And you are to name him John. ¹⁴You will have great joy and gladness, and many will rejoice with you at his birth, ¹⁵for he will be great in the eyes of the Lord. He must never touch wine or hard liquor, and he will be filled with the Holy Spirit, even before his birth.* ¹⁶And he will persuade many Israelites to turn to the Lord their God. ¹⁷He will be a man with the spirit and power of Elijah, the prophet of old. He will precede the coming of the Lord, preparing the people for his arrival. He will turn the hearts of the fathers to their children, and he will change disobedient minds to accept godly wisdom."*

¹⁸Zechariah said to the angel, "How can I know this will happen? I'm an old man now, and my wife is also well along in years."

¹⁹Then the angel said, "I am Gabriel! I stand in the very presence of God. It was he who sent me to bring you this good news! ²⁰And now, since you didn't believe what I said, you won't be able to speak until the child is born. For my words will certainly come true at the proper time."

²¹Meanwhile, the people were waiting for Zechariah to come out, wondering why he was taking so long. ²²When he finally did come out, he couldn't speak to them. Then they realized from his gestures that he must have seen a vision in the Temple sanctuary.

²³He stayed at the Temple until his term of service was over, and then he returned home. ²⁴Soon afterward his wife, Elizabeth, became pregnant and went into seclusion for five months. ²⁵"How kind the Lord is!" she exclaimed. "He has taken away my disgrace of having no children!"

The Birth of Jesus Foretold

²⁶In the sixth month of Elizabeth's pregnancy, God sent the angel Gabriel to Nazareth, a village in Galilee, ²⁷to a virgin named Mary. She was engaged to be married to a man named Joseph, a descendant of King David. ²⁸Gabriel appeared to her and said, "Greetings, favored woman! The Lord is with you!*"

²⁹Confused and disturbed, Mary tried to think what the angel could mean. ³⁰"Don't be frightened, Mary," the angel told her, "for God has decided to bless you! ³¹You will become pregnant and have a son, and you are to name him Jesus. ³²He will be very great and will be called the Son of the Most High. And the Lord God will give him the throne of his ancestor David. ³³And he will reign over Israel* forever; his Kingdom will never end!"

³⁴Mary asked the angel, "But how can I have a baby? I am a virgin."

1:15 Or *even from birth.*   1:17 See Mal 4:5-6.   1:28 Some manuscripts add *Blessed are you among women.*   1:33 Greek *over the house of Jacob.*

35The angel replied, "The Holy Spirit will come upon you, and the power of the Most High will overshadow you. So the baby born to you will be holy, and he will be called the Son of God. 36What's more, your relative Elizabeth has become pregnant in her old age! People used to say she was barren, but she's already in her sixth month. 37For nothing is impossible with God."

38Mary responded, "I am the Lord's servant, and I am willing to accept whatever he wants. May everything you have said come true." And then the angel left.

Mary Visits Elizabeth

39A few days later Mary hurried to the hill country of Judea, to the town 40where Zechariah lived. She entered the house and greeted Elizabeth. 41At the sound of Mary's greeting, Elizabeth's child leaped within her, and Elizabeth was filled with the Holy Spirit.

42Elizabeth gave a glad cry and exclaimed to Mary, "You are blessed by God above all other women, and your child is blessed. 43What an honor this is, that the mother of my Lord should visit me! 44When you came in and greeted me, my baby jumped for joy the instant I heard your voice! 45You are blessed, because you believed that the Lord would do what he said."

The Magnificat: Mary's Song of Praise

46Mary responded,

"Oh, how I praise the Lord.
47 How I rejoice in God my Savior!
48 For he took notice of his lowly servant girl,
        and now generation after generation
        will call me blessed.
49 For he, the Mighty One, is holy,
        and he has done great things for me.
50 His mercy goes on from generation to generation,
        to all who fear him.
51 His mighty arm does tremendous things!
        How he scatters the proud and haughty ones!
52 He has taken princes from their thrones
        and exalted the lowly.
53 He has satisfied the hungry with good things
        and sent the rich away with empty hands.
54 And how he has helped his servant Israel!
        He has not forgotten his promise to be merciful.
55 For he promised our ancestors—Abraham and his children—
        to be merciful to them forever."

56Mary stayed with Elizabeth about three months and then went back to her own home.

The Birth of John the Baptist

57Now it was time for Elizabeth's baby to be born, and it was a boy. 58The word spread quickly to her neighbors and relatives that the Lord had been very kind to her, and everyone rejoiced with her.

59When the baby was eight days old, all the relatives and friends came for the circumcision ceremony. They wanted to name him Zechariah, after his father. 60But Elizabeth said, "No! His name is John!"

61 "What?" they exclaimed. "There is no one in all your family by that name." 62So they asked the baby's father, communicating to him by making gestures. 63He motioned for a writing tablet, and to everyone's surprise he wrote, "His name is John!" 64Instantly Zechariah could speak again, and he began praising God.

65Wonder fell upon the whole neighborhood, and the news of what had happened spread throughout the Judean hills. 66Everyone who heard about it reflected on these events and asked, "I wonder what this child will turn out to be? For the hand of the Lord is surely upon him in a special way."

Zechariah's Prophecy

67Then his father, Zechariah, was filled with the Holy Spirit and gave this prophecy:

68 "Praise the Lord, the God of Israel,
    because he has visited his people and redeemed them.
69 He has sent us a mighty Savior
    from the royal line of his servant David,
70 just as he promised
    through his holy prophets long ago.
71 Now we will be saved from our enemies
    and from all who hate us.
72 He has been merciful to our ancestors
    by remembering his sacred covenant with them,
73   the covenant he gave to our ancestor Abraham.
74 We have been rescued from our enemies,
    so we can serve God without fear,
75   in holiness and righteousness forever.

76 "And you, my little son,
    will be called the prophet of the Most High,
    because you will prepare the way for the Lord.
77 You will tell his people how to find salvation
    through forgiveness of their sins.
78 Because of God's tender mercy,
    the light from heaven is about to break upon us,
79 to give light to those who sit in darkness and in the shadow of
    death,
    and to guide us to the path of peace."

80John grew up and became strong in spirit. Then he lived out in the wilderness until he began his public ministry to Israel.

CHAPTER 2

The Birth of Jesus

At that time the Roman emperor, Augustus, decreed that a census should be taken throughout the Roman Empire. 2(This was the first census taken when Quirinius was governor of Syria.) 3All returned to their own towns to register for this census. 4And because Joseph was a descendant of King David, he had to go to Bethlehem in Judea, David's ancient home. He traveled there from the village of Nazareth in Galilee. 5He took with him Mary, his fiancée, who was obviously pregnant by this time.

6And while they were there, the time came for her baby to be born. 7She gave birth to her first child, a son. She wrapped him snugly in strips of cloth and laid him in a manger, because there was no room for them in the village inn.

The Shepherds and Angels

8That night some shepherds were in the fields outside the village, guarding their flocks of sheep. 9Suddenly, an angel of the Lord appeared among them, and the radiance of the Lord's glory surrounded them. They were terribly frightened, 10but the angel reassured them. "Don't be afraid!" he said. "I bring you good news of great joy for everyone! 11The Savior—yes, the Messiah, the Lord—has been born tonight in Bethlehem, the city of David! 12And this is how you will recognize him: You will find a baby lying in a manger, wrapped snugly in strips of cloth!"

13Suddenly, the angel was joined by a vast host of others—the armies of heaven—praising God:

14 "Glory to God in the highest heaven,
and peace on earth to all whom God favors.*"

15When the angels had returned to heaven, the shepherds said to each other, "Come on, let's go to Bethlehem! Let's see this wonderful thing that has happened, which the Lord has told us about."

16They ran to the village and found Mary and Joseph. And there was the baby, lying in the manger. 17Then the shepherds told everyone what had happened and what the angel had said to them about this child. 18All who heard the shepherds' story were astonished, 19but Mary quietly treasured these things in her heart and thought about them often. 20The shepherds went back to their fields and flocks, glorifying and praising God for what the angels had told them, and because they had seen the child, just as the angel had said.

Jesus Is Presented in the Temple

21Eight days later, when the baby was circumcised, he was named Jesus, the name given him by the angel even before he was conceived.

22Then it was time for the purification offering, as required by the law of Moses after the birth of a child; so his parents took him to Jerusalem to present him to the Lord. 23The law of the Lord says, "If a woman's first child is a boy, he must be dedicated to the Lord."* 24So they offered a sacrifice according to what was required in the law of the Lord—"either a pair of turtledoves or two young pigeons."*

The Prophecy of Simeon

25Now there was a man named Simeon who lived in Jerusalem. He was a righteous man and very devout. He was filled with the Holy Spirit, and he eagerly expected the Messiah to come and rescue Israel. 26The Holy Spirit had revealed to him that he would not die until he had seen the Lord's Messiah. 27That day the Spirit led him to the Temple. So when Mary and Joseph came to present the baby

2:14 Or and peace on earth for all those pleasing God. Some manuscripts read and peace on earth, goodwill among people.   2:23 Exod 13:2.   2:24 Lev 12:8.

Jesus to the Lord as the law required, [28]Simeon was there. He took the child in his arms and praised God, saying,

[29] "Lord, now I can die in peace!
　　As you promised me,
[30] I have seen the Savior
[31] 　you have given to all people.
[32] He is a light to reveal God to the nations,
　　and he is the glory of your people Israel!"

[33]Joseph and Mary were amazed at what was being said about Jesus. [34]Then Simeon blessed them, and he said to Mary, "This child will be rejected by many in Israel, and it will be their undoing. But he will be the greatest joy to many others. [35]Thus, the deepest thoughts of many hearts will be revealed. And a sword will pierce your very soul."

The Prophecy of Anna

[36]Anna, a prophet, was also there in the Temple. She was the daughter of Phanuel, of the tribe of Asher, and was very old. She was a widow, for her husband had died when they had been married only seven years. [37]She was now eighty-four years old. She never left the Temple but stayed there day and night, worshiping God with fasting and prayer. [38]She came along just as Simeon was talking with Mary and Joseph, and she began praising God. She talked about Jesus to everyone who had been waiting for the promised King to come and deliver Jerusalem.

[39]When Jesus' parents had fulfilled all the requirements of the law of the Lord, they returned home to Nazareth in Galilee. [40]There the child grew up healthy and strong. He was filled with wisdom beyond his years, and God placed his special favor upon him.

Jesus Speaks with the Teachers

[41]Every year Jesus' parents went to Jerusalem for the Passover festival. [42]When Jesus was twelve years old, they attended the festival as usual. [43]After the celebration was over, they started home to Nazareth, but Jesus stayed behind in Jerusalem. His parents didn't miss him at first, [44]because they assumed he was with friends among the other travelers. But when he didn't show up that evening, they started to look for him among their relatives and friends. [45]When they couldn't find him, they went back to Jerusalem to search for him there. [46]Three days later they finally discovered him. He was in the Temple, sitting among the religious teachers, discussing deep questions with them. [47]And all who heard him were amazed at his understanding and his answers.

[48]His parents didn't know what to think. "Son!" his mother said to him. "Why have you done this to us? Your father and I have been frantic, searching for you everywhere."

[49]"But why did you need to search?" he asked. "You should have known that I would be in my Father's house."* [50]But they didn't understand what he meant.

[51]Then he returned to Nazareth with them and was obedient to them; and his mother stored all these things in her heart. [52]So Jesus

2:49 Or *"Didn't you realize that I should be involved with my Father's affairs?"*

grew both in height and in wisdom, and he was loved by God and by all who knew him.

CHAPTER 3
John the Baptist Prepares the Way
It was now the fifteenth year of the reign of Tiberius, the Roman emperor. Pilate was governor over Judea; Herod Antipas was ruler* over Galilee; his brother Philip was ruler* over Iturea and Traconitis; Lysanias was ruler over Abilene. ²Annas and Caiaphas were the high priests. At this time a message from God came to John son of Zechariah, who was living out in the wilderness. ³Then John went from place to place on both sides of the Jordan River, preaching that people should be baptized to show that they had turned from their sins and turned to God to be forgiven.* ⁴Isaiah had spoken of John when he said,

"He is a voice shouting in the wilderness:
'Prepare a pathway for the Lord's coming!
   Make a straight road for him!
⁵ Fill in the valleys,
   and level the mountains and hills!
Straighten the curves,
   and smooth out the rough places!
⁶ And then all people will see
   the salvation sent from God.'"*

⁷Here is a sample of John's preaching to the crowds that came for baptism: "You brood of snakes! Who warned you to flee God's coming judgment? ⁸Prove by the way you live that you have really turned from your sins and turned to God. Don't just say, 'We're safe—we're the descendants of Abraham.' That proves nothing. God can change these stones here into children of Abraham. ⁹Even now the ax of God's judgment is poised, ready to sever your roots. Yes, every tree that does not produce good fruit will be chopped down and thrown into the fire."

¹⁰The crowd asked, "What should we do?"

¹¹John replied, "If you have two coats, give one to the poor. If you have food, share it with those who are hungry."

¹²Even corrupt tax collectors came to be baptized and asked, "Teacher, what should we do?"

¹³"Show your honesty," he replied. "Make sure you collect no more taxes than the Roman government requires you to."

¹⁴"What should we do?" asked some soldiers.

John replied, "Don't extort money, and don't accuse people of things you know they didn't do. And be content with your pay."

¹⁵Everyone was expecting the Messiah to come soon, and they were eager to know whether John might be the Messiah. ¹⁶John answered their questions by saying, "I baptize with* water; but someone is coming soon who is greater than I am—so much greater that I am not even worthy to be his slave.* He will baptize you with the Holy Spirit and with fire.* ¹⁷He is ready to separate

---

3:1a Greek *Herod was tetrarch.* Herod Antipas was a son of King Herod.   3:1b Greek *tetrarch;* also in 3:19.   3:3 Greek *preaching a baptism of repentance for the forgiveness of sins.*   3:4-6 Isa 40:3-5.   3:16a Or *in.*   3:16b Greek *to untie his sandals.*   3:16c Or *in the Holy Spirit and in fire.*

the chaff from the grain with his winnowing fork. Then he will clean up the threshing area, storing the grain in his barn but burning the chaff with never-ending fire." [18]John used many such warnings as he announced the Good News to the people.

[19]John also publicly criticized Herod Antipas, ruler of Galilee, for marrying Herodias, his brother's wife, and for many other wrongs he had done. [20]So Herod put John in prison, adding this sin to his many others.

The Baptism of Jesus

[21]One day when the crowds were being baptized, Jesus himself was baptized. As he was praying, the heavens opened, [22]and the Holy Spirit descended on him in the form of a dove. And a voice from heaven said, "You are my beloved Son, and I am fully pleased with you.*"

The Record of Jesus' Ancestors

[23]Jesus was about thirty years old when he began his public ministry.

Jesus was known as the son of Joseph.
Joseph was the son of Heli.
[24] Heli was the son of Matthat.
Matthat was the son of Levi.
Levi was the son of Melki.
Melki was the son of Jannai.
Jannai was the son of Joseph.
[25] Joseph was the son of Mattathias.
Mattathias was the son of Amos.
Amos was the son of Nahum.
Nahum was the son of Esli.
Esli was the son of Naggai.
[26] Naggai was the son of Maath.
Maath was the son of Mattathias.
Mattathias was the son of Semein.
Semein was the son of Josech.
Josech was the son of Joda.
[27] Joda was the son of Joanan.
Joanan was the son of Rhesa.
Rhesa was the son of Zerubbabel.
Zerubbabel was the son of Shealtiel.
Shealtiel was the son of Neri.
[28] Neri was the son of Melki.
Melki was the son of Addi.
Addi was the son of Cosam.
Cosam was the son of Elmadam.
Elmadam was the son of Er.
[29] Er was the son of Joshua.
Joshua was the son of Eliezer.
Eliezer was the son of Jorim.
Jorim was the son of Matthat.
Matthat was the son of Levi.
[30] Levi was the son of Simeon.

3:22 Some manuscripts read *and today I have become your Father.*

Simeon was the son of Judah.
Judah was the son of Joseph.
Joseph was the son of Jonam.
Jonam was the son of Eliakim.
31 Eliakim was the son of Melea.
Melea was the son of Menna.
Menna was the son of Mattatha.
Mattatha was the son of Nathan.
Nathan was the son of David.
32 David was the son of Jesse.
Jesse was the son of Obed.
Obed was the son of Boaz.
Boaz was the son of Salmon.*
Salmon was the son of Nahshon.
33 Nahshon was the son of Amminadab.
Amminadab was the son of Admin.
Admin was the son of Arni.*
Arni was the son of Hezron.
Hezron was the son of Perez.
Perez was the son of Judah.
34 Judah was the son of Jacob.
Jacob was the son of Isaac.
Isaac was the son of Abraham.
Abraham was the son of Terah.
Terah was the son of Nahor.
35 Nahor was the son of Serug.
Serug was the son of Reu.
Reu was the son of Peleg.
Peleg was the son of Eber.
Eber was the son of Shelah.
36 Shelah was the son of Cainan.
Cainan was the son of Arphaxad.
Arphaxad was the son of Shem.
Shem was the son of Noah.
Noah was the son of Lamech.
37 Lamech was the son of Methuselah.
Methuselah was the son of Enoch.
Enoch was the son of Jared.
Jared was the son of Mahalalel.
Mahalalel was the son of Kenan.
38 Kenan was the son of Enosh.*
Enosh was the son of Seth.
Seth was the son of Adam.
Adam was the son of God.

CHAPTER 4

The Temptation of Jesus

Then Jesus, full of the Holy Spirit, left the Jordan River. He was led by the Spirit to go out into the wilderness, 2where the Devil tempted him for forty days. He ate nothing all that time and was very hungry.

3:32 Greek *Sala;* see Ruth 4:22.　　**3:33** *Arni* is the same person as Ram; see 1 Chr 2:9-10.
3:38 Greek *Enos;* see Gen 5:6.

³Then the Devil said to him, "If you are the Son of God, change this stone into a loaf of bread."

⁴But Jesus told him, "No! The Scriptures say, 'People need more than bread for their life.'*"

⁵Then the Devil took him up and revealed to him all the kingdoms of the world in a moment of time. ⁶The Devil told him, "I will give you the glory of these kingdoms and authority over them—because they are mine to give to anyone I please. ⁷I will give it all to you if you will bow down and worship me."

⁸Jesus replied, "The Scriptures say,

'You must worship the Lord your God;
    serve only him.'*"

⁹Then the Devil took him to Jerusalem, to the highest point of the Temple, and said, "If you are the Son of God, jump off! ¹⁰For the Scriptures say,

'He orders his angels to protect and guard you.
¹¹ And they will hold you with their hands
    to keep you from striking your foot on a stone.'*"

¹²Jesus responded, "The Scriptures also say, 'Do not test the Lord your God.'*"

¹³When the Devil had finished tempting Jesus, he left him until the next opportunity came.

Jesus Rejected at Nazareth

¹⁴Then Jesus returned to Galilee, filled with the Holy Spirit's power. Soon he became well known throughout the surrounding country. ¹⁵He taught in their synagogues and was praised by everyone.

¹⁶When he came to the village of Nazareth, his boyhood home, he went as usual to the synagogue on the Sabbath and stood up to read the Scriptures. ¹⁷The scroll containing the messages of Isaiah the prophet was handed to him, and he unrolled the scroll to the place where it says:

18 "The Spirit of the Lord is upon me,
    for he has appointed me to preach Good News to the poor.
He has sent me to proclaim
    that captives will be released,
    that the blind will see,
    that the downtrodden will be freed from their oppressors,
19   and that the time of the Lord's favor has come.*"

²⁰He rolled up the scroll, handed it back to the attendant, and sat down. Everyone in the synagogue stared at him intently. ²¹Then he said, "This Scripture has come true today before your very eyes!"

²²All who were there spoke well of him and were amazed by the gracious words that fell from his lips. "How can this be?" they asked. "Isn't this Joseph's son?"

²³Then he said, "Probably you will quote me that proverb, 'Physician, heal yourself'—meaning, 'Why don't you do miracles

4:4 Deut 8:3.   4:8 Deut 6:13.   4:10-11 Ps 91:11-12.   4:12 Deut 6:16.   4:18-19 Or *and to proclaim the acceptable year of the Lord.* Isa 61:1-2.

here in your hometown like those you did in Capernaum?' ²⁴But the truth is, no prophet is accepted in his own hometown.

²⁵"Certainly there were many widows in Israel who needed help in Elijah's time, when there was no rain for three and a half years and hunger stalked the land. ²⁶Yet Elijah was not sent to any of them. He was sent instead to a widow of Zarephath—a foreigner in the land of Sidon. ²⁷Or think of the prophet Elisha, who healed Naaman, a Syrian, rather than the many lepers in Israel who needed help."

²⁸When they heard this, the people in the synagogue were furious. ²⁹Jumping up, they mobbed him and took him to the edge of the hill on which the city was built. They intended to push him over the cliff, ³⁰but he slipped away through the crowd and left them.

Jesus Casts Out a Demon

³¹Then Jesus went to Capernaum, a town in Galilee, and taught there in the synagogue every Sabbath day. ³²There, too, the people were amazed at the things he said, because he spoke with authority.

³³Once when he was in the synagogue, a man possessed by a demon began shouting at Jesus, ³⁴"Go away! Why are you bothering us, Jesus of Nazareth? Have you come to destroy us? I know who you are—the Holy One sent from God."

³⁵Jesus cut him short. "Be silent!" he told the demon. "Come out of the man!" The demon threw the man to the floor as the crowd watched; then it left him without hurting him further.

³⁶Amazed, the people exclaimed, "What authority and power this man's words possess! Even evil spirits obey him and flee at his command!" ³⁷The story of what he had done spread like wildfire throughout the whole region.

Jesus Heals Many People

³⁸After leaving the synagogue that day, Jesus went to Simon's home, where he found Simon's mother-in-law very sick with a high fever. "Please heal her," everyone begged. ³⁹Standing at her bedside, he spoke to the fever, rebuking it, and immediately her temperature returned to normal. She got up at once and prepared a meal for them.

⁴⁰As the sun went down that evening, people throughout the village brought sick family members to Jesus. No matter what their diseases were, the touch of his hand healed every one. ⁴¹Some were possessed by demons; and the demons came out at his command, shouting, "You are the Son of God." But because they knew he was the Messiah, he stopped them and told them to be silent.

Jesus Continues to Preach

⁴²Early the next morning Jesus went out into the wilderness. The crowds searched everywhere for him, and when they finally found him, they begged him not to leave them. ⁴³But he replied, "I must preach the Good News of the Kingdom of God in other places, too, because that is why I was sent." ⁴⁴So he continued to travel around, preaching in synagogues throughout Judea.*

4:44 Some manuscripts read *Galilee*.

CHAPTER 5

The First Disciples

One day as Jesus was preaching on the shore of the Sea of Galilee,* great crowds pressed in on him to listen to the word of God. 2He noticed two empty boats at the water's edge, for the fishermen had left them and were washing their nets. 3Stepping into one of the boats, Jesus asked Simon,* its owner, to push it out into the water. So he sat in the boat and taught the crowds from there.

4When he had finished speaking, he said to Simon, "Now go out where it is deeper and let down your nets, and you will catch many fish."

5"Master," Simon replied, "we worked hard all last night and didn't catch a thing. But if you say so, we'll try again." 6And this time their nets were so full they began to tear! 7A shout for help brought their partners in the other boat, and soon both boats were filled with fish and on the verge of sinking.

8When Simon Peter realized what had happened, he fell to his knees before Jesus and said, "Oh, Lord, please leave me—I'm too much of a sinner to be around you." 9For he was awestruck by the size of their catch, as were the others with him. 10His partners, James and John, the sons of Zebedee, were also amazed.

Jesus replied to Simon, "Don't be afraid! From now on you'll be fishing for people!" 11And as soon as they landed, they left everything and followed Jesus.

Jesus Heals a Man with Leprosy

12In one of the villages, Jesus met a man with an advanced case of leprosy. When the man saw Jesus, he fell to the ground, face down in the dust, begging to be healed. "Lord," he said, "if you want to, you can make me well again."

13Jesus reached out and touched the man. "I want to," he said. "Be healed!" And instantly the leprosy disappeared. 14Then Jesus instructed him not to tell anyone what had happened. He said, "Go right to the priest and let him examine you. Take along the offering required in the law of Moses for those who have been healed of leprosy, so everyone will have proof of your healing." 15Yet despite Jesus' instructions, the report of his power spread even faster, and vast crowds came to hear him preach and to be healed of their diseases. 16But Jesus often withdrew to the wilderness for prayer.

Jesus Heals a Paralyzed Man

17One day while Jesus was teaching, some Pharisees and teachers of religious law were sitting nearby. (It seemed that these men showed up from every village in all Galilee and Judea, as well as from Jerusalem.) And the Lord's healing power was strongly with Jesus. 18Some men came carrying a paralyzed man on a sleeping mat. They tried to push through the crowd to Jesus, 19but they couldn't reach him. So they went up to the roof, took off some tiles, and lowered the sick man down into the crowd, still on his mat, right in front of Jesus. 20Seeing their faith, Jesus said to the man, "Son, your sins are forgiven."

5:1 Greek *Lake Gennesaret,* another name for the Sea of Galilee.   5:3 *Simon* is called *Peter* in 6:14 and thereafter.

21 "Who does this man think he is?" the Pharisees and teachers of religious law said to each other. "This is blasphemy! Who but God can forgive sins?"

22 Jesus knew what they were thinking, so he asked them, "Why do you think this is blasphemy? 23 Is it easier to say, 'Your sins are forgiven' or 'Get up and walk'? 24 I will prove that I, the Son of Man, have the authority on earth to forgive sins." Then Jesus turned to the paralyzed man and said, "Stand up, take your mat, and go on home, because you are healed!"

25 And immediately, as everyone watched, the man jumped to his feet, picked up his mat, and went home praising God. 26 Everyone was gripped with great wonder and awe. And they praised God, saying over and over again, "We have seen amazing things today."

Jesus Calls Levi (Matthew)

27 Later, as Jesus left the town, he saw a tax collector named Levi sitting at his tax-collection booth. "Come, be my disciple!" Jesus said to him. 28 So Levi got up, left everything, and followed him.

29 Soon Levi held a banquet in his home with Jesus as the guest of honor. Many of Levi's fellow tax collectors and other guests were there. 30 But the Pharisees and their teachers of religious law complained bitterly to Jesus' disciples, "Why do you eat and drink with such scum*?"

31 Jesus answered them, "Healthy people don't need a doctor—sick people do. 32 I have come to call sinners to turn from their sins, not to spend my time with those who think they are already good enough."

A Discussion about Fasting

33 The religious leaders complained that Jesus' disciples were feasting instead of fasting. "John the Baptist's disciples always fast and pray," they declared, "and so do the disciples of the Pharisees. Why are yours always feasting?"

34 Jesus asked, "Do wedding guests fast while celebrating with the groom? 35 Someday he will be taken away from them, and then they will fast.

36 Then Jesus gave them this illustration: "No one tears a piece of cloth from a new garment and uses it to patch an old garment. For then the new garment would be torn, and the patch wouldn't even match the old garment. 37 And no one puts new wine into old wineskins. The new wine would burst the old skins, spilling the wine and ruining the skins. 38 New wine must be put into new wineskins. 39 But no one who drinks the old wine seems to want the fresh and the new. 'The old is better,' they say."

CHAPTER 6

A Discussion about the Sabbath

One Sabbath day as Jesus was walking through some grainfields, his disciples broke off heads of wheat, rubbed off the husks in their hands, and ate the grains. 2 But some Pharisees said, "You shouldn't be doing that! It's against the law to work by harvesting grain on the Sabbath."

3 Jesus replied, "Haven't you ever read in the Scriptures what

5:30 Greek *with tax collectors and sinners.*

King David did when he and his companions were hungry? ⁴He went into the house of God, ate the special bread reserved for the priests alone, and then gave some to his friends. That was breaking the law, too." ⁵And Jesus added, "I, the Son of Man, am master even of the Sabbath."

Jesus Heals on the Sabbath

⁶On another Sabbath day, a man with a deformed right hand was in the synagogue while Jesus was teaching. ⁷The teachers of religious law and the Pharisees watched closely to see whether Jesus would heal the man on the Sabbath, because they were eager to find some legal charge to bring against him. ⁸But Jesus knew their thoughts. He said to the man with the deformed hand, "Come and stand here where everyone can see." So the man came forward. ⁹Then Jesus said to his critics, "I have a question for you. Is it legal to do good deeds on the Sabbath, or is it a day for doing harm? Is this a day to save life or to destroy it?" ¹⁰He looked around at them one by one and then said to the man, "Reach out your hand." The man reached out his hand, and it became normal again! ¹¹At this, the enemies of Jesus were wild with rage and began to discuss what to do with him.

Jesus Chooses the Twelve Apostles

¹²One day soon afterward Jesus went to a mountain to pray, and he prayed to God all night. ¹³At daybreak he called together all of his disciples and chose twelve of them to be apostles. Here are their names:

¹⁴ Simon (he also called him Peter),
   Andrew (Peter's brother),
   James,
   John,
   Philip,
   Bartholomew,
¹⁵ Matthew,
   Thomas,
   James (son of Alphaeus),
   Simon (the Zealot),
¹⁶ Judas (son of James),
   Judas Iscariot (who later betrayed him).

Crowds Follow Jesus

¹⁷When they came down the slopes of the mountain, the disciples stood with Jesus on a large, level area, surrounded by many of his followers and by the crowds. There were people from all over Judea and from Jerusalem and from as far north as the seacoasts of Tyre and Sidon. ¹⁸They had come to hear him and to be healed, and Jesus cast out many evil spirits. ¹⁹Everyone was trying to touch him, because healing power went out from him, and they were all cured.

The Beatitudes

²⁰Then Jesus turned to his disciples and said,

"God blesses you who are poor,
   for the Kingdom of God is given to you.
²¹ God blesses you who are hungry now,
   for you will be satisfied.

God blesses you who weep now,
for the time will come when you will laugh with joy.
22 God blesses you who are hated and excluded and mocked and cursed
because you are identified with me, the Son of Man.

23 "When that happens, rejoice! Yes, leap for joy! For a great reward awaits you in heaven. And remember, the ancient prophets were also treated that way by your ancestors.

Sorrows Foretold

24 "What sorrows await you who are rich,
for you have your only happiness now.
25 What sorrows await you who are satisfied and prosperous now,
for a time of awful hunger is before you.
What sorrows await you who laugh carelessly,
for your laughing will turn to mourning and sorrow.
26 What sorrows await you who are praised by the crowds,
for their ancestors also praised false prophets.

Love for Enemies

27 "But if you are willing to listen, I say, love your enemies. Do good to those who hate you. 28 Pray for the happiness of those who curse you. Pray for those who hurt you. 29 If someone slaps you on one cheek, turn the other cheek. If someone demands your coat, offer your shirt also. 30 Give what you have to anyone who asks you for it; and when things are taken away from you, don't try to get them back. 31 Do for others as you would like them to do for you.

32 "Do you think you deserve credit merely for loving those who love you? Even the sinners do that! 33 And if you do good only to those who do good to you, is that so wonderful? Even sinners do that much! 34 And if you lend money only to those who can repay you, what good is that? Even sinners will lend to their own kind for a full return.

35 "Love your enemies! Do good to them! Lend to them! And don't be concerned that they might not repay. Then your reward from heaven will be very great, and you will truly be acting as children of the Most High, for he is kind to the unthankful and to those who are wicked. 36 You must be compassionate, just as your Father is compassionate.

Don't Condemn Others

37 "Stop judging others, and you will not be judged. Stop criticizing others, or it will all come back on you. If you forgive others, you will be forgiven. 38 If you give, you will receive. Your gift will return to you in full measure, pressed down, shaken together to make room for more, and running over. Whatever measure you use in giving—large or small—it will be used to measure what is given back to you."

39 Then Jesus gave the following illustration: "What good is it for one blind person to lead another? The first one will fall into a ditch and pull the other down also. 40 A student is not greater than the teacher. But the student who works hard will become like the teacher. 41 "And why worry about a speck in your friend's eye* when you

6:41 Greek *your brother's eye;* also in 6:42.

have a log in your own? ⁴²How can you think of saying, 'Friend,*
let me help you get rid of the speck in your eye,' when you can't
see past the log in your own eye? Hypocrite! First get rid of the log
from your own eye; then perhaps you will see well enough to deal
with the speck in your friend's eye.

The Tree and Its Fruit

⁴³"A good tree can't produce bad fruit, and a bad tree can't produce
good fruit. ⁴⁴A tree is identified by the kind of fruit it produces. Figs
never grow on thornbushes or grapes on bramble bushes. ⁴⁵A good
person produces good deeds from a good heart, and an evil person
produces evil deeds from an evil heart. Whatever is in your heart
determines what you say.

Building on a Solid Foundation

⁴⁶"So why do you call me 'Lord,' when you won't obey me? ⁴⁷I will
show you what it's like when someone comes to me, listens to my
teaching, and then obeys me. ⁴⁸It is like a person who builds a
house on a strong foundation laid upon the underlying rock.
When the floodwaters rise and break against the house, it stands
firm because it is well built. ⁴⁹But anyone who listens and doesn't
obey is like a person who builds a house without a foundation.
When the floods sweep down against that house, it will crumble
into a heap of ruins."

CHAPTER 7

Faith of the Roman Officer

When Jesus had finished saying all this, he went back to Capernaum. ²Now the highly valued slave of a Roman officer was sick
and near death. ³When the officer heard about Jesus, he sent some
respected Jewish leaders to ask him to come and heal his slave. ⁴So
they earnestly begged Jesus to come with them and help the man.
"If anyone deserves your help, it is he," they said, ⁵"for he loves
the Jews and even built a synagogue for us."

⁶So Jesus went with them. But just before they arrived at the house,
the officer sent some friends to say, "Lord, don't trouble yourself by
coming to my home, for I am not worthy of such an honor. ⁷I am not
even worthy to come and meet you. Just say the word from where you
are, and my servant will be healed. ⁸I know because I am under the
authority of my superior officers, and I have authority over my
soldiers. I only need to say, 'Go,' and they go, or 'Come,' and they
come. And if I say to my slaves, 'Do this or that,' they do it."

⁹When Jesus heard this, he was amazed. Turning to the crowd,
he said, "I tell you, I haven't seen faith like this in all the land of
Israel!" ¹⁰And when the officer's friends returned to his house, they
found the slave completely healed.

Jesus Raises a Widow's Son

¹¹Soon afterward Jesus went with his disciples to the village of
Nain, with a great crowd following him. ¹²A funeral procession was
coming out as he approached the village gate. The boy who had
died was the only son of a widow, and many mourners from the
village were with her. ¹³When the Lord saw her, his heart overflowed with compassion. "Don't cry!" he said. ¹⁴Then he walked

6:42 Greek *Brother.*

over to the coffin and touched it, and the bearers stopped. "Young man," he said, "get up." ¹⁵Then the dead boy sat up and began to talk to those around him! And Jesus gave him back to his mother.

¹⁶Great fear swept the crowd, and they praised God, saying, "A mighty prophet has risen among us," and "We have seen the hand of God at work today." ¹⁷The report of what Jesus had done that day spread all over Judea and even out across its borders.

Jesus and John the Baptist

¹⁸The disciples of John the Baptist told John about everything Jesus was doing. So John called for two of his disciples, ¹⁹and he sent them to the Lord to ask him, "Are you the Messiah we've been expecting, or should we keep looking for someone else?"

²⁰John's two disciples found Jesus and said to him, "John the Baptist sent us to ask, 'Are you the Messiah we've been expecting, or should we keep looking for someone else?'"

²¹At that very time, he cured many people of their various diseases, and he cast out evil spirits and restored sight to the blind. ²²Then he told John's disciples, "Go back to John and tell him what you have seen and heard—the blind see, the lame walk, the lepers are cured, the deaf hear, the dead are raised to life, and the Good News is being preached to the poor. ²³And tell him, 'God blesses those who are not offended by me.*'"

²⁴After they left, Jesus talked to the crowd about John. "Who is this man in the wilderness that you went out to see? Did you find him weak as a reed, moved by every breath of wind? ²⁵Or were you expecting to see a man dressed in expensive clothes? No, people who wear beautiful clothes and live in luxury are found in palaces, not in the wilderness. ²⁶Were you looking for a prophet? Yes, and he is more than a prophet. ²⁷John is the man to whom the Scriptures refer when they say,

'Look, I am sending my messenger before you,
    and he will prepare your way before you.'*

²⁸I tell you, of all who have ever lived, none is greater than John. Yet even the most insignificant person in the Kingdom of God is greater than he is!"

²⁹When they heard this, all the people, including the unjust tax collectors, agreed that God's plan was right,* for they had been baptized by John. ³⁰But the Pharisees and experts in religious law had rejected God's plan for them, for they had refused John's baptism.

³¹"How shall I describe this generation?" Jesus asked. "With what will I compare them? ³²They are like a group of children playing a game in the public square. They complain to their friends, 'We played wedding songs, and you weren't happy, so we played funeral songs, but you weren't sad.' ³³For John the Baptist didn't drink wine and he often fasted, and you say, 'He's demon possessed.' ³⁴And I, the Son of Man, feast and drink, and you say, 'He's a glutton and a drunkard, and a friend of the worst sort of sinners!' ³⁵But wisdom is shown to be right by the lives of those who follow it.*"

7:23 Or *who don't fall away because of me.*   7:27 Mal 3:1.   7:29 Or *praised God.*
7:35 Or *But wisdom is justified by all her children.*

Jesus Anointed by a Sinful Woman

³⁶One of the Pharisees asked Jesus to come to his home for a meal, so Jesus accepted the invitation and sat down to eat. ³⁷A certain immoral woman heard he was there and brought a beautiful jar* filled with expensive perfume. ³⁸Then she knelt behind him at his feet, weeping. Her tears fell on his feet, and she wiped them off with her hair. Then she kept kissing his feet and putting perfume on them.

³⁹When the Pharisee who was the host saw what was happening and who the woman was, he said to himself, "This proves that Jesus is no prophet. If God had really sent him, he would know what kind of woman is touching him. She's a sinner!"

⁴⁰Then Jesus spoke up and answered his thoughts. "Simon," he said to the Pharisee, "I have something to say to you."

"All right, Teacher," Simon replied, "go ahead."

⁴¹Then Jesus told him this story: "A man loaned money to two people—five hundred pieces of silver* to one and fifty pieces to the other. ⁴²But neither of them could repay him, so he kindly forgave them both, canceling their debts. Who do you suppose loved him more after that?"

⁴³Simon answered, "I suppose the one for whom he canceled the larger debt."

"That's right," Jesus said. ⁴⁴Then he turned to the woman and said to Simon, "Look at this woman kneeling here. When I entered your home, you didn't offer me water to wash the dust from my feet, but she has washed them with her tears and wiped them with her hair. ⁴⁵You didn't give me a kiss of greeting, but she has kissed my feet again and again from the time I first came in. ⁴⁶You neglected the courtesy of olive oil to anoint my head, but she has anointed my feet with rare perfume. ⁴⁷I tell you, her sins—and they are many—have been forgiven, so she has shown me much love. But a person who is forgiven little shows only little love."

⁴⁸Then Jesus said to the woman, "Your sins are forgiven."

⁴⁹The men at the table said among themselves, "Who does this man think he is, going around forgiving sins?"

⁵⁰And Jesus said to the woman, "Your faith has saved you; go in peace."

CHAPTER 8

Women Who Followed Jesus

Not long afterward Jesus began a tour of the nearby cities and villages to announce the Good News concerning the Kingdom of God. He took his twelve disciples with him, ²along with some women he had healed and from whom he had cast out evil spirits. Among them were Mary Magdalene, from whom he had cast out seven demons; ³Joanna, the wife of Chuza, Herod's business manager; Susanna; and many others who were contributing from their own resources to support Jesus and his disciples.

Story of the Farmer Scattering Seed

⁴One day Jesus told this story to a large crowd that had gathered from many towns to hear him: ⁵"A farmer went out to plant some

---

7:37 Greek *an alabaster jar.* 7:41 Greek *500 denarii.* A denarius was the equivalent of a full day's wage.

seed. As he scattered it across his field, some seed fell on a footpath, where it was stepped on, and the birds came and ate it. 6Other seed fell on shallow soil with underlying rock. This seed began to grow, but soon it withered and died for lack of moisture. 7Other seed fell among thorns that shot up and choked out the tender blades. 8Still other seed fell on fertile soil. This seed grew and produced a crop one hundred times as much as had been planted." When he had said this, he called out, "Anyone who is willing to hear should listen and understand!"

9His disciples asked him what the story meant. 10He replied, "You have been permitted to understand the secrets of the Kingdom of God. But I am using these stories to conceal everything about it from outsiders, so that the Scriptures might be fulfilled:

'They see what I do,
  but they don't really see;
they hear what I say,
  but they don't understand.'*

11"This is the meaning of the story: The seed is God's message. 12The seed that fell on the hard path represents those who hear the message, but then the Devil comes and steals it away and prevents them from believing and being saved. 13The rocky soil represents those who hear the message with joy. But like young plants in such soil, their roots don't go very deep. They believe for a while, but they wilt when the hot winds of testing blow. 14The thorny ground represents those who hear and accept the message, but all too quickly the message is crowded out by the cares and riches and pleasures of this life. And so they never grow into maturity. 15But the good soil represents honest, good-hearted people who hear God's message, cling to it, and steadily produce a huge harvest.

Illustration of the Lamp

16"No one would light a lamp and then cover it up or put it under a bed. No, lamps are mounted in the open, where they can be seen by those entering the house. 17For everything that is hidden or secret will eventually be brought to light and made plain to all. 18So be sure to pay attention to what you hear. To those who are open to my teaching, more understanding will be given. But to those who are not listening, even what they think they have will be taken away from them."

The True Family of Jesus

19Once when Jesus' mother and brothers came to see him, they couldn't get to him because of the crowds. 20Someone told Jesus, "Your mother and your brothers are outside, and they want to see you."

21Jesus replied, "My mother and my brothers are all those who hear the message of God and obey it."

Jesus Calms the Storm

22One day Jesus said to his disciples, "Let's cross over to the other side of the lake." So they got into a boat and started out. 23On the way across, Jesus lay down for a nap, and while he was sleeping the

8:10 Isa 6:9.

wind began to rise. A fierce storm developed that threatened to swamp them, and they were in real danger.

²⁴The disciples woke him up, shouting, "Master, Master, we're going to drown!"

So Jesus rebuked the wind and the raging waves. The storm stopped and all was calm! ²⁵Then he asked them, "Where is your faith?"

And they were filled with awe and amazement. They said to one another, "Who is this man, that even the winds and waves obey him?"

Jesus Heals a Demon-Possessed Man

²⁶So they arrived in the land of the Gerasenes,* across the lake from Galilee. ²⁷As Jesus was climbing out of the boat, a man who was possessed by demons came out to meet him. Homeless and naked, he had lived in a cemetery for a long time. ²⁸As soon as he saw Jesus, he shrieked and fell to the ground before him, screaming, "Why are you bothering me, Jesus, Son of the Most High God? Please, I beg you, don't torture me!" ²⁹For Jesus had already commanded the evil spirit to come out of him. This spirit had often taken control of the man. Even when he was shackled with chains, he simply broke them and rushed out into the wilderness, completely under the demon's power.

³⁰"What is your name?" Jesus asked.

"Legion," he replied—for the man was filled with many demons. ³¹The demons kept begging Jesus not to send them into the Bottomless Pit. ³²A large herd of pigs was feeding on the hillside nearby, and the demons pleaded with him to let them enter into the pigs. Jesus gave them permission. ³³So the demons came out of the man and entered the pigs, and the whole herd plunged down the steep hillside into the lake, where they drowned.

³⁴When the herdsmen saw it, they fled to the nearby city and the surrounding countryside, spreading the news as they ran. ³⁵A crowd soon gathered around Jesus, for they wanted to see for themselves what had happened. And they saw the man who had been possessed by demons sitting quietly at Jesus' feet, clothed and sane. And the whole crowd was afraid. ³⁶Then those who had seen what happened told the others how the demon-possessed man had been healed. ³⁷And all the people in that region begged Jesus to go away and leave them alone, for a great wave of fear swept over them.

So Jesus returned to the boat and left, crossing back to the other side of the lake. ³⁸The man who had been demon possessed begged to go, too, but Jesus said, ³⁹"No, go back to your family and tell them all the wonderful things God has done for you." So he went all through the city telling about the great thing Jesus had done for him.

Jesus Heals in Response to Faith

⁴⁰On the other side of the lake the crowds received Jesus with open arms because they had been waiting for him. ⁴¹And now a man named Jairus, a leader of the local synagogue, came and fell down

8:26 Some manuscripts read *Gadarenes*; other manuscripts read *Gergesenes*. See Matt 8:28; Mark 5:1.

at Jesus' feet, begging him to come home with him. [42]His only child was dying, a little girl twelve years old.

As Jesus went with him, he was surrounded by the crowds. [43]And there was a woman in the crowd who had had a hemorrhage for twelve years. She had spent everything she had on doctors* and still could find no cure. [44]She came up behind Jesus and touched the fringe of his robe. Immediately, the bleeding stopped.

[45]"Who touched me?" Jesus asked.

Everyone denied it, and Peter said, "Master, this whole crowd is pressing up against you."

[46]But Jesus told him, "No, someone deliberately touched me, for I felt healing power go out from me." [47]When the woman realized that Jesus knew, she began to tremble and fell to her knees before him. The whole crowd heard her explain why she had touched him and that she had been immediately healed. [48]"Daughter," he said to her, "your faith has made you well. Go in peace."

[49]While he was still speaking to her, a messenger arrived from Jairus's home with the message, "Your little girl is dead. There's no use troubling the Teacher now."

[50]But when Jesus heard what had happened, he said to Jairus, "Don't be afraid. Just trust me, and she will be all right."

[51]When they arrived at the house, Jesus wouldn't let anyone go in with him except Peter, James, John, and the little girl's father and mother. [52]The house was filled with people weeping and wailing, but he said, "Stop the weeping! She isn't dead; she is only asleep."

[53]But the crowd laughed at him because they all knew she had died. [54]Then Jesus took her by the hand and said in a loud voice, "Get up, my child!" [55]And at that moment her life returned, and she immediately stood up! Then Jesus told them to give her something to eat. [56]Her parents were overwhelmed, but Jesus insisted that they not tell anyone what had happened.

CHAPTER 9

Jesus Sends Out the Twelve Apostles

One day Jesus called together his twelve apostles and gave them power and authority to cast out demons and to heal all diseases. [2]Then he sent them out to tell everyone about the coming of the Kingdom of God and to heal the sick. [3]"Don't even take along a walking stick," he instructed them, "nor a traveler's bag, nor food, nor money. Not even an extra coat. [4]When you enter each village, be a guest in only one home. [5]If the people of the village won't receive your message when you enter it, shake off its dust from your feet as you leave. It is a sign that you have abandoned that village to its fate."

[6]So they began their circuit of the villages, preaching the Good News and healing the sick.

Herod's Confusion

[7]When reports of Jesus' miracles reached Herod Antipas,* he was worried and puzzled because some were saying, "This is John the

---

8:43 Some manuscripts omit *She had spent everything she had on doctors.* 9:7 Greek *Herod the tetrarch.* He was a son of King Herod and was ruler over one of the four districts in Palestine.

Baptist come back to life again." [8]Others were saying, "It is Elijah or some other ancient prophet risen from the dead."

[9]"I beheaded John," Herod said, "so who is this man about whom I hear such strange stories?" And he tried to see him.

Jesus Feeds Five Thousand

[10]When the apostles returned, they told Jesus everything they had done. Then he slipped quietly away with them toward the town of Bethsaida. [11]But the crowds found out where he was going, and they followed him. And he welcomed them, teaching them about the Kingdom of God and curing those who were ill. [12]Late in the afternoon the twelve disciples came to him and said, "Send the crowds away to the nearby villages and farms, so they can find food and lodging for the night. There is nothing to eat here in this deserted place."

[13]But Jesus said, "You feed them."

"Impossible!" they protested. "We have only five loaves of bread and two fish. Or are you expecting us to go and buy enough food for this whole crowd?" [14]For there were about five thousand men there.

"Just tell them to sit down on the ground in groups of about fifty each," Jesus replied. [15]So the people all sat down. [16]Jesus took the five loaves and two fish, looked up toward heaven, and asked God's blessing on the food. Breaking the loaves into pieces, he kept giving the bread and fish to the disciples to give to the people. [17]They all ate as much as they wanted, and they picked up twelve baskets of leftovers!

Peter's Declaration about Jesus

[18]One day as Jesus was alone, praying, he came over to his disciples and asked them, "Who do people say I am?"

[19]"Well," they replied, "some say John the Baptist, some say Elijah, and others say you are one of the other ancient prophets risen from the dead."

[20]Then he asked them, "Who do you say I am?"

Peter replied, "You are the Messiah sent from God!"

Jesus Predicts His Death

[21]Jesus warned them not to tell anyone about this. [22]"For I, the Son of Man, must suffer many terrible things," he said. "I will be rejected by the leaders, the leading priests, and the teachers of religious law. I will be killed, but three days later I will be raised from the dead."

[23]Then he said to the crowd, "If any of you wants to be my follower, you must put aside your selfish ambition, shoulder your cross daily, and follow me. [24]If you try to keep your life for yourself, you will lose it. But if you give up your life for me, you will find true life. [25]And how do you benefit if you gain the whole world but lose or forfeit your own soul in the process? [26]If a person is ashamed of me and my message, I, the Son of Man, will be ashamed of that person when I return in my glory and in the glory of the Father and the holy angels. [27]And I assure you that some of you standing here right now will not die before you see the Kingdom of God."

The Transfiguration

28About eight days later Jesus took Peter, James, and John to a mountain to pray. 29And as he was praying, the appearance of his face changed, and his clothing became dazzling white. 30Then two men, Moses and Elijah, appeared and began talking with Jesus. 31They were glorious to see. And they were speaking of how he was about to fulfill God's plan by dying in Jerusalem.

32Peter and the others were very drowsy and had fallen asleep. Now they woke up and saw Jesus' glory and the two men standing with him. 33As Moses and Elijah were starting to leave, Peter, not even knowing what he was saying, blurted out, "Master, this is wonderful! We will make three shrines*—one for you, one for Moses, and one for Elijah." 34But even as he was saying this, a cloud came over them; and terror gripped them as it covered them.

35Then a voice from the cloud said, "This is my Son, my Chosen One.* Listen to him." 36When the voice died away, Jesus was there alone. They didn't tell anyone what they had seen until long after this happened.

Jesus Heals a Demon-Possessed Boy

37The next day, after they had come down the mountain, a huge crowd met Jesus. 38A man in the crowd called out to him, "Teacher, look at my boy, who is my only son. 39An evil spirit keeps seizing him, making him scream. It throws him into convulsions so that he foams at the mouth. It is always hitting and injuring him. It hardly ever leaves him alone. 40I begged your disciples to cast the spirit out, but they couldn't do it."

41"You stubborn, faithless people," Jesus said, "how long must I be with you and put up with you? Bring him here." 42As the boy came forward, the demon knocked him to the ground and threw him into a violent convulsion. But Jesus rebuked the evil spirit and healed the boy. Then he gave him back to his father. 43Awe gripped the people as they saw this display of God's power.

Jesus Again Predicts His Death

While everyone was marveling over all the wonderful things he was doing, Jesus said to his disciples, 44"Listen to me and remember what I say. The Son of Man is going to be betrayed." 45But they didn't know what he meant. Its significance was hidden from them, so they could not understand it, and they were afraid to ask him about it.

The Greatest in the Kingdom

46Then there was an argument among them as to which of them would be the greatest. 47But Jesus knew their thoughts, so he brought a little child to his side. 48Then he said to them, "Anyone who welcomes a little child like this on my behalf welcomes me, and anyone who welcomes me welcomes my Father who sent me. Whoever is the least among you is the greatest."

Using the Name of Jesus

49John said to Jesus, "Master, we saw someone using your name to cast out demons. We tried to stop him because he isn't in our group."

9:33 Or shelters; Greek reads tabernacles. 9:35 Some manuscripts read This is my beloved Son.

⁵⁰But Jesus said, "Don't stop him! Anyone who is not against you is for you."

Opposition from Samaritans

⁵¹As the time drew near for his return to heaven, Jesus resolutely set out for Jerusalem. ⁵²He sent messengers ahead to a Samaritan village to prepare for his arrival. ⁵³But they were turned away. The people of the village refused to have anything to do with Jesus because he had resolved to go to Jerusalem. ⁵⁴When James and John heard about it, they said to Jesus, "Lord, should we order down fire from heaven to burn them up*?" ⁵⁵But Jesus turned and rebuked them.* ⁵⁶So they went on to another village.

The Cost of Following Jesus

⁵⁷As they were walking along someone said to Jesus, "I will follow you no matter where you go."

⁵⁸But Jesus replied, "Foxes have dens to live in, and birds have nests, but I, the Son of Man, have no home of my own, not even a place to lay my head."

⁵⁹He said to another person, "Come, be my disciple."

The man agreed, but he said, "Lord, first let me return home and bury my father."

⁶⁰Jesus replied, "Let those who are spiritually dead care for their own dead.* Your duty is to go and preach the coming of the Kingdom of God."

⁶¹Another said, "Yes, Lord, I will follow you, but first let me say good-bye to my family."

⁶²But Jesus told him, "Anyone who puts a hand to the plow and then looks back is not fit for the Kingdom of God."

CHAPTER 10

Jesus Sends Out His Disciples

The Lord now chose seventy-two* other disciples and sent them on ahead in pairs to all the towns and villages he planned to visit. ²These were his instructions to them: "The harvest is so great, but the workers are so few. Pray to the Lord who is in charge of the harvest, and ask him to send out more workers for his fields. ³Go now, and remember that I am sending you out as lambs among wolves. ⁴Don't take along any money, or a traveler's bag, or even an extra pair of sandals. And don't stop to greet anyone on the road.

⁵"Whenever you enter a home, give it your blessing. ⁶If those who live there are worthy, the blessing will stand; if they are not, the blessing will return to you. ⁷When you enter a town, don't move around from home to home. Stay in one place, eating and drinking what they provide. Don't hesitate to accept hospitality, because those who work deserve their pay.

⁸"If a town welcomes you, eat whatever is set before you ⁹and heal the sick. As you heal them, say, 'The Kingdom of God is near you now.' ¹⁰But if a town refuses to welcome you, go out into its streets and say, ¹¹'We wipe the dust of your town from our feet as

9:54 Some manuscripts add *as Elijah did.* 9:55 Some manuscripts add *And he said, "You don't realize what your hearts are like.* 9:56*For the Son of Man has not come to destroy men's lives, but to save them."* 9:60 Greek *Let the dead bury their own dead.* 10:1 Some manuscripts read *70;* also in 10:17.

a public announcement of your doom. And don't forget the Kingdom of God is near!' ¹²The truth is, even wicked Sodom will be better off than such a town on the judgment day.

¹³"What horrors await you, Korazin and Bethsaida! For if the miracles I did in you had been done in wicked Tyre and Sidon, their people would have sat in deep repentance long ago, clothed in sackcloth and throwing ashes on their heads to show their remorse. ¹⁴Yes, Tyre and Sidon will be better off on the judgment day than you. ¹⁵And you people of Capernaum, will you be exalted to heaven? No, you will be brought down to the place of the dead.*"

¹⁶Then he said to the disciples, "Anyone who accepts your message is also accepting me. And anyone who rejects you is rejecting me. And anyone who rejects me is rejecting God who sent me."

¹⁷When the seventy-two disciples returned, they joyfully reported to him, "Lord, even the demons obey us when we use your name!"

¹⁸"Yes," he told them, "I saw Satan falling from heaven as a flash of lightning! ¹⁹And I have given you authority over all the power of the enemy, and you can walk among snakes and scorpions and crush them. Nothing will injure you. ²⁰But don't rejoice just because evil spirits obey you; rejoice because your names are registered as citizens of heaven."

Jesus' Prayer of Thanksgiving

²¹Then Jesus was filled with the joy of the Holy Spirit and said, "O Father, Lord of heaven and earth, thank you for hiding the truth from those who think themselves so wise and clever, and for revealing it to the childlike. Yes, Father, it pleased you to do it this way.

²²"My Father has given me authority over everything. No one really knows the Son except the Father, and no one really knows the Father except the Son and those to whom the Son chooses to reveal him."

²³Then when they were alone, he turned to the disciples and said, "How privileged you are to see what you have seen. ²⁴I tell you, many prophets and kings have longed to see and hear what you have seen and heard, but they could not."

The Most Important Commandment

²⁵One day an expert in religious law stood up to test Jesus by asking him this question: "Teacher, what must I do to receive eternal life?"

²⁶Jesus replied, "What does the law of Moses say? How do you read it?"

²⁷The man answered, "'You must love the Lord your God with all your heart, all your soul, all your strength, and all your mind.' And, 'Love your neighbor as yourself.'"*

²⁸"Right!" Jesus told him. "Do this and you will live!"

²⁹The man wanted to justify his actions, so he asked Jesus, "And who is my neighbor?"

Story of the Good Samaritan

³⁰Jesus replied with an illustration: "A Jewish man was traveling on a trip from Jerusalem to Jericho, and he was attacked by bandits.

10:15 Greek *to Hades.*   **10:27** Deut 6:5; Lev 19:18.

They stripped him of his clothes and money, beat him up, and left him half dead beside the road.

³¹ "By chance a Jewish priest came along; but when he saw the man lying there, he crossed to the other side of the road and passed him by. ³²A Temple assistant* walked over and looked at him lying there, but he also passed by on the other side.

³³ "Then a despised Samaritan came along, and when he saw the man, he felt deep pity. ³⁴Kneeling beside him, the Samaritan soothed his wounds with medicine and bandaged them. Then he put the man on his own donkey and took him to an inn, where he took care of him. ³⁵The next day he handed the innkeeper two pieces of silver* and told him to take care of the man. 'If his bill runs higher than that,' he said, 'I'll pay the difference the next time I am here.'

³⁶ "Now which of these three would you say was a neighbor to the man who was attacked by bandits?" Jesus asked.

³⁷The man replied, "The one who showed him mercy."

Then Jesus said, "Yes, now go and do the same."

Jesus Visits Martha and Mary

³⁸As Jesus and the disciples continued on their way to Jerusalem, they came to a village where a woman named Martha welcomed them into her home. ³⁹Her sister, Mary, sat at the Lord's feet, listening to what he taught. ⁴⁰But Martha was worrying over the big dinner she was preparing. She came to Jesus and said, "Lord, doesn't it seem unfair to you that my sister just sits here while I do all the work? Tell her to come and help me."

⁴¹But the Lord said to her, "My dear Martha, you are so upset over all these details! ⁴²There is really only one thing worth being concerned about. Mary has discovered it—and I won't take it away from her."

CHAPTER 11

Teaching about Prayer

Once when Jesus had been out praying, one of his disciples came to him as he finished and said, "Lord, teach us to pray, just as John taught his disciples."

²He said, "This is how you should pray:

"Father, may your name be honored.
May your Kingdom come soon.
³ Give us our food day by day.
⁴ And forgive us our sins—
just as we forgive those who have sinned against us.
And don't let us yield to temptation.*"

⁵Then, teaching them more about prayer, he used this illustration: "Suppose you went to a friend's house at midnight, wanting to borrow three loaves of bread. You would say to him, ⁶'A friend of mine has just arrived for a visit, and I have nothing for him to eat.' ⁷He would call out from his bedroom, 'Don't bother me. The door is locked for the night, and we are all in bed. I can't help you

---

10:32 Greek *A Levite.*   10:35 Greek *2 denarii.* A denarius was the equivalent of a full day's wage.   11:2-4 Some manuscripts add additional portions of the Lord's Prayer as it reads in Matt 6:9-13.

this time.' ⁸But I tell you this—though he won't do it as a friend, if you keep knocking long enough, he will get up and give you what you want so his reputation won't be damaged.*

⁹"And so I tell you, keep on asking, and you will be given what you ask for. Keep on looking, and you will find. Keep on knocking, and the door will be opened. ¹⁰For everyone who asks, receives. Everyone who seeks, finds. And the door is opened to everyone who knocks.

¹¹"You fathers—if your children ask* for a fish, do you give them a snake instead? ¹²Or if they ask for an egg, do you give them a scorpion? Of course not! ¹³If you sinful people know how to give good gifts to your children, how much more will your heavenly Father give the Holy Spirit to those who ask him."

Jesus and the Prince of Demons

¹⁴One day Jesus cast a demon out of a man who couldn't speak, and the man's voice returned to him. The crowd was amazed, ¹⁵but some said, "No wonder he can cast out demons. He gets his power from Satan,* the prince of demons!" ¹⁶Trying to test Jesus, others asked for a miraculous sign from heaven to see if he was from God.

¹⁷He knew their thoughts, so he said, "Any kingdom at war with itself is doomed. A divided home is also doomed. ¹⁸You say I am empowered by the prince of demons.* But if Satan is fighting against himself by empowering me to cast out his demons, how can his kingdom survive? ¹⁹And if I am empowered by the prince of demons, what about your own followers? They cast out demons, too, so they will judge you for what you have said. ²⁰But if I am casting out demons by the power of God, then the Kingdom of God has arrived among you. ²¹For when Satan,* who is completely armed, guards his palace, it is safe—²²until someone who is stronger attacks and overpowers him, strips him of his weapons, and carries off his belongings.

²³"Anyone who isn't helping me opposes me, and anyone who isn't working with me is actually working against me.

²⁴"When an evil spirit leaves a person, it goes into the desert, searching for rest. But when it finds none, it says, 'I will return to the person I came from.' ²⁵So it returns and finds that its former home is all swept and clean. ²⁶Then the spirit finds seven other spirits more evil than itself, and they all enter the person and live there. And so that person is worse off than before."

²⁷As he was speaking, a woman in the crowd called out, "God bless your mother—the womb from which you came, and the breasts that nursed you!"

²⁸He replied, "But even more blessed are all who hear the word of God and put it into practice."

The Sign of Jonah

²⁹As the crowd pressed in on Jesus, he said, "These are evil times, and this evil generation keeps asking me to show them a miraculous sign. But the only sign I will give them is the sign of the prophet Jonah. ³⁰What happened to him was a sign to the people

11:8 Greek *in order to avoid shame,* or *because of [your] persistence.*   **11:11** Some manuscripts add *for bread, do you give them a stone? Or if they ask.*   **11:15** Greek *Beelzeboul.*   **11:18** Greek *by Beelzeboul;* also in 11:19.   **11:21** Greek *the strong one.*

of Nineveh that God had sent him. What happens to me will be a sign that God has sent me, the Son of Man, to these people.

³¹ "The queen of Sheba* will rise up against this generation on judgment day and condemn it, because she came from a distant land to hear the wisdom of Solomon. And now someone greater than Solomon is here—and you refuse to listen to him. ³²The people of Nineveh, too, will rise up against this generation on judgment day and condemn it, because they repented at the preaching of Jonah. And now someone greater than Jonah is here—and you refuse to repent.

Receiving the Light

³³ "No one lights a lamp and then hides it or puts it under a basket. Instead, it is put on a lampstand to give light to all who enter the room. ³⁴Your eye is a lamp for your body. A pure eye lets sunshine into your soul. But an evil eye shuts out the light and plunges you into darkness. ³⁵Make sure that the light you think you have is not really darkness. ³⁶If you are filled with light, with no dark corners, then your whole life will be radiant, as though a floodlight is shining on you."

Jesus Criticizes the Religious Leaders

³⁷As Jesus was speaking, one of the Pharisees invited him home for a meal. So he went in and took his place at the table. ³⁸His host was amazed to see that he sat down to eat without first performing the ceremonial washing required by Jewish custom. ³⁹Then the Lord said to him, "You Pharisees are so careful to clean the outside of the cup and the dish, but inside you are still filthy—full of greed and wickedness! ⁴⁰Fools! Didn't God make the inside as well as the outside? ⁴¹So give to the needy what you greedily possess, and you will be clean all over.

⁴²"But how terrible it will be for you Pharisees! For you are careful to tithe even the tiniest part of your income,* but you completely forget about justice and the love of God. You should tithe, yes, but you should not leave undone the more important things.

⁴³ "How terrible it will be for you Pharisees! For how you love the seats of honor in the synagogues and the respectful greetings from everyone as you walk through the markets! ⁴⁴Yes, how terrible it will be for you. For you are like hidden graves in a field. People walk over them without knowing the corruption they are stepping on."

⁴⁵ "Teacher," said an expert in religious law, "you have insulted us, too, in what you just said."

⁴⁶"Yes," said Jesus, "how terrible it will be for you experts in religious law! For you crush people beneath impossible religious demands, and you never lift a finger to help ease the burden. ⁴⁷How terrible it will be for you! For you build tombs for the very prophets your ancestors killed long ago. ⁴⁸Murderers! You agree with your ancestors that what they did was right. You would have done the same yourselves. ⁴⁹This is what God in his wisdom said about you:* 'I will send prophets and apostles to them, and they will kill some and persecute the others.'

⁵⁰ "And you of this generation will be held responsible for the

11:31 Greek *the queen of the south.*   11:42 Greek *to tithe the mint and the rue and every herb.*
11:49 Greek *Therefore, the wisdom of God said.*

murder of all God's prophets from the creation of the world—
⁵¹from the murder of Abel to the murder of Zechariah, who was killed between the altar and the sanctuary. Yes, it will surely be charged against you.

⁵²"How terrible it will be for you experts in religious law! For you hide the key to knowledge from the people. You don't enter the Kingdom yourselves, and you prevent others from entering."

⁵³As Jesus finished speaking, the Pharisees and teachers of religious law were furious. From that time on they grilled him with many hostile questions, ⁵⁴trying to trap him into saying something they could use against him.

CHAPTER 12

A Warning against Hypocrisy

Meanwhile, the crowds grew until thousands were milling about and crushing each other. Jesus turned first to his disciples and warned them, "Beware of the yeast of the Pharisees—beware of their hypocrisy. ²The time is coming when everything will be revealed; all that is secret will be made public. ³Whatever you have said in the dark will be heard in the light, and what you have whispered behind closed doors will be shouted from the housetops for all to hear!

⁴"Dear friends, don't be afraid of those who want to kill you. They can only kill the body; they cannot do any more to you. ⁵But I'll tell you whom to fear. Fear God, who has the power to kill people and then throw them into hell.

⁶"What is the price of five sparrows? A couple of pennies? Yet God does not forget a single one of them. ⁷And the very hairs on your head are all numbered. So don't be afraid; you are more valuable to him than a whole flock of sparrows.

⁸"And I assure you of this: If anyone acknowledges me publicly here on earth, I, the Son of Man, will openly acknowledge that person in the presence of God's angels. ⁹But if anyone denies me here on earth, I will deny that person before God's angels. ¹⁰Yet those who speak against the Son of Man may be forgiven, but anyone who speaks blasphemies against the Holy Spirit will never be forgiven.

¹¹"And when you are brought to trial in the synagogues and before rulers and authorities, don't worry about what to say in your defense, ¹²for the Holy Spirit will teach you what needs to be said even as you are standing there."

Story of the Rich Fool

¹³Then someone called from the crowd, "Teacher, please tell my brother to divide our father's estate with me."

¹⁴Jesus replied, "Friend, who made me a judge over you to decide such things as that?" ¹⁵Then he said, "Beware! Don't be greedy for what you don't have. Real life is not measured by how much we own."

¹⁶And he gave an illustration: "A rich man had a fertile farm that produced fine crops. ¹⁷In fact, his barns were full to overflowing. ¹⁸So he said, 'I know! I'll tear down my barns and build bigger ones. Then I'll have room enough to store everything. ¹⁹And I'll sit

back and say to myself, My friend, you have enough stored away for years to come. Now take it easy! Eat, drink, and be merry!'

²⁰"But God said to him, 'You fool! You will die this very night. Then who will get it all?'

²¹"Yes, a person is a fool to store up earthly wealth but not have a rich relationship with God."

Teaching about Money and Possessions

²²Then turning to his disciples, Jesus said, "So I tell you, don't worry about everyday life—whether you have enough food to eat or clothes to wear. ²³For life consists of far more than food and clothing. ²⁴Look at the ravens. They don't need to plant or harvest or put food in barns because God feeds them. And you are far more valuable to him than any birds! ²⁵Can all your worries add a single moment to your life? Of course not! ²⁶And if worry can't do little things like that, what's the use of worrying over bigger things?

²⁷"Look at the lilies and how they grow. They don't work or make their clothing, yet Solomon in all his glory was not dressed as beautifully as they are. ²⁸And if God cares so wonderfully for flowers that are here today and gone tomorrow, won't he more surely care for you? You have so little faith! ²⁹And don't worry about food—what to eat and drink. Don't worry whether God will provide it for you. ³⁰These things dominate the thoughts of most people, but your Father already knows your needs. ³¹He will give you all you need from day to day if you make the Kingdom of God your primary concern.

³²"So don't be afraid, little flock. For it gives your Father great happiness to give you the Kingdom.

³³"Sell what you have and give to those in need. This will store up treasure for you in heaven! And the purses of heaven have no holes in them. Your treasure will be safe—no thief can steal it and no moth can destroy it. ³⁴Wherever your treasure is, there your heart and thoughts will also be.

Be Ready for the Lord's Coming

³⁵"Be dressed for service and well prepared, ³⁶as though you were waiting for your master to return from the wedding feast. Then you will be ready to open the door and let him in the moment he arrives and knocks. ³⁷There will be special favor for those who are ready and waiting for his return. I tell you, he himself will seat them, put on an apron, and serve them as they sit and eat! ³⁸He may come in the middle of the night or just before dawn.* But whenever he comes, there will be special favor for his servants who are ready!

³⁹"Know this: A homeowner who knew exactly when a burglar was coming would not permit the house to be broken into. ⁴⁰You must be ready all the time, for the Son of Man will come when least expected."

⁴¹Peter asked, "Lord, is this illustration just for us or for everyone?"

⁴²And the Lord replied, "I'm talking to any faithful, sensible servant to whom the master gives the responsibility of managing his household and feeding his family. ⁴³If the master returns and

12:38 Greek *in the second or third watch.*

finds that the servant has done a good job, there will be a reward. ⁴⁴I assure you, the master will put that servant in charge of all he owns. ⁴⁵But if the servant thinks, 'My master won't be back for a while,' and begins oppressing the other servants, partying, and getting drunk—⁴⁶well, the master will return unannounced and unexpected. He will tear the servant apart and banish him with the unfaithful. ⁴⁷The servant will be severely punished, for though he knew his duty, he refused to do it.

⁴⁸"But people who are not aware that they are doing wrong will be punished only lightly. Much is required from those to whom much is given, and much more is required from those to whom much more is given.

Jesus Causes Division

⁴⁹"I have come to bring fire to the earth, and I wish that my task were already completed! ⁵⁰There is a terrible baptism ahead of me, and I am under a heavy burden until it is accomplished. ⁵¹Do you think I have come to bring peace to the earth? No, I have come to bring strife and division! ⁵²From now on families will be split apart, three in favor of me, and two against—or the other way around. ⁵³There will be a division between father and son, mother and daughter, mother-in-law and daughter-in-law."

⁵⁴Then Jesus turned to the crowd and said, "When you see clouds beginning to form in the west, you say, 'Here comes a shower.' And you are right. ⁵⁵When the south wind blows, you say, 'Today will be a scorcher.' And it is. ⁵⁶You hypocrites! You know how to interpret the appearance of the earth and the sky, but you can't interpret these present times.

⁵⁷"Why can't you decide for yourselves what is right? ⁵⁸If you are on the way to court and you meet your accuser, try to settle the matter before it reaches the judge, or you may be sentenced and handed over to an officer and thrown in jail. ⁵⁹And if that happens, you won't be free again until you have paid the last penny."

CHAPTER 13

A Call to Repentance

About this time Jesus was informed that Pilate had murdered some people from Galilee as they were sacrificing at the Temple in Jerusalem. ²"Do you think those Galileans were worse sinners than other people from Galilee?" he asked. "Is that why they suffered? ³Not at all! And you will also perish unless you turn from your evil ways and turn to God. ⁴And what about the eighteen men who died when the Tower of Siloam fell on them? Were they the worst sinners in Jerusalem? ⁵No, and I tell you again that unless you repent, you will also perish."

Illustration of the Barren Fig Tree

⁶Then Jesus used this illustration: "A man planted a fig tree in his garden and came again and again to see if there was any fruit on it, but he was always disappointed. ⁷Finally, he said to his gardener, 'I've waited three years, and there hasn't been a single fig! Cut it down. It's taking up space we can use for something else.'

⁸"The gardener answered, 'Give it one more chance. Leave it

another year, and I'll give it special attention and plenty of fertilizer. ⁹If we get figs next year, fine. If not, you can cut it down.'".

Jesus Heals on the Sabbath

¹⁰One Sabbath day as Jesus was teaching in a synagogue, ¹¹he saw a woman who had been crippled by an evil spirit. She had been bent double for eighteen years and was unable to stand up straight. ¹²When Jesus saw her, he called her over and said, "Woman, you are healed of your sickness!" ¹³Then he touched her, and instantly she could stand straight. How she praised and thanked God!

¹⁴But the leader in charge of the synagogue was indignant that Jesus had healed her on the Sabbath day. "There are six days of the week for working," he said to the crowd. "Come on those days to be healed, not on the Sabbath."

¹⁵But the Lord replied, "You hypocrite! You work on the Sabbath day! Don't you untie your ox or your donkey from their stalls on the Sabbath and lead them out for water? ¹⁶Wasn't it necessary for me, even on the Sabbath day, to free this dear woman* from the bondage in which Satan has held her for eighteen years?" ¹⁷This shamed his enemies. And all the people rejoiced at the wonderful things he did.

Illustration of the Mustard Seed

¹⁸Then Jesus said, "What is the Kingdom of God like? How can I illustrate it? ¹⁹It is like a tiny mustard seed planted in a garden; it grows and becomes a tree, and the birds come and find shelter among its branches."

Illustration of the Yeast

²⁰He also asked, "What else is the Kingdom of God like? ²¹It is like yeast used by a woman making bread. Even though she used a large amount* of flour, the yeast permeated every part of the dough."

The Narrow Door

²²Jesus went through the towns and villages, teaching as he went, always pressing on toward Jerusalem. ²³Someone asked him, "Lord, will only a few be saved?"

He replied, ²⁴"The door to heaven is narrow. Work hard to get in, because many will try to enter, ²⁵but when the head of the house has locked the door, it will be too late. Then you will stand outside knocking and pleading, 'Lord, open the door for us!' But he will reply, 'I do not know you.' ²⁶You will say, 'But we ate and drank with you, and you taught in our streets.' ²⁷And he will reply, 'I tell you, I do not know you. Go away, all you who do evil.'

²⁸"And there will be great weeping and gnashing of teeth, for you will see Abraham, Isaac, Jacob, and all the prophets within the Kingdom of God, but you will be thrown out. ²⁹Then people will come from all over the world to take their places in the Kingdom of God. ³⁰And note this: Some who are despised now will be greatly honored then; and some who are greatly honored now will be despised then.*"

Jesus Grieves over Jerusalem

³¹A few minutes later some Pharisees said to him, "Get out of here if you want to live, because Herod Antipas wants to kill you!"

13:16 Greek *this woman, a daughter of Abraham.*   13:21 Greek *3 measures.*   13:30 Greek *Some who are last who will be first, and some who are first will be last.*

³²Jesus replied, "Go tell that fox that I will keep on casting out demons and doing miracles of healing today and tomorrow; and the third day I will accomplish my purpose. ³³Yes, today, tomorrow, and the next day I must proceed on my way. For it wouldn't do for a prophet of God to be killed except in Jerusalem!

³⁴"O Jerusalem, Jerusalem, the city that kills the prophets and stones God's messengers! How often I have wanted to gather your children together as a hen protects her chicks beneath her wings, but you wouldn't let me. ³⁵And now look, your house is left to you empty. And you will never see me again until you say, 'Bless the one who comes in the name of the Lord!'* "

CHAPTER 14

Jesus Heals on the Sabbath

One Sabbath day Jesus was in the home of a leader of the Pharisees. The people were watching him closely, ²because there was a man there whose arms and legs were swollen.* ³Jesus asked the Pharisees and experts in religious law, "Well, is it permitted in the law to heal people on the Sabbath day, or not?" ⁴When they refused to answer, Jesus touched the sick man and healed him and sent him away. ⁵Then he turned to them and asked, "Which of you does work on the Sabbath? If your son* or your cow falls into a pit, don't you proceed at once to get him out?" ⁶Again they had no answer.

Jesus Teaches about Humility

⁷When Jesus noticed that all who had come to the dinner were trying to sit near the head of the table, he gave them this advice: ⁸"If you are invited to a wedding feast, don't always head for the best seat. What if someone more respected than you has also been invited? ⁹The host will say, 'Let this person sit here instead.' Then you will be embarrassed and will have to take whatever seat is left at the foot of the table!

¹⁰"Do this instead—sit at the foot of the table. Then when your host sees you, he will come and say, 'Friend, we have a better place than this for you!' Then you will be honored in front of all the other guests. ¹¹For the proud will be humbled, but the humble will be honored."

¹²Then he turned to his host. "When you put on a luncheon or a dinner," he said, "don't invite your friends, brothers, relatives, and rich neighbors. For they will repay you by inviting you back. ¹³Instead, invite the poor, the crippled, the lame, and the blind. ¹⁴Then at the resurrection of the godly, God will reward you for inviting those who could not repay you."

Story of the Great Feast

¹⁵Hearing this, a man sitting at the table with Jesus exclaimed, "What a privilege it would be to have a share in the Kingdom of God!"

¹⁶Jesus replied with this illustration: "A man prepared a great feast and sent out many invitations. ¹⁷When all was ready, he sent his servant around to notify the guests that it was time for them to come. ¹⁸But they all began making excuses. One said he had just bought a field and wanted to inspect it, so he asked to be excused.

13:35 Ps 118:26.   14:2 Traditionally translated *who had dropsy.*   14:5 Some manuscripts read *donkey.*

¹⁹Another said he had just bought five pair of oxen and wanted to try them out. ²⁰Another had just been married, so he said he couldn't come.

²¹"The servant returned and told his master what they had said. His master was angry and said, 'Go quickly into the streets and alleys of the city and invite the poor, the crippled, the lame, and the blind.' ²²After the servant had done this, he reported, 'There is still room for more.' ²³So his master said, 'Go out into the country lanes and behind the hedges and urge anyone you find to come, so that the house will be full. ²⁴For none of those I invited first will get even the smallest taste of what I had prepared for them.'"

The Cost of Being a Disciple

²⁵Great crowds were following Jesus. He turned around and said to them, ²⁶"If you want to be my follower you must love me more than* your own father and mother, wife and children, brothers and sisters—yes, more than your own life. Otherwise, you cannot be my disciple. ²⁷And you cannot be my disciple if you do not carry your own cross and follow me.

²⁸"But don't begin until you count the cost. For who would begin construction of a building without first getting estimates and then checking to see if there is enough money to pay the bills? ²⁹Otherwise, you might complete only the foundation before running out of funds. And then how everyone would laugh at you! ³⁰They would say, 'There's the person who started that building and ran out of money before it was finished!'

³¹"Or what king would ever dream of going to war without first sitting down with his counselors and discussing whether his army of ten thousand is strong enough to defeat the twenty thousand soldiers who are marching against him? ³²If he is not able, then while the enemy is still far away, he will send a delegation to discuss terms of peace. ³³So no one can become my disciple without giving up everything for me.

³⁴"Salt is good for seasoning. But if it loses its flavor, how do you make it salty again? ³⁵Flavorless salt is good neither for the soil nor for fertilizer. It is thrown away. Anyone who is willing to hear should listen and understand!"

CHAPTER 15

Story of the Lost Sheep

Tax collectors and other notorious sinners often came to listen to Jesus teach. ²This made the Pharisees and teachers of religious law complain that he was associating with such despicable people—even eating with them!

³So Jesus used this illustration: ⁴"If you had one hundred sheep, and one of them strayed away and was lost in the wilderness, wouldn't you leave the ninety-nine others to go and search for the lost one until you found it? ⁵And then you would joyfully carry it home on your shoulders. ⁶When you arrived, you would call together your friends and neighbors to rejoice with you because your lost sheep was found. ⁷In the same way, heaven will be happier over one lost sinner who returns to God than over ninety-nine others who are righteous and haven't strayed away!

14:26 Greek *you must hate.*

Story of the Lost Coin

8 "Or suppose a woman has ten valuable silver coins* and loses one. Won't she light a lamp and look in every corner of the house and sweep every nook and cranny until she finds it? 9And when she finds it, she will call in her friends and neighbors to rejoice with her because she has found her lost coin. 10In the same way, there is joy in the presence of God's angels when even one sinner repents."

Story of the Lost Son

11To illustrate the point further, Jesus told them this story: "A man had two sons. 12The younger son told his father, 'I want my share of your estate now, instead of waiting until you die.' So his father agreed to divide his wealth between his sons.

13 "A few days later this younger son packed all his belongings and took a trip to a distant land, and there he wasted all his money on wild living. 14About the time his money ran out, a great famine swept over the land, and he began to starve. 15He persuaded a local farmer to hire him to feed his pigs. 16The boy became so hungry that even the pods he was feeding the pigs looked good to him. But no one gave him anything.

17 "When he finally came to his senses, he said to himself, 'At home even the hired men have food enough to spare, and here I am, dying of hunger! 18I will go home to my father and say, "Father, I have sinned against both heaven and you, 19and I am no longer worthy of being called your son. Please take me on as a hired man."'

20 "So he returned home to his father. And while he was still a long distance away, his father saw him coming. Filled with love and compassion, he ran to his son, embraced him, and kissed him. 21His son said to him, 'Father, I have sinned against both heaven and you, and I am no longer worthy of being called your son.*'

22 "But his father said to the servants, 'Quick! Bring the finest robe in the house and put it on him. Get a ring for his finger, and sandals for his feet. 23And kill the calf we have been fattening in the pen. We must celebrate with a feast, 24for this son of mine was dead and has now returned to life. He was lost, but now he is found.' So the party began.

25 "Meanwhile, the older son was in the fields working. When he returned home, he heard music and dancing in the house, 26and he asked one of the servants what was going on. 27'Your brother is back,' he was told, 'and your father has killed the calf we were fattening and has prepared a great feast. We are celebrating because of his safe return.'

28 "The older brother was angry and wouldn't go in. His father came out and begged him, 29but he replied, 'All these years I've worked hard for you and never once refused to do a single thing you told me to. And in all that time you never gave me even one young goat for a feast with my friends. 30Yet when this son of yours comes back after squandering your money on prostitutes, you celebrate by killing the finest calf we have.'

31 "His father said to him, 'Look, dear son, you and I are very

15:8 Greek *10 drachmas.* A drachma was the equivalent of a full day's wage.   15:21 Some manuscripts add *Please take me on as a hired man.*

close, and everything I have is yours. ³²We had to celebrate this happy day. For your brother was dead and has come back to life! He was lost, but now he is found!'"

C H A P T E R   1 6
Story of the Shrewd Manager
Jesus told this story to his disciples: "A rich man hired a manager to handle his affairs, but soon a rumor went around that the manager was thoroughly dishonest. ²So his employer called him in and said, 'What's this I hear about your stealing from me? Get your report in order, because you are going to be dismissed.'

³"The manager thought to himself, 'Now what? I'm through here, and I don't have the strength to go out and dig ditches, and I'm too proud to beg. ⁴I know just the thing! And then I'll have plenty of friends to take care of me when I leave!'

⁵"So he invited each person who owed money to his employer to come and discuss the situation. He asked the first one, 'How much do you owe him?' ⁶The man replied, 'I owe him eight hundred gallons of olive oil.' So the manager told him, 'Tear up that bill and write another one for four hundred gallons.*'

⁷"'And how much do you owe my employer?' he asked the next man. 'A thousand bushels of wheat,' was the reply. 'Here,' the manager said, 'take your bill and replace it with one for only eight hundred bushels.*'

⁸"The rich man had to admire the dishonest rascal for being so shrewd. And it is true that the citizens of this world are more shrewd than the godly are. ⁹I tell you, use your worldly resources to benefit others and make friends. In this way, your generosity stores up a reward for you in heaven.*

¹⁰"Unless you are faithful in small matters, you won't be faithful in large ones. If you cheat even a little, you won't be honest with greater responsibilities. ¹¹And if you are untrustworthy about worldly wealth, who will trust you with the true riches of heaven? ¹²And if you are not faithful with other people's money, why should you be trusted with money of your own?

¹³"No one can serve two masters. For you will hate one and love the other, or be devoted to one and despise the other. You cannot serve both God and money."

¹⁴The Pharisees, who dearly loved their money, naturally scoffed at all this. ¹⁵Then he said to them, "You like to look good in public, but God knows your evil hearts. What this world honors is an abomination in the sight of God.

¹⁶"Until John the Baptist began to preach, the laws of Moses and the messages of the prophets were your guides. But now the Good News of the Kingdom of God is preached, and eager multitudes are forcing their way in. ¹⁷But that doesn't mean that the law has lost its force in even the smallest point. It is stronger and more permanent than heaven and earth.

¹⁸"Anyone who divorces his wife and marries someone else commits adultery, and anyone who marries a divorced woman commits adultery."

16:6 Greek *100 baths . . . 50 [baths].*   **16:7** Greek *100 korous . . . 80 [korous].*   **16:9** Or *Then when you run out at the end of this life, your friends will welcome you into eternal homes.*

The Rich Man and Lazarus

[19]Jesus said, "There was a certain rich man who was splendidly clothed and who lived each day in luxury. [20]At his door lay a diseased beggar named Lazarus. [21]As Lazarus lay there longing for scraps from the rich man's table, the dogs would come and lick his open sores. [22]Finally, the beggar died and was carried by the angels to be with Abraham.* The rich man also died and was buried, [23]and his soul went to the place of the dead.* There, in torment, he saw Lazarus in the far distance with Abraham.

[24]The rich man shouted, 'Father Abraham, have some pity! Send Lazarus over here to dip the tip of his finger in water and cool my tongue, because I am in anguish in these flames.'

[25]But Abraham said to him, 'Son, remember that during your lifetime you had everything you wanted, and Lazarus had nothing. So now he is here being comforted, and you are in anguish. [26]And besides, there is a great chasm separating us. Anyone who wanted to cross over to you from here is stopped at its edge, and no one there can cross over to us.'

[27]Then the rich man said, 'Please, Father Abraham, send him to my father's home. [28]For I have five brothers, and I want him to warn them about this place of torment so they won't have to come here when they die.'

[29]But Abraham said, 'Moses and the prophets have warned them. Your brothers can read their writings anytime they want to.'

[30]The rich man replied, 'No, Father Abraham! But if someone is sent to them from the dead, then they will turn from their sins.'

[31]But Abraham said, 'If they won't listen to Moses and the prophets, they won't listen even if someone rises from the dead.'"

CHAPTER 17

Teachings about Forgiveness and Faith

One day Jesus said to his disciples, "There will always be temptations to sin, but how terrible it will be for the person who does the tempting. [2]It would be far better to be thrown into the sea with a large millstone tied around the neck than to face the punishment in store for harming one of these little ones. [3]I am warning you! If another believer* sins, rebuke him; then if he repents, forgive him. [4]Even if he wrongs you seven times a day and each time turns again and asks forgiveness, forgive him."

[5]One day the apostles said to the Lord, "We need more faith; tell us how to get it."

[6]"Even if you had faith as small as a mustard seed," the Lord answered, "you could say to this mulberry tree, 'May God uproot you and throw you into the sea,' and it would obey you!

[7]"When a servant comes in from plowing or taking care of sheep, he doesn't just sit down and eat. [8]He must first prepare his master's meal and serve him his supper before eating his own. [9]And the servant is not even thanked, because he is merely doing what he is supposed to do. [10]In the same way, when you obey me you should say, 'We are not worthy of praise. We are servants who have simply done our duty.'"

16:22 Greek *into Abraham's bosom.*   16:23 Greek *to Hades.*   17:3 Greek *your brother.*

Ten Healed of Leprosy

11As Jesus continued on toward Jerusalem, he reached the border between Galilee and Samaria. 12As he entered a village there, ten lepers stood at a distance, 13crying out, "Jesus, Master, have mercy on us!"

14He looked at them and said, "Go show yourselves to the priests." And as they went, their leprosy disappeared.

15One of them, when he saw that he was healed, came back to Jesus, shouting, "Praise God, I'm healed!" 16He fell face down on the ground at Jesus' feet, thanking him for what he had done. This man was a Samaritan.

17Jesus asked, "Didn't I heal ten men? Where are the other nine? 18Does only this foreigner return to give glory to God?" 19And Jesus said to the man, "Stand up and go. Your faith has made you well."

The Coming of the Kingdom

20One day the Pharisees asked Jesus, "When will the Kingdom of God come?"

Jesus replied, "The Kingdom of God isn't ushered in with visible signs.* 21You won't be able to say, 'Here it is!' or 'It's over there!' For the Kingdom of God is among you.*"

22Later he talked again about this with his disciples. "The time is coming when you will long to share in the days of the Son of Man, but you won't be able to," he said. 23"Reports will reach you that the Son of Man has returned and that he is in this place or that. Don't believe such reports or go out to look for him. 24For when the Son of Man returns, you will know it beyond all doubt. It will be as evident as the lightning that flashes across the sky. 25But first the Son of Man must suffer terribly* and be rejected by this generation.

26"When the Son of Man returns, the world will be like the people were in Noah's day. 27In those days before the flood, the people enjoyed banquets and parties and weddings right up to the time Noah entered his boat and the flood came to destroy them all.

28"And the world will be as it was in the days of Lot. People went about their daily business—eating and drinking, buying and selling, farming and building—29until the morning Lot left Sodom. Then fire and burning sulfur rained down from heaven and destroyed them all. 30Yes, it will be 'business as usual' right up to the hour when the Son of Man returns.* 31On that day a person outside the house* must not go into the house to pack. A person in the field must not return to town. 32Remember what happened to Lot's wife! 33Whoever clings to this life will lose it, and whoever loses this life will save it. 34That night two people will be asleep in one bed; one will be taken away, and the other will be left. 35Two women will be grinding flour together at the mill; one will be taken, the other left.*"

37"Lord, where will this happen?" the disciples asked.

Jesus replied, "Just as the gathering of vultures shows there is a carcass nearby, so these signs indicate that the end is near."*

17:20 Or *by your speculations.*   17:21 Or *within you.*   17:25 Or *suffer many things.*
17:30 Or *on the day the Son of Man is revealed.*   17:31 Greek *on the roof.*   17:35 Some manuscripts add verse 36, *Two men will be working in the field; one will be taken, the other left.*   17:37 Greek *Wherever the carcass is, the vultures gather.*

CHAPTER 18

Story of the Persistent Widow

One day Jesus told his disciples a story to illustrate their need for constant prayer and to show them that they must never give up. 2"There was a judge in a certain city," he said, "who was a godless man with great contempt for everyone. 3A widow of that city came to him repeatedly, appealing for justice against someone who had harmed her. 4The judge ignored her for a while, but eventually she wore him out. 'I fear neither God nor man,' he said to himself, 5'but this woman is driving me crazy. I'm going to see that she gets justice, because she is wearing me out with her constant requests!'"

6Then the Lord said, "Learn a lesson from this evil judge. 7Even he rendered a just decision in the end, so don't you think God will surely give justice to his chosen people who plead with him day and night? Will he keep putting them off? 8I tell you, he will grant justice to them quickly! But when I, the Son of Man, return, how many will I find who have faith?"

Story of the Pharisee and Tax Collector

9Then Jesus told this story to some who had great self-confidence and scorned everyone else: 10"Two men went to the Temple to pray. One was a Pharisee, and the other was a dishonest tax collector. 11The proud Pharisee stood by himself and prayed this prayer: 'I thank you, God, that I am not a sinner like everyone else, especially like that tax collector over there! For I never cheat, I don't sin, I don't commit adultery, 12I fast twice a week, and I give you a tenth of my income.'

13"But the tax collector stood at a distance and dared not even lift his eyes to heaven as he prayed. Instead, he beat his chest in sorrow, saying, 'O God, be merciful to me, for I am a sinner.' 14I tell you, this sinner, not the Pharisee, returned home justified before God. For the proud will be humbled, but the humble will be honored."

Jesus Blesses the Children

15One day some parents brought their little children to Jesus so he could touch them and bless them, but the disciples told them not to bother him. 16Then Jesus called for the children and said to the disciples, "Let the children come to me. Don't stop them! For the Kingdom of God belongs to such as these. 17I assure you, anyone who doesn't have their kind of faith will never get into the Kingdom of God."

The Rich Man

18Once a religious leader asked Jesus this question: "Good teacher, what should I do to get eternal life?"

19"Why do you call me good?" Jesus asked him. "Only God is truly good. 20But as for your question, you know the commandments: 'Do not commit adultery. Do not murder. Do not steal. Do not testify falsely. Honor your father and mother.'*"

21The man replied, "I've obeyed all these commandments since I was a child."

22"There is still one thing you lack," Jesus said. "Sell all you have

18:20 Exod 20:12-16; Deut 5:16-20.

and give the money to the poor, and you will have treasure in heaven. Then come, follow me." ²³But when the man heard this, he became sad because he was very rich.

²⁴Jesus watched him go and then said to his disciples, "How hard it is for rich people to get into the Kingdom of God! ²⁵It is easier for a camel to go through the eye of a needle than for a rich person to enter the Kingdom of God!"

²⁶Those who heard this said, "Then who in the world can be saved?"

²⁷He replied, "What is impossible from a human perspective is possible with God."

²⁸Peter said, "We have left our homes and followed you."

²⁹"Yes," Jesus replied, "and I assure you, everyone who has given up house or wife or brothers or parents or children, for the sake of the Kingdom of God, ³⁰will be repaid many times over in this life, as well as receiving eternal life in the world to come."

Jesus Again Predicts His Death

³¹Gathering the twelve disciples around him, Jesus told them, "As you know, we are going to Jerusalem. And when we get there, all the predictions of the ancient prophets concerning the Son of Man will come true. ³²He will be handed over to the Romans to be mocked, treated shamefully, and spit upon. ³³They will whip him and kill him, but on the third day he will rise again."

³⁴But they didn't understand a thing he said. Its significance was hidden from them, and they failed to grasp what he was talking about.

Jesus Heals a Blind Beggar

³⁵As they approached Jericho, a blind beggar was sitting beside the road. ³⁶When he heard the noise of a crowd going past, he asked what was happening. ³⁷They told him that Jesus of Nazareth was going by. ³⁸So he began shouting, "Jesus, Son of David, have mercy on me!" ³⁹The crowds ahead of Jesus tried to hush the man, but he only shouted louder, "Son of David, have mercy on me!"

⁴⁰When Jesus heard him, he stopped and ordered that the man be brought to him. ⁴¹Then Jesus asked the man, "What do you want me to do for you?"

"Lord," he pleaded, "I want to see!"

⁴²And Jesus said, "All right, you can see! Your faith has healed you." ⁴³Instantly the man could see, and he followed Jesus, praising God. And all who saw it praised God, too.

CHAPTER 19

Jesus and Zacchaeus

Jesus entered Jericho and made his way through the town. ²There was a man there named Zacchaeus. He was one of the most influential Jews in the Roman tax-collecting business, and he had become very rich. ³He tried to get a look at Jesus, but he was too short to see over the crowds. ⁴So he ran ahead and climbed a sycamore tree beside the road, so he could watch from there.

⁵When Jesus came by, he looked up at Zacchaeus and called him by name. "Zacchaeus!" he said. "Quick, come down! For I must be a guest in your home today."

⁶Zacchaeus quickly climbed down and took Jesus to his house in great excitement and joy. ⁷But the crowds were displeased. "He has gone to be the guest of a notorious sinner," they grumbled.

⁸Meanwhile, Zacchaeus stood there and said to the Lord, "I will give half my wealth to the poor, Lord, and if I have overcharged people on their taxes, I will give them back four times as much!"

⁹Jesus responded, "Salvation has come to this home today, for this man has shown himself to be a son of Abraham. ¹⁰And I, the Son of Man, have come to seek and save those like him who are lost."

Story of the Ten Servants

¹¹The crowd was listening to everything Jesus said. And because he was nearing Jerusalem, he told a story to correct the impression that the Kingdom of God would begin right away. ¹²He said, "A nobleman was called away to a distant empire to be crowned king and then return. ¹³Before he left, he called together ten servants and gave them ten pounds of silver* to invest for him while he was gone. ¹⁴But his people hated him and sent a delegation after him to say they did not want him to be their king.

¹⁵"When he returned, the king called in the servants to whom he had given the money. He wanted to find out what they had done with the money and what their profits were. ¹⁶The first servant reported a tremendous gain—ten times as much as the original amount! ¹⁷'Well done!' the king exclaimed. 'You are a trustworthy servant. You have been faithful with the little I entrusted to you, so you will be governor of ten cities as your reward.'

¹⁸"The next servant also reported a good gain—five times the original amount. ¹⁹'Well done!' the king said. 'You can be governor over five cities.'

²⁰"But the third servant brought back only the original amount of money and said, 'I hid it and kept it safe. ²¹I was afraid because you are a hard man to deal with, taking what isn't yours and harvesting crops you didn't plant.'

²²" 'You wicked servant!' the king roared. 'Hard, am I? If you knew so much about me and how tough I am, ²³why didn't you deposit the money in the bank so I could at least get some interest on it?' ²⁴Then turning to the others standing nearby, the king ordered, 'Take the money from this servant, and give it to the one who earned the most.'

²⁵" 'But, master,' they said, 'that servant has enough already!'

²⁶" 'Yes,' the king replied, 'but to those who use well what they are given, even more will be given. But from those who are unfaithful,* even what little they have will be taken away. ²⁷And now about these enemies of mine who didn't want me to be their king—bring them in and execute them right here in my presence.'"

The Triumphal Entry

²⁸After telling this story, Jesus went on toward Jerusalem, walking ahead of his disciples. ²⁹As they came to the towns of Bethphage and Bethany, on the Mount of Olives, he sent two disciples ahead. ³⁰"Go into that village over there," he told them, "and as you enter

19:13 Greek *10 minas;* 1 mina was worth about 3 months' wages.   19:26 Or *who have nothing.*

it, you will see a colt tied there that has never been ridden. Untie it and bring it here. ³¹If anyone asks what you are doing, just say, 'The Lord needs it.'"

³²So they went and found the colt, just as Jesus had said. ³³And sure enough, as they were untying it, the owners asked them, "Why are you untying our colt?"

³⁴And the disciples simply replied, "The Lord needs it." ³⁵So they brought the colt to Jesus and threw their garments over it for him to ride on.

³⁶Then the crowds spread out their coats on the road ahead of Jesus. ³⁷As they reached the place where the road started down from the Mount of Olives, all of his followers began to shout and sing as they walked along, praising God for all the wonderful miracles they had seen.

³⁸ "Bless the King who comes in the name of the Lord!

Peace in heaven

and glory in highest heaven!"*

³⁹But some of the Pharisees among the crowd said, "Teacher, rebuke your followers for saying things like that!"

⁴⁰He replied, "If they kept quiet, the stones along the road would burst into cheers!"

Jesus Weeps over Jerusalem

⁴¹But as they came closer to Jerusalem and Jesus saw the city ahead, he began to cry. ⁴²"I wish that even today you would find the way of peace. But now it is too late, and peace is hidden from you. ⁴³Before long your enemies will build ramparts against your walls and encircle you and close in on you. ⁴⁴They will crush you to the ground, and your children with you. Your enemies will not leave a single stone in place, because you have rejected the opportunity God offered you."

Jesus Clears the Temple

⁴⁵Then Jesus entered the Temple and began to drive out the merchants from their stalls. ⁴⁶He told them, "The Scriptures declare, 'My Temple will be a place of prayer,' but you have turned it into a den of thieves."*

⁴⁷After that, he taught daily in the Temple, but the leading priests, the teachers of religious law, and the other leaders of the people began planning how to kill him. ⁴⁸But they could think of nothing, because all the people hung on every word he said.

CHAPTER 20
The Authority of Jesus Challenged

One day as Jesus was teaching and preaching the Good News in the Temple, the leading priests and teachers of religious law and other leaders came up to him. ²They demanded, "By whose authority did you drive out the merchants from the Temple?* Who gave you such authority?"

³"Let me ask you a question first," he replied. ⁴"Did John's baptism come from heaven, or was it merely human?"

⁵They talked it over among themselves. "If we say it was from heaven, he will ask why we didn't believe him. ⁶But if we say it was

19:38 Pss 118:26; 148:1.   19:46 Isa 56:7; Jer 7:11.   20:2 Or *By whose authority do you do these things?*

merely human, the people will stone us, because they are convinced he was a prophet." ⁷Finally they replied, "We don't know."

⁸And Jesus responded, "Then I won't answer your question either."

Story of the Evil Farmers

⁹Now Jesus turned to the people again and told them this story: "A man planted a vineyard, leased it out to tenant farmers, and moved to another country for several years. ¹⁰At grape-picking time, he sent one of his servants to collect his share of the crop. But the farmers attacked the servant, beat him up, and sent him back empty-handed. ¹¹So the owner sent another servant, but the same thing happened; he was beaten up and treated shamefully, and he went away empty-handed. ¹²A third man was sent and the same thing happened. He, too, was wounded and chased away.

¹³" 'What will I do?' the owner asked himself. 'I know! I'll send my cherished son. Surely they will respect him.'

¹⁴"But when the farmers saw his son, they said to each other, 'Here comes the heir to this estate. Let's kill him and get the estate for ourselves!' ¹⁵So they dragged him out of the vineyard and murdered him.

"What do you suppose the owner of the vineyard will do to those farmers?" Jesus asked. ¹⁶"I'll tell you—he will come and kill them all and lease the vineyard to others."

"But God forbid that such a thing should ever happen," his listeners protested.

¹⁷Jesus looked at them and said, "Then what do the Scriptures mean?

'The stone rejected by the builders
　has now become the cornerstone.'*

¹⁸All who stumble over that stone will be broken to pieces, and it will crush anyone on whom it falls."

¹⁹When the teachers of religious law and the leading priests heard this story, they wanted to arrest Jesus immediately because they realized he was pointing at them—that they were the farmers in the story. But they were afraid there would be a riot if they arrested him.

Taxes for Caesar

²⁰Watching for their opportunity, the leaders sent secret agents pretending to be honest men. They tried to get Jesus to say something that could be reported to the Roman governor so he would arrest Jesus. ²¹They said, "Teacher, we know that you speak and teach what is right and are not influenced by what others think. You sincerely teach the ways of God. ²²Now tell us—is it right to pay taxes to the Roman government or not?"

²³He saw through their trickery and said, ²⁴"Show me a Roman coin.* Whose picture and title are stamped on it?"

"Caesar's," they replied.

²⁵"Well then," he said, "give to Caesar what belongs to him. But everything that belongs to God must be given to God." ²⁶So they failed to trap him in the presence of the people. Instead, they were amazed by his answer, and they were silenced.

20:17 Ps 118:22.　20:24 Greek *a denarius.*

Discussion about Resurrection

27Then some Sadducees stepped forward—a group of Jews who say there is no resurrection after death. 28They posed this question: "Teacher, Moses gave us a law that if a man dies, leaving a wife but no children, his brother should marry the widow and have a child who will be the brother's heir.* 29Well, there were seven brothers. The oldest married and then died without children. 30His brother married the widow, but he also died. Still no children. 31And so it went, one after the other, until each of the seven had married her and died, leaving no children. 32Finally, the woman died, too. 33So tell us, whose wife will she be in the resurrection? For all seven were married to her!"

34Jesus replied, "Marriage is for people here on earth. 35But that is not the way it will be in the age to come. For those worthy of being raised from the dead won't be married then. 36And they will never die again. In these respects they are like angels. They are children of God raised up to new life. 37But now, as to whether the dead will be raised—even Moses proved this when he wrote about the burning bush. Long after Abraham, Isaac, and Jacob had died, he referred to the Lord* as 'the God of Abraham, the God of Isaac, and the God of Jacob.'* 38So he is the God of the living, not the dead. They are all alive to him."

39"Well said, Teacher!" remarked some of the teachers of religious law who were standing there. 40And that ended their questions; no one dared to ask any more.

Whose Son Is the Messiah?

41Then Jesus presented them with a question. "Why is it," he asked, "that the Messiah is said to be the son of David? 42For David himself wrote in the book of Psalms:

'The Lord said to my Lord,
Sit in honor at my right hand
43   until I humble your enemies,
     making them a footstool under your feet.'*

44Since David called him Lord, how can he be his son at the same time?"

45Then, with the crowds listening, he turned to his disciples and said, 46"Beware of these teachers of religious law! For they love to parade in flowing robes and to have everyone bow to them as they walk in the marketplaces. And how they love the seats of honor in the synagogues and at banquets. 47But they shamelessly cheat widows out of their property, and then, to cover up the kind of people they really are, they make long prayers in public. Because of this, their punishment will be the greater."

CHAPTER 21

The Widow's Offering

While Jesus was in the Temple, he watched the rich people putting their gifts into the collection box. 2Then a poor widow came by and dropped in two pennies.* 3"I assure you," he said, "this poor widow has given more than all the rest of them. 4For they have

20:28 Deut 25:5-6.   20:37a Greek *when he wrote about the bush. He referred to the Lord.*
20:37b Exod 3:6.   20:42-43 Ps 110:1.   21:2 Greek *2 lepta.*

given a tiny part of their surplus, but she, poor as she is, has given everything she has."

Jesus Foretells the Future

5Some of his disciples began talking about the beautiful stonework of the Temple and the memorial decorations on the walls. But Jesus said, 6"The time is coming when all these things will be so completely demolished that not one stone will be left on top of another."

7"Teacher," they asked, "when will all this take place? And will there be any sign ahead of time?"

8He replied, "Don't let anyone mislead you. For many will come in my name, claiming to be the Messiah* and saying, 'The time has come!' But don't believe them. 9And when you hear of wars and insurrections, don't panic. Yes, these things must come, but the end won't follow immediately." 10Then he added, "Nations and kingdoms will proclaim war against each other. 11There will be great earthquakes, and there will be famines and epidemics in many lands, and there will be terrifying things and great miraculous signs in the heavens.

12"But before all this occurs, there will be a time of great persecution. You will be dragged into synagogues and prisons, and you will be accused before kings and governors of being my followers. 13This will be your opportunity to tell them about me. 14So don't worry about how to answer the charges against you, 15for I will give you the right words and such wisdom that none of your opponents will be able to reply! 16Even those closest to you—your parents, brothers, relatives, and friends—will betray you. And some of you will be killed. 17And everyone will hate you because of your allegiance to me. 18But not a hair of your head will perish! 19By standing firm, you will win your souls.

20"And when you see Jerusalem surrounded by armies, then you will know that the time of its destruction has arrived. 21Then those in Judea must flee to the hills. Let those in Jerusalem escape, and those outside the city should not enter it for shelter. 22For those will be days of God's vengeance, and the prophetic words of the Scriptures will be fulfilled. 23How terrible it will be for pregnant women and for mothers nursing their babies. For there will be great distress in the land and wrath upon this people. 24They will be brutally killed by the sword or sent away as captives to all the nations of the world. And Jerusalem will be conquered and trampled down by the Gentiles until the age of the Gentiles comes to an end.

25"And there will be strange events in the skies—signs in the sun, moon, and stars. And down here on earth the nations will be in turmoil, perplexed by the roaring seas and strange tides. 26The courage of many people will falter because of the fearful fate they see coming upon the earth, because the stability of the very heavens will be broken up. 27Then everyone will see the Son of Man arrive on the clouds with power and great glory.* 28So when all these things begin to happen, stand straight and look up, for your salvation is near!"

21:8 Greek *name, saying, 'I am.'*   21:27 See Dan 7:13.

²⁹Then he gave them this illustration: "Notice the fig tree, or any other tree. ³⁰When the leaves come out, you know without being told that summer is near. ³¹Just so, when you see the events I've described taking place, you can be sure that the Kingdom of God is near. ³²I assure you, this generation* will not pass from the scene until all these events have taken place. ³³Heaven and earth will disappear, but my words will remain forever.

³⁴"Watch out! Don't let me find you living in careless ease and drunkenness, and filled with the worries of this life. Don't let that day catch you unaware, ³⁵as in a trap. For that day will come upon everyone living on the earth. ³⁶Keep a constant watch. And pray that, if possible, you may escape these horrors and stand before the Son of Man."

³⁷Every day Jesus went to the Temple to teach, and each evening he returned to spend the night on the Mount of Olives. ³⁸The crowds gathered early each morning to hear him.

CHAPTER 22

Judas Agrees to Betray Jesus

The Festival of Unleavened Bread, which begins with the Passover celebration, was drawing near. ²The leading priests and teachers of religious law were actively plotting Jesus' murder. But they wanted to kill him without starting a riot, a possibility they greatly feared.

³Then Satan entered into Judas Iscariot, who was one of the twelve disciples, ⁴and he went over to the leading priests and captains of the Temple guard to discuss the best way to betray Jesus to them. ⁵They were delighted that he was ready to help them, and they promised him a reward. ⁶So he began looking for an opportunity to betray Jesus so they could arrest him quietly when the crowds weren't around.

The Last Supper

⁷Now the Festival of Unleavened Bread arrived, when the Passover lambs were sacrificed. ⁸Jesus sent Peter and John ahead and said, "Go and prepare the Passover meal, so we can eat it together."

⁹"Where do you want us to go?" they asked him.

¹⁰He replied, "As soon as you enter Jerusalem, a man carrying a pitcher of water will meet you. Follow him. At the house he enters, ¹¹say to the owner, 'The Teacher asks, Where is the guest room where I can eat the Passover meal with my disciples?' ¹²He will take you upstairs to a large room that is already set up. That is the place. Go ahead and prepare our supper there." ¹³They went off to the city and found everything just as Jesus had said, and they prepared the Passover supper there.

¹⁴Then at the proper time Jesus and the twelve apostles sat down together at the table. ¹⁵Jesus said, "I have looked forward to this hour with deep longing, anxious to eat this Passover meal with you before my suffering begins. ¹⁶For I tell you now that I won't eat it again until it comes to fulfillment in the Kingdom of God."

¹⁷Then he took a cup of wine, and when he had given thanks for it, he said, "Take this and share it among yourselves. ¹⁸For I will not drink wine again until the Kingdom of God has come."

21:32 Or *this age,* or *this nation.*

¹⁹Then he took a loaf of bread; and when he had thanked God for it, he broke it in pieces and gave it to the disciples, saying, "This is my body, given for you. Do this in remembrance of me." ²⁰After supper he took another cup of wine and said, "This wine is the token of God's new covenant to save you—an agreement sealed with the blood I will pour out for you.*

²¹"But here at this table, sitting among us as a friend, is the man who will betray me. ²²For I, the Son of Man, must die since it is part of God's plan. But how terrible it will be for my betrayer!" ²³Then the disciples began to ask each other which of them would ever do such a thing.

²⁴And they began to argue among themselves as to who would be the greatest in the coming Kingdom. ²⁵Jesus told them, "In this world the kings and great men order their people around, and yet they are called 'friends of the people.' ²⁶But among you, those who are the greatest should take the lowest rank, and the leader should be like a servant. ²⁷Normally the master sits at the table and is served by his servants. But not here! For I am your servant. ²⁸You have remained true to me in my time of trial. ²⁹And just as my Father has granted me a Kingdom, I now grant you the right ³⁰to eat and drink at my table in that Kingdom. And you will sit on thrones, judging the twelve tribes of Israel.

Jesus Predicts Peter's Denial

³¹"Simon, Simon, Satan has asked to have all of you, to sift you like wheat. ³²But I have pleaded in prayer for you, Simon, that your faith should not fail. So when you have repented and turned to me again, strengthen and build up your brothers."

³³Peter said, "Lord, I am ready to go to prison with you, and even to die with you."

³⁴But Jesus said, "Peter, let me tell you something. The rooster will not crow tomorrow morning until you have denied three times that you even know me."

³⁵Then Jesus asked them, "When I sent you out to preach the Good News and you did not have money, a traveler's bag, or extra clothing, did you lack anything?"

"No," they replied.

³⁶"But now," he said, "take your money and a traveler's bag. And if you don't have a sword, sell your clothes and buy one! ³⁷For the time has come for this prophecy about me to be fulfilled: 'He was counted among those who were rebels.'* Yes, everything written about me by the prophets will come true."

³⁸"Lord," they replied, "we have two swords among us."

"That's enough," he said.

Jesus Prays on the Mount of Olives

³⁹Then, accompanied by the disciples, Jesus left the upstairs room and went as usual to the Mount of Olives. ⁴⁰There he told them, "Pray that you will not be overcome by temptation."

⁴¹He walked away, about a stone's throw, and knelt down and prayed, ⁴²"Father, if you are willing, please take this cup of suffering away from me. Yet I want your will, not mine." ⁴³Then an angel

22:19-20 Some manuscripts omit 22:19b-20, *given for you . . . I will pour out for you.*
22:37 Isa 53:12.

from heaven appeared and strengthened him. ⁴⁴He prayed more fervently, and he was in such agony of spirit that his sweat fell to the ground like great drops of blood.* ⁴⁵At last he stood up again and returned to the disciples, only to find them asleep, exhausted from grief. ⁴⁶"Why are you sleeping?" he asked. "Get up and pray. Otherwise temptation will overpower you."

Jesus Is Betrayed and Arrested

⁴⁷But even as he said this, a mob approached, led by Judas, one of his twelve disciples. Judas walked over to Jesus and greeted him with a kiss. ⁴⁸But Jesus said, "Judas, how can you betray me, the Son of Man, with a kiss?"

⁴⁹When the other disciples saw what was about to happen, they exclaimed, "Lord, should we fight? We brought the swords!" ⁵⁰And one of them slashed at the high priest's servant and cut off his right ear.

⁵¹But Jesus said, "Don't resist anymore." And he touched the place where the man's ear had been and healed him. ⁵²Then Jesus spoke to the leading priests and captains of the Temple guard and the other leaders who headed the mob. "Am I some dangerous criminal," he asked, "that you have come armed with swords and clubs to arrest me? ⁵³Why didn't you arrest me in the Temple? I was there every day. But this is your moment, the time when the power of darkness reigns."

Peter Denies Jesus

⁵⁴So they arrested him and led him to the high priest's residence, and Peter was following far behind. ⁵⁵The guards lit a fire in the courtyard and sat around it, and Peter joined them there. ⁵⁶A servant girl noticed him in the firelight and began staring at him. Finally she said, "This man was one of Jesus' followers!"

⁵⁷Peter denied it. "Woman," he said, "I don't even know the man!"

⁵⁸After a while someone else looked at him and said, "You must be one of them!"

"No, man, I'm not!" Peter replied.

⁵⁹About an hour later someone else insisted, "This must be one of Jesus' disciples because he is a Galilean, too."

⁶⁰But Peter said, "Man, I don't know what you are talking about." And as soon as he said these words, the rooster crowed. ⁶¹At that moment the Lord turned and looked at Peter. Then Peter remembered that the Lord had said, "Before the rooster crows tomorrow morning, you will deny me three times." ⁶²And Peter left the courtyard, crying bitterly.

⁶³Now the guards in charge of Jesus began mocking and beating him. ⁶⁴They blindfolded him; then they hit him and asked, "Who hit you that time, you prophet?" ⁶⁵And they threw all sorts of terrible insults at him.

Jesus before the Council

⁶⁶At daybreak all the leaders of the people assembled, including the leading priests and the teachers of religious law. Jesus was led before this high council,* ⁶⁷and they said, "Tell us if you are the Messiah."

22:43-44 These verses are not included in many ancient manuscripts. 22:66 Greek *before their Sanhedrin.*

But he replied, "If I tell you, you won't believe me. [68]And if I ask you a question, you won't answer. [69]But the time is soon coming when I, the Son of Man, will be sitting at God's right hand in the place of power."*

[70]They all shouted, "Then you claim you are the Son of God?"

And he replied, "You are right in saying that I am."

[71]"What need do we have for other witnesses?" they shouted. "We ourselves heard him say it."

CHAPTER 23

Jesus' Trial before Pilate

Then the entire council took Jesus over to Pilate, the Roman governor. [2]They began at once to state their case: "This man has been leading our people to ruin by telling them not to pay their taxes to the Roman government and by claiming he is the Messiah, a king."

[3]So Pilate asked him, "Are you the King of the Jews?"

Jesus replied, "Yes, it is as you say."

[4]Pilate turned to the leading priests and to the crowd and said, "I find nothing wrong with this man!"

[5]Then they became desperate. "But he is causing riots everywhere he goes, all over Judea, from Galilee to Jerusalem!"

[6]"Oh, is he a Galilean?" Pilate asked. [7]When they answered that he was, Pilate sent him to Herod Antipas, because Galilee was under Herod's jurisdiction, and Herod happened to be in Jerusalem at the time.

[8]Herod was delighted at the opportunity to see Jesus, because he had heard about him and had been hoping for a long time to see him perform a miracle. [9]He asked Jesus question after question, but Jesus refused to answer. [10]Meanwhile, the leading priests and the teachers of religious law stood there shouting their accusations. [11]Now Herod and his soldiers began mocking and ridiculing Jesus. Then they put a royal robe on him and sent him back to Pilate. [12]Herod and Pilate, who had been enemies before, became friends that day.

[13]Then Pilate called together the leading priests and other religious leaders, along with the people, [14]and he announced his verdict. "You brought this man to me, accusing him of leading a revolt. I have examined him thoroughly on this point in your presence and find him innocent. [15]Herod came to the same conclusion and sent him back to us. Nothing this man has done calls for the death penalty. [16]So I will have him flogged, but then I will release him."*

[18]Then a mighty roar rose from the crowd, and with one voice they shouted, "Kill him, and release Barabbas to us!" [19](Barabbas was in prison for murder and for taking part in an insurrection in Jerusalem against the government.) [20]Pilate argued with them, because he wanted to release Jesus. [21]But they shouted, "Crucify him! Crucify him!"

[22]For the third time he demanded, "Why? What crime has he committed? I have found no reason to sentence him to death. I will therefore flog him and let him go."

22:69 See Ps 110:1. **23:16** Some manuscripts add verse 17, *For it was necessary for him to release one [prisoner] for them during the feast.*

²³But the crowd shouted louder and louder for Jesus' death, and their voices prevailed. ²⁴So Pilate sentenced Jesus to die as they demanded. ²⁵As they had requested, he released Barabbas, the man in prison for insurrection and murder. But he delivered Jesus over to them to do as they wished.

The Crucifixion

²⁶As they led Jesus away, Simon of Cyrene,* who was coming in from the country just then, was forced to follow Jesus and carry his cross. ²⁷Great crowds trailed along behind, including many grief-stricken women. ²⁸But Jesus turned and said to them, "Daughters of Jerusalem, don't weep for me, but weep for yourselves and for your children. ²⁹For the days are coming when they will say, 'Fortunate indeed are the women who are childless, the wombs that have not borne a child and the breasts that have never nursed.' ³⁰People will beg the mountains to fall on them and the hills to bury them. ³¹For if these things are done when the tree is green, what will happen when it is dry?*"

³²Two others, both criminals, were led out to be executed with him. ³³Finally, they came to a place called The Skull.* All three were crucified there—Jesus on the center cross, and the two criminals on either side.

³⁴Jesus said, "Father, forgive these people, because they don't know what they are doing."* And the soldiers gambled for his clothes by throwing dice.*

³⁵The crowd watched, and the leaders laughed and scoffed. "He saved others," they said, "let him save himself if he is really God's Chosen One, the Messiah." ³⁶The soldiers mocked him, too, by offering him a drink of sour wine. ³⁷They called out to him, "If you are the King of the Jews, save yourself!" ³⁸A signboard was nailed to the cross above him with these words: "This is the King of the Jews."

³⁹One of the criminals hanging beside him scoffed, "So you're the Messiah, are you? Prove it by saving yourself—and us, too, while you're at it!"

⁴⁰But the other criminal protested, "Don't you fear God even when you are dying? ⁴¹We deserve to die for our evil deeds, but this man hasn't done anything wrong." ⁴²Then he said, "Jesus, remember me when you come into your Kingdom."

⁴³And Jesus replied, "I assure you, today you will be with me in paradise."

The Death of Jesus

⁴⁴By this time it was noon, and darkness fell across the whole land until three o'clock. ⁴⁵The light from the sun was gone. And suddenly, the thick veil hanging in the Temple was torn apart. ⁴⁶Then Jesus shouted, "Father, I entrust my spirit into your hands!"* And with those words he breathed his last.

⁴⁷When the captain of the Roman soldiers handling the executions saw what had happened, he praised God and said, "Surely this man was innocent.*" ⁴⁸And when the crowd that came to see

23:26 Cyrene was a city in northern Africa. 23:31 Or If these things are done to me, the living tree, what will happen to you, the dry tree? 23:33 Sometimes rendered Calvary, which comes from the Latin word for "skull." 23:34a This sentence is not included in many ancient manuscripts. 23:34b Greek by casting lots. See Ps 22:18. 23:46 Ps 31:5. 23:47 Or righteous.

the crucifixion saw all that had happened, they went home in deep sorrow.* 49But Jesus' friends, including the women who had followed him from Galilee, stood at a distance watching.

The Burial of Jesus

50Now there was a good and righteous man named Joseph. He was a member of the Jewish high council, 51but he had not agreed with the decision and actions of the other religious leaders. He was from the town of Arimathea in Judea, and he had been waiting for the Kingdom of God to come. 52He went to Pilate and asked for Jesus' body. 53Then he took the body down from the cross and wrapped it in a long linen cloth and laid it in a new tomb that had been carved out of rock. 54This was done late on Friday afternoon, the day of preparation* for the Sabbath.

55As his body was taken away, the women from Galilee followed and saw the tomb where they placed his body. 56Then they went home and prepared spices and ointments to embalm him. But by the time they were finished it was the Sabbath, so they rested all that day as required by the law.

CHAPTER 24

The Resurrection

But very early on Sunday morning* the women came to the tomb, taking the spices they had prepared. 2They found that the stone covering the entrance had been rolled aside. 3So they went in, but they couldn't find the body of the Lord Jesus. 4They were puzzled, trying to think what could have happened to it. Suddenly, two men appeared to them, clothed in dazzling robes. 5The women were terrified and bowed low before them. Then the men asked, "Why are you looking in a tomb for someone who is alive? 6He isn't here! He has risen from the dead! Don't you remember what he told you back in Galilee, 7that the Son of Man must be betrayed into the hands of sinful men and be crucified, and that he would rise again the third day?"

8Then they remembered that he had said this. 9So they rushed back to tell his eleven disciples—and everyone else—what had happened. 10The women who went to the tomb were Mary Magdalene, Joanna, Mary the mother of James, and several others. They told the apostles what had happened, 11but the story sounded like nonsense, so they didn't believe it. 12However, Peter ran to the tomb to look. Stooping, he peered in and saw the empty linen wrappings; then he went home again, wondering what had happened.*

The Walk to Emmaus

13That same day two of Jesus' followers were walking to the village of Emmaus, seven miles* out of Jerusalem. 14As they walked along they were talking about everything that had happened. 15Suddenly, Jesus himself came along and joined them and began walking beside them. 16But they didn't know who he was, because God kept them from recognizing him.

17"You seem to be in a deep discussion about something," he said. "What are you so concerned about?"

23:48 Greek *beating their breasts.*   23:54 Greek *on the day of preparation.*   24:1 Greek *But on the first day of the week, very early in the morning.*   24:12 Some manuscripts do not include this verse.   24:13 Greek *60 stadia* [11.1 kilometers].

They stopped short, sadness written across their faces. 18Then one of them, Cleopas, replied, "You must be the only person in Jerusalem who hasn't heard about all the things that have happened there the last few days."

19"What things?" Jesus asked.

"The things that happened to Jesus, the man from Nazareth," they said. "He was a prophet who did wonderful miracles. He was a mighty teacher, highly regarded by both God and all the people. 20But our leading priests and other religious leaders arrested him and handed him over to be condemned to death, and they crucified him. 21We had thought he was the Messiah who had come to rescue Israel. That all happened three days ago. 22Then some women from our group of his followers were at his tomb early this morning, and they came back with an amazing report. 23They said his body was missing, and they had seen angels who told them Jesus is alive! 24Some of our men ran out to see, and sure enough, Jesus' body was gone, just as the women had said."

25Then Jesus said to them, "You are such foolish people! You find it so hard to believe all that the prophets wrote in the Scriptures. 26Wasn't it clearly predicted by the prophets that the Messiah would have to suffer all these things before entering his time of glory?" 27Then Jesus quoted passages from the writings of Moses and all the prophets, explaining what all the Scriptures said about himself.

28By this time they were nearing Emmaus and the end of their journey. Jesus would have gone on, 29but they begged him to stay the night with them, since it was getting late. So he went home with them. 30As they sat down to eat, he took a small loaf of bread, asked God's blessing on it, broke it, then gave it to them. 31Suddenly, their eyes were opened, and they recognized him. And at that moment he disappeared!

32They said to each other, "Didn't our hearts feel strangely warm as he talked with us on the road and explained the Scriptures to us?" 33And within the hour they were on their way back to Jerusalem, where the eleven disciples and the other followers of Jesus were gathered. When they arrived, they were greeted with the report, 34"The Lord has really risen! He appeared to Peter*!"

Jesus Appears to the Disciples

35Then the two from Emmaus told their story of how Jesus had appeared to them as they were walking along the road and how they had recognized him as he was breaking the bread. 36And just as they were telling about it, Jesus himself was suddenly standing there among them. He said, "Peace be with you."* 37But the whole group was terribly frightened, thinking they were seeing a ghost! 38"Why are you frightened?" he asked. "Why do you doubt who I am?" 39Look at my hands. Look at my feet. You can see that it's really me. Touch me and make sure that I am not a ghost, because ghosts don't have bodies, as you see that I do!" 40As he spoke, he held out his hands for them to see, and he showed them his feet.*

41Still they stood there doubting, filled with joy and wonder.

24:34 Greek *Simon.*   24:36 Some manuscripts do not include *He said, "Peace be with you."*   24:40 Some manuscripts do not include this verse.

Then he asked them, "Do you have anything here to eat?" 42They gave him a piece of broiled fish, 43and he ate it as they watched.

44Then he said, "When I was with you before, I told you that everything written about me by Moses and the prophets and in the Psalms must all come true." 45Then he opened their minds to understand these many Scriptures. 46And he said, "Yes, it was written long ago that the Messiah must suffer and die and rise again from the dead on the third day. 47With my authority, take this message of repentance to all the nations, beginning in Jerusalem: 'There is forgiveness of sins for all who turn to me.' 48You are witnesses of all these things.

49"And now I will send the Holy Spirit, just as my Father promised. But stay here in the city until the Holy Spirit comes and fills you with power from heaven."

The Ascension

50Then Jesus led them to Bethany, and lifting his hands to heaven, he blessed them. 51While he was blessing them, he left them and was taken up to heaven.* 52They worshiped him and* then returned to Jerusalem filled with great joy. 53And they spent all of their time in the Temple, praising God.

24:51 Some manuscripts do not include *and was taken up to heaven.*   24:52 Some manuscripts do not include *worshiped him and.*

JOHN

CHAPTER 1

Christ, the Eternal Word

In the beginning the Word already existed. He was with God, and he was God. 2He was in the beginning with God. 3He created everything there is. Nothing exists that he didn't make. 4Life itself was in him, and this life gives light to everyone. 5The light shines through the darkness, and the darkness can never extinguish it.

6God sent John the Baptist 7to tell everyone about the light so that everyone might believe because of his testimony. 8John himself was not the light; he was only a witness to the light. 9The one who is the true light, who gives light to everyone, was going to come into the world.

10But although the world was made through him, the world didn't recognize him when he came. 11Even in his own land and among his own people, he was not accepted. 12But to all who believed him and accepted him, he gave the right to become children of God. 13They are reborn! This is not a physical birth resulting from human passion or plan—this rebirth comes from God.

14So the Word became human and lived here on earth among us. He was full of unfailing love and faithfulness.* And we have seen his glory, the glory of the only Son of the Father.

15John pointed him out to the people. He shouted to the crowds,

1:14 Greek *grace and truth;* also in 1:17.

"This is the one I was talking about when I said, 'Someone is coming who is far greater than I am, for he existed long before I did.'"

16We have all benefited from the rich blessings he brought to us—one gracious blessing after another.* 17For the law was given through Moses; God's unfailing love and faithfulness came through Jesus Christ. 18No one has ever seen God. But his only Son, who is himself God,* is near to the Father's heart; he has told us about him.

The Testimony of John the Baptist

19This was the testimony of John when the Jewish leaders sent priests and Temple assistants* from Jerusalem to ask John whether he claimed to be the Messiah. 20He flatly denied it. "I am not the Messiah," he said.

21"Well then, who are you?" they asked. "Are you Elijah?"

"No," he replied.

"Are you the Prophet?"*

"No."

22"Then who are you? Tell us, so we can give an answer to those who sent us. What do you have to say about yourself?"

23John replied in the words of Isaiah:

"I am a voice shouting in the wilderness,
    'Prepare a straight pathway for the Lord's coming!'"*

24Then those who were sent by the Pharisees 25asked him, "If you aren't the Messiah or Elijah or the Prophet, what right do you have to baptize?"

26John told them, "I baptize with* water, but right here in the crowd is someone you do not know, 27who will soon begin his ministry. I am not even worthy to be his slave.*" 28This incident took place at Bethany, a village east of the Jordan River, where John was baptizing.

Jesus, the Lamb of God

29The next day John saw Jesus coming toward him and said, "Look! There is the Lamb of God who takes away the sin of the world! 30He is the one I was talking about when I said, 'Soon a man is coming who is far greater than I am, for he existed long before I did.' 31I didn't know he was the one, but I have been baptizing with water in order to point him out to Israel."

32Then John said, "I saw the Holy Spirit descending like a dove from heaven and resting upon him. 33I didn't know he was the one, but when God sent me to baptize with water, he told me, 'When you see the Holy Spirit descending and resting upon someone, he is the one you are looking for. He is the one who baptizes with the Holy Spirit.' 34I saw this happen to Jesus, so I testify that he is the Son of God.*"

The First Disciples

35The following day, John was again standing with two of his disciples. 36As Jesus walked by, John looked at him and then

1:16 Greek *grace upon grace.* 1:18 Some manuscripts read *his one and only Son.*
1:19 Greek *and Levites.* 1:21 See Deut 18:15, 18; Mal 4:5-6. 1:23 Isa 40:3. 1:26 Or *in;* also in 1:31, 33. 1:27 Greek *to untie his sandals.* 1:34 Some manuscripts read *the chosen One of God.*

declared, "Look! There is the Lamb of God!" [37]Then John's two disciples turned and followed Jesus.

[38]Jesus looked around and saw them following. "What do you want?" he asked them.

They replied, "Rabbi" (which means Teacher), "where are you staying?"

[39]"Come and see," he said. It was about four o'clock in the afternoon when they went with him to the place, and they stayed there the rest of the day.

[40]Andrew, Simon Peter's brother, was one of these men who had heard what John said and then followed Jesus. [41]The first thing Andrew did was to find his brother, Simon, and tell him, "We have found the Messiah" (which means the Christ).

[42]Then Andrew brought Simon to meet Jesus. Looking intently at Simon, Jesus said, "You are Simon, the son of John—but you will be called Cephas" (which means Peter*).

[43]The next day Jesus decided to go to Galilee. He found Philip and said to him, "Come, be my disciple." [44]Philip was from Bethsaida, Andrew and Peter's hometown.

[45]Philip went off to look for Nathanael and told him, "We have found the very person Moses and the prophets wrote about! His name is Jesus, the son of Joseph from Nazareth."

[46]"Nazareth!" exclaimed Nathanael. "Can anything good come from there?"

"Just come and see for yourself," Philip said.

[47]As they approached, Jesus said, "Here comes an honest man—a true son of Israel."

[48]"How do you know about me?" Nathanael asked.

And Jesus replied, "I could see you under the fig tree before Philip found you."

[49]Nathanael replied, "Teacher, you are the Son of God—the King of Israel!"

[50]Jesus asked him, "Do you believe all this just because I told you I had seen you under the fig tree? You will see greater things than this." [51]Then he said, "The truth is, you will all see heaven open and the angels of God going up and down upon the Son of Man."*

CHAPTER 2

The Wedding at Cana

The next day* Jesus' mother was a guest at a wedding celebration in the village of Cana in Galilee. [2]Jesus and his disciples were also invited to the celebration. [3]The wine supply ran out during the festivities, so Jesus' mother spoke to him about the problem. "They have no more wine," she told him.

[4]"How does that concern you and me?" Jesus asked. "My time has not yet come."

[5]But his mother told the servants, "Do whatever he tells you."

[6]Six stone waterpots were standing there; they were used for Jewish ceremonial purposes and held twenty to thirty gallons* each. [7]Jesus told the servants, "Fill the jars with water." When the

1:42 The names *Cephas* and *Peter* both mean "rock."   1:51 See Gen 28:10-17, the account of Jacob's ladder.   2:1 Greek *On the third day;* see 1:35, 43.   2:6 Greek *2 or 3 measures* [75 to 113 liters].

exception

jars had been filled to the brim, [8]he said, "Dip some out and take it to the master of ceremonies." So they followed his instructions.

[9]When the master of ceremonies tasted the water that was now wine, not knowing where it had come from (though, of course, the servants knew), he called the bridegroom over. [10]"Usually a host serves the best wine first," he said. "Then, when everyone is full and doesn't care, he brings out the less expensive wines. But you have kept the best until now!"

[11]This miraculous sign at Cana in Galilee was Jesus' first display of his glory. And his disciples believed in him.

[12]After the wedding he went to Capernaum for a few days with his mother, his brothers, and his disciples.

Jesus Clears the Temple

[13]It was time for the annual Passover celebration, and Jesus went to Jerusalem. [14]In the Temple area he saw merchants selling cattle, sheep, and doves for sacrifices; and he saw money changers behind their counters. [15]Jesus made a whip from some ropes and chased them all out of the Temple. He drove out the sheep and oxen, scattered the money changers' coins over the floor, and turned over their tables. [16]Then, going over to the people who sold doves, he told them, "Get these things out of here. Don't turn my Father's house into a marketplace!"

[17]Then his disciples remembered this prophecy from the Scriptures: "Passion for God's house burns within me."*

[18]"What right do you have to do these things?" the Jewish leaders demanded. "If you have this authority from God, show us a miraculous sign to prove it."

[19]"All right," Jesus replied. "Destroy this temple, and in three days I will raise it up."

[20]"What!" they exclaimed. "It took forty-six years to build this Temple, and you can do it in three days?" [21]But by "this temple," Jesus meant his body. [22]After he was raised from the dead, the disciples remembered that he had said this. And they believed both Jesus and the Scriptures.

[23]Because of the miraculous signs he did in Jerusalem at the Passover celebration, many people were convinced that he was indeed the Messiah. [24]But Jesus didn't trust them, because he knew what people were really like. [25]No one needed to tell him about human nature.

CHAPTER 3

Jesus and Nicodemus

After dark one evening, a Jewish religious leader named Nicodemus, a Pharisee, [2]came to speak with Jesus. "Teacher," he said, "we all know that God has sent you to teach us. Your miraculous signs are proof enough that God is with you."

[3]Jesus replied, "I assure you, unless you are born again,* you can never see the Kingdom of God."

[4]"What do you mean?" exclaimed Nicodemus. "How can an old man go back into his mother's womb and be born again?"

[5]Jesus replied, "The truth is, no one can enter the Kingdom of

2:17 Or *"Concern for God's house will be my undoing."* Ps 69:9. **3:3** Or *born from above;* also in 3:7.

God without being born of water and the Spirit.* 6Humans can reproduce only human life, but the Holy Spirit gives new life from heaven. 7So don't be surprised at my statement that you* must be born again. 8Just as you can hear the wind but can't tell where it comes from or where it is going, so you can't explain how people are born of the Spirit."

9"What do you mean?" Nicodemus asked.

10Jesus replied, "You are a respected Jewish teacher, and yet you don't understand these things? 11I assure you, I am telling you what we know and have seen, and yet you won't believe us. 12But if you don't even believe me when I tell you about things that happen here on earth, how can you possibly believe if I tell you what is going on in heaven? 13For only I, the Son of Man,* have come to earth and will return to heaven again. 14And as Moses lifted up the bronze snake on a pole in the wilderness, so I, the Son of Man, must be lifted up on a pole,* 15so that everyone who believes in me will have eternal life.

16"For God so loved the world that he gave his only Son, so that everyone who believes in him will not perish but have eternal life. 17God did not send his Son into the world to condemn it, but to save it.

18"There is no judgment awaiting those who trust him. But those who do not trust him have already been judged for not believing in the only Son of God. 19Their judgment is based on this fact: The light from heaven came into the world, but they loved the darkness more than the light, for their actions were evil. 20They hate the light because they want to sin in the darkness. They stay away from the light for fear their sins will be exposed and they will be punished. 21But those who do what is right come to the light gladly, so everyone can see that they are doing what God wants."

John the Baptist Exalts Jesus

22Afterward Jesus and his disciples left Jerusalem, but they stayed in Judea for a while and baptized there.

23At this time John the Baptist was baptizing at Aenon, near Salim, because there was plenty of water there and people kept coming to him for baptism. 24This was before John was put into prison. 25At that time a certain Jew began an argument with John's disciples over ceremonial cleansing. 26John's disciples came to him and said, "Teacher, the man you met on the other side of the Jordan River, the one you said was the Messiah, is also baptizing people. And everybody is going over there instead of coming here to us."

27John replied, "God in heaven appoints each person's work. 28You yourselves know how plainly I told you that I am not the Messiah. I am here to prepare the way for him—that is all. 29The bride will go where the bridegroom is. A bridegroom's friend rejoices with him. I am the bridegroom's friend, and I am filled with joy at his success. 30He must become greater and greater, and I must become less and less.

3:5 Or *spirit.* The Greek word for *Spirit* can also be translated *wind;* see 3:8.   3:7 The Greek word for *you* is plural; also in 3:12.   3:13 Some manuscripts add *who lives in heaven.*   3:14 Greek *must be lifted up.*

31 "He has come from above and is greater than anyone else. I am of the earth, and my understanding is limited to the things of earth, but he has come from heaven.* 32 He tells what he has seen and heard, but how few believe what he tells them! 33 Those who believe him discover that God is true. 34 For he is sent by God. He speaks God's words, for God's Spirit is upon him without measure or limit. 35 The Father loves his Son, and he has given him authority over everything. 36 And all who believe in God's Son have eternal life. Those who don't obey the Son will never experience eternal life, but the wrath of God remains upon them."

CHAPTER 4
Jesus and the Samaritan Woman

Jesus* learned that the Pharisees had heard, "Jesus is baptizing and making more disciples than John" 2 (though Jesus himself didn't baptize them—his disciples did). 3 So he left Judea to return to Galilee.

4 He had to go through Samaria on the way. 5 Eventually he came to the Samaritan village of Sychar, near the parcel of ground that Jacob gave to his son Joseph. 6 Jacob's well was there; and Jesus, tired from the long walk, sat wearily beside the well about noon-time. 7 Soon a Samaritan woman came to draw water, and Jesus said to her, "Please give me a drink." 8 He was alone at the time because his disciples had gone into the village to buy some food.

9 The woman was surprised, for Jews refuse to have anything to do with Samaritans. She said to Jesus, "You are a Jew, and I am a Samaritan woman. Why are you asking me for a drink?"

10 Jesus replied, "If you only knew the gift God has for you and who I am, you would ask me, and I would give you living water."

11 "But sir, you don't have a rope or a bucket," she said, "and this is a very deep well. Where would you get this living water? 12 And besides, are you greater than our ancestor Jacob who gave us this well? How can you offer better water than he and his sons and his cattle enjoyed?"

13 Jesus replied, "People soon become thirsty again after drinking this water. 14 But the water I give them takes away thirst altogether. It becomes a perpetual spring within them, giving them eternal life."

15 "Please, sir," the woman said, "give me some of that water! Then I'll never be thirsty again, and I won't have to come here to haul water."

16 "Go and get your husband," Jesus told her.

17 "I don't have a husband," the woman replied.

Jesus said, "You're right! You don't have a husband—18 for you have had five husbands, and you aren't even married to the man you're living with now."

19 "Sir," the woman said, "you must be a prophet. 20 So tell me, why is it that you Jews insist that Jerusalem is the only place of worship, while we Samaritans claim it is here at Mount Gerizim,* where our ancestors worshiped?"

21 Jesus replied, "Believe me, the time is coming when it will no longer matter whether you worship the Father here or in Jerusalem.

3:31 Some manuscripts omit *but he has come from heaven.* 4:1 Some manuscripts read *The Lord.* 4:20 Greek *on this mountain.*

22You Samaritans know so little about the one you worship, while we Jews know all about him, for salvation comes through the Jews. 23But the time is coming and is already here when true worshipers will worship the Father in spirit and in truth. The Father is looking for anyone who will worship him that way. 24For God is Spirit, so those who worship him must worship in spirit and in truth."

25The woman said, "I know the Messiah will come—the one who is called Christ. When he comes, he will explain everything to us."

26Then Jesus told her, "I am the Messiah!"*

27Just then his disciples arrived. They were astonished to find him talking to a woman, but none of them asked him why he was doing it or what they had been discussing. 28The woman left her water jar beside the well and went back to the village and told everyone, 29"Come and meet a man who told me everything I ever did! Can this be the Messiah?" 30So the people came streaming from the village to see him.

31Meanwhile, the disciples were urging Jesus to eat. 32"No," he said, "I have food you don't know about."

33"Who brought it to him?" the disciples asked each other.

34Then Jesus explained: "My nourishment comes from doing the will of God, who sent me, and from finishing his work. 35Do you think the work of harvesting will not begin until the summer ends four months from now? Look around you! Vast fields are ripening all around us and are ready now for the harvest. 36The harvesters are paid good wages, and the fruit they harvest is people brought to eternal life. What joy awaits both the planter and the harvester alike! 37You know the saying, 'One person plants and someone else harvests.' And it's true. 38I sent you to harvest where you didn't plant; others had already done the work, and you will gather the harvest."

Many Samaritans Believe

39Many Samaritans from the village believed in Jesus because the woman had said, "He told me everything I ever did!" 40When they came out to see him, they begged him to stay at their village. So he stayed for two days, 41long enough for many of them to hear his message and believe. 42Then they said to the woman, "Now we believe because we have heard him ourselves, not just because of what you told us. He is indeed the Savior of the world."

Jesus Heals an Official's Son

43At the end of the two days' stay, Jesus went on into Galilee. 44He had previously said, "A prophet is honored everywhere except in his own country." 45The Galileans welcomed him, for they had been in Jerusalem at the Passover celebration and had seen all his miraculous signs.

46In the course of his journey through Galilee, he arrived at the town of Cana, where he had turned the water into wine. There was a government official in the city of Capernaum whose son was very sick. 47When he heard that Jesus had come from Judea and was traveling in Galilee, he went over to Cana. He found Jesus and

4:26 Greek *"I am, the one speaking to you."*

begged him to come to Capernaum with him to heal his son, who was about to die.

⁴⁸Jesus asked, "Must I do miraculous signs and wonders before you people will believe in me?"

⁴⁹The official pleaded, "Lord, please come now before my little boy dies."

⁵⁰Then Jesus told him, "Go back home. Your son will live!" And the man believed Jesus' word and started home.

⁵¹While he was on his way, some of his servants met him with the news that his son was alive and well. ⁵²He asked them when the boy had begun to feel better, and they replied, "Yesterday afternoon at one o'clock his fever suddenly disappeared!" ⁵³Then the father realized it was the same time that Jesus had told him, "Your son will live." And the officer and his entire household believed in Jesus. ⁵⁴This was Jesus' second miraculous sign in Galilee after coming from Judea.

CHAPTER 5

Jesus Heals a Lame Man

Afterward Jesus returned to Jerusalem for one of the Jewish holy days. ²Inside the city, near the Sheep Gate, was the pool of Bethesda,* with five covered porches. ³Crowds of sick people—blind, lame, or paralyzed—lay on the porches.* ⁵One of the men lying there had been sick for thirty-eight years. ⁶When Jesus saw him and knew how long he had been ill, he asked him, "Would you like to get well?"

⁷"I can't, sir," the sick man said, "for I have no one to help me into the pool when the water is stirred up. While I am trying to get there, someone else always gets in ahead of me."

⁸Jesus told him, "Stand up, pick up your sleeping mat, and walk!"

⁹Instantly, the man was healed! He rolled up the mat and began walking! But this miracle happened on the Sabbath day. ¹⁰So the Jewish leaders objected. They said to the man who was cured, "You can't work on the Sabbath! It's illegal to carry that sleeping mat!"

¹¹He replied, "The man who healed me said to me, 'Pick up your sleeping mat and walk.'"

¹²"Who said such a thing as that?" they demanded.

¹³The man didn't know, for Jesus had disappeared into the crowd. ¹⁴But afterward Jesus found him in the Temple and told him, "Now you are well; so stop sinning, or something even worse may happen to you." ¹⁵Then the man went to find the Jewish leaders and told them it was Jesus who had healed him.

Jesus Claims to Be the Son of God

¹⁶So the Jewish leaders began harassing Jesus for breaking the Sabbath rules. ¹⁷But Jesus replied, "My Father never stops working, so why should I?" ¹⁸So the Jewish leaders tried all the more to kill him. In addition to disobeying the Sabbath rules, he had spoken of God as his Father, thereby making himself equal with God.

¹⁹Jesus replied, "I assure you, the Son can do nothing by him-

5:2 Some manuscripts read *Beth-zatha*; other manuscripts read *Bethsaida*. 5:3 Some manuscripts add *waiting for a certain movement of the water,* ⁴*for an angel of the Lord came from time to time and stirred up the water. And the first person to step down into it afterward was healed.*

self. He does only what he sees the Father doing. Whatever the Father does, the Son also does. ²⁰For the Father loves the Son and tells him everything he is doing, and the Son will do far greater things than healing this man. You will be astonished at what he does. ²¹He will even raise from the dead anyone he wants to, just as the Father does. ²²And the Father leaves all judgment to his Son, ²³so that everyone will honor the Son, just as they honor the Father. But if you refuse to honor the Son, then you are certainly not honoring the Father who sent him.

²⁴"I assure you, those who listen to my message and believe in God who sent me have eternal life. They will never be condemned for their sins, but they have already passed from death into life.

²⁵"And I assure you that the time is coming, in fact it is here, when the dead will hear my voice—the voice of the Son of God. And those who listen will live. ²⁶The Father has life in himself, and he has granted his Son to have life in himself. ²⁷And he has given him authority to judge all mankind because he is the Son of Man. ²⁸Don't be so surprised! Indeed, the time is coming when all the dead in their graves will hear the voice of God's Son, ²⁹and they will rise again. Those who have done good will rise to eternal life, and those who have continued in evil will rise to judgment. ³⁰But I do nothing without consulting the Father. I judge as I am told. And my judgment is absolutely just, because it is according to the will of God who sent me; it is not merely my own.

Witnesses to Jesus

³¹"If I were to testify on my own behalf, my testimony would not be valid. ³²But someone else is also testifying about me, and I can assure you that everything he says about me is true. ³³In fact, you sent messengers to listen to John the Baptist, and he preached the truth. ³⁴But the best testimony about me is not from a man, though I have reminded you about John's testimony so you might be saved. ³⁵John shone brightly for a while, and you benefited and rejoiced. ³⁶But I have a greater witness than John—my teachings and my miracles. They have been assigned to me by the Father, and they testify that the Father has sent me. ³⁷And the Father himself has also testified about me. You have never heard his voice or seen him face to face, ³⁸and you do not have his message in your hearts, because you do not believe me—the one he sent to you.

³⁹"You search the Scriptures because you believe they give you eternal life. But the Scriptures point to me! ⁴⁰Yet you refuse to come to me so that I can give you this eternal life.

⁴¹"Your approval or disapproval means nothing to me, ⁴²because I know you don't have God's love within you. ⁴³For I have come to you representing my Father, and you refuse to welcome me, even though you readily accept others who represent only themselves. ⁴⁴No wonder you can't believe! For you gladly honor each other, but you don't care about the honor that comes from God alone.

⁴⁵"Yet it is not I who will accuse you of this before the Father. Moses will accuse you! Yes, Moses, on whom you set your hopes. ⁴⁶But if you had believed Moses, you would have believed me because he wrote about me. ⁴⁷And since you don't believe what he wrote, how will you believe what I say?"

CHAPTER 6
Jesus Feeds Five Thousand

After this, Jesus crossed over the Sea of Galilee, also known as the Sea of Tiberias. ²And a huge crowd kept following him wherever he went, because they saw his miracles as he healed the sick. ³Then Jesus went up into the hills and sat down with his disciples around him. ⁴(It was nearly time for the annual Passover celebration.) ⁵Jesus soon saw a great crowd of people climbing the hill, looking for him. Turning to Philip, he asked, "Philip, where can we buy bread to feed all these people?" ⁶He was testing Philip, for he already knew what he was going to do.

⁷Philip replied, "It would take a small fortune* to feed them!"

⁸Then Andrew, Simon Peter's brother, spoke up. ⁹"There's a young boy here with five barley loaves and two fish. But what good is that with this huge crowd?"

¹⁰"Tell everyone to sit down," Jesus ordered. So all of them—the men alone numbered five thousand—sat down on the grassy slopes. ¹¹Then Jesus took the loaves, gave thanks to God, and passed them out to the people. Afterward he did the same with the fish. And they all ate until they were full. ¹²"Now gather the leftovers," Jesus told his disciples, "so that nothing is wasted." ¹³There were only five barley loaves to start with, but twelve baskets were filled with the pieces of bread the people did not eat!

¹⁴When the people saw this miraculous sign, they exclaimed, "Surely, he is the Prophet* we have been expecting!" ¹⁵Jesus saw that they were ready to take him by force and make him king, so he went higher into the hills alone.

Jesus Walks on Water

¹⁶That evening his disciples went down to the shore to wait for him. ¹⁷But as darkness fell and Jesus still hadn't come back, they got into the boat and headed out across the lake toward Capernaum. ¹⁸Soon a gale swept down upon them as they rowed, and the sea grew very rough. ¹⁹They were three or four miles* out when suddenly they saw Jesus walking on the water toward the boat. They were terrified, ²⁰but he called out to them, "I am here! Don't be afraid." ²¹Then they were eager to let him in, and immediately the boat arrived at their destination!

Jesus, the Bread of Life

²²The next morning, back across the lake, crowds began gathering on the shore, waiting to see Jesus. For they knew that he and his disciples had come over together and that the disciples had gone off in their boat, leaving him behind. ²³Several boats from Tiberias landed near the place where the Lord had blessed the bread and the people had eaten. ²⁴When the crowd saw that Jesus wasn't there, nor his disciples, they got into the boats and went across to Capernaum to look for him. ²⁵When they arrived and found him, they asked, "Teacher, how did you get here?"

²⁶Jesus replied, "The truth is, you want to be with me because I fed you, not because you saw the miraculous sign. ²⁷But you shouldn't be so concerned about perishable things like food.

6:7 Greek *200 denarii.* A denarius was the equivalent of a full day's wage.   6:14 See Deut 18:15, 18.   6:19 Greek *25 or 30 stadia* [4.6 or 5.5 kilometers].

Spend your energy seeking the eternal life that I, the Son of Man, can give you. For God the Father has sent me for that very purpose."

²⁸They replied, "What does God want us to do?"

²⁹Jesus told them, "This is what God wants you to do: Believe in the one he has sent."

³⁰They replied, "You must show us a miraculous sign if you want us to believe in you. What will you do for us? ³¹After all, our ancestors ate manna while they journeyed through the wilderness! As the Scriptures say, 'Moses gave them bread from heaven to eat.'*"

³²Jesus said, "I assure you, Moses didn't give them bread from heaven. My Father did. And now he offers you the true bread from heaven. ³³The true bread of God is the one who comes down from heaven and gives life to the world."

³⁴"Sir," they said, "give us that bread every day of our lives."

³⁵Jesus replied, "I am the bread of life. No one who comes to me will ever be hungry again. Those who believe in me will never thirst. ³⁶But you haven't believed in me even though you have seen me. ³⁷However, those the Father has given me will come to me, and I will never reject them. ³⁸For I have come down from heaven to do the will of God who sent me, not to do what I want. ³⁹And this is the will of God, that I should not lose even one of all those he has given me, but that I should raise them to eternal life at the last day. ⁴⁰For it is my Father's will that all who see his Son and believe in him should have eternal life—that I should raise them at the last day."

⁴¹Then the people* began to murmur in disagreement because he had said, "I am the bread from heaven." ⁴²They said, "This is Jesus, the son of Joseph. We know his father and mother. How can he say, 'I came down from heaven'?"

⁴³But Jesus replied, "Don't complain about what I said. ⁴⁴For people can't come to me unless the Father who sent me draws them to me, and at the last day I will raise them from the dead. ⁴⁵As it is written in the Scriptures, 'They will all be taught by God.'* Everyone who hears and learns from the Father comes to me. ⁴⁶(Not that anyone has ever seen the Father; only I, who was sent from God, have seen him.)

⁴⁷"I assure you, anyone who believes in me already has eternal life. ⁴⁸Yes, I am the bread of life! ⁴⁹Your ancestors ate manna in the wilderness, but they all died. ⁵⁰However, the bread from heaven gives eternal life to everyone who eats it. ⁵¹I am the living bread that came down out of heaven. Anyone who eats this bread will live forever; this bread is my flesh, offered so the world may live."

⁵²Then the people began arguing with each other about what he meant. "How can this man give us his flesh to eat?" they asked.

⁵³So Jesus said again, "I assure you, unless you eat the flesh of the Son of Man and drink his blood, you cannot have eternal life within you. ⁵⁴But those who eat my flesh and drink my blood have eternal life, and I will raise them at the last day. ⁵⁵For my flesh is the true food, and my blood is the true drink. ⁵⁶All who eat my flesh and drink my blood remain in me, and I in them. ⁵⁷I live by the power of the living Father who sent me; in the same way, those who partake of me will live because of me. ⁵⁸I am the true bread

6:31 Exod 16:4; Ps 78:24.   **6:41** Greek *Jewish people;* also in 6:52.   **6:45** Isa 54:13.

from heaven. Anyone who eats this bread will live forever and not die as your ancestors did, even though they ate the manna."

⁵⁹He said these things while he was teaching in the synagogue in Capernaum.

Many Disciples Desert Jesus

⁶⁰Even his disciples said, "This is very hard to understand. How can anyone accept it?"

⁶¹Jesus knew within himself that his disciples were complaining, so he said to them, "Does this offend you? ⁶²Then what will you think if you see me, the Son of Man, return to heaven again? ⁶³It is the Spirit who gives eternal life. Human effort accomplishes nothing. And the very words I have spoken to you are spirit and life. ⁶⁴But some of you don't believe me." (For Jesus knew from the beginning who didn't believe, and he knew who would betray him.) ⁶⁵Then he said, "That is what I meant when I said that people can't come to me unless the Father brings them to me."

⁶⁶At this point many of his disciples turned away and deserted him. ⁶⁷Then Jesus turned to the Twelve and asked, "Are you going to leave, too?"

⁶⁸Simon Peter replied, "Lord, to whom would we go? You alone have the words that give eternal life. ⁶⁹We believe them, and we know you are the Holy One of God."

⁷⁰Then Jesus said, "I chose the twelve of you, but one is a devil." ⁷¹He was speaking of Judas, son of Simon Iscariot, one of the Twelve, who would betray him.

CHAPTER 7

Jesus and His Brothers

After this, Jesus stayed in Galilee, going from village to village. He wanted to stay out of Judea where the Jewish leaders were plotting his death. ²But soon it was time for the Festival of Shelters, ³and Jesus' brothers urged him to go to Judea for the celebration. "Go where your followers can see your miracles!" they scoffed. ⁴"You can't become a public figure if you hide this! If you can do such wonderful things, prove it to the world!" ⁵For even his brothers didn't believe in him.

⁶Jesus replied, "Now is not the right time for me to go. But you can go anytime, and it will make no difference. ⁷The world can't hate you, but it does hate me because I accuse it of sin and evil. ⁸You go on. I am not yet* ready to go to this festival, because my time has not yet come." ⁹So Jesus remained in Galilee.

Jesus Teaches Openly at the Temple

¹⁰But after his brothers had left for the festival, Jesus also went, though secretly, staying out of public view. ¹¹The Jewish leaders tried to find him at the festival and kept asking if anyone had seen him. ¹²There was a lot of discussion about him among the crowds. Some said, "He's a wonderful man," while others said, "He's nothing but a fraud, deceiving the people." ¹³But no one had the courage to speak favorably about him in public, for they were afraid of getting in trouble with the Jewish leaders.

¹⁴Then, midway through the festival, Jesus went up to the

7:8 Some manuscripts omit *yet.*

Temple and began to teach. 15The Jewish leaders were surprised when they heard him. "How does he know so much when he hasn't studied everything we've studied?" they asked.

16So Jesus told them, "I'm not teaching my own ideas, but those of God who sent me. 17Anyone who wants to do the will of God will know whether my teaching is from God or is merely my own. 18Those who present their own ideas are looking for praise for themselves, but those who seek to honor the one who sent them are good and genuine. 19None of you obeys the law of Moses! In fact, you are trying to kill me."

20The crowd replied, "You're demon possessed! Who's trying to kill you?"

21Jesus replied, "I worked on the Sabbath by healing a man, and you were offended. 22But you work on the Sabbath, too, when you obey Moses' law of circumcision. (Actually, this tradition of circumcision is older than the law of Moses; it goes back to Abraham.) 23For if the correct time for circumcising your son falls on the Sabbath, you go ahead and do it, so as not to break the law of Moses. So why should I be condemned for making a man completely well on the Sabbath? 24Think this through and you will see that I am right."

Is Jesus the Messiah?

25Some of the people who lived there in Jerusalem said among themselves, "Isn't this the man they are trying to kill? 26But here he is, speaking in public, and they say nothing to him. Can it be that our leaders know that he really is the Messiah? 27But how could he be? For we know where this man comes from. When the Messiah comes, he will simply appear; no one will know where he comes from."

28While Jesus was teaching in the Temple, he called out, "Yes, you know me, and you know where I come from. But I represent one you don't know, and he is true. 29I know him because I have come from him, and he sent me to you." 30Then the leaders tried to arrest him; but no one laid a hand on him, because his time had not yet come.

31Many among the crowds at the Temple believed in him. "After all," they said, "would you expect the Messiah to do more miraculous signs than this man has done?"

32When the Pharisees heard that the crowds were murmuring such things, they and the leading priests sent Temple guards to arrest Jesus. 33But Jesus told them, "I will be here a little longer. Then I will return to the one who sent me. 34You will search for me but not find me. And you won't be able to come where I am."

35The Jewish leaders were puzzled by this statement. "Where is he planning to go?" they asked. "Maybe he is thinking of leaving the country and going to the Jews in other lands, or maybe even to the Gentiles! 36What does he mean when he says, 'You will search for me but not find me,' and 'You won't be able to come where I am'?"

Jesus Promises Living Water

37On the last day, the climax of the festival, Jesus stood and shouted to the crowds, "If you are thirsty, come to me! 38If you believe in me, come and drink! For the Scriptures declare that rivers of living water will flow out from within."* 39(When he said

7:37-38 Or *"Let anyone who is thirsty come to me and drink.* 38*For the Scriptures declare that rivers of living water will flow from the heart of those who believe in me."*

"living water," he was speaking of the Spirit, who would be given to everyone believing in him. But the Spirit had not yet been given, because Jesus had not yet entered into his glory.)

Division and Unbelief

⁴⁰When the crowds heard him say this, some of them declared, "This man surely is the Prophet."* ⁴¹Others said, "He is the Messiah." Still others said, "But he can't be! Will the Messiah come from Galilee? ⁴²For the Scriptures clearly state that the Messiah will be born of the royal line of David, in Bethlehem, the village where King David was born."* ⁴³So the crowd was divided in their opinion about him. ⁴⁴And some wanted him arrested, but no one touched him.

⁴⁵The Temple guards who had been sent to arrest him returned to the leading priests and Pharisees. "Why didn't you bring him in?" they demanded.

⁴⁶"We have never heard anyone talk like this!" the guards responded.

⁴⁷"Have you been led astray, too?" the Pharisees mocked. ⁴⁸"Is there a single one of us rulers or Pharisees who believes in him? ⁴⁹These ignorant crowds do, but what do they know about it? A curse on them anyway!"

⁵⁰Nicodemus, the leader who had met with Jesus earlier, then spoke up. ⁵¹"Is it legal to convict a man before he is given a hearing?" he asked.

⁵²They replied, "Are you from Galilee, too? Search the Scriptures and see for yourself—no prophet ever comes from Galilee!"

[*The most ancient Greek manuscripts do not include John 7:53–8:11.*]

⁵³Then the meeting broke up and everybody went home.

CHAPTER 8

A Woman Caught in Adultery

Jesus returned to the Mount of Olives, ²but early the next morning he was back again at the Temple. A crowd soon gathered, and he sat down and taught them. ³As he was speaking, the teachers of religious law and Pharisees brought a woman they had caught in the act of adultery. They put her in front of the crowd.

⁴"Teacher," they said to Jesus, "this woman was caught in the very act of adultery. ⁵The law of Moses says to stone her. What do you say?"

⁶They were trying to trap him into saying something they could use against him, but Jesus stooped down and wrote in the dust with his finger. ⁷They kept demanding an answer, so he stood up again and said, "All right, stone her. But let those who have never sinned throw the first stones!" ⁸Then he stooped down again and wrote in the dust.

⁹When the accusers heard this, they slipped away one by one, beginning with the oldest, until only Jesus was left in the middle of the crowd with the woman. ¹⁰Then Jesus stood up again and said to her, "Where are your accusers? Didn't even one of them condemn you?"

7:40 See Deut 18:15, 18.   7:42 See Mic 5:2.

11"No, Lord," she said.

And Jesus said, "Neither do I. Go and sin no more."

Jesus, the Light of the World

12Jesus said to the people, "I am the light of the world. If you follow me, you won't be stumbling through the darkness, because you will have the light that leads to life."

13The Pharisees replied, "You are making false claims about yourself!"

14Jesus told them, "These claims are valid even though I make them about myself. For I know where I came from and where I am going, but you don't know this about me. 15You judge me with all your human limitations,* but I am not judging anyone. 16And if I did, my judgment would be correct in every respect because I am not alone—I have with me the Father who sent me. 17Your own law says that if two people agree about something, their witness is accepted as fact.* 18I am one witness, and my Father who sent me is the other."

19"Where is your father?" they asked.

Jesus answered, "Since you don't know who I am, you don't know who my Father is. If you knew me, then you would know my Father, too." 20Jesus made these statements while he was teaching in the section of the Temple known as the Treasury. But he was not arrested, because his time had not yet come.

The Unbelieving People Warned

21Later Jesus said to them again, "I am going away. You will search for me and die in your sin. You cannot come where I am going."

22The Jewish leaders asked, "Is he planning to commit suicide? What does he mean, 'You cannot come where I am going'?"

23Then he said to them, "You are from below; I am from above. You are of this world; I am not. 24That is why I said that you will die in your sins; for unless you believe that I am who I say I am, you will die in your sins."

25"Tell us who you are," they demanded.

Jesus replied, "I am the one I have always claimed to be.* 26I have much to say about you and much to condemn, but I won't. For I say only what I have heard from the one who sent me, and he is true." 27But they still didn't understand that he was talking to them about his Father.

28So Jesus said, "When you have lifted up the Son of Man on the cross, then you will realize that I am he and that I do nothing on my own, but I speak what the Father taught me. 29And the one who sent me is with me—he has not deserted me. For I always do those things that are pleasing to him." 30Then many who heard him say these things believed in him.

Jesus and Abraham

31Jesus said to the people* who believed in him, "You are truly my disciples if you keep obeying my teachings. 32And you will know the truth, and the truth will set you free."

33"But we are descendants of Abraham," they said. "We have

8:15 Or *judge me by human standards.* 8:17 See Deut 19:15. 8:25 Or *"Why do I speak to you at all?"* 8:31 Greek *Jewish people;* also in 8:48, 52, 57.

never been slaves to anyone on earth. What do you mean, 'set free'?"

³⁴Jesus replied, "I assure you that everyone who sins is a slave of sin. ³⁵A slave is not a permanent member of the family, but a son is part of the family forever. ³⁶So if the Son sets you free, you will indeed be free. ³⁷Yes, I realize that you are descendants of Abraham. And yet some of you are trying to kill me because my message does not find a place in your hearts. ³⁸I am telling you what I saw when I was with my Father. But you are following the advice of your father."

³⁹"Our father is Abraham," they declared.

"No," Jesus replied, "for if you were children of Abraham, you would follow his good example.* ⁴⁰I told you the truth I heard from God, but you are trying to kill me. Abraham wouldn't do a thing like that. ⁴¹No, you are obeying your real father when you act that way."

They replied, "We were not born out of wedlock! Our true Father is God himself."

⁴²Jesus told them, "If God were your Father, you would love me, because I have come to you from God. I am not here on my own, but he sent me. ⁴³Why can't you understand what I am saying? It is because you are unable to do so! ⁴⁴For you are the children of your father the Devil, and you love to do the evil things he does. He was a murderer from the beginning and has always hated the truth. There is no truth in him. When he lies, it is consistent with his character; for he is a liar and the father of lies. ⁴⁵So when I tell the truth, you just naturally don't believe me! ⁴⁶Which of you can truthfully accuse me of sin? And since I am telling you the truth, why don't you believe me? ⁴⁷Anyone whose Father is God listens gladly to the words of God. Since you don't, it proves you aren't God's children."

⁴⁸The people retorted, "You Samaritan devil! Didn't we say all along that you were possessed by a demon?"

⁴⁹"No," Jesus said, "I have no demon in me. For I honor my Father—and you dishonor me. ⁵⁰And though I have no wish to glorify myself, God wants to glorify me. Let him be the judge. ⁵¹I assure you, anyone who obeys my teaching will never die!"

⁵²The people said, "Now we know you are possessed by a demon. Even Abraham and the prophets died, but you say that those who obey your teaching will never die! ⁵³Are you greater than our father Abraham, who died? Are you greater than the prophets, who died? Who do you think you are?"

⁵⁴Jesus answered, "If I am merely boasting about myself, it doesn't count. But it is my Father who says these glorious things about me. You say, 'He is our God,' ⁵⁵but you do not even know him. I know him. If I said otherwise, I would be as great a liar as you! But it is true—I know him and obey him. ⁵⁶Your ancestor Abraham rejoiced as he looked forward to my coming. He saw it and was glad."

⁵⁷The people said, "You aren't even fifty years old. How can you say you have seen Abraham?*"

8:39 Some manuscripts read *if you are children of Abraham, follow his example.*
8:57 Some manuscripts read *How can you say Abraham has seen you?*

⁵⁸Jesus answered, "The truth is, I existed before Abraham was even born!"* ⁵⁹At that point they picked up stones to kill him. But Jesus hid himself from them and left the Temple.

CHAPTER 9

Jesus Heals a Man Born Blind

As Jesus was walking along, he saw a man who had been blind from birth. ²"Teacher," his disciples asked him, "why was this man born blind? Was it a result of his own sins or his parents'?"

³"It was not because of his sins or his parents' sins," Jesus answered. "He was born blind so the power of God could be seen in him. ⁴All of us must quickly carry out the tasks assigned us by the one who sent me, because there is little time left before the night falls and all work comes to an end. ⁵But while I am still here in the world, I am the light of the world."

⁶Then he spit on the ground, made mud with the saliva, and smoothed the mud over the blind man's eyes. ⁷He told him, "Go and wash in the pool of Siloam" (Siloam means Sent). So the man went and washed, and came back seeing!

⁸His neighbors and others who knew him as a blind beggar asked each other, "Is this the same man—that beggar?" ⁹Some said he was, and others said, "No, but he surely looks like him!"

And the beggar kept saying, "I am the same man!"

¹⁰They asked, "Who healed you? What happened?"

¹¹He told them, "The man they call Jesus made mud and smoothed it over my eyes and told me, 'Go to the pool of Siloam and wash off the mud.' I went and washed, and now I can see!"

¹²"Where is he now?" they asked.

"I don't know," he replied.

¹³Then they took the man to the Pharisees. ¹⁴Now as it happened, Jesus had healed the man on a Sabbath. ¹⁵The Pharisees asked the man all about it. So he told them, "He smoothed the mud over my eyes, and when it was washed away, I could see!"

¹⁶Some of the Pharisees said, "This man Jesus is not from God, for he is working on the Sabbath." Others said, "But how could an ordinary sinner do such miraculous signs?" So there was a deep division of opinion among them.

¹⁷Then the Pharisees once again questioned the man who had been blind and demanded, "This man who opened your eyes— who do you say he is?"

The man replied, "I think he must be a prophet."

¹⁸The Jewish leaders wouldn't believe he had been blind, so they called in his parents. ¹⁹They asked them, "Is this your son? Was he born blind? If so, how can he see?"

²⁰His parents replied, "We know this is our son and that he was born blind, ²¹but we don't know how he can see or who healed him. He is old enough to speak for himself. Ask him." ²²They said this because they were afraid of the Jewish leaders, who had announced that anyone saying Jesus was the Messiah would be expelled from the synagogue. ²³That's why they said, "He is old enough to speak for himself. Ask him."

²⁴So for the second time they called in the man who had been

8:58 Or *"Truly, truly, before Abraham was, I am."*

blind and told him, "Give glory to God by telling the truth,* because we know Jesus is a sinner."

²⁵"I don't know whether he is a sinner," the man replied. "But I know this: I was blind, and now I can see!"

²⁶"But what did he do?" they asked. "How did he heal you?"

²⁷"Look!" the man exclaimed. "I told you once. Didn't you listen? Why do you want to hear it again? Do you want to become his disciples, too?"

²⁸Then they cursed him and said, "You are his disciple, but we are disciples of Moses. ²⁹We know God spoke to Moses, but as for this man, we don't know anything about him."

³⁰"Why, that's very strange!" the man replied. "He healed my eyes, and yet you don't know anything about him! ³¹Well, God doesn't listen to sinners, but he is ready to hear those who worship him and do his will. ³²Never since the world began has anyone been able to open the eyes of someone born blind. ³³If this man were not from God, he couldn't do it."

³⁴"You were born in sin!" they answered. "Are you trying to teach us?" And they threw him out of the synagogue.

Spiritual Blindness

³⁵When Jesus heard what had happened, he found the man and said, "Do you believe in the Son of Man*?"

³⁶The man answered, "Who is he, sir, because I would like to."

³⁷"You have seen him," Jesus said, "and he is speaking to you!"

³⁸"Yes, Lord," the man said, "I believe!" And he worshiped Jesus.

³⁹Then Jesus told him, "I have come to judge the world. I have come to give sight to the blind and to show those who think they see that they are blind."

⁴⁰The Pharisees who were standing there heard him and asked, "Are you saying we are blind?"

⁴¹"If you were blind, you wouldn't be guilty," Jesus replied. "But you remain guilty because you claim you can see.

CHAPTER 10

The Good Shepherd and His Sheep

"I assure you, anyone who sneaks over the wall of a sheepfold, rather than going through the gate, must surely be a thief and a robber! ²For a shepherd enters through the gate. ³The gatekeeper opens the gate for him, and the sheep hear his voice and come to him. He calls his own sheep by name and leads them out. ⁴After he has gathered his own flock, he walks ahead of them, and they follow him because they recognize his voice. ⁵They won't follow a stranger; they will run from him because they don't recognize his voice."

⁶Those who heard Jesus use this illustration didn't understand what he meant, ⁷so he explained it to them. "I assure you, I am the gate for the sheep," he said. ⁸"All others who came before me were thieves and robbers. But the true sheep did not listen to them. ⁹Yes, I am the gate. Those who come in through me will be saved. Wherever they go, they will find green pastures. ¹⁰The thief's

9:24 Or *Give glory to God, not to Jesus;* Greek reads *Give glory to God.*   9:35 Some manuscripts read *the Son of God.*

purpose is to steal and kill and destroy. My purpose is to give life in all its fullness.

¹¹"I am the good shepherd. The good shepherd lays down his life for the sheep. ¹²A hired hand will run when he sees a wolf coming. He will leave the sheep because they aren't his and he isn't their shepherd. And so the wolf attacks them and scatters the flock. ¹³The hired hand runs away because he is merely hired and has no real concern for the sheep.

¹⁴"I am the good shepherd; I know my own sheep, and they know me, ¹⁵just as my Father knows me and I know the Father. And I lay down my life for the sheep. ¹⁶I have other sheep, too, that are not in this sheepfold. I must bring them also, and they will listen to my voice; and there will be one flock with one shepherd.

¹⁷"The Father loves me because I lay down my life that I may have it back again. ¹⁸No one can take my life from me. I lay down my life voluntarily. For I have the right to lay it down when I want to and also the power to take it again. For my Father has given me this command."

¹⁹When he said these things, the people* were again divided in their opinions about him. ²⁰Some of them said, "He has a demon, or he's crazy. Why listen to a man like that?" ²¹Others said, "This doesn't sound like a man possessed by a demon! Can a demon open the eyes of the blind?"

Jesus Claims to Be the Son of God

²²It was now winter, and Jesus was in Jerusalem at the time of Hanukkah.* ²³He was at the Temple, walking through the section known as Solomon's Colonnade. ²⁴The Jewish leaders surrounded him and asked, "How long are you going to keep us in suspense? If you are the Messiah, tell us plainly."

²⁵Jesus replied, "I have already told you, and you don't believe me. The proof is what I do in the name of my Father. ²⁶But you don't believe me because you are not part of my flock. ²⁷My sheep recognize my voice; I know them, and they follow me. ²⁸I give them eternal life, and they will never perish. No one will snatch them away from me, ²⁹for my Father has given them to me, and he is more powerful than anyone else. So no one can take them from me. ³⁰The Father and I are one."

³¹Once again the Jewish leaders picked up stones to kill him. ³²Jesus said, "At my Father's direction I have done many things to help the people. For which one of these good deeds are you killing me?"

³³They replied, "Not for any good work, but for blasphemy, because you, a mere man, have made yourself God."

³⁴Jesus replied, "It is written in your own law that God said to certain leaders of the people, 'I say, you are gods!'* ³⁵And you know that the Scriptures cannot be altered. So if those people, who received God's message, were called 'gods,' ³⁶why do you call it blasphemy when the Holy One who was sent into the world by the Father says, 'I am the Son of God'? ³⁷Don't believe me unless I carry out my Father's work. ³⁸But if I do his work, believe in what I have done, even if you don't believe me. Then you will realize that the Father is in me, and I am in the Father."

10:19 Greek *Jewish people.*   **10:22** Or *the Festival of Dedication.*   **10:34** Ps 82:6.

³⁹Once again they tried to arrest him, but he got away and left them. ⁴⁰He went beyond the Jordan River to stay near the place where John was first baptizing. ⁴¹And many followed him. "John didn't do miracles," they remarked to one another, "but all his predictions about this man have come true." ⁴²And many believed in him there.

CHAPTER 11

The Death of Lazarus

A man named Lazarus was sick. He lived in Bethany with his sisters, Mary and Martha. ²This is the Mary who poured the expensive perfume on the Lord's feet and wiped them with her hair.* Her brother, Lazarus, was sick. ³So the two sisters sent a message to Jesus telling him, "Lord, the one you love is very sick."

⁴But when Jesus heard about it he said, "Lazarus's sickness will not end in death. No, it is for the glory of God. I, the Son of God, will receive glory from this." ⁵Although Jesus loved Martha, Mary, and Lazarus, ⁶he stayed where he was for the next two days and did not go to them. ⁷Finally after two days, he said to his disciples, "Let's go to Judea again."

⁸But his disciples objected. "Teacher," they said, "only a few days ago the Jewish leaders in Judea were trying to kill you. Are you going there again?"

⁹Jesus replied, "There are twelve hours of daylight every day. As long as it is light, people can walk safely. They can see because they have the light of this world. ¹⁰Only at night is there danger of stumbling because there is no light." ¹¹Then he said, "Our friend Lazarus has fallen asleep, but now I will go and wake him up."

¹²The disciples said, "Lord, if he is sleeping, that means he is getting better!" ¹³They thought Jesus meant Lazarus was having a good night's rest, but Jesus meant Lazarus had died.

¹⁴Then he told them plainly, "Lazarus is dead. ¹⁵And for your sake, I am glad I wasn't there, because this will give you another opportunity to believe in me. Come, let's go see him."

¹⁶Thomas, nicknamed the Twin,* said to his fellow disciples, "Let's go, too—and die with Jesus."

¹⁷When Jesus arrived at Bethany, he was told that Lazarus had already been in his grave for four days. ¹⁸Bethany was only a few miles* down the road from Jerusalem, ¹⁹and many of the people* had come to pay their respects and console Martha and Mary on their loss. ²⁰When Martha got word that Jesus was coming, she went to meet him. But Mary stayed at home. ²¹Martha said to Jesus, "Lord, if you had been here, my brother would not have died. ²²But even now I know that God will give you whatever you ask."

²³Jesus told her, "Your brother will rise again."

²⁴"Yes," Martha said, "when everyone else rises, on resurrection day."

²⁵Jesus told her, "I am the resurrection and the life.* Those who believe in me, even though they die like everyone else, will live again. ²⁶They are given eternal life for believing in me and will never perish. Do you believe this, Martha?"

11:2 This incident is recorded in chapter 12.　11:16 Greek *the one who was called Didymus.*
11:18 Greek *was about 15 stadia* [about 2.8 kilometers].　11:19 Greek *Jewish people; also*
11:31, 33, 36, 45, 54.　11:25 Some manuscripts do not include *and the life.*

27"Yes, Lord," she told him. "I have always believed you are the Messiah, the Son of God, the one who has come into the world from God." 28Then she left him and returned to Mary. She called Mary aside from the mourners and told her, "The Teacher is here and wants to see you." 29So Mary immediately went to him.

30Now Mary had stayed outside the village, at the place where Martha met him. 31When the people who were at the house trying to console Mary saw her leave so hastily, they assumed she was going to Lazarus's grave to weep. So they followed her there. 32When Mary arrived and saw Jesus, she fell down at his feet and said, "Lord, if you had been here, my brother would not have died."

33When Jesus saw her weeping and saw the other people wailing with her, he was moved with indignation and was deeply troubled. 34"Where have you put him?" he asked them.

They told him, "Lord, come and see." 35Then Jesus wept. 36The people who were standing nearby said, "See how much he loved him." 37But some said, "This man healed a blind man. Why couldn't he keep Lazarus from dying?"

Jesus Raises Lazarus from the Dead

38And again Jesus was deeply troubled. Then they came to the grave. It was a cave with a stone rolled across its entrance. 39"Roll the stone aside," Jesus told them.

But Martha, the dead man's sister, said, "Lord, by now the smell will be terrible because he has been dead for four days."

40Jesus responded, "Didn't I tell you that you will see God's glory if you believe?" 41So they rolled the stone aside. Then Jesus looked up to heaven and said, "Father, thank you for hearing me. 42You always hear me, but I said it out loud for the sake of all these people standing here, so they will believe you sent me." 43Then Jesus shouted, "Lazarus, come out!" 44And Lazarus came out, bound in graveclothes, his face wrapped in a headcloth. Jesus told them, "Unwrap him and let him go!"

The Plot to Kill Jesus

45Many of the people who were with Mary believed in Jesus when they saw this happen. 46But some went to the Pharisees and told them what Jesus had done. 47Then the leading priests and Pharisees called the high council* together to discuss the situation. "What are we going to do?" they asked each other. "This man certainly performs many miraculous signs. 48If we leave him alone, the whole nation will follow him, and then the Roman army will come and destroy both our Temple and our nation."

49And one of them, Caiaphas, who was high priest that year, said, "How can you be so stupid? 50Why should the whole nation be destroyed? Let this one man die for the people."

51This prophecy that Jesus should die for the entire nation came from Caiaphas in his position as high priest. He didn't think of it himself; he was inspired to say it. 52It was a prediction that Jesus' death would be not for Israel only, but for the gathering together of all the children of God scattered around the world.

53So from that time on the Jewish leaders began to plot Jesus' death. 54As a result, Jesus stopped his public ministry among the

11:47 Greek *the Sanhedrin.*

people and left Jerusalem. He went to a place near the wilderness, to the village of Ephraim, and stayed there with his disciples.

⁵⁵It was now almost time for the celebration of Passover, and many people from the country arrived in Jerusalem several days early so they could go through the cleansing ceremony before the Passover began. ⁵⁶They wanted to see Jesus, and as they talked in the Temple, they asked each other, "What do you think? Will he come for the Passover?" ⁵⁷Meanwhile, the leading priests and Pharisees had publicly announced that anyone seeing Jesus must report him immediately so they could arrest him.

CHAPTER 12

Jesus Anointed at Bethany

Six days before the Passover ceremonies began, Jesus arrived in Bethany, the home of Lazarus—the man he had raised from the dead. ²A dinner was prepared in Jesus' honor. Martha served, and Lazarus sat at the table with him. ³Then Mary took a twelve-ounce jar* of expensive perfume made from essence of nard, and she anointed Jesus' feet with it and wiped his feet with her hair. And the house was filled with fragrance.

⁴But Judas Iscariot, one of his disciples—the one who would betray him—said, ⁵"That perfume was worth a small fortune.* It should have been sold and the money given to the poor." ⁶Not that he cared for the poor—he was a thief who was in charge of the disciples' funds, and he often took some for his own use.

⁷Jesus replied, "Leave her alone. She did it in preparation for my burial. ⁸You will always have the poor among you, but I will not be here with you much longer."

⁹When all the people* heard of Jesus' arrival, they flocked to see him and also to see Lazarus, the man Jesus had raised from the dead. ¹⁰Then the leading priests decided to kill Lazarus, too, ¹¹for it was because of him that many of the people had deserted them and believed in Jesus.

The Triumphal Entry

¹²The next day, the news that Jesus was on the way to Jerusalem swept through the city. A huge crowd of Passover visitors ¹³took palm branches and went down the road to meet him. They shouted,

"Praise God!*
Bless the one who comes in the name of the Lord!
Hail to the King of Israel!"*

¹⁴Jesus found a young donkey and sat on it, fulfilling the prophecy that said:

¹⁵ "Don't be afraid, people of Israel.*
Look, your King is coming,
    sitting on a donkey's colt."*

¹⁶His disciples didn't realize at the time that this was a fulfillment of prophecy. But after Jesus entered into his glory, they remembered that these Scriptures had come true before their eyes.

12:3 Greek *took 1 litra* [327 grams].   12:5 Greek *300 denarii.* A denarius was equivalent to a full day's wage.   12:9 Greek *Jewish people;* also in 12:11.   12:13a Greek *Hosanna,* an exclamation of praise that literally means "save now."   12:13b Ps 118:25-26; Zeph 3:15.   12:15a Greek *daughter of Zion.*   12:15b Zech 9:9.

17Those in the crowd who had seen Jesus call Lazarus back to life were telling others all about it. 18That was the main reason so many went out to meet him—because they had heard about this mighty miracle. 19Then the Pharisees said to each other, "We've lost. Look, the whole world has gone after him!"

Jesus Predicts His Death

20Some Greeks who had come to Jerusalem to attend the Passover 21paid a visit to Philip, who was from Bethsaida in Galilee. They said, "Sir, we want to meet Jesus." 22Philip told Andrew about it, and they went together to ask Jesus.

23Jesus replied, "The time has come for the Son of Man to enter into his glory. 24The truth is, a kernel of wheat must be planted in the soil. Unless it dies it will be alone—a single seed. But its death will produce many new kernels—a plentiful harvest of new lives. 25Those who love their life in this world will lose it. Those who despise their life in this world will keep it for eternal life. 26All those who want to be my disciples must come and follow me, because my servants must be where I am. And if they follow me, the Father will honor them. 27Now my soul is deeply troubled. Should I pray, 'Father, save me from what lies ahead'? But that is the very reason why I came! 28Father, bring glory to your name."

Then a voice spoke from heaven, saying, "I have already brought it glory, and I will do it again." 29When the crowd heard the voice, some thought it was thunder, while others declared an angel had spoken to him.

30Then Jesus told them, "The voice was for your benefit, not mine. 31The time of judgment for the world has come, when the prince of this world* will be cast out. 32And when I am lifted up on the cross,* I will draw everyone to myself." 33He said this to indicate how he was going to die.

34"Die?" asked the crowd. "We understood from Scripture that the Messiah would live forever. Why are you saying the Son of Man will die? Who is this Son of Man you are talking about?"

35Jesus replied, "My light will shine out for you just a little while longer. Walk in it while you can, so you will not stumble when the darkness falls. If you walk in the darkness, you cannot see where you are going. 36Believe in the light while there is still time; then you will become children of the light." After saying these things, Jesus went away and was hidden from them.

The Unbelief of the People

37But despite all the miraculous signs he had done, most of the people did not believe in him. 38This is exactly what Isaiah the prophet had predicted:

"Lord, who has believed our message?
     To whom will the Lord reveal his saving power?"*

39But the people couldn't believe, for as Isaiah also said,

40 "The Lord has blinded their eyes
     and hardened their hearts—

12:31 *The prince of this world* is a name for Satan.   **12:32** *Greek lifted up from the earth.*
12:38 Isa 53:1.

so their eyes cannot see,
and their hearts cannot understand,
and they cannot turn to me
and let me heal them."*

⁴¹Isaiah was referring to Jesus when he made this prediction, because he was given a vision of the Messiah's glory. ⁴²Many people, including some of the Jewish leaders, believed in him. But they wouldn't admit it to anyone because of their fear that the Pharisees would expel them from the synagogue. ⁴³For they loved human praise more than the praise of God.

⁴⁴Jesus shouted to the crowds, "If you trust me, you are really trusting God who sent me. ⁴⁵For when you see me, you are seeing the one who sent me. ⁴⁶I have come as a light to shine in this dark world, so that all who put their trust in me will no longer remain in the darkness. ⁴⁷If anyone hears me and doesn't obey me, I am not his judge—for I have come to save the world and not to judge it. ⁴⁸But all who reject me and my message will be judged at the day of judgment by the truth I have spoken. ⁴⁹I don't speak on my own authority. The Father who sent me gave me his own instructions as to what I should say. ⁵⁰And I know his instructions lead to eternal life; so I say whatever the Father tells me to say!"

CHAPTER 13

Jesus Washes His Disciples' Feet

Before the Passover celebration, Jesus knew that his hour had come to leave this world and return to his Father. He now showed the disciples the full extent of his love.* ²It was time for supper, and the Devil had already enticed Judas, son of Simon Iscariot, to carry out his plan to betray Jesus. ³Jesus knew that the Father had given him authority over everything and that he had come from God and would return to God. ⁴So he got up from the table, took off his robe, wrapped a towel around his waist, ⁵and poured water into a basin. Then he began to wash the disciples' feet and to wipe them with the towel he had around him.

⁶When he came to Simon Peter, Peter said to him, "Lord, why are you going to wash my feet?"

⁷Jesus replied, "You don't understand now why I am doing it; someday you will."

⁸"No," Peter protested, "you will never wash my feet!"

Jesus replied, "But if I don't wash you, you won't belong to me."

⁹Simon Peter exclaimed, "Then wash my hands and head as well, Lord, not just my feet!"

¹⁰Jesus replied, "A person who has bathed all over does not need to wash, except for the feet,* to be entirely clean. And you are clean, but that isn't true of everyone here." ¹¹For Jesus knew who would betray him. That is what he meant when he said, "Not all of you are clean."

¹²After washing their feet, he put on his robe again and sat down and asked, "Do you understand what I was doing? ¹³You call me 'Teacher' and 'Lord,' and you are right, because it is true. ¹⁴And since I, the Lord and Teacher, have washed your feet, you ought to

12:40 Isa 6:10.   13:1 Or *He loved his disciples to the very end.*   13:10 Some manuscripts do not include *except for the feet.*

wash each other's feet. [15]I have given you an example to follow. Do as I have done to you. [16]How true it is that a servant is not greater than the master. Nor are messengers more important than the one who sends them. [17]You know these things—now do them! That is the path of blessing.

Jesus Predicts His Betrayal

[18]"I am not saying these things to all of you; I know so well each one of you I chose. The Scriptures declare, 'The one who shares my food has turned against me,'* and this will soon come true. [19]I tell you this now, so that when it happens you will believe I am the Messiah. [20]Truly, anyone who welcomes my messenger is welcoming me, and anyone who welcomes me is welcoming the Father who sent me."

[21]Now Jesus was in great anguish of spirit, and he exclaimed, "The truth is, one of you will betray me!"

[22]The disciples looked at each other, wondering whom he could mean. [23]One of Jesus' disciples, the one Jesus loved, was sitting next to Jesus at the table.* [24]Simon Peter motioned to him to ask who would do this terrible thing. [25]Leaning toward Jesus, he asked, "Lord, who is it?"

[26]Jesus said, "It is the one to whom I give the bread dipped in the sauce." And when he had dipped it, he gave it to Judas, son of Simon Iscariot. [27]As soon as Judas had eaten the bread, Satan entered into him. Then Jesus told him, "Hurry. Do it now." [28]None of the others at the table knew what Jesus meant. [29]Since Judas was their treasurer, some thought Jesus was telling him to go and pay for the food or to give some money to the poor. [30]So Judas left at once, going out into the night.

Jesus Predicts Peter's Denial

[31]As soon as Judas left the room, Jesus said, "The time has come for me, the Son of Man, to enter into my glory, and God will receive glory because of all that happens to me. [32]And God will bring* me into my glory very soon. [33]Dear children, how brief are these moments before I must go away and leave you! Then, though you search for me, you cannot come to me—just as I told the Jewish leaders. [34]So now I am giving you a new commandment: Love each other. Just as I have loved you, you should love each other. [35]Your love for one another will prove to the world that you are my disciples."

[36]Simon Peter said, "Lord, where are you going?"

And Jesus replied, "You can't go with me now, but you will follow me later."

[37]"But why can't I come now, Lord?" he asked. "I am ready to die for you."

[38]Jesus answered, "Die for me? No, before the rooster crows tomorrow morning, you will deny three times that you even know me.

CHAPTER 14

Jesus, the Way to the Father

"Don't be troubled. You trust God, now trust in me. [2]There are many rooms in my Father's home, and I am going to prepare a

---

13:18 Ps 41:9. 13:23 Greek *was reclining on Jesus' bosom.* The "disciple whom Jesus loved" was probably John. 13:32 Some manuscripts read *And if God is glorified in him [the Son of Man], God will bring.*

place for you. If this were not so, I would tell you plainly. ³When everything is ready, I will come and get you, so that you will always be with me where I am. ⁴And you know where I am going and how to get there."

⁵"No, we don't know, Lord," Thomas said. "We haven't any idea where you are going, so how can we know the way?"

⁶Jesus told him, "I am the way, the truth, and the life. No one can come to the Father except through me. ⁷If you had known who I am, then you would have known who my Father is.* From now on you know him and have seen him!"

⁸Philip said, "Lord, show us the Father and we will be satisfied."

⁹Jesus replied, "Philip, don't you even yet know who I am, even after all the time I have been with you? Anyone who has seen me has seen the Father! So why are you asking to see him? ¹⁰Don't you believe that I am in the Father and the Father is in me? The words I say are not my own, but my Father who lives in me does his work through me. ¹¹Just believe that I am in the Father and the Father is in me. Or at least believe because of what you have seen me do.

¹²"The truth is, anyone who believes in me will do the same works I have done, and even greater works, because I am going to be with the Father. ¹³You can ask for anything in my name, and I will do it, because the work of the Son brings glory to the Father. ¹⁴Yes, ask anything in my name, and I will do it!

Jesus Promises the Holy Spirit

¹⁵"If you love me, obey my commandments. ¹⁶And I will ask the Father, and he will give you another Counselor,* who will never leave you. ¹⁷He is the Holy Spirit, who leads into all truth. The world at large cannot receive him, because it isn't looking for him and doesn't recognize him. But you do, because he lives with you now and later will be in you. ¹⁸No, I will not abandon you as orphans—I will come to you. ¹⁹In just a little while the world will not see me again, but you will. For I will live again, and you will, too. ²⁰When I am raised to life again, you will know that I am in my Father, and you are in me, and I am in you. ²¹Those who obey my commandments are the ones who love me. And because they love me, my Father will love them, and I will love them. And I will reveal myself to each one of them."

²²Judas (not Judas Iscariot, but the other disciple with that name) said to him, "Lord, why are you going to reveal yourself only to us and not to the world at large?"

²³Jesus replied, "All those who love me will do what I say. My Father will love them, and we will come to them and live with them. ²⁴Anyone who doesn't love me will not do what I say. And remember, my words are not my own. This message is from the Father who sent me. ²⁵I am telling you these things now while I am still with you. ²⁶But when the Father sends the Counselor as my representative—and by the Counselor I mean the Holy Spirit—he will teach you everything and will remind you of everything I myself have told you.

²⁷"I am leaving you with a gift—peace of mind and heart. And

14:7 Some manuscripts read *If you really have known me, you will know who my Father is.*
14:16 Or *Comforter*, or *Encourager*, or *Advocate*. Greek *Paraclete*; also in 14:26.

the peace I give isn't like the peace the world gives. So don't be troubled or afraid. 28Remember what I told you: I am going away, but I will come back to you again. If you really love me, you will be very happy for me, because now I can go to the Father, who is greater than I am. 29I have told you these things before they happen so that you will believe when they do happen.

30"I don't have much more time to talk to you, because the prince of this world approaches. He has no power over me, 31but I will do what the Father requires of me, so that the world will know that I love the Father. Come, let's be going.

CHAPTER 15
Jesus, the True Vine

"I am the true vine, and my Father is the gardener. 2He cuts off every branch that doesn't produce fruit, and he prunes the branches that do bear fruit so they will produce even more. 3You have already been pruned for greater fruitfulness by the message I have given you. 4Remain in me, and I will remain in you. For a branch cannot produce fruit if it is severed from the vine, and you cannot be fruitful apart from me.

5"Yes, I am the vine; you are the branches. Those who remain in me, and I in them, will produce much fruit. For apart from me you can do nothing. 6Anyone who parts from me is thrown away like a useless branch and withers. Such branches are gathered into a pile to be burned. 7But if you stay joined to me and my words remain in you, you may ask any request you like, and it will be granted! 8My true disciples produce much fruit. This brings great glory to my Father.

9"I have loved you even as the Father has loved me. Remain in my love. 10When you obey me, you remain in my love, just as I obey my Father and remain in his love. 11I have told you this so that you will be filled with my joy. Yes, your joy will overflow! 12I command you to love each other in the same way that I love you. 13And here is how to measure it—the greatest love is shown when people lay down their lives for their friends. 14You are my friends if you obey me. 15I no longer call you servants, because a master doesn't confide in his servants. Now you are my friends, since I have told you everything the Father told me. 16You didn't choose me. I chose you. I appointed you to go and produce fruit that will last, so that the Father will give you whatever you ask for, using my name. 17I command you to love each other.

The World's Hatred

18"When the world hates you, remember it hated me before it hated you. 19The world would love you if you belonged to it, but you don't. I chose you to come out of the world, and so it hates you. 20Do you remember what I told you? 'A servant is not greater than the master.' Since they persecuted me, naturally they will persecute you. And if they had listened to me, they would listen to you! 21The people of the world will hate you because you belong to me, for they don't know God who sent me. 22They would not be guilty if I had not come and spoken to them. But now they have no excuse for their sin. 23Anyone who hates me hates my Father, too. 24If I hadn't done such miraculous signs among them that no one else could do, they would not be counted guilty. But as it is, they saw all that I did and yet hated both of us—me and my Father. 25This has fulfilled what the Scriptures said: 'They hated me without cause.'*

26"But I will send you the Counselor*—the Spirit of truth. He will come to you from the Father and will tell you all about me. 27And you must also tell others about me because you have been with me from the beginning.

CHAPTER 16

"I have told you these things so that you won't fall away. 2For you will be expelled from the synagogues, and the time is coming when those who kill you will think they are doing God a service. 3This is because they have never known the Father or me. 4Yes, I'm telling you these things now, so that when they happen, you will remember I warned you. I didn't tell you earlier because I was going to be with you for a while longer.

The Work of the Holy Spirit

5"But now I am going away to the one who sent me, and none of you has asked me where I am going. 6Instead, you are very sad. 7But it is actually best for you that I go away, because if I don't, the Counselor* won't come. If I do go away, he will come because I will send him to you. 8And when he comes, he will convince the world of its sin, and of God's righteousness, and of the coming judgment. 9The world's sin is unbelief in me. 10Righteousness is available because I go to the Father, and you will see me no more. 11Judgment will come because the prince of this world has already been judged.

12"Oh, there is so much more I want to tell you, but you can't bear it now. 13When the Spirit of truth comes, he will guide you into all truth. He will not be presenting his own ideas; he will be telling you what he has heard. He will tell you about the future. 14He will bring me glory by revealing to you whatever he receives from me. 15All that the Father has is mine; this is what I mean when I say that the Spirit will reveal to you whatever he receives from me.

Sadness Will Be Turned to Joy

16"In just a little while I will be gone, and you won't see me anymore. Then, just a little while after that, you will see me again."

17The disciples asked each other, "What does he mean when he says, 'You won't see me, and then you will see me'? And what does he mean when he says, 'I am going to the Father'? 18And what does he mean by 'a little while'? We don't understand."

19Jesus realized they wanted to ask him, so he said, "Are you asking yourselves what I meant? I said in just a little while I will be gone, and you won't see me anymore. Then, just a little while after that, you will see me again. 20Truly, you will weep and mourn over what is going to happen to me, but the world will rejoice. You will grieve, but your grief will suddenly turn to wonderful joy when you see me again. 21It will be like a woman experiencing the pains of labor. When her child is born, her anguish gives place to joy because she has brought a new person into the world. 22You have sorrow now, but I will see you again; then you will rejoice, and no

15:25 Pss 35:19; 69:4.   15:26 Or *Comforter*, or *Encourager*, or *Advocate*. Greek *Paraclete*.
16:7 Or *Comforter*, or *Encourager*, or *Advocate*. Greek *Paraclete*.

one can rob you of that joy. 23At that time you won't need to ask me for anything. The truth is, you can go directly to the Father and ask him, and he will grant your request because you use my name. 24You haven't done this before. Ask, using my name, and you will receive, and you will have abundant joy.

25"I have spoken of these matters in parables, but the time will come when this will not be necessary, and I will tell you plainly all about the Father. 26Then you will ask in my name. I'm not saying I will ask the Father on your behalf, 27for the Father himself loves you dearly because you love me and believe that I came from God. 28Yes, I came from the Father into the world, and I will leave the world and return to the Father."

29Then his disciples said, "At last you are speaking plainly and not in parables. 30Now we understand that you know everything and don't need anyone to tell you anything.* From this we believe that you came from God."

31Jesus asked, "Do you finally believe? 32But the time is coming—in fact, it is already here—when you will be scattered, each one going his own way, leaving me alone. Yet I am not alone because the Father is with me. 33I have told you all this so that you may have peace in me. Here on earth you will have many trials and sorrows. But take heart, because I have overcome the world."

CHAPTER 17

The Prayer of Jesus

When Jesus had finished saying all these things, he looked up to heaven and said, "Father, the time has come. Glorify your Son so he can give glory back to you. 2For you have given him authority over everyone in all the earth. He gives eternal life to each one you have given him. 3And this is the way to have eternal life—to know you, the only true God, and Jesus Christ, the one you sent to earth. 4I brought glory to you here on earth by doing everything you told me to do. 5And now, Father, bring me into the glory we shared before the world began.

6"I have told these men about you. They were in the world, but then you gave them to me. Actually, they were always yours, and you gave them to me; and they have kept your word. 7Now they know that everything I have is a gift from you, 8for I have passed on to them the words you gave me; and they accepted them and know that I came from you, and they believe you sent me.

9"My prayer is not for the world, but for those you have given me, because they belong to you. 10And all of them, since they are mine, belong to you; and you have given them back to me, so they are my glory! 11Now I am departing the world; I am leaving them behind and coming to you. Holy Father, keep them and care for them—all those you have given me—so that they will be united just as we are. 12During my time here, I have kept them safe.* I guarded them so that not one was lost, except the one headed for destruction, as the Scriptures foretold.

13"And now I am coming to you. I have told them many things while I was with them so they would be filled with my joy. 14I have given them your word. And the world hates them because they do

16:30 Or *don't need that anyone should ask you anything.* 17:12 Greek *I have kept in your name those whom you have given me.*

not belong to the world, just as I do not. [15]I'm not asking you to take them out of the world, but to keep them safe from the evil one. [16]They are not part of this world any more than I am. [17]Make them pure and holy by teaching them your words of truth. [18]As you sent me into the world, I am sending them into the world. [19]And I give myself entirely to you so they also might be entirely yours.

[20]"I am praying not only for these disciples but also for all who will ever believe in me because of their testimony. [21]My prayer for all of them is that they will be one, just as you and I are one, Father—that just as you are in me and I am in you, so they will be in us, and the world will believe you sent me.

[22]"I have given them the glory you gave me, so that they may be one, as we are—[23]I in them and you in me, all being perfected into one. Then the world will know that you sent me and will understand that you love them as much as you love me. [24]Father, I want these whom you've given me to be with me, so they can see my glory. You gave me the glory because you loved me even before the world began!

[25]"O righteous Father, the world doesn't know you, but I do; and these disciples know you sent me. [26]And I have revealed you to them and will keep on revealing you. I will do this so that your love for me may be in them and I in them."

CHAPTER 18
Jesus Is Betrayed and Arrested

After saying these things, Jesus crossed the Kidron Valley with his disciples and entered a grove of olive trees. [2]Judas, the betrayer, knew this place, because Jesus had gone there many times with his disciples. [3]The leading priests and Pharisees had given Judas a battalion of Roman soldiers and Temple guards to accompany him. Now with blazing torches, lanterns, and weapons, they arrived at the olive grove.

[4]Jesus fully realized all that was going to happen to him. Stepping forward to meet them, he asked, "Whom are you looking for?"

[5]"Jesus of Nazareth," they replied.

"I am he,"* Jesus said. Judas was standing there with them when Jesus identified himself. [6]And as he said, "I am he," they all fell backward to the ground! [7]Once more he asked them, "Whom are you searching for?"

And again they replied, "Jesus of Nazareth."

[8]"I told you that I am he," Jesus said. "And since I am the one you want, let these others go." [9]He did this to fulfill his own statement: "I have not lost a single one of those you gave me."*

[10]Then Simon Peter drew a sword and slashed off the right ear of Malchus, the high priest's servant. [11]But Jesus said to Peter, "Put your sword back into its sheath. Shall I not drink from the cup the Father has given me?"

Annas Questions Jesus

[12]So the soldiers, their commanding officer, and the Temple guards arrested Jesus and tied him up. [13]First they took him to Annas, the father-in-law of Caiaphas, the high priest that year. [14]Caiaphas was the one who had told the other Jewish leaders, "Better that one should die for all."

18:5 Greek *I am;* also in 18:6, 8.   18:9 See John 6:39 and 17:12.

Peter's First Denial

15Simon Peter followed along behind, as did another of the disciples. That other disciple was acquainted with the high priest, so he was allowed to enter the courtyard with Jesus. 16Peter stood outside the gate. Then the other disciple spoke to the woman watching at the gate, and she let Peter in. 17The woman asked Peter, "Aren't you one of Jesus' disciples?"

"No," he said, "I am not."

18The guards and the household servants were standing around a charcoal fire they had made because it was cold. And Peter stood there with them, warming himself.

The High Priest Questions Jesus

19Inside, the high priest began asking Jesus about his followers and what he had been teaching them. 20Jesus replied, "What I teach is widely known, because I have preached regularly in the synagogues and the Temple. I have been heard by people* everywhere, and I teach nothing in private that I have not said in public. 21Why are you asking me this question? Ask those who heard me. They know what I said."

22One of the Temple guards standing there struck Jesus on the face. "Is that the way to answer the high priest?" he demanded.

23Jesus replied, "If I said anything wrong, you must give evidence for it. Should you hit a man for telling the truth?"

24Then Annas bound Jesus and sent him to Caiaphas, the high priest.

Peter's Second and Third Denials

25Meanwhile, as Simon Peter was standing by the fire, they asked him again, "Aren't you one of his disciples?"

"I am not," he said.

26But one of the household servants of the high priest, a relative of the man whose ear Peter had cut off, asked, "Didn't I see you out there in the olive grove with Jesus?" 27Again Peter denied it. And immediately a rooster crowed.

Jesus' Trial before Pilate

28Jesus' trial before Caiaphas ended in the early hours of the morning. Then he was taken to the headquarters of the Roman governor. His accusers didn't go in themselves because it would defile them, and they wouldn't be allowed to celebrate the Passover feast. 29So Pilate, the governor, went out to them and asked, "What is your charge against this man?"

30"We wouldn't have handed him over to you if he weren't a criminal!" they retorted.

31"Then take him away and judge him by your own laws," Pilate told them.

"Only the Romans are permitted to execute someone," the Jewish leaders replied. 32This fulfilled Jesus' prediction about the way he would die.*

33Then Pilate went back inside and called for Jesus to be brought to him. "Are you the King of the Jews?" he asked him.

18:20 Greek *Jewish people;* also in 18:38.   **18:32** See John 12:32-33.

34Jesus replied, "Is this your own question, or did others tell you about me?"

35"Am I a Jew?" Pilate asked. "Your own people and their leading priests brought you here. Why? What have you done?"

36Then Jesus answered, "I am not an earthly king. If I were, my followers would have fought when I was arrested by the Jewish leaders. But my Kingdom is not of this world."

37Pilate replied, "You are a king then?"

"You say that I am a king, and you are right," Jesus said. "I was born for that purpose. And I came to bring truth to the world. All who love the truth recognize that what I say is true."

38"What is truth?" Pilate asked. Then he went out again to the people and told them, "He is not guilty of any crime. 39But you have a custom of asking me to release someone from prison each year at Passover. So if you want me to, I'll release the King of the Jews."

40But they shouted back, "No! Not this man, but Barabbas!" (Barabbas was a criminal.)

CHAPTER 19

Jesus Sentenced to Death

Then Pilate had Jesus flogged with a lead-tipped whip. 2The soldiers made a crown of long, sharp thorns and put it on his head, and they put a royal purple robe on him. 3"Hail! King of the Jews!" they mocked, and they hit him with their fists.

4Pilate went outside again and said to the people, "I am going to bring him out to you now, but understand clearly that I find him not guilty." 5Then Jesus came out wearing the crown of thorns and the purple robe. And Pilate said, "Here is the man!"

6When they saw him, the leading priests and Temple guards began shouting, "Crucify! Crucify!"

"You crucify him," Pilate said. "I find him not guilty."

7The Jewish leaders replied, "By our laws he ought to die because he called himself the Son of God."

8When Pilate heard this, he was more frightened than ever. 9He took Jesus back into the headquarters again and asked him, "Where are you from?" But Jesus gave no answer. 10"You won't talk to me?" Pilate demanded. "Don't you realize that I have the power to release you or to crucify you?"

11Then Jesus said, "You would have no power over me at all unless it were given to you from above. So the one who brought me to you has the greater sin."

12Then Pilate tried to release him, but the Jewish leaders told him, "If you release this man, you are not a friend of Caesar. Anyone who declares himself a king is a rebel against Caesar."

13When they said this, Pilate brought Jesus out to them again. Then Pilate sat down on the judgment seat on the platform that is called the Stone Pavement (in Hebrew, *Gabbatha*). 14It was now about noon of the day of preparation for the Passover. And Pilate said to the people,* "Here is your king!"

15"Away with him," they yelled. "Away with him—crucify him!"

"What? Crucify your king?" Pilate asked.

"We have no king but Caesar," the leading priests shouted back.

19:14 Greek *Jewish people;* also in 19:20.

16Then Pilate gave Jesus to them to be crucified.

The Crucifixion

So they took Jesus and led him away. 17Carrying the cross by himself, Jesus went to the place called Skull Hill (in Hebrew, *Golgotha*). 18There they crucified him. There were two others crucified with him, one on either side, with Jesus between them. 19And Pilate posted a sign over him that read, "Jesus of Nazareth, the King of the Jews." 20The place where Jesus was crucified was near the city; and the sign was written in Hebrew, Latin, and Greek, so that many people could read it.

21Then the leading priests said to Pilate, "Change it from 'The King of the Jews' to 'He said, I am King of the Jews.'"

22Pilate replied, "What I have written, I have written. It stays exactly as it is."

23When the soldiers had crucified Jesus, they divided his clothes among the four of them. They also took his robe, but it was seamless, woven in one piece from the top. 24So they said, "Let's not tear it but throw dice* to see who gets it." This fulfilled the Scripture that says, "They divided my clothes among themselves and threw dice for my robe."* So that is what they did.

25 Standing near the cross were Jesus' mother, and his mother's sister, Mary (the wife of Clopas), and Mary Magdalene 26When Jesus saw his mother standing there beside the disciple he loved, he said to her, "Woman, he is your son." 27And he said to this disciple, "She is your mother." And from then on this disciple took her into his home.

The Death of Jesus

28Jesus knew that everything was now finished, and to fulfill the Scriptures he said, "I am thirsty."* 29A jar of sour wine was sitting there, so they soaked a sponge in it, put it on a hyssop branch, and held it up to his lips. 30When Jesus had tasted it, he said, "It is finished!" Then he bowed his head and gave up his spirit.

31The Jewish leaders didn't want the victims hanging there the next day, which was the Sabbath (and a very special Sabbath at that, because it was the Passover), so they asked Pilate to hasten their deaths by ordering that their legs be broken. Then their bodies could be taken down. 32So the soldiers came and broke the legs of the two men crucified with Jesus. 33But when they came to Jesus, they saw that he was dead already, so they didn't break his legs. 34One of the soldiers, however, pierced his side with a spear, and blood and water flowed out. 35This report is from an eyewitness giving an accurate account; it is presented so that you also can believe. 36These things happened in fulfillment of the Scriptures that say, "Not one of his bones will be broken,"* 37and "They will look on him whom they pierced."*

The Burial of Jesus

38Afterward Joseph of Arimathea, who had been a secret disciple of Jesus (because he feared the Jewish leaders), asked Pilate for permission to take Jesus' body down. When Pilate gave him permission, he came and took the body away. 39Nicodemus, the man

19:24a Greek *cast lots.*   **19:24b** Ps 22:18.   **19:28** See Pss 22:15; 69:21.   **19:36** Exod 12:46; Num 9:12; Ps 34:20.   **19:37** Zech 12:10.

who had come to Jesus at night, also came, bringing about seventy-five pounds* of embalming ointment made from myrrh and aloes. ⁴⁰Together they wrapped Jesus' body in a long linen cloth with the spices, as is the Jewish custom of burial. ⁴¹The place of crucifixion was near a garden, where there was a new tomb, never used before. ⁴²And so, because it was the day of preparation before the Passover and since the tomb was close at hand, they laid Jesus there.

CHAPTER 20

The Resurrection

Early Sunday morning,* while it was still dark, Mary Magdalene came to the tomb and found that the stone had been rolled away from the entrance. ²She ran and found Simon Peter and the other disciple, the one whom Jesus loved. She said, "They have taken the Lord's body out of the tomb, and I don't know where they have put him!"

³Peter and the other disciple ran to the tomb to see. ⁴The other disciple outran Peter and got there first. ⁵He stooped and looked in and saw the linen cloth lying there, but he didn't go in. ⁶Then Simon Peter arrived and went inside. He also noticed the linen wrappings lying there, ⁷while the cloth that had covered Jesus' head was folded up and lying to the side. ⁸Then the other disciple also went in, and he saw and believed—⁹for until then they hadn't realized that the Scriptures said he would rise from the dead. ¹⁰Then they went home.

Jesus Appears to Mary Magdalene

¹¹Mary was standing outside the tomb crying, and as she wept, she stooped and looked in. ¹²She saw two white-robed angels sitting at the head and foot of the place where the body of Jesus had been lying. ¹³"Why are you crying?" the angels asked her.

"Because they have taken away my Lord," she replied, "and I don't know where they have put him."

¹⁴She glanced over her shoulder and saw someone standing behind her. It was Jesus, but she didn't recognize him. ¹⁵"Why are you crying?" Jesus asked her. "Who are you looking for?"

She thought he was the gardener. "Sir," she said, "if you have taken him away, tell me where you have put him, and I will go and get him."

¹⁶"Mary!" Jesus said.

She turned toward him and exclaimed, "Teacher!"*

¹⁷"Don't cling to me," Jesus said, "for I haven't yet ascended to the Father. But go find my brothers and tell them that I am ascending to my Father and your Father, my God and your God."

¹⁸Mary Magdalene found the disciples and told them, "I have seen the Lord!" Then she gave them his message.

Jesus Appears to His Disciples

¹⁹That evening, on the first day of the week, the disciples were meeting behind locked doors because they were afraid of the Jewish leaders. Suddenly, Jesus was standing there among them! "Peace be with you," he said. ²⁰As he spoke, he held out his hands for them to see, and he showed them his side. They were filled with joy when they saw their Lord! ²¹He spoke to them again and said, "Peace be with you. As the Father has sent me, so I send you."

19:39 Greek *100 litras* [32.7 kilograms].   20:1 Greek *On the first day of the week.*
20:16 Greek *and said in Hebrew, "Rabboni," which means "Teacher."*

22Then he breathed on them and said to them, "Receive the Holy Spirit. 23If you forgive anyone's sins, they are forgiven. If you refuse to forgive them, they are unforgiven."

Jesus Appears to Thomas

24One of the disciples, Thomas (nicknamed the Twin*), was not with the others when Jesus came. 25They told him, "We have seen the Lord!" But he replied, "I won't believe it unless I see the nail wounds in his hands, put my fingers into them, and place my hand into the wound in his side."

26Eight days later the disciples were together again, and this time Thomas was with them. The doors were locked; but suddenly, as before, Jesus was standing among them. He said, "Peace be with you." 27Then he said to Thomas, "Put your finger here and see my hands. Put your hand into the wound in my side. Don't be faithless any longer. Believe!"

28"My Lord and my God!" Thomas exclaimed.

29Then Jesus told him, "You believe because you have seen me. Blessed are those who haven't seen me and believe anyway."

Purpose of the Book

30Jesus' disciples saw him do many other miraculous signs besides the ones recorded in this book. 31But these are written so that you may believe* that Jesus is the Messiah, the Son of God, and that by believing in him you will have life.

CHAPTER 21

Jesus Appears to Seven Disciples

Later Jesus appeared again to the disciples beside the Sea of Galilee.* This is how it happened. 2Several of the disciples were there—Simon Peter, Thomas (nicknamed the Twin*), Nathanael from Cana in Galilee, the sons of Zebedee, and two other disciples.

3Simon Peter said, "I'm going fishing."

"We'll come, too," they all said. So they went out in the boat, but they caught nothing all night.

4At dawn the disciples saw Jesus standing on the beach, but they couldn't see who he was. 5He called out, "Friends, have you caught any fish?"

"No," they replied.

6Then he said, "Throw out your net on the right-hand side of the boat, and you'll get plenty of fish!" So they did, and they couldn't draw in the net because there were so many fish in it.

7Then the disciple whom Jesus loved said to Peter, "It is the Lord!" When Simon Peter heard that it was the Lord, he put on his tunic (for he had stripped for work), jumped into the water, and swam ashore. 8The others stayed with the boat and pulled the loaded net to the shore, for they were only out about three hundred feet.* 9When they got there, they saw that a charcoal fire was burning and fish were frying over it, and there was bread.

10"Bring some of the fish you've just caught," Jesus said. 11So Simon Peter went aboard and dragged the net to the shore. There were 153 large fish, and yet the net hadn't torn.

20:24 Greek *the one who was called Didymus.*   20:31 Some manuscripts read *may continue to believe.*   21:1 Greek *Sea of Tiberias,* another name for the Sea of Galilee.   21:2 Greek *the one who was called Didymus.*   21:8 Greek *200 cubits* [90 meters].

[12]"Now come and have some breakfast!" Jesus said. And no one dared ask him if he really was the Lord because they were sure of it. [13]Then Jesus served them the bread and the fish. [14]This was the third time Jesus had appeared to his disciples since he had been raised from the dead.

Jesus Challenges Peter

[15]After breakfast Jesus said to Simon Peter, "Simon son of John, do you love me more than these?"

"Yes, Lord," Peter replied, "you know I love you."

"Then feed my lambs," Jesus told him.

[16]Jesus repeated the question: "Simon son of John, do you love me?"

"Yes, Lord," Peter said, "you know I love you."

"Then take care of my sheep," Jesus said.

[17]Once more he asked him, "Simon son of John, do you love me?"

Peter was grieved that Jesus asked the question a third time. He said, "Lord, you know everything. You know I love you."

Jesus said, "Then feed my sheep. [18]The truth is, when you were young, you were able to do as you liked and go wherever you wanted to. But when you are old, you will stretch out your hands, and others will direct you and take you where you don't want to go." [19]Jesus said this to let him know what kind of death he would die to glorify God. Then Jesus told him, "Follow me."

[20]Peter turned around and saw the disciple Jesus loved following them—the one who had leaned over to Jesus during supper and asked, "Lord, who among us will betray you?" [21]Peter asked Jesus, "What about him, Lord?"

[22]Jesus replied, "If I want him to remain alive until I return, what is that to you? You follow me." [23]So the rumor spread among the community of believers* that that disciple wouldn't die. But that isn't what Jesus said at all. He only said, "If I want him to remain alive until I return, what is that to you?"

Conclusion

[24]This is that disciple who saw these events and recorded them here. And we all know that his account of these things is accurate.

[25]And I suppose that if all the other things Jesus did were written down, the whole world could not contain the books.

21:23 Greek *the brothers.*

ACTS

CHAPTER 1

The Promise of the Holy Spirit

Dear Theophilus:

In my first book* I told you about everything Jesus began to do and teach [2]until the day he ascended to heaven after giving his chosen

1:1 The reference is to the book of Luke.

apostles further instructions from the Holy Spirit. ³During the forty days after his crucifixion, he appeared to the apostles from time to time and proved to them in many ways that he was actually alive. On these occasions he talked to them about the Kingdom of God.

⁴In one of these meetings as he was eating a meal with them, he told them, "Do not leave Jerusalem until the Father sends you what he promised. Remember, I have told you about this before. ⁵John baptized with* water, but in just a few days you will be baptized with the Holy Spirit."

The Ascension of Jesus

⁶When the apostles were with Jesus, they kept asking him, "Lord, are you going to free Israel now and restore our kingdom?"

⁷"The Father sets those dates," he replied, "and they are not for you to know. ⁸But when the Holy Spirit has come upon you, you will receive power and will tell people about me everywhere—in Jerusalem, throughout Judea, in Samaria, and to the ends of the earth."

⁹It was not long after he said this that he was taken up into the sky while they were watching, and he disappeared into a cloud. ¹⁰As they were straining their eyes to see him, two white-robed men suddenly stood there among them. ¹¹They said, "Men of Galilee, why are you standing here staring at the sky? Jesus has been taken away from you into heaven. And someday, just as you saw him go, he will return!"

Matthias Replaces Judas

¹²The apostles were at the Mount of Olives when this happened, so they walked the half mile* back to Jerusalem. ¹³Then they went to the upstairs room of the house where they were staying. Here is the list of those who were present:

Peter,
John,
James,
Andrew,
Philip,
Thomas,
Bartholomew,
Matthew,
James (son of Alphaeus),
Simon (the Zealot),
and Judas (son of James).

¹⁴They all met together continually for prayer, along with Mary the mother of Jesus, several other women, and the brothers of Jesus.

¹⁵During this time, on a day when about 120 believers* were present, Peter stood up and addressed them as follows:

¹⁶"Brothers, it was necessary for the Scriptures to be fulfilled concerning Judas, who guided the Temple police to arrest Jesus. This was predicted long ago by the Holy Spirit, speaking through King David. ¹⁷Judas was one of us, chosen to share in the ministry with us."

¹⁸(Judas bought a field with the money he received for his treachery, and falling there, he burst open, spilling out his intestines. ¹⁹The news of his death spread rapidly among all the people

1:5 Or *in;* also in 1:5b.   1:12 Greek *a Sabbath day's journey.*   1:15 Greek *brothers.*

of Jerusalem, and they gave the place the Aramaic name *Akeldama*, which means "Field of Blood.")

20Peter continued, "This was predicted in the book of Psalms, where it says, 'Let his home become desolate, with no one living in it.' And again, 'Let his position be given to someone else.'*

21"So now we must choose another man to take Judas's place. It must be someone who has been with us all the time that we were with the Lord Jesus—22from the time he was baptized by John until the day he was taken from us into heaven. Whoever is chosen will join us as a witness of Jesus' resurrection."

23So they nominated two men: Joseph called Barsabbas (also known as Justus) and Matthias. 24Then they all prayed for the right man to be chosen. "O Lord," they said, "you know every heart. Show us which of these men you have chosen 25as an apostle to replace Judas the traitor in this ministry, for he has deserted us and gone where he belongs." 26Then they cast lots, and in this way Matthias was chosen and became an apostle with the other eleven.

CHAPTER 2

The Holy Spirit Comes

On the day of Pentecost, seven weeks after Jesus' resurrection,* the believers were meeting together in one place. 2Suddenly, there was a sound from heaven like the roaring of a mighty windstorm in the skies above them, and it filled the house where they were meeting. 3Then, what looked like flames or tongues of fire appeared and settled on each of them. 4And everyone present was filled with the Holy Spirit and began speaking in other languages,* as the Holy Spirit gave them this ability.

5Godly Jews from many nations were living in Jerusalem at that time. 6When they heard this sound, they came running to see what it was all about, and they were bewildered to hear their own languages being spoken by the believers.

7They were beside themselves with wonder. "How can this be?" they exclaimed. "These people are all from Galilee, 8and yet we hear them speaking the languages of the lands where we were born! 9Here we are—Parthians, Medes, Elamites, people from Mesopotamia, Judea, Cappadocia, Pontus, the province of Asia, 10Phrygia, Pamphylia, Egypt, and the areas of Libya toward Cyrene, visitors from Rome (both Jews and converts to Judaism), 11Cretans, and Arabians. And we all hear these people speaking in our own languages about the wonderful things God has done!" 12They stood there amazed and perplexed. "What can this mean?" they asked each other. 13But others in the crowd were mocking. "They're drunk, that's all!" they said.

Peter Preaches to a Crowd

14Then Peter stepped forward with the eleven other apostles and shouted to the crowd, "Listen carefully, all of you, fellow Jews and residents of Jerusalem! Make no mistake about this. 15Some of you are saying these people are drunk. It isn't true! It's much too early for that. People don't get drunk by nine o'clock in the morning.

1:20 Pss 69:25; 109:8.   2:1 Greek *When the day of Pentecost arrived.* This annual celebration came 50 days after the Passover ceremonies. See Lev 23:16.   2:4 Or *in other tongues.*

16No, what you see this morning was predicted centuries ago by the prophet Joel:

17 'In the last days, God said,
  I will pour out my Spirit upon all people.
  Your sons and daughters will prophesy,
    your young men will see visions,
    and your old men will dream dreams.
18 In those days I will pour out my Spirit
    upon all my servants, men and women alike,
    and they will prophesy.
19 And I will cause wonders in the heavens above
    and signs on the earth below—
    blood and fire and clouds of smoke.
20 The sun will be turned into darkness,
    and the moon will turn bloodred,
    before that great and glorious day of the Lord arrives.
21 And anyone who calls on the name of the Lord
    will be saved.'*

22"People of Israel, listen! God publicly endorsed Jesus of Nazareth by doing wonderful miracles, wonders, and signs through him, as you well know. 23But you followed God's prearranged plan. With the help of lawless Gentiles, you nailed him to the cross and murdered him. 24However, God released him from the horrors of death and raised him back to life again, for death could not keep him in its grip. 25King David said this about him:

'I know the Lord is always with me.
    I will not be shaken, for he is right beside me.
26 No wonder my heart is filled with joy,
    and my mouth shouts his praises!
    My body rests in hope.
27 For you will not leave my soul among the dead*
    or allow your Holy One to rot in the grave.
28 You have shown me the way of life,
    and you will give me wonderful joy in your presence.'*

29"Dear brothers, think about this! David wasn't referring to himself when he spoke these words I have quoted, for he died and was buried, and his tomb is still here among us. 30But he was a prophet, and he knew God had promised with an oath that one of David's own descendants would sit on David's throne as the Messiah. 31David was looking into the future and predicting the Messiah's resurrection. He was saying that the Messiah would not be left among the dead and that his body would not rot in the grave.

32"This prophecy was speaking of Jesus, whom God raised from the dead, and we all are witnesses of this. 33Now he sits on the throne of highest honor in heaven, at God's right hand. And the Father, as he had promised, gave him the Holy Spirit to pour out upon us, just as you see and hear today. 34For David himself never ascended into heaven, yet he said,

2:17-21 Joel 2:28-32.   **2:27** Greek *in Hades*; also in 2:31.   **2:25-28** Ps 16:8-11.

'The LORD said to my Lord,
   Sit in honor at my right hand
35   until I humble your enemies,
      making them a footstool under your feet.'*

36 So let it be clearly known by everyone in Israel that God has made this Jesus whom you crucified to be both Lord and Messiah!"

37 Peter's words convicted them deeply, and they said to him and to the other apostles, "Brothers, what should we do?"

38 Peter replied, "Each of you must turn from your sins and turn to God, and be baptized in the name of Jesus Christ for the forgiveness of your sins. Then you will receive the gift of the Holy Spirit. 39 This promise is to you and to your children, and even to the Gentiles*—all who have been called by the Lord our God." 40 Then Peter continued preaching for a long time, strongly urging all his listeners, "Save yourselves from this generation that has gone astray!"

41 Those who believed what Peter said were baptized and added to the church—about three thousand in all. 42 They joined with the other believers and devoted themselves to the apostles' teaching and fellowship, sharing in the Lord's Supper and in prayer.

The Believers Meet Together

43 A deep sense of awe came over them all, and the apostles performed many miraculous signs and wonders. 44 And all the believers met together constantly and shared everything they had. 45 They sold their possessions and shared the proceeds with those in need. 46 They worshiped together at the Temple each day, met in homes for the Lord's Supper, and shared their meals with great joy and generosity—47 all the while praising God and enjoying the goodwill of all the people. And each day the Lord added to their group those who were being saved.

CHAPTER 3

Peter Heals a Crippled Beggar

Peter and John went to the Temple one afternoon to take part in the three o'clock prayer service. 2 As they approached the Temple, a man lame from birth was being carried in. Each day he was put beside the Temple gate, the one called the Beautiful Gate, so he could beg from the people going into the Temple. 3 When he saw Peter and John about to enter, he asked them for some money.

4 Peter and John looked at him intently, and Peter said, "Look at us!" 5 The lame man looked at them eagerly, expecting a gift. 6 But Peter said, "I don't have any money for you. But I'll give you what I have. In the name of Jesus Christ of Nazareth, get up and walk!"

7 Then Peter took the lame man by the right hand and helped him up. And as he did, the man's feet and anklebones were healed and strengthened. 8 He jumped up, stood on his feet, and began to walk! Then, walking, leaping, and praising God, he went into the Temple with them.

9 All the people saw him walking and heard him praising God. 10 When they realized he was the lame beggar they had seen so often at the Beautiful Gate, they were absolutely astounded! 11 They

2:34-35 Ps 110:1.   2:39 Greek *to those far away.*

all rushed out to Solomon's Colonnade, where he was holding tightly to Peter and John. Everyone stood there in awe of the wonderful thing that had happened.

Peter Preaches in the Temple

12Peter saw his opportunity and addressed the crowd. "People of Israel," he said, "what is so astounding about this? And why look at us as though we had made this man walk by our own power and godliness? 13For it is the God of Abraham, the God of Isaac, the God of Jacob, the God of all our ancestors who has brought glory to his servant Jesus by doing this. This is the same Jesus whom you handed over and rejected before Pilate, despite Pilate's decision to release him. 14You rejected this holy, righteous one and instead demanded the release of a murderer. 15You killed the author of life, but God raised him to life. And we are witnesses of this fact!

16"The name of Jesus has healed this man—and you know how lame he was before. Faith in Jesus' name has caused this healing before your very eyes.

17"Friends,* I realize that what you did to Jesus was done in ignorance; and the same can be said of your leaders. 18But God was fulfilling what all the prophets had declared about the Messiah beforehand—that he must suffer all these things. 19Now turn from your sins and turn to God, so you can be cleansed of your sins. 20Then wonderful times of refreshment will come from the presence of the Lord, and he will send Jesus your Messiah to you again. 21For he must remain in heaven until the time for the final restoration of all things, as God promised long ago through his prophets. 22Moses said, 'The Lord your God will raise up a Prophet like me from among your own people. Listen carefully to everything he tells you.'* 23Then Moses said, 'Anyone who will not listen to that Prophet will be cut off from God's people and utterly destroyed.'*

24"Starting with Samuel, every prophet spoke about what is happening today. 25You are the children of those prophets, and you are included in the covenant God promised to your ancestors. For God said to Abraham, 'Through your descendants all the families on earth will be blessed.'* 26When God raised up his servant, he sent him first to you people of Israel, to bless you by turning each of you back from your sinful ways."

CHAPTER 4

Peter and John before the Council

While Peter and John were speaking to the people, the leading priests, the captain of the Temple guard, and some of the Sadducees came over to them. 2They were very disturbed that Peter and John were claiming, on the authority of Jesus, that there is a resurrection of the dead. 3They arrested them and, since it was already evening, jailed them until morning. 4But many of the people who heard their message believed it, so that the number of believers totaled about five thousand men, not counting women and children.*

5The next day the council of all the rulers and elders and teachers of religious law met in Jerusalem. 6Annas the high priest was there, along with Caiaphas, John, Alexander, and other relatives of the

3:17 Greek *Brothers.*   **3:22** Deut 18:15.   **3:23** Deut 18:19; Lev 23:29.   **3:25** Gen 22:18.
4:4 Greek *5,000 adult males.*

high priest. [7]They brought in the two disciples and demanded, "By what power, or in whose name, have you done this?"

[8]Then Peter, filled with the Holy Spirit, said to them, "Leaders and elders of our nation, [9]are we being questioned because we've done a good deed for a crippled man? Do you want to know how he was healed? [10]Let me clearly state to you and to all the people of Israel that he was healed in the name and power of Jesus Christ from Nazareth, the man you crucified, but whom God raised from the dead. [11]For Jesus is the one referred to in the Scriptures, where it says,

'The stone that you builders rejected
    has now become the cornerstone.'*

[12]There is salvation in no one else! There is no other name in all of heaven for people to call on to save them."

[13]The members of the council were amazed when they saw the boldness of Peter and John, for they could see that they were ordinary men who had had no special training. They also recognized them as men who had been with Jesus. [14]But since the man who had been healed was standing right there among them, the council had nothing to say. [15]So they sent Peter and John out of the council chamber* and conferred among themselves.

[16]"What should we do with these men?" they asked each other. "We can't deny they have done a miraculous sign, and everybody in Jerusalem knows about it. [17]But perhaps we can stop them from spreading their propaganda. We'll warn them not to speak to anyone in Jesus' name again." [18]So they called the apostles back in and told them never again to speak or teach about Jesus.

[19]But Peter and John replied, "Do you think God wants us to obey you rather than him? [20]We cannot stop telling about the wonderful things we have seen and heard."

[21]The council then threatened them further, but they finally let them go because they didn't know how to punish them without starting a riot. For everyone was praising God [22]for this miraculous sign—the healing of a man who had been lame for more than forty years.

The Believers Pray for Courage

[23]As soon as they were freed, Peter and John found the other believers and told them what the leading priests and elders had said. [24]Then all the believers were united as they lifted their voices in prayer: "O Sovereign Lord, Creator of heaven and earth, the sea, and everything in them—[25]you spoke long ago by the Holy Spirit through our ancestor King David, your servant, saying,

'Why did the nations rage?
    Why did the people waste their time with futile plans?
[26] The kings of the earth prepared for battle;
        the rulers gathered together
    against the Lord
        and against his Messiah.'*

[27]"That is what has happened here in this city! For Herod Antipas, Pontius Pilate the governor, the Gentiles, and the people

4:11 Ps 118:22.   **4:15** Greek *the Sanhedrin.*   **4:25-26** Ps 2:1-2.

of Israel were all united against Jesus, your holy servant, whom you anointed. 28In fact, everything they did occurred according to your eternal will and plan. 29And now, O Lord, hear their threats, and give your servants great boldness in their preaching. 30Send your healing power; may miraculous signs and wonders be done through the name of your holy servant Jesus."

31After this prayer, the building where they were meeting shook, and they were all filled with the Holy Spirit. And they preached God's message with boldness.

The Believers Share Their Possessions

32All the believers were of one heart and mind, and they felt that what they owned was not their own; they shared everything they had. 33And the apostles gave powerful witness to the resurrection of the Lord Jesus, and God's great favor was upon them all. 34There was no poverty among them, because people who owned land or houses sold them 35and brought the money to the apostles to give to others in need.

36For instance, there was Joseph, the one the apostles nick-named Barnabas (which means "Son of Encouragement"). He was from the tribe of Levi and came from the island of Cyprus. 37He sold a field he owned and brought the money to the apostles for those in need.

CHAPTER 5

Ananias and Sapphira

There was also a man named Ananias who, with his wife, Sapphira, sold some property. 2He brought part of the money to the apostles, but he claimed it was the full amount. His wife had agreed to this deception.

3Then Peter said, "Ananias, why has Satan filled your heart? You lied to the Holy Spirit, and you kept some of the money for yourself. 4The property was yours to sell or not sell, as you wished. And after selling it, the money was yours to give away. How could you do a thing like this? You weren't lying to us but to God."

5As soon as Ananias heard these words, he fell to the floor and died. Everyone who heard about it was terrified. 6Then some young men wrapped him in a sheet and took him out and buried him.

7About three hours later his wife came in, not knowing what had happened. 8Peter asked her, "Was this the price you and your husband received for your land?"

"Yes," she replied, "that was the price."

9And Peter said, "How could the two of you even think of doing a thing like this—conspiring together to test the Spirit of the Lord? Just outside that door are the young men who buried your husband, and they will carry you out, too."

10Instantly, she fell to the floor and died. When the young men came in and saw that she was dead, they carried her out and buried her beside her husband. 11Great fear gripped the entire church and all others who heard what had happened.

The Apostles Heal Many

12Meanwhile, the apostles were performing many miraculous signs and wonders among the people. And the believers were meeting regularly at the Temple in the area known as Solomon's Colonnade. [13]No one else dared to join them, though everyone had high regard for them. [14]And more and more people believed and were brought to the Lord—crowds of both men and women. [15]As a result of the apostles' work, sick people were brought out into the streets on beds and mats so that Peter's shadow might fall across some of them as he went by. [16]Crowds came in from the villages around Jerusalem, bringing their sick and those possessed by evil spirits, and they were all healed.

The Apostles Meet Opposition

[17]The high priest and his friends, who were Sadducees, reacted with violent jealousy. [18]They arrested the apostles and put them in the jail. [19]But an angel of the Lord came at night, opened the gates of the jail, and brought them out. Then he told them, [20]"Go to the Temple and give the people this message of life!" [21]So the apostles entered the Temple about daybreak and immediately began teaching.

When the high priest and his officials arrived, they convened the high council,* along with all the elders of Israel. Then they sent for the apostles to be brought for trial. [22]But when the Temple guards went to the jail, the men were gone. So they returned to the council and reported, [23]"The jail was locked, with the guards standing outside, but when we opened the gates, no one was there!"

[24]When the captain of the Temple guard and the leading priests heard this, they were perplexed, wondering where it would all end. [25]Then someone arrived with the news that the men they had jailed were out in the Temple, teaching the people.

[26]The captain went with his Temple guards and arrested them, but without violence, for they were afraid the people would kill them if they treated the apostles roughly. [27]Then they brought the apostles in before the council. [28]"Didn't we tell you never again to teach in this man's name?" the high priest demanded. "Instead, you have filled all Jerusalem with your teaching about Jesus, and you intend to blame us for his death!"

[29]But Peter and the apostles replied, "We must obey God rather than human authority. [30]The God of our ancestors raised Jesus from the dead after you killed him by crucifying him. [31]Then God put him in the place of honor at his right hand as Prince and Savior. He did this to give the people of Israel an opportunity to turn from their sins and turn to God so their sins would be forgiven. [32]We are witnesses of these things and so is the Holy Spirit, who is given by God to those who obey him."

[33]At this, the high council was furious and decided to kill them. [34]But one member had a different perspective. He was a Pharisee named Gamaliel, who was an expert on religious law and was very popular with the people. He stood up and ordered that the apostles be sent outside the council chamber for a while. [35]Then he addressed his colleagues as follows: "Men of Israel, take care what you are planning to do to these men! [36]Some time ago there was that fellow Theudas, who pretended to be someone great. About four hundred others joined him, but he was killed, and his follow-

5:21 Greek *Sanhedrin*; also in 5:27, 41.

ers went their various ways. The whole movement came to nothing. 37After him, at the time of the census, there was Judas of Galilee. He got some people to follow him, but he was killed, too, and all his followers were scattered.

38"So my advice is, leave these men alone. If they are teaching and doing these things merely on their own, it will soon be overthrown. 39But if it is of God, you will not be able to stop them. You may even find yourselves fighting against God."

40The council accepted his advice. They called in the apostles and had them flogged. Then they ordered them never again to speak in the name of Jesus, and they let them go. 41The apostles left the high council rejoicing that God had counted them worthy to suffer dishonor for the name of Jesus. 42And every day, in the Temple and in their homes,* they continued to teach and preach this message: "The Messiah you are looking for is Jesus."

CHAPTER 6

Seven Men Chosen to Serve

But as the believers* rapidly multiplied, there were rumblings of discontent. Those who spoke Greek complained against those who spoke Hebrew, saying that their widows were being discriminated against in the daily distribution of food. 2So the Twelve called a meeting of all the believers.

"We apostles should spend our time preaching and teaching the word of God, not administering a food program," they said. 3"Now look around among yourselves, brothers, and select seven men who are well respected and are full of the Holy Spirit and wisdom. We will put them in charge of this business. 4Then we can spend our time in prayer and preaching and teaching the word."

5This idea pleased the whole group, and they chose the following: Stephen (a man full of faith and the Holy Spirit), Philip, Procorus, Nicanor, Timon, Parmenas, and Nicolas of Antioch (a Gentile convert to the Jewish faith, who had now become a Christian). 6These seven were presented to the apostles, who prayed for them as they laid their hands on them.

7God's message was preached in ever-widening circles. The number of believers greatly increased in Jerusalem, and many of the Jewish priests were converted, too.

Stephen Is Arrested

8Stephen, a man full of God's grace and power, performed amazing miracles and signs among the people. 9But one day some men from the Synagogue of Freed Slaves, as it was called, started to debate with him. They were Jews from Cyrene, Alexandria, Cilicia, and the province of Asia. 10None of them was able to stand against the wisdom and Spirit by which Stephen spoke.

11So they persuaded some men to lie about Stephen, saying, "We heard him blaspheme Moses, and even God." 12Naturally, this roused the crowds, the elders, and the teachers of religious law. So they arrested Stephen and brought him before the high council.* 13The lying witnesses said, "This man is always speaking against the Temple and against the law of Moses. 14We have heard

5:42 Greek *from house to house.* 6:1 Greek *disciples;* also in 6:2, 7. 6:12 Greek *Sanhedrin;* also in 6:15.

him say that this Jesus of Nazareth will destroy the Temple and change the customs Moses handed down to us." 15At this point everyone in the council stared at Stephen because his face became as bright as an angel's.

CHAPTER 7

Stephen Addresses the Council

Then the high priest asked Stephen, "Are these accusations true?"

2This was Stephen's reply: "Brothers and honorable fathers, listen to me. Our glorious God appeared to our ancestor Abraham in Mesopotamia before he moved to Haran.* 3God told him, 'Leave your native land and your relatives, and come to the land that I will show you.' * 4So Abraham left the land of the Chaldeans and lived in Haran until his father died. Then God brought him here to the land where you now live. 5But God gave him no inheritance here, not even one square foot of land. God did promise, however, that eventually the whole country would belong to Abraham and his descendants—though he had no children yet. 6But God also told him that his descendants would live in a foreign country where they would be mistreated as slaves for four hundred years. 7'But I will punish the nation that enslaves them,' God told him, 'and in the end they will come out and worship me in this place.' * 8God also gave Abraham the covenant of circumcision at that time. And so Isaac, Abraham's son, was circumcised when he was eight days old. Isaac became the father of Jacob, and Jacob was the father of the twelve patriarchs of the Jewish nation.

9"These sons of Jacob were very jealous of their brother Joseph, and they sold him to be a slave in Egypt. But God was with him 10and delivered him from his anguish. And God gave him favor before Pharaoh, king of Egypt. God also gave Joseph unusual wisdom, so that Pharaoh appointed him governor over all of Egypt and put him in charge of all the affairs of the palace.

11"But a famine came upon Egypt and Canaan. There was great misery for our ancestors, as they ran out of food. 12Jacob heard that there was still grain in Egypt, so he sent his sons* to buy some. 13The second time they went, Joseph revealed his identity to his brothers, and they were introduced to Pharaoh. 14Then Joseph sent for his father, Jacob, and all his relatives to come to Egypt, seventy-five persons in all. 15So Jacob went to Egypt. He died there, as did all his sons. 16All of them were taken to Shechem and buried in the tomb Abraham had bought from the sons of Hamor in Shechem.

17"As the time drew near when God would fulfill his promise to Abraham, the number of our people in Egypt greatly increased. 18But then a new king came to the throne of Egypt who knew nothing about Joseph. 19This king plotted against our people and forced parents to abandon their newborn babies so they would die.

20"At that time Moses was born—a beautiful child in God's eyes. His parents cared for him at home for three months. 21When at last they had to abandon him, Pharaoh's daughter found him and raised him as her own son. 22Moses was taught all the wisdom of the Egyptians, and he became mighty in both speech and action.

7:2 *Mesopotamia* was the region now called Iraq. *Haran* was a city in what is now called Syria.   7:3 Gen 12:1.   7:5-7 Gen 12:7; 15:13-14; Exod 3:12.   7:12 Greek *our fathers;* also in 7:15.

²³"One day when he was forty years old, he decided to visit his relatives, the people of Israel. ²⁴During this visit, he saw an Egyptian mistreating a man of Israel. So Moses came to his defense and avenged him, killing the Egyptian. ²⁵Moses assumed his brothers would realize that God had sent him to rescue them, but they didn't.

²⁶"The next day he visited them again and saw two men of Israel fighting. He tried to be a peacemaker. 'Men,' he said, 'you are brothers. Why are you hurting each other?'

²⁷"But the man in the wrong pushed Moses aside and told him to mind his own business. 'Who made you a ruler and judge over us?' he asked. ²⁸'Are you going to kill me as you killed that Egyptian yesterday?' ²⁹When Moses heard that, he fled the country and lived as a foreigner in the land of Midian, where his two sons were born.

³⁰"Forty years later, in the desert near Mount Sinai, an angel appeared to Moses in the flame of a burning bush. ³¹Moses saw it and wondered what it was. As he went to see, the voice of the Lord called out to him, ³²'I am the God of your ancestors—the God of Abraham, Isaac, and Jacob.' Moses shook with terror and dared not look.

³³"And the Lord said to him, 'Take off your sandals, for you are standing on holy ground. ³⁴You can be sure that I have seen the misery of my people in Egypt. I have heard their cries. So I have come to rescue them. Now go, for I will send you to Egypt.'* ³⁵And so God sent back the same man his people had previously rejected by demanding, 'Who made you a ruler and judge over us?' Through the angel who appeared to him in the burning bush, Moses was sent to be their ruler and savior. ³⁶And by means of many miraculous signs and wonders, he led them out of Egypt, through the Red Sea, and back and forth through the wilderness for forty years.

³⁷"Moses himself told the people of Israel, 'God will raise up a Prophet like me from among your own people.'* ³⁸Moses was with the assembly of God's people in the wilderness. He was the mediator between the people of Israel and the angel who gave him life-giving words on Mount Sinai to pass on to us.

³⁹"But our ancestors rejected Moses and wanted to return to Egypt. ⁴⁰They told Aaron, 'Make us some gods who can lead us, for we don't know what has become of this Moses, who brought us out of Egypt.' ⁴¹So they made an idol shaped like a calf, and they sacrificed to it and rejoiced in this thing they had made. ⁴²Then God turned away from them and gave them up to serve the sun, moon, and stars as their gods! In the book of the prophets it is written,

'Was it to me you were bringing sacrifices
    during those forty years in the wilderness, Israel?
⁴³ No, your real interest was in your pagan gods—
    the shrine of Molech,
    the star god Rephan,
    and the images you made to worship them.
So I will send you into captivity
    far away in Babylon.'*

⁴⁴"Our ancestors carried the Tabernacle* with them through the wilderness. It was constructed in exact accordance with the plan

7:31-34 Exod 3:5-10.   **7:37** Deut 18:15.   **7:42-43** Amos 5:25-27.   **7:44** Greek *the tent of witness.*

shown to Moses by God. [45] Years later, when Joshua led the battles against the Gentile nations that God drove out of this land, the Tabernacle was taken with them into their new territory. And it was used there until the time of King David.

[46] "David found favor with God and asked for the privilege of building a permanent Temple for the God of Jacob.* [47] But it was Solomon who actually built it. [48] However, the Most High doesn't live in temples made by human hands. As the prophet says,

[49] 'Heaven is my throne,
  and the earth is my footstool.
Could you ever build me a temple as good as that?'
  asks the Lord.
'Could you build a dwelling place for me?
[50] Didn't I make everything in heaven and earth?'*

[51] "You stubborn people! You are heathen at heart and deaf to the truth. Must you forever resist the Holy Spirit? But your ancestors did, and so do you! [52] Name one prophet your ancestors didn't persecute! They even killed the ones who predicted the coming of the Righteous One—the Messiah whom you betrayed and murdered. [53] You deliberately disobeyed God's law, though you received it from the hands of angels.*"

[54] The Jewish leaders were infuriated by Stephen's accusation, and they shook their fists in rage.* [55] But Stephen, full of the Holy Spirit, gazed steadily upward into heaven and saw the glory of God, and he saw Jesus standing in the place of honor at God's right hand. [56] And he told them, "Look, I see the heavens opened and the Son of Man standing in the place of honor at God's right hand!"

[57] Then they put their hands over their ears, and drowning out his voice with their shouts, they rushed at him. [58] They dragged him out of the city and began to stone him. The official witnesses took off their coats and laid them at the feet of a young man named Saul.*

[59] And as they stoned him, Stephen prayed, "Lord Jesus, receive my spirit." [60] And he fell to his knees, shouting, "Lord, don't charge them with this sin!" And with that, he died.

CHAPTER 8

Saul was one of the official witnesses at the killing of Stephen.

Persecution Scatters the Believers

A great wave of persecution began that day, sweeping over the church in Jerusalem, and all the believers except the apostles fled into Judea and Samaria. [2] (Some godly men came and buried Stephen with loud weeping.) [3] Saul was going everywhere to devastate the church. He went from house to house, dragging out both men and women to throw them into jail.

Philip Preaches in Samaria

[4] But the believers who had fled Jerusalem went everywhere preaching the Good News about Jesus. [5] Philip, for example, went to the city of Samaria and told the people there about the Messiah. [6] Crowds listened intently to what he had to say because of the

7:46 Some manuscripts read *the house of Jacob.*   7:49-50 Isa 66:1-2.   7:53 Greek *received the Law as it was ordained by angels.*   7:54 Greek *they were grinding their teeth against him.*   7:58 *Saul* is later called *Paul;* see 13:9.

miracles he did. [7]Many evil spirits were cast out, screaming as they left their victims. And many who had been paralyzed or lame were healed. [8]So there was great joy in that city.

[9]A man named Simon had been a sorcerer there for many years, claiming to be someone great. [10]The Samaritan people, from the least to the greatest, often spoke of him as "the Great One—the Power of God." [11]He was very influential because of the magic he performed. [12]But now the people believed Philip's message of Good News concerning the Kingdom of God and the name of Jesus Christ. As a result, many men and women were baptized. [13]Then Simon himself believed and was baptized. He began following Philip wherever he went, and he was amazed by the great miracles and signs Philip performed.

[14]When the apostles back in Jerusalem heard that the people of Samaria had accepted God's message, they sent Peter and John there. [15]As soon as they arrived, they prayed for these new Christians to receive the Holy Spirit. [16]The Holy Spirit had not yet come upon any of them, for they had only been baptized in the name of the Lord Jesus. [17]Then Peter and John laid their hands upon these believers, and they received the Holy Spirit.

[18]When Simon saw that the Holy Spirit was given when the apostles placed their hands upon people's heads, he offered money to buy this power. [19]"Let me have this power, too," he exclaimed, "so that when I lay my hands on people, they will receive the Holy Spirit!"

[20]But Peter replied, "May your money perish with you for thinking God's gift can be bought! [21]You can have no part in this, for your heart is not right before God. [22]Turn from your wickedness and pray to the Lord. Perhaps he will forgive your evil thoughts, [23]for I can see that you are full of bitterness and held captive by sin."

[24]"Pray to the Lord for me," Simon exclaimed, "that these terrible things won't happen to me!"

[25]After testifying and preaching the word of the Lord in Samaria, Peter and John returned to Jerusalem. And they stopped in many Samaritan villages along the way to preach the Good News to them, too.

Philip and the Ethiopian Eunuch

[26]As for Philip, an angel of the Lord said to him, "Go south* down the desert road that runs from Jerusalem to Gaza." [27]So he did, and he met the treasurer of Ethiopia, a eunuch of great authority under the queen of Ethiopia.* The eunuch had gone to Jerusalem to worship, [28]and he was now returning. Seated in his carriage, he was reading aloud from the book of the prophet Isaiah.

[29]The Holy Spirit said to Philip, "Go over and walk along beside the carriage."

[30]Philip ran over and heard the man reading from the prophet Isaiah; so he asked, "Do you understand what you are reading?"

[31]The man replied, "How can I, when there is no one to instruct me?" And he begged Philip to come up into the carriage and sit with him. [32]The passage of Scripture he had been reading was this:

8:26 Or *Go at noon.* 8:27 Greek *under the Candace, the queen of Ethiopia.*

"He was led as a sheep to the slaughter.
And as a lamb is silent before the shearers,
he did not open his mouth.
33 He was humiliated and received no justice.
Who can speak of his descendants?
For his life was taken from the earth."*

34The eunuch asked Philip, "Was Isaiah talking about himself or someone else?" 35So Philip began with this same Scripture and then used many others to tell him the Good News about Jesus.

36As they rode along, they came to some water, and the eunuch said, "Look! There's some water! Why can't I be baptized?"* 38He ordered the carriage to stop, and they went down into the water, and Philip baptized him.

39When they came up out of the water, the Spirit of the Lord caught Philip away. The eunuch never saw him again but went on his way rejoicing. 40Meanwhile, Philip found himself farther north at the city of Azotus! He preached the Good News there and in every city along the way until he came to Caesarea.

CHAPTER 9
Saul's Conversion

Meanwhile, Saul was uttering threats with every breath. He was eager to destroy the Lord's followers,* so he went to the high priest. 2He requested letters addressed to the synagogues in Damascus, asking their cooperation in the arrest of any followers of the Way he found there. He wanted to bring them—both men and women—back to Jerusalem in chains.

3As he was nearing Damascus on this mission, a brilliant light from heaven suddenly beamed down upon him! 4He fell to the ground and heard a voice saying to him, "Saul! Saul! Why are you persecuting me?"

5"Who are you, sir?" Saul asked.

And the voice replied, "I am Jesus, the one you are persecuting! 6Now get up and go into the city, and you will be told what you are to do."

7The men with Saul stood speechless with surprise, for they heard the sound of someone's voice, but they saw no one! 8As Saul picked himself up off the ground, he found that he was blind. 9So his companions led him by the hand to Damascus. He remained there blind for three days. And all that time he went without food and water.

10Now there was a believer* in Damascus named Ananias. The Lord spoke to him in a vision, calling, "Ananias!"

"Yes, Lord!" he replied.

11The Lord said, "Go over to Straight Street, to the house of Judas. When you arrive, ask for Saul of Tarsus. He is praying to me right now. 12I have shown him a vision of a man named Ananias coming in and laying his hands on him so that he can see again."

13"But Lord," exclaimed Ananias, "I've heard about the terrible things this man has done to the believers in Jerusalem! 14And we

---

8:32-33 Isa 53:7-8. 8:36 Some manuscripts add verse 37, *"You can,"* Philip answered, *"if you believe with all your heart."* And the eunuch replied, *"I believe that Jesus Christ is the Son of God."* 9:1 Greek *disciples.* 9:10 Greek *disciple;* also in 9:36.

hear that he is authorized by the leading priests to arrest every believer in Damascus."

15But the Lord said, "Go and do what I say. For Saul is my chosen instrument to take my message to the Gentiles and to kings, as well as to the people of Israel. 16And I will show him how much he must suffer for me."

17So Ananias went and found Saul. He laid his hands on him and said, "Brother Saul, the Lord Jesus, who appeared to you on the road, has sent me so that you may get your sight back and be filled with the Holy Spirit." 18Instantly something like scales fell from Saul's eyes, and he regained his sight. Then he got up and was baptized. 19Afterward he ate some food and was strengthened.

Saul in Damascus and Jerusalem

Saul stayed with the believers* in Damascus for a few days. 20And immediately he began preaching about Jesus in the synagogues, saying, "He is indeed the Son of God!"

21All who heard him were amazed. "Isn't this the same man who persecuted Jesus' followers with such devastation in Jerusalem?" they asked. "And we understand that he came here to arrest them and take them in chains to the leading priests."

22Saul's preaching became more and more powerful, and the Jews in Damascus couldn't refute his proofs that Jesus was indeed the Messiah. 23After a while the Jewish leaders decided to kill him. 24But Saul was told about their plot, and that they were watching for him day and night at the city gate so they could murder him. 25So during the night, some of the other believers* let him down in a large basket through an opening in the city wall.

26When Saul arrived in Jerusalem, he tried to meet with the believers, but they were all afraid of him. They thought he was only pretending to be a believer! 27Then Barnabas brought him to the apostles and told them how Saul had seen the Lord on the way to Damascus. Barnabas also told them what the Lord had said to Saul and how he boldly preached in the name of Jesus in Damascus. 28Then the apostles accepted Saul, and after that he was constantly with them in Jerusalem, preaching boldly in the name of the Lord. 29He debated with some Greek-speaking Jews, but they plotted to murder him. 30When the believers* heard about it, however, they took him to Caesarea and sent him on to his hometown of Tarsus.

31The church then had peace throughout Judea, Galilee, and Samaria, and it grew in strength and numbers. The believers were walking in the fear of the Lord and in the comfort of the Holy Spirit.

Peter Heals Aeneas and Raises Dorcas

32Peter traveled from place to place to visit the believers, and in his travels he came to the Lord's people in the town of Lydda. 33There he met a man named Aeneas, who had been paralyzed and bed-ridden for eight years. 34Peter said to him, "Aeneas, Jesus Christ heals you! Get up and make your bed!" And he was healed instantly. 35Then the whole population of Lydda and Sharon turned to the Lord when they saw Aeneas walking around.

9:19 Greek *disciples;* also in 9:26.   9:25 Greek *his disciples.*   9:30 Greek *brothers.*

36There was a believer in Joppa named Tabitha (which in Greek is Dorcas*). She was always doing kind things for others and helping the poor. 37About this time she became ill and died. Her friends prepared her for burial and laid her in an upstairs room. 38But they had heard that Peter was nearby at Lydda, so they sent two men to beg him, "Please come as soon as possible!"

39So Peter returned with them; and as soon as he arrived, they took him to the upstairs room. The room was filled with widows who were weeping and showing him the coats and other garments Dorcas had made for them. 40But Peter asked them all to leave the room; then he knelt and prayed. Turning to the body he said, "Get up, Tabitha." And she opened her eyes! When she saw Peter, she sat up! 41He gave her his hand and helped her up. Then he called in the widows and all the believers, and he showed them that she was alive.

42The news raced through the whole town, and many believed in the Lord. 43And Peter stayed a long time in Joppa, living with Simon, a leatherworker.

CHAPTER 10

Cornelius Calls for Peter

In Caesarea there lived a Roman army officer named Cornelius, who was a captain of the Italian Regiment. 2He was a devout man who feared the God of Israel, as did his entire household. He gave generously to charity and was a man who regularly prayed to God. 3One afternoon about three o'clock, he had a vision in which he saw an angel of God coming toward him. "Cornelius!" the angel said.

4Cornelius stared at him in terror. "What is it, sir?" he asked the angel.

And the angel replied, "Your prayers and gifts to the poor have not gone unnoticed by God! 5Now send some men down to Joppa to find a man named Simon Peter. 6He is staying with Simon, a leatherworker who lives near the shore. Ask him to come and visit you."

7As soon as the angel was gone, Cornelius called two of his household servants and a devout soldier, one of his personal attendants. 8He told them what had happened and sent them off to Joppa.

Peter Visits Cornelius

9The next day as Cornelius's messengers were nearing the city, Peter went up to the flat roof to pray. It was about noon, 10and he was hungry. But while lunch was being prepared, he fell into a trance. 11He saw the sky open, and something like a large sheet was let down by its four corners. 12In the sheet were all sorts of animals, reptiles, and birds. 13Then a voice said to him, "Get up, Peter; kill and eat them."

14"Never, Lord," Peter declared. "I have never in all my life eaten anything forbidden by our Jewish laws.*"

15The voice spoke again, "If God says something is acceptable, don't say it isn't."* 16The same vision was repeated three times. Then the sheet was pulled up again to heaven.

17Peter was very perplexed. What could the vision mean? Just

9:36 The names *Tabitha* in Aramaic and *Dorcas* in Greek both mean "gazelle."
10:14 Greek *anything common and unclean.* 10:15 Greek *"What God calls clean you must not call unclean."*

then the men sent by Cornelius found the house and stood outside at the gate. ¹⁸They asked if this was the place where Simon Peter was staying. ¹⁹Meanwhile, as Peter was puzzling over the vision, the Holy Spirit said to him, "Three men have come looking for you. ²⁰Go down and go with them without hesitation. All is well, for I have sent them."

²¹So Peter went down and said, "I'm the man you are looking for. Why have you come?"

²²They said, "We were sent by Cornelius, a Roman officer. He is a devout man who fears the God of Israel and is well respected by all the Jews. A holy angel instructed him to send for you so you can go to his house and give him a message." ²³So Peter invited the men to be his guests for the night. The next day he went with them, accompanied by some other believers* from Joppa.

²⁴They arrived in Caesarea the following day. Cornelius was waiting for him and had called together his relatives and close friends to meet Peter. ²⁵As Peter entered his home, Cornelius fell to the floor before him in worship. ²⁶But Peter pulled him up and said, "Stand up! I'm a human being like you!" ²⁷So Cornelius got up, and they talked together and went inside where the others were assembled.

²⁸Peter told them, "You know it is against the Jewish laws for me to come into a Gentile home like this. But God has shown me that I should never think of anyone as impure. ²⁹So I came as soon as I was sent for. Now tell me why you sent for me."

³⁰Cornelius replied, "Four days ago I was praying in my house at three o'clock in the afternoon. Suddenly, a man in dazzling clothes was standing in front of me. ³¹He told me, 'Cornelius, your prayers have been heard, and your gifts to the poor have been noticed by God! ³²Now send some men to Joppa and summon Simon Peter. He is staying in the home of Simon, a leatherworker who lives near the shore.' ³³So I sent for you at once, and it was good of you to come. Now here we are, waiting before God to hear the message the Lord has given you."

The Gentiles Hear the Good News

³⁴Then Peter replied, "I see very clearly that God doesn't show partiality. ³⁵In every nation he accepts those who fear him and do what is right. ³⁶I'm sure you have heard about the Good News for the people of Israel—that there is peace with God through Jesus Christ, who is Lord of all. ³⁷You know what happened all through Judea, beginning in Galilee after John the Baptist began preaching. ³⁸And no doubt you know that God anointed Jesus of Nazareth with the Holy Spirit and with power. Then Jesus went around doing good and healing all who were oppressed by the Devil, for God was with him.

³⁹"And we apostles are witnesses of all he did throughout Israel and in Jerusalem. They put him to death by crucifying him, ⁴⁰but God raised him to life three days later. Then God allowed him to appear, ⁴¹not to the general public,* but to us whom God had chosen beforehand to be his witnesses. We were those who ate and drank with him after he rose from the dead. ⁴²And he ordered us

10:23 Greek *brothers.* **10:41** Greek *the people.*

to preach everywhere and to testify that Jesus is ordained of God to be the judge of all—the living and the dead. 43He is the one all the prophets testified about, saying that everyone who believes in him will have their sins forgiven through his name."

The Gentiles Receive the Holy Spirit

44Even as Peter was saying these things, the Holy Spirit fell upon all who had heard the message. 45The Jewish believers who came with Peter were amazed that the gift of the Holy Spirit had been poured out upon the Gentiles, too. 46And there could be no doubt about it, for they heard them speaking in tongues and praising God.

Then Peter asked, 47"Can anyone object to their being baptized, now that they have received the Holy Spirit just as we did?" 48So he gave orders for them to be baptized in the name of Jesus Christ. Afterward Cornelius asked him to stay with them for several days.

CHAPTER 11

Peter Explains His Actions

Soon the news reached the apostles and other believers* in Judea that the Gentiles had received the word of God. 2But when Peter arrived back in Jerusalem, some of the Jewish believers* criticized him. 3"You entered the home of Gentiles* and even ate with them!" they said.

4Then Peter told them exactly what had happened. 5"One day in Joppa," he said, "while I was praying, I went into a trance and saw a vision. Something like a large sheet was let down by its four corners from the sky. And it came right down to me. 6When I looked inside the sheet, I saw all sorts of small animals, wild animals, reptiles, and birds that we are not allowed to eat. 7And I heard a voice say, 'Get up, Peter; kill and eat them.'

8"'Never, Lord,' I replied. 'I have never eaten anything forbidden by our Jewish laws.*'

9"But the voice from heaven came again, 'If God says something is acceptable, don't say it isn't.'*

10"This happened three times before the sheet and all it contained was pulled back up to heaven. 11Just then three men who had been sent from Caesarea arrived at the house where I was staying. 12The Holy Spirit told me to go with them and not to worry about their being Gentiles. These six brothers here accompanied me, and we soon arrived at the home of the man who had sent for us. 13He told us how an angel had appeared to him in his home and had told him, 'Send messengers to Joppa to find Simon Peter. 14He will tell you how you and all your household will be saved!'

15"Well, I began telling them the Good News, but just as I was getting started, the Holy Spirit fell on them, just as he fell on us at the beginning. 16Then I thought of the Lord's words when he said, 'John baptized with* water, but you will be baptized with the Holy Spirit.' 17And since God gave these Gentiles the same gift he gave us when we believed in the Lord Jesus Christ, who was I to argue?"

18When the others heard this, all their objections were answered

11:1 Greek *brothers.*   11:2 Greek *those of the circumcision.*   11:3 Greek *of uncircumcised men.*   11:8 Greek *anything common or unclean.*   11:9 Greek *'What God calls clean you must not call unclean.'*   11:16 Or *in;* also in 11:16b.

and they began praising God. They said, "God has also given the Gentiles the privilege of turning from sin and receiving eternal life."

The Church in Antioch of Syria

19Meanwhile, the believers who had fled from Jerusalem during the persecution after Stephen's death traveled as far as Phoenicia, Cyprus, and Antioch of Syria. They preached the Good News, but only to Jews. 20However, some of the believers who went to Antioch from Cyprus and Cyrene began preaching to Gentiles* about the Lord Jesus. 21The power of the Lord was upon them, and large numbers of these Gentiles believed and turned to the Lord.

22When the church at Jerusalem heard what had happened, they sent Barnabas to Antioch. 23When he arrived and saw this proof of God's favor, he was filled with joy, and he encouraged the believers to stay true to the Lord. 24Barnabas was a good man, full of the Holy Spirit and strong in faith. And large numbers of people were brought to the Lord.

25Then Barnabas went on to Tarsus to find Saul. 26When he found him, he brought him back to Antioch. Both of them stayed there with the church for a full year, teaching great numbers of people. (It was there at Antioch that the believers* were first called Christians.)

27During this time, some prophets traveled from Jerusalem to Antioch. 28One of them named Agabus stood up in one of the meetings to predict by the Spirit that a great famine was coming upon the entire Roman world. (This was fulfilled during the reign of Claudius.) 29So the believers in Antioch decided to send relief to the brothers and sisters* in Judea, everyone giving as much as they could. 30This they did, entrusting their gifts to Barnabas and Saul to take to the elders of the church in Jerusalem.

CHAPTER 12

James Is Killed and Peter Is Imprisoned

About that time King Herod Agrippa* began to persecute some believers in the church. 2He had the apostle James (John's brother) killed with a sword. 3When Herod saw how much this pleased the Jewish leaders, he arrested Peter during the Passover celebration* 4and imprisoned him, placing him under the guard of four squads of four soldiers each. Herod's intention was to bring Peter out for public trial after the Passover. 5But while Peter was in prison, the church prayed very earnestly for him.

Peter's Miraculous Escape from Prison

6The night before Peter was to be placed on trial, he was asleep, chained between two soldiers, with others standing guard at the prison gate. 7Suddenly, there was a bright light in the cell, and an angel of the Lord stood before Peter. The angel tapped him on the side to awaken him and said, "Quick! Get up!" And the chains fell off his wrists. 8Then the angel told him, "Get dressed and put on your sandals." And he did. "Now put on your coat and follow me," the angel ordered.

9So Peter left the cell, following the angel. But all the time he

11:20 Greek *the Greeks;* other manuscripts read *the Hellenists.* 11:26 Greek *disciples;* also in 11:29. 11:29 Greek *the brothers.* 12:1 Greek *Herod the king.* He was the nephew of Herod Antipas and a grandson of Herod the Great. 12:3 Greek *the days of unleavened bread.*

thought it was a vision. He didn't realize it was really happening. [10]They passed the first and second guard posts and came to the iron gate to the street, and this opened to them all by itself. So they passed through and started walking down the street, and then the angel suddenly left him.

[11]Peter finally realized what had happened. "It's really true!" he said to himself. "The Lord has sent his angel and saved me from Herod and from what the Jews were hoping to do to me!"

[12]After a little thought, he went to the home of Mary, the mother of John Mark, where many were gathered for prayer. [13]He knocked at the door in the gate, and a servant girl named Rhoda came to open it. [14]When she recognized Peter's voice, she was so overjoyed that, instead of opening the door, she ran back inside and told everyone, "Peter is standing at the door!"

[15]"You're out of your mind," they said. When she insisted, they decided, "It must be his angel."

[16]Meanwhile, Peter continued knocking. When they finally went out and opened the door, they were amazed. [17]He motioned for them to quiet down and told them what had happened and how the Lord had led him out of jail. "Tell James and the other brothers what happened," he said. And then he went to another place.

[18]At dawn, there was a great commotion among the soldiers about what had happened to Peter. [19]Herod Agrippa ordered a thorough search for him. When he couldn't be found, Herod interrogated the guards and sentenced them to death. Afterward Herod left Judea to stay in Caesarea for a while.

The Death of Herod Agrippa

[20]Now Herod was very angry with the people of Tyre and Sidon. So they sent a delegation to make peace with him because their cities were dependent upon Herod's country for their food. They made friends with Blastus, Herod's personal assistant, [21]and an appointment with Herod was granted. When the day arrived, Herod put on his royal robes, sat on his throne, and made a speech to them. [22]The people gave him a great ovation, shouting, "It is the voice of a god, not of a man!"

[23]Instantly, an angel of the Lord struck Herod with a sickness, because he accepted the people's worship instead of giving the glory to God. So he was consumed with worms and died.

[24]But God's Good News was spreading rapidly, and there were many new believers.

[25]When Barnabas and Saul had finished their mission in Jerusalem, they returned to Antioch, taking John Mark with them.

CHAPTER 13

Barnabas and Saul Are Sent Out

Among the prophets and teachers of the church at Antioch of Syria were Barnabas, Simeon (called "the black man"*), Lucius (from Cyrene), Manaen (the childhood companion of King Herod Antipas*), and Saul. [2]One day as these men were worshiping the Lord and fasting, the Holy Spirit said, "Dedicate Barnabas and Saul for the special work I have for them." [3]So after more fasting and prayer, the men laid their hands on them and sent them on their way.

13:1a Greek *who was called Niger.*   13:1b Greek *Herod the tetrarch.*

Paul's First Missionary Journey

[4]Sent out by the Holy Spirit, Saul and Barnabas went down to the seaport of Seleucia and then sailed for the island of Cyprus. [5]There, in the town of Salamis, they went to the Jewish synagogues and preached the word of God. (John Mark went with them as their assistant.)

[6]Afterward they preached from town to town across the entire island until finally they reached Paphos, where they met a Jewish sorcerer, a false prophet named Bar-Jesus. [7]He had attached himself to the governor, Sergius Paulus, a man of considerable insight and understanding. The governor invited Barnabas and Saul to visit him, for he wanted to hear the word of God. [8]But Elymas, the sorcerer (as his name means in Greek), interfered and urged the governor to pay no attention to what Saul and Barnabas said. He was trying to turn the governor away from the Christian faith.

[9]Then Saul, also known as Paul, filled with the Holy Spirit, looked the sorcerer in the eye and said, [10]"You son of the Devil, full of every sort of trickery and villainy, enemy of all that is good, will you never stop perverting the true ways of the Lord? [11]And now the Lord has laid his hand of punishment upon you, and you will be stricken awhile with blindness." Instantly mist and darkness fell upon him, and he began wandering around begging for someone to take his hand and lead him. [12]When the governor saw what had happened, he believed and was astonished at what he learned about the Lord.

Paul Preaches in Antioch of Pisidia

[13]Now Paul and those with him left Paphos by ship for Pamphylia,* landing at the port town of Perga. There John Mark left them and returned to Jerusalem. [14]But Barnabas and Paul traveled inland to Antioch of Pisidia.*

On the Sabbath they went to the synagogue for the services. [15]After the usual readings from the books of Moses and from the Prophets, those in charge of the service sent them this message: "Brothers, if you have any word of encouragement for us, come and give it!"

[16]So Paul stood, lifted his hand to quiet them, and started speaking. "People of Israel," he said, "and you devout Gentiles who fear the God of Israel, listen to me.

[17]"The God of this nation of Israel chose our ancestors and made them prosper in Egypt. Then he powerfully led them out of their slavery. [18]He put up with them* through forty years of wandering around in the wilderness. [19]Then he destroyed seven nations in Canaan and gave their land to Israel as an inheritance. [20]All this took about 450 years. After that, judges ruled until the time of Samuel the prophet. [21]Then the people begged for a king, and God gave them Saul son of Kish, a man of the tribe of Benjamin, who reigned for forty years. [22]But God removed him from the kingship and replaced him with David, a man about whom God said, 'David son of Jesse is a man after my own heart, for he will do everything I want him to.'*

[23]"And it is one of King David's descendants, Jesus, who is God's

13:13-14 Pamphylia and Pisidia were districts in the land now called Turkey.
13:18 Other manuscripts read He cared for them; compare Deut 1:31.
13:22 1 Sam 13:14.

promised Savior of Israel! 24But before he came, John the Baptist preached the need for everyone in Israel to turn from sin and turn to God and be baptized. 25As John was finishing his ministry he asked, 'Do you think I am the Messiah? No! But he is coming soon—and I am not even worthy to be his slave.*'

26"Brothers—you sons of Abraham, and also all of you devout Gentiles who fear the God of Israel—this salvation is for us! 27The people in Jerusalem and their leaders fulfilled prophecy by condemning Jesus to death. They didn't recognize him or realize that he is the one the prophets had written about, though they hear the prophets' words read every Sabbath. 28They found no just cause to execute him, but they asked Pilate to have him killed anyway.

29"When they had fulfilled all the prophecies concerning his death, they took him down from the cross and placed him in a tomb. 30But God raised him from the dead! 31And he appeared over a period of many days to those who had gone with him from Galilee to Jerusalem—these are his witnesses to the people of Israel.

32"And now Barnabas and I are here to bring you this Good News. God's promise to our ancestors has come true in our own time, 33in that God raised Jesus. This is what the second psalm is talking about when it says concerning Jesus,

'You are my Son.
    Today I have become your Father.*'

34For God had promised to raise him from the dead, never again to die. This is stated in the Scripture that says, 'I will give you the sacred blessings I promised to David.'* 35Another psalm explains more fully, saying, 'You will not allow your Holy One to rot in the grave.'* 36Now this is not a reference to David, for after David had served his generation according to the will of God, he died and was buried, and his body decayed. 37No, it was a reference to someone else—someone whom God raised and whose body did not decay.

38"Brothers, listen! In this man Jesus there is forgiveness for your sins. 39Everyone who believes in him is freed from all guilt and declared right with God—something the Jewish law could never do. 40Be careful! Don't let the prophets' words apply to you. For they said,

41 'Look you mockers,
        be amazed and die!
    For I am doing something in your own day,
        something you wouldn't believe
    even if someone told you about it.'*"

42As Paul and Barnabas left the synagogue that day, the people asked them to return again and speak about these things the next week. 43Many Jews and godly converts to Judaism who worshiped at the synagogue followed Paul and Barnabas, and the two men urged them, "By God's grace, remain faithful."

Paul Turns to the Gentiles

44The following week almost the entire city turned out to hear them preach the word of the Lord. 45But when the Jewish leaders

13:25 Greek *to untie his sandals.*   13:33 Or *Today I reveal you as my Son.* Ps 2:7.
13:34 Isa 55:3.   13:35 Ps 16:10.   13:41 Hab 1:5.

saw the crowds, they were jealous; so they slandered Paul and argued against whatever he said.

⁴⁶Then Paul and Barnabas spoke out boldly and declared, "It was necessary that this Good News from God be given first to you Jews. But since you have rejected it and judged yourselves unworthy of eternal life—well, we will offer it to Gentiles. ⁴⁷For this is as the Lord commanded us when he said,

'I have made you a light to the Gentiles,
  to bring salvation to the farthest corners of the earth.'*"

⁴⁸When the Gentiles heard this, they were very glad and thanked the Lord for his message; and all who were appointed to eternal life became believers. ⁴⁹So the Lord's message spread throughout that region.

⁵⁰Then the Jewish leaders stirred up both the influential religious women and the leaders of the city, and they incited a mob against Paul and Barnabas and ran them out of town. ⁵¹But they shook off the dust of their feet against them and went to the city of Iconium. ⁵²And the believers* were filled with joy and with the Holy Spirit.

CHAPTER 14

Paul and Barnabas in Iconium

In Iconium,* Paul and Barnabas went together to the synagogue and preached with such power that a great number of both Jews and Gentiles believed. ²But the Jews who spurned God's message stirred up distrust among the Gentiles against Paul and Barnabas, saying all sorts of evil things about them. ³The apostles stayed there a long time, preaching boldly about the grace of the Lord. The Lord proved their message was true by giving them power to do miraculous signs and wonders. ⁴But the people of the city were divided in their opinion about them. Some sided with the Jews, and some with the apostles.

⁵A mob of Gentiles and Jews, along with their leaders, decided to attack and stone them. ⁶When the apostles learned of it, they fled for their lives. They went to the region of Lycaonia, to the cities of Lystra and Derbe and the surrounding area, ⁷and they preached the Good News there.

Paul and Barnabas in Lystra and Derbe

⁸While they were at Lystra, Paul and Barnabas came upon a man with crippled feet. He had been that way from birth, so he had never walked. ⁹He was listening as Paul preached, and Paul noticed him and realized he had faith to be healed. ¹⁰So Paul called to him in a loud voice, "Stand up!" And the man jumped to his feet and started walking.

¹¹When the listening crowd saw what Paul had done, they shouted in their local dialect, "These men are gods in human bodies!" ¹²They decided that Barnabas was the Greek god Zeus and that Paul, because he was the chief speaker, was Hermes. ¹³The temple of Zeus was located on the outskirts of the city. The priest

---

13:47 Isa 49:6.   **13:52** Greek *the disciples.*   **14:1** *Iconium,* as well as *Lystra* and *Derbe* (14:6), were cities in the land now called Turkey.

of the temple and the crowd brought oxen and wreaths of flowers, and they prepared to sacrifice to the apostles at the city gates.

14But when Barnabas and Paul heard what was happening, they tore their clothing in dismay and ran out among the people, shouting, 15"Friends,* why are you doing this? We are merely human beings like yourselves! We have come to bring you the Good News that you should turn from these worthless things to the living God, who made heaven and earth, the sea, and everything in them. 16In earlier days he permitted all the nations to go their own ways, 17but he never left himself without a witness. There were always reminders, such as sending you rain and good crops and giving you food and joyful hearts." 18But even so, Paul and Barnabas could scarcely restrain the people from sacrificing to them.

19Now some Jews arrived from Antioch and Iconium and turned the crowds into a murderous mob. They stoned Paul and dragged him out of the city, apparently dead. 20But as the believers* stood around him, he got up and went back into the city. The next day he left with Barnabas for Derbe.

Paul and Barnabas Return to Antioch of Syria

21After preaching the Good News in Derbe and making many disciples, Paul and Barnabas returned again to Lystra, Iconium, and Antioch of Pisidia, 22where they strengthened the believers. They encouraged them to continue in the faith, reminding them that they must enter into the Kingdom of God through many tribulations. 23Paul and Barnabas also appointed elders in every church and prayed for them with fasting, turning them over to the care of the Lord, in whom they had come to trust. 24Then they traveled back through Pisidia to Pamphylia. 25They preached again in Perga, then went on to Attalia.

26Finally, they returned by ship to Antioch of Syria, where their journey had begun and where they had been committed to the grace of God for the work they had now completed. 27Upon arriving in Antioch, they called the church together and reported about their trip, telling all that God had done and how he had opened the door of faith to the Gentiles, too. 28And they stayed there with the believers in Antioch for a long time.

CHAPTER 15

The Council at Jerusalem

While Paul and Barnabas were at Antioch of Syria, some men from Judea arrived and began to teach the Christians*: "Unless you keep the ancient Jewish custom of circumcision taught by Moses, you cannot be saved." 2Paul and Barnabas, disagreeing with them, argued forcefully and at length. Finally, Paul and Barnabas were sent to Jerusalem, accompanied by some local believers, to talk to the apostles and elders about this question. 3The church sent the delegates to Jerusalem, and they stopped along the way in Phoenicia and Samaria to visit the believers.* They told them—much to everyone's joy—that the Gentiles, too, were being converted.

4When they arrived in Jerusalem, Paul and Barnabas were welcomed by the whole church, including the apostles and elders.

14:15 Greek *Men.*   14:20 Greek *disciples;* also in 14:22, 28.   15:1 Greek *brothers;* also in 15:32, 33.   15:3 Greek *brothers;* also in 15:23, 36, 40.

They reported on what God had been doing through their ministry. [5]But then some of the men who had been Pharisees before their conversion stood up and declared that all Gentile converts must be circumcised and be required to follow the law of Moses.

[6]So the apostles and church elders got together to decide this question. [7]At the meeting, after a long discussion, Peter stood and addressed them as follows: "Brothers, you all know that God chose me from among you some time ago to preach to the Gentiles so that they could hear the Good News and believe. [8]God, who knows people's hearts, confirmed that he accepts them by giving them the Holy Spirit, just as he gave him to us. [9]He made no distinction between us and them, for he also cleansed their hearts through faith. [10]Why are you now questioning God's way by burdening the Gentile believers* with a yoke that neither we nor our ancestors were able to bear? [11]We believe that we are all saved the same way, by the special favor of the Lord Jesus."

[12]There was no further discussion, and everyone listened as Barnabas and Paul told about the miraculous signs and wonders God had done through them among the Gentiles.

[13]When they had finished, James stood and said, "Brothers, listen to me. [14]Peter* has told you about the time God first visited the Gentiles to take from them a people for himself. [15]And this conversion of Gentiles agrees with what the prophets predicted. For instance, it is written:

[16] 'Afterward I will return,
and I will restore the fallen kingdom of David.
From the ruins I will rebuild it,
and I will restore it,
[17] so that the rest of humanity might find the Lord,
including the Gentiles—
all those I have called to be mine.
This is what the Lord says,
[18] he who made these things known long ago.'*

[19]And so my judgment is that we should stop troubling the Gentiles who turn to God, [20]except that we should write to them and tell them to abstain from eating meat sacrificed to idols, from sexual immorality, and from consuming blood or eating the meat of strangled animals. [21]For these laws of Moses have been preached in Jewish synagogues in every city on every Sabbath for many generations."

The Letter for Gentile Believers

[22]Then the apostles and elders and the whole church in Jerusalem chose delegates, and they sent them to Antioch of Syria with Paul and Barnabas to report on this decision. The men chosen were two of the church leaders*—Judas (also called Barsabbas) and Silas. [23]This is the letter they took along with them:

"This letter is from the apostles and elders, your brothers in Jerusalem. It is written to the Gentile believers in Antioch, Syria, and Cilicia. Greetings!

[24]"We understand that some men from here have troubled

15:10 Greek *disciples.*   15:14 Greek *Simon.*   15:16-18 Amos 9:11-12; Isa 45:21.
15:22 Greek *were leaders among the brothers.*

you and upset you with their teaching, but they had no such instructions from us. 25So it seemed good to us, having unanimously agreed on our decision, to send you these official representatives, along with our beloved Barnabas and Paul, 26who have risked their lives for the sake of our Lord Jesus Christ. 27So we are sending Judas and Silas to tell you what we have decided concerning your question.

28"For it seemed good to the Holy Spirit and to us to lay no greater burden on you than these requirements: 29You must abstain from eating food offered to idols, from consuming blood or eating the meat of strangled animals, and from sexual immorality. If you do this, you will do well. Farewell."

30The four messengers went at once to Antioch, where they called a general meeting of the Christians and delivered the letter. 31And there was great joy throughout the church that day as they read this encouraging message.

32Then Judas and Silas, both being prophets, spoke extensively to the Christians, encouraging and strengthening their faith. 33They stayed for a while, and then Judas and Silas were sent back to Jerusalem, with the blessings of the Christians, to those who had sent them.* 35Paul and Barnabas stayed in Antioch to assist many others who were teaching and preaching the word of the Lord there.

Paul and Barnabas Separate

36After some time Paul said to Barnabas, "Let's return to each city where we previously preached the word of the Lord, to see how the new believers are getting along." 37Barnabas agreed and wanted to take along John Mark. 38But Paul disagreed strongly, since John Mark had deserted them in Pamphylia and had not shared in their work. 39Their disagreement over this was so sharp that they separated. Barnabas took John Mark with him and sailed for Cyprus. 40Paul chose Silas, and the believers sent them off, entrusting them to the Lord's grace. 41So they traveled throughout Syria and Cilicia to strengthen the churches there.

CHAPTER 16

Paul's Second Missionary Journey

Paul and Silas went first to Derbe and then on to Lystra. There they met Timothy, a young disciple whose mother was a Jewish believer, but whose father was a Greek. 2Timothy was well thought of by the believers* in Lystra and Iconium, 3so Paul wanted him to join them on their journey. In deference to the Jews of the area, he arranged for Timothy to be circumcised before they left, for everyone knew that his father was a Greek. 4Then they went from town to town, explaining the decision regarding the commandments that were to be obeyed, as decided by the apostles and elders in Jerusalem. 5So the churches were strengthened in their faith and grew daily in numbers.

A Call from Macedonia

6Next Paul and Silas traveled through the area of Phrygia and Galatia, because the Holy Spirit had told them not to go into the

15:33 Some manuscripts add verse 34, *But Silas decided to stay there.* 16:2 Greek *brothers;* also in 16:40.

province of Asia at that time. ⁷Then coming to the borders of Mysia, they headed for the province of Bithynia,* but again the Spirit of Jesus did not let them go. ⁸So instead, they went on through Mysia to the city of Troas.

⁹That night Paul had a vision. He saw a man from Macedonia in northern Greece, pleading with him, "Come over here and help us." ¹⁰So we* decided to leave for Macedonia at once, for we could only conclude that God was calling us to preach the Good News there.

Lydia of Philippi Believes in Jesus

¹¹We boarded a boat at Troas and sailed straight across to the island of Samothrace, and the next day we landed at Neapolis. ¹²From there we reached Philippi, a major city of the district of Macedonia and a Roman colony; we stayed there several days.

¹³On the Sabbath we went a little way outside the city to a riverbank, where we supposed that some people met for prayer, and we sat down to speak with some women who had come together. ¹⁴One of them was Lydia from Thyatira, a merchant of expensive purple cloth. She was a worshiper of God. As she listened to us, the Lord opened her heart, and she accepted what Paul was saying. ¹⁵She was baptized along with other members of her household, and she asked us to be her guests. "If you agree that I am faithful to the Lord," she said, "come and stay at my home." And she urged us until we did.

Paul and Silas in Prison

¹⁶One day as we were going down to the place of prayer, we met a demon-possessed slave girl. She was a fortune-teller who earned a lot of money for her masters. ¹⁷She followed along behind us shouting, "These men are servants of the Most High God, and they have come to tell you how to be saved."

¹⁸This went on day after day until Paul got so exasperated that he turned and spoke to the demon within her. "I command you in the name of Jesus Christ to come out of her," he said. And instantly it left her.

¹⁹Her masters' hopes of wealth were now shattered, so they grabbed Paul and Silas and dragged them before the authorities at the marketplace. ²⁰"The whole city is in an uproar because of these Jews!" they shouted. ²¹"They are teaching the people to do things that are against Roman customs."

²²A mob quickly formed against Paul and Silas, and the city officials ordered them stripped and beaten with wooden rods. ²³They were severely beaten, and then they were thrown into prison. The jailer was ordered to make sure they didn't escape. ²⁴So he took no chances but put them into the inner dungeon and clamped their feet in the stocks.

²⁵Around midnight, Paul and Silas were praying and singing hymns to God, and the other prisoners were listening. ²⁶Suddenly, there was a great earthquake, and the prison was shaken to its foundations. All the doors flew open, and the chains of every prisoner fell off! ²⁷The jailer woke up to see the prison doors wide open. He

16:6-7 *Phrygia, Galatia, Asia, Mysia,* and *Bithynia* were all districts in the land now called Turkey. **16:10** Luke, the writer of this book, here joined Paul and accompanied him on his journey.

assumed the prisoners had escaped, so he drew his sword to kill himself. 28But Paul shouted to him, "Don't do it! We are all here!"

29Trembling with fear, the jailer called for lights and ran to the dungeon and fell down before Paul and Silas. 30He brought them out and asked, "Sirs, what must I do to be saved?"

31They replied, "Believe on the Lord Jesus and you will be saved, along with your entire household." 32Then they shared the word of the Lord with him and all who lived in his household. 33That same hour the jailer washed their wounds, and he and everyone in his household were immediately baptized. 34Then he brought them into his house and set a meal before them. He and his entire household rejoiced because they all believed in God.

35The next morning the city officials sent the police to tell the jailer, "Let those men go!" 36So the jailer told Paul, "You and Silas are free to leave. Go in peace."

37But Paul replied, "They have publicly beaten us without trial and jailed us—and we are Roman citizens. So now they want us to leave secretly? Certainly not! Let them come themselves to release us!"

38When the police made their report, the city officials were alarmed to learn that Paul and Silas were Roman citizens. 39They came to the jail and apologized to them. Then they brought them out and begged them to leave the city. 40Paul and Silas then returned to the home of Lydia, where they met with the believers and encouraged them once more before leaving town.

CHAPTER 17

Paul Preaches in Thessalonica

Now Paul and Silas traveled through the towns of Amphipolis and Apollonia and came to Thessalonica, where there was a Jewish synagogue. 2As was Paul's custom, he went to the synagogue service, and for three Sabbaths in a row he interpreted the Scriptures to the people. 3He was explaining and proving the prophecies about the sufferings of the Messiah and his rising from the dead. He said, "This Jesus I'm telling you about is the Messiah." 4Some who listened were persuaded and became converts, including a large number of godly Greek men and also many important women of the city.*

5But the Jewish leaders were jealous, so they gathered some worthless fellows from the streets to form a mob and start a riot. They attacked the home of Jason, searching for Paul and Silas so they could drag them out to the crowd.* 6Not finding them there, they dragged out Jason and some of the other believers* instead and took them before the city council. "Paul and Silas have turned the rest of the world upside down, and now they are here disturbing our city," they shouted. 7"And Jason has let them into his home. They are all guilty of treason against Caesar, for they profess allegiance to another king, Jesus."

8The people of the city, as well as the city officials, were thrown into turmoil by these reports. 9But the officials released Jason and the other believers after they had posted bail.

17:4 Some manuscripts read *many of the wives of the leading men.*   17:5 Or *the city council.* 17:6 Greek *brothers;* also in 17:10, 14.

Paul and Silas in Berea

[10]That very night the believers sent Paul and Silas to Berea. When they arrived there, they went to the synagogue. [11]And the people of Berea were more open-minded than those in Thessalonica, and they listened eagerly to Paul's message. They searched the Scriptures day after day to check up on Paul and Silas, to see if they were really teaching the truth. [12]As a result, many Jews believed, as did some of the prominent Greek women and many men.

[13]But when some Jews in Thessalonica learned that Paul was preaching the word of God in Berea, they went there and stirred up trouble. [14]The believers acted at once, sending Paul on to the coast, while Silas and Timothy remained behind. [15]Those escorting Paul went with him to Athens; then they returned to Berea with a message for Silas and Timothy to hurry and join him.

Paul Preaches in Athens

[16]While Paul was waiting for them in Athens, he was deeply troubled by all the idols he saw everywhere in the city. [17]He went to the synagogue to debate with the Jews and the God-fearing Gentiles, and he spoke daily in the public square to all who happened to be there.

[18]He also had a debate with some of the Epicurean and Stoic philosophers. When he told them about Jesus and his resurrection, they said, "This babbler has picked up some strange ideas." Others said, "He's pushing some foreign religion."

[19]Then they took him to the Council of Philosophers.* "Come and tell us more about this new religion," they said. [20]"You are saying some rather startling things, and we want to know what it's all about." [21](It should be explained that all the Athenians as well as the foreigners in Athens seemed to spend all their time discussing the latest ideas.)

[22]So Paul, standing before the Council,* addressed them as follows: "Men of Athens, I notice that you are very religious, [23]for as I was walking along I saw your many altars. And one of them had this inscription on it—'To an Unknown God.' You have been worshiping him without knowing who he is, and now I wish to tell you about him.

[24]"He is the God who made the world and everything in it. Since he is Lord of heaven and earth, he doesn't live in man-made temples, [25]and human hands can't serve his needs—for he has no needs. He himself gives life and breath to everything, and he satisfies every need there is. [26]From one man he created all the nations throughout the whole earth. He decided beforehand which should rise and fall, and he determined their boundaries.

[27]"His purpose in all of this was that the nations should seek after God and perhaps feel their way toward him and find him— though he is not far from any one of us. [28]For in him we live and move and exist. As one of your own poets says, 'We are his offspring.' [29]And since this is true, we shouldn't think of God as an idol designed by craftsmen from gold or silver or stone. [30]God overlooked people's former ignorance about these things, but now he commands everyone everywhere to turn away from idols and turn to him.* [31]For he has set a day for judging the world with

17:19 Greek *the Areopagus.*   17:22 Or *in the middle of Mars Hill;* Greek reads *in the middle of the Areopagus.*   17:30 Greek *everywhere to repent.*

justice by the man he has appointed, and he proved to everyone who this is by raising him from the dead."

³²When they heard Paul speak of the resurrection of a person who had been dead, some laughed, but others said, "We want to hear more about this later." ³³That ended Paul's discussion with them, ³⁴but some joined him and became believers. Among them were Dionysius, a member of the Council,* a woman named Damaris, and others.

CHAPTER 18

Paul Meets Priscilla and Aquila in Corinth

Then Paul left Athens and went to Corinth.* ²There he became acquainted with a Jew named Aquila, born in Pontus, who had recently arrived from Italy with his wife, Priscilla. They had been expelled from Italy as a result of Claudius Caesar's order to deport all Jews from Rome. ³Paul lived and worked with them, for they were tentmakers* just as he was.

⁴Each Sabbath found Paul at the synagogue, trying to convince the Jews and Greeks alike. ⁵And after Silas and Timothy came down from Macedonia, Paul spent his full time preaching and testifying to the Jews, telling them, "The Messiah you are looking for is Jesus." ⁶But when the Jews opposed him and insulted him, Paul shook the dust from his robe and said, "Your blood be upon your own heads—I am innocent. From now on I will go to the Gentiles."

⁷After that he stayed with Titius Justus, a Gentile who worshiped God and lived next door to the synagogue. ⁸Crispus, the leader of the synagogue, and all his household believed in the Lord. Many others in Corinth also became believers and were baptized.

⁹One night the Lord spoke to Paul in a vision and told him, "Don't be afraid! Speak out! Don't be silent! ¹⁰For I am with you, and no one will harm you because many people here in this city belong to me." ¹¹So Paul stayed there for the next year and a half, teaching the word of God.

¹²But when Gallio became governor of Achaia, some Jews rose in concerted action against Paul and brought him before the governor for judgment. ¹³They accused Paul of "persuading people to worship God in ways that are contrary to the law." ¹⁴But just as Paul started to make his defense, Gallio turned to Paul's accusers and said, "Listen, you Jews, if this were a case involving some wrongdoing or a serious crime, I would be obliged to listen to you. ¹⁵But since it is merely a question of words and names and your Jewish laws, you take care of it. I refuse to judge such matters." ¹⁶And he drove them out of the courtroom. ¹⁷The mob had grabbed Sosthenes, the leader of the synagogue, and had beaten him right there in the courtroom. But Gallio paid no attention.

Paul Returns to Antioch of Syria

¹⁸Paul stayed in Corinth for some time after that and then said good-bye to the brothers and sisters* and sailed for the coast of Syria, taking Priscilla and Aquila with him. (Earlier, at Cenchrea, Paul had shaved his head according to Jewish custom, for he had

17:34 Greek an Areopagite.   18:1 Athens and Corinth were major cities in Achaia, the region on the southern end of the Greek peninsula.   18:3 Or leatherworkers.
18:18 Greek brothers; also in 18:27.

taken a vow.) ¹⁹When they arrived at the port of Ephesus, Paul left the others behind. But while he was there, he went to the synagogue to debate with the Jews. ²⁰They asked him to stay longer, but he declined. ²¹So he left, saying, "I will come back later,* God willing." Then he set sail from Ephesus. ²²The next stop was at the port of Caesarea. From there he went up and visited the church at Jerusalem* and then went back to Antioch.

²³After spending some time in Antioch, Paul went back to Galatia and Phrygia, visiting all the believers,* encouraging them and helping them to grow in the Lord.

Apollos Instructed at Ephesus

²⁴Meanwhile, a Jew named Apollos, an eloquent speaker who knew the Scriptures well, had just arrived in Ephesus from Alexandria in Egypt. ²⁵He had been taught the way of the Lord and talked to others with great enthusiasm and accuracy about Jesus. However, he knew only about John's baptism. ²⁶When Priscilla and Aquila heard him preaching boldly in the synagogue, they took him aside and explained the way of God more accurately.

²⁷Apollos had been thinking about going to Achaia, and the brothers and sisters in Ephesus encouraged him in this. They wrote to the believers in Achaia, asking them to welcome him. When he arrived there, he proved to be of great benefit to those who, by God's grace, had believed. ²⁸He refuted all the Jews with powerful arguments in public debate. Using the Scriptures, he explained to them, "The Messiah you are looking for is Jesus."

CHAPTER 19

Paul's Third Missionary Journey

While Apollos was in Corinth, Paul traveled through the interior provinces. Finally, he came to Ephesus, where he found several believers.* ²"Did you receive the Holy Spirit when you believed?" he asked them.

"No," they replied, "we don't know what you mean. We haven't even heard that there is a Holy Spirit."

³"Then what baptism did you experience?" he asked.

And they replied, "The baptism of John."

⁴Paul said, "John's baptism was to demonstrate a desire to turn from sin and turn to God. John himself told the people to believe in Jesus, the one John said would come later."

⁵As soon as they heard this, they were baptized in the name of the Lord Jesus. ⁶Then when Paul laid his hands on them, the Holy Spirit came on them, and they spoke in other tongues and prophesied. ⁷There were about twelve men in all.

Paul Ministers in Ephesus

⁸Then Paul went to the synagogue and preached boldly for the next three months, arguing persuasively about the Kingdom of God. ⁹But some rejected his message and publicly spoke against the Way, so Paul left the synagogue and took the believers with him. Then he began preaching daily at the lecture hall of Tyrannus. ¹⁰This went on for the next two years, so that people throughout the province of Asia—both Jews and Greeks—heard the Lord's message.

18:21 Some manuscripts read *"I must by all means be at Jerusalem for the upcoming festival, but I will come back later."* 18:22 Greek *the church.* 18:23 Greek *disciples;* also in 18:27. 19:1 Greek *disciples;* also in 19:9, 30.

¹¹God gave Paul the power to do unusual miracles, ¹²so that even when handkerchiefs, or cloths that had touched his skin were placed on sick people, they were healed of their diseases, and any evil spirits within them came out.

¹³A team of Jews who were traveling from town to town casting out evil spirits tried to use the name of the Lord Jesus. The incantation they used was this: "I command you by Jesus, whom Paul preaches, to come out!" ¹⁴Seven sons of Sceva, a leading priest, were doing this. ¹⁵But when they tried it on a man possessed by an evil spirit, the spirit replied, "I know Jesus, and I know Paul. But who are you?" ¹⁶And he leaped on them and attacked them with such violence that they fled from the house, naked and badly injured.

¹⁷The story of what happened spread quickly all through Ephesus, to Jews and Greeks alike. A solemn fear descended on the city, and the name of the Lord Jesus was greatly honored. ¹⁸Many who became believers confessed their sinful practices. ¹⁹A number of them who had been practicing magic brought their incantation books and burned them at a public bonfire. The value of the books was several million dollars.* ²⁰So the message about the Lord spread widely and had a powerful effect.

The Riot in Ephesus

²¹Afterward Paul felt impelled by the Holy Spirit* to go over to Macedonia and Achaia before returning to Jerusalem. "And after that," he said, "I must go on to Rome!" ²²He sent his two assistants, Timothy and Erastus, on ahead to Macedonia while he stayed awhile longer in the province of Asia.

²³But about that time, serious trouble developed in Ephesus concerning the Way. ²⁴It began with Demetrius, a silversmith who had a large business manufacturing silver shrines of the Greek goddess Artemis.* He kept many craftsmen busy. ²⁵He called the craftsmen together, along with others employed in related trades, and addressed them as follows:

"Gentlemen, you know that our wealth comes from this business. ²⁶As you have seen and heard, this man Paul has persuaded many people that handmade gods aren't gods at all. And this is happening not only here in Ephesus but throughout the entire province! ²⁷Of course, I'm not just talking about the loss of public respect for our business. I'm also concerned that the temple of the great goddess Artemis will lose its influence and that Artemis—this magnificent goddess worshiped throughout the province of Asia and all around the world—will be robbed of her prestige!"

²⁸At this their anger boiled, and they began shouting, "Great is Artemis of the Ephesians!" ²⁹A crowd began to gather, and soon the city was filled with confusion. Everyone rushed to the amphitheater, dragging along Gaius and Aristarchus, who were Paul's traveling companions from Macedonia. ³⁰Paul wanted to go in, but the believers wouldn't let him. ³¹Some of the officials of the province, friends of Paul, also sent a message to him, begging him not to risk his life by entering the amphitheater.

³²Inside, the people were all shouting, some one thing and some another. Everything was in confusion. In fact, most of them didn't

19:19 Greek *50,000 pieces of silver*, each of which was the equivalent of a day's wage. **19:21** Or *purposed in his spirit.* **19:24** *Artemis* is otherwise known as Diana.

even know why they were there. ³³Alexander was thrust forward by some of the Jews, who encouraged him to explain the situation. He motioned for silence and tried to speak in defense. ³⁴But when the crowd realized he was a Jew, they started shouting again and kept it up for two hours: "Great is Artemis of the Ephesians! Great is Artemis of the Ephesians!"

³⁵At last the mayor was able to quiet them down enough to speak. "Citizens of Ephesus," he said. "Everyone knows that Ephesus is the official guardian of the temple of the great Artemis, whose image fell down to us from heaven. ³⁶Since this is an indisputable fact, you shouldn't be disturbed, no matter what is said. Don't do anything rash. ³⁷You have brought these men here, but they have stolen nothing from the temple and have not spoken against our goddess. ³⁸If Demetrius and the craftsmen have a case against them, the courts are in session and the judges can take the case at once. Let them go through legal channels. ³⁹And if there are complaints about other matters, they can be settled in a legal assembly. ⁴⁰I am afraid we are in danger of being charged with rioting by the Roman government, since there is no cause for all this commotion. And if Rome demands an explanation, we won't know what to say." ⁴¹Then he dismissed them, and they dispersed.

CHAPTER 20

Paul Goes to Macedonia and Greece

When it was all over, Paul sent for the believers* and encouraged them. Then he said good-bye and left for Macedonia. ²Along the way, he encouraged the believers in all the towns he passed through. Then he traveled down to Greece, ³where he stayed for three months. He was preparing to sail back to Syria when he discovered a plot by some Jews against his life, so he decided to return through Macedonia.

⁴Several men were traveling with him. They were Sopater of Berea, the son of Pyrrhus; Aristarchus and Secundus, from Thessalonica; Gaius, from Derbe; Timothy; and Tychicus and Trophimus, who were from the province of Asia. ⁵They went ahead and waited for us at Troas. ⁶As soon as the Passover season* ended, we boarded a ship at Philippi in Macedonia and five days later arrived in Troas, where we stayed a week.

Paul's Final Visit to Troas

⁷On the first day of the week, we gathered to observe the Lord's Supper.* Paul was preaching; and since he was leaving the next day, he talked until midnight. ⁸The upstairs room where we met was lighted with many flickering lamps. ⁹As Paul spoke on and on, a young man named Eutychus, sitting on the windowsill, became very drowsy. Finally, he sank into a deep sleep and fell three stories to his death below. ¹⁰Paul went down, bent over him, and took him into his arms. "Don't worry," he said, "he's alive!" ¹¹Then they all went back upstairs and ate the Lord's Supper together.* And Paul continued talking to them until dawn; then he left. ¹²Meanwhile, the young man was taken home unhurt, and everyone was greatly relieved.

20:1 Greek *disciples.* **20:6** Greek *the days of unleavened bread.* **20:7** Greek *to break bread.* **20:11** Greek *broke the bread.*

Paul Meets the Ephesian Elders

13Paul went by land to Assos, where he had arranged for us to join him, and we went on ahead by ship. 14He joined us there and we sailed together to Mitylene. 15The next day we passed the island of Kios. The following day, we crossed to the island of Samos. And a day later we arrived at Miletus.

16Paul had decided against stopping at Ephesus this time because he didn't want to spend further time in the province of Asia. He was hurrying to get to Jerusalem, if possible, for the Festival of Pentecost. 17But when we landed at Miletus, he sent a message to the elders of the church at Ephesus, asking them to come down to meet him.

18When they arrived he declared, "You know that from the day I set foot in the province of Asia until now 19I have done the Lord's work humbly—yes, and with tears. I have endured the trials that came to me from the plots of the Jews. 20Yet I never shrank from telling you the truth, either publicly or in your homes. 21I have had one message for Jews and Gentiles alike—the necessity of turning from sin and turning to God, and of faith in our Lord Jesus.

22"And now I am going to Jerusalem, drawn there irresistibly by the Holy Spirit,* not knowing what awaits me, 23except that the Holy Spirit has told me in city after city that jail and suffering lie ahead. 24But my life is worth nothing unless I use it for doing the work assigned me by the Lord Jesus—the work of telling others the Good News about God's wonderful kindness and love.

25"And now I know that none of you to whom I have preached the Kingdom will ever see me again. 26Let me say plainly that I have been faithful. No one's damnation can be blamed on me,* 27for I didn't shrink from declaring all that God wants for you.

28"And now beware! Be sure that you feed and shepherd God's flock—his church, purchased with his blood—over whom the Holy Spirit has appointed you as elders.* 29I know full well that false teachers, like vicious wolves, will come in among you after I leave, not sparing the flock. 30Even some of you will distort the truth in order to draw a following. 31Watch out! Remember the three years I was with you—my constant watch and care over you night and day, and my many tears for you.

32"And now I entrust you to God and the word of his grace—his message that is able to build you up and give you an inheritance with all those he has set apart for himself.

33"I have never coveted anyone's money or fine clothing. 34You know that these hands of mine have worked to pay my own way, and I have even supplied the needs of those who were with me. 35And I have been a constant example of how you can help the poor by working hard. You should remember the words of the Lord Jesus: 'It is more blessed to give than to receive.' "

36When he had finished speaking, he knelt and prayed with them. 37They wept aloud as they embraced him in farewell, 38sad most of all because he had said that they would never see him again. Then they accompanied him down to the ship.

20:22 Or *by my spirit, or by an inner compulsion;* Greek reads *by the spirit.*   20:26 Greek *I am innocent of the blood of all.*   20:28 Greek *overseers.*

CHAPTER 21

Paul's Journey to Jerusalem

After saying farewell to the Ephesian elders, we sailed straight to the island of Cos. The next day we reached Rhodes and then went to Patara. ²There we boarded a ship sailing for the Syrian province of Phoenicia. ³We sighted the island of Cyprus, passed it on our left, and landed at the harbor of Tyre, in Syria, where the ship was to unload. ⁴We went ashore, found the local believers,* and stayed with them a week. These disciples prophesied through the Holy Spirit that Paul should not go on to Jerusalem. ⁵When we returned to the ship at the end of the week, the entire congregation, including wives and children, came down to the shore with us. There we knelt, prayed, ⁶and said our farewells. Then we went aboard, and they returned home.

⁷The next stop after leaving Tyre was Ptolemais, where we greeted the brothers and sisters* but stayed only one day. ⁸We then went on to Caesarea and stayed at the home of Philip the Evangelist, one of the seven men who had been chosen to distribute food. ⁹He had four unmarried daughters who had the gift of prophecy.

¹⁰During our stay of several days, a man named Agabus, who also had the gift of prophecy, arrived from Judea. ¹¹When he visited us, he took Paul's belt and bound his own feet and hands with it. Then he said, "The Holy Spirit declares, 'So shall the owner of this belt be bound by the Jewish leaders in Jerusalem and turned over to the Romans.'" ¹²When we heard this, we who were traveling with him, as well as the local believers, begged Paul not to go on to Jerusalem.

¹³But he said, "Why all this weeping? You are breaking my heart! For I am ready not only to be jailed at Jerusalem but also to die for the sake of the Lord Jesus." ¹⁴When it was clear that we couldn't persuade him, we gave up and said, "The will of the Lord be done."

Paul Arrives at Jerusalem

¹⁵Shortly afterward we packed our things and left for Jerusalem. ¹⁶Some believers from Caesarea accompanied us, and they took us to the home of Mnason, a man originally from Cyprus and one of the early disciples. ¹⁷All the brothers and sisters in Jerusalem welcomed us cordially.

¹⁸The next day Paul went in with us to meet with James, and all the elders of the Jerusalem church were present. ¹⁹After greetings were exchanged, Paul gave a detailed account of the things God had accomplished among the Gentiles through his ministry.

²⁰After hearing this, they praised God. But then they said, "You know, dear brother, how many thousands of Jews have also believed, and they all take the law of Moses very seriously. ²¹Our Jewish Christians here at Jerusalem have been told that you are teaching all the Jews living in the Gentile world to turn their backs on the laws of Moses. They say that you teach people not to circumcise their children or follow other Jewish customs. ²²Now what can be done? For they will certainly hear that you have come.

²³"Here's our suggestion. We have four men here who have taken a vow and are preparing to shave their heads. ²⁴Go with them to the Temple and join them in the purification ceremony, and pay for

21:4 Greek *disciples*; also in 21:16. 21:7 Greek *brothers*; also in 21:17.

them to have their heads shaved. Then everyone will know that the rumors are all false and that you yourself observe the Jewish laws.

25"As for the Gentile Christians, all we ask of them is what we already told them in a letter: They should not eat food offered to idols, nor consume blood, nor eat meat from strangled animals, and they should stay away from all sexual immorality."

Paul Is Arrested

26So Paul agreed to their request, and the next day he went through the purification ritual with the men and went to the Temple. Then he publicly announced the date when their vows would end and sacrifices would be offered for each of them.

27The seven days were almost ended when some Jews from the province of Asia saw Paul in the Temple and roused a mob against him. They grabbed him, 28yelling, "Men of Israel! Help! This is the man who teaches against our people and tells everybody to disobey the Jewish laws. He speaks against the Temple—and he even defiles it by bringing Gentiles in!" 29(For earlier that day they had seen him in the city with Trophimus, a Gentile from Ephesus,* and they assumed Paul had taken him into the Temple.)

30The whole population of the city was rocked by these accusations, and a great riot followed. Paul was dragged out of the Temple, and immediately the gates were closed behind him. 31As they were trying to kill him, word reached the commander of the Roman regiment that all Jerusalem was in an uproar. 32He immediately called out his soldiers and officers and ran down among the crowd. When the mob saw the commander and the troops coming, they stopped beating Paul. 33The commander arrested him and ordered him bound with two chains. Then he asked the crowd who he was and what he had done. 34Some shouted one thing and some another. He couldn't find out the truth in all the uproar and confusion, so he ordered Paul to be taken to the fortress. 35As they reached the stairs, the mob grew so violent the soldiers had to lift Paul to their shoulders to protect him. 36And the crowd followed behind shouting, "Kill him, kill him!"

Paul Speaks to the Crowd

37As Paul was about to be taken inside, he said to the commander, "May I have a word with you?"

"Do you know Greek?" the commander asked, surprised. 38"Aren't you the Egyptian who led a rebellion some time ago and took four thousand members of the Assassins out into the desert?"

39"No," Paul replied, "I am a Jew from Tarsus in Cilicia, which is an important city. Please, let me talk to these people." 40The commander agreed, so Paul stood on the stairs and motioned to the people to be quiet. Soon a deep silence enveloped the crowd, and he addressed them in their own language, Aramaic.*

CHAPTER 22

"Brothers and esteemed fathers," Paul said, "listen to me as I offer my defense." 2When they heard him speaking in their own language,* the silence was even greater. 3"I am a Jew, born in Tarsus, a city in Cilicia, and I was brought up and educated here in

21:29 Greek *Trophimus, the Ephesian.* 21:40 Or *Hebrew.* 22:2 Greek *in Aramaic.*

Jerusalem under Gamaliel. At his feet I learned to follow our Jewish laws and customs very carefully. I became very zealous to honor God in everything I did, just as all of you are today. 4And I persecuted the followers of the Way, hounding some to death, binding and delivering both men and women to prison. 5The high priest and the whole council of leaders can testify that this is so. For I received letters from them to our Jewish brothers in Damascus, authorizing me to bring the Christians from there to Jerusalem, in chains, to be punished.

6"As I was on the road, nearing Damascus, about noon a very bright light from heaven suddenly shone around me. 7I fell to the ground and heard a voice saying to me, 'Saul, Saul, why are you persecuting me?'

8" 'Who are you, sir?' I asked. And he replied, 'I am Jesus of Nazareth, the one you are persecuting.' 9The people with me saw the light but didn't hear the voice.

10"I said, 'What shall I do, Lord?' And the Lord told me, 'Get up and go into Damascus, and there you will be told all that you are to do.'

11"I was blinded by the intense light and had to be led into Damascus by my companions. 12A man named Ananias lived there. He was a godly man in his devotion to the law, and he was well thought of by all the Jews of Damascus. 13He came to me and stood beside me and said, 'Brother Saul, receive your sight.' And that very hour I could see him!

14"Then he told me, 'The God of our ancestors has chosen you to know his will and to see the Righteous One and hear him speak. 15You are to take his message everywhere, telling the whole world what you have seen and heard. 16And now, why delay? Get up and be baptized, and have your sins washed away, calling on the name of the Lord.'

17"One day after I returned to Jerusalem, I was praying in the Temple, and I fell into a trance. 18I saw a vision of Jesus saying to me, 'Hurry! Leave Jerusalem, for the people here won't believe you when you give them your testimony about me.'

19" 'But Lord,' I argued, 'they certainly know that I imprisoned and beat those in every synagogue who believed on you. 20And when your witness Stephen was killed, I was standing there agreeing. I kept the coats they laid aside as they stoned him.'

21"But the Lord said to me, 'Leave Jerusalem, for I will send you far away to the Gentiles!' "

22The crowd listened until Paul came to that word; then with one voice they shouted, "Away with such a fellow! Kill him! He isn't fit to live!" 23They yelled, threw off their coats, and tossed handfuls of dust into the air.

Paul Reveals His Roman Citizenship

24The commander brought Paul inside and ordered him lashed with whips to make him confess his crime. He wanted to find out why the crowd had become so furious. 25As they tied Paul down to lash him, Paul said to the officer standing there, "Is it legal for you to whip a Roman citizen who hasn't even been tried?"

26The officer went to the commander and asked, "What are you doing? This man is a Roman citizen!"

²⁷So the commander went over and asked Paul, "Tell me, are you a Roman citizen?"

"Yes, I certainly am," Paul replied.

²⁸"I am, too," the commander muttered, "and it cost me plenty!"

"But I am a citizen by birth!"

²⁹The soldiers who were about to interrogate Paul quickly withdrew when they heard he was a Roman citizen, and the commander was frightened because he had ordered him bound and whipped.

Paul before the High Council

³⁰The next day the commander freed Paul from his chains and ordered the leading priests into session with the Jewish high council.* He had Paul brought in before them to try to find out what the trouble was all about.

CHAPTER 23

Gazing intently at the high council,* Paul began: "Brothers, I have always lived before God in all good conscience!"

²Instantly Ananias the high priest commanded those close to Paul to slap him on the mouth. ³But Paul said to him, "God will slap you, you whitewashed wall! What kind of judge are you to break the law yourself by ordering me struck like that?"

⁴Those standing near Paul said to him, "Is that the way to talk to God's high priest?"

⁵"I'm sorry, brothers. I didn't realize he was the high priest," Paul replied, "for the Scriptures say, 'Do not speak evil of anyone who rules over you.'*"

⁶Paul realized that some members of the high council were Sadducees and some were Pharisees, so he shouted, "Brothers, I am a Pharisee, as were all my ancestors! And I am on trial because my hope is in the resurrection of the dead!"

⁷This divided the council—the Pharisees against the Sadducees—⁸for the Sadducees say there is no resurrection or angels or spirits, but the Pharisees believe in all of these. ⁹So a great clamor arose. Some of the teachers of religious law who were Pharisees jumped up to argue that Paul was all right. "We see nothing wrong with him," they shouted. "Perhaps a spirit or an angel spoke to him." ¹⁰The shouting grew louder and louder, and the men were tugging at Paul from both sides, pulling him this way and that. Finally, the commander, fearing they would tear him apart, ordered his soldiers to take him away from them and bring him back to the fortress.

¹¹That night the Lord appeared to Paul and said, "Be encouraged, Paul. Just as you have told the people about me here in Jerusalem, you must preach the Good News in Rome."

The Plan to Kill Paul

¹²The next morning a group of Jews got together and bound themselves with an oath to neither eat nor drink until they had killed Paul. ¹³There were more than forty of them. ¹⁴They went to the leading priests and other leaders and told them what they had done. "We have bound ourselves under oath to neither eat nor

22:30 Greek *Sanhedrin*.   23:1 Greek *Sanhedrin*; also in 23:6, 15, 20, 28.
23:5 Exod 22:28.

drink until we have killed Paul. [15] You and the high council should tell the commander to bring Paul back to the council again," they requested. "Pretend you want to examine his case more fully. We will kill him on the way."

[16] But Paul's nephew heard of their plan and went to the fortress and told Paul. [17] Paul called one of the officers and said, "Take this young man to the commander. He has something important to tell him."

[18] So the officer did, explaining, "Paul, the prisoner, called me over and asked me to bring this young man to you because he has something to tell you."

[19] The commander took him by the arm, led him aside, and asked, "What is it you want to tell me?"

[20] Paul's nephew told him, "Some Jews are going to ask you to bring Paul before the Jewish high council tomorrow, pretending they want to get some more information. [21] But don't do it! There are more than forty men hiding along the way ready to jump him and kill him. They have vowed not to eat or drink until they kill him. They are ready, expecting you to agree to their request."

[22] "Don't let a soul know you told me this," the commander warned the young man as he sent him away.

Paul Is Sent to Caesarea

[23] Then the commander called two of his officers and ordered, "Get two hundred soldiers ready to leave for Caesarea at nine o'clock tonight. Also take two hundred spearmen and seventy horsemen. [24] Provide horses for Paul to ride, and get him safely to Governor Felix." [25] Then he wrote this letter to the governor:

[26] "From Claudius Lysias, to his Excellency, Governor Felix. Greetings! [27] This man was seized by some Jews, and they were about to kill him when I arrived with the troops. When I learned that he was a Roman citizen, I removed him to safety. [28] Then I took him to their high council to try to find out what he had done. [29] I soon discovered it was something regarding their religious law—certainly nothing worthy of imprisonment or death. [30] But when I was informed of a plot to kill him, I immediately sent him on to you. I have told his accusers to bring their charges before you."

[31] So that night, as ordered, the soldiers took Paul as far as Antipatris. [32] They returned to the fortress the next morning, while the horsemen took him on to Caesarea. [33] When they arrived in Caesarea, they presented Paul and the letter to Governor Felix. [34] He read it and then asked Paul what province he was from. "Cilicia," Paul answered.

[35] "I will hear your case myself when your accusers arrive," the governor told him. Then the governor ordered him kept in the prison at Herod's headquarters.

CHAPTER 24

Paul Appears before Felix

Five days later Ananias, the high priest, arrived with some of the Jewish leaders and the lawyer* Tertullus, to press charges against

24:1 Greek *some elders and an orator.*

Paul. ²When Paul was called in, Tertullus laid charges against Paul in the following address to the governor:

"Your Excellency, you have given peace to us Jews and have enacted reforms for us. ³And for all of this we are very grateful to you. ⁴But lest I bore you, kindly give me your attention for only a moment as I briefly outline our case against this man. ⁵For we have found him to be a troublemaker, a man who is constantly inciting the Jews throughout the world to riots and rebellions against the Roman government. He is a ringleader of the sect known as the Nazarenes. ⁶Moreover he was trying to defile the Temple when we arrested him.* ⁸You can find out the truth of our accusations by examining him yourself." ⁹Then the other Jews chimed in, declaring that everything Tertullus said was true.

¹⁰Now it was Paul's turn. The governor motioned for him to rise and speak. Paul said, "I know, sir, that you have been a judge of Jewish affairs for many years, and this gives me confidence as I make my defense. ¹¹You can quickly discover that it was no more than twelve days ago that I arrived in Jerusalem to worship at the Temple. ¹²I didn't argue with anyone in the Temple, nor did I incite a riot in any synagogue or on the streets of the city. ¹³These men certainly cannot prove the things they accuse me of doing.

¹⁴"But I admit that I follow the Way, which they call a sect. I worship the God of our ancestors, and I firmly believe the Jewish law and everything written in the books of prophecy. ¹⁵I have hope in God, just as these men do, that he will raise both the righteous and the ungodly. ¹⁶Because of this, I always try to maintain a clear conscience before God and everyone else.

¹⁷"After several years away, I returned to Jerusalem with money to aid my people and to offer sacrifices to God. ¹⁸My accusers saw me in the Temple as I was completing a purification ritual. There was no crowd around me and no rioting. ¹⁹But some Jews from the province of Asia were there—and they ought to be here to bring charges if they have anything against me! ²⁰Ask these men here what wrongdoing the Jewish high council* found in me, ²¹except for one thing I said when I shouted out, 'I am on trial before you today because I believe in the resurrection of the dead!'"

²²Felix, who was quite familiar with the Way, adjourned the hearing and said, "Wait until Lysias, the garrison commander, arrives. Then I will decide the case." ²³He ordered an officer to keep Paul in custody but to give him some freedom and allow his friends to visit him and take care of his needs.

²⁴A few days later Felix came with his wife, Drusilla, who was Jewish. Sending for Paul, they listened as he told them about faith in Christ Jesus. ²⁵As he reasoned with them about righteousness and self-control and the judgment to come, Felix was terrified. "Go away for now," he replied. "When it is more convenient, I'll call for you again." ²⁶He also hoped that Paul would bribe him, so he sent for him quite often and talked with him.

²⁷Two years went by in this way; then Felix was succeeded by Porcius Festus. And because Felix wanted to gain favor with the Jewish leaders, he left Paul in prison.

24:6 Some manuscripts add *We would have judged him by our law,* ⁷*but Lysias, the commander of the garrison, came and took him violently away from us,* ⁸*commanding his accusers to come before you.* **24:20** Greek *Sanhedrin.*

CHAPTER 25

Paul Appears before Festus

Three days after Festus arrived in Caesarea to take over his new responsibilities, he left for Jerusalem, ²where the leading priests and other Jewish leaders met with him and made their accusations against Paul. ³They asked Festus as a favor to transfer Paul to Jerusalem. (Their plan was to waylay and kill him.) ⁴But Festus replied that Paul was at Caesarea and he himself would be returning there soon. ⁵So he said, "Those of you in authority can return with me. If Paul has done anything wrong, you can make your accusations."

⁶Eight or ten days later he returned to Caesarea, and on the following day Paul's trial began. ⁷On Paul's arrival in court, the Jewish leaders from Jerusalem gathered around and made many serious accusations they couldn't prove. ⁸Paul denied the charges. "I am not guilty," he said. "I have committed no crime against the Jewish laws or the Temple or the Roman government."

⁹Then Festus, wanting to please the Jews, asked him, "Are you willing to go to Jerusalem and stand trial before me there?"

¹⁰But Paul replied, "No! This is the official Roman court, so I ought to be tried right here. You know very well I am not guilty. ¹¹If I have done something worthy of death, I don't refuse to die. But if I am innocent, neither you nor anyone else has a right to turn me over to these men to kill me. I appeal to Caesar!"

¹²Festus conferred with his advisers and then replied, "Very well! You have appealed to Caesar, and to Caesar you shall go!"

¹³A few days later King Agrippa and his sister, Bernice,* to pay their respects to Festus. ¹⁴During their stay of several days, Festus discussed Paul's case with the king. "There is a prisoner here," he told him, "whose case was left for me by Felix. ¹⁵When I was in Jerusalem, the leading priests and other Jewish leaders pressed charges against him and asked me to sentence him. ¹⁶Of course, I quickly pointed out to them that Roman law does not convict people without a trial. They are given an opportunity to defend themselves face to face with their accusers.

¹⁷"When they came here for the trial, I called the case the very next day and ordered Paul brought in. ¹⁸But the accusations made against him weren't at all what I expected. ¹⁹It was something about their religion and about someone called Jesus who died, but whom Paul insists is alive. ²⁰I was perplexed as to how to conduct an investigation of this kind, and I asked him whether he would be willing to stand trial on these charges in Jerusalem. ²¹But Paul appealed to the emperor. So I ordered him back to jail until I could arrange to send him to Caesar."

²²"I'd like to hear the man myself," Agrippa said.

And Festus replied, "You shall—tomorrow!"

Paul Speaks to Agrippa

²³So the next day Agrippa and Bernice arrived at the auditorium with great pomp, accompanied by military officers and prominent men of the city. Festus ordered that Paul be brought in. ²⁴Then Festus said, "King Agrippa and all present, this is the man whose death is

25:13 Greek *Agrippa the king and Bernice arrived.*

demanded both by the local Jews and by those in Jerusalem. ²⁵But in my opinion he has done nothing worthy of death. However, he appealed his case to the emperor, and I decided to send him. ²⁶But what shall I write the emperor? For there is no real charge against him. So I have brought him before all of you, and especially you, King Agrippa, so that after we examine him, I might have something to write. ²⁷For it doesn't seem reasonable to send a prisoner to the emperor without specifying the charges against him!"

CHAPTER 26

Then Agrippa said to Paul, "You may speak in your defense."

So Paul, with a gesture of his hand, started his defense: ²"I am fortunate, King Agrippa, that you are the one hearing my defense against all these accusations made by the Jewish leaders, ³for I know you are an expert on Jewish customs and controversies. Now please listen to me patiently!

⁴"As the Jewish leaders are well aware, I was given a thorough Jewish training from my earliest childhood among my own people and in Jerusalem. ⁵If they would admit it, they know that I have been a member of the Pharisees, the strictest sect of our religion. ⁶Now I am on trial because I am looking forward to the fulfillment of God's promise made to our ancestors. ⁷In fact, that is why the twelve tribes of Israel worship God night and day, and they share the same hope I have. Yet, O king, they say it is wrong for me to have this hope! ⁸Why does it seem incredible to any of you that God can raise the dead?

⁹"I used to believe that I ought to do everything I could to oppose the followers of Jesus of Nazareth.* ¹⁰Authorized by the leading priests, I caused many of the believers in Jerusalem to be sent to prison. And I cast my vote against them when they were condemned to death. ¹¹Many times I had them whipped in the synagogues to try to get them to curse Christ. I was so violently opposed to them I even hounded them in distant cities of foreign lands.

¹²"One day I was on such a mission to Damascus, armed with the authority and commission of the leading priests. ¹³About noon, Your Majesty, a light from heaven brighter than the sun shone down on me and my companions. ¹⁴We all fell down, and I heard a voice saying to me in Aramaic,* 'Saul, Saul, why are you persecuting me? It is hard for you to fight against my will.*'

¹⁵" 'Who are you, sir?' I asked.

"And the Lord replied, 'I am Jesus, the one you are persecuting. ¹⁶Now stand up! For I have appeared to you to appoint you as my servant and my witness. You are to tell the world about this experience and about other times I will appear to you. ¹⁷And I will protect you from both your own people and the Gentiles. Yes, I am going to send you to the Gentiles, ¹⁸to open their eyes so they may turn from darkness to light, and from the power of Satan to God. Then they will receive forgiveness for their sins and be given a place among God's people, who are set apart by faith in me.'

¹⁹"And so, O King Agrippa, I was not disobedient to that vision from heaven. ²⁰I preached first to those in Damascus, then in Jerusa-

---

26:9 Greek oppose the name of Jesus the Nazarene. 26:14a Or Hebrew. 26:14b Greek It is hard for you to kick against the oxgoads.

lem and throughout all Judea, and also to the Gentiles, that all must turn from their sins and turn to God—and prove they have changed by the good things they do. 21Some Jews arrested me in the Temple for preaching this, and they tried to kill me. 22But God protected me so that I am still alive today to tell these facts to everyone, from the least to the greatest. I teach nothing except what the prophets and Moses said would happen—23that the Messiah would suffer and be the first to rise from the dead as a light to Jews and Gentiles alike."

24Suddenly, Festus shouted, "Paul, you are insane. Too much study has made you crazy!"

25But Paul replied, "I am not insane, Most Excellent Festus. I am speaking the sober truth. 26And King Agrippa knows about these things. I speak frankly, for I am sure these events are all familiar to him, for they were not done in a corner! 27King Agrippa, do you believe the prophets? I know you do—"

28Agrippa interrupted him. "Do you think you can make me a Christian so quickly?"*

29Paul replied, "Whether quickly or not, I pray to God that both you and everyone here in this audience might become the same as I am, except for these chains."

30Then the king, the governor, Bernice, and all the others stood and left. 31As they talked it over they agreed, "This man hasn't done anything worthy of death or imprisonment." 32And Agrippa said to Festus, "He could be set free if he hadn't appealed to Caesar!"

CHAPTER 27

Paul Sails for Rome

When the time came, we set sail for Italy. Paul and several other prisoners were placed in the custody of an army officer named Julius, a captain of the Imperial Regiment. 2And Aristarchus, a Macedonian from Thessalonica, was also with us. We left on a boat whose home port was Adramyttium; it was scheduled to make several stops at ports along the coast of the province of Asia.

3The next day when we docked at Sidon, Julius was very kind to Paul and let him go ashore to visit with friends so they could provide for his needs. 4Putting out to sea from there, we encountered headwinds that made it difficult to keep the ship on course, so we sailed north of Cyprus between the island and the mainland. 5We passed along the coast of the provinces of Cilicia and Pamphylia, landing at Myra, in the province of Lycia. 6There the officer found an Egyptian ship from Alexandria that was bound for Italy, and he put us on board.

7We had several days of rough sailing, and after great difficulty we finally neared Cnidus. But the wind was against us, so we sailed down to the leeward side of Crete, past the cape of Salmone. 8We struggled along the coast with great difficulty and finally arrived at Fair Havens, near the city of Lasea. 9We had lost a lot of time. The weather was becoming dangerous for long voyages by then because it was so late in the fall,* and Paul spoke to the ship's officers about it.

10"Sirs," he said, "I believe there is trouble ahead if we go on—shipwreck, loss of cargo, injuries, and danger to our lives."

26:28 Or "A little more, and your arguments would make me a Christian." 27:9 Greek because the fast was now already gone by. This fast happened on the Day of Atonement (Yom Kippur), which occurred in late September or early October.

[11]But the officer in charge of the prisoners listened more to the ship's captain and the owner than to Paul. [12]And since Fair Havens was an exposed harbor—a poor place to spend the winter—most of the crew wanted to go to Phoenix, farther up the coast of Crete, and spend the winter there. Phoenix was a good harbor with only a southwest and northwest exposure.

The Storm at Sea

[13]When a light wind began blowing from the south, the sailors thought they could make it. So they pulled up anchor and sailed along close to shore. [14]But the weather changed abruptly, and a wind of typhoon strength (a "northeaster," they called it) caught the ship and blew it out to sea. [15]They couldn't turn the ship into the wind, so they gave up and let it run before the gale.

[16]We sailed behind a small island named Cauda,* where with great difficulty we hoisted aboard the lifeboat that was being towed behind us. [17]Then we banded the ship with ropes to strengthen the hull. The sailors were afraid of being driven across to the sandbars of Syrtis off the African coast, so they lowered the sea anchor and were thus driven before the wind.

[18]The next day, as gale-force winds continued to batter the ship, the crew began throwing the cargo overboard. [19]The following day they even threw out the ship's equipment and anything else they could lay their hands on. [20]The terrible storm raged unabated for many days, blotting out the sun and the stars, until at last all hope was gone.

[21]No one had eaten for a long time. Finally, Paul called the crew together and said, "Men, you should have listened to me in the first place and not left Fair Havens. You would have avoided all this injury and loss. [22]But take courage! None of you will lose your lives, even though the ship will go down. [23]For last night an angel of the God to whom I belong and whom I serve stood beside me, [24]and he said, 'Don't be afraid, Paul, for you will surely stand trial before Caesar! What's more, God in his goodness has granted safety to everyone sailing with you.' [25]So take courage! For I believe God. It will be just as he said. [26]But we will be shipwrecked on an island."

The Shipwreck

[27]About midnight on the fourteenth night of the storm, as we were being driven across the Sea of Adria,* the sailors sensed land was near. [28]They took soundings and found the water was only 120 feet deep. A little later they sounded again and found only 90 feet.* [29]At this rate they were afraid we would soon be driven against the rocks along the shore, so they threw out four anchors from the stern and prayed for daylight. [30]Then the sailors tried to abandon the ship; they lowered the lifeboat as though they were going to put anchors from the prow. [31]But Paul said to the commanding officer and the soldiers, "You will all die unless the sailors stay aboard." [32]So the soldiers cut the ropes and let the boat fall off.

[33]As the darkness gave way to the early morning light, Paul begged everyone to eat. "You haven't touched food for two weeks," he said. [34]"Please eat something now for your own good. For not a hair of your heads will perish." [35]Then he took some bread, gave thanks to

27:16 Some manuscripts read *Clauda.*   27:27 The *Sea of Adria* is in the central Mediterranean; it is not to be confused with the Adriatic Sea.   27:28 Greek *20 fathoms . . . 15 fathoms* [37 meters . . . 27 meters].

God before them all, and broke off a piece and ate it. ³⁶Then everyone was encouraged, ³⁷and all 276 of us began eating—for that is the number we had aboard. ³⁸After eating, the crew lightened the ship further by throwing the cargo of wheat overboard.

³⁹When morning dawned, they didn't recognize the coastline, but they saw a bay with a beach and wondered if they could get between the rocks and get the ship safely to shore. ⁴⁰So they cut off the anchors and left them in the sea. Then they lowered the rudders, raised the foresail, and headed toward shore. ⁴¹But the ship hit a shoal and ran aground. The bow of the ship stuck fast, while the stern was repeatedly smashed by the force of the waves and began to break apart.

⁴²The soldiers wanted to kill the prisoners to make sure they didn't swim ashore and escape. ⁴³But the commanding officer wanted to spare Paul, so he didn't let them carry out their plan. Then he ordered all who could swim to jump overboard first and make for land, ⁴⁴and he told the others to try for it on planks and debris from the broken ship. So everyone escaped safely ashore!

CHAPTER 28

Paul on the Island of Malta

Once we were safe on shore, we learned that we were on the island of Malta. ²The people of the island were very kind to us. It was cold and rainy, so they built a fire on the shore to welcome us and warm us.

³As Paul gathered an armful of sticks and was laying them on the fire, a poisonous snake, driven out by the heat, fastened itself onto his hand. ⁴The people of the island saw it hanging there and said to each other, "A murderer, no doubt! Though he escaped the sea, justice will not permit him to live." ⁵But Paul shook off the snake into the fire and was unharmed. ⁶The people waited for him to swell up or suddenly drop dead. But when they had waited a long time and saw no harm come to him, they changed their minds and decided he was a god.

⁷Near the shore where we landed was an estate belonging to Publius, the chief official of the island. He welcomed us courteously and fed us for three days. ⁸As it happened, Publius's father was ill with fever and dysentery. Paul went in and prayed for him, and laying his hands on him, he healed him. ⁹Then all the other sick people on the island came and were cured. ¹⁰As a result we were showered with honors, and when the time came to sail, people put on board all sorts of things we would need for the trip.

Paul Arrives at Rome

¹¹It was three months after the shipwreck that we set sail on another ship that had wintered at the island—an Alexandrian ship with the twin gods* as its figurehead. ¹²Our first stop was Syracuse,* where we stayed three days. ¹³From there we sailed across to Rhegium.* A day later a south wind began blowing, so the following day we sailed up the coast to Puteoli. ¹⁴There we found some believers,* who invited us to stay with them seven days. And so we came to Rome. ¹⁵The brothers and sisters* in Rome had heard we were coming,

28:11 The *twin gods* were the Roman gods Castor and Pollux.   28:12 *Syracuse* was on the island of Sicily.   28:13 *Rhegium* was on the southern tip of Italy.   28:14 Greek *brothers.*   28:15a Greek *brothers.*

and they came to meet us at the Forum* on the Appian Way. Others joined us at The Three Taverns.* When Paul saw them, he thanked God and took courage.

16When we arrived in Rome, Paul was permitted to have his own private lodging, though he was guarded by a soldier.

Paul Preaches at Rome under Guard

17Three days after Paul's arrival, he called together the local Jewish leaders. He said to them, "Brothers, I was arrested in Jerusalem and handed over to the Roman government, even though I had done nothing against our people or the customs of our ancestors. 18The Romans tried me and wanted to release me, for they found no cause for the death sentence. 19But when the Jewish leaders protested the decision, I felt it necessary to appeal to Caesar, even though I had no desire to press charges against my own people. 20I asked you to come here today so we could get acquainted and so I could tell you that I am bound with this chain because I believe that the hope of Israel—the Messiah—has already come."

21They replied, "We have heard nothing against you. We have had no letters from Judea or reports from anyone who has arrived here. 22But we want to hear what you believe, for the only thing we know about these Christians* is that they are denounced everywhere."

23So a time was set, and on that day a large number of people came to Paul's house. He told them about the Kingdom of God and taught them about Jesus from the Scriptures—from the five books of Moses and the books of the prophets. He began lecturing in the morning and went on into the evening. 24Some believed and some didn't. 25But after they had argued back and forth among themselves, they left with this final word from Paul: "The Holy Spirit was right when he said to our ancestors through Isaiah the prophet,

26 'Go and say to my people,
You will hear my words,
     but you will not understand;
you will see what I do,
     but you will not perceive its meaning.
27 For the hearts of these people are hardened,
     and their ears cannot hear,
     and they have closed their eyes—
so their eyes cannot see,
     and their ears cannot hear,
     and their hearts cannot understand,
and they cannot turn to me
     and let me heal them.'*

28So I want you to realize that this salvation from God is also available to the Gentiles, and they will accept it."*

30For the next two years, Paul lived in his own rented house.* He welcomed all who visited him, 31proclaiming the Kingdom of God with all boldness and teaching about the Lord Jesus Christ. And no one tried to stop him.

28:15b *The Forum* was about 43 miles (70 kilometers) from Rome.   **28:15c** *The Three Taverns* was about 35 miles (57 kilometers) from Rome.   **28:22** Greek *this sect.*   **28:26-27** Isa 6:9-10.   **28:28** Some manuscripts add verse 29, *And when he had said these words, the Jews departed, greatly disagreeing with each other.*   **28:30** Or *at his own expense.*

ROMANS

CHAPTER 1

Greetings from Paul

This letter is from Paul, Jesus Christ's slave, chosen by God to be an apostle and sent out to preach his Good News. ²This Good News was promised long ago by God through his prophets in the holy Scriptures. ³It is the Good News about his Son, Jesus, who came as a man, born into King David's royal family line. ⁴And Jesus Christ our Lord was shown to be the Son of God when God powerfully raised him from the dead by means of the Holy Spirit.* ⁵Through Christ, God has given us the privilege and authority to tell Gentiles everywhere what God has done for them, so that they will believe and obey him, bringing glory to his name.

⁶You are among those who have been called to belong to Jesus Christ, ⁷dear friends in Rome. God loves you dearly, and he has called you to be his very own people.

May grace and peace be yours from God our Father and the Lord Jesus Christ.

God's Good News

⁸Let me say first of all that your faith in God is becoming known throughout the world. How I thank God through Jesus Christ for each one of you. ⁹God knows how often I pray for you. Day and night I bring you and your needs in prayer to God, whom I serve with all my heart* by telling others the Good News about his Son.

¹⁰One of the things I always pray for is the opportunity, God willing, to come at last to see you. ¹¹For I long to visit you so I can share a spiritual blessing with you that will help you grow strong in the Lord. ¹²I'm eager to encourage you in your faith, but I also want to be encouraged by yours. In this way, each of us will be a blessing to the other.

¹³I want you to know, dear brothers and sisters,* that I planned many times to visit you, but I was prevented until now. I want to work among you and see good results, just as I have done among other Gentiles. ¹⁴For I have a great sense of obligation to people in our culture and to people in other cultures,* to the educated and uneducated alike. ¹⁵So I am eager to come to you in Rome, too, to preach God's Good News.

¹⁶For I am not ashamed of this Good News about Christ. It is the power of God at work, saving everyone who believes—Jews first and also Gentiles. ¹⁷This Good News tells us how God makes us right in his sight. This is accomplished from start to finish by faith. As the Scriptures say, "It is through faith that a righteous person has life."*

1:4 Or *the Spirit of holiness.*   1:9 Or *in my spirit.*   1:13 Greek *brothers.*   1:14 Greek *to Greeks and to barbarians.*   1:17 Hab 2:4.

God's Anger at Sin

18But God shows his anger from heaven against all sinful, wicked people who push the truth away from themselves.* 19For the truth about God is known to them instinctively.* God has put this knowledge in their hearts. 20From the time the world was created, people have seen the earth and sky and all that God made. They can clearly see his invisible qualities—his eternal power and divine nature. So they have no excuse whatsoever for not knowing God.

21Yes, they knew God, but they wouldn't worship him as God or even give him thanks. And they began to think up foolish ideas of what God was like. The result was that their minds became dark and confused. 22Claiming to be wise, they became utter fools instead. 23And instead of worshiping the glorious, ever-living God, they worshiped idols made to look like mere people, or birds and animals and snakes.

24So God let them go ahead and do whatever shameful things their hearts desired. As a result, they did vile and degrading things with each other's bodies. 25Instead of believing what they knew was the truth about God, they deliberately chose to believe lies. So they worshiped the things God made but not the Creator himself, who is to be praised forever. Amen.

26That is why God abandoned them to their shameful desires. Even the women turned against the natural way to have sex and instead indulged in sex with each other. 27And the men, instead of having normal sexual relationships with women, burned with lust for each other. Men did shameful things with other men and, as a result, suffered within themselves the penalty they so richly deserved.

28When they refused to acknowledge God, he abandoned them to their evil minds and let them do things that should never be done. 29Their lives became full of every kind of wickedness, sin, greed, hate, envy, murder, fighting, deception, malicious behavior, and gossip. 30They are backstabbers, haters of God, insolent, proud, and boastful. They are forever inventing new ways of sinning and are disobedient to their parents. 31They refuse to understand, break their promises, and are heartless and unforgiving. 32They are fully aware of God's death penalty for those who do these things, yet they go right ahead and do them anyway. And, worse yet, they encourage others to do them, too.

CHAPTER 2

God's Judgment of Sin

You may be saying, "What terrible people you have been talking about!" But you are just as bad, and you have no excuse! When you say they are wicked and should be punished, you are condemning yourself, for you do these very same things. 2And we know that God, in his justice, will punish anyone who does such things. 3Do you think that God will judge and condemn others for doing them and not judge you when you do them, too? 4Don't you realize how kind, tolerant, and patient God is with you? Or don't you care? Can't you see how kind he has been in giving you time to turn from your sin?

5But no, you won't listen. So you are storing up terrible punish-

1:18 Or *who prevent the truth from being known.*   1:19 Greek *is manifest in them.*

ment for yourself because of your stubbornness in refusing to turn from your sin. For there is going to come a day of judgment when God, the just judge of all the world, [6]will judge all people according to what they have done. [7]He will give eternal life to those who persist in doing what is good, seeking after the glory and honor and immortality that God offers. [8]But he will pour out his anger and wrath on those who live for themselves, who refuse to obey the truth and practice evil deeds. [9]There will be trouble and calamity for everyone who keeps on sinning—for the Jew first and also for the Gentile. [10]But there will be glory and honor and peace from God for all who do good—for the Jew first and also for the Gentile. [11]For God does not show favoritism.

[12]God will punish the Gentiles when they sin, even though they never had God's written law. And he will punish the Jews when they sin, for they do have the law. [13]For it is not merely knowing the law that brings God's approval. Those who obey the law will be declared right in God's sight. [14]Even when Gentiles, who do not have God's written law, instinctively follow what the law says, they show that in their hearts they know right from wrong. [15]They demonstrate that God's law is written within them, for their own consciences either accuse them or tell them they are doing what is right. [16]The day will surely come when God, by Jesus Christ, will judge everyone's secret life. This is my message.

The Jews and the Law

[17]If you are a Jew, you are relying on God's law for your special relationship with him. You boast that all is well between yourself and God. [18]Yes, you know what he wants; you know right from wrong because you have been taught his law. [19]You are convinced that you are a guide for the blind and a beacon light for people who are lost in darkness without God. [20]You think you can instruct the ignorant and teach children the ways of God. For you are certain that in God's law you have complete knowledge and truth.

[21]Well then, if you teach others, why don't you teach yourself? You tell others not to steal, but do you steal? [22]You say it is wrong to commit adultery, but do you do it? You condemn idolatry, but do you steal from pagan temples? [23]You are so proud of knowing the law, but you dishonor God by breaking it. [24]No wonder the Scriptures say, "The world blasphemes the name of God because of you."*

[25]The Jewish ceremony of circumcision is worth something only if you obey God's law. But if you don't obey God's law, you are no better off than an uncircumcised Gentile. [26]And if the Gentiles obey God's law, won't God give them all the rights and honors of being his own people? [27]In fact, uncircumcised Gentiles who keep God's law will be much better off than you Jews who are circumcised and know so much about God's law but don't obey it.

[28]For you are not a true Jew just because you were born of Jewish parents or because you have gone through the Jewish ceremony of circumcision. [29]No, a true Jew is one whose heart is right with God. And true circumcision is not a cutting of the body but a change of

2:24 Isa 52:5.

heart produced by God's Spirit. Whoever has that kind of change seeks praise from God, not from people.

CHAPTER 3
God Remains Faithful

Then what's the advantage of being a Jew? Is there any value in the Jewish ceremony of circumcision? [2] Yes, being a Jew has many advantages. First of all, the Jews were entrusted with the whole revelation of God.*

[3] True, some of them were unfaithful; but just because they broke their promises, does that mean God will break his promises? [4] Of course not! Though everyone else in the world is a liar, God is true. As the Scriptures say, "He will be proved right in what he says, and he will win his case in court."*

[5] "But," some say, "our sins serve a good purpose, for people will see God's goodness when he declares us sinners to be innocent. Isn't it unfair, then, for God to punish us?" (That is actually the way some people talk.) [6] Of course not! If God is not just, how is he qualified to judge the world? [7] "But," some might still argue, "how can God judge and condemn me as a sinner if my dishonesty highlights his truthfulness and brings him more glory?" [8] If you follow that kind of thinking, however, you might as well say that the more we sin the better it is! Those who say such things deserve to be condemned, yet some slander me by saying this is what I preach!

All People Are Sinners

[9] Well then, are we Jews better than others?* No, not at all, for we have already shown that all people, whether Jews or Gentiles, are under the power of sin. [10] As the Scriptures say,

"No one is good—
not even one.
[11] No one has real understanding;
no one is seeking God.
[12] All have turned away from God;
all have gone wrong.
No one does good,
not even one."*
[13] "Their talk is foul, like the stench from an open grave.
Their speech is filled with lies."
"The poison of a deadly snake drips from their lips."*
[14] "Their mouths are full of cursing and bitterness."*
[15] "They are quick to commit murder.
[16] Wherever they go, destruction and misery follow them.
[17] They do not know what true peace is."*
[18] "They have no fear of God to restrain them."*

[19] Obviously, the law applies to those to whom it was given, for its purpose is to keep people from having excuses and to bring the entire world into judgment before God. [20] For no one can ever be made right in God's sight by doing what his law commands. For

3:2 Greek *the oracles of God.* 3:4 Ps 51:4. 3:9 Greek *Are we better?* 3:10-12 Pss 14:1-3; 53:1-3. 3:13 Pss 5:9; 140:3. 3:14 Ps 10:7. 3:15-17 Isa 59:7-8. 3:18 Ps 36:1.

the more we know God's law, the clearer it becomes that we aren't obeying it.

Christ Took Our Punishment

21But now God has shown us a different way of being right in his sight—not by obeying the law but by the way promised in the Scriptures long ago. 22We are made right in God's sight when we trust in Jesus Christ to take away our sins. And we all can be saved in this same way, no matter who we are or what we have done.

23For all have sinned; all fall short of God's glorious standard. 24Yet now God in his gracious kindness declares us not guilty. He has done this through Christ Jesus, who has freed us by taking away our sins. 25For God sent Jesus to take the punishment for our sins and to satisfy God's anger against us. We are made right with God when we believe that Jesus shed his blood, sacrificing his life for us. God was being entirely fair and just when he did not punish those who sinned in former times. 26And he is entirely fair and just in this present time when he declares sinners to be right in his sight because they believe in Jesus.

27Can we boast, then, that we have done anything to be accepted by God? No, because our acquittal is not based on our good deeds. It is based on our faith. 28So we are made right with God through faith and not by obeying the law.

29After all, God is not the God of the Jews only, is he? Isn't he also the God of the Gentiles? Of course he is. 30There is only one God, and there is only one way of being accepted by him. He makes people right with himself only by faith, whether they are Jews or Gentiles. 31Well then, if we emphasize faith, does this mean that we can forget about the law? Of course not! In fact, only when we have faith do we truly fulfill the law.

C H A P T E R 4

The Faith of Abraham

Abraham was, humanly speaking, the founder of our Jewish nation. What were his experiences concerning this question of being saved by faith? 2Was it because of his good deeds that God accepted him? If so, he would have had something to boast about. But from God's point of view Abraham had no basis at all for pride. 3For the Scriptures tell us, "Abraham believed God, so God declared him to be righteous."*

4When people work, their wages are not a gift. Workers earn what they receive. 5But people are declared righteous because of their faith, not because of their work.

6King David spoke of this, describing the happiness of an undeserving sinner who is declared to be righteous:

7 "Oh, what joy for those whose disobedience is forgiven,
  whose sins are put out of sight.
8 Yes, what joy for those
  whose sin is no longer counted against them by the Lord."*

9Now then, is this blessing only for the Jews, or is it for Gentiles, too? Well, what about Abraham? We have been saying he was declared righteous by God because of his faith. 10But how did his

4:3 Gen 15:6.   4:7-8 Ps 32:1-2.

faith help him? Was he declared righteous only after he had been circumcised, or was it before he was circumcised? The answer is that God accepted him first, and then he was circumcised later!

¹¹The circumcision ceremony was a sign that Abraham already had faith and that God had already accepted him and declared him to be righteous—even before he was circumcised. So Abraham is the spiritual father of those who have faith but have not been circumcised. They are made right with God by faith. ¹²And Abraham is also the spiritual father of those who have been circumcised, but only if they have the same kind of faith Abraham had before he was circumcised.

¹³It is clear, then, that God's promise to give the whole earth to Abraham and his descendants was not based on obedience to God's law, but on the new relationship with God that comes by faith. ¹⁴So if you claim that God's promise is for those who obey God's law and think they are "good enough" in God's sight, then you are saying that faith is useless. And in that case, the promise is also meaningless. ¹⁵But the law brings punishment on those who try to obey it. (The only way to avoid breaking the law is to have no law to break!)

¹⁶So that's why faith is the key! God's promise is given to us as a free gift. And we are certain to receive it, whether or not we follow Jewish customs, if we have faith like Abraham's. For Abraham is the father of all who believe. ¹⁷That is what the Scriptures mean when God told him, "I have made you the father of many nations."* This happened because Abraham believed in the God who brings the dead back to life and who brings into existence what didn't exist before.

¹⁸When God promised Abraham that he would become the father of many nations, Abraham believed him. God had also said, "Your descendants will be as numerous as the stars,"* even though such a promise seemed utterly impossible! ¹⁹And Abraham's faith did not weaken, even though he knew that he was too old to be a father at the age of one hundred and that Sarah, his wife, had never been able to have children.

²⁰Abraham never wavered in believing God's promise. In fact, his faith grew stronger, and in this he brought glory to God. ²¹He was absolutely convinced that God was able to do anything he promised. ²²And because of Abraham's faith, God declared him to be righteous.

²³Now this wonderful truth—that God declared him to be righteous—wasn't just for Abraham's benefit. ²⁴It was for us, too, assuring us that God will also declare us to be righteous if we believe in God, who brought Jesus our Lord back from the dead. ²⁵He was handed over to die because of our sins, and he was raised from the dead to make us right with God.

CHAPTER 5

Faith Brings Joy

Therefore, since we have been made right in God's sight by faith, we have peace with God because of what Jesus Christ our Lord has done for us. ²Because of our faith, Christ has brought us into this

4:17 Gen 17:5.   **4:18** Gen 15:5.

place of highest privilege where we now stand, and we confidently and joyfully look forward to sharing God's glory.

[3] We can rejoice, too, when we run into problems and trials, for we know that they are good for us—they help us learn to endure. [4] And endurance develops strength of character in us, and character strengthens our confident expectation of salvation. [5] And this expectation will not disappoint us. For we know how dearly God loves us, because he has given us the Holy Spirit to fill our hearts with his love.

[6] When we were utterly helpless, Christ came at just the right time and died for us sinners. [7] Now, no one is likely to die for a good person, though someone might be willing to die for a person who is especially good. [8] But God showed his great love for us by sending Christ to die for us while we were still sinners. [9] And since we have been made right in God's sight by the blood of Christ, he will certainly save us from God's judgment. [10] For since we were restored to friendship with God by the death of his Son while we were still his enemies, we will certainly be delivered from eternal punishment by his life. [11] So now we can rejoice in our wonderful new relationship with God—all because of what our Lord Jesus Christ has done for us in making us friends of God.

Adam and Christ Contrasted

[12] When Adam sinned, sin entered the entire human race. Adam's sin brought death, so death spread to everyone, for everyone sinned. [13] Yes, people sinned even before the law was given. And though there was no law to break, since it had not yet been given, [14] they all died anyway—even though they did not disobey an explicit commandment of God, as Adam did. What a contrast between Adam and Christ, who was yet to come! [15] And what a difference between our sin and God's generous gift of forgiveness. For this one man, Adam, brought death to many through his sin. But this other man, Jesus Christ, brought forgiveness to many through God's bountiful gift. [16] And the result of God's gracious gift is very different from the result of that one man's sin. For Adam's sin led to condemnation, but we have the free gift of being accepted by God, even though we are guilty of many sins. [17] The sin of this one man, Adam, caused death to rule over us, but all who receive God's wonderful, gracious gift of righteousness will live in triumph over sin and death through this one man, Jesus Christ.

[18] Yes, Adam's one sin brought condemnation upon everyone, but Christ's one act of righteousness makes all people right in God's sight and gives them life. [19] Because one person disobeyed God, many people became sinners. But because one other person obeyed God, many people will be made right in God's sight.

[20] God's law was given so that all people could see how sinful they were. But as people sinned more and more, God's wonderful kindness became more abundant. [21] So just as sin ruled over all people and brought them to death, now God's wonderful kindness rules instead, giving us right standing with God and resulting in eternal life through Jesus Christ our Lord.

what does that say to you?

CHAPTER 6

Sin's Power Is Broken

Well then, should we keep on sinning so that God can show us more and more kindness and forgiveness? ²Of course not! Since we have died to sin, how can we continue to live in it? ³Or have you forgotten that when we became Christians and were baptized to become one with Christ Jesus, we died with him? ⁴For we died and were buried with Christ by baptism. And just as Christ was raised from the dead by the glorious power of the Father, now we also may live new lives.

⁵Since we have been united with him in his death, we will also be raised as he was. ⁶Our old sinful selves were crucified with Christ so that sin might lose its power in our lives. We are no longer slaves to sin. ⁷For when we died with Christ we were set free from the power of sin. ⁸And since we died with Christ, we know we will also share his new life. ⁹We are sure of this because Christ rose from the dead, and he will never die again. Death no longer has any power over him. ¹⁰He died once to defeat sin, and now he lives for the glory of God. ¹¹So you should consider yourselves dead to sin and able to live for the glory of God through Christ Jesus.

¹²Do not let sin control the way you live;* do not give in to its lustful desires. ¹³Do not let any part of your body become a tool of wickedness, to be used for sinning. Instead, give yourselves completely to God since you have been given new life. And use your whole body as a tool to do what is right for the glory of God. ¹⁴Sin is no longer your master, for you are no longer subject to the law, which enslaves you to sin. Instead, you are free by God's grace.

Freedom to Obey God

¹⁵So since God's grace has set us free from the law, does this mean we can go on sinning? Of course not! ¹⁶Don't you realize that whatever you choose to obey becomes your master? You can choose sin, which leads to death, or you can choose to obey God and receive his approval. ¹⁷Thank God! Once you were slaves of sin, but now you have obeyed with all your heart the new teaching God has given you. ¹⁸Now you are free from sin, your old master, and you have become slaves to your new master, righteousness.

¹⁹I speak this way, using the illustration of slaves and masters, because it is easy to understand. Before, you let yourselves be slaves of impurity and lawlessness. Now you must choose to be slaves of righteousness so that you will become holy.

²⁰In those days, when you were slaves of sin, you weren't concerned with doing what was right. ²¹And what was the result? It was not good, since now you are ashamed of the things you used to do, things that end in eternal doom. ²²But now you are free from the power of sin and have become slaves of God. Now you do those things that lead to holiness and result in eternal life. ²³For the wages of sin is death, but the free gift of God is eternal life through Christ Jesus our Lord.

CHAPTER 7

No Longer Bound to the Law

Now, dear brothers and sisters*—you who are familiar with the law—don't you know that the law applies only to a person who is

6:12 Or *Do not let sin reign in your body, which is subject to death.* 7:1 Greek *brothers.*

still living? ²Let me illustrate. When a woman marries, the law binds her to her husband as long as he is alive. But if he dies, the laws of marriage no longer apply to her. ³So while her husband is alive, she would be committing adultery if she married another man. But if her husband dies, she is free from that law and does not commit adultery when she remarries.

⁴So this is the point: The law no longer holds you in its power, because you died to its power when you died with Christ on the cross. And now you are united with the one who was raised from the dead. As a result, you can produce good fruit, that is, good deeds for God. ⁵When we were controlled by our old nature, sinful desires were at work within us, and the law aroused these evil desires that produced sinful deeds, resulting in death. ⁶But now we have been released from the law, for we died with Christ, and we are no longer captive to its power. Now we can really serve God, not in the old way by obeying the letter of the law, but in the new way, by the Spirit.

God's Law Reveals Our Sin

⁷Well then, am I suggesting that the law of God is evil? Of course not! The law is not sinful, but it was the law that showed me my sin. I would never have known that coveting is wrong if the law had not said, "Do not covet."* ⁸But sin took advantage of this law and aroused all kinds of forbidden desires within me! If there were no law, sin would not have that power.

⁹I felt fine when I did not understand what the law demanded. But when I learned the truth, I realized I had broken the law and was a sinner, doomed to die. ¹⁰So the good law, which was supposed to show me the way of life, instead gave me the death penalty. ¹¹Sin took advantage of the law and fooled me; it took the good law and used it to make me guilty of death. ¹²But still, the law itself is holy and right and good.

¹³But how can that be? Did the law, which is good, cause my doom? Of course not! Sin used what was good to bring about my condemnation. So we can see how terrible sin really is. It uses God's good commandment for its own evil purposes.

Struggling with Sin

¹⁴The law is good, then. The trouble is not with the law but with me, because I am sold into slavery, with sin as my master. ¹⁵I don't understand myself at all, for I really want to do what is right, but I don't do it. Instead, I do the very thing I hate. ¹⁶I know perfectly well that what I am doing is wrong, and my bad conscience shows that I agree that the law is good. ¹⁷But I can't help myself, because it is sin inside me that makes me do these evil things.

¹⁸I know I am rotten through and through so far as my old sinful nature is concerned. No matter which way I turn, I can't make myself do right. I want to, but I can't. ¹⁹When I want to do good, I don't. And when I try not to do wrong, I do it anyway. ²⁰But if I am doing what I don't want to do, I am not really the one doing it; the sin within me is doing it.

²¹It seems to be a fact of life that when I want to do what is right, I inevitably do what is wrong. ²²I love God's law with all my heart.

7:7 Exod 20:17; Deut 5:21.

23But there is another law at work within me that is at war with my mind. This law wins the fight and makes me a slave to the sin that is still within me. 24Oh, what a miserable person I am! Who will free me from this life that is dominated by sin?* 25Thank God! The answer is in Jesus Christ our Lord. So you see how it is: In my mind I really want to obey God's law, but because of my sinful nature I am a slave to sin.

CHAPTER 8

Life in the Spirit

So now there is no condemnation for those who belong to Christ Jesus. 2For the power* of the life-giving Spirit has freed you* through Christ Jesus from the power of sin that leads to death. 3The law of Moses could not save us, because of our sinful nature. But God put into effect a different plan to save us. He sent his own Son in a human body like ours, except that ours are sinful. God destroyed sin's control over us by giving his Son as a sacrifice for our sins. 4He did this so that the requirement of the law would be fully accomplished for us* who no longer follow our sinful nature but instead follow the Spirit.

5Those who are dominated by the sinful nature think about sinful things, but those who are controlled by the Holy Spirit think about things that please the Spirit. 6If your sinful nature controls your mind, there is death. But if the Holy Spirit controls your mind, there is life and peace. 7For the sinful nature is always hostile to God. It never did obey God's laws, and it never will. 8That's why those who are still under the control of their sinful nature can never please God.

9But you are not controlled by your sinful nature. You are controlled by the Spirit if you have the Spirit of God living in you. (And remember that those who do not have the Spirit of Christ living in them are not Christians at all.) 10Since Christ lives in you, even though your body will die because of sin, your spirit is alive* because you have been made right with God. 11The Spirit of God, who raised Jesus from the dead, lives in you. And just as he raised Christ from the dead, he will give life to your mortal body by this same Spirit living within you.

12So, dear brothers and sisters,* you have no obligation whatsoever to do what your sinful nature urges you to do. 13For if you keep on following it, you will perish. But if through the power of the Holy Spirit you turn from it* and its evil deeds, you will live. 14For all who are led by the Spirit of God are children* of God.

15So you should not be like cowering, fearful slaves. You should behave instead like God's very own children, adopted into his family*—calling him "Father, dear Father."* 16For his Holy Spirit speaks to us deep in our hearts and tells us that we are God's children. 17And since we are his children, we will share his treasures—for everything God gives to his Son, Christ, is ours, too. But if we are to share his glory, we must also share his suffering.

7:24 Greek *from this body of death?* 8:2a Greek *the law;* also in 8:2b. 8:2b Some manuscripts read *me.* 8:4 Or *accomplished by us.* 8:10 Or *the Spirit will bring you eternal life.* 8:12 Greek *brothers;* also in 8:29. 8:13 Greek *put it to death.* 8:14 Greek *sons;* also in 8:19. 8:15a Greek *You received a spirit of sonship.* 8:15b Greek "*Abba, Father.*" *Abba* is an Aramaic term for "father."

The Future Glory

[18]Yet what we suffer now is nothing compared to the glory he will give us later. [19]For all creation is waiting eagerly for that future day when God will reveal who his children really are. [20]Against its will, everything on earth was subjected to God's curse. [21]All creation anticipates the day when it will join God's children in glorious freedom from death and decay. [22]For we know that all creation has been groaning as in the pains of childbirth right up to the present time. [23]And even we Christians, although we have the Holy Spirit within us as a foretaste of future glory, also groan to be released from pain and suffering. We, too, wait anxiously for that day when God will give us our full rights as his children,* including the new bodies he has promised us. [24]Now that we are saved, we eagerly look forward to this freedom. For if you already have something, you don't need to hope for it. [25]But if we look forward to something we don't have yet, we must wait patiently and confidently.

[26]And the Holy Spirit helps us in our distress. For we don't even know what we should pray for, nor how we should pray. But the Holy Spirit prays for us with groanings that cannot be expressed in words. [27]And the Father who knows all hearts knows what the Spirit is saying, for the Spirit pleads for us believers in harmony with God's own will. [28]And we know that God causes everything to work together* for the good of those who love God and are called according to his purpose for them. [29]For God knew his people in advance, and he chose them to become like his Son, so that his Son would be the firstborn, with many brothers and sisters. [30]And having chosen them, he called them to come to him. And he gave them right standing with himself, and he promised them his glory.

Nothing Can Separate Us from God's Love

[31]What can we say about such wonderful things as these? If God is for us, who can ever be against us? [32]Since God did not spare even his own Son but gave him up for us all, won't God, who gave us Christ, also give us everything else?

[33]Who dares accuse us whom God has chosen for his own? Will God? No! He is the one who has given us right standing with himself. [34]Who then will condemn us? Will Christ Jesus? No, for he is the one who died for us and was raised to life for us and is sitting at the place of highest honor next to God, pleading for us.

[35]Can anything ever separate us from Christ's love? Does it mean he no longer loves us if we have trouble or calamity, or are persecuted, or are hungry or cold or in danger or threatened with death? [36](Even the Scriptures say, "For your sake we are killed every day; we are being slaughtered like sheep."*) [37]No, despite all these things, overwhelming victory is ours through Christ, who loved us.

[38]And I am convinced that nothing can ever separate us from his love. Death can't, and life can't. The angels can't, and the demons can't. Our fears for today, our worries about tomorrow, and even the powers of hell can't keep God's love away. [39]Whether we are high above the sky or in the deepest ocean, nothing in all creation will ever be able to separate us from the love of God that is revealed in Christ Jesus our Lord.

8:23 Greek *wait anxiously for sonship.* **8:28** Some manuscripts read *And we know that everything works together.* **8:36** Ps 44:22.

CHAPTER 9

God's Selection of Israel

In the presence of Christ, I speak with utter truthfulness—I do not lie—and my conscience and the Holy Spirit confirm that what I am saying is true. ²My heart is filled with bitter sorrow and unending grief ³for my people, my Jewish brothers and sisters.* I would be willing to be forever cursed—cut off from Christ!—if that would save them. ⁴They are the people of Israel, chosen to be God's special children.* God revealed his glory to them. He made covenants with them and gave his law to them. They have the privilege of worshiping him and receiving his wonderful promises. ⁵Their ancestors were great people of God, and Christ himself was a Jew as far as his human nature is concerned. And he is God, who rules over everything and is worthy of eternal praise! Amen.*

⁶Well then, has God failed to fulfill his promise to the Jews? No, for not everyone born into a Jewish family is truly a Jew! ⁷Just the fact that they are descendants of Abraham doesn't make them truly Abraham's children. For the Scriptures say, "Isaac is the son through whom your descendants will be counted,"* though Abraham had other children, too. ⁸This means that Abraham's physical descendants are not necessarily children of God. It is the children of the promise who are considered to be Abraham's children. ⁹For God had promised, "Next year I will return, and Sarah will have a son."*

¹⁰This son was our ancestor Isaac. When he grew up, he married Rebekah, who gave birth to twins. ¹¹But before they were born, before they had done anything good or bad, she received a message from God. (This message proves that God chooses according to his own plan, ¹²not according to our good or bad works.) She was told, "The descendants of your older son will serve the descendants of your younger son."* ¹³In the words of the Scriptures, "I loved Jacob, but I rejected Esau."*

¹⁴What can we say? Was God being unfair? Of course not! ¹⁵For God said to Moses,

"I will show mercy to anyone I choose,
    and I will show compassion to anyone I choose."*

¹⁶So receiving God's promise is not up to us. We can't get it by choosing it or working hard for it. God will show mercy to anyone he chooses.

¹⁷For the Scriptures say that God told Pharaoh, "I have appointed you for the very purpose of displaying my power in you, and so that my fame might spread throughout the earth."* ¹⁸So you see, God shows mercy to some just because he wants to, and he chooses to make some people refuse to listen.

¹⁹Well then, you might say, "Why does God blame people for not listening? Haven't they simply done what he made them do?" ²⁰No, don't say that. Who are you, a mere human being, to criticize God? Should the thing that was created say to the one who made it, "Why have you made me like this?" ²¹When a potter makes jars out of clay, doesn't he have a right to use the same lump

9:3 Greek *my brothers.* 9:4 Greek *chosen for sonship.* 9:5 Or *May God, who rules over everything, be praised forever. Amen.* 9:7 Gen 21:12. 9:9 Gen 18:10, 14. 9:12 Gen 25:23. 9:13 Mal 1:2-3. 9:15 Exod 33:19. 9:17 Exod 9:16.

of clay to make one jar for decoration and another to throw garbage into? ²²God has every right to exercise his judgment and his power, but he also has the right to be very patient with those who are the objects of his judgment and are fit only for destruction. ²³He also has the right to pour out the riches of his glory upon those he prepared to be the objects of his mercy—²⁴even upon us, whom he selected, both from the Jews and from the Gentiles.

²⁵Concerning the Gentiles, God says in the prophecy of Hosea,

"Those who were not my people,
    I will now call my people.
And I will love those
    whom I did not love before."*

²⁶And,

"Once they were told,
    'You are not my people.'
But now he will say,
    'You are children of the living God.'* "

²⁷Concerning Israel, Isaiah the prophet cried out,

"Though the people of Israel are as numerous as the sand on
    the seashore,
    only a small number will be saved.
²⁸ For the Lord will carry out his sentence upon the earth
    quickly and with finality."*

²⁹And Isaiah said in another place,

"If the Lord Almighty
    had not spared a few of us,
we would have been wiped out
    as completely as Sodom and Gomorrah."*

Israel's Unbelief

³⁰Well then, what shall we say about these things? Just this: The Gentiles have been made right with God by faith, even though they were not seeking him. ³¹But the Jews, who tried so hard to get right with God by keeping the law, never succeeded. ³²Why not? Because they were trying to get right with God by keeping the law and being good instead of by depending on faith. They stumbled over the great rock in their path. ³³God warned them of this in the Scriptures when he said,

"I am placing a stone in Jerusalem* that causes people to stumble,
    and a rock that makes them fall.*
But anyone who believes in him
    will not be disappointed.*"

CHAPTER 10

Dear brothers and sisters,* the longing of my heart and my prayer to God is that the Jewish people might be saved. ²I know what enthusiasm they have for God, but it is misdirected zeal. ³For they

9:25 Hos 2:23.   9:26 Greek *You are sons of the living God.* Hos 1:10.   9:27-28 Isa 10:22-23.   9:29 Isa 1:9.   9:33a Greek *in Zion.*   9:33b Isa 8:14.   9:33c Or *will not be put to shame.* Isa 28:16.   10:1 Greek *Brothers.*

don't understand God's way of making people right with himself. Instead, they are clinging to their own way of getting right with God by trying to keep the law. They won't go along with God's way. [4]For Christ has accomplished the whole purpose* of the law. All who believe in him are made right with God.

Salvation Is for Everyone

[5]For Moses wrote that the law's way of making a person right with God requires obedience to all of its commands.* [6]But the way of getting right with God through faith says, "You don't need to go to heaven" (to find Christ and bring him down to help you). [7]And it says, "You don't need to go to the place of the dead" (to bring Christ back to life again). [8]Salvation that comes from trusting Christ—which is the message we preach—is already within easy reach. In fact, the Scriptures say, "The message is close at hand; it is on your lips and in your heart."*

[9]For if you confess with your mouth that Jesus is Lord and believe in your heart that God raised him from the dead, you will be saved. [10]For it is by believing in your heart that you are made right with God, and it is by confessing with your mouth that you are saved. [11]As the Scriptures tell us, "Anyone who believes in him will not be disappointed.*" [12]Jew and Gentile are the same in this respect. They all have the same Lord, who generously gives his riches to all who ask for them. [13]For "Anyone who calls on the name of the Lord will be saved."*

[14]But how can they call on him to save them unless they believe in him? And how can they believe in him if they have never heard about him? And how can they hear about him unless someone tells them? [15]And how will anyone go and tell them without being sent? That is what the Scriptures mean when they say, "How beautiful are the feet of those who bring good news!"*

[16]But not everyone welcomes the Good News, for Isaiah the prophet said, "Lord, who has believed our message?"* [17]Yet faith comes from listening to this message of good news—the Good News about Christ.

[18]But what about the Jews? Have they actually heard the message? Yes, they have:

"The message of God's creation has gone out to everyone,
    and its words to all the world."*

[19]But did the people of Israel really understand? Yes, they did, for even in the time of Moses, God had said,

"I will rouse your jealousy by blessing other nations.
    I will make you angry by blessing the foolish Gentiles."*

[20]And later Isaiah spoke boldly for God:

"I was found by people
    who were not looking for me.
I showed myself to those
    who were not asking for me."*

10:4 Or *the end.*   **10:5** Lev 18:5.   **10:6-8** Deut 30:12-14.   **10:11** Or *will not be put to shame.* Isa 28:16.   **10:13** Joel 2:32.   **10:15** Isa 52:7.   **10:16** Isa 53:1.   **10:18** Ps 19:4.   **10:19** Deut 32:21.   **10:20** Isa 65:1.

21But regarding Israel, God said,

"All day long I opened my arms to them,
    but they kept disobeying me and arguing with me."*

CHAPTER 11

God's Mercy on Israel

I ask, then, has God rejected his people, the Jews? Of course not!
Remember that I myself am a Jew, a descendant of Abraham and a
member of the tribe of Benjamin.

2No, God has not rejected his own people, whom he chose from
the very beginning. Do you remember what the Scriptures say
about this? Elijah the prophet complained to God about the
people of Israel and said, 3 "Lord, they have killed your prophets
and torn down your altars. I alone am left, and now they are trying
to kill me, too."*

4And do you remember God's reply? He said, "You are not the
only one left. I have seven thousand others who have never bowed
down to Baal!"*

5It is the same today, for not all the Jews have turned away from
God. A few* are being saved as a result of God's kindness in
choosing them. 6And if they are saved by God's kindness, then it
is not by their good works. For in that case, God's wonderful
kindness would not be what it really is—free and undeserved.

7So this is the situation: Most of the Jews have not found the
favor of God they are looking for so earnestly. A few have—the
ones God has chosen—but the rest were made unresponsive. 8As
the Scriptures say,

"God has put them into a deep sleep.
To this very day he has shut their eyes so they do not see,
    and closed their ears so they do not hear."*

9David spoke of this same thing when he said,

"Let their bountiful table become a snare,
    a trap that makes them think all is well.
    Let their blessings cause them to stumble.
10 Let their eyes go blind so they cannot see,
    and let their backs grow weaker and weaker."*

11Did God's people stumble and fall beyond recovery? Of course
not! His purpose was to make his salvation available to the Gentiles, and then the Jews would be jealous and want it for themselves. 12Now if the Gentiles were enriched because the Jews turned
down God's offer of salvation, think how much greater a blessing
the world will share when the Jews finally accept it.

13I am saying all of this especially for you Gentiles. God has
appointed me as the apostle to the Gentiles. I lay great stress on
this, 14for I want to find a way to make the Jews want what you
Gentiles have, and in that way I might save some of them. 15For
since the Jews' rejection meant that God offered salvation to the
rest of the world, how much more wonderful their acceptance will
be. It will be life for those who were dead! 16And since Abraham

10:21 Isa 65:2. **11:3** 1 Kgs 19:10, 14. **11:4** 1 Kgs 19:18. **11:5** Greek *A remnant.*
11:8 Deut 29:4; Isa 29:10. **11:9-10** Ps 69:22-23.

and the other patriarchs were holy, their children will also be holy.* For if the roots of the tree are holy, the branches will be, too.

17But some of these branches from Abraham's tree, some of the Jews, have been broken off. And you Gentiles, who were branches from a wild olive tree, were grafted in. So now you also receive the blessing God has promised Abraham and his children, sharing in God's rich nourishment of his special olive tree. 18But you must be careful not to brag about being grafted in to replace the branches that were broken off. Remember, you are just a branch, not the root.

19"Well," you may say, "those branches were broken off to make room for me." 20Yes, but remember—those branches, the Jews, were broken off because they didn't believe God, and you are there because you do believe. Don't think highly of yourself, but fear what could happen. 21For if God did not spare the branches he put there in the first place, he won't spare you either.

22Notice how God is both kind and severe. He is severe to those who disobeyed, but kind to you as you continue to trust in his kindness. But if you stop trusting, you also will be cut off. 23And if the Jews turn from their unbelief, God will graft them back into the tree again. He has the power to do it.

24For if God was willing to take you who were, by nature, branches from a wild olive tree and graft you into his own good tree—a very unusual thing to do—he will be far more eager to graft the Jews back into the tree where they belong.

God's Mercy Is for Everyone

25I want you to understand this mystery, dear brothers and sisters,* so that you will not feel proud and start bragging. Some of the Jews have hard hearts, but this will last only until the complete number of Gentiles comes to Christ. 26And so all Israel will be saved. Do you remember what the prophets said about this?

"A Deliverer will come from Jerusalem,*
	and he will turn Israel* from all ungodliness.
27 And then I will keep my covenant with them
	and take away their sins."*

28Many of the Jews are now enemies of the Good News. But this has been to your benefit, for God has given his gifts to you Gentiles. Yet the Jews are still his chosen people because of his promises to Abraham, Isaac, and Jacob. 29For God's gifts and his call can never be withdrawn. 30Once, you Gentiles were rebels against God, but when the Jews refused his mercy, God was merciful to you instead. 31And now, in the same way, the Jews are the rebels, and God's mercy has come to you. But someday they,* too, will share in God's mercy. 32For God has imprisoned all people in their own disobedience so he could have mercy on everyone.

33Oh, what a wonderful God we have! How great are his riches and wisdom and knowledge! How impossible it is for us to understand his decisions and his methods! 34For who can know what the Lord is thinking? Who knows enough to be his counselor?* 35And

11:16 Greek *If the dough offered as firstfruits is holy, so is the whole lump.*   11:25 Greek *brothers.*
11:26a Greek *from Zion.*   11:26b Greek *Jacob.*   11:26-27 Isa 59:20-21.   11:31 Some
manuscripts read *But now they;* other manuscripts read *But they.*   11:34 See Isa 40:13.

who could ever give him so much that he would have to pay it back? ³⁶For everything comes from him; everything exists by his power and is intended for his glory. To him be glory evermore. Amen.

CHAPTER 12

A Living Sacrifice to God

And so, dear brothers and sisters,* I plead with you to give your bodies to God. Let them be a living and holy sacrifice—the kind he will accept. When you think of what he has done for you, is this too much to ask? ²Don't copy the behavior and customs of this world, but let God transform you into a new person by changing the way you think. Then you will know what God wants you to do, and you will know how good and pleasing and perfect his will really is.

³As God's messenger, I give each of you this warning: Be honest in your estimate of yourselves, measuring your value by how much faith God has given you. ⁴Just as our bodies have many parts and each part has a special function, ⁵so it is with Christ's body. We are all parts of his one body, and each of us has different work to do. And since we are all one body in Christ, we belong to each other, and each of us needs all the others.

⁶God has given each of us the ability to do certain things well. So if God has given you the ability to prophesy, speak out when you have faith that God is speaking through you. ⁷If your gift is that of serving others, serve them well. If you are a teacher, do a good job of teaching. ⁸If your gift is to encourage others, do it! If you have money, share it generously. If God has given you leadership ability, take the responsibility seriously. And if you have a gift for showing kindness to others, do it gladly.

⁹Don't just pretend that you love others. Really love them. Hate what is wrong. Stand on the side of the good. ¹⁰Love each other with genuine affection,* and take delight in honoring each other. ¹¹Never be lazy in your work, but serve the Lord enthusiastically.

¹²Be glad for all God is planning for you. Be patient in trouble, and always be prayerful. ¹³When God's children are in need, be the one to help them out. And get into the habit of inviting guests home for dinner or, if they need lodging, for the night.

¹⁴If people persecute you because you are a Christian, don't curse them; pray that God will bless them. ¹⁵When others are happy, be happy with them. If they are sad, share their sorrow. ¹⁶Live in harmony with each other. Don't try to act important, but enjoy the company of ordinary people. And don't think you know it all!

¹⁷Never pay back evil for evil to anyone. Do things in such a way that everyone can see that you are honorable. ¹⁸Do your part to live in peace with everyone, as much as possible.

¹⁹Dear friends, never avenge yourselves. Leave that to God. For it is written,

"I will take vengeance;
    I will repay those who deserve it,"*
    says the Lord.

12:1 Greek *brothers.*   12:10 Greek *with brotherly love.*   12:19 Deut 32:35.

²⁰Instead, do what the Scriptures say:

"If your enemies are hungry, feed them.
If they are thirsty, give them something to drink,
    and they will be ashamed of what they have done to you."*

²¹Don't let evil get the best of you, but conquer evil by doing good.

CHAPTER 13

Respect for Authority

Obey the government, for God is the one who put it there. All governments have been placed in power by God. ²So those who refuse to obey the laws of the land are refusing to obey God, and punishment will follow. ³For the authorities do not frighten people who are doing right, but they frighten those who do wrong. So do what they say, and you will get along well. ⁴The authorities are sent by God to help you. But if you are doing something wrong, of course you should be afraid, for you will be punished. The authorities are established by God for that very purpose, to punish those who do wrong. ⁵So you must obey the government for two reasons: to keep from being punished and to keep a clear conscience.

⁶Pay your taxes, too, for these same reasons. For government workers need to be paid so they can keep on doing the work God intended them to do. ⁷Give to everyone what you owe them: Pay your taxes and import duties, and give respect and honor to all to whom it is due.

Love Fulfills God's Requirements

⁸Pay all your debts, except the debt of love for others. You can never finish paying that! If you love your neighbor, you will fulfill all the requirements of God's law. ⁹For the commandments against adultery and murder and stealing and coveting—and any other commandment—are all summed up in this one commandment: "Love your neighbor as yourself."* ¹⁰Love does no wrong to anyone, so love satisfies all of God's requirements.

¹¹Another reason for right living is that you know how late it is; time is running out. Wake up, for the coming of our salvation is nearer now than when we first believed. ¹²The night is almost gone; the day of salvation will soon be here. So don't live in darkness. Get rid of your evil deeds. Shed them like dirty clothes. Clothe yourselves with the armor of right living, as those who live in the light. ¹³We should be decent and true in everything we do, so that everyone can approve of our behavior. Don't participate in wild parties and getting drunk, or in adultery and immoral living, or in fighting and jealousy. ¹⁴But let the Lord Jesus Christ take control of you, and don't think of ways to indulge your evil desires.

CHAPTER 14

The Danger of Criticism

Accept Christians who are weak in faith, and don't argue with them about what they think is right or wrong. ²For instance, one person believes it is all right to eat anything. But another believer who has a sensitive conscience will eat only vegetables. ³Those who think it is all right to eat anything must not look down on those who

12:20 Greek *and you will heap burning coals on their heads.* Prov 25:21-22.   13:9 Lev 19:18.

won't. And those who won't eat certain foods must not condemn those who do, for God has accepted them. 4Who are you to condemn God's servants? They are responsible to the Lord, so let him tell them whether they are right or wrong. The Lord's power will help them do as they should.

5In the same way, some think one day is more holy than another day, while others think every day is alike. Each person should have a personal conviction about this matter. 6Those who have a special day for worshiping the Lord are trying to honor him. Those who eat all kinds of food do so to honor the Lord, since they give thanks to God before eating. And those who won't eat everything also want to please the Lord and give thanks to God. 7For we are not our own masters when we live or when we die. 8While we live, we live to please the Lord. And when we die, we go to be with the Lord. So in life and in death, we belong to the Lord. 9Christ died and rose again for this very purpose, so that he might be Lord of those who are alive and of those who have died.

10So why do you condemn another Christian*? Why do you look down on another Christian? Remember, each of us will stand personally before the judgment seat of God. 11For the Scriptures say,

" 'As surely as I live,' says the Lord,
'every knee will bow to me
    and every tongue will confess allegiance to God.' " *

12Yes, each of us will have to give a personal account to God. 13So don't condemn each other anymore. Decide instead to live in such a way that you will not put an obstacle in another Christian's path.

14I know and am perfectly sure on the authority of the Lord Jesus that no food, in and of itself, is wrong to eat. But if someone believes it is wrong, then for that person it is wrong. 15And if another Christian is distressed by what you eat, you are not acting in love if you eat it. Don't let your eating ruin someone for whom Christ died. 16Then you will not be condemned for doing something you know is all right.

17For the Kingdom of God is not a matter of what we eat or drink, but of living a life of goodness and peace and joy in the Holy Spirit. 18If you serve Christ with this attitude, you will please God. And other people will approve of you, too. 19So then, let us aim for harmony in the church and try to build each other up.

20Don't tear apart the work of God over what you eat. Remember, there is nothing wrong with these things in themselves. But it is wrong to eat anything if it makes another person stumble. 21Don't eat meat or drink wine or do anything else if it might cause another Christian to stumble. 22You may have the faith to believe that there is nothing wrong with what you are doing, but keep it between yourself and God. Blessed are those who do not condemn themselves by doing something they know is all right. 23But if people have doubts about whether they should eat something, they shouldn't eat it. They would be condemned for not acting in faith before God. If you do anything you believe is not right, you are sinning.

14:10 Greek *your brother;* also in 14:10b, 13, 15, 21.   **14:11** Isa 45:23.

CHAPTER 15

Living to Please Others

We may know that these things make no difference, but we cannot just go ahead and do them to please ourselves. We must be considerate of the doubts and fears of those who think these things are wrong. ²We should please others. If we do what helps them, we will build them up in the Lord. ³For even Christ didn't please himself. As the Scriptures say, "Those who insult you are also insulting me."* ⁴Such things were written in the Scriptures long ago to teach us. They give us hope and encouragement as we wait patiently for God's promises.

⁵May God, who gives this patience and encouragement, help you live in complete harmony with each other—each with the attitude of Christ Jesus toward the other. ⁶Then all of you can join together with one voice, giving praise and glory to God, the Father of our Lord Jesus Christ.

⁷So accept each other just as Christ has accepted you; then God will be glorified. ⁸Remember that Christ came as a servant to the Jews to show that God is true to the promises he made to their ancestors. ⁹And he came so the Gentiles might also give glory to God for his mercies to them. That is what the psalmist meant when he wrote:

"I will praise you among the Gentiles;
  I will sing praises to your name."*

¹⁰And in another place it is written,

"Rejoice, O you Gentiles,
  along with his people, the Jews."*

¹¹And yet again,

"Praise the Lord, all you Gentiles;
  praise him, all you people of the earth."*

¹²And the prophet Isaiah said,

"The heir to David's throne* will come,
  and he will rule over the Gentiles.
  They will place their hopes on him."*

¹³So I pray that God, who gives you hope, will keep you happy and full of peace as you believe in him. May you overflow with hope through the power of the Holy Spirit.

Paul's Reason for Writing

¹⁴I am fully convinced, dear brothers and sisters,* that you are full of goodness. You know these things so well that you are able to teach others all about them. ¹⁵Even so, I have been bold enough to emphasize some of these points, knowing that all you need is this reminder from me. For I am, by God's grace, ¹⁶a special messenger from Christ Jesus to you Gentiles. I bring you the Good News and offer you up as a fragrant sacrifice to God so that you might be pure and pleasing to him by the Holy Spirit. ¹⁷So it is right for me to be enthusiastic about all Christ Jesus has done

15:3 Ps 69:9. 15:9 Ps 18:49. 15:10 Deut 32:43. 15:11 Ps 117:1. 15:12a Greek *The root of Jesse.* 15:12b Isa 11:10. 15:14 Greek *brothers*; also in 15:30.

through me in my service to God. [18]I dare not boast of anything else. I have brought the Gentiles to God by my message and the way I lived before them. [19]I have won them over by the miracles done through me as signs from God—all by the power of God's Spirit. In this way, I have fully presented the Good News of Christ all the way from Jerusalem clear over into Illyricum.*

[20]My ambition has always been to preach the Good News where the name of Christ has never been heard, rather than where a church has already been started by someone else. [21]I have been following the plan spoken of in the Scriptures, where it says,

"Those who have never been told about him will see,
 and those who have never heard of him will understand."*

[22]In fact, my visit to you has been delayed so long because I have been preaching in these places.

Paul's Travel Plans

[23]But now I have finished my work in these regions, and after all these long years of waiting, I am eager to visit you. [24]I am planning to go to Spain, and when I do, I will stop off in Rome. And after I have enjoyed your fellowship for a little while, you can send me on my way again.

[25]But before I come, I must go down to Jerusalem to take a gift to the Christians there. [26]For you see, the believers in Greece* have eagerly taken up an offering for the Christians in Jerusalem, who are going through such hard times. [27]They were very glad to do this because they feel they owe a real debt to them. Since the Gentiles received the wonderful spiritual blessings of the Good News from the Jewish Christians, they feel the least they can do in return is help them financially. [28]As soon as I have delivered this money and completed this good deed of theirs, I will come to see you on my way to Spain. [29]And I am sure that when I come, Christ will give me a great blessing for you.

[30]Dear brothers and sisters, I urge you in the name of our Lord Jesus Christ to join me in my struggle by praying to God for me. Do this because of your love for me, given to you by the Holy Spirit. [31]Pray that I will be rescued from those in Judea who refuse to obey God. Pray also that the Christians there will be willing to accept the donation I am bringing them. [32]Then, by the will of God, I will be able to come to you with a happy heart, and we will be an encouragement to each other.

[33]And now may God, who gives us his peace, be with you all. Amen.

CHAPTER 16

Paul Greets His Friends

Our sister Phoebe, a deacon in the church in Cenchrea, will be coming to see you soon. [2]Receive her in the Lord, as one who is worthy of high honor. Help her in every way you can, for she has helped many in their needs, including me.

[3]Greet Priscilla and Aquila. They have been co-workers in my ministry for Christ Jesus. [4]In fact, they risked their lives for me. I

15:19 *Illyricum* was a region northeast of Italy.   **15:21** Isa 52:15.   **15:26** Greek *Macedonia and Achaia,* the northern and southern regions of Greece.

am not the only one who is thankful to them; so are all the Gentile churches. 5Please give my greetings to the church that meets in their home.

Greet my dear friend Epenetus. He was the very first person to become a Christian in the province of Asia. 6Give my greetings to Mary, who has worked so hard for your benefit. 7Then there are Andronicus and Junia,* my relatives,* who were in prison with me. They are respected among the apostles and became Christians before I did. Please give them my greetings. 8Say hello to Ampliatus, whom I love as one of the Lord's own children, 9and Urbanus, our co-worker in Christ, and beloved Stachys.

10Give my greetings to Apelles, a good man whom Christ approves. And give my best regards to the members of the household of Aristobulus. 11Greet Herodion, my relative.* Greet the Christians in the household of Narcissus. 12Say hello to Tryphena and Tryphosa, the Lord's workers, and to dear Persis, who has worked so hard for the Lord. 13Greet Rufus, whom the Lord picked out to be his very own; and also his dear mother, who has been a mother to me.

14And please give my greetings to Asyncritus, Phlegon, Hermes, Patrobas, Hermas, and the brothers and sisters* who are with them. 15Give my greetings to Philologus, Julia, Nereus and his sister, and to Olympas and all the other believers who are with them. 16Greet each other in Christian love.* All the churches of Christ send you their greetings.

Paul's Final Instructions

17And now I make one more appeal, my dear brothers and sisters. Watch out for people who cause divisions and upset people's faith by teaching things that are contrary to what you have been taught. Stay away from them. 18Such people are not serving Christ our Lord; they are serving their own personal interests. By smooth talk and glowing words they deceive innocent people. 19But everyone knows that you are obedient to the Lord. This makes me very happy. I want you to see clearly what is right and to stay innocent of any wrong. 20The God of peace will soon crush Satan under your feet. May the grace of our Lord Jesus Christ be with you.

21Timothy, my fellow worker, and Lucius, Jason, and Sosipater, my relatives, send you their good wishes.

22I, Tertius, the one who is writing this letter for Paul, send my greetings, too, as a Christian brother.

23Gaius says hello to you. I am his guest, and the church meets here in his home. Erastus, the city treasurer, sends you his greetings, and so does Quartus, a Christian brother.*

25God is able to make you strong, just as the Good News says. It is the message about Jesus Christ and his plan for you Gentiles, a plan kept secret from the beginning of time. 26But now as the prophets* foretold and as the eternal God has commanded, this message is made known to all Gentiles everywhere, so that they might believe and obey Christ. 27To God, who alone is wise, be the glory forever through Jesus Christ. Amen.

16:7a Or *Junias;* some manuscripts read *Julia.* 16:7b Or *compatriots;* also in 16:21.
16:11 Or *compatriot.* 16:14 Greek *brothers;* also in 16:17. 16:16 Greek *with a sacred kiss.*
16:23 Some manuscripts add verse 24, *May the grace of our Lord Jesus Christ be with you all.
Amen.* 16:26 Greek *the prophetic writings.*

1 CORINTHIANS

CHAPTER 1

Greetings from Paul

This letter is from Paul, chosen by the will of God to be an apostle of Christ Jesus, and from our brother Sosthenes.

2 We are writing to the church of God in Corinth, you who have been called by God to be his own holy people. He made you holy by means of Christ Jesus, just as he did all Christians everywhere—whoever calls upon the name of Jesus Christ, our Lord and theirs.

3 May God our Father and the Lord Jesus Christ give you his grace and peace.

Paul Gives Thanks to God

4 I can never stop thanking God for all the generous gifts he has given you, now that you belong to Christ Jesus. 5 He has enriched your church with the gifts of eloquence and every kind of knowledge. 6 This shows that what I told you about Christ is true. 7 Now you have every spiritual gift you need as you eagerly wait for the return of our Lord Jesus Christ. 8 He will keep you strong right up to the end, and he will keep you free from all blame on the great day when our Lord Jesus Christ returns. 9 God will surely do this for you, for he always does just what he says, and he is the one who invited you into this wonderful friendship with his Son, Jesus Christ our Lord.

Divisions in the Church

10 Now, dear brothers and sisters,* I appeal to you by the authority of the Lord Jesus Christ to stop arguing among yourselves. Let there be real harmony so there won't be divisions in the church. I plead with you to be of one mind, united in thought and purpose. 11 For some members of Chloe's household have told me about your arguments, dear brothers and sisters. 12 Some of you are saying, "I am a follower of Paul." Others are saying, "I follow Apollos," or "I follow Peter,*" or "I follow only Christ." 13 Can Christ be divided into pieces?

Was I, Paul, crucified for you? Were any of you baptized in the name of Paul? 14 I thank God that I did not baptize any of you except Crispus and Gaius, 15 for now no one can say they were baptized in my name. 16 (Oh yes, I also baptized the household of Stephanas. I don't remember baptizing anyone else.) 17 For Christ didn't send me to baptize, but to preach the Good News—and not with clever speeches and high-sounding ideas, for fear that the cross of Christ would lose its power.

The Wisdom of God

18 I know very well how foolish the message of the cross sounds to those who are on the road to destruction. But we who are being

1:10 Greek *brothers;* also in 1:11, 26.   1:12 Greek *Cephas.*

saved recognize this message as the very power of God. ¹⁹As the Scriptures say,

"I will destroy human wisdom
and discard their most brilliant ideas."*

²⁰So where does this leave the philosophers, the scholars, and the world's brilliant debaters? God has made them all look foolish and has shown their wisdom to be useless nonsense. ²¹Since God in his wisdom saw to it that the world would never find him through human wisdom, he has used our foolish preaching to save all who believe. ²²God's way seems foolish to the Jews because they want a sign from heaven to prove it is true. And it is foolish to the Greeks because they believe only what agrees with their own wisdom. ²³So when we preach that Christ was crucified, the Jews are offended, and the Gentiles say it's all nonsense. ²⁴But to those called by God to salvation, both Jews and Gentiles,* Christ is the mighty power of God and the wonderful wisdom of God. ²⁵This "foolish" plan of God is far wiser than the wisest of human plans, and God's weakness is far stronger than the greatest of human strength.

²⁶Remember, dear brothers and sisters, that few of you were wise in the world's eyes, or powerful, or wealthy when God called you. ²⁷Instead, God deliberately chose things the world considers foolish in order to shame those who think they are wise. And he chose those who are powerless to shame those who are powerful. ²⁸God chose things despised by the world, things counted as nothing at all, and used them to bring to nothing what the world considers important, ²⁹so that no one can ever boast in the presence of God.

³⁰God alone made it possible for you to be in Christ Jesus. For our benefit God made Christ to be wisdom itself. He is the one who made us acceptable to God. He made us pure and holy, and he gave himself to purchase our freedom. ³¹As the Scriptures say,

"The person who wishes to boast
should boast only of what the Lord has done."*

CHAPTER 2

Paul Preaches Wisdom

Dear brothers and sisters,* when I first came to you I didn't use lofty words and brilliant ideas to tell you God's message.* ²For I decided to concentrate only on Jesus Christ and his death on the cross. ³I came to you in weakness—timid and trembling. ⁴And my message and my preaching were very plain. I did not use wise and persuasive speeches, but the Holy Spirit was powerful among you. ⁵I did this so that you might trust the power of God rather than human wisdom.

⁶Yet when I am among mature Christians, I do speak with words of wisdom, but not the kind of wisdom that belongs to this world, and not the kind that appeals to the rulers of this world, who are being brought to nothing. ⁷No, the wisdom we speak of is the secret wisdom of God,* which was hidden in former times, though he made it for our benefit before the world began. ⁸But the rulers of this world have not understood it; if they had, they would never

1:19 Isa 29:14.   1:24 Greek *Greeks*.   1:31 Jer 9:24.   2:1a Greek *Brothers*.   2:1b Greek *mystery*; other manuscripts read *testimony*.   2:7 Greek *we speak God's wisdom in a mystery*.

have crucified our glorious Lord. 9That is what the Scriptures mean when they say,

> "No eye has seen, no ear has heard,
>   and no mind has imagined
> what God has prepared
>   for those who love him."*

10But we know these things because God has revealed them to us by his Spirit, and his Spirit searches out everything and shows us even God's deep secrets. 11No one can know what anyone else is really thinking except that person alone, and no one can know God's thoughts except God's own Spirit. 12And God has actually given us his Spirit (not the world's spirit) so we can know the wonderful things God has freely given us. 13When we tell you this, we do not use words of human wisdom. We speak words given to us by the Spirit, using the Spirit's words to explain spiritual truths.* 14But people who aren't Christians can't understand these truths from God's Spirit. It all sounds foolish to them because only those who have the Spirit can understand what the Spirit means. 15We who have the Spirit understand these things, but others can't understand us at all. 16How could they? For,

> "Who can know what the Lord is thinking?
>   Who can give him counsel?"*

But we can understand these things, for we have the mind of Christ.

CHAPTER 3
Paul and Apollos, Servants of Christ
Dear brothers and sisters,* when I was with you I couldn't talk to you as I would to mature Christians. I had to talk as though you belonged to this world or as though you were infants in the Christian life.* 2I had to feed you with milk and not with solid food, because you couldn't handle anything stronger. And you still aren't ready, 3for you are still controlled by your own sinful desires. You are jealous of one another and quarrel with each other. Doesn't that prove you are controlled by your own desires? You are acting like people who don't belong to the Lord. 4When one of you says, "I am a follower of Paul," and another says, "I prefer Apollos," aren't you acting like those who are not Christians?*

5Who is Apollos, and who is Paul, that we should be the cause of such quarrels? Why, we're only servants. Through us God caused you to believe. Each of us did the work the Lord gave us. 6My job was to plant the seed in your hearts, and Apollos watered it, but it was God, not we, who made it grow. 7The ones who do the planting or watering aren't important, but God is important because he is the one who makes the seed grow. 8The one who plants and the one who waters work as a team with the same purpose. Yet they will be rewarded individually, according to their own hard work. 9We work together as partners who belong to God. You are God's field, God's building—not ours.

10Because of God's special favor to me, I have laid the foundation

2:9 Isa 64:4.   2:13 Or *explaining spiritual truths in spiritual language,* or *explaining spiritual truths to spiritual people.*   2:16 Isa 40:13.   3:1a Greek *Brothers.*   3:1b Greek *in Christ.*
3:4 Greek *aren't you merely human?*

like an expert builder. Now others are building on it. But whoever is building on this foundation must be very careful. 11For no one can lay any other foundation than the one we already have—Jesus Christ. 12Now anyone who builds on that foundation may use gold, silver, jewels, wood, hay, or straw. 13But there is going to come a time of testing at the judgment day to see what kind of work each builder has done. Everyone's work will be put through the fire to see whether or not it keeps its value. 14If the work survives the fire, that builder will receive a reward. 15But if the work is burned up, the builder will suffer great loss. The builders themselves will be saved, but like someone escaping through a wall of flames.

16Don't you realize that all of you together are the temple of God and that the Spirit of God lives in* you? 17God will bring ruin upon anyone who ruins this temple. For God's temple is holy, and you Christians are that temple.

18Stop fooling yourselves. If you think you are wise by this world's standards, you will have to become a fool so you can become wise by God's standards. 19For the wisdom of this world is foolishness to God. As the Scriptures say,

"God catches those who think they are wise
    in their own cleverness."*

20And again,

"The Lord knows the thoughts of the wise,
    that they are worthless."*

21So don't take pride in following a particular leader. Everything belongs to you: 22Paul and Apollos and Peter*; the whole world and life and death; the present and the future. Everything belongs to you, 23and you belong to Christ, and Christ belongs to God.

CHAPTER 4

Paul and the Corinthians

So look at Apollos and me as mere servants of Christ who have been put in charge of explaining God's secrets. 2Now, a person who is put in charge as a manager must be faithful. 3What about me? Have I been faithful? Well, it matters very little what you or anyone else thinks. I don't even trust my own judgment on this point. 4My conscience is clear, but that isn't what matters. It is the Lord himself who will examine me and decide.

5So be careful not to jump to conclusions before the Lord returns as to whether or not someone is faithful. When the Lord comes, he will bring our deepest secrets to light and will reveal our private motives. And then God will give to everyone whatever praise is due.

6Dear brothers and sisters,* I have used Apollos and myself to illustrate what I've been saying. If you pay attention to the Scriptures,* you won't brag about one of your leaders at the expense of another. 7What makes you better than anyone else? What do you have that God hasn't given you? And if all you have is from God, why boast as though you have accomplished something on your own?

3:16 Or *among.* **3:19** Job 5:13. **3:20** Ps 94:11. **3:22** Greek *Cephas.* **4:6a** Greek *Brothers.* **4:6b** Or *You must learn not to go beyond "what is written," so that.*

8You think you already have everything you need! You are already rich! Without us you have become kings! I wish you really were on your thrones already, for then we would be reigning with you! 9But sometimes I think God has put us apostles on display, like prisoners of war at the end of a victor's parade, condemned to die. We have become a spectacle to the entire world—to people and angels alike.

10Our dedication to Christ makes us look like fools, but you are so wise! We are weak, but you are so powerful! You are well thought of, but we are laughed at. 11To this very hour we go hungry and thirsty, without enough clothes to keep us warm. We have endured many beatings, and we have no homes of our own. 12We have worked wearily with our own hands to earn our living. We bless those who curse us. We are patient with those who abuse us. 13We respond gently when evil things are said about us. Yet we are treated like the world's garbage, like everybody's trash—right up to the present moment.

14I am not writing these things to shame you, but to warn you as my beloved children. 15For even if you had ten thousand others to teach you about Christ, you have only one spiritual father. For I became your father in Christ Jesus when I preached the Good News to you. 16So I ask you to follow my example and do as I do.

17That is the very reason I am sending Timothy—to help you do this. For he is my beloved and trustworthy child in the Lord. He will remind you of what I teach about Christ Jesus in all the churches wherever I go.

18I know that some of you have become arrogant, thinking I will never visit you again. 19But I will come—and soon—if the Lord will let me, and then I'll find out whether these arrogant people are just big talkers or whether they really have God's power. 20For the Kingdom of God is not just fancy talk; it is living by God's power. 21Which do you choose? Should I come with punishment and scolding, or should I come with quiet love and gentleness?

CHAPTER 5

Paul Condemns Spiritual Pride

I can hardly believe the report about the sexual immorality going on among you, something so evil that even the pagans don't do it. I am told that you have a man in your church who is living in sin with his father's wife. 2And you are so proud of yourselves! Why aren't you mourning in sorrow and shame? And why haven't you removed this man from your fellowship?

3Even though I am not there with you in person, I am with you in the Spirit.* Concerning the one who has done this, I have already passed judgment 4in the name of the Lord Jesus. You are to call a meeting of the church,* and I will be there in spirit, and the power of the Lord Jesus will be with you as you meet. 5Then you must cast this man out of the church and into Satan's hands, so that his sinful nature will be destroyed* and he himself* will be saved when the Lord returns.

6How terrible that you should boast about your spirituality, and

5:3 Or *in spirit.* 5:4 Or *In the name of the Lord Jesus, you are to call a meeting of the church.* 5:5a Or *so that he will die;* Greek reads *for the destruction of the flesh.* 5:5b Greek *and the spirit.*

yet you let this sort of thing go on. Don't you realize that if even one person is allowed to go on sinning, soon all will be affected? [7]Remove this wicked person from among you so that you can stay pure.* Christ, our Passover Lamb, has been sacrificed for us. [8]So let us celebrate the festival, not by eating the old bread* of wickedness and evil, but by eating the new bread* of purity and truth.

[9]When I wrote to you before, I told you not to associate with people who indulge in sexual sin. [10]But I wasn't talking about unbelievers who indulge in sexual sin, or who are greedy or are swindlers or idol worshipers. You would have to leave this world to avoid people like that. [11]What I meant was that you are not to associate with anyone who claims to be a Christian* yet indulges in sexual sin, or is greedy, or worships idols, or is abusive, or a drunkard, or a swindler. Don't even eat with such people.

[12]It isn't my responsibility to judge outsiders, but it certainly is your job to judge those inside the church who are sinning in these ways. [13]God will judge those on the outside; but as the Scriptures say, "You must remove the evil person from among you."*

CHAPTER 6

Avoiding Lawsuits with Christians

When you have something against another Christian, why do you file a lawsuit and ask a secular court to decide the matter, instead of taking it to other Christians to decide who is right? [2]Don't you know that someday we Christians are going to judge the world? And since you are going to judge the world, can't you decide these little things among yourselves? [3]Don't you realize that we Christians will judge angels? So you should surely be able to resolve ordinary disagreements here on earth. [4]If you have legal disputes about such matters, why do you go to outside judges who are not respected by the church? [5]I am saying this to shame you. Isn't there anyone in all the church who is wise enough to decide these arguments? [6]But instead, one Christian* sues another—right in front of unbelievers!

[7]To have such lawsuits at all is a real defeat for you. Why not just accept the injustice and leave it at that? Why not let yourselves be cheated? [8]But instead, you yourselves are the ones who do wrong and cheat even your own Christian brothers and sisters.*

Avoiding Sexual Sin

[9]Don't you know that those who do wrong will have no share in the Kingdom of God? Don't fool yourselves. Those who indulge in sexual sin, who are idol worshipers, adulterers, male prostitutes, homosexuals, [10]thieves, greedy people, drunkards, abusers, and swindlers—none of these will have a share in the Kingdom of God. [11]There was a time when some of you were just like that, but now your sins have been washed away,* and you have been set apart for God. You have been made right with God because of what the Lord Jesus Christ and the Spirit of our God have done for you.

[12]You may say, "I am allowed to do anything." But I reply, "Not

---

5:6-7 Greek *Don't you realize that even a little leaven spreads quickly through the whole batch of dough?* [7]*Purge out the old leaven so that you can be a new batch of dough, just as you are already unleavened.* 5:8a Greek *not with old leaven.* 5:8b Greek *but with unleavened [bread].* 5:11 Greek *a brother.* 5:13 Deut 17:7. 6:6 Greek *one brother.* 6:8 Greek *brothers.* 6:11 Or *you have been cleansed.*

everything is good for you." And even though "I am allowed to do anything," I must not become a slave to anything. 13You say, "Food is for the stomach, and the stomach is for food." This is true, though someday God will do away with both of them. But our bodies were not made for sexual immorality. They were made for the Lord, and the Lord cares about our bodies. 14And God will raise our bodies from the dead by his marvelous power, just as he raised our Lord from the dead. 15Don't you realize that your bodies are actually parts of Christ? Should a man take his body, which belongs to Christ, and join it to a prostitute? Never! 16And don't you know that if a man joins himself to a prostitute, he becomes one body with her? For the Scriptures say, "The two are united into one."* 17But the person who is joined to the Lord becomes one spirit with him.

18Run away from sexual sin! No other sin so clearly affects the body as this one does. For sexual immorality is a sin against your own body. 19Or don't you know that your body is the temple of the Holy Spirit, who lives in you and was given to you by God? You do not belong to yourself, 20for God bought you with a high price. So you must honor God with your body.

CHAPTER 7

Instruction on Marriage

Now about the questions you asked in your letter. Yes, it is good to live a celibate life. 2But because there is so much sexual immorality, each man should have his own wife, and each woman should have her own husband.

3The husband should not deprive his wife of sexual intimacy, which is her right as a married woman, nor should the wife deprive her husband. 4The wife gives authority over her body to her husband, and the husband also gives authority over his body to his wife. 5So do not deprive each other of sexual relations. The only exception to this rule would be the agreement of both husband and wife to refrain from sexual intimacy for a limited time, so they can give themselves more completely to prayer. Afterward they should come together again so that Satan won't be able to tempt them because of their lack of self-control. 6This is only my suggestion. It's not meant to be an absolute rule. 7I wish everyone could get along without marrying, just as I do. But we are not all the same. God gives some the gift of marriage, and to others he gives the gift of singleness.

8Now I say to those who aren't married and to widows—it's better to stay unmarried, just as I am. 9But if they can't control themselves, they should go ahead and marry. It's better to marry than to burn with lust.

10Now, for those who are married I have a command that comes not from me, but from the Lord.* A wife must not leave her husband. 11But if she does leave him, let her remain single or else go back to him. And the husband must not leave his wife.

12Now, I will speak to the rest of you, though I do not have a direct command from the Lord. If a Christian man* has a wife who is an unbeliever and she is willing to continue living with him, he

6:16 Gen 2:24.   7:10 See Matt 5:32; 19:9; Mark 10:11-12; Luke 16:18.   7:12 Greek *a brother.*

must not leave her. 13And if a Christian woman has a husband who is an unbeliever, and he is willing to continue living with her, she must not leave him. 14For the Christian wife brings holiness to her marriage, and the Christian husband brings holiness to his marriage. Otherwise, your children would not have a godly influence, but now they are set apart for him. 15(But if the husband or wife who isn't a Christian insists on leaving, let them go. In such cases the Christian husband or wife is not required to stay with them, for God wants his children to live in peace.) 16You wives must remember that your husbands might be converted because of you. And you husbands must remember that your wives might be converted because of you.

17You must accept whatever situation the Lord has put you in, and continue on as you were when God first called you. This is my rule for all the churches. 18For instance, a man who was circumcised before he became a believer should not try to reverse it. And the man who was uncircumcised when he became a believer should not be circumcised now. 19For it makes no difference whether or not a man has been circumcised. The important thing is to keep God's commandments.

20You should continue on as you were when God called you. 21Are you a slave? Don't let that worry you—but if you get a chance to be free, take it. 22And remember, if you were a slave when the Lord called you, the Lord has now set you free from the awful power of sin. And if you were free when the Lord called you, you are now a slave of Christ. 23God purchased you at a high price. Don't be enslaved by the world.* 24So, dear brothers and sisters,* whatever situation you were in when you became a believer, stay there in your new relationship with God.

25Now, about the young women who are not yet married. I do not have a command from the Lord for them. But the Lord in his kindness has given me wisdom that can be trusted, and I will share it with you. 26Because of the present crisis,* I think it is best to remain just as you are. 27If you have a wife, do not end the marriage. If you do not have a wife, do not get married. 28But if you do get married, it is not a sin. And if a young woman gets married, it is not a sin. However, I am trying to spare you the extra problems that come with marriage.

29Now let me say this, dear brothers and sisters: The time that remains is very short, so husbands should not let marriage be their major concern. 30Happiness or sadness or wealth should not keep anyone from doing God's work. 31Those in frequent contact with the things of the world should make good use of them without becoming attached to them, for this world and all it contains will pass away. 32In everything you do, I want you to be free from the concerns of this life. An unmarried man can spend his time doing the Lord's work and thinking how to please him. 33But a married man can't do that so well. He has to think about his earthly responsibilities and how to please his wife. 34His interests are divided. In the same way, a woman who is no longer married or has never been married can be more devoted to the Lord in body

7:23 Greek *don't become slaves of people.*   7:24 Greek *brothers;* also in 7:29.   7:26 Or *pressures of life.*

and in spirit, while the married woman must be concerned about her earthly responsibilities and how to please her husband.

³⁵I am saying this for your benefit, not to place restrictions on you. I want you to do whatever will help you serve the Lord best, with as few distractions as possible. ³⁶But if a man thinks he ought to marry his fiancée because he has trouble controlling his passions and time is passing, it is all right; it is not a sin. Let them marry. ³⁷But if he has decided firmly not to marry and there is no urgency and he can control his passion, he does well not to marry. ³⁸So the person who marries does well, and the person who doesn't marry does even better.

³⁹A wife is married to her husband as long as he lives. If her husband dies, she is free to marry whomever she wishes, but this must be a marriage acceptable to the Lord.* ⁴⁰But in my opinion it will be better for her if she doesn't marry again, and I think I am giving you counsel from God's Spirit when I say this.

CHAPTER 8

Food Sacrificed to Idols

Now let's talk about food that has been sacrificed to idols. You think that everyone should agree with your perfect knowledge. While knowledge may make us feel important, it is love that really builds up the church. ²Anyone who claims to know all the answers doesn't really know very much. ³But the person who loves God is the one God knows and cares for.

⁴So now, what about it? Should we eat meat that has been sacrificed to idols? Well, we all know that an idol is not really a god and that there is only one God and no other. ⁵According to some people, there are many so-called gods and many lords, both in heaven and on earth. ⁶But we know that there is only one God, the Father, who created everything, and we exist for him. And there is only one Lord, Jesus Christ, through whom God made everything and through whom we have been given life.

⁷However, not all Christians realize this. Some are accustomed to thinking of idols as being real, so when they eat food that has been offered to idols, they think of it as the worship of real gods, and their weak consciences are violated. ⁸It's true that we can't win God's approval by what we eat. We don't miss out on anything if we don't eat it, and we don't gain anything if we do. ⁹But you must be careful with this freedom of yours. Do not cause a brother or sister with a weaker conscience to stumble.

¹⁰You see, this is what can happen: Weak Christians who think it is wrong to eat this food will see you eating in the temple of an idol. You know there's nothing wrong with it, but they will be encouraged to violate their conscience by eating food that has been dedicated to the idol. ¹¹So because of your superior knowledge, a weak Christian,* for whom Christ died, will be destroyed. ¹²And you are sinning against Christ when you sin against other Christians* by encouraging them to do something they believe is wrong. ¹³If what I eat is going to make another Christian sin, I will never eat meat again as long as I live—for I don't want to make another Christian stumble.

7:39 Or *but only to a Christian;* Greek reads *but only in the Lord.*   **8:11** Greek *brother;* also in 8:13.   **8:12** Greek *brothers.*

CHAPTER 9
Paul Gives Up His Rights

Do I not have as much freedom as anyone else?* Am I not an apostle? Haven't I seen Jesus our Lord with my own eyes? Isn't it because of my hard work that you are in the Lord? ²Even if others think I am not an apostle, I certainly am to you, for you are living proof that I am the Lord's apostle.

³This is my answer to those who question my authority as an apostle.* ⁴Don't we have the right to live in your homes and share your meals? ⁵Don't we have the right to bring a Christian wife* along with us as the other disciples and the Lord's brothers and Peter* do? ⁶Or is it only Barnabas and I who have to work to support ourselves? ⁷What soldier has to pay his own expenses? And have you ever heard of a farmer who harvests his crop and doesn't have the right to eat some of it? What shepherd takes care of a flock of sheep and isn't allowed to drink some of the milk? ⁸And this isn't merely human opinion. Doesn't God's law say the same thing? ⁹For the law of Moses says, "Do not keep an ox from eating as it treads out the grain."* Do you suppose God was thinking only about oxen when he said this? ¹⁰Wasn't he also speaking to us? Of course he was. Just as farm workers who plow fields and thresh the grain expect a share of the harvest, Christian workers should be paid by those they serve.

¹¹We have planted good spiritual seed among you. Is it too much to ask, in return, for mere food and clothing? ¹²If you support others who preach to you, shouldn't we have an even greater right to be supported? Yet we have never used this right. We would rather put up with anything than put an obstacle in the way of the Good News about Christ.

¹³Don't you know that those who work in the Temple get their meals from the food brought to the Temple as offerings? And those who serve at the altar get a share of the sacrificial offerings. ¹⁴In the same way, the Lord gave orders that those who preach the Good News should be supported by those who benefit from it. ¹⁵Yet I have never used any of these rights. And I am not writing this to suggest that I would like to start now. In fact, I would rather die than lose my distinction of preaching without charge. ¹⁶For preaching the Good News is not something I can boast about. I am compelled by God to do it. How terrible for me if I didn't do it!

¹⁷If I were doing this of my own free will, then I would deserve payment. But God has chosen me and given me this sacred trust, and I have no choice. ¹⁸What then is my pay? It is the satisfaction I get from preaching the Good News without expense to anyone, never demanding my rights as a preacher.

¹⁹This means I am not bound to obey people just because they pay me, yet I have become a servant of everyone so that I can bring them to Christ. ²⁰When I am with the Jews, I become one of them so that I can bring them to Christ. When I am with those who follow the Jewish laws, I do the same, even though I am not subject to the law, so that I can bring them to Christ. ²¹When I am with the Gentiles who do not have the Jewish law,* I fit in with them as much

9:1 Greek *Am I not free?*   9:3 Greek *those who examine me.*   9:5a Greek *a sister, a wife.*
9:5b Greek *Cephas.*   9:9 Deut 25:4.   9:21 Greek *those without the law.*

as I can. In this way, I gain their confidence and bring them to Christ. But I do not discard the law of God; I obey the law of Christ.

²²When I am with those who are oppressed, I share their oppression so that I might bring them to Christ. Yes, I try to find common ground with everyone so that I might bring them to Christ. ²³I do all this to spread the Good News, and in doing so I enjoy its blessings.

²⁴Remember that in a race everyone runs, but only one person gets the prize. You also must run in such a way that you will win. ²⁵All athletes practice strict self-control. They do it to win a prize that will fade away, but we do it for an eternal prize. ²⁶So I run straight to the goal with purpose in every step. I am not like a boxer who misses his punches.* ²⁷I discipline my body like an athlete, training it to do what it should. Otherwise, I fear that after preaching to others I myself might be disqualified.

CHAPTER 10
Warnings against Idolatry

I don't want you to forget, dear brothers and sisters,* what happened to our ancestors in the wilderness long ago. God guided all of them by sending a cloud that moved along ahead of them, and he brought them all safely through the waters of the sea on dry ground. ²As followers of Moses, they were all baptized in the cloud and the sea. ³And all of them ate the same miraculous* food, ⁴and all of them drank the same miraculous water. For they all drank from the miraculous rock that traveled with them, and that rock was Christ. ⁵Yet after all this, God was not pleased with most of them, and he destroyed them in the wilderness.

⁶These events happened as a warning to us, so that we would not crave evil things as they did ⁷or worship idols as some of them did. For the Scriptures say, "The people celebrated with feasting and drinking, and they indulged themselves in pagan revelry."* ⁸And we must not engage in sexual immorality as some of them did, causing 23,000 of them to die in one day. ⁹Nor should we put Christ* to the test, as some of them did and then died from snakebites. ¹⁰And don't grumble as some of them did, for that is why God sent his angel of death to destroy them. ¹¹All these events happened to them as examples for us. They were written down to warn us, who live at the time when this age is drawing to a close.

¹²If you think you are standing strong, be careful, for you, too, may fall into the same sin. ¹³But remember that the temptations that come into your life are no different from what others experience. And God is faithful. He will keep the temptation from becoming so strong that you can't stand up against it. When you are tempted, he will show you a way out so that you will not give in to it.

¹⁴So, my dear friends, flee from the worship of idols. ¹⁵You are reasonable people. Decide for yourselves if what I am about to say is true. ¹⁶When we bless the cup at the Lord's Table, aren't we sharing in the benefits of the blood of Christ? And when we break the loaf of bread, aren't we sharing in the benefits of the body of Christ? ¹⁷And we all eat from one loaf, showing that we are one

9:26 Or *I am not just shadowboxing.*   10:1 Greek *brothers.*   10:3 Greek *spiritual;* also in 10:4.
10:7 Exod 32:6.   10:9 Some manuscripts read *the Lord.*

body. ¹⁸And think about the nation of Israel; all who eat the sacrifices are united by that act.

¹⁹What am I trying to say? Am I saying that the idols to whom the pagans bring sacrifices are real gods and that these sacrifices are of some value? ²⁰No, not at all. What I am saying is that these sacrifices are offered to demons, not to God. And I don't want any of you to be partners with demons. ²¹You cannot drink from the cup of the Lord and from the cup of demons, too. You cannot eat at the Lord's Table and at the table of demons, too. ²²What? Do you dare to rouse the Lord's jealousy as Israel did? Do you think we are stronger than he is?

²³You say, "I am allowed to do anything"—but not everything is helpful. You say, "I am allowed to do anything"—but not everything is beneficial. ²⁴Don't think only of your own good. Think of other Christians and what is best for them.

²⁵Here's what you should do. You may eat any meat that is sold in the marketplace. Don't ask whether or not it was offered to idols, and then your conscience won't be bothered. ²⁶For "the earth is the Lord's, and everything in it."*

²⁷If someone who isn't a Christian asks you home for dinner, go ahead; accept the invitation if you want to. Eat whatever is offered to you and don't ask any questions about it. Your conscience should not be bothered by this. ²⁸But suppose someone warns you that this meat has been offered to an idol. Don't eat it, out of consideration for the conscience of the one who told you. ²⁹It might not be a matter of conscience for you, but it is for the other person.

Now, why should my freedom be limited by what someone else thinks? ³⁰If I can thank God for the food and enjoy it, why should I be condemned for eating it? ³¹Whatever you eat or drink or whatever you do, you must do all for the glory of God. ³²Don't give offense to Jews or Gentiles or the church of God. ³³That is the plan I follow, too. I try to please everyone in everything I do. I don't just do what I like or what is best for me, but what is best for them so they may be saved.

CHAPTER 11

And you should follow my example, just as I follow Christ's.

Instructions for Public Worship

²I am so glad, dear friends, that you always keep me in your thoughts and you are following the Christian teaching I passed on to you. ³But there is one thing I want you to know: A man is responsible to Christ, a woman is responsible to her husband, and Christ is responsible to God. ⁴A man dishonors Christ* if he covers his head while praying or prophesying. ⁵But a woman dishonors her husband* if she prays or prophesies without a covering on her head, for this is the same as shaving her head. ⁶Yes, if she refuses to wear a head covering, she should cut off all her hair. And since it is shameful for a woman to have her hair cut or her head shaved, then she should wear a covering.* ⁷A man should not wear anything on his head when worshiping, for man is God's glory, made

10:26 Ps 24:1. 11:4 Greek *his head.* 11:5 Greek *her head.* 11:6 Or *then she should have long hair.*

in God's own image, but woman is the glory of man. [8]For the first man didn't come from woman, but the first woman came from man. [9]And man was not made for woman's benefit, but woman was made for man. [10]So a woman should wear a covering on her head as a sign of authority because the angels are watching.

[11]But in relationships among the Lord's people, women are not independent of men, and men are not independent of women. [12]For although the first woman came from man, all men have been born from women ever since, and everything comes from God.

[13]What do you think about this? Is it right for a woman to pray to God in public without covering her head? [14]Isn't it obvious that it's disgraceful for a man to have long hair? [15]And isn't it obvious that long hair is a woman's pride and joy? For it has been given to her as a covering. [16]But if anyone wants to argue about this, all I can say is that we have no other custom than this, and all the churches of God feel the same way about it.

Order at the Lord's Supper

[17]But now when I mention this next issue, I cannot praise you. For it sounds as if more harm than good is done when you meet together. [18]First of all, I hear that there are divisions among you when you meet as a church, and to some extent I believe it. [19]But, of course, there must be divisions among you so that those of you who are right will be recognized!

[20]It's not the Lord's Supper you are concerned about when you come together. [21]For I am told that some of you hurry to eat your own meal without sharing with others. As a result, some go hungry while others get drunk. [22]What? Is this really true? Don't you have your own homes for eating and drinking? Or do you really want to disgrace the church of God and shame the poor? What am I supposed to say about these things? Do you want me to praise you? Well, I certainly do not!

[23]For this is what the Lord himself said, and I pass it on to you just as I received it. On the night when he was betrayed, the Lord Jesus took a loaf of bread, [24]and when he had given thanks, he broke it and said, "This is my body, which is given* for you. Do this in remembrance of me." [25]In the same way, he took the cup of wine after supper, saying, "This cup is the new covenant between God and you, sealed by the shedding of my blood. Do this in remembrance of me as often as you drink it." [26]For every time you eat this bread and drink this cup, you are announcing the Lord's death until he comes again.

[27]So if anyone eats this bread or drinks this cup of the Lord unworthily, that person is guilty of sinning against the body and the blood of the Lord. [28]That is why you should examine yourself before eating the bread and drinking from the cup. [29]For if you eat the bread or drink the cup unworthily, not honoring the body of Christ,* you are eating and drinking God's judgment upon yourself. [30]That is why many of you are weak and sick and some have even died.

[31]But if we examine ourselves, we will not be examined by God and judged in this way. [32]But when we are judged and disciplined

11:24 Some manuscripts read *broken.*   **11:29** Greek *the body;* some manuscripts read *the Lord's body.*

by the Lord, we will not be condemned with the world. [33]So, dear brothers and sisters,* when you gather for the Lord's Supper, wait for each other. [34]If you are really hungry, eat at home so you won't bring judgment upon yourselves when you meet together.

I'll give you instructions about the other matters after I arrive.

CHAPTER 12
Spiritual Gifts

And now, dear brothers and sisters,* I will write about the special abilities the Holy Spirit gives to each of us, for I must correct your misunderstandings about them. [2]You know that when you were still pagans you were led astray and swept along in worshiping speechless idols. [3]So I want you to know how to discern what is truly from God: No one speaking by the Spirit of God can curse Jesus, and no one is able to say, "Jesus is Lord," except by the Holy Spirit.

[4]Now there are different kinds of spiritual gifts, but it is the same Holy Spirit who is the source of them all. [5]There are different kinds of service in the church, but it is the same Lord we are serving. [6]There are different ways God works in our lives, but it is the same God who does the work through all of us. [7]A spiritual gift is given to each of us as a means of helping the entire church.

[8]To one person the Spirit gives the ability to give wise advice; to another he gives the gift of special knowledge. [9]The Spirit gives special faith to another, and to someone else he gives the power to heal the sick. [10]He gives one person the power to perform miracles, and to another the ability to prophesy. He gives someone else the ability to know whether it is really the Spirit of God or another spirit that is speaking. Still another person is given the ability to speak in unknown languages,* and another is given the ability to interpret what is being said. [11]It is the one and only Holy Spirit who distributes these gifts. He alone decides which gift each person should have.

One Body with Many Parts

[12]The human body has many parts, but the many parts make up only one body. So it is with the body of Christ. [13]Some of us are Jews, some are Gentiles, some are slaves, and some are free. But we have all been baptized into Christ's body by one Spirit, and we have all received the same Spirit.*

[14]Yes, the body has many different parts, not just one part. [15]If the foot says, "I am not a part of the body because I am not a hand," that does not make it any less a part of the body. [16]And if the ear says, "I am not part of the body because I am only an ear and not an eye," would that make it any less a part of the body? [17]Suppose the whole body were an eye—then how would you hear? Or if your whole body were just one big ear, how could you smell anything?

[18]But God made our bodies with many parts, and he has put each part just where he wants it. [19]What a strange thing a body would be if it had only one part! [20]Yes, there are many parts, but

11:33 Greek *brothers.* **12:1** Greek *brothers.* **12:10** Or *in tongues;* also in 12:28, 30.
12:13 Greek *we were all given one Spirit to drink.*

only one body. [21]The eye can never say to the hand, "I don't need you." The head can't say to the feet, "I don't need you."

[22]In fact, some of the parts that seem weakest and least important are really the most necessary. [23]And the parts we regard as less honorable are those we clothe with the greatest care. So we carefully protect from the eyes of others those parts that should not be seen, [24]while other parts do not require this special care. So God has put the body together in such a way that extra honor and care are given to those parts that have less dignity. [25]This makes for harmony among the members, so that all the members care for each other equally. [26]If one part suffers, all the parts suffer with it, and if one part is honored, all the parts are glad.

[27]Now all of you together are Christ's body, and each one of you is a separate and necessary part of it. [28]Here is a list of some of the members that God has placed in the body of Christ:

first are apostles,
second are prophets,
third are teachers,
then those who do miracles,
those who have the gift of healing,
those who can help others,
those who can get others to work together,
those who speak in unknown languages.

[29]Is everyone an apostle? Of course not. Is everyone a prophet? No. Are all teachers? Does everyone have the power to do miracles? [30]Does everyone have the gift of healing? Of course not. Does God give all of us the ability to speak in unknown languages? Can everyone interpret unknown languages? No! [31]And in any event, you should desire the most helpful gifts.

Love Is the Greatest

First, however, let me tell you about something else that is better than any of them!

CHAPTER 13

If I could speak in any language in heaven or on earth* but didn't love others, I would only be making meaningless noise like a loud gong or a clanging cymbal. [2]If I had the gift of prophecy, and if I knew all the mysteries of the future and knew everything about everything, but didn't love others, what good would I be? And if I had the gift of faith so that I could speak to a mountain and make it move, without love I would be no good to anybody. [3]If I gave everything I have to the poor and even sacrificed my body, I could boast about it;* but if I didn't love others, I would be of no value whatsoever.

[4]Love is patient and kind. Love is not jealous or boastful or proud [5]or rude. Love does not demand its own way. Love is not irritable, and it keeps no record of when it has been wronged. [6]It is never glad about injustice but rejoices whenever the truth wins out. [7]Love never gives up, never loses faith, is always hopeful, and endures through every circumstance.

13:1 Greek *in tongues of people and angels.*   **13:3** Some manuscripts read *and even gave my body to be burned.*

8Love will last forever, but prophecy and speaking in unknown languages* and special knowledge will all disappear. 9Now we know only a little, and even the gift of prophecy reveals little! 10But when the end comes, these special gifts will all disappear.

11It's like this: When I was a child, I spoke and thought and reasoned as a child does. But when I grew up, I put away childish things. 12Now we see things imperfectly as in a poor mirror, but then we will see everything with perfect clarity.* All that I know now is partial and incomplete, but then I will know everything completely, just as God knows me now.

13There are three things that will endure—faith, hope, and love—and the greatest of these is love.

CHAPTER 14

The Gifts of Tongues and Prophecy

Let love be your highest goal, but also desire the special abilities the Spirit gives, especially the gift of prophecy. 2For if your gift is the ability to speak in tongues,* you will be talking to God but not to people, since they won't be able to understand you. You will be speaking by the power of the Spirit, but it will all be mysterious. 3But one who prophesies is helping others grow in the Lord, encouraging and comforting them. 4A person who speaks in tongues is strengthened personally in the Lord, but one who speaks a word of prophecy strengthens the entire church.

5I wish you all had the gift of speaking in tongues, but even more I wish you were all able to prophesy. For prophecy is a greater and more useful gift than speaking in tongues, unless someone interprets what you are saying so that the whole church can get some good out of it.

6Dear brothers and sisters,* if I should come to you talking in an unknown language,* how would that help you? But if I bring you some revelation or some special knowledge or some prophecy or some teaching—that is what will help you. 7Even musical instruments like the flute or the harp, though they are lifeless, are examples of the need for speaking in plain language. For no one will recognize the melody unless the notes are played clearly. 8And if the bugler doesn't sound a clear call, how will the soldiers know they are being called to battle? 9And it's the same for you. If you talk to people in a language they don't understand, how will they know what you mean? You might as well be talking to an empty room.

10There are so many different languages in the world, and all are excellent for those who understand them, 11but to me they mean nothing. I will not understand people who speak those languages, and they will not understand me. 12Since you are so eager to have spiritual gifts, ask God for those that will be of real help to the whole church.

13So anyone who has the gift of speaking in tongues should pray also for the gift of interpretation in order to tell people plainly what has been said. 14For if I pray in tongues, my spirit is praying, but I don't understand what I am saying.

13:8 Or *in tongues.* **13:12** Greek *see face to face.* **14:2** Or *in unknown languages;* also in 14:4, 5, 13, 14, 18, 22, 28, 39. **14:6a** Greek *brothers;* also in 14:20, 26, 39. **14:6b** Or *in tongues;* also in 14:19, 23, 26, 27.

¹⁵Well then, what shall I do? I will do both. I will pray in the spirit,* and I will pray in words I understand. I will sing in the spirit, and I will sing in words I understand. ¹⁶For if you praise God only in the spirit, how can those who don't understand you praise God along with you? How can they join you in giving thanks when they don't understand what you are saying? ¹⁷You will be giving thanks very nicely, no doubt, but it doesn't help the other people present.

¹⁸I thank God that I speak in tongues more than all of you. ¹⁹But in a church meeting I would much rather speak five understandable words that will help others than ten thousand words in an unknown language.

²⁰Dear brothers and sisters, don't be childish in your understanding of these things. Be innocent as babies when it comes to evil, but be mature and wise in understanding matters of this kind. ²¹It is written in the Scriptures,*

"I will speak to my own people
    through unknown languages
    and through the lips of foreigners.
But even then, they will not listen to me,"*
    says the Lord.

²²So you see that speaking in tongues is a sign, not for believers, but for unbelievers; prophecy, however, is for the benefit of believers, not unbelievers. ²³Even so, if unbelievers or people who don't understand these things come into your meeting and hear everyone talking in an unknown language, they will think you are crazy. ²⁴But if all of you are prophesying, and unbelievers or people who don't understand these things come into your meeting, they will be convicted of sin, and they will be condemned by what you say. ²⁵As they listen, their secret thoughts will be laid bare, and they will fall down on their knees and worship God, declaring, "God is really here among you."

A Call to Orderly Worship

²⁶Well, my brothers and sisters, let's summarize what I am saying. When you meet, one will sing, another will teach, another will tell some special revelation God has given, one will speak in an unknown language, while another will interpret what is said. But everything that is done must be useful to all and build them up in the Lord. ²⁷No more than two or three should speak in an unknown language. They must speak one at a time, and someone must be ready to interpret what they are saying. ²⁸But if no one is present who can interpret, they must be silent in your church meeting and speak in tongues to God privately.

²⁹Let two or three prophesy, and let the others evaluate what is said. ³⁰But if someone is prophesying and another person receives a revelation from the Lord, the one who is speaking must stop. ³¹In this way, all who prophesy will have a turn to speak, one after the other, so that everyone will learn and be encouraged. ³²Remember that people who prophesy are in control of their spirit and can wait

14:15 Or *in the Spirit;* also in 14:15b, 16.   **14:21a** Greek *in the law.*   **14:21b** Isa 28:11-12.

their turn. ³³For God is not a God of disorder but of peace, as in all the other churches.

³⁴Women should be silent during the church meetings. It is not proper for them to speak. They should be submissive, just as the law says. ³⁵If they have any questions to ask, let them ask their husbands at home, for it is improper for women to speak in church meetings.*

³⁶Do you think that the knowledge of God's word begins and ends with you Corinthians? Well, you are mistaken! ³⁷If you claim to be a prophet or think you are very spiritual, you should recognize that what I am saying is a command from the Lord himself. ³⁸But if you do not recognize this, you will not be recognized.*

³⁹So, dear brothers and sisters, be eager to prophesy, and don't forbid speaking in tongues. ⁴⁰But be sure that everything is done properly and in order.

CHAPTER 15

The Resurrection of Christ

Now let me remind you, dear brothers and sisters,* of the Good News I preached to you before. You welcomed it then and still do now, for your faith is built on this wonderful message. ²And it is this Good News that saves you if you firmly believe it—unless, of course, you believed something that was never true in the first place.

³I passed on to you what was most important and what had also been passed on to me—that Christ died for our sins, just as the Scriptures said. ⁴He was buried, and he was raised from the dead on the third day, as the Scriptures said. ⁵He was seen by Peter* and then by the twelve apostles. ⁶After that, he was seen by more than five hundred of his followers* at one time, most of whom are still alive, though some have died by now. ⁷Then he was seen by James and later by all the apostles. ⁸Last of all, I saw him, too, long after the others, as though I had been born at the wrong time. ⁹For I am the least of all the apostles, and I am not worthy to be called an apostle after the way I persecuted the church of God.

¹⁰But whatever I am now, it is all because God poured out his special favor on me—and not without results. For I have worked harder than all the other apostles, yet it was not I but God who was working through me by his grace. ¹¹So it makes no difference whether I preach or they preach. The important thing is that you believed what we preached to you.

The Resurrection of the Dead

¹²But tell me this—since we preach that Christ rose from the dead, why are some of you saying there will be no resurrection of the dead? ¹³For if there is no resurrection of the dead, then Christ has not been raised either. ¹⁴And if Christ was not raised, then all our preaching is useless, and your trust in God is useless. ¹⁵And we apostles would all be lying about God, for we have

14:33 The phrase *as in all the other churches* could be joined to the beginning of 14:34. 14:35 Some manuscripts place verses 34-35 after 14:40. 14:38 Some manuscripts read *If you are ignorant of this, stay in your ignorance.* 15:1 Greek *brothers;* also in 15:31, 50, 58. 15:5 Greek *Cephas.* 15:6 Greek *the brothers.*

said that God raised Christ from the grave, but that can't be true if there is no resurrection of the dead. ¹⁶If there is no resurrection of the dead, then Christ has not been raised. ¹⁷And if Christ has not been raised, then your faith is useless, and you are still under condemnation for your sins. ¹⁸In that case, all who have died believing in Christ have perished! ¹⁹And if we have hope in Christ only for this life, we are the most miserable people in the world.

²⁰But the fact is that Christ has been raised from the dead. He has become the first of a great harvest of those who will be raised to life again.

²¹So you see, just as death came into the world through a man, Adam, now the resurrection from the dead has begun through another man, Christ. ²²Everyone dies because all of us are related to Adam, the first man. But all who are related to Christ, the other man, will be given new life. ²³But there is an order to this resurrection: Christ was raised first; then when Christ comes back, all his people will be raised.

²⁴After that the end will come, when he will turn the Kingdom over to God the Father, having put down all enemies of every kind.* ²⁵For Christ must reign until he humbles all his enemies beneath his feet. ²⁶And the last enemy to be destroyed is death. ²⁷For the Scriptures say, "God has given him authority over all things."* (Of course, when it says "authority over all things," it does not include God himself, who gave Christ his authority.) ²⁸Then, when he has conquered all things, the Son will present himself to God, so that God, who gave his Son authority over all things, will be utterly supreme over everything everywhere.

²⁹If the dead will not be raised, then what point is there in people being baptized for those who are dead? Why do it unless the dead will someday rise again?

³⁰And why should we ourselves be continually risking our lives, facing death hour by hour? ³¹For I swear, dear brothers and sisters, I face death daily. This is as certain as my pride in what the Lord Jesus Christ has done in you. ³²And what value was there in fighting wild beasts—those men of Ephesus*—if there will be no resurrection from the dead? If there is no resurrection,

"Let's feast and get drunk,
   for tomorrow we die!"*

³³Don't be fooled by those who say such things, for "bad company corrupts good character." ³⁴Come to your senses and stop sinning. For to your shame I say that some of you don't even know God.

The Resurrection Body

³⁵But someone may ask, "How will the dead be raised? What kind of bodies will they have?" ³⁶What a foolish question! When you put a seed into the ground, it doesn't grow into a plant unless it dies first. ³⁷And what you put in the ground is not the plant that will grow, but only a dry little seed of wheat or

15:24 Greek *every ruler and every authority and power.*   **15:27** Ps 8:6.   **15:32a** Greek *fighting wild beasts in Ephesus.*   **15:32b** Isa 22:13.

whatever it is you are planting. [38]Then God gives it a new body—just the kind he wants it to have. A different kind of plant grows from each kind of seed. [39]And just as there are different kinds of seeds and plants, so also there are different kinds of flesh—whether of humans, animals, birds, or fish.

[40]There are bodies in the heavens, and there are bodies on earth. The glory of the heavenly bodies is different from the beauty of the earthly bodies. [41]The sun has one kind of glory, while the moon and stars each have another kind. And even the stars differ from each other in their beauty and brightness.

[42]It is the same way for the resurrection of the dead. Our earthly bodies, which die and decay, will be different when they are resurrected, for they will never die. [43]Our bodies now disappoint us, but when they are raised, they will be full of glory. They are weak now, but when they are raised, they will be full of power. [44]They are natural human bodies now, but when they are raised, they will be spiritual bodies. For just as there are natural bodies, so also there are spiritual bodies.

[45]The Scriptures tell us, "The first man, Adam, became a living person."* But the last Adam—that is, Christ—is a life-giving Spirit. [46]What came first was the natural body, then the spiritual body comes later. [47]Adam, the first man, was made from the dust of the earth, while Christ, the second man, came from heaven. [48]Every human being has an earthly body just like Adam's, but our heavenly bodies will be just like Christ's. [49]Just as we are now like Adam, the man of the earth, so we will someday be like Christ, the man from heaven.

[50]What I am saying, dear brothers and sisters, is that flesh and blood cannot inherit the Kingdom of God. These perishable bodies of ours are not able to live forever.

[51]But let me tell you a wonderful secret God has revealed to us. Not all of us will die, but we will all be transformed. [52]It will happen in a moment, in the blinking of an eye, when the last trumpet is blown. For when the trumpet sounds, the Christians who have died* will be raised with transformed bodies. And then we who are living will be transformed so that we will never die. [53]For our perishable earthly bodies must be transformed into heavenly bodies that will never die.

[54]When this happens—when our perishable earthly bodies have been transformed into heavenly bodies that will never die—then at last the Scriptures will come true:

"Death is swallowed up in victory."*
[55] O death, where is your victory?
 O death, where is your sting?"*

[56]For sin is the sting that results in death, and the law gives sin its power. [57]How we thank God, who gives us victory over sin and death through Jesus Christ our Lord!

[58]So, my dear brothers and sisters, be strong and steady, always enthusiastic about the Lord's work, for you know that nothing you do for the Lord is ever useless.

15:45 Gen 2:7.   **15:52** Greek *the dead.*   **15:54** Isa 25:8.   **15:55** Hos 13:14.

CHAPTER 16

The Collection for Jerusalem

Now about the money being collected for the Christians in Jerusalem: You should follow the same procedures I gave to the churches in Galatia. ²On every Lord's Day,* each of you should put aside some amount of money in relation to what you have earned and save it for this offering. Don't wait until I get there and then try to collect it all at once. ³When I come I will write letters of recommendation for the messengers you choose to deliver your gift to Jerusalem. ⁴And if it seems appropriate for me also to go along, then we can travel together.

Paul's Final Instructions

⁵I am coming to visit you after I have been to Macedonia, for I am planning to travel through Macedonia. ⁶It could be that I will stay awhile with you, perhaps all winter, and then you can send me on my way to the next destination. ⁷This time I don't want to make just a short visit and then go right on. I want to come and stay awhile, if the Lord will let me. ⁸In the meantime, I will be staying here at Ephesus until the Festival of Pentecost, ⁹for there is a wide-open door for a great work here, and many people are responding. But there are many who oppose me.

¹⁰When Timothy comes, treat him with respect. He is doing the Lord's work, just as I am. ¹¹Don't let anyone despise him. Send him on his way with your blessings when he returns to me. I am looking forward to seeing him soon, along with the other brothers.

¹²Now about our brother Apollos—I urged him to join the other brothers when they visit you, but he was not willing to come right now. He will be seeing you later, when the time is right.

¹³Be on guard. Stand true to what you believe. Be courageous. Be strong. ¹⁴And everything you do must be done with love.

¹⁵You know that Stephanas and his household were the first to become Christians in Greece,* and they are spending their lives in service to other Christians. I urge you, dear brothers and sisters,* ¹⁶to respect them fully and others like them who serve with such real devotion. ¹⁷I am so glad that Stephanas, Fortunatus, and Achaicus have come here. They have been making up for the help you weren't here to give me. ¹⁸They have been a wonderful encouragement to me, as they have been to you, too. You must give proper honor to all who serve as well.

Paul's Final Greetings

¹⁹The churches here in the province of Asia* greet you heartily in the Lord, along with Aquila and Priscilla and all the others who gather in their home for church meetings. ²⁰All the brothers and sisters here have asked me to greet you for them. Greet each other in Christian love.*

²¹Here is my greeting, which I write with my own hand—PAUL.

²²If anyone does not love the Lord, that person is cursed. Our Lord, come!*

²³May the grace of the Lord Jesus be with you.

²⁴My love to all of you in Christ Jesus.*

16:2 Greek *every first day of the week.*   16:15a Greek *were the firstfruits in Achaia,* the southern region of the Greek peninsula.   16:15b Greek *brothers;* also in 16:20.
16:19 *Asia* was a Roman province in what is now western Turkey.   16:20 Greek *with a sacred kiss.*   16:22 From Aramaic, *Marana tha.*   16:24 Some manuscripts add *Amen.*

2 CORINTHIANS

CHAPTER 1

Greetings from Paul

This letter is from Paul, appointed by God to be an apostle of Christ Jesus, and from our dear brother Timothy.

We are writing to God's church in Corinth and to all the Christians throughout Greece.*

²May God our Father and the Lord Jesus Christ give you his grace and peace.

God Offers Comfort to All

³All praise to the God and Father of our Lord Jesus Christ. He is the source* of every mercy and the God who comforts us. ⁴He comforts us in all our troubles so that we can comfort others. When others are troubled, we will be able to give them the same comfort God has given us. ⁵You can be sure that the more we suffer for Christ, the more God will shower us with his comfort through Christ. ⁶So when we are weighed down with troubles, it is for your benefit and salvation! For when God comforts us, it is so that we, in turn, can be an encouragement to you. Then you can patiently endure the same things we suffer. ⁷We are confident that as you share in suffering, you will also share God's comfort.

⁸I think you ought to know, dear brothers and sisters,* about the trouble we went through in the province of Asia. We were crushed and completely overwhelmed, and we thought we would never live through it. ⁹In fact, we expected to die. But as a result, we learned not to rely on ourselves, but on God who can raise the dead. ¹⁰And he did deliver us from mortal danger. And we are confident that he will continue to deliver us. ¹¹He will rescue us because you are helping by praying for us. As a result, many will give thanks to God because so many people's prayers for our safety have been answered.

Paul's Change of Plans

¹²We can say with confidence and a clear conscience that we have been honest* and sincere in all our dealings. We have depended on God's grace, not on our own earthly wisdom. That is how we have acted toward everyone, and especially toward you. ¹³My letters have been straightforward, and there is nothing written between the lines and nothing you can't understand. I hope someday you will fully understand us, ¹⁴even if you don't fully understand us now. Then on the day when our Lord Jesus comes back again, you will be proud of us in the same way we are proud of you.

¹⁵Since I was so sure of your understanding and trust, I wanted to give you a double blessing. ¹⁶I wanted to stop and see you on

1:1 Greek *Achaia*, the southern region of the Greek peninsula.   1:3 Greek *the Father*.
1:8 Greek *brothers*.   1:12 Some manuscripts read *holy*.

my way to Macedonia and again on my return trip. Then you could send me on my way to Judea.

[17]You may be asking why I changed my plan. Hadn't I made up my mind yet? Or am I like people of the world who say yes when they really mean no? [18]As surely as God is true, I am not that sort of person. My yes means yes [19]because Jesus Christ, the Son of God, never wavers between yes and no. He is the one whom Timothy, Silas,* and I preached to you, and he is the divine Yes—God's affirmation. [20]For all of God's promises have been fulfilled in him. That is why we say "Amen" when we give glory to God through Christ. [21]It is God who gives us, along with you, the ability to stand firm for Christ.* He has commissioned us, [22]and he has identified us as his own by placing the Holy Spirit in our hearts as the first installment of everything he will give us.

[23]Now I call upon God as my witness that I am telling the truth. The reason I didn't return to Corinth was to spare you from a severe rebuke. [24]But that does not mean we want to tell you exactly how to put your faith into practice.* We want to work together with you so you will be full of joy as you stand firm in your faith.

CHAPTER 2

So I said to myself, "No, I won't do it. I won't make them unhappy with another painful visit." [2]For if I cause you pain and make you sad, who is going to make me glad? [3]That is why I wrote as I did in my last letter, so that when I do come, I will not be made sad by the very ones who ought to give me the greatest joy. Surely you know that my happiness depends on your happiness. [4]How painful it was to write that letter! Heartbroken, I cried over it. I didn't want to hurt you, but I wanted you to know how very much I love you.

Forgiveness for the Sinner

[5]I am not overstating it when I say that the man who caused all the trouble hurt your entire church more than he hurt me. [6]He was punished enough when most of you were united in your judgment against him. [7]Now it is time to forgive him and comfort him. Otherwise he may become so discouraged that he won't be able to recover. [8]Now show him that you still love him.

[9]I wrote to you as I did to find out how far you would go in obeying me. [10]When you forgive this man, I forgive him, too. And when I forgive him (for whatever is to be forgiven), I do so with Christ's authority for your benefit, [11]so that Satan will not outsmart us. For we are very familiar with his evil schemes.

Ministers of the New Covenant

[12]Well, when I came to the city of Troas to preach the Good News of Christ, the Lord gave me tremendous opportunities. [13]But I couldn't rest because my dear brother Titus hadn't yet arrived with a report from you. So I said good-bye and went on to Macedonia to find him.

[14]But thanks be to God, who made us his captives and leads us along in Christ's triumphal procession. Now wherever we go he uses us to tell others about the Lord and to spread the Good News like a sweet perfume. [15]Our lives are a fragrance presented by

1:19 Greek *Silvanus.*   1:21 Or *who has identified us and you as genuine Christians.*
1:24 Greek *want to lord it over your faith.*

Christ to God. But this fragrance is perceived differently by those being saved and by those perishing. 16To those who are perishing we are a fearful smell of death and doom. But to those who are being saved we are a life-giving perfume. And who is adequate for such a task as this? 17You see, we are not like those hucksters—and there are many of them—who preach just to make money. We preach God's message with sincerity and with Christ's authority. And we know that the God who sent us is watching us.

CHAPTER 3

Are we beginning again to tell you how good we are? Some people need to bring letters of recommendation with them or ask you to write letters of recommendation for them. 2But the only letter of recommendation we need is you yourselves! Your lives are a letter written in our* hearts, and everyone can read it and recognize our good work among you. 3Clearly, you are a letter from Christ prepared by us. It is written not with pen and ink, but with the Spirit of the living God. It is carved not on stone, but on human hearts.

4We are confident of all this because of our great trust in God through Christ. 5It is not that we think we can do anything of lasting value by ourselves. Our only power and success come from God. 6He is the one who has enabled us to represent his new covenant. This is a covenant, not of written laws, but of the Spirit. The old way ends in death; in the new way, the Holy Spirit gives life.

The Glory of the New Covenant

7That old system of law etched in stone led to death, yet it began with such glory that the people of Israel could not bear to look at Moses' face. For his face shone with the glory of God, even though the brightness was already fading away. 8Shouldn't we expect far greater glory when the Holy Spirit is giving life? 9If the old covenant, which brings condemnation, was glorious, how much more glorious is the new covenant, which makes us right with God! 10In fact, that first glory was not glorious at all compared with the overwhelming glory of the new covenant. 11So if the old covenant, which has been set aside, was full of glory, then the new covenant, which remains forever, has far greater glory.

12Since this new covenant gives us such confidence, we can be very bold. 13We are not like Moses, who put a veil over his face so the people of Israel would not see the glory fading away. 14But the people's minds were hardened, and even to this day whenever the old covenant is being read, a veil covers their minds so they cannot understand the truth. And this veil can be removed only by believing in Christ. 15Yes, even today when they read Moses' writings, their hearts are covered with that veil, and they do not understand.

16But whenever anyone turns to the Lord, then the veil is taken away. 17Now, the Lord is the Spirit, and wherever the Spirit of the Lord is, he gives freedom. 18And all of us have had that veil removed so that we can be mirrors that brightly reflect* the glory of the Lord. And as the Spirit of the Lord works within us, we become more and more like him and reflect his glory even more.

3:2 Some manuscripts read *your.* 3:18 Or *so that we can see in a mirror.*

CHAPTER 4

Treasure in Perishable Containers

And so, since God in his mercy has given us this wonderful ministry, we never give up. ²We reject all shameful and underhanded methods. We do not try to trick anyone, and we do not distort the word of God. We tell the truth before God, and all who are honest know that.

³If the Good News we preach is veiled from anyone, it is a sign that they are perishing. ⁴Satan, the god of this evil world, has blinded the minds of those who don't believe, so they are unable to see the glorious light of the Good News that is shining upon them. They don't understand the message we preach about the glory of Christ, who is the exact likeness of God.

⁵We don't go around preaching about ourselves; we preach Christ Jesus, the Lord. All we say about ourselves is that we are your servants because of what Jesus has done for us. ⁶For God, who said, "Let there be light in the darkness," has made us understand that this light is the brightness of the glory of God that is seen in the face of Jesus Christ.

⁷But this precious treasure—this light and power that now shine within us—is held in perishable containers, that is, in our weak bodies.* So everyone can see that our glorious power is from God and is not our own.

⁸We are pressed on every side by troubles, but we are not crushed and broken. We are perplexed, but we don't give up and quit. ⁹We are hunted down, but God never abandons us. We get knocked down, but we get up again and keep going. ¹⁰Through suffering, these bodies of ours constantly share in the death of Jesus so that the life of Jesus may also be seen in our bodies.

¹¹Yes, we live under constant danger of death because we serve Jesus, so that the life of Jesus will be obvious in our dying bodies. ¹²So we live in the face of death, but it has resulted in eternal life for you.

¹³But we continue to preach because we have the same kind of faith the psalmist had when he said, "I believed in God, and so I speak."* ¹⁴We know that the same God who raised our Lord Jesus will also raise us with Jesus and present us to himself along with you. ¹⁵All of these things are for your benefit. And as God's grace brings more and more people to Christ, there will be great thanksgiving, and God will receive more and more glory.

¹⁶That is why we never give up. Though our bodies are dying, our spirits are* being renewed every day. ¹⁷For our present troubles are quite small and won't last very long. Yet they produce for us an immeasurably great glory that will last forever! ¹⁸So we don't look at the troubles we can see right now; rather, we look forward to what we have not yet seen. For the troubles we see will soon be over, but the joys to come will last forever.

CHAPTER 5

New Bodies

For we know that when this earthly tent we live in is taken down—when we die and leave these bodies—we will have a home in heaven, an eternal body made for us by God himself and not by human hands. ²We grow weary in our present bodies, and we long

4:7 Greek *But we have this treasure in earthen vessels.*   4:13 Ps 116:10.   4:16 Greek *our inner being is.*

for the day when we will put on our heavenly bodies like new clothing. ³For we will not be spirits without bodies, but we will put on new heavenly bodies. ⁴Our dying bodies make us groan and sigh, but it's not that we want to die and have no bodies at all. We want to slip into our new bodies so that these dying bodies will be swallowed up by everlasting life. ⁵God himself has prepared us for this, and as a guarantee he has given us his Holy Spirit.

⁶So we are always confident, even though we know that as long as we live in these bodies we are not at home with the Lord. ⁷That is why we live by believing and not by seeing. ⁸Yes, we are fully confident, and we would rather be away from these bodies, for then we will be at home with the Lord. ⁹So our aim is to please him always, whether we are here in this body or away from this body. ¹⁰For we must all stand before Christ to be judged. We will each receive whatever we deserve for the good or evil we have done in our bodies.

We Are God's Ambassadors

¹¹It is because we know this solemn fear of the Lord that we work so hard to persuade others. God knows we are sincere, and I hope you know this, too. ¹²Are we trying to pat ourselves on the back again? No, we are giving you a reason to be proud of us, so you can answer those who brag about having a spectacular ministry rather than having a sincere heart before God. ¹³If it seems that we are crazy, it is to bring glory to God. And if we are in our right minds, it is for your benefit. ¹⁴Whatever we do, it is because Christ's love controls us.* Since we believe that Christ died for everyone, we also believe that we have all died to the old life we used to live.* ¹⁵He died for everyone so that those who receive his new life will no longer live to please themselves. Instead, they will live to please Christ, who died and was raised for them.

¹⁶So we have stopped evaluating others by what the world thinks about them. Once I mistakenly thought of Christ that way, as though he were merely a human being. How differently I think about him now! ¹⁷What this means is that those who become Christians become new persons. They are not the same anymore, for the old life is gone. A new life has begun!

¹⁸All this newness of life is from God, who brought us back to himself through what Christ did. And God has given us the task of reconciling people to him. ¹⁹For God was in Christ, reconciling the world to himself, no longer counting people's sins against them. This is the wonderful message he has given us to tell others. ²⁰We are Christ's ambassadors, and God is using us to speak to you. We urge you, as though Christ himself were here pleading with you, "Be reconciled to God!" ²¹For God made Christ, who never sinned, to be the offering for our sin, so that we could be made right with God through Christ.

CHAPTER 6

As God's partners,* we beg you not to reject this marvelous message of God's great kindness. ²For God says,

"At just the right time, I heard you.
    On the day of salvation, I helped you."*

5:14a Or urges us on. 5:14b Greek Since one died on behalf of all, then all died. 6:1 Or As we work together. 6:2 Isa 49:8.

Indeed, God is ready to help you right now. Today is the day of salvation.

Paul's Hardships

³We try to live in such a way that no one will be hindered from finding the Lord by the way we act, and so no one can find fault with our ministry. ⁴In everything we do we try to show that we are true ministers of God. We patiently endure troubles and hardships and calamities of every kind. ⁵We have been beaten, been put in jail, faced angry mobs, worked to exhaustion, endured sleepless nights, and gone without food. ⁶We have proved ourselves by our purity, our understanding, our patience, our kindness, our sincere love, and the power of the Holy Spirit.* ⁷We have faithfully preached the truth. God's power has been working in us. We have righteousness as our weapon, both to attack and to defend ourselves. ⁸We serve God whether people honor us or despise us, whether they slander us or praise us. We are honest, but they call us impostors. ⁹We are well known, but we are treated as unknown. We live close to death, but here we are, still alive. We have been beaten within an inch of our lives. ¹⁰Our hearts ache, but we always have joy. We are poor, but we give spiritual riches to others. We own nothing, and yet we have everything.

¹¹Oh, dear Corinthian friends! We have spoken honestly with you. Our hearts are open to you. ¹²If there is a problem between us, it is not because of a lack of love on our part, but because you have withheld your love from us. ¹³I am talking now as I would to my own children. Open your hearts to us!

The Temple of the Living God

¹⁴Don't team up with those who are unbelievers. How can goodness be a partner with wickedness? How can light live with darkness? ¹⁵What harmony can there be between Christ and the Devil*? How can a believer be a partner with an unbeliever? ¹⁶And what union can there be between God's temple and idols? For we are the temple of the living God. As God said:

"I will live in them
    and walk among them.
I will be their God,
    and they will be my people.*
¹⁷ Therefore, come out from them
    and separate yourselves from them, says the Lord.
Don't touch their filthy things,
    and I will welcome you.*
¹⁸ And I will be your Father,
    and you will be my sons and daughters,
    says the Lord Almighty.*"

CHAPTER 7

Because we have these promises, dear friends, let us cleanse ourselves from everything that can defile our body or spirit. And let us work toward complete purity because we fear God.

6:6 Or *the holiness of spirit.*   **6:15** Greek *and Beliar.*   **6:16** Lev 26:12; Ezek 37:27.
6:17 Isa 52:11; Ezek 20:34.   **6:18** 2 Sam 7:14.

Paul's Joy at the Church's Repentance

2Please open your hearts to us. We have not done wrong to anyone. We have not led anyone astray. We have not taken advantage of anyone. 3I'm not saying this to condemn you, for I said before that you are in our hearts forever. We live or die together with you. 4I have the highest confidence in you, and my pride in you is great. You have greatly encouraged me; you have made me happy despite all our troubles.

5When we arrived in Macedonia there was no rest for us. Outside there was conflict from every direction, and inside there was fear. 6But God, who encourages those who are discouraged, encouraged us by the arrival of Titus. 7His presence was a joy, but so was the news he brought of the encouragement he received from you. When he told me how much you were looking forward to my visit, and how sorry you were about what had happened, and how loyal your love is for me, I was filled with joy!

8I am no longer sorry that I sent that letter to you, though I was sorry for a time, for I know that it was painful to you for a little while. 9Now I am glad I sent it, not because it hurt you, but because the pain caused you to have remorse and change your ways. It was the kind of sorrow God wants his people to have, so you were not harmed by us in any way. 10For God can use sorrow in our lives to help us turn away from sin and seek salvation. We will never regret that kind of sorrow. But sorrow without repentance is the kind that results in death.

11Just see what this godly sorrow produced in you! Such earnestness, such concern to clear yourselves, such indignation, such alarm, such longing to see me, such zeal, and such a readiness to punish the wrongdoer. You showed that you have done everything you could to make things right. 12My purpose was not to write about who did the wrong or who was wronged. I wrote to you so that in the sight of God you could show how much you really do care for us. 13We have been encouraged by this.

In addition to our own encouragement, we were especially delighted to see how happy Titus was at the way you welcomed him and set his mind at ease. 14I had told him how proud I was of you—and you didn't disappoint me. I have always told you the truth, and now my boasting to Titus has also proved true! 15Now he cares for you more than ever when he remembers the way you listened to him and welcomed him with such respect and deep concern. 16I am very happy now because I have complete confidence in you.

CHAPTER 8

A Call to Generous Giving

Now I want to tell you, dear brothers and sisters,* what God in his kindness has done for the churches in Macedonia. 2Though they have been going through much trouble and hard times, their wonderful joy and deep poverty have overflowed in rich generosity. 3For I can testify that they gave not only what they could afford but far more. And they did it of their own free will. 4They begged us again and again for the gracious privilege of sharing in the gift for the Christians in Jerusalem. 5Best of all, they went beyond our

8:1 Greek *brothers.*

highest hopes, for their first action was to dedicate themselves to the Lord and to us for whatever directions God might give them.

[6]So we have urged Titus, who encouraged your giving in the first place, to return to you and encourage you to complete your share in this ministry of giving. [7]Since you excel in so many ways—you have so much faith, such gifted speakers, such knowledge, such enthusiasm, and such love for us*—now I want you to excel also in this gracious ministry of giving. [8]I am not saying you must do it, even though the other churches are eager to do it. This is one way to prove your love is real.

[9]You know how full of love and kindness our Lord Jesus Christ was. Though he was very rich, yet for your sakes he became poor, so that by his poverty he could make you rich.

[10]I suggest that you finish what you started a year ago, for you were the first to propose this idea, and you were the first to begin doing something about it. [11]Now you should carry this project through to completion just as enthusiastically as you began it. Give whatever you can according to what you have. [12]If you are really eager to give, it isn't important how much you are able to give. God wants you to give what you have, not what you don't have. [13]Of course, I don't mean you should give so much that you suffer from having too little. I only mean that there should be some equality. [14]Right now you have plenty and can help them. Then at some other time they can share with you when you need it. In this way, everyone's needs will be met. [15]Do you remember what the Scriptures say about this? "Those who gathered a lot had nothing left over, and those who gathered only a little had enough."*

Titus and His Companions

[16]I am thankful to God that he has given Titus the same enthusiasm for you that I have. [17]He welcomed our request that he visit you again. In fact, he himself was eager to go and see you. [18]We are also sending another brother with Titus. He is highly praised in all the churches as a preacher of the Good News. [19]He was appointed by the churches to accompany us as we take the offering to Jerusalem*—a service that glorifies the Lord and shows our eagerness to help. [20]By traveling together we will guard against any suspicion, for we are anxious that no one should find fault with the way we are handling this generous gift. [21]We are careful to be honorable before the Lord, but we also want everyone else to know we are honorable.

[22]And we are also sending with them another brother who has been thoroughly tested and has shown how earnest he is on many occasions. He is now even more enthusiastic because of his increased confidence in you. [23]If anyone asks about Titus, say that he is my partner who works with me to help you. And these brothers are representatives* of the churches. They are splendid examples of those who bring glory to Christ. [24]So show them your love, and prove to all the churches that our boasting about you is justified.

8:7 Some manuscripts read *love from us to you.*   **8:15** Exod 16:18.   **8:19** See 1 Cor 16:3-4.   **8:23** Greek *apostles.*

CHAPTER 9

The Collection for Christians in Jerusalem

I really don't need to write to you about this gift for the Christians in Jerusalem.* ²For I know how eager you are to help, and I have been boasting to our friends in Macedonia that you Christians in Greece* were ready to send an offering a year ago. In fact, it was your enthusiasm that stirred up many of them to begin helping. ³But I am sending these brothers just to be sure that you really are ready, as I told them you would be, with your money all collected. I don't want it to turn out that I was wrong in my boasting about you. ⁴I would be humiliated—and so would you—if some Macedonian Christians came with me, only to find that you still weren't ready after all I had told them! ⁵So I thought I should send these brothers ahead of me to make sure the gift you promised is ready. But I want it to be a willing gift, not one given under pressure.

⁶Remember this—a farmer who plants only a few seeds will get a small crop. But the one who plants generously will get a generous crop. ⁷You must each make up your own mind as to how much you should give. Don't give reluctantly or in response to pressure. For God loves the person who gives cheerfully. ⁸And God will generously provide all you need. Then you will always have everything you need and plenty left over to share with others. ⁹As the Scriptures say,

"Godly people give generously to the poor.
     Their good deeds will never be forgotten."*

¹⁰For God is the one who gives seed to the farmer and then bread to eat. In the same way, he will give you many opportunities to do good, and he will produce a great harvest of generosity* in you. ¹¹Yes, you will be enriched so that you can give even more generously. And when we take your gifts to those who need them, they will break out in thanksgiving to God. ¹²So two good things will happen—the needs of the Christians in Jerusalem will be met, and they will joyfully express their thanksgiving to God. ¹³You will be glorifying God through your generous gifts. For your generosity to them will prove that you are obedient to the Good News of Christ. ¹⁴And they will pray for you with deep affection because of the wonderful grace of God shown through you.

¹⁵Thank God for his Son—a gift too wonderful for words!*

CHAPTER 10

Paul Defends His Authority

Now I, Paul, plead with you. I plead with the gentleness and kindness that Christ himself would use, even though some of you say I am bold in my letters but timid in person. ²I hope it won't be necessary, but when I come I may have to be very bold with those who think we act from purely human motives. ³We are human, but we don't wage war with human plans and methods. ⁴We use God's mighty weapons, not mere worldly weapons, to knock down the Devil's strongholds. ⁵With these weapons we break down every proud argument that keeps people from knowing God. With these

---

9:1 Greek about the offering for the saints.   9:2 Greek Achaia, the southern region of the Greek peninsula.   9:9 Ps 112:9.   9:10 Greek righteousness.   9:15 Greek Thank God for his indescribable gift.

weapons we conquer their rebellious ideas, and we teach them to obey Christ. 6And we will punish those who remained disobedient after the rest of you became loyal and obedient.

7The trouble with you is that you make your decisions on the basis of appearance.* You must recognize that we belong to Christ just as much as those who proudly declare that they belong to Christ. 8I may seem to be boasting too much about the authority given to us by the Lord. But this authority is to build you up, not to tear you down. And I will not be put to shame by having my work among you destroyed.

9Now this is not just an attempt to frighten you by my letters. 10For some say, "Don't worry about Paul. His letters are demanding and forceful, but in person he is weak, and his speeches are really bad!" 11The ones who say this must realize that we will be just as demanding and forceful in person as we are in our letters.

12Oh, don't worry; I wouldn't dare say that I am as wonderful as these other men who tell you how important they are! But they are only comparing themselves with each other, and measuring themselves by themselves. What foolishness!

13But we will not boast of authority we do not have. Our goal is to stay within the boundaries of God's plan for us, and this plan includes our working there with you. 14We are not going too far when we claim authority over you, for we were the first to travel all the way to you with the Good News of Christ. 15Nor do we claim credit for the work someone else has done. Instead, we hope that your faith will grow and that our work among you will be greatly enlarged. 16Then we will be able to go and preach the Good News in other places that are far beyond you, where no one else is working. Then there will be no question about being in someone else's territory. 17As the Scriptures say,

"The person who wishes to boast
    should boast only of what the Lord has done."*

18When people boast about themselves, it doesn't count for much. But when the Lord commends someone, that's different!

CHAPTER 11

Paul and the False Apostles

I hope you will be patient with me as I keep on talking like a fool. Please bear with me. 2I am jealous for you with the jealousy of God himself. For I promised you as a pure bride* to one husband, Christ. 3But I fear that somehow you will be led away from your pure and simple devotion to Christ, just as Eve was deceived by the serpent. 4You seem to believe whatever anyone tells you, even if they preach about a different Jesus than the one we preach, or a different Spirit than the one you received, or a different kind of gospel than the one you believed. 5But I don't think I am inferior to these "super apostles." 6I may not be a trained speaker, but I know what I am talking about. I think you realize this by now, for we have proved it again and again.

7Did I do wrong when I humbled myself and honored you by preaching God's Good News to you without expecting anything in

10:7 Or *Look at the obvious facts.*   **10:17** Jer 9:24.   **11:2** Greek *a virgin.*

return? [8]I "robbed" other churches by accepting their contributions so I could serve you at no cost. [9]And when I was with you and didn't have enough to live on, I did not ask you to help me. For the brothers who came from Macedonia brought me another gift. I have never yet asked you for any support, and I never will. [10]As surely as the truth of Christ is in me, I will never stop boasting about this all over Greece.* [11]Why? Because I don't love you? God knows I do.

[12]But I will continue doing this to cut the ground out from under the feet of those who boast that their work is just like ours. [13]These people are false apostles. They have fooled you by disguising themselves as apostles of Christ. [14]But I am not surprised! Even Satan can disguise himself as an angel of light. [15]So it is no wonder his servants can also do it by pretending to be godly ministers. In the end they will get every bit of punishment their wicked deeds deserve.

Paul's Many Trials

[16]Once again, don't think that I have lost my wits to talk like this. But even if you do, listen to me, as you would to a foolish person, while I also boast a little. [17]Such bragging is not something the Lord wants, but I am acting like a fool. [18]And since others boast about their human achievements, I will, too. [19]After all, you, who think you are so wise, enjoy listening to fools! [20]You put up with it when they make you their slaves, take everything you have, take advantage of you, put on airs, and slap you in the face. [21]I'm ashamed to say that we were not strong enough to do that!

But whatever they dare to boast about—I'm talking like a fool again—I can boast about it, too. [22]They say they are Hebrews, do they? So am I. And they say they are Israelites? So am I. And they are descendants of Abraham? So am I. [23]They say they serve Christ? I know I sound like a madman, but I have served him far more! I have worked harder, been put in jail more often, been whipped times without number, and been faced death again and again. [24]Five different times the Jews gave me thirty-nine lashes. [25]Three times I was beaten with rods. Once I was stoned. Three times I was shipwrecked. Once I spent a whole night and a day adrift at sea. [26]I have traveled many weary miles. I have faced danger from flooded rivers and from robbers. I have faced danger from my own people, the Jews, as well as from the Gentiles. I have faced danger in the cities, in the deserts, and on the stormy seas. And I have faced danger from men who claim to be Christians but are not.* [27]I have lived with weariness and pain and sleepless nights. Often I have been hungry and thirsty and have gone without food. Often I have shivered with cold, without enough clothing to keep me warm.

[28]Then, besides all this, I have the daily burden of how the churches are getting along. [29]Who is weak without my feeling that weakness? Who is led astray, and I do not burn with anger?

[30]If I must boast, I would rather boast about the things that show how weak I am. [31]God, the Father of our Lord Jesus, who is to be praised forever, knows I tell the truth. [32]When I was in Damascus, the governor under King Aretas kept guards at the city gates to catch me. [33]But I was lowered in a basket through a window in the city wall, and that's how I got away!

11:10 Greek *Achaia.* **11:26** Greek *from false brothers.*

CHAPTER 12

Paul's Vision and His Thorn in the Flesh

This boasting is all so foolish, but let me go on. Let me tell about the visions and revelations I received from the Lord. [2]I* was caught up into the third heaven fourteen years ago. [3]Whether my body was there or just my spirit, I don't know; only God knows. [4]But I do know that I* was caught up into paradise and heard things so astounding that they cannot be told. [5]That experience is something worth boasting about, but I am not going to do it. I am going to boast only about my weaknesses. [6]I have plenty to boast about and would be no fool in doing it, because I would be telling the truth. But I won't do it. I don't want anyone to think more highly of me than what they can actually see in my life and in my message, [7]even though I have received wonderful revelations from God. But to keep me from getting puffed up, I was given a thorn in my flesh, a messenger from Satan to torment me and keep me from getting proud.

[8]Three different times I begged the Lord to take it away. [9]Each time he said, "My gracious favor is all you need. My power works best in your weakness." So now I am glad to boast about my weaknesses, so that the power of Christ may work through me. [10]Since I know it is all for Christ's good, I am quite content with my weaknesses and with insults, hardships, persecutions, and calamities. For when I am weak, then I am strong.

Paul's Concern for the Corinthians

[11]You have made me act like a fool—boasting like this. You ought to be writing commendations for me, for I am not at all inferior to these "super apostles," even though I am nothing at all. [12]When I was with you, I certainly gave you every proof that I am truly an apostle, sent to you by God himself. For I patiently did many signs and wonders and miracles among you. [13]The only thing I didn't do, which I do in the other churches, was to become a burden to you. Please forgive me for this wrong!

[14]Now I am coming to you for the third time, and I will not be a burden to you. I don't want what you have; I want you. And anyway, little children don't pay for their parents' food. It's the other way around; parents supply food for their children. [15]I will gladly spend myself and all I have for your spiritual good, even though it seems that the more I love you, the less you love me.

[16]Some of you admit I was not a burden to you. But they still think I was sneaky and took advantage of you by trickery. [17]But how? Did any of the men I sent to you take advantage of you? [18]When I urged Titus to visit you and sent our other brother with him, did Titus take advantage of you? No, of course not! For we both have the same Spirit and walk in each other's steps, doing things the same way.

[19]Perhaps you think we are saying all this just to defend ourselves. That isn't it at all. We tell you this as Christ's servants, and we know that God is listening. Everything we do, dear friends, is for your benefit. [20]For I am afraid that when I come to visit you I won't like what I find, and then you won't like my response. I am afraid that I will find quarreling, jealousy, outbursts of anger, selfishness, backstabbing, gossip, conceit, and disorderly behavior.

12:2 Greek *I know a man in Christ who.* 12:4 Greek *he.*

21 Yes, I am afraid that when I come, God will humble me again because of you. And I will have to grieve because many of you who sinned earlier have not repented of your impurity, sexual immorality, and eagerness for lustful pleasure.

CHAPTER 13
Paul's Final Advice

This is the third time I am coming to visit you. As the Scriptures say, "The facts of every case must be established by the testimony of two or three witnesses." * 2 I have already warned those who had been sinning when I was there on my second visit. Now I again warn them and all others, just as I did before, that this next time I will not spare them.

3 I will give you all the proof you want that Christ speaks through me. Christ is not weak in his dealings with you; he is a mighty power among you. 4 Although he died on the cross in weakness, he now lives by the mighty power of God. We, too, are weak, but we live in him and have God's power—the power we use in dealing with you.

5 Examine yourselves to see if your faith is really genuine. Test yourselves. If you cannot tell that Jesus Christ is among you, * it means you have failed the test. 6 I hope you recognize that we have passed the test and are approved by God.

7 We pray to God that you will not do anything wrong. We pray this, not to show that our ministry to you has been successful, but because we want you to do right even if we ourselves seem to have failed. 8 Our responsibility is never to oppose the truth, but to stand for the truth at all times. 9 We are glad to be weak, if you are really strong. What we pray for is your restoration to maturity.

10 I am writing this to you before I come, hoping that I won't need to deal harshly with you when I do come. For I want to use the authority the Lord has given me to build you up, not to tear you down.

Paul's Final Greetings

11 Dear brothers and sisters, * I close my letter with these last words: Rejoice. Change your ways. Encourage each other. Live in harmony and peace. Then the God of love and peace will be with you.

12 Greet each other in Christian love. * All the Christians here send you their greetings.

13 May the grace of our Lord Jesus Christ, the love of God, and the fellowship of the Holy Spirit be with you all.

13:1 Deut 19:15.   **13:5** Or *in you.*   **13:11** Greek *Brothers.*   **13:12** Greek *with a sacred kiss.*

GALATIANS

CHAPTER 1
Greetings from Paul

This letter is from Paul, an apostle. I was not appointed by any group or by human authority. My call is from Jesus Christ himself and from God the Father, who raised Jesus from the dead.

²All the brothers and sisters* here join me in sending greetings to the churches of Galatia.

³May grace and peace be yours from God our Father and from the Lord Jesus Christ. ⁴He died for our sins, just as God our Father planned, in order to rescue us from this evil world in which we live. ⁵That is why all glory belongs to God through all the ages of eternity. Amen.

There Is Only One Good News

⁶I am shocked that you are turning away so soon from God, who in his love and mercy called you to share the eternal life he gives through Christ. You are already following a different way ⁷that pretends to be the Good News but is not the Good News at all. You are being fooled by those who twist and change the truth concerning Christ.

⁸Let God's curse fall on anyone, including myself, who preaches any other message than the one we told you about. Even if an angel comes from heaven and preaches any other message, let him be forever cursed. ⁹I will say it again: If anyone preaches any other gospel than the one you welcomed, let God's curse fall upon that person.

¹⁰Obviously, I'm not trying to be a people pleaser! No, I am trying to please God. If I were still trying to please people, I would not be Christ's servant.

Paul's Message Comes from Christ

¹¹Dear brothers and sisters, I solemnly assure you that the Good News of salvation which I preach is not based on mere human reasoning or logic. ¹²For my message came by a direct revelation from Jesus Christ himself. No one else taught me.

¹³You know what I was like when I followed the Jewish religion—how I violently persecuted the Christians.* I did my best to get rid of them. ¹⁴I was one of the most religious Jews of my own age, and I tried as hard as possible to follow all the old traditions of my religion.

¹⁵But then something happened! For it pleased God in his kindness to choose me and call me, even before I was born! What undeserved mercy! ¹⁶Then he revealed his Son to me* so that I could proclaim the Good News about Jesus to the Gentiles. When all this happened to me, I did not rush out to consult with anyone else; ¹⁷nor did I go up to Jerusalem to consult with those who were apostles before I was. No, I went away into Arabia and later returned to the city of Damascus. ¹⁸It was not until three years later that I finally went to Jerusalem for a visit with Peter* and stayed there with him for fifteen days. ¹⁹And the only other apostle I met at that time was James, our Lord's brother. ²⁰You must believe what I am saying, for I declare before God that I am not lying. ²¹Then after this visit, I went north into the provinces of Syria and Cilicia. ²²And still the Christians in the churches in Judea didn't know me personally. ²³All they knew was that people were saying, "The one who used to persecute us now preaches the very faith he tried to destroy!" ²⁴And they gave glory to God because of me.

1:2 Greek *brothers;* also in 1:11.   1:13 Greek *the church of God.*   1:16 Or *in me.*
1:18 Greek *Cephas.*

CHAPTER 2

The Apostles Accept Paul

Then fourteen years later I went back to Jerusalem again, this time with Barnabas; and Titus came along, too. ²I went there because God revealed to me that I should go. While I was there I talked privately with the leaders of the church. I wanted them to understand what I had been preaching to the Gentiles. I wanted to make sure they did not disagree, or my ministry would have been useless. ³And they did agree. They did not even demand that my companion Titus be circumcised, though he was a Gentile.*

⁴Even that question wouldn't have come up except for some so-called Christians there—false ones, really*—who came to spy on us and see our freedom in Christ Jesus. They wanted to force us, like slaves, to follow their Jewish regulations. ⁵But we refused to listen to them for a single moment. We wanted to preserve the truth of the Good News for you.

⁶And the leaders of the church who were there had nothing to add to what I was preaching. (By the way, their reputation as great leaders made no difference to me, for God has no favorites.) ⁷They saw that God had given me the responsibility of preaching the Good News to the Gentiles, just as he had given Peter the responsibility of preaching to the Jews. ⁸For the same God who worked through Peter for the benefit of the Jews worked through me for the benefit of the Gentiles. ⁹In fact, James, Peter,* and John, who were known as pillars of the church, recognized the gift God had given me, and they accepted Barnabas and me as their co-workers. They encouraged us to keep preaching to the Gentiles, while they continued their work with the Jews. ¹⁰The only thing they suggested was that we remember to help the poor, and I have certainly been eager to do that.

Paul Confronts Peter

¹¹But when Peter came to Antioch, I had to oppose him publicly, speaking strongly against what he was doing, for it was very wrong. ¹²When he first arrived, he ate with the Gentile Christians, who don't bother with circumcision. But afterward, when some Jewish friends of James came, Peter wouldn't eat with the Gentiles anymore because he was afraid of what these legalists would say. ¹³Then the other Jewish Christians followed Peter's hypocrisy, and even Barnabas was influenced to join them in their hypocrisy.

¹⁴When I saw that they were not following the truth of the Good News, I said to Peter in front of all the others, "Since you, a Jew by birth, have discarded the Jewish laws and are living like a Gentile, why are you trying to make these Gentiles obey the Jewish laws you abandoned? ¹⁵You and I are Jews by birth, not 'sinners' like the Gentiles. ¹⁶And yet we Jewish Christians know that we become right with God, not by doing what the law commands, but by faith in Jesus Christ. So we have believed in Christ Jesus, that we might be accepted by God because of our faith in Christ—and not because we have obeyed the law. For no one will ever be saved by obeying the law."*

¹⁷But what if we seek to be made right with God through faith

2:3 Greek *a Greek.* 2:4 Greek *some false brothers.* 2:9 Greek *Cephas;* also in 2:11, 14. 2:16 Some translators hold that the quotation extends through verse 14; others through verse 16; and still others through verse 21.

in Christ and then find out that we are still sinners? Has Christ led us into sin? Of course not! 18Rather, I make myself guilty if I rebuild the old system I already tore down. 19For when I tried to keep the law, I realized I could never earn God's approval. So I died to the law so that I might live for God. I have been crucified with Christ. 20I myself no longer live, but Christ lives in me. So I live my life in this earthly body by trusting in the Son of God, who loved me and gave himself for me. 21I am not one of those who treats the grace of God as meaningless. For if we could be saved by keeping the law, then there was no need for Christ to die.

CHAPTER 3
The Law and Faith in Christ

Oh, foolish Galatians! What magician has cast an evil spell on you? For you used to see the meaning of Jesus Christ's death as clearly as though I had shown you a signboard with a picture of Christ dying on the cross. 2Let me ask you this one question: Did you receive the Holy Spirit by keeping the law? Of course not, for the Holy Spirit came upon you only after you believed the message you heard about Christ. 3Have you lost your senses? After starting your Christian lives in the Spirit, why are you now trying to become perfect by your own human effort? 4You have suffered so much for the Good News. Surely it was not in vain, was it? Are you now going to just throw it all away?

5I ask you again, does God give you the Holy Spirit and work miracles among you because you obey the law of Moses? Of course not! It is because you believe the message you heard about Christ.

6In the same way, "Abraham believed God, so God declared him righteous because of his faith."* 7The real children of Abraham, then, are all those who put their faith in God.

8What's more, the Scriptures looked forward to this time when God would accept the Gentiles, too, on the basis of their faith. God promised this good news to Abraham long ago when he said, "All nations will be blessed through you."* 9And so it is: All who put their faith in Christ share the same blessing Abraham received because of his faith.

10But those who depend on the law to make them right with God are under his curse, for the Scriptures say, "Cursed is everyone who does not observe and obey all these commands that are written in God's Book of the Law."* 11Consequently, it is clear that no one can ever be right with God by trying to keep the law. For the Scriptures say, "It is through faith that a righteous person has life."* 12How different from this way of faith is the way of law, which says, "If you wish to find life by obeying the law, you must obey all of its commands."* 13But Christ has rescued us from the curse pronounced by the law. When he was hung on the cross, he took upon himself the curse for our wrongdoing. For it is written in the Scriptures, "Cursed is everyone who is hung on a tree."* 14Through the work of Christ Jesus, God has blessed the Gentiles with the same blessing he promised to Abraham, and we Christians receive the promised Holy Spirit through faith.

3:6 Gen 15:6.   3:8 Gen 12:3; 18:18; 22:18.   3:10 Deut 27:26.   3:11 Hab 2:4.
3:12 Lev 18:5.   3:13 Deut 21:23.

The Law and God's Promises

15Dear brothers and sisters,* here's an example from everyday life. Just as no one can set aside or amend an irrevocable agreement, so it is in this case. 16God gave the promise to Abraham and his child.* And notice that it doesn't say the promise was to his children,* as if it meant many descendants. But the promise was to his child—and that, of course, means Christ. 17This is what I am trying to say: The agreement God made with Abraham could not be canceled 430 years later when God gave the law to Moses. God would be breaking his promise. 18For if the inheritance could be received only by keeping the law, then it would not be the result of accepting God's promise. But God gave it to Abraham as a promise.

19Well then, why was the law given? It was given to show people how guilty they are. But this system of law was to last only until the coming of the child to whom God's promise was made. And there is this further difference. God gave his laws to angels to give to Moses, who was the mediator between God and the people. 20Now a mediator is needed if two people enter into an agreement, but God acted on his own when he made his promise to Abraham.

21Well then, is there a conflict between God's law and God's promises? Absolutely not! If the law could have given us new life, we could have been made right with God by obeying it. 22But the Scriptures have declared that we are all prisoners of sin, so the only way to receive God's promise is to believe in Jesus Christ.

23Until faith in Christ was shown to us as the way of becoming right with God, we were guarded by the law. We were kept in protective custody, so to speak, until we could put our faith in the coming Savior.

God's Children through Faith

24Let me put it another way. The law was our guardian and teacher to lead us until Christ came. So now, through faith in Christ, we are made right with God. 25But now that faith in Christ has come, we no longer need the law as our guardian. 26So you are all children* of God through faith in Christ Jesus. 27And all who have been united with Christ in baptism have been made like him. 28There is no longer Jew or Gentile,* slave or free, male or female. For you are all Christians—you are one in Christ Jesus. 29And now that you belong to Christ, you are the true children of Abraham. You are his heirs, and now all the promises God gave to him belong to you.

CHAPTER 4

Think of it this way. If a father dies and leaves great wealth for his young children, those children are not much better off than slaves until they grow up, even though they actually own everything their father had. 2They have to obey their guardians until they reach whatever age their father set.

3And that's the way it was with us before Christ came. We were slaves to the spiritual powers of this world. 4But when the right time came, God sent his Son, born of a woman, subject to the law. 5God sent him to buy freedom for us who were slaves to the law, so that he could adopt us as his very own children.* 6And because

3:15 Greek *Brothers.* **3:16a** Greek *seed;* also in 3:16c, 19. See Gen 12:7. **3:16b** Greek *seeds.* **3:26** Greek *sons.* **3:28** Greek *Jew or Greek.* **4:5** Greek *sons,* also in 4:6.

you Gentiles have become his children, God has sent the Spirit of his Son into your hearts, and now you can call God your dear Father.* 7Now you are no longer a slave but God's own child.* And since you are his child, everything he has belongs to you.

Paul's Concern for the Galatians

8Before you Gentiles knew God, you were slaves to so-called gods that do not even exist. 9And now that you have found God (or should I say, now that God has found you), why do you want to go back again and become slaves once more to the weak and useless spiritual powers of this world? 10You are trying to find favor with God by what you do or don't do on certain days or months or seasons or years. 11I fear for you. I am afraid that all my hard work for you was worth nothing. 12Dear brothers and sisters,* I plead with you to live as I do in freedom from these things, for I have become like you Gentiles were—free from the law.

You did not mistreat me when I first preached to you. 13Surely you remember that I was sick when I first brought you the Good News of Christ. 14But even though my sickness was revolting to you, you did not reject me and turn me away. No, you took me in and cared for me as though I were an angel from God or even Christ Jesus himself. 15Where is that joyful spirit we felt together then? In those days, I know you would gladly have taken out your own eyes and given them to me if it had been possible. 16Have I now become your enemy because I am telling you the truth?

17Those false teachers who are so anxious to win your favor are not doing it for your good. They are trying to shut you off from me so that you will pay more attention to them. 18Now it's wonderful if you are eager to do good, and especially when I am not with you. 19But oh, my dear children! I feel as if I am going through labor pains for you again, and they will continue until Christ is fully developed in your lives. 20How I wish I were there with you right now, so that I could be more gentle with you. But at this distance I frankly don't know what else to do.

Abraham's Two Children

21Listen to me, you who want to live under the law. Do you know what the law really says? 22The Scriptures say that Abraham had two sons, one from his slave-wife and one from his freeborn wife.* 23The son of the slave-wife was born in a human attempt to bring about the fulfillment of God's promise. But the son of the freeborn wife was born as God's own fulfillment of his promise.

24Now these two women serve as an illustration of God's two covenants. Hagar, the slave-wife, represents Mount Sinai where people first became enslaved to the law. 25And now Jerusalem is just like Mount Sinai in Arabia, because she and her children live in slavery. 26But Sarah, the free woman, represents the heavenly Jerusalem. And she is our mother. 27That is what Isaiah meant when he prophesied,

"Rejoice, O childless woman!
   Break forth into loud and joyful song,
      even though you never gave birth to a child.

4:6 Greek *into your hearts, crying, "Abba, Father." Abba* is an Aramaic term for "Father." 4:7 Greek *son;* also in 4:7b. 4:12 Greek *brothers;* also in 4:28, 31. 4:22 See Gen 16:15; 21:2-3.

For the woman who could bear no children
now has more than all the other women!"*

28And you, dear brothers and sisters, are children of the promise, just like Isaac. 29And we who are born of the Holy Spirit are persecuted by those who want us to keep the law, just as Isaac, the child of promise, was persecuted by Ishmael, the son of the slave-wife.

30 But what do the Scriptures say about that? " Get rid of the slave and her son, for the son of the slave woman will not share the family inheritance with the free woman's son."* 31So, dear brothers and sisters, we are not children of the slave woman, obligated to the law. We are children of the free woman, acceptable to God because of our faith.

CHAPTER 5

Freedom in Christ

So Christ has really set us free. Now make sure that you stay free, and don't get tied up again in slavery to the law.

2Listen! I, Paul, tell you this: If you are counting on circumcision to make you right with God, then Christ cannot help you. 3I'll say it again. If you are trying to find favor with God by being circumcised, you must obey all of the regulations in the whole law of Moses. 4For if you are trying to make yourselves right with God by keeping the law, you have been cut off from Christ! You have fallen away from God's grace.

5But we who live by the Spirit eagerly wait to receive everything promised to us who are right with God through faith. 6For when we place our faith in Christ Jesus, it makes no difference to God whether we are circumcised or not circumcised. What is important is faith expressing itself in love.

7You were getting along so well. Who has interfered with you to hold you back from following the truth? 8It certainly isn't God, for he is the one who called you to freedom. 9But it takes only one wrong person among you to infect all the others—a little yeast spreads quickly through the whole batch of dough! 10I am trusting the Lord to bring you back to believing as I do about these things. God will judge that person, whoever it is, who has been troubling and confusing you.

11Dear brothers and sisters,* if I were still preaching that you must be circumcised—as some say I do—why would the Jews persecute me? The fact that I am still being persecuted proves that I am still preaching salvation through the cross of Christ alone. 12I only wish that those troublemakers who want to mutilate you by circumcision would mutilate themselves.*

13For you have been called to live in freedom—not freedom to satisfy your sinful nature, but freedom to serve one another in love. 14For the whole law can be summed up in this one command: "Love your neighbor as yourself."* 15But if instead of showing love among yourselves you are always biting and devouring one another, watch out! Beware of destroying one another.

Living by the Spirit's Power

16So I advise you to live according to your new life in the Holy Spirit. Then you won't be doing what your sinful nature craves.

4:27 Isa 54:1.   4:30 Gen 21:10.   5:11 Greek *Brothers.*   5:12 Or *castrate themselves;* Greek reads *cut themselves off.*   5:14 Lev 19:18.

¹⁷The old sinful nature loves to do evil, which is just opposite from what the Holy Spirit wants. And the Spirit gives us desires that are opposite from what the sinful nature desires. These two forces are constantly fighting each other, and your choices are never free from this conflict. ¹⁸But when you are directed by the Holy Spirit, you are no longer subject to the law.

¹⁹When you follow the desires of your sinful nature, your lives will produce these evil results: sexual immorality, impure thoughts, eagerness for lustful pleasure, ²⁰idolatry, participation in demonic activities, hostility, quarreling, jealousy, outbursts of anger, selfish ambition, divisions, the feeling that everyone is wrong except those in your own little group, ²¹envy, drunkenness, wild parties, and other kinds of sin. Let me tell you again, as I have before, that anyone living that sort of life will not inherit the Kingdom of God.

²²But when the Holy Spirit controls our lives, he will produce this kind of fruit in us: love, joy, peace, patience, kindness, goodness, faithfulness, ²³gentleness, and self-control. Here there is no conflict with the law.

²⁴Those who belong to Christ Jesus have nailed the passions and desires of their sinful nature to his cross and crucified them there. ²⁵If we are living now by the Holy Spirit, let us follow the Holy Spirit's leading in every part of our lives. ²⁶Let us not become conceited, or irritate one another, or be jealous of one another.

CHAPTER 6

We Reap What We Sow

Dear brothers and sisters, if another Christian* is overcome by some sin, you who are godly should gently and humbly help that person back onto the right path. And be careful not to fall into the same temptation yourself. ²Share each other's troubles and problems, and in this way obey the law of Christ. ³If you think you are too important to help someone in need, you are only fooling yourself. You are really a nobody.

⁴Be sure to do what you should, for then you will enjoy the personal satisfaction of having done your work well, and you won't need to compare yourself to anyone else. ⁵For we are each responsible for our own conduct.

⁶Those who are taught the word of God should help their teachers by paying them.

⁷Don't be misled. Remember that you can't ignore God and get away with it. You will always reap what you sow! ⁸Those who live only to satisfy their own sinful desires will harvest the consequences of decay and death. But those who live to please the Spirit will harvest everlasting life from the Spirit. ⁹So don't get tired of doing what is good. Don't get discouraged and give up, for we will reap a harvest of blessing at the appropriate time. ¹⁰Whenever we have the opportunity, we should do good to everyone, especially to our Christian brothers and sisters.

Paul's Final Advice

¹¹Notice what large letters I use as I write these closing words in my own handwriting. ¹²Those who are trying to force you to be

6:1 Greek *Brothers, if a man.*

circumcised are doing it for just one reason. They don't want to be persecuted for teaching that the cross of Christ alone can save. [13]And even those who advocate circumcision don't really keep the whole law. They only want you to be circumcised so they can brag about it and claim you as their disciples.

[14]As for me, God forbid that I should boast about anything except the cross of our Lord Jesus Christ. Because of that cross,* my interest in this world died long ago, and the world's interest in me is also long dead. [15]It doesn't make any difference now whether we have been circumcised or not. What counts is whether we really have been changed into new and different people. [16]May God's mercy and peace be upon all those who live by this principle. They are the new people of God.*

[17]From now on, don't let anyone trouble me with these things. For I bear on my body the scars that show I belong to Jesus.

[18]My dear brothers and sisters,* may the grace of our Lord Jesus Christ be with you all. Amen.

6:14 Or *Because of him.*   6:16 Greek *the Israel of God.*   6:18 Greek *Brothers.*

EPHESIANS

CHAPTER 1
Greetings from Paul
This letter is from Paul, chosen by God to be an apostle of Christ Jesus.

It is written to God's holy people in Ephesus,* who are faithful followers of Christ Jesus.

[2]May grace and peace be yours, sent to you from God our Father and Jesus Christ our Lord.

Spiritual Blessings
[3]How we praise God, the Father of our Lord Jesus Christ, who has blessed us with every spiritual blessing in the heavenly realms because we belong to Christ. [4]Long ago, even before he made the world, God loved us and chose us in Christ to be holy and without fault in his eyes. [5]His unchanging plan has always been to adopt us into his own family by bringing us to himself through Jesus Christ. And this gave him great pleasure.

[6]So we praise God for the wonderful kindness he has poured out on us because we belong to his dearly loved Son. [7]He is so rich in kindness that he purchased our freedom through the blood of his Son, and our sins are forgiven. [8]He has showered his kindness on us, along with all wisdom and understanding.

[9]God's secret plan has now been revealed to us; it is a plan centered on Christ, designed long ago according to his good pleasure. [10]And this is his plan: At the right time he will bring everything together under the authority of Christ—everything in

1:1 Some manuscripts do not include *in Ephesus.*

heaven and on earth. [11]Furthermore, because of Christ, we have received an inheritance from God,* for he chose us from the beginning, and all things happen just as he decided long ago. [12]God's purpose was that we who were the first to trust in Christ should praise our glorious God. [13]And now you also have heard the truth, the Good News that God saves you. And when you believed in Christ, he identified you as his own by giving you the Holy Spirit, whom he promised long ago. [14]The Spirit is God's guarantee that he will give us everything he promised and that he has purchased us to be his own people. This is just one more reason for us to praise our glorious God.

Paul's Prayer for Spiritual Wisdom

[15]Ever since I first heard of your strong faith in the Lord Jesus and your love for Christians everywhere, [16]I have never stopped thanking God for you. I pray for you constantly, [17]asking God, the glorious Father of our Lord Jesus Christ, to give you spiritual wisdom and understanding, so that you might grow in your knowledge of God. [18]I pray that your hearts will be flooded with light so that you can understand the wonderful future he has promised to those he called. I want you to realize what a rich and glorious inheritance he has given to his people.*

[19]I pray that you will begin to understand the incredible greatness of his power for us who believe him. This is the same mighty power [20]that raised Christ from the dead and seated him in the place of honor at God's right hand in the heavenly realms. [21]Now he is far above any ruler or authority or power or leader or anything else in this world or in the world to come. [22]And God has put all things under the authority of Christ, and he gave him this authority for the benefit of the church. [23]And the church is his body; it is filled by Christ, who fills everything everywhere with his presence.

CHAPTER 2

Made Alive with Christ

Once you were dead, doomed forever because of your many sins. [2]You used to live just like the rest of the world, full of sin, obeying Satan, the mighty prince of the power of the air. He is the spirit at work in the hearts of those who refuse to obey God. [3]All of us used to live that way, following the passions and desires of our evil nature. We were born with an evil nature, and we were under God's anger just like everyone else.

[4]But God is so rich in mercy, and he loved us so very much, [5]that even while we were dead because of our sins, he gave us life when he raised Christ from the dead. (It is only by God's special favor that you have been saved!) [6]For he raised us from the dead along with Christ, and we are seated with him in the heavenly realms— all because we are one with Christ Jesus. [7]And so God can always point to us as examples of the incredible wealth of his favor and kindness toward us, as shown in all he has done for us through Christ Jesus.

[8]God saved you by his special favor when you believed. And you can't take credit for this; it is a gift from God. [9]Salvation is not a

---

1:11 Or *we have become God's inheritance.*   1:18 Or *realize how much God has been honored by acquiring his people.*

reward for the good things we have done, so none of us can boast about it. [10]For we are God's masterpiece. He has created us anew in Christ Jesus, so that we can do the good things he planned for us long ago.

Oneness and Peace in Christ

[11]Don't forget that you Gentiles used to be outsiders by birth. You were called "the uncircumcised ones" by the Jews, who were proud of their circumcision, even though it affected only their bodies and not their hearts. [12]In those days you were living apart from Christ. You were excluded from God's people, Israel, and you did not know the promises God had made to them. You lived in this world without God and without hope. [13]But now you belong to Christ Jesus. Though you once were far away from God, now you have been brought near to him because of the blood of Christ.

[14]For Christ himself made peace between us Jews and you Gentiles by making us all one people. He has broken down the wall of hostility that used to separate us. [15]By his death he ended the whole system of Jewish law that excluded the Gentiles. His purpose was to make peace between Jews and Gentiles by creating in himself one new person from the two groups. [16]Together as one body, Christ reconciled both groups to God by means of his death, and our hostility toward each other was put to death. [17]He has brought this Good News of peace to you Gentiles who were far away from him, and to us Jews who were near. [18]Now all of us, both Jews and Gentiles, may come to the Father through the same Holy Spirit because of what Christ has done for us.

A Temple for the Lord

[19]So now you Gentiles are no longer strangers and foreigners. You are citizens along with all of God's holy people. You are members of God's family. [20]We are his house, built on the foundation of the apostles and the prophets. And the cornerstone is Christ Jesus himself. [21]We who believe are carefully joined together, becoming a holy temple for the Lord. [22]Through him you Gentiles are also joined together as part of this dwelling where God lives by his Spirit.

CHAPTER 3

God's Secret Plan Revealed

I, Paul, am a prisoner of Christ Jesus because of my preaching to you Gentiles. [2]As you already know, God has given me this special ministry of announcing his favor to you Gentiles. [3]As I briefly mentioned earlier in this letter, God himself revealed his secret plan to me. [4]As you read what I have written, you will understand what I know about this plan regarding Christ. [5]God did not reveal it to previous generations, but now he has revealed it by the Holy Spirit to his holy apostles and prophets.

[6]And this is the secret plan: The Gentiles have an equal share with the Jews in all the riches inherited by God's children. Both groups have believed the Good News, and both are part of the same body and enjoy together the promise of blessings through Christ Jesus. [7]By God's special favor and mighty power, I have been given the wonderful privilege of serving him by spreading this Good News.

[8]Just think! Though I did nothing to deserve it, and though I am

the least deserving Christian there is, I was chosen for this special joy of telling the Gentiles about the endless treasures available to them in Christ. [9]I was chosen to explain to everyone this plan that God, the Creator of all things, had kept secret from the beginning.

[10]God's purpose was to show his wisdom in all its rich variety to all the rulers and authorities in the heavenly realms. They will see this when Jews and Gentiles are joined together in his church. [11]This was his plan from all eternity, and it has now been carried out through Christ Jesus our Lord.

[12]Because of Christ and our faith in him, we can now come fearlessly into God's presence, assured of his glad welcome. [13]So please don't despair because of what they are doing to me here. It is for you that I am suffering, so you should feel honored and encouraged.

Paul's Prayer for Spiritual Empowering

[14]When I think of the wisdom and scope of God's plan, I fall to my knees and pray to the Father,* [15]the Creator of everything in heaven and on earth. [16]I pray that from his glorious, unlimited resources he will give you mighty inner strength through his Holy Spirit. [17]And I pray that Christ will be more and more at home in your hearts as you trust in him. May your roots go down deep into the soil of God's marvelous love. [18]And may you have the power to understand, as all God's people should, how wide, how long, how high, and how deep his love really is. [19]May you experience the love of Christ, though it is so great you will never fully understand it. Then you will be filled with the fullness of life and power that comes from God.

[20]Now glory be to God! By his mighty power at work within us, he is able to accomplish infinitely more than we would ever dare to ask or hope. [21]May he be given glory in the church and in Christ Jesus forever and ever through endless ages. Amen.

CHAPTER 4

Unity in the Body

Therefore I, a prisoner for serving the Lord, beg you to lead a life worthy of your calling, for you have been called by God. [2]Be humble and gentle. Be patient with each other, making allowance for each other's faults because of your love. [3]Always keep yourselves united in the Holy Spirit, and bind yourselves together with peace.

[4]We are all one body, we have the same Spirit, and we have all been called to the same glorious future. [5]There is only one Lord, one faith, one baptism, [6]and there is only one God and Father, who is over us all and in us all and living through us all. [7]However, he has given each one of us a special gift according to the generosity of Christ. [8]That is why the Scriptures say,

" When he ascended to the heights,
 he led a crowd of captives
 and gave gifts to his people."*

[9]Notice that it says "he ascended." This means that Christ first came down to the lowly world in which we live.* [10]The same one

---

3:14 Some manuscripts read *the Father of our Lord Jesus Christ.* **4:8** Ps 68:18. **4:9** Or *to the lowest parts of the earth.*

who came down is the one who ascended higher than all the heavens, so that his rule might fill the entire universe.

¹¹He is the one who gave these gifts to the church: the apostles, the prophets, the evangelists, and the pastors and teachers. ¹²Their responsibility is to equip God's people to do his work and build up the church, the body of Christ, ¹³until we come to such unity in our faith and knowledge of God's Son that we will be mature and full grown in the Lord, measuring up to the full stature of Christ.

¹⁴Then we will no longer be like children, forever changing our minds about what we believe because someone has told us something different or because someone has cleverly lied to us and made the lie sound like the truth. ¹⁵Instead, we will hold to the truth in love, becoming more and more in every way like Christ, who is the head of his body, the church. ¹⁶Under his direction, the whole body is fitted together perfectly. As each part does its own special work, it helps the other parts grow, so that the whole body is healthy and growing and full of love.

Living as Children of Light

¹⁷With the Lord's authority let me say this: Live no longer as the ungodly* do, for they are hopelessly confused. ¹⁸Their closed minds are full of darkness; they are far away from the life of God because they have shut their minds and hardened their hearts against him. ¹⁹They don't care anymore about right and wrong, and they have given themselves over to immoral ways. Their lives are filled with all kinds of impurity and greed.

²⁰But that isn't what you were taught when you learned about Christ. ²¹Since you have heard all about him and have learned the truth that is in Jesus, ²²throw off your old evil nature and your former way of life, which is rotten through and through, full of lust and deception. ²³Instead, there must be a spiritual renewal of your thoughts and attitudes. ²⁴You must display a new nature because you are a new person, created in God's likeness—righteous, holy, and true.

²⁵So put away all falsehood and "tell your neighbor the truth"* because we belong to each other. ²⁶And "don't sin by letting anger gain control over you."* Don't let the sun go down while you are still angry, ²⁷for anger gives a mighty foothold to the Devil.

²⁸If you are a thief, stop stealing. Begin using your hands for honest work, and then give generously to others in need. ²⁹Don't use foul or abusive language. Let everything you say be good and helpful, so that your words will be an encouragement to those who hear them.

³⁰And do not bring sorrow to God's Holy Spirit by the way you live. Remember, he is the one who has identified you as his own, guaranteeing that you will be saved on the day of redemption.

³¹Get rid of all bitterness, rage, anger, harsh words, and slander, as well as all types of malicious behavior. ³²Instead, be kind to each other, tenderhearted, forgiving one another, just as God through Christ has forgiven you.

4:17 Greek *Gentiles.*   4:25 Zech 8:16.   4:26 Ps 4:4.

CHAPTER 5

Living in the Light

Follow God's example in everything you do, because you are his dear children. ²Live a life filled with love for others, following the example of Christ, who loved you and gave himself as a sacrifice to take away your sins. And God was pleased, because that sacrifice was like sweet perfume to him.

³Let there be no sexual immorality, impurity, or greed among you. Such sins have no place among God's people. ⁴Obscene stories, foolish talk, and coarse jokes—these are not for you. Instead, let there be thankfulness to God. ⁵You can be sure that no immoral, impure, or greedy person will inherit the Kingdom of Christ and of God. For a greedy person is really an idolater who worships the things of this world. ⁶Don't be fooled by those who try to excuse these sins, for the terrible anger of God comes upon all those who disobey him. ⁷Don't participate in the things these people do. ⁸For though your hearts were once full of darkness, now you are full of light from the Lord, and your behavior should show it! ⁹For this light within you produces only what is good and right and true.

¹⁰Try to find out what is pleasing to the Lord. ¹¹Take no part in the worthless deeds of evil and darkness; instead, rebuke and expose them. ¹²It is shameful even to talk about the things that ungodly people do in secret. ¹³But when the light shines on them, it becomes clear how evil these things are. ¹⁴And where your light shines, it will expose their evil deeds. This is why it is said,

"Awake, O sleeper,
   rise up from the dead,
   and Christ will give you light."

Living by the Spirit's Power

¹⁵So be careful how you live, not as fools but as those who are wise. ¹⁶Make the most of every opportunity for doing good in these evil days. ¹⁷Don't act thoughtlessly, but try to understand what the Lord wants you to do. ¹⁸Don't be drunk with wine, because that will ruin your life. Instead, let the Holy Spirit fill and control you. ¹⁹Then you will sing psalms and hymns and spiritual songs among yourselves, making music to the Lord in your hearts. ²⁰And you will always give thanks for everything to God the Father in the name of our Lord Jesus Christ.

Spirit-Guided Relationships: Wives and Husbands

²¹And further, you will submit to one another out of reverence for Christ. ²²You wives will submit to your husbands as you do to the Lord. ²³For a husband is the head of his wife as Christ is the head of his body, the church; he gave his life to be her Savior. ²⁴As the church submits to Christ, so you wives must submit to your husbands in everything.

²⁵And you husbands must love your wives with the same love Christ showed the church. He gave up his life for her ²⁶to make her holy and clean, washed by baptism and God's word. * ²⁷He did this to present her to himself as a glorious church without a spot or wrinkle or any other blemish. Instead, she will be holy and without

5:26 Greek *having cleansed her by the washing of water with the word.*

fault. [28]In the same way, husbands ought to love their wives as they love their own bodies. For a man is actually loving himself when he loves his wife. [29]No one hates his own body but lovingly cares for it, just as Christ cares for his body, which is the church. [30]And we are his body.

[31]As the Scriptures say, "A man leaves his father and mother and is joined to his wife, and the two are united into one."* [32]This is a great mystery, but it is an illustration of the way Christ and the church are one. [33]So again I say, each man must love his wife as he loves himself, and the wife must respect her husband.

CHAPTER 6
Children and Parents
Children, obey your parents because you belong to the Lord, for this is the right thing to do. [2]"Honor your father and mother." This is the first of the Ten Commandments that ends with a promise: [3]And this is the promise: If you honor your father and mother, "you will live a long life, full of blessing."*

[4]And now a word to you fathers. Don't make your children angry by the way you treat them. Rather, bring them up with the discipline and instruction approved by the Lord.

Slaves and Masters
[5]Slaves, obey your earthly masters with deep respect and fear. Serve them sincerely as you would serve Christ. [6]Work hard, but not just to please your masters when they are watching. As slaves of Christ, do the will of God with all your heart. [7]Work with enthusiasm, as though you were working for the Lord rather than for people. [8]Remember that the Lord will reward each one of us for the good we do, whether we are slaves or free.

[9]And in the same way, you masters must treat your slaves right. Don't threaten them; remember, you both have the same Master in heaven, and he has no favorites.

The Whole Armor of God
[10]A final word: Be strong with the Lord's mighty power. [11]Put on all of God's armor so that you will be able to stand firm against all strategies and tricks of the Devil. [12]For we are not fighting against people made of flesh and blood, but against the evil rulers and authorities of the unseen world, against those mighty powers of darkness who rule this world, and against wicked spirits in the heavenly realms.

[13]Use every piece of God's armor to resist the enemy in the time of evil, so that after the battle you will still be standing firm. [14]Stand your ground, putting on the sturdy belt of truth and the body armor of God's righteousness. [15]For shoes, put on the peace that comes from the Good News, so that you will be fully prepared.* [16]In every battle you will need faith as your shield to stop the fiery arrows aimed at you by Satan.* [17]Put on salvation as your helmet, and take the sword of the Spirit, which is the word of God. [18]Pray at all times and on every occasion in the power of the Holy Spirit. Stay alert and be persistent in your prayers for all Christians everywhere.

5:31 Gen 2:24   **6:2-3** Exod 20:12; Deut 5:16.   **6:15** Or *For shoes, put on the readiness to preach the Good News of peace with God.*   **6:16** Greek *by the evil one.*

¹⁹And pray for me, too. Ask God to give me the right words as I boldly explain God's secret plan that the Good News is for the Gentiles, too.* ²⁰I am in chains now for preaching this message as God's ambassador. But pray that I will keep on speaking boldly for him, as I should.

Final Greetings

²¹Tychicus, a much loved brother and faithful helper in the Lord's work, will tell you all about how I am getting along. ²²I am sending him to you for just this purpose. He will let you know how we are, and he will encourage you.

²³May God give you peace, dear brothers and sisters,* and love with faith, from God the Father and the Lord Jesus Christ. ²⁴May God's grace be upon all who love our Lord Jesus Christ with an undying love.

6:19 Greek *explain the mystery of the gospel.*   **6:23** Greek *brothers.*

PHILIPPINANS

CHAPTER 1

Greetings from Paul

This letter is from Paul and Timothy, slaves of Christ Jesus.

It is written to all of God's people in Philippi, who believe in Christ Jesus, and to the elders* and deacons.

²May God our Father and the Lord Jesus Christ give you grace and peace.

Paul's Thanksgiving and Prayer

³Every time I think of you, I give thanks to my God. ⁴I always pray for you, and I make my requests with a heart full of joy ⁵because you have been my partners in spreading the Good News about Christ from the time you first heard it until now. ⁶And I am sure that God, who began the good work within you, will continue his work until it is finally finished on that day when Christ Jesus comes back again.

⁷It is right that I should feel as I do about all of you, for you have a very special place in my heart. We have shared together the blessings of God, both when I was in prison and when I was out, defending the truth and telling others the Good News. ⁸God knows how much I love you and long for you with the tender compassion of Christ Jesus. ⁹I pray that your love for each other will overflow more and more, and that you will keep on growing in your knowledge and understanding. ¹⁰For I want you to understand what really matters, so that you may live pure and blameless lives until Christ returns. ¹¹May you always be filled with the fruit of your salvation*—those good things that are produced in your life by Jesus Christ—for this will bring much glory and praise to God.

1:1 Greek *overseers.*   **1:11** Greek *the fruit of righteousness.*

Paul's Joy That Christ Is Preached

¹²And I want you to know, dear brothers and sisters*, that everything that has happened to me here has helped to spread the Good News. ¹³For everyone here, including all the soldiers in the palace guard, knows that I am in chains because of Christ. ¹⁴And because of my imprisonment, many of the Christians* here have gained confidence and become more bold in telling others about Christ.

¹⁵Some are preaching out of jealousy and rivalry. But others preach about Christ with pure motives. ¹⁶They preach because they love me, for they know the Lord brought me here to defend the Good News. ¹⁷Those others do not have pure motives as they preach about Christ. They preach with selfish ambition, not sincerely, intending to make my chains more painful to me. ¹⁸But whether or not their motives are pure, the fact remains that the message about Christ is being preached, so I rejoice. And I will continue to rejoice. ¹⁹For I know that as you pray for me and as the Spirit of Jesus Christ helps me, this will all turn out for my deliverance.

Paul's Life for Christ

²⁰For I live in eager expectation and hope that I will never do anything that causes me shame, but that I will always be bold for Christ, as I have been in the past, and that my life will always honor Christ, whether I live or I die. ²¹For to me, living is for Christ, and dying is even better. ²²Yet if I live, that means fruitful service for Christ. I really don't know which is better. ²³I'm torn between two desires: Sometimes I want to live, and sometimes I long to go and be with Christ. That would be far better for me, ²⁴but it is better for you that I live.

²⁵I am convinced of this, so I will continue with you so that you will grow and experience the joy of your faith. ²⁶Then when I return to you, you will have even more reason to boast about what Christ Jesus has done for me.

Live as Citizens of Heaven

²⁷But whatever happens to me, you must live in a manner worthy of the Good News about Christ, as citizens of heaven. Then, whether I come and see you again or only hear about you, I will know that you are standing side by side, fighting together for the Good News. ²⁸Don't be intimidated by your enemies. This will be a sign to them that they are going to be destroyed, but that you are going to be saved, even by God himself. ²⁹For you have been given not only the privilege of trusting in Christ but also the privilege of suffering for him. ³⁰We are in this fight together. You have seen me suffer for him in the past, and you know that I am still in the midst of this great struggle.

CHAPTER 2

Unity through Humility

Is there any encouragement from belonging to Christ? Any comfort from his love? Any fellowship together in the Spirit? Are your hearts tender and sympathetic? ²Then make me truly happy by

1:12 Greek *brothers*. 1:14 Greek *brothers in the Lord.*

agreeing wholeheartedly with each other, loving one another, and working together with one heart and purpose.

³Don't be selfish; don't live to make a good impression on others. Be humble, thinking of others as better than yourself. ⁴Don't think only about your own affairs, but be interested in others, too, and what they are doing.

Christ's Humility and Exaltation

⁵Your attitude should be the same that Christ Jesus had. ⁶Though he was God, he did not demand and cling to his rights as God. ⁷He made himself nothing;* he took the humble position of a slave and appeared in human form.* ⁸And in human form he obediently humbled himself even further by dying a criminal's death on a cross. ⁹Because of this, God raised him up to the heights of heaven and gave him a name that is above every other name, ¹⁰so that at the name of Jesus every knee will bow, in heaven and on earth and under the earth, ¹¹and every tongue will confess that Jesus Christ is Lord, to the glory of God the Father.

Shine Brightly for Christ

¹²Dearest friends, you were always so careful to follow my instructions when I was with you. And now that I am away you must be even more careful to put into action God's saving work in your lives, obeying God with deep reverence and fear. ¹³For God is working in you, giving you the desire to obey him and the power to do what pleases him.

¹⁴In everything you do, stay away from complaining and arguing, ¹⁵so that no one can speak a word of blame against you. You are to live clean, innocent lives as children of God in a dark world full of crooked and perverse people. Let your lives shine brightly before them. ¹⁶Hold tightly to the word of life, so that when Christ returns, I will be proud that I did not lose the race and that my work was not useless. ¹⁷But even if my life is to be poured out like a drink offering to complete the sacrifice of your faithful service (that is, if I am to die for you), I will rejoice, and I want to share my joy with all of you. ¹⁸And you should be happy about this and rejoice with me.

Paul Commends Timothy

¹⁹If the Lord Jesus is willing, I hope to send Timothy to you soon. Then when he comes back, he can cheer me up by telling me how you are getting along. ²⁰I have no one else like Timothy, who genuinely cares about your welfare. ²¹All the others care only for themselves and not for what matters to Jesus Christ. ²²But you know how Timothy has proved himself. Like a son with his father, he has helped me in preaching the Good News. ²³I hope to send him to you just as soon as I find out what is going to happen to me here. ²⁴And I have confidence from the Lord that I myself will come to see you soon.

Paul Commends Epaphroditus

²⁵Meanwhile, I thought I should send Epaphroditus back to you. He is a true brother, a faithful worker, and a courageous soldier. And he was your messenger to help me in my need. ²⁶Now I am

2:7a Or *He laid aside his mighty power and glory.* **2:7b** Greek *and was born in the likeness of men and was found in appearance as a man.*

sending him home again, for he has been longing to see you, and he was very distressed that you heard he was ill. ²⁷And he surely was ill; in fact, he almost died. But God had mercy on him—and also on me, so that I would not have such unbearable sorrow.

²⁸So I am all the more anxious to send him back to you, for I know you will be glad to see him, and that will lighten all my cares. ²⁹Welcome him with Christian love* and with great joy, and be sure to honor people like him. ³⁰For he risked his life for the work of Christ, and he was at the point of death while trying to do for me the things you couldn't do because you were far away.

CHAPTER 3
The Priceless Gain of Knowing Christ

Whatever happens, dear brothers and sisters,* may the Lord give you joy. I never get tired of telling you this. I am doing this for your own good.

²Watch out for those dogs, those wicked men and their evil deeds, those mutilators who say you must be circumcised to be saved. ³For we who worship God in the Spirit* are the only ones who are truly circumcised. We put no confidence in human effort. Instead, we boast about what Christ has done for us.

⁴Yet I could have confidence in myself if anyone could. If others have reason for confidence in their own efforts, I have even more! ⁵For I was circumcised when I was eight days old, having been born into a pure-blooded Jewish family that is a branch of the tribe of Benjamin. So I am a real Jew if there ever was one! What's more, I was a member of the Pharisees, who demand the strictest obedience to the Jewish law. ⁶And zealous? Yes, in fact, I harshly persecuted the church. And I obeyed the Jewish law so carefully that I was never accused of any fault.

⁷I once thought all these things were so very important, but now I consider them worthless because of what Christ has done. ⁸Yes, everything else is worthless when compared with the priceless gain of knowing Christ Jesus my Lord. I have discarded everything else, counting it all as garbage, so that I may have Christ ⁹and become one with him. I no longer count on my own goodness or my ability to obey God's law, but I trust Christ to save me. For God's way of making us right with himself depends on faith. ¹⁰As a result, I can really know Christ and experience the mighty power that raised him from the dead. I can learn what it means to suffer with him, sharing in his death, ¹¹so that, somehow, I can experience the resurrection from the dead!

Pressing toward the Goal

¹²I don't mean to say that I have already achieved these things or that I have already reached perfection! But I keep working toward that day when I will finally be all that Christ Jesus saved me for and wants me to be. ¹³No, dear brothers and sisters, I am still not all I should be,* but I am focusing all my energies on this one thing: Forgetting the past and looking forward to what lies ahead, ¹⁴I strain to reach the end of the race and receive the

2:29 Greek *in the Lord.*   3:1 Greek *brothers;* also in 3:13, 17.   3:3 Or *in spirit;* some manuscripts read *worship by the Spirit of God.*   3:13 Some manuscripts read *I am not all I should be.*

prize for which God, through Christ Jesus, is calling us up to heaven.*

15I hope all of you who are mature Christians will agree on these things. If you disagree on some point, I believe God will make it plain to you. 16But we must be sure to obey the truth we have learned already.

17Dear brothers and sisters, pattern your lives after mine, and learn from those who follow our example. 18For I have told you often before, and I say it again with tears in my eyes, that there are many whose conduct shows they are really enemies of the cross of Christ. 19Their future is eternal destruction. Their god is their appetite, they brag about shameful things, and all they think about is this life here on earth. 20But we are citizens of heaven, where the Lord Jesus Christ lives. And we are eagerly waiting for him to return as our Savior. 21He will take these weak mortal bodies of ours and change them into glorious bodies like his own, using the same mighty power that he will use to conquer everything, everywhere.

CHAPTER 4

Dear brothers and sisters,* I love you and long to see you, for you are my joy and the reward for my work. So please stay true to the Lord, my dear friends.

Paul's Final Thoughts

2And now I want to plead with those two women, Euodia and Syntyche. Please, because you belong to the Lord, settle your disagreement. 3And I ask you, my true teammate,* to help these women, for they worked hard with me in telling others the Good News. And they worked with Clement and the rest of my co-workers, whose names are written in the Book of Life.

4Always be full of joy in the Lord. I say it again—rejoice! 5Let everyone see that you are considerate in all you do. Remember, the Lord is coming soon.

6Don't worry about anything; instead, pray about everything. Tell God what you need, and thank him for all he has done. 7If you do this, you will experience God's peace, which is far more wonderful than the human mind can understand. His peace will guard your hearts and minds as you live in Christ Jesus.

8And now, dear brothers and sisters, let me say one more thing as I close this letter. Fix your thoughts on what is true and honorable and right. Think about things that are pure and lovely and admirable. Think about things that are excellent and worthy of praise. 9Keep putting into practice all you learned from me and heard from me and saw me doing, and the God of peace will be with you.

Paul's Thanks for Their Gifts

10How grateful I am, and how I praise the Lord that you are concerned about me again. I know you have always been concerned for me, but for a while you didn't have the chance to help me. 11Not that I was ever in need, for I have learned how to get along happily whether I have much or little. 12I know how to live on almost nothing or with everything. I have learned the secret of living in every situation, whether it is with a full stomach or empty,

3:14 Or *from heaven.*   4:1 Greek *brothers;* also in 4:8.   4:3 Greek *true yokefellow,* or *loyal Syzygus.*

with plenty or little. ¹³For I can do everything with the help of Christ who gives me the strength I need. ¹⁴But even so, you have done well to share with me in my present difficulty.

¹⁵As you know, you Philippians were the only ones who gave me financial help when I brought you the Good News and then traveled on from Macedonia. No other church did this. ¹⁶Even when I was in Thessalonica you sent help more than once. ¹⁷I don't say this because I want a gift from you. What I want is for you to receive a well-earned reward because of your kindness.

¹⁸At the moment I have all I need—more than I need! I am generously supplied with the gifts you sent me with Epaphroditus. They are a sweet-smelling sacrifice that is acceptable to God and pleases him. ¹⁹And this same God who takes care of me will supply all your needs from his glorious riches, which have been given to us in Christ Jesus. ²⁰Now glory be to God our Father forever and ever. Amen.

Paul's Final Greetings

²¹Give my greetings to all the Christians there. The brothers who are with me here send you their greetings. ²²And all the other Christians send their greetings, too, especially those who work in Caesar's palace.

²³May the grace of the Lord Jesus Christ be with your spirit.

COLOSSIANS

CHAPTER 1

Greetings from Paul

This letter is from Paul, chosen by God to be an apostle of Christ Jesus, and from our brother Timothy.

²It is written to God's holy people in the city of Colosse, who are faithful brothers and sisters* in Christ.

May God our Father give you grace and peace.

Paul's Thanksgiving and Prayer

³We always pray for you, and we give thanks to God the Father of our Lord Jesus Christ, ⁴for we have heard that you trust in Christ Jesus and that you love all of God's people. ⁵You do this because you are looking forward to the joys of heaven—as you have been ever since you first heard the truth of the Good News. ⁶This same Good News that came to you is going out all over the world. It is changing lives everywhere, just as it changed yours that very first day you heard and understood the truth about God's great kindness to sinners.

⁷Epaphras, our much loved co-worker, was the one who brought you the Good News. He is Christ's faithful servant, and he is helping us in your place.* ⁸He is the one who told us about the great love for others that the Holy Spirit has given you.

1:2 Greek *faithful brothers.* 1:7 Greek *he is ministering on your behalf;* other manuscripts read *he is ministering on our behalf.*

⁹So we have continued praying for you ever since we first heard about you. We ask God to give you a complete understanding of what he wants to do in your lives, and we ask him to make you wise with spiritual wisdom. ¹⁰Then the way you live will always honor and please the Lord, and you will continually do good, kind things for others. All the while, you will learn to know God better and better.

¹¹We also pray that you will be strengthened with his glorious power so that you will have all the patience and endurance you need. May you be filled with joy, ¹²always thanking the Father, who has enabled you to share the inheritance that belongs to God's holy people, who live in the light. ¹³For he has rescued us from the one who rules in the kingdom of darkness, and he has brought us into the Kingdom of his dear Son. ¹⁴God has purchased our freedom with his blood* and has forgiven all our sins.

Christ Is Supreme

¹⁵Christ is the visible image of the invisible God. He existed before God made anything at all and is supreme over all creation.* ¹⁶Christ is the one through whom God created everything in heaven and earth. He made the things we can see and the things we can't see—kings, kingdoms, rulers, and authorities. Everything has been created through him and for him. ¹⁷He existed before everything else began, and he holds all creation together.

¹⁸Christ is the head of the church, which is his body. He is the first of all who will rise from the dead,* so he is first in everything. ¹⁹For God in all his fullness was pleased to live in Christ, ²⁰and by him God reconciled everything to himself. He made peace with everything in heaven and on earth by means of his blood on the cross. ²¹This includes you who were once so far away from God. You were his enemies, separated from him by your evil thoughts and actions, ²²yet now he has brought you back as his friends. He has done this through his death on the cross in his own human body. As a result, he has brought you into the very presence of God, and you are holy and blameless as you stand before him without a single fault. ²³But you must continue to believe this truth and stand in it firmly. Don't drift away from the assurance you received when you heard the Good News. The Good News has been preached all over the world, and I, Paul, have been appointed by God to proclaim it.

Paul's Work for the Church

²⁴I am glad when I suffer for you in my body, for I am completing what remains of Christ's sufferings for his body, the church. ²⁵God has given me the responsibility of serving his church by proclaiming his message in all its fullness to you Gentiles. ²⁶This message was kept secret for centuries and generations past, but now it has been revealed to his own holy people. ²⁷For it has pleased God to tell his people that the riches and glory of Christ are for you Gentiles, too. For this is the secret: Christ lives in you, and this is your assurance that you will share in his glory.

²⁸So everywhere we go, we tell everyone about Christ. We warn

1:14 Some manuscripts do not include *with his blood.*   1:15 Greek *He is the firstborn of all creation.*   1:18 Greek *He is the beginning, the firstborn from the dead.*

them and teach them with all the wisdom God has given us, for we want to present them to God, perfect* in their relationship to Christ. 29I work very hard at this, as I depend on Christ's mighty power that works within me.

CHAPTER 2

I want you to know how much I have agonized for you and for the church at Laodicea, and for many other friends who have never known me personally. 2My goal is that they will be encouraged and knit together by strong ties of love. I want them to have full confidence because they have complete understanding of God's secret plan, which is Christ himself. 3In him lie hidden all the treasures of wisdom and knowledge.

4I am telling you this so that no one will be able to deceive you with persuasive arguments. 5For though I am far away from you, my heart is with you. And I am very happy because you are living as you should and because of your strong faith in Christ.

Freedom from Rules and New Life in Christ

6And now, just as you accepted Christ Jesus as your Lord, you must continue to live in obedience to him. 7Let your roots grow down into him and draw up nourishment from him, so you will grow in faith, strong and vigorous in the truth you were taught. Let your lives overflow with thanksgiving for all he has done.

8Don't let anyone lead you astray with empty philosophy and high-sounding nonsense that come from human thinking and from the evil powers of this world,* and not from Christ. 9For in Christ the fullness of God lives in a human body,* 10and you are complete through your union with Christ. He is the Lord over every ruler and authority in the universe.

11When you came to Christ, you were "circumcised," but not by a physical procedure. It was a spiritual procedure—the cutting away of your sinful nature. 12For you were buried with Christ when you were baptized. And with him you were raised to a new life because you trusted the mighty power of God, who raised Christ from the dead.

13You were dead because of your sins and because your sinful nature was not yet cut away. Then God made you alive with Christ. He forgave all our sins. 14He canceled the record that contained the charges against us. He took it and destroyed it by nailing it to Christ's cross. 15In this way, God disarmed the evil rulers and authorities. He shamed them publicly by his victory over them on the cross of Christ.

16So don't let anyone condemn you for what you eat or drink, or for not celebrating certain holy days or new-moon ceremonies or Sabbaths. 17For these rules were only shadows of the real thing, Christ himself. 18Don't let anyone condemn you by insisting on self-denial. And don't let anyone say you must worship angels, even though they say they have had visions about this. These people claim to be so humble, but their sinful minds have made them proud. 19But they are not connected to Christ, the head of the body. For we are joined together in his body by his strong sinews, and we grow only as we get our nourishment and strength from God.

1:28 Or *mature.*   2:8 Or *from the basic principles of this world;* also in 2:20.   2:9 Greek *in him dwells all the fullness of the Godhead bodily.*

²⁰You have died with Christ, and he has set you free from the evil powers of this world. So why do you keep on following rules of the world, such as, ²¹"Don't handle, don't eat, don't touch." ²²Such rules are mere human teaching about things that are gone as soon as we use them. ²³These rules may seem wise because they require strong devotion, humility, and severe bodily discipline. But they have no effect when it comes to conquering a person's evil thoughts and desires.

CHAPTER 3

Living the New Life

Since you have been raised to new life with Christ, set your sights on the realities of heaven, where Christ sits at God's right hand in the place of honor and power. ²Let heaven fill your thoughts. Do not think only about things down here on earth. ³For you died when Christ died, and your real life is hidden with Christ in God. ⁴And when Christ, who is your* real life, is revealed to the whole world, you will share in all his glory.

⁵So put to death the sinful, earthly things lurking within you. Have nothing to do with sexual sin, impurity, lust, and shameful desires. Don't be greedy for the good things of this life, for that is idolatry. ⁶God's terrible anger will come upon those who do such things. ⁷You used to do them when your life was still part of this world. ⁸But now is the time to get rid of anger, rage, malicious behavior, slander, and dirty language. ⁹Don't lie to each other, for you have stripped off your old evil nature and all its wicked deeds. ¹⁰In its place you have clothed yourselves with a brand-new nature that is continually being renewed as you learn more and more about Christ, who created this new nature within you. ¹¹In this new life, it doesn't matter if you are a Jew or a Gentile,* circumcised or uncircumcised, barbaric, uncivilized,* slave, or free. Christ is all that matters, and he lives in all of us.

¹²Since God chose you to be the holy people whom he loves, you must clothe yourselves with tenderhearted mercy, kindness, humility, gentleness, and patience. ¹³You must make allowance for each other's faults and forgive the person who offends you. Remember, the Lord forgave you, so you must forgive others. ¹⁴And the most important piece of clothing you must wear is love. Love is what binds us all together in perfect harmony. ¹⁵And let the peace that comes from Christ rule in your hearts. For as members of one body you are all called to live in peace. And always be thankful.

¹⁶Let the words of Christ, in all their richness, live in your hearts and make you wise. Use his words to teach and counsel each other. Sing psalms and hymns and spiritual songs to God with thankful hearts. ¹⁷And whatever you do or say, let it be as a representative of the Lord Jesus, all the while giving thanks through him to God the Father.

Instructions for Christian Households

¹⁸You wives must submit to your husbands, as is fitting for those who belong to the Lord. ¹⁹And you husbands must love your wives and never treat them harshly.

²⁰You children must always obey your parents, for this is what pleases the Lord. ²¹Fathers, don't aggravate your children. If you do, they will become discouraged and quit trying.

3:4 Some manuscripts read *our.*   **3:11a** Greek *Greek.*   **3:11b** Greek *Barbarian, Scythian.*

²²You slaves must obey your earthly masters in everything you do. Try to please them all the time, not just when they are watching you. Obey them willingly because of your reverent fear of the Lord. ²³Work hard and cheerfully at whatever you do, as though you were working for the Lord rather than for people. ²⁴Remember that the Lord will give you an inheritance as your reward, and the Master you are serving is Christ. ²⁵But if you do what is wrong, you will be paid back for the wrong you have done. For God has no favorites who can get away with evil.

CHAPTER 4

You slave owners must be just and fair to your slaves. Remember that you also have a Master—in heaven.

An Encouragement for Prayer

²Devote yourselves to prayer with an alert mind and a thankful heart. ³Don't forget to pray for us, too, that God will give us many opportunities to preach about his secret plan—that Christ is also for you Gentiles. That is why I am here in chains. ⁴Pray that I will proclaim this message as clearly as I should.

⁵Live wisely among those who are not Christians, and make the most of every opportunity. ⁶Let your conversation be gracious and effective so that you will have the right answer for everyone.

Paul's Final Instructions and Greetings

⁷Tychicus, a much loved brother, will tell you how I am getting along. He is a faithful helper who serves the Lord with me. ⁸I have sent him on this special trip to let you know how we are doing and to encourage you. ⁹I am also sending Onesimus, a faithful and much loved brother, one of your own people. He and Tychicus will give you all the latest news.

¹⁰Aristarchus, who is in prison with me, sends you his greetings, and so does Mark, Barnabas's cousin. And as you were instructed before, make Mark welcome if he comes your way. ¹¹Jesus (the one we call Justus) also sends his greetings. These are the only Jewish Christians among my co-workers; they are working with me here for the Kingdom of God. And what a comfort they have been!

¹²Epaphras, from your city, a servant of Christ Jesus, sends you his greetings. He always prays earnestly for you, asking God to make you strong and perfect, fully confident of the whole will of God. ¹³I can assure you that he has agonized for you and also for the Christians in Laodicea and Hierapolis.

¹⁴Dear Doctor Luke sends his greetings, and so does Demas. ¹⁵Please give my greetings to our Christian brothers and sisters* at Laodicea, and to Nympha and those who meet in her house.

¹⁶After you have read this letter, pass it on to the church at Laodicea so they can read it, too. And you should read the letter I wrote to them. ¹⁷And say to Archippus, "Be sure to carry out the work the Lord gave you."

¹⁸Here is my greeting in my own handwriting—PAUL.
Remember my chains.
May the grace of God be with you.

4:15 Greek *brothers*.

1 THESSALONIANS

CHAPTER 1

Greetings from Paul

This letter is from Paul, Silas,* and Timothy.

It is written to the church in Thessalonica, you who belong to God the Father and the Lord Jesus Christ.

May his grace and peace be yours.

The Faith of the Thessalonian Believers

2 We always thank God for all of you and pray for you constantly. 3 As we talk to our God and Father about you, we think of your faithful work, your loving deeds, and your continual anticipation of the return of our Lord Jesus Christ.

4 We know that God loves you, dear brothers and sisters,* and that he chose you to be his own people. 5 For when we brought you the Good News, it was not only with words but also with power, for the Holy Spirit gave you full assurance that what we said was true. And you know that the way we lived among you was further proof of the truth of our message. 6 So you received the message with joy from the Holy Spirit in spite of the severe suffering it brought you. In this way, you imitated both us and the Lord. 7 As a result, you yourselves became an example to all the Christians in Greece.* 8 And now the word of the Lord is ringing out from you to people everywhere, even beyond Greece, for wherever we go we find people telling us about your faith in God. We don't need to tell them about it, 9 for they themselves keep talking about the wonderful welcome you gave us and how you turned away from idols to serve the true and living God. 10 And they speak of how you are looking forward to the coming of God's Son from heaven— Jesus, whom God raised from the dead. He is the one who has rescued us from the terrors of the coming judgment.

CHAPTER 2

Paul Remembers His Visit

You yourselves know, dear brothers and sisters,* that our visit to you was not a failure. 2 You know how badly we had been treated at Philippi just before we came to you and how much we suffered there. Yet our God gave us the courage to declare his Good News to you boldly, even though we were surrounded by many who opposed us. 3 So you can see that we were not preaching with any deceit or impure purposes or trickery.

4 For we speak as messengers who have been approved by God to be entrusted with the Good News. Our purpose is to please God, not people. He is the one who examines the motives of our hearts. 5 Never once did we try to win you with flattery, as you very well

---

1:1 Greek *Silvanus.*　1:4 Greek *brothers.*　1:7 Greek *Macedonia and Achaia,* the northern and southern regions of Greece; also in 1:8.　2:1 Greek *brothers;* also in 2:9, 14, 17.

know. And God is our witness that we were not just pretending to be your friends so you would give us money! 6As for praise, we have never asked for it from you or anyone else. 7As apostles of Christ we certainly had a right to make some demands of you, but we were as gentle among you as a mother* feeding and caring for her own children. 8We loved you so much that we gave you not only God's Good News but our own lives, too.

9Don't you remember, dear brothers and sisters, how hard we worked among you? Night and day we toiled to earn a living so that our expenses would not be a burden to anyone there as we preached God's Good News among you. 10You yourselves are our witnesses—and so is God—that we were pure and honest and faultless toward all of you believers. 11And you know that we treated each of you as a father treats his own children. 12We pleaded with you, encouraged you, and urged you to live your lives in a way that God would consider worthy. For he called you into his Kingdom to share his glory.

13And we will never stop thanking God that when we preached his message to you, you didn't think of the words we spoke as being just our own. You accepted what we said as the very word of God—which, of course, it was. And this word continues to work in you who believe.

14And then, dear brothers and sisters, you suffered persecution from your own countrymen. In this way, you imitated the believers in God's churches in Judea who, because of their belief in Christ Jesus, suffered from their own people, the Jews.

15For some of the Jews had killed their own prophets, and some even killed the Lord Jesus. Now they have persecuted us and driven us out. They displease God and oppose everyone 16by trying to keep us from preaching the Good News to the Gentiles, for fear some might be saved. By doing this, they continue to pile up their sins. But the anger of God has caught up with them at last.

Timothy's Good Report about the Church

17Dear brothers and sisters, after we were separated from you for a little while (though our hearts never left you), we tried very hard to come back because of our intense longing to see you again. 18We wanted very much to come, and I, Paul, tried again and again, but Satan prevented us. 19After all, what gives us hope and joy, and what is our proud reward and crown? It is you! Yes, you will bring us much joy as we stand together before our Lord Jesus when he comes back again. 20For you are our pride and joy.

CHAPTER 3

Finally, when we could stand it no longer, we decided that I should stay alone in Athens, 2and we sent Timothy to visit you. He is our co-worker for God and our brother in proclaiming the Good News of Christ. We sent him to strengthen you, to encourage you in your faith, 3and to keep you from becoming disturbed by the troubles you were going through. But, of course, you know that such troubles are going to happen to us Christians. 4Even while we were

2:7 Some manuscripts read *we were as infants among you; we were as a mother.*

with you, we warned you that troubles would soon come—and they did, as you well know.

⁵That is why, when I could bear it no longer, I sent Timothy to find out whether your faith was still strong. I was afraid that the Tempter had gotten the best of you and that all our work had been useless. ⁶Now Timothy has just returned, bringing the good news that your faith and love are as strong as ever. He reports that you remember our visit with joy and that you want to see us just as much as we want to see you. ⁷So we have been greatly comforted, dear brothers and sisters,* in all of our own crushing troubles and suffering, because you have remained strong in your faith. ⁸It gives us new life, knowing you remain strong in the Lord.

⁹How we thank God for you! Because of you we have great joy in the presence of God. ¹⁰Night and day we pray earnestly for you, asking God to let us see you again to fill up anything that may still be missing in your faith.

¹¹May God himself, our Father, and our Lord Jesus make it possible for us to come to you very soon. ¹²And may the Lord make your love grow and overflow to each other and to everyone else, just as our love overflows toward you. ¹³As a result, Christ will make your hearts strong, blameless, and holy when you stand before God our Father on that day when our Lord Jesus comes with all those who belong to him.

CHAPTER 4

Live to Please God

Finally, dear brothers and sisters,* we urge you in the name of the Lord Jesus to live in a way that pleases God, as we have taught you. You are doing this already, and we encourage you to do so more and more. ²For you remember what we taught you in the name of the Lord Jesus. ³God wants you to be holy, so you should keep clear of all sexual sin. ⁴Then each of you will control your body* and live in holiness and honor—⁵not in lustful passion as the pagans do, in their ignorance of God and his ways.

⁶Never cheat a Christian brother in this matter by taking his wife, for the Lord avenges all such sins, as we have solemnly warned you before. ⁷God has called us to be holy, not to live impure lives. ⁸Anyone who refuses to live by these rules is not disobeying human rules but is rejecting God, who gives his Holy Spirit to you.

⁹But I don't need to write to you about the Christian love* that should be shown among God's people. For God himself has taught you to love one another. ¹⁰Indeed, your love is already strong toward all the Christians* in all of Macedonia. Even so, dear brothers and sisters, we beg you to love them more and more. ¹¹This should be your ambition: to live a quiet life, minding your own business and working with your hands, just as we commanded you before. ¹²As a result, people who are not Christians will respect the way you live, and you will not need to depend on others to meet your financial needs.

3:7 Greek *brothers.*   4:1 Greek *brothers;* also in 4:10, 13.   4:4 Or *will know how to take a wife for himself;* Greek reads *will know how to possess his own vessel.*   4:9 Greek *brotherly love.*   4:10 Greek *the brothers.*

The Hope of the Resurrection

13And now, brothers and sisters, I want you to know what will happen to the Christians who have died so you will not be full of sorrow like people who have no hope. 14For since we believe that Jesus died and was raised to life again, we also believe that when Jesus comes, God will bring back with Jesus all the Christians who have died.

15I can tell you this directly from the Lord: We who are still living when the Lord returns will not rise to meet him ahead of those who are in their graves. 16For the Lord himself will come down from heaven with a commanding shout, with the call of the archangel, and with the trumpet call of God. First, all the Christians who have died will rise from their graves. 17Then, together with them, we who are still alive and remain on the earth will be caught up in the clouds to meet the Lord in the air and remain with him forever. 18So comfort and encourage each other with these words.

CHAPTER 5

I really don't need to write to you about how and when all this will happen, dear brothers and sisters.* 2For you know quite well that the day of the Lord will come unexpectedly, like a thief in the night. 3When people are saying, "All is well; everything is peaceful and secure," then disaster will fall upon them as suddenly as a woman's birth pains begin when her child is about to be born. And there will be no escape.

4But you aren't in the dark about these things, dear brothers and sisters, and you won't be surprised when the day of the Lord comes like a thief. 5For you are all children of the light and of the day; we don't belong to darkness and night. 6So be on your guard, not asleep like the others. Stay alert and be sober. 7Night is the time for sleep and the time when people get drunk. 8But let us who live in the light think clearly, protected by the body armor of faith and love, and wearing as our helmet the confidence of our salvation. 9For God decided to save us through our Lord Jesus Christ, not to pour out his anger on us. 10He died for us so that we can live with him forever, whether we are dead or alive at the time of his return. 11So encourage each other and build each other up, just as you are already doing.

Paul's Final Advice

12Dear brothers and sisters, honor those who are your leaders in the Lord's work. They work hard among you and warn you against all that is wrong. 13Think highly of them and give them your wholehearted love because of their work. And remember to live peaceably with each other.

14Brothers and sisters, we urge you to warn those who are lazy. Encourage those who are timid. Take tender care of those who are weak. Be patient with everyone.

15See that no one pays back evil for evil, but always try to do good to each other and to everyone else.

16Always be joyful. 17Keep on praying. 18No matter what happens, always be thankful, for this is God's will for you who belong to Christ Jesus.

19Do not stifle the Holy Spirit. 20Do not scoff at prophecies, 21but test everything that is said. Hold on to what is good. 22Keep away from every kind of evil.

5:1 Greek *brothers;* also in 5:4, 12, 14, 25, 26, 27.

Paul's Final Greetings

23Now may the God of peace make you holy in every way, and may your whole spirit and soul and body be kept blameless until that day when our Lord Jesus Christ comes again. 24God, who calls you, is faithful; he will do this.

25Dear brothers and sisters, pray for us.

26Greet all the brothers and sisters in Christian love.*

27I command you in the name of the Lord to read this letter to all the brothers and sisters.

28And may the grace of our Lord Jesus Christ be with all of you.

5:26 Greek *with a holy kiss.*

2 THESSALONIANS

CHAPTER 1

Greetings from Paul

This letter is from Paul, Silas,* and Timothy.

It is written to the church in Thessalonica, you who belong to God our Father and the Lord Jesus Christ.

2May God our Father and the Lord Jesus Christ give you grace and peace.

Encouragement during Persecution

3Dear brothers and sisters,* we always thank God for you, as is right, for we are thankful that your faith is flourishing and you are all growing in love for each other. 4We proudly tell God's other churches about your endurance and faithfulness in all the persecutions and hardships you are suffering. 5But God will use this persecution to show his justice. For he will make you worthy of his Kingdom, for which you are suffering, 6and in his justice he will punish those who persecute you. 7And God will provide rest for you who are being persecuted and also for us when the Lord Jesus appears from heaven. He will come with his mighty angels, 8in flaming fire, bringing judgment on those who don't know God and on those who refuse to obey the Good News of our Lord Jesus. 9They will be punished with everlasting destruction, forever separated from the Lord and from his glorious power 10when he comes to receive glory and praise from his holy people. And you will be among those praising him on that day, for you believed what we testified about him.

11And so we keep on praying for you, that our God will make you worthy of the life to which he called you. And we pray that God, by his power, will fulfill all your good intentions and faithful deeds. 12Then everyone will give honor to the name of our Lord Jesus because of you, and you will be honored along with him. This is all made possible because of the undeserved favor of our God and Lord, Jesus Christ.*

1:1 Greek *Silvanus.*   1:3 Greek *Brothers.*   1:12 Or *of our God and the Lord Jesus Christ.*

CHAPTER 2

Events prior to the Lord's Second Coming

And now, brothers and sisters,* let us tell you about the coming again of our Lord Jesus Christ and how we will be gathered together to meet him. ²Please don't be so easily shaken and troubled by those who say that the day of the Lord has already begun. Even if they claim to have had a vision, a revelation, or a letter supposedly from us, don't believe them. ³Don't be fooled by what they say.

For that day will not come until there is a great rebellion against God and the man of lawlessness is revealed—the one who brings destruction.* ⁴He will exalt himself and defy every god there is and tear down every object of adoration and worship. He will position himself in the temple of God, claiming that he himself is God. ⁵Don't you remember that I told you this when I was with you? ⁶And you know what is holding him back, for he can be revealed only when his time comes.

⁷For this lawlessness is already at work secretly, and it will remain secret until the one who is holding it back steps out of the way. ⁸Then the man of lawlessness will be revealed, whom the Lord Jesus will consume with the breath of his mouth and destroy by the splendor of his coming. ⁹This evil man will come to do the work of Satan with counterfeit power and signs and miracles. ¹⁰He will use every kind of wicked deception to fool those who are on their way to destruction because they refuse to believe the truth that would save them. ¹¹So God will send great deception upon them, and they will believe all these lies. ¹²Then they will be condemned for not believing the truth and for enjoying the evil they do.

Believers Should Stand Firm

¹³As for us, we always thank God for you, dear brothers and sisters loved by the Lord. We are thankful that God chose you to be among the first* to experience salvation, a salvation that came through the Spirit who makes you holy and by your belief in the truth. ¹⁴He called you to salvation when we told you the Good News; now you can share in the glory of our Lord Jesus Christ.

¹⁵With all these things in mind, dear brothers and sisters, stand firm and keep a strong grip on everything we taught you both in person and by letter.

¹⁶May our Lord Jesus Christ and God our Father, who loved us and in his special favor gave us everlasting comfort and good hope, ¹⁷comfort your hearts and give you strength in every good thing you do and say.

CHAPTER 3

Paul's Request for Prayer

Finally, dear brothers and sisters,* I ask you to pray for us. Pray first that the Lord's message will spread rapidly and be honored wherever it goes, just as when it came to you. ²Pray, too, that we will be saved from wicked and evil people, for not everyone believes in the Lord. ³But the Lord is faithful; he will make you strong and guard you from the evil one.* ⁴And we are confident in the Lord that you

2:1 Greek *brothers*; also in 2:13, 15.   2:3 Greek *the son of destruction*.   2:13 Some manuscripts read *God chose you from the very beginning*.   3:1 Greek *brothers*; also in 3:6, 13.   3:3 Or *from evil*.

are practicing the things we commanded you, and that you always will. [5]May the Lord bring you into an ever deeper understanding of the love of God and the endurance that comes from Christ.

An Exhortation to Proper Living

[6]And now, dear brothers and sisters, we give you this command with the authority of our Lord Jesus Christ: Stay away from any Christian* who lives in idleness and doesn't follow the tradition of hard work we gave you. [7]For you know that you ought to follow our example. We were never lazy when we were with you. [8]We never accepted food from anyone without paying for it. We worked hard day and night so that we would not be a burden to any of you. [9]It wasn't that we didn't have the right to ask you to feed us, but we wanted to give you an example to follow. [10]Even while we were with you, we gave you this rule: "Whoever does not work should not eat."

[11]Yet we hear that some of you are living idle lives, refusing to work and wasting time meddling in other people's business. [12]In the name of the Lord Jesus Christ, we appeal to such people—no, we command them: Settle down and get to work. Earn your own living. [13]And I say to the rest of you, dear brothers and sisters, never get tired of doing good.

[14]Take note of those who refuse to obey what we say in this letter. Stay away from them so they will be ashamed. [15]Don't think of them as enemies, but speak to them as you would to a Christian who needs to be warned.

Paul's Final Greetings

[16]May the Lord of peace himself always give you his peace no matter what happens. The Lord be with you all.

[17]Now here is my greeting, which I write with my own hand— PAUL. I do this at the end of all my letters to prove that they really are from me.

[18]May the grace of our Lord Jesus Christ be with you all.

3:6 Greek *brother*; also in 3:15.

1 TIMOTHY

CHAPTER 1

Greetings from Paul

This letter is from Paul, an apostle of Christ Jesus, appointed by the command of God our Savior and by Christ Jesus our hope.

[2]It is written to Timothy, my true child in the faith.

May God our Father and Christ Jesus our Lord give you grace, mercy, and peace.

Warnings against False Teachings

[3]When I left for Macedonia, I urged you to stay there in Ephesus and stop those who are teaching wrong doctrine. [4]Don't let people waste time in endless speculation over myths and spiritual

pedigrees.* For these things only cause arguments; they don't help people live a life of faith in God.* 5The purpose of my instruction is that all the Christians there would be filled with love that comes from a pure heart, a clear conscience, and sincere faith.

6But some teachers have missed this whole point. They have turned away from these things and spend their time arguing and talking foolishness. 7They want to be known as teachers of the law of Moses, but they don't know what they are talking about, even though they seem so confident. 8We know these laws are good when they are used as God intended. 9But they were not made for people who do what is right. They are for people who are disobedient and rebellious, who are ungodly and sinful, who consider nothing sacred and defile what is holy, who murder their father or mother or other people. 10These laws are for people who are sexually immoral, for homosexuals and slave traders, for liars and oath breakers, and for those who do anything else that contradicts the right teaching 11that comes from the glorious Good News entrusted to me by our blessed God.

Paul's Gratitude for God's Mercy

12How thankful I am to Christ Jesus our Lord for considering me trustworthy and appointing me to serve him, 13even though I used to scoff at the name of Christ. I hunted down his people, harming them in every way I could. But God had mercy on me because I did it in ignorance and unbelief. 14Oh, how kind and gracious the Lord was! He filled me completely with faith and the love of Christ Jesus.

15This is a true saying, and everyone should believe it: Christ Jesus came into the world to save sinners—and I was the worst of them all. 16But that is why God had mercy on me, so that Christ Jesus could use me as a prime example of his great patience with even the worst sinners. Then others will realize that they, too, can believe in him and receive eternal life. 17Glory and honor to God forever and ever. He is the eternal King, the unseen one who never dies; he alone is God. Amen.

Timothy's Responsibility

18Timothy, my son, here are my instructions for you, based on the prophetic words spoken about you earlier. May they give you the confidence to fight well in the Lord's battles. 19Cling tightly to your faith in Christ, and always keep your conscience clear. For some people have deliberately violated their consciences; as a result, their faith has been shipwrecked. 20Hymenaeus and Alexander are two examples of this. I turned them over to Satan so they would learn not to blaspheme God.

CHAPTER 2

Instructions about Worship

I urge you, first of all, to pray for all people. As you make your requests, plead for God's mercy upon them, and give thanks. 2Pray this way for kings and all others who are in authority, so that we can live in peace and quietness, in godliness and dignity. 3This is good and pleases God our Savior, 4for he wants everyone to be saved and to understand the truth. 5For there is only one God and

1:4a *Greek in myths and endless genealogies, which cause speculation.* 1:4b *Greek a stewardship of God in faith.*

one Mediator who can reconcile God and people. He is the man Christ Jesus. [6]He gave his life to purchase freedom for everyone. This is the message that God gave to the world at the proper time. [7]And I have been chosen—this is the absolute truth—as a preacher and apostle to teach the Gentiles about faith and truth.

[8]So wherever you assemble, I want men to pray with holy hands lifted up to God, free from anger and controversy. [9]And I want women to be modest in their appearance. They should wear decent and appropriate clothing and not draw attention to themselves by the way they fix their hair or by wearing gold or pearls or expensive clothes. [10]For women who claim to be devoted to God should make themselves attractive by the good things they do.

[11]Women should listen and learn quietly and submissively. [12]I do not let women teach men or have authority over them. Let them listen quietly. [13]For God made Adam first, and afterward he made Eve. [14]And it was the woman, not Adam, who was deceived by Satan, and sin was the result. [15]But women will be saved through childbearing* and by continuing to live in faith, love, holiness, and modesty.

CHAPTER 3

Leaders in the Church

It is a true saying that if someone wants to be an elder,* he desires an honorable responsibility. [2]For an elder must be a man whose life cannot be spoken against. He must be faithful to his wife.* He must exhibit self-control, live wisely, and have a good reputation. He must enjoy having guests in his home and must be able to teach. [3]He must not be a heavy drinker or be violent. He must be gentle, peace loving, and not one who loves money. [4]He must manage his own family well, with children who respect and obey him. [5]For if a man cannot manage his own household, how can he take care of God's church?

[6]An elder must not be a new Christian, because he might be proud of being chosen so soon, and the Devil will use that pride to make him fall.* [7]Also, people outside the church must speak well of him so that he will not fall into the Devil's trap and be disgraced.

[8]In the same way, deacons must be people who are respected and have integrity. They must not be heavy drinkers and must not be greedy for money. [9]They must be committed to the revealed truths of the Christian faith and must live with a clear conscience. [10]Before they are appointed as deacons, they should be given other responsibilities in the church as a test of their character and ability. If they do well, then they may serve as deacons.

[11]In the same way, their wives* must be respected and must not speak evil of others. They must exercise self-control and be faithful in everything they do.

[12]A deacon must be faithful to his wife, and he must manage his children and household well. [13]Those who do well as deacons will be rewarded with respect from others and will have increased confidence in their faith in Christ Jesus.

2:15 Or *will be saved by accepting their role as mothers,* or *will be saved by the birth of the Child.*   3:1 Greek *overseer;* also in 3:2.   3:2 Greek *be the husband of one wife;* also in 3:12.   3:6 Or *He might fall into the same judgment as the Devil.*   3:11 Or *the women deacons.* The Greek word can be translated *women* or *wives.*

The Truths of Our Faith

¹⁴I am writing these things to you now, even though I hope to be with you soon, ¹⁵so that if I can't come for a while, you will know how people must conduct themselves in the household of God. This is the church of the living God, which is the pillar and support of the truth.

¹⁶Without question, this is the great mystery of our faith:

Christ* appeared in the flesh
  and was shown to be righteous by the Spirit.*
He was seen by angels
  and was announced to the nations.
He was believed on in the world
  and was taken up into heaven.*

CHAPTER 4

Warnings against False Teachers

Now the Holy Spirit tells us clearly that in the last times some will turn away from what we believe; they will follow lying spirits and teachings that come from demons. ²These teachers are hypocrites and liars. They pretend to be religious, but their consciences are dead.*

³They will say it is wrong to be married and wrong to eat certain foods. But God created those foods to be eaten with thanksgiving by people who know and believe the truth. ⁴Since everything God created is good, we should not reject any of it. We may receive it gladly, with thankful hearts. ⁵For we know it is made holy by the word of God and prayer.

A Good Servant of Christ Jesus

⁶If you explain this to the brothers and sisters,* you will be doing your duty as a worthy servant of Christ Jesus, one who is fed by the message of faith and the true teaching you have followed. ⁷Do not waste time arguing over godless ideas and old wives' tales. Spend your time and energy in training yourself for spiritual fitness. ⁸Physical exercise has some value, but spiritual exercise is much more important, for it promises a reward in both this life and the next. ⁹This is true, and everyone should accept it. ¹⁰We work hard and suffer much* in order that people will believe the truth, for our hope is in the living God, who is the Savior of all people, and particularly of those who believe.

¹¹Teach these things and insist that everyone learn them. ¹²Don't let anyone think less of you because you are young. Be an example to all believers in what you teach, in the way you live, in your love, your faith, and your purity. ¹³Until I get there, focus on reading the Scriptures to the church, encouraging the believers, and teaching them.

¹⁴Do not neglect the spiritual gift you received through the prophecies spoken to you when the elders of the church laid their hands on you. ¹⁵Give your complete attention to these matters. Throw yourself into your tasks so that everyone will see your progress. ¹⁶Keep a close watch on yourself and on your teaching.

3:16a Greek *Who;* some manuscripts read *God.*   **3:16b** Or *in his spirit.*   **3:16c** Greek *in glory.*   **4:2** Greek *are seared.*   **4:6** Greek *brothers.*   **4:10** Some manuscripts read *and strive.*

Stay true to what is right, and God will save you and those who hear you.

CHAPTER 5

Never speak harshly to an older man,* but appeal to him respectfully as though he were your own father. Talk to the younger men as you would to your own brothers. ²Treat the older women as you would your mother, and treat the younger women with all purity as your own sisters.

Advice about Widows, Elders, and Slaves

³The church should care for any widow who has no one else to care for her. ⁴But if she has children or grandchildren, their first responsibility is to show godliness at home and repay their parents by taking care of them. This is something that pleases God very much.

⁵But a woman who is a true widow, one who is truly alone in this world, has placed her hope in God. Night and day she asks God for help and spends much time in prayer. ⁶But the widow who lives only for pleasure is spiritually dead. ⁷Give these instructions to the church so that the widows you support* will not be criticized.

⁸But those who won't care for their own relatives, especially those living in the same household, have denied what we believe. Such people are worse than unbelievers.

⁹A widow who is put on the list for support must be a woman who is at least sixty years old and was faithful to her husband.* ¹⁰She must be well respected by everyone because of the good she has done. Has she brought up her children well? Has she been kind to strangers? Has she served other Christians humbly?* Has she helped those who are in trouble? Has she always been ready to do good?

¹¹The younger widows should not be on the list, because their physical desires will overpower their devotion to Christ and they will want to remarry. ¹²Then they would be guilty of breaking their previous pledge. ¹³Besides, they are likely to become lazy and spend their time gossiping from house to house, getting into other people's business and saying things they shouldn't. ¹⁴So I advise these younger widows to marry again, have children, and take care of their own homes. Then the enemy will not be able to say anything against them. ¹⁵For I am afraid that some of them have already gone astray and now follow Satan.

¹⁶If a Christian woman has relatives who are widows, she must take care of them and not put the responsibility on the church. Then the church can care for widows who are truly alone.

¹⁷Elders who do their work well should be paid well,* especially those who work hard at both preaching and teaching. ¹⁸For the Scripture says, "Do not keep an ox from eating as it treads out the grain." And in another place, "Those who work deserve their pay!"*

¹⁹Do not listen to complaints against an elder unless there are two or three witnesses to accuse him. ²⁰Anyone who sins should be rebuked in front of the whole church so that others will have a proper fear of God.

²¹I solemnly command you in the presence of God and Christ

5:1 Or *an elder.* 5:7 Or *so the church;* Greek reads *so they.* 5:9 Greek *was the wife of one man.* 5:10 Greek *Has she washed the feet of saints?* 5:17 Greek *should receive double honor.* 5:18 Deut 25:4; Luke 10:7.

Jesus and the holy angels to obey these instructions without taking sides or showing special favor to anyone. 22Never be in a hurry about appointing an elder. Do not participate in the sins of others. Keep yourself pure.

23Don't drink only water. You ought to drink a little wine for the sake of your stomach because you are sick so often.

24Remember that some people lead sinful lives, and everyone knows they will be judged. But there are others whose sin will not be revealed until later. 25In the same way, everyone knows how much good some people do, but there are others whose good deeds won't be known until later.

CHAPTER 6

Christians who are slaves should give their masters full respect so that the name of God and his teaching will not be shamed. 2If your master is a Christian, that is no excuse for being disrespectful. You should work all the harder because you are helping another believer* by your efforts.

False Teaching and True Riches

Teach these truths, Timothy, and encourage everyone to obey them. 3Some false teachers may deny these things, but these are the sound, wholesome teachings of the Lord Jesus Christ, and they are the foundation for a godly life. 4Anyone who teaches anything different is both conceited and ignorant. Such a person has an unhealthy desire to quibble over the meaning of words. This stirs up arguments ending in jealousy, fighting, slander, and evil suspicions. 5These people always cause trouble. Their minds are corrupt, and they don't tell the truth. To them religion is just a way to get rich.

6Yet true religion with contentment is great wealth. 7After all, we didn't bring anything with us when we came into the world, and we certainly cannot carry anything with us when we die. 8So if we have enough food and clothing, let us be content. 9But people who long to be rich fall into temptation and are trapped by many foolish and harmful desires that plunge them into ruin and destruction. 10For the love of money is at the root of all kinds of evil. And some people, craving money, have wandered from the faith and pierced themselves with many sorrows.

Paul's Final Instructions

11But you, Timothy, belong to God; so run from all these evil things, and follow what is right and good. Pursue a godly life, along with faith, love, perseverance, and gentleness. 12Fight the good fight for what we believe. Hold tightly to the eternal life that God has given you, which you have confessed so well before many witnesses. 13And I command you before God, who gives life to all, and before Christ Jesus, who gave a good testimony before Pontius Pilate, 14that you obey his commands with all purity. Then no one can find fault with you from now until our Lord Jesus Christ returns. 15For at the right time Christ will be revealed from heaven by the blessed and only almighty God, the King of kings and Lord of lords. 16He alone can never die, and he lives in light so brilliant

6:2 Greek a brother.

that no human can approach him. No one has ever seen him, nor ever will. To him be honor and power forever. Amen.

¹⁷Tell those who are rich in this world not to be proud and not to trust in their money, which will soon be gone. But their trust should be in the living God, who richly gives us all we need for our enjoyment. ¹⁸Tell them to use their money to do good. They should be rich in good works and should give generously to those in need, always being ready to share with others whatever God has given them. ¹⁹By doing this they will be storing up their treasure as a good foundation for the future so that they may take hold of real life.

²⁰Timothy, guard what God has entrusted to you. Avoid godless, foolish discussions with those who oppose you with their so-called knowledge. ²¹Some people have wandered from the faith by following such foolishness.

May God's grace be with you all.

2 TIMOTHY

CHAPTER 1

Greetings from Paul

This letter is from Paul, an apostle of Christ Jesus by God's will, sent out to tell others about the life he has promised through faith in Christ Jesus.

²It is written to Timothy, my dear son.

May God our Father and Christ Jesus our Lord give you grace, mercy, and peace.

Encouragement to Be Faithful

³Timothy, I thank God for you. He is the God I serve with a clear conscience, just as my ancestors did. Night and day I constantly remember you in my prayers. ⁴I long to see you again, for I remember your tears as we parted. And I will be filled with joy when we are together again.

⁵I know that you sincerely trust the Lord, for you have the faith of your mother, Eunice, and your grandmother, Lois. ⁶This is why I remind you to fan into flames the spiritual gift God gave you when I laid my hands on you. ⁷For God has not given us a spirit of fear and timidity, but of power, love, and self-discipline. ⁸So you must never be ashamed to tell others about our Lord. And don't be ashamed of me, either, even though I'm in prison for Christ. With the strength God gives you, be ready to suffer with me for the proclamation of the Good News.

⁹It is God who saved us and chose us to live a holy life. He did this not because we deserved it, but because that was his plan long before the world began—to show his love and kindness to us through Christ Jesus. ¹⁰And now he has made all of this plain to us by the coming of Christ Jesus, our Savior, who broke the power of death and showed us the way to everlasting life through the Good

News. [11]And God chose me to be a preacher, an apostle, and a teacher of this Good News.

[12]And that is why I am suffering here in prison. But I am not ashamed of it, for I know the one in whom I trust, and I am sure that he is able to guard what I have entrusted to him* until the day of his return.

[13]Hold on to the pattern of right teaching you learned from me. And remember to live in the faith and love that you have in Christ Jesus. [14]With the help of the Holy Spirit who lives within us, carefully guard what has been entrusted to you.

[15]As you know, all the Christians who came here from the province of Asia have deserted me; even Phygelus and Hermogenes are gone. [16]May the Lord show special kindness to Onesiphorus and all his family because he often visited and encouraged me. He was never ashamed of me because I was in prison. [17]When he came to Rome, he searched everywhere until he found me. [18]May the Lord show him special kindness on the day of Christ's return. And you know how much he helped me at Ephesus.

CHAPTER 2

A Good Soldier of Christ Jesus

Timothy, my dear son, be strong with the special favor God gives you in Christ Jesus. [2]You have heard me teach many things that have been confirmed by many reliable witnesses. Teach these great truths to trustworthy people who are able to pass them on to others.

[3]Endure suffering along with me, as a good soldier of Christ Jesus. [4]And as Christ's soldier, do not let yourself become tied up in the affairs of this life, for then you cannot satisfy the one who has enlisted you in his army. [5]Follow the Lord's rules for doing his work, just as an athlete either follows the rules or is disqualified and wins no prize. [6]Hardworking farmers are the first to enjoy the fruit of their labor. [7]Think about what I am saying. The Lord will give you understanding in all these things.

[8]Never forget that Jesus Christ was a man born into King David's family and that he was raised from the dead. This is the Good News I preach. [9]And because I preach this Good News, I am suffering and have been chained like a criminal. But the word of God cannot be chained. [10]I am willing to endure anything if it will bring salvation and eternal glory in Christ Jesus to those God has chosen.

[11]This is a true saying:

If we die with him,
     we will also live with him.
[12] If we endure hardship,
     we will reign with him.
If we deny him,
     he will deny us.
[13] If we are unfaithful,
     he remains faithful,
     for he cannot deny himself.

An Approved Worker

[14]Remind everyone of these things, and command them in God's name to stop fighting over words. Such arguments are useless, and

1:12 Or *what has been entrusted to me.*

they can ruin those who hear them. 15Work hard so God can approve you. Be a good worker, one who does not need to be ashamed and who correctly explains the word of truth. 16Avoid godless, foolish discussions that lead to more and more ungodliness. 17This kind of talk spreads like cancer. Hymenaeus and Philetus are examples of this. 18They have left the path of truth, preaching the lie that the resurrection of the dead has already occurred; and they have undermined the faith of some.

19But God's truth stands firm like a foundation stone with this inscription: "The Lord knows those who are his,"* and "Those who claim they belong to the Lord must turn away from all wickedness."*

20In a wealthy home some utensils are made of gold and silver, and some are made of wood and clay. The expensive utensils are used for special occasions, and the cheap ones are for everyday use. 21If you keep yourself pure, you will be a utensil God can use for his purpose. Your life will be clean, and you will be ready for the Master to use you for every good work.

22Run from anything that stimulates youthful lust. Follow anything that makes you want to do right. Pursue faith and love and peace, and enjoy the companionship of those who call on the Lord with pure hearts.

23Again I say, don't get involved in foolish, ignorant arguments that only start fights. 24The Lord's servants must not quarrel but must be kind to everyone. They must be able to teach effectively and be patient with difficult people. 25They should gently teach those who oppose the truth. Perhaps God will change those people's hearts, and they will believe the truth. 26Then they will come to their senses and escape from the Devil's trap. For they have been held captive by him to do whatever he wants.

CHAPTER 3

The Dangers of the Last Days

You should also know this, Timothy, that in the last days there will be very difficult times. 2For people will love only themselves and their money. They will be boastful and proud, scoffing at God, disobedient to their parents, and ungrateful. They will consider nothing sacred. 3They will be unloving and unforgiving; they will slander others and have no self-control; they will be cruel and have no interest in what is good. 4They will betray their friends, be reckless, be puffed up with pride, and love pleasure rather than God. 5They will act as if they are religious, but they will reject the power that could make them godly. You must stay away from people like that.

6They are the kind who work their way into people's homes and win the confidence of* vulnerable women who are burdened with the guilt of sin and controlled by many desires. 7Such women are forever following new teachings, but they never understand the truth. 8And these teachers fight the truth just as Jannes and Jambres fought against Moses. Their minds are depraved, and their faith is counterfeit. 9But they won't get away with this for long. Someday

2:19a Num 16:5.   2:19b See Isa 52:11.   3:6 Greek *and take captive.*

everyone will recognize what fools they are, just as happened with Jannes and Jambres.

Paul's Charge to Timothy

[10]But you know what I teach, Timothy, and how I live, and what my purpose in life is. You know my faith and how long I have suffered. You know my love and my patient endurance. [11]You know how much persecution and suffering I have endured. You know all about how I was persecuted in Antioch, Iconium, and Lystra—but the Lord delivered me from all of it. [12]Yes, and everyone who wants to live a godly life in Christ Jesus will suffer persecution. [13]But evil people and impostors will flourish. They will go on deceiving others, and they themselves will be deceived.

[14]But you must remain faithful to the things you have been taught. You know they are true, for you know you can trust those who taught you. [15]You have been taught the holy Scriptures from childhood, and they have given you the wisdom to receive the salvation that comes by trusting in Christ Jesus. [16]All Scripture is inspired by God and is useful to teach us what is true and to make us realize what is wrong in our lives. It straightens us out and teaches us to do what is right. [17]It is God's way of preparing us in every way, fully equipped for every good thing God wants us to do.

CHAPTER 4

And so I solemnly urge you before God and before Christ Jesus— who will someday judge the living and the dead when he appears to set up his Kingdom: [2]Preach the word of God. Be persistent, whether the time is favorable or not. Patiently correct, rebuke, and encourage your people with good teaching.

[3]For a time is coming when people will no longer listen to right teaching. They will follow their own desires and will look for teachers who will tell them whatever they want to hear. [4]They will reject the truth and follow strange myths.

[5]But you should keep a clear mind in every situation. Don't be afraid of suffering for the Lord. Work at bringing others to Christ. Complete the ministry God has given you.

Paul's Final Words

[6]As for me, my life has already been poured out as an offering to God. The time of my death is near. [7]I have fought a good fight, I have finished the race, and I have remained faithful. [8]And now the prize awaits me—the crown of righteousness that the Lord, the righteous Judge, will give me on that great day of his return. And the prize is not just for me but for all who eagerly look forward to his glorious return.

[9]Please come as soon as you can. [10]Demas has deserted me because he loves the things of this life and has gone to Thessalonica. Crescens has gone to Galatia, and Titus has gone to Dalmatia. [11]Only Luke is with me. Bring Mark with you when you come, for he will be helpful to me. [12]I sent Tychicus to Ephesus. [13]When you come, be sure to bring the coat I left with Carpus at Troas. Also bring my books, and especially my papers.*

[14]Alexander the coppersmith has done me much harm, but the

4:13 Greek *especially the parchments.*

Lord will judge him for what he has done. ¹⁵Be careful of him, for he fought against everything we said.

¹⁶The first time I was brought before the judge, no one was with me. Everyone had abandoned me. I hope it will not be counted against them. ¹⁷But the Lord stood with me and gave me strength, that I might preach the Good News in all its fullness for all the Gentiles to hear. And he saved me from certain death.* ¹⁸Yes, and the Lord will deliver me from every evil attack and will bring me safely to his heavenly Kingdom. To God be the glory forever and ever. Amen.

Paul's Final Greetings

¹⁹Give my greetings to Priscilla and Aquila and those living at the household of Onesiphorus. ²⁰Erastus stayed at Corinth, and I left Trophimus sick at Miletus.

²¹Hurry so you can get here before winter. Eubulus sends you greetings, and so do Pudens, Linus, Claudia, and all the brothers and sisters.*

²²May the Lord be with your spirit. Grace be with you all.

4:17 Greek *from the mouth of a lion.*   4:21 Greek *brothers.*

TITUS

CHAPTER 1

Greetings from Paul

This letter is from Paul, a slave of God and an apostle of Jesus Christ. I have been sent to bring faith to those God has chosen and to teach them to know the truth that shows them how to live godly lives. ²This truth gives them the confidence of eternal life, which God promised them before the world began—and he cannot lie. ³And now at the right time he has revealed this Good News, and we announce it to everyone. It is by the command of God our Savior that I have been trusted to do this work for him.

⁴This letter is written to Titus, my true child in the faith that we share.

May God the Father and Christ Jesus our Savior give you grace and peace.

Titus's Work in Crete

⁵I left you on the island of Crete so you could complete our work there and appoint elders in each town as I instructed you. ⁶An elder must be well thought of for his good life. He must be faithful to his wife,* and his children must be believers who are not wild or rebellious. ⁷An elder* must live a blameless life because he is God's minister. He must not be arrogant or quick-tempered; he must not be a heavy drinker, violent, or greedy for money. ⁸He must enjoy having guests in his home and must love all that is good. He must

1:6 Or *have only one wife,* or *be married only once;* Greek reads *be the husband of one wife.*
1:7 Greek *overseer.*

live wisely and be fair. He must live a devout and disciplined life. ⁹He must have a strong and steadfast belief in the trustworthy message he was taught; then he will be able to encourage others with right teaching and show those who oppose it where they are wrong.

¹⁰For there are many who rebel against right teaching; they engage in useless talk and deceive people. This is especially true of those who insist on circumcision for salvation. ¹¹They must be silenced. By their wrong teaching, they have already turned whole families away from the truth. Such teachers only want your money. ¹²One of their own men, a prophet from Crete, has said about them, "The people of Crete are all liars; they are cruel animals and lazy gluttons." ¹³This is true. So rebuke them as sternly as necessary to make them strong in the faith. ¹⁴They must stop listening to Jewish myths and the commands of people who have turned their backs on the truth.

¹⁵Everything is pure to those whose hearts are pure. But nothing is pure to those who are corrupt and unbelieving, because their minds and consciences are defiled. ¹⁶Such people claim they know God, but they deny him by the way they live. They are despicable and disobedient, worthless for doing anything good.

CHAPTER 2

Promote Right Teaching

But as for you, promote the kind of living that reflects right teaching. ² Teach the older men to exercise self-control, to be worthy of respect, and to live wisely. They must have strong faith and be filled with love and patience.

³ Similarly, teach the older women to live in a way that is appropriate for someone serving the Lord. They must not go around speaking evil of others and must not be heavy drinkers. Instead, they should teach others what is good. ⁴ These older women must train the younger women to love their husbands and their children, ⁵ to live wisely and be pure, to take care of their homes, to do good, and to be submissive to their husbands. Then they will not bring shame on the word of God.

⁶In the same way, encourage the young men to live wisely in all they do. ⁷And you yourself must be an example to them by doing good deeds of every kind. Let everything you do reflect the integrity and seriousness of your teaching. ⁸Let your teaching be so correct that it can't be criticized. Then those who want to argue will be ashamed because they won't have anything bad to say about us.

⁹Slaves must obey their masters and do their best to please them. They must not talk back ¹⁰or steal, but they must show themselves to be entirely trustworthy and good. Then they will make the teaching about God our Savior attractive in every way.

¹¹For the grace of God has been revealed, bringing salvation to all people. ¹²And we are instructed to turn from godless living and sinful pleasures. We should live in this evil world with self-control, right conduct, and devotion to God, ¹³while we look forward to that wonderful event when the glory of our great God and Savior, Jesus Christ, will be revealed. ¹⁴He gave his life to free us from every kind of sin, to cleanse us, and to make us his very own people, totally committed to doing what is right. ¹⁵You must teach these things and encourage your people to do them, correcting them

when necessary. You have the authority to do this, so don't let anyone ignore you or disregard what you say.

CHAPTER 3

Do What Is Good

Remind your people to submit to the government and its officers. They should be obedient, always ready to do what is good. ²They must not speak evil of anyone, and they must avoid quarreling. Instead, they should be gentle and show true humility to everyone.

³Once we, too, were foolish and disobedient. We were misled by others and became slaves to many wicked desires and evil pleasures. Our lives were full of evil and envy. We hated others, and they hated us.

⁴But then God our Savior showed us his kindness and love. ⁵He saved us, not because of the good things we did, but because of his mercy. He washed away our sins and gave us a new life through the Holy Spirit.* ⁶He generously poured out the Spirit upon us because of what Jesus Christ our Savior did. ⁷He declared us not guilty because of his great kindness. And now we know that we will inherit eternal life. ⁸These things I have told you are all true. I want you to insist on them so that everyone who trusts in God will be careful to do good deeds all the time. These things are good and beneficial for everyone.

Paul's Final Remarks and Greetings

⁹Do not get involved in foolish discussions about spiritual pedigrees* or in quarrels and fights about obedience to Jewish laws. These kinds of things are useless and a waste of time. ¹⁰If anyone is causing divisions among you, give a first and second warning. After that, have nothing more to do with that person. ¹¹For people like that have turned away from the truth. They are sinning, and they condemn themselves.

¹²I am planning to send either Artemas or Tychicus to you. As soon as one of them arrives, do your best to meet me at Nicopolis as quickly as you can, for I have decided to stay there for the winter. ¹³Do everything you can to help Zenas the lawyer and Apollos with their trip. See that they are given everything they need. ¹⁴For our people should not have unproductive lives. They must learn to do good by helping others who have urgent needs.

¹⁵Everybody here sends greetings. Please give my greetings to all of the believers who love us.

May God's grace be with you all.

3:5 Greek *He saved us through the washing of regeneration and renewing of the Holy Spirit.*
3:9 Greek *discussions and genealogies.*

PHILEMON

Greetings from Paul

This letter is from Paul, in prison for preaching the Good News about Christ Jesus, and from our brother Timothy.

It is written to Philemon, our much loved co-worker, [2]and to our sister Apphia and to Archippus, a fellow soldier of the cross. I am also writing to the church that meets in your house.

[3]May God our Father and the Lord Jesus Christ give you grace and peace.

Paul's Thanksgiving and Prayer

[4]I always thank God when I pray for you, Philemon, [5]because I keep hearing of your trust in the Lord Jesus and your love for all of God's people. [6]You are generous because of your faith. And I am praying that you will really put your generosity to work, for in so doing you will come to an understanding of all the good things we can do for Christ. [7]I myself have gained much joy and comfort from your love, my brother, because your kindness has so often refreshed the hearts of God's people.

Paul's Appeal for Onesimus

[8]That is why I am boldly asking a favor of you. I could demand it in the name of Christ because it is the right thing for you to do, [9]but because of our love, I prefer just to ask you. So take this as a request from your friend Paul, an old man, now in prison for the sake of Christ Jesus.

[10]My plea is that you show kindness to Onesimus. I think of him as my own son because he became a believer as a result of my ministry here in prison. [11]Onesimus* hasn't been of much use to you in the past, but now he is very useful to both of us. [12]I am sending him back to you, and with him comes my own heart.

[13]I really wanted to keep him here with me while I am in these chains for preaching the Good News, and he would have helped me on your behalf. [14]But I didn't want to do anything without your consent. And I didn't want you to help because you were forced to do it but because you wanted to. [15]Perhaps you could think of it this way: Onesimus ran away for a little while so you could have him back forever. [16]He is no longer just a slave; he is a beloved brother, especially to me. Now he will mean much more to you, both as a slave and as a brother in the Lord.

[17]So if you consider me your partner, give him the same welcome you would give me if I were coming. [18]If he has harmed you in any way or stolen anything from you, charge me for it. [19]I, Paul, write this in my own handwriting: "I will repay it." And I won't mention that you owe me your very soul!

[20]Yes, dear brother, please do me this favor for the Lord's sake. Give me this encouragement in Christ. [21]I am confident as I write this letter that you will do what I ask and even more!

[22]Please keep a guest room ready for me, for I am hoping that God will answer your prayers and let me return to you soon.

Paul's Final Greetings

[23] Epaphras, my fellow prisoner in Christ Jesus, sends you his greetings. [24] So do Mark, Aristarchus, Demas, and Luke, my co-workers.

[25]The grace of the Lord Jesus Christ be with your spirit.

11 *Onesimus* means "useful."

HEBREWS

CHAPTER 1

Jesus Christ Is God's Son

Long ago God spoke many times and in many ways to our ancestors through the prophets. ²But now in these final days, he has
spoken to us through his Son. God promised everything to the Son
as an inheritance, and through the Son he made the universe and
everything in it. ³The Son reflects God's own glory, and everything
about him represents God exactly. He sustains the universe by the
mighty power of his command. After he died to cleanse us from
the stain of sin, he sat down in the place of honor at the right hand
of the majestic God of heaven.

Christ Is Greater Than the Angels

⁴This shows that God's Son is far greater than the angels, just as the
name God gave him is far greater than their names. ⁵For God never
said to any angel what he said to Jesus:

> "You are my Son.
>   Today I have become your Father.*"

And again God said,

> "I will be his Father,
>   and he will be my Son."*

⁶And then, when he presented his honored* Son to the world, God
said, "Let all the angels of God worship him."* ⁷God calls his
angels

> "messengers swift as the wind,
>   and servants made of flaming fire."*

⁸But to his Son he says,

> "Your throne, O God, endures forever and ever.
>   Your royal power is expressed in righteousness.
> ⁹ You love what is right and hate what is wrong.
>   Therefore God, your God, has anointed you,
>   pouring out the oil of joy on you more than on anyone else."*

¹⁰And,

> "Lord, in the beginning you laid the foundation of the earth,
>   and the heavens are the work of your hands.
> ¹¹ Even they will perish, but you remain forever.
>   They will wear out like old clothing.
> ¹² You will roll them up like an old coat.
>   They will fade away like old clothing.

1:5a Or *Today I reveal you as my Son.* Ps 2:7.   1:5b 2 Sam 7:14.   1:6a Greek *firstborn.*
1:6b Deut 32:43.   1:7 Ps 104:4.   1:8-9 Ps 45:6-7.

But you are always the same;
  you will never grow old."*

13And God never said to an angel, as he did to his Son,

"Sit in honor at my right hand
  until I humble your enemies,
  making them a footstool under your feet."*

14But angels are only servants. They are spirits sent from God to care for those who will receive salvation.

CHAPTER 2

A Warning against Drifting Away

So we must listen very carefully to the truth we have heard, or we may drift away from it. 2The message God delivered through angels has always proved true, and the people were punished for every violation of the law and every act of disobedience. 3What makes us think that we can escape if we are indifferent to this great salvation that was announced by the Lord Jesus himself? It was passed on* to us by those who heard him speak, 4and God verified the message by signs and wonders and various miracles and by giving gifts of the Holy Spirit whenever he chose to do so.

Jesus, the Man

5And furthermore, the future world we are talking about will not be controlled by angels. 6For somewhere in the Scriptures it says,

"What is man that you should think of him,
  and the son of man* that you should care for him?
7 For a little while you made him lower than the angels,
  and you crowned him with glory and honor.*
8 You gave him authority over all things."*

Now when it says "all things," it means nothing is left out. But we have not yet seen all of this happen. 9What we do see is Jesus, who "for a little while was made lower than the angels" and now is "crowned with glory and honor" because he suffered death for us. Yes, by God's grace, Jesus tasted death for everyone in all the world. 10And it was only right that God—who made everything and for whom everything was made—should bring his many children into glory. Through the suffering of Jesus, God made him a perfect leader, one fit to bring them into their salvation.

11So now Jesus and the ones he makes holy have the same Father. That is why Jesus is not ashamed to call them his brothers and sisters.* 12For he said to God,

"I will declare the wonder of your name to my brothers and
  sisters.*
  I will praise you among all your people."

13 He also said, "I will put my trust in him." And in the same context he said, "Here I am—together with the children God has given me."*

1:10-12 Ps 102:25-27. 1:13 Ps 110:1. 2:3 Or *and confirmed.* 2:6 Or *Son of Man.* 2:7 Some manuscripts add *You put him in charge of everything you made.* 2:6-8 Ps 8:4-6. 2:11 Greek *his brothers;* also in 2:17. 2:12 Greek *my brothers.* Ps 22:22. 2:13 Isa 8:17-18.

14Because God's children are human beings—made of flesh and blood—Jesus also became flesh and blood by being born in human form. For only as a human being could he die, and only by dying could he break the power of the Devil, who had the power of death. 15Only in this way could he deliver those who have lived all their lives as slaves to the fear of dying.

16 We all know that Jesus came to help the descendants of Abraham, not to help the angels. 17Therefore, it was necessary for Jesus to be in every respect like us, his brothers and sisters, so that he could be our merciful and faithful High Priest before God. He then could offer a sacrifice that would take away the sins of the people. 18Since he himself has gone through suffering and temptation, he is able to help us when we are being tempted.

CHAPTER 3

Jesus Is Greater Than Moses

And so, dear brothers and sisters who belong to God* and are bound for heaven, think about this Jesus whom we declare to be God's Messenger and High Priest. 2For he was faithful to God, who appointed him, just as Moses served faithfully and was entrusted with God's entire house. 3But Jesus deserves far more glory than Moses, just as a person who builds a fine house deserves more praise than the house itself. 4For every house has a builder, but God is the one who made everything.

5Moses was certainly faithful in God's house, but only as a servant. His work was an illustration of the truths God would reveal later. 6But Christ, the faithful Son, was in charge of the entire household. And we are God's household, if we keep up our courage and remain confident in our hope in Christ. 7That is why the Holy Spirit says,

"Today you must listen to his voice.
8 Don't harden your hearts against him
    as Israel did when they rebelled,
    when they tested God's patience in the wilderness.
9 There your ancestors tried my patience,
    even though they saw my miracles for forty years.
10 So I was angry with them, and I said,
    'Their hearts always turn away from me.
    They refuse to do what I tell them.'
11 So in my anger I made a vow:
    'They will never enter my place of rest.'"*

12Be careful then, dear brothers and sisters.* Make sure that your own hearts are not evil and unbelieving, turning you away from the living God. 13You must warn each other every day, as long as it is called "today," so that none of you will be deceived by sin and hardened against God. 14For if we are faithful to the end, trusting God just as firmly as when we first believed, we will share in all that belongs to Christ. 15But never forget the warning:

"Today you must listen to his voice.
    Don't harden your hearts against him
    as Israel did when they rebelled."*

3:1 Greek *And so, holy brothers.*   **3:7-11** Ps 95:7-11.   **3:12** Greek *brothers.*   **3:15** Ps 95:7-8.

¹⁶And who were those people who rebelled against God, even though they heard his voice? Weren't they the ones Moses led out of Egypt? ¹⁷And who made God angry for forty years? Wasn't it the people who sinned, whose bodies fell in the wilderness? ¹⁸And to whom was God speaking when he vowed that they would never enter his place of rest? He was speaking to those who disobeyed him. ¹⁹So we see that they were not allowed to enter his rest because of their unbelief.

CHAPTER 4

Promised Rest for God's People

God's promise of entering his place of rest still stands, so we ought to tremble with fear that some of you might fail to get there. ²For this Good News—that God has prepared a place of rest—has been announced to us just as it was to them. But it did them no good because they didn't believe what God told them.* ³For only we who believe can enter his place of rest. As for those who didn't believe, God said,

"In my anger I made a vow:
  'They will never enter my place of rest,' "*

even though his place of rest has been ready since he made the world. ⁴We know it is ready because the Scriptures mention the seventh day, saying, "On the seventh day God rested from all his work."* ⁵But in the other passage God said, "They will never enter my place of rest."* ⁶So God's rest is there for people to enter. But those who formerly heard the Good News failed to enter because they disobeyed God. ⁷So God set another time for entering his place of rest, and that time is today. God announced this through David a long time later in the words already quoted:

"Today you must listen to his voice.
  Don't harden your hearts against him."*

⁸This new place of rest was not the land of Canaan, where Joshua led them. If it had been, God would not have spoken later about another day of rest. ⁹So there is a special rest* still waiting for the people of God. ¹⁰For all who enter into God's rest will find rest from their labors, just as God rested after creating the world. ¹¹Let us do our best to enter that place of rest. For anyone who disobeys God, as the people of Israel did, will fall.

¹²For the word of God is full of living power. It is sharper than the sharpest knife, cutting deep into our innermost thoughts and desires. It exposes us for what we really are. ¹³Nothing in all creation can hide from him. Everything is naked and exposed before his eyes. This is the God to whom we must explain all that we have done.

Christ Is Our High Priest

¹⁴That is why we have a great High Priest who has gone to heaven, Jesus the Son of God. Let us cling to him and never stop trusting him. ¹⁵This High Priest of ours understands our weaknesses, for he faced all of the same temptations we do, yet he did not sin. ¹⁶So let

4:2 Some manuscripts read *they didn't share the faith of those who listened [to God].*
4:3 Ps 95:11. 4:4 Gen 2:2. 4:5 Ps 95:11. 4:7 Ps 95:7-8. 4:9 Or *Sabbath rest.*

us come boldly to the throne of our gracious God. There we will receive his mercy, and we will find grace to help us when we need it.

CHAPTER 5

Now a high priest is a man chosen to represent other human beings in their dealings with God. He presents their gifts to God and offers their sacrifices for sins. ²And because he is human, he is able to deal gently with the people, though they are ignorant and wayward. For he is subject to the same weaknesses they have. ³That is why he has to offer sacrifices, both for their sins and for his own sins. ⁴And no one can become a high priest simply because he wants such an honor. He has to be called by God for this work, just as Aaron was.

⁵That is why Christ did not exalt himself to become High Priest. No, he was chosen by God, who said to him,

"You are my Son.
Today I have become your Father.*"

⁶And in another passage God said to him,

"You are a priest forever
in the line of Melchizedek."*

⁷While Jesus was here on earth, he offered prayers and pleadings, with a loud cry and tears, to the one who could deliver him out of death. And God heard his prayers because of his reverence for God. ⁸So even though Jesus was God's Son, he learned obedience from the things he suffered. ⁹In this way, God qualified him as a perfect High Priest, and he became the source of eternal salvation for all those who obey him. ¹⁰And God designated him to be a High Priest in the line of Melchizedek.

A Call to Spiritual Growth

¹¹There is so much more we would like to say about this. But you don't seem to listen, so it's hard to make you understand. ¹²You have been Christians a long time now, and you ought to be teaching others. Instead, you need someone to teach you again the basic things a beginner must learn about the Scriptures.* You are like babies who drink only milk and cannot eat solid food. ¹³And a person who is living on milk isn't very far along in the Christian life and doesn't know much about doing what is right. ¹⁴Solid food is for those who are mature, who have trained themselves to recognize the difference between right and wrong and then do what is right.

CHAPTER 6

So let us stop going over the basics of Christianity* again and again. Let us go on instead and become mature in our understanding. Surely we don't need to start all over again with the importance of turning away from evil deeds and placing our faith in God. ²You don't need further instruction about baptisms, the laying on of hands, the resurrection of the dead, and eternal judgment. ³And so, God willing, we will move forward to further understanding.

5:5 Or *Today I reveal you as my Son.* Ps 2:7. **5:6** Ps 110:4. **5:12** Or *about the oracles of God.* **6:1** Or *the basics about Christ.*

4For it is impossible to restore to repentance those who were once enlightened—those who have experienced the good things of heaven and shared in the Holy Spirit, 5who have tasted the goodness of the word of God and the power of the age to come—6and who then turn away from God. It is impossible to bring such people to repentance again because they are nailing the Son of God to the cross again by rejecting him, holding him up to public shame.

7When the ground soaks up the rain that falls on it and bears a good crop for the farmer, it has the blessing of God. 8But if a field bears thistles and thorns, it is useless. The farmer will condemn that field and burn it.

9 Dear friends, even though we are talking like this, we really don't believe that it applies to you. We are confident that you are meant for better things, things that come with salvation. 10For God is not unfair. He will not forget how hard you have worked for him and how you have shown your love to him by caring for other Christians, as you still do. 11Our great desire is that you will keep right on loving others as long as life lasts, in order to make certain that what you hope for will come true. 12Then you will not become spiritually dull and indifferent. Instead, you will follow the example of those who are going to inherit God's promises because of their faith and patience.

God's Promises Bring Hope

13For example, there was God's promise to Abraham. Since there was no one greater to swear by, God took an oath in his own name, saying:

14 "I will certainly bless you richly,
   and I will multiply your descendants into countless
      millions."*

15Then Abraham waited patiently, and he received what God had promised.

16When people take an oath, they call on someone greater than themselves to hold them to it. And without any question that oath is binding. 17God also bound himself with an oath, so that those who received the promise could be perfectly sure that he would never change his mind. 18So God has given us both his promise and his oath. These two things are unchangeable because it is impossible for God to lie. Therefore, we who have fled to him for refuge can take new courage, for we can hold on to his promise with confidence.

19This confidence is like a strong and trustworthy anchor for our souls. It leads us through the curtain of heaven into God's inner sanctuary. 20Jesus has already gone in there for us. He has become our eternal High Priest in the line of Melchizedek.

CHAPTER 7

Melchizedek Is Compared to Abraham

This Melchizedek was king of the city of Salem and also a priest of God Most High. When Abraham was returning home after winning a great battle against many kings, Melchizedek met him and blessed him. 2Then Abraham took a tenth of all he had won in the

6:14 Gen 22:17.

battle and gave it to Melchizedek. His name means "king of justice." He is also "king of peace" because *Salem* means "peace." [3]There is no record of his father or mother or any of his ancestors— no beginning or end to his life. He remains a priest forever, resembling the Son of God.

[4]Consider then how great this Melchizedek was. Even Abraham, the great patriarch of Israel, recognized how great Melchizedek was by giving him a tenth of what he had taken in battle. [5]Now the priests, who are descendants of Levi, are commanded in the law of Moses to collect a tithe from all the people, even though they are their own relatives.* [6]But Melchizedek, who was not even related to Levi, collected a tenth from Abraham. And Melchizedek placed a blessing upon Abraham, the one who had already received the promises of God. [7]And without question, the person who has the power to bless is always greater than the person who is blessed.

[8]In the case of Jewish priests, tithes are paid to men who will die. But Melchizedek is greater than they are, because we are told that he lives on. [9]In addition, we might even say that Levi's descendants, the ones who collect the tithe, paid a tithe to Melchizedek through their ancestor Abraham. [10]For although Levi wasn't born yet, the seed from which he came was in Abraham's loins when Melchizedek collected the tithe from him.

[11]And finally, if the priesthood of Levi could have achieved God's purposes—and it was that priesthood on which the law was based—why did God need to send a different priest from the line of Melchizedek, instead of from the line of Levi and Aaron?*

[12]And when the priesthood is changed, the law must also be changed to permit it. [13]For the one we are talking about belongs to a different tribe, whose members do not serve at the altar. [14]What I mean is, our Lord came from the tribe of Judah, and Moses never mentioned Judah in connection with the priesthood.

Christ Is like Melchizedek

[15]The change in God's law is even more evident from the fact that a different priest, who is like Melchizedek, has now come. [16]He became a priest, not by meeting the old requirement of belonging to the tribe of Levi, but by the power of a life that cannot be destroyed. [17]And the psalmist pointed this out when he said of Christ,

> "You are a priest forever
> in the line of Melchizedek."*

[18]Yes, the old requirement about the priesthood was set aside because it was weak and useless. [19]For the law made nothing perfect, and now a better hope has taken its place. And that is how we draw near to God.

[20]God took an oath that Christ would always be a priest, but he never did this for any other priest. [21]Only to Jesus did he say,

> "The Lord has taken an oath
> and will not break his vow:
> 'You are a priest forever.'"*

7:5 Greek *their brothers, who are descendants of Abraham.*   7:11 Greek *according to the order of Aaron.*   7:17 Ps 110:4.   7:21 Ps 110:4.

22Because of God's oath, it is Jesus who guarantees the effectiveness of this better covenant.

23Another difference is that there were many priests under the old system. When one priest died, another had to take his place. 24But Jesus remains a priest forever; his priesthood will never end. 25Therefore he is able, once and forever, to save* everyone who comes to God through him. He lives forever to plead with God on their behalf.

26He is the kind of high priest we need because he is holy and blameless, unstained by sin. He has now been set apart from sinners, and he has been given the highest place of honor in heaven. 27He does not need to offer sacrifices every day like the other high priests. They did this for their own sins first and then for the sins of the people. But Jesus did this once for all when he sacrificed himself on the cross. 28Those who were high priests under the law of Moses were limited by human weakness. But after the law was given, God appointed his Son with an oath, and his Son has been made perfect forever.

CHAPTER 8

Christ Is Our High Priest

Here is the main point: Our High Priest sat down in the place of highest honor in heaven, at God's right hand. 2There he ministers in the sacred tent, the true place of worship that was built by the Lord and not by human hands.

3And since every high priest is required to offer gifts and sacrifices, our High Priest must make an offering, too. 4If he were here on earth, he would not even be a priest, since there already are priests who offer the gifts required by the law of Moses. 5They serve in a place of worship that is only a copy, a shadow of the real one in heaven. For when Moses was getting ready to build the Tabernacle, God gave him this warning: "Be sure that you make everything according to the design I have shown you here on the mountain."* 6But our High Priest has been given a ministry that is far superior to the ministry of those who serve under the old laws, for he is the one who guarantees for us a better covenant with God, based on better promises.

7If the first covenant had been faultless, there would have been no need for a second covenant to replace it. 8But God himself found fault with the old one when he said:

"The day will come, says the Lord,
  when I will make a new covenant
  with the people of Israel and Judah.
9 This covenant will not be like the one
    I made with their ancestors
  when I took them by the hand
    and led them out of the land of Egypt.
They did not remain faithful to my covenant,
  so I turned my back on them, says the Lord.
10 But this is the new covenant I will make
    with the people of Israel on that day, says the Lord:
  I will put my laws in their minds
    so they will understand them,

7:25 Or *able to save completely.*   8:5 Exod 25:40; 26:30.

and I will write them on their hearts
  so they will obey them.
I will be their God,
  and they will be my people.
¹¹ And they will not need to teach their neighbors,
  nor will they need to teach their family,
  saying, 'You should know the Lord.'
For everyone, from the least to the greatest,
  will already know me.
¹² And I will forgive their wrongdoings,
  and I will never again remember their sins."*

¹³When God speaks of a new covenant, it means he has made the first one obsolete. It is now out of date and ready to be put aside.

CHAPTER 9
Old Rules about Worship
Now in that first covenant between God and Israel, there were regulations for worship and a sacred tent here on earth. ²There were two rooms in this tent. In the first room were a lampstand, a table, and loaves of holy bread on the table. This was called the Holy Place. ³Then there was a curtain, and behind the curtain was the second room called the Most Holy Place. ⁴In that room were a gold incense altar and a wooden chest called the Ark of the Covenant, which was covered with gold on all sides. Inside the Ark were a gold jar containing some manna, Aaron's staff that sprouted leaves, and the stone tablets of the covenant with the Ten Commandments written on them. ⁵The glorious cherubim were above the Ark. Their wings were stretched out over the Ark's cover, the place of atonement. But we cannot explain all of these things now.

⁶When these things were all in place, the priests went in and out of the first room* regularly as they performed their religious duties. ⁷But only the high priest goes into the Most Holy Place, and only once a year, and always with blood, which he offers to God to cover his own sins and the sins the people have committed in ignorance. ⁸By these regulations the Holy Spirit revealed that the Most Holy Place was not open to the people as long as the first room and the entire system it represents were still in use.

⁹This is an illustration pointing to the present time. For the gifts and sacrifices that the priests offer are not able to cleanse the consciences of the people who bring them. ¹⁰For that old system deals only with food and drink and ritual washing—external regulations that are in effect only until their limitations can be corrected.

Christ Is the Perfect Sacrifice
¹¹ So Christ has now become the High Priest over all the good things that have come. He has entered that great, perfect sanctuary in heaven, not made by human hands and not part of this created world. ¹²Once for all time he took blood into that Most Holy Place, but not the blood of goats and calves. He took his own blood, and with it he secured our salvation forever.

¹³Under the old system, the blood of goats and bulls and the

8:8-12 Jer 31:31-34.   9:6 Greek *first tent; also in 9:8.*

ashes of a young cow could cleanse people's bodies from ritual defilement. 14Just think how much more the blood of Christ will purify our hearts from deeds that lead to death so that we can worship the living God. For by the power of the eternal Spirit, Christ offered himself to God as a perfect sacrifice for our sins. 15That is why he is the one who mediates the new covenant between God and people, so that all who are invited can receive the eternal inheritance God has promised them. For Christ died to set them free from the penalty of the sins they had committed under that first covenant.

16 Now when someone dies and leaves a will, no one gets anything until it is proved that the person who wrote the will* is dead.* 17The will goes into effect only after the death of the person who wrote it. While the person is still alive, no one can use the will to get any of the things promised to them.

18That is why blood was required under the first covenant as a proof of death. 19For after Moses had given the people all of God's laws, he took the blood of calves and goats, along with water, and sprinkled both the book of God's laws and all the people, using branches of hyssop bushes and scarlet wool. 20Then he said, "This blood confirms the covenant God has made with you."* 21And in the same way, he sprinkled blood on the sacred tent and on everything used for worship. 22In fact, we can say that according to the law of Moses, nearly everything was purified by sprinkling with blood. Without the shedding of blood, there is no forgiveness of sins.

23That is why the earthly tent and everything in it—which were copies of things in heaven—had to be purified by the blood of animals. But the real things in heaven had to be purified with far better sacrifices than the blood of animals.

24For Christ has entered into heaven itself to appear now before God as our Advocate.* He did not go into the earthly place of worship, for that was merely a copy of the real Temple in heaven. 25Nor did he enter heaven to offer himself again and again, like the earthly high priest who enters the Most Holy Place year after year to offer the blood of an animal. 26If that had been necessary, he would have had to die again and again, ever since the world began. But no! He came once for all time, at the end of the age, to remove the power of sin forever by his sacrificial death for us.

27And just as it is destined that each person dies only once and after that comes judgment, 28so also Christ died only once as a sacrifice to take away the sins of many people. He will come again but not to deal with our sins again. This time he will bring salvation to all those who are eagerly waiting for him.

CHAPTER 10
Christ's Sacrifice Once for All
The old system in the law of Moses was only a shadow of the things to come, not the reality of the good things Christ has done for us. The sacrifices under the old system were repeated again and again, year after year, but they were never able to provide perfect cleansing for those who came to worship. 2If they could

9:16a Or covenant. 9:16b Or Now when someone makes a covenant, it is necessary to ratify it with the death of a sacrifice. 9:20 Exod 24:8. 9:24 Greek on our behalf.

have provided perfect cleansing, the sacrifices would have stopped, for the worshipers would have been purified once for all time, and their feelings of guilt would have disappeared.

³ But just the opposite happened. Those yearly sacrifices reminded them of their sins year after year. ⁴For it is not possible for the blood of bulls and goats to take away sins. ⁵That is why Christ, when he came into the world, said,

"You did not want animal sacrifices and grain offerings.
But you have given me a body so that I may obey you.
⁶ No, you were not pleased with animals burned on the altar
or with other offerings for sin.
⁷ Then I said, 'Look, I have come to do your will, O God—
just as it is written about me in the Scriptures.' "*

⁸Christ said, "You did not want animal sacrifices or grain offerings or animals burned on the altar or other offerings for sin, nor were you pleased with them" (though they are required by the law of Moses). ⁹Then he added, "Look, I have come to do your will." He cancels the first covenant in order to establish the second. ¹⁰And what God wants is for us to be made holy by the sacrifice of the body of Jesus Christ once for all time.

¹¹Under the old covenant, the priest stands before the altar day after day, offering sacrifices that can never take away sins. ¹²But our High Priest offered himself to God as one sacrifice for sins, good for all time. Then he sat down at the place of highest honor at God's right hand. ¹³There he waits until his enemies are humbled as a footstool under his feet. ¹⁴For by that one offering he perfected forever all those whom he is making holy.

¹⁵And the Holy Spirit also testifies that this is so. First he says,

¹⁶ "This is the new covenant I will make
with my people on that day, says the Lord:
I will put my laws in their hearts
so they will understand them,
and I will write them on their minds
so they will obey them."

¹⁷Then he adds,

"I will never again remember
their sins and lawless deeds."*

¹⁸Now when sins have been forgiven, there is no need to offer any more sacrifices.

A Call to Persevere

¹⁹And so, dear brothers and sisters,* we can boldly enter heaven's Most Holy Place because of the blood of Jesus. ²⁰This is the new, life-giving way that Christ has opened up for us through the sacred curtain, by means of his death for us.*

²¹And since we have a great High Priest who rules over God's people, ²²let us go right into the presence of God, with true hearts fully trusting him. For our evil consciences have been sprinkled

10:5-7 Ps 40:6-8.   10:16-17 Jer 31:33-34.   10:19 Greek *brothers.*   10:20 Greek *his flesh.*

with Christ's blood to make us clean, and our bodies have been washed with pure water.

²³Without wavering, let us hold tightly to the hope we say we have, for God can be trusted to keep his promise. ²⁴Think of ways to encourage one another to outbursts of love and good deeds. ²⁵And let us not neglect our meeting together, as some people do, but encourage and warn each other, especially now that the day of his coming back again is drawing near.

²⁶Dear friends, if we deliberately continue sinning after we have received a full knowledge of the truth, there is no other sacrifice that will cover these sins. ²⁷There will be nothing to look forward to but the terrible expectation of God's judgment and the raging fire that will consume his enemies. ²⁸Anyone who refused to obey the law of Moses was put to death without mercy on the testimony of two or three witnesses. ²⁹Think how much more terrible the punishment will be for those who have trampled on the Son of God and have treated the blood of the covenant as if it were common and unholy. Such people have insulted and enraged the Holy Spirit who brings God's mercy to his people.

³⁰For we know the one who said,

"I will take vengeance.
 I will repay those who deserve it."

He also said,

"The Lord will judge his own people."*

³¹It is a terrible thing to fall into the hands of the living God.

³²Don't ever forget those early days when you first learned about Christ. Remember how you remained faithful even though it meant terrible suffering. ³³Sometimes you were exposed to public ridicule and were beaten, and sometimes you helped others who were suffering the same things. ³⁴You suffered along with those who were thrown into jail. When all you owned was taken from you, you accepted it with joy. You knew you had better things waiting for you in eternity.

³⁵Do not throw away this confident trust in the Lord, no matter what happens. Remember the great reward it brings you! ³⁶Patient endurance is what you need now, so you will continue to do God's will. Then you will receive all that he has promised.

³⁷ "For in just a little while,
  the Coming One will come and not delay.
³⁸ And a righteous person will live by faith.
  But I will have no pleasure in anyone who turns away."*

³⁹But we are not like those who turn their backs on God and seal their fate. We have faith that assures our salvation.

CHAPTER 11
Great Examples of Faith

What is faith? It is the confident assurance that what we hope for is going to happen. It is the evidence of things we cannot yet see. ²God gave his approval to people in days of old because of their faith.

10:30 Deut 32:35-36. **10:37-38** Hab 2:3-4.

³By faith we understand that the entire universe was formed at God's command, that what we now see did not come from anything that can be seen.

⁴It was by faith that Abel brought a more acceptable offering to God than Cain did. God accepted Abel's offering to show that he was a righteous man. And although Abel is long dead, he still speaks to us because of his faith.

⁵It was by faith that Enoch was taken up to heaven without dying—"suddenly he disappeared because God took him."* But before he was taken up, he was approved as pleasing to God. ⁶So, you see, it is impossible to please God without faith. Anyone who wants to come to him must believe that there is a God and that he rewards those who sincerely seek him.

⁷It was by faith that Noah built an ark to save his family from the flood. He obeyed God, who warned him about something that had never happened before. By his faith he condemned the rest of the world and was made right in God's sight.

⁸It was by faith that Abraham obeyed when God called him to leave home and go to another land that God would give him as his inheritance. He went without knowing where he was going. ⁹And even when he reached the land God promised him, he lived there by faith—for he was like a foreigner, living in a tent. And so did Isaac and Jacob, to whom God gave the same promise. ¹⁰Abraham did this because he was confidently looking forward to a city with eternal foundations, a city designed and built by God.

¹¹It was by faith that Sarah together with Abraham was able to have a child, even though they were too old and Sarah was barren. Abraham believed that God would keep his promise.* ¹²And so a whole nation came from this one man, Abraham, who was too old to have any children—a nation with so many people that, like the stars of the sky and the sand on the seashore, there is no way to count them.

¹³All these faithful ones died without receiving what God had promised them, but they saw it all from a distance and welcomed the promises of God. They agreed that they were no more than foreigners and nomads here on earth. ¹⁴And obviously people who talk like that are looking forward to a country they can call their own. ¹⁵If they had meant the country they came from, they would have found a way to go back. ¹⁶But they were looking for a better place, a heavenly homeland. That is why God is not ashamed to be called their God, for he has prepared a heavenly city for them.

¹⁷It was by faith that Abraham offered Isaac as a sacrifice when God was testing him. Abraham, who had received God's promises, was ready to sacrifice his only son, Isaac, ¹⁸ though God had promised him, "Isaac is the son through whom your descendants will be counted."* Abraham assumed that if Isaac died, God was able to bring him back to life again. And in a sense, Abraham did receive his son back from the dead.

²⁰It was by faith that Isaac blessed his two sons, Jacob and Esau. He had confidence in what God was going to do in the future.

11:5 Gen 5:24.   **11:11** Some manuscripts read *It was by faith that Sarah was able to have a child, even though she was too old and barren. Sarah believed that God would keep his promise.* **11:18** Gen 21:12.

²¹It was by faith that Jacob, when he was old and dying, blessed each of Joseph's sons and bowed in worship as he leaned on his staff.

²²And it was by faith that Joseph, when he was about to die, confidently spoke of God's bringing the people of Israel out of Egypt. He was so sure of it that he commanded them to carry his bones with them when they left!

²³It was by faith that Moses' parents hid him for three months. They saw that God had given them an unusual child, and they were not afraid of what the king might do.

²⁴It was by faith that Moses, when he grew up, refused to be treated as the son of Pharaoh's daughter. ²⁵He chose to share the oppression of God's people instead of enjoying the fleeting pleasures of sin. ²⁶He thought it was better to suffer for the sake of the Messiah than to own the treasures of Egypt, for he was looking ahead to the great reward that God would give him. ²⁷It was by faith that Moses left the land of Egypt. He was not afraid of the king. Moses kept right on going because he kept his eyes on the one who is invisible. ²⁸It was by faith that Moses commanded the people of Israel to keep the Passover and to sprinkle blood on the doorposts so that the angel of death would not kill their firstborn sons.

²⁹It was by faith that the people of Israel went right through the Red Sea as though they were on dry ground. But when the Egyptians followed, they were all drowned.

³⁰It was by faith that the people of Israel marched around Jericho seven days, and the walls came crashing down.

³¹It was by faith that Rahab the prostitute did not die with all the others in her city who refused to obey God. For she had given a friendly welcome to the spies.

³²Well, how much more do I need to say? It would take too long to recount the stories of the faith of Gideon, Barak, Samson, Jephthah, David, Samuel, and all the prophets. ³³By faith these people overthrew kingdoms, ruled with justice, and received what God had promised them. They shut the mouths of lions, ³⁴quenched the flames of fire, and escaped death by the edge of the sword. Their weakness was turned to strength. They became strong in battle and put whole armies to flight. ³⁵Women received their loved ones back again from death.

But others trusted God and were tortured, preferring to die rather than turn from God and be free. They placed their hope in the resurrection to a better life. ³⁶Some were mocked, and their backs were cut open with whips. Others were chained in dungeons. ³⁷Some died by stoning, and some were sawed in half; others were killed with the sword. Some went about in skins of sheep and goats, hungry and oppressed and mistreated. ³⁸They were too good for this world. They wandered over deserts and mountains, hiding in caves and holes in the ground.

³⁹All of these people we have mentioned received God's approval because of their faith, yet none of them received all that God had promised. ⁴⁰For God had far better things in mind for us that would also benefit them, for they can't receive the prize at the end of the race until we finish the race.*

11:40 Greek *for us, for they apart from us can't finish.*

CHAPTER 12

God's Discipline Proves His Love

Therefore, since we are surrounded by such a huge crowd of witnesses to the life of faith, let us strip off every weight that slows us down, especially the sin that so easily hinders our progress. And let us run with endurance the race that God has set before us. ²We do this by keeping our eyes on Jesus, on whom our faith depends from start to finish.* He was willing to die a shameful death on the cross because of the joy he knew would be his afterward. Now he is seated in the place of highest honor beside God's throne in heaven. ³Think about all he endured when sinful people did such terrible things to him, so that you don't become weary and give up. ⁴After all, you have not yet given your lives in your struggle against sin.

⁵And have you entirely forgotten the encouraging words God spoke to you, his children? He said,

"My child, don't ignore it when the Lord disciplines you,
  and don't be discouraged when he corrects you.
⁶ For the Lord disciplines those he loves,
  and he punishes those he accepts as his children."*

⁷ As you endure this divine discipline, remember that God is treating you as his own children. Whoever heard of a child who was never disciplined? ⁸If God doesn't discipline you as he does all of his children, it means that you are illegitimate and are not really his children after all. ⁹ Since we respect our earthly fathers who disciplined us, should we not all the more cheerfully submit to the discipline of our heavenly Father and live forever*?

¹⁰For our earthly fathers disciplined us for a few years, doing the best they knew how. But God's discipline is always right and good for us because it means we will share in his holiness. ¹¹No discipline is enjoyable while it is happening—it is painful! But afterward there will be a quiet harvest of right living for those who are trained in this way.

¹²So take a new grip with your tired hands and stand firm on your shaky legs. ¹³Mark out a straight path for your feet. Then those who follow you, though they are weak and lame, will not stumble and fall but will become strong.

A Call to Listen to God

¹⁴Try to live in peace with everyone, and seek to live a clean and holy life, for those who are not holy will not see the Lord. ¹⁵Look after each other so that none of you will miss out on the special favor of God. Watch out that no bitter root of unbelief rises up among you, for whenever it springs up, many are corrupted by its poison. ¹⁶Make sure that no one is immoral or godless like Esau. He traded his birthright as the oldest son for a single meal. ¹⁷And afterward, when he wanted his father's blessing, he was rejected. It was too late for repentance, even though he wept bitter tears.

¹⁸ You have not come to a physical mountain, to a place of flaming fire, darkness, gloom, and whirlwind, as the Israelites did at Mount Sinai when God gave them his laws. ¹⁹For they heard an awesome trumpet blast and a voice with a message so terrible that

12:2 Or *Jesus, the Originator and Perfecter of our faith.*   12:5-6 Prov 3:11-12.   12:9 Or *really live.*

they begged God to stop speaking. [20]They staggered back under God's command: "If even an animal touches the mountain, it must be stoned to death."* [21]Moses himself was so frightened at the sight that he said, "I am terrified and trembling."*

[22]No, you have come to Mount Zion, to the city of the living God, the heavenly Jerusalem, and to thousands of angels in joyful assembly. [23]You have come to the assembly of God's firstborn children, whose names are written in heaven. You have come to God himself, who is the judge of all people. And you have come to the spirits of the redeemed in heaven who have now been made perfect. [24]You have come to Jesus, the one who mediates the new covenant between God and people, and to the sprinkled blood, which graciously forgives instead of crying out for vengeance as the blood of Abel did.

[25]See to it that you obey God, the one who is speaking to you. For if the people of Israel did not escape when they refused to listen to Moses, the earthly messenger, how terrible our danger if we reject the One who speaks to us from heaven! [26]When God spoke from Mount Sinai his voice shook the earth, but now he makes another promise: "Once again I will shake not only the earth but the heavens also."* [27]This means that the things on earth will be shaken, so that only eternal things will be left.

[28]Since we are receiving a kingdom that cannot be destroyed, let us be thankful and please God by worshiping him with holy fear and awe. [29]For our God is a consuming fire.

CHAPTER 13
Concluding Words

Continue to love each other with true Christian love.* [2]Don't forget to show hospitality to strangers, for some who have done this have entertained angels without realizing it! [3]Don't forget about those in prison. Suffer with them as though you were there yourself. Share the sorrow of those being mistreated, as though you feel their pain in your own bodies.

[4]Give honor to marriage, and remain faithful to one another in marriage. God will surely judge people who are immoral and those who commit adultery.

[5]Stay away from the love of money; be satisfied with what you have. For God has said,

"I will never fail you.
  I will never forsake you."*

[6]That is why we can say with confidence,

"The Lord is my helper,
  so I will not be afraid.
  What can mere mortals do to me?"*

[7]Remember your leaders who first taught you the word of God. Think of all the good that has come from their lives, and trust the Lord as they do.

[8]Jesus Christ is the same yesterday, today, and forever. [9]So do not be attracted by strange, new ideas. Your spiritual strength comes

12:20 Exod 19:13.   **12:21** Deut 9:19.   **12:26** Hag 2:6.   **13:1** Greek *with brotherly love.*
13:5 Deut 31:6, 8.   **13:6** Ps 118:6.

from God's special favor, not from ceremonial rules about food, which don't help those who follow them.

¹⁰We have an altar from which the priests in the Temple on earth have no right to eat. ¹¹Under the system of Jewish laws, the high priest brought the blood of animals into the Holy Place as a sacrifice for sin, but the bodies of the animals were burned outside the camp. ¹²So also Jesus suffered and died outside the city gates in order to make his people holy by shedding his own blood. ¹³So let us go out to him outside the camp and bear the disgrace he bore. ¹⁴For this world is not our home; we are looking forward to our city in heaven, which is yet to come.

¹⁵With Jesus' help, let us continually offer our sacrifice of praise to God by proclaiming the glory of his name. ¹⁶Don't forget to do good and to share what you have with those in need, for such sacrifices are very pleasing to God.

¹⁷Obey your spiritual leaders and do what they say. Their work is to watch over your souls, and they know they are accountable to God. Give them reason to do this joyfully and not with sorrow. That would certainly not be for your benefit.

¹⁸Pray for us, for our conscience is clear and we want to live honorably in everything we do. ¹⁹I especially need your prayers right now so that I can come back to you soon.

²⁰⁻²¹And now, may the God of peace, who brought again from the dead our Lord Jesus, equip you with all you need for doing his will. May he produce in you, through the power of Jesus Christ, all that is pleasing to him. Jesus is the great Shepherd of the sheep by an everlasting covenant, signed with his blood. To him be glory forever and ever. Amen.

²²I urge you, dear brothers and sisters,* please listen carefully to what I have said in this brief letter.

²³I want you to know that our brother Timothy is now out of jail. If he comes here soon, I will bring him with me to see you.

²⁴Give my greetings to all your leaders and to the other believers there. The Christians from Italy send you their greetings.

²⁵May God's grace be with you all.

13:22 Greek *brothers.*

JAMES

CHAPTER 1

Greetings from James

This letter is from James, a slave of God and of the Lord Jesus Christ. It is written to Jewish Christians scattered among the nations.* Greetings!

Faith and Endurance

²Dear brothers and sisters,* whenever trouble comes your way, let it be an opportunity for joy. ³For when your faith is tested, your

1:1 Greek *To the twelve tribes in the dispersion.*   1:2 Greek *brothers;* also in 1:16, 19.

endurance has a chance to grow. ⁴ So let it grow, for when your endurance is fully developed, you will be strong in character and ready for anything.

⁵ If you need wisdom—if you want to know what God wants you to do—ask him, and he will gladly tell you. He will not resent your asking. ⁶ But when you ask him, be sure that you really expect him to answer, for a doubtful mind is as unsettled as a wave of the sea that is driven and tossed by the wind. ⁷ People like that should not expect to receive anything from the Lord. ⁸ They can't make up their minds. They waver back and forth in everything they do.

⁹ Christians who are* poor should be glad, for God has honored them. ¹⁰ And those who are rich should be glad, for God has humbled them. They will fade away like a flower in the field. ¹¹ The hot sun rises and dries up the grass; the flower withers, and its beauty fades away. So also, wealthy people will fade away with all of their achievements.

¹² God blesses the people who patiently endure testing. Afterward they will receive the crown of life that God has promised to those who love him. ¹³ And remember, no one who wants to do wrong should ever say, "God is tempting me." God is never tempted to do wrong, and he never tempts anyone else either. ¹⁴ Temptation comes from the lure of our own evil desires. These evil desires lead to evil actions, and evil actions lead to death. ¹⁶ So don't be misled, my dear brothers and sisters.

¹⁷ Whatever is good and perfect comes to us from God above, who created all heaven's lights.* Unlike them, he never changes or casts shifting shadows. ¹⁸ In his goodness he chose to make us his own children by giving us his true word. And we, out of all creation, became his choice possession.

Listening and Doing

¹⁹ My dear brothers and sisters, be quick to listen, slow to speak, and slow to get angry. ²⁰ Your anger can never make things right in God's sight.

²¹ So get rid of all the filth and evil in your lives, and humbly accept the message God has planted in your hearts, for it is strong enough to save your souls.

²² And remember, it is a message to obey, not just to listen to. If you don't obey, you are only fooling yourself. ²³ For if you just listen and don't obey, it is like looking at your face in a mirror but doing nothing to improve your appearance. ²⁴ You see yourself, walk away, and forget what you look like. ²⁵ But if you keep looking steadily into God's perfect law—the law that sets you free—and if you do what it says and don't forget what you heard, then God will bless you for doing it.

²⁶ If you claim to be religious but don't control your tongue, you are just fooling yourself, and your religion is worthless. ²⁷ Pure and lasting religion in the sight of God our Father means that we must care for orphans and widows in their troubles, and refuse to let the world corrupt us.

1:9 Greek *The brother who is.*   1:17 Greek *from above, from the Father of lights.*

CHAPTER 2

A Warning against Prejudice

My dear brothers and sisters,* how can you claim that you have faith in our glorious Lord Jesus Christ if you favor some people more than others?

² For instance, suppose someone comes into your meeting* dressed in fancy clothes and expensive jewelry, and another comes in who is poor and dressed in shabby clothes. ³If you give special attention and a good seat to the rich person, but you say to the poor one, "You can stand over there, or else sit on the floor"—well, ⁴doesn't this discrimination show that you are guided by wrong motives?

⁵Listen to me, dear brothers and sisters. Hasn't God chosen the poor in this world to be rich in faith? Aren't they the ones who will inherit the kingdom God promised to those who love him? ⁶And yet, you insult the poor man! Isn't it the rich who oppress you and drag you into court? ⁷Aren't they the ones who slander Jesus Christ, whose noble name you bear?

⁸ Yes indeed, it is good when you truly obey our Lord's royal command found in the Scriptures: "Love your neighbor as yourself."* ⁹ But if you pay special attention to the rich, you are committing a sin, for you are guilty of breaking that law.

¹⁰And the person who keeps all of the laws except one is as guilty as the person who has broken all of God's laws. ¹¹For the same God who said, "Do not commit adultery," also said, "Do not murder."* So if you murder someone, you have broken the entire law, even if you do not commit adultery.

¹²So whenever you speak, or whatever you do, remember that you will be judged by the law of love, the law that set you free. ¹³For there will be no mercy for you if you have not been merciful to others. But if you have been merciful, then God's mercy toward you will win out over his judgment against you.

Faith without Good Deeds Is Dead

¹⁴Dear brothers and sisters, what's the use of saying you have faith if you don't prove it by your actions? That kind of faith can't save anyone. ¹⁵Suppose you see a brother or sister who needs food or clothing, ¹⁶and you say, "Well, good-bye and God bless you; stay warm and eat well"—but then you don't give that person any food or clothing. What good does that do?

¹⁷So you see, it isn't enough just to have faith. Faith that doesn't show itself by good deeds is no faith at all—it is dead and useless.

¹⁸Now someone may argue, "Some people have faith; others have good deeds." I say, "I can't see your faith if you don't have good deeds, but I will show you my faith through my good deeds."

¹⁹Do you still think it's enough just to believe that there is one God? Well, even the demons believe this, and they tremble in terror! ²⁰Fool! When will you ever learn that faith that does not result in good deeds is useless?

²¹Don't you remember that our ancestor Abraham was declared right with God because of what he did when he offered his son Isaac on the altar? ²²You see, he was trusting God so much that he

---

2:1 Greek *brothers*; also in 2:5, 14.   **2:2** Greek *synagogue*.   **2:8** Lev 19:18.   **2:11** Exod 20:13-14; Deut 5:17-18.

was willing to do whatever God told him to do. His faith was made complete by what he did—by his actions. 23 And so it happened just as the Scriptures say: "Abraham believed God, so God declared him to be righteous."* He was even called "the friend of God."* 24 So you see, we are made right with God by what we do, not by faith alone.

25 Rahab the prostitute is another example of this. She was made right with God by her actions—when she hid those messengers and sent them safely away by a different road. 26 Just as the body is dead without a spirit, so also faith is dead without good deeds.

CHAPTER 3

Controlling the Tongue

Dear brothers and sisters,* not many of you should become teachers in the church, for we who teach will be judged by God with greater strictness.

2 We all make many mistakes, but those who control their tongues can also control themselves in every other way. 3 We can make a large horse turn around and go wherever we want by means of a small bit in its mouth. 4 And a tiny rudder makes a huge ship turn wherever the pilot wants it to go, even though the winds are strong. 5 So also, the tongue is a small thing, but what enormous damage it can do. A tiny spark can set a great forest on fire. 6 And the tongue is a flame of fire. It is full of wickedness that can ruin your whole life. It can turn the entire course of your life into a blazing flame of destruction, for it is set on fire by hell itself.

7 People can tame all kinds of animals and birds and reptiles and fish, 8 but no one can tame the tongue. It is an uncontrollable evil, full of deadly poison. 9 Sometimes it praises our Lord and Father, and sometimes it breaks out into curses against those who have been made in the image of God. 10 And so blessing and cursing come pouring out of the same mouth. Surely, my brothers and sisters, this is not right! 11 Does a spring of water bubble out with both fresh water and bitter water? 12 Can you pick olives from a fig tree or figs from a grapevine? No, and you can't draw fresh water from a salty pool.

True Wisdom Comes from God

13 If you are wise and understand God's ways, live a life of steady goodness so that only good deeds will pour forth. And if you don't brag about the good you do, then you will be truly wise! 14 But if you are bitterly jealous and there is selfish ambition in your hearts, don't brag about being wise. That is the worst kind of lie. 15 For jealousy and selfishness are not God's kind of wisdom. Such things are earthly, unspiritual, and motivated by the Devil. 16 For wherever there is jealousy and selfish ambition, there you will find disorder and every kind of evil.

17 But the wisdom that comes from heaven is first of all pure. It is also peace loving, gentle at all times, and willing to yield to others. It is full of mercy and good deeds. It shows no partiality and is always sincere. 18 And those who are peacemakers will plant seeds of peace and reap a harvest of goodness.

2:23a Gen 15:6. 2:23b See Isa 41:8. 3:1 Greek *brothers*; also in 3:10.

CHAPTER 4
Drawing Close to God

What is causing the quarrels and fights among you? Isn't it the whole army of evil desires at war within you? ²You want what you don't have, so you scheme and kill to get it. You are jealous for what others have, and you can't possess it, so you fight and quarrel to take it away from them. And yet the reason you don't have what you want is that you don't ask God for it. ³And even when you do ask, you don't get it because your whole motive is wrong—you want only what will give you pleasure.

⁴ You adulterers! Don't you realize that friendship with this world makes you an enemy of God? I say it again, that if your aim is to enjoy this world, you can't be a friend of God. ⁵What do you think the Scriptures mean when they say that the Holy Spirit, whom God has placed within us, jealously longs for us to be faithful*? ⁶He gives us more and more strength to stand against such evil desires. As the Scriptures say,

"God sets himself against the proud,
   but he shows favor to the humble."*

⁷So humble yourselves before God. Resist the Devil, and he will flee from you. ⁸Draw close to God, and God will draw close to you. Wash your hands, you sinners; purify your hearts, you hypocrites. ⁹Let there be tears for the wrong things you have done. Let there be sorrow and deep grief. Let there be sadness instead of laughter, and gloom instead of joy. ¹⁰When you bow down before the Lord and admit your dependence on him, he will lift you up and give you honor.

Warning against Judging Others

¹¹Don't speak evil against each other, my dear brothers and sisters.* If you criticize each other and condemn each other, then you are criticizing and condemning God's law. But you are not a judge who can decide whether the law is right or wrong. Your job is to obey it. ¹²God alone, who made the law, can rightly judge among us. He alone has the power to save or to destroy. So what right do you have to condemn your neighbor?

Warning about Self-Confidence

¹³ Look here, you people who say, "Today or tomorrow we are going to a certain town and will stay there a year. We will do business there and make a profit." ¹⁴How do you know what will happen tomorrow? For your life is like the morning fog—it's here a little while, then it's gone. ¹⁵What you ought to say is, "If the Lord wants us to, we will live and do this or that." ¹⁶Otherwise you will be boasting about your own plans, and all such boasting is evil.

¹⁷Remember, it is sin to know what you ought to do and then not do it.

CHAPTER 5
Warning to the Rich

Look here, you rich people, weep and groan with anguish because of all the terrible troubles ahead of you. ²Your wealth is rotting away, and your fine clothes are moth-eaten rags. ³Your gold and

4:5 Or *the spirit that God placed within us tends to envy,* or *the Holy Spirit, whom God has placed within us, opposes our envy.* 4:6 Prov 3:34. 4:11 Greek *brothers.*

silver have become worthless. The very wealth you were counting on will eat away your flesh in hell.* This treasure you have accumulated will stand as evidence against you on the day of judgment. ⁴For listen! Hear the cries of the field workers whom you have cheated of their pay. The wages you held back cry out against you. The cries of the reapers have reached the ears of the Lord Almighty.

⁵You have spent your years on earth in luxury, satisfying your every whim. Now your hearts are nice and fat, ready for the slaughter. ⁶You have condemned and killed good people who had no power to defend themselves against you.

Patience in Suffering

⁷Dear brothers and sisters,* you must be patient as you wait for the Lord's return. Consider the farmers who eagerly look for the rains in the fall and in the spring. They patiently wait for the precious harvest to ripen. ⁸You, too, must be patient. And take courage, for the coming of the Lord is near.

⁹Don't grumble about each other, my brothers and sisters, or God will judge you. For look! The great Judge is coming. He is standing at the door!

¹⁰For examples of patience in suffering, dear brothers and sisters, look at the prophets who spoke in the name of the Lord. ¹¹We give great honor to those who endure under suffering. Job is an example of a man who endured patiently. From his experience we see how the Lord's plan finally ended in good, for he is full of tenderness and mercy.

¹²But most of all, my brothers and sisters, never take an oath, by heaven or earth or anything else. Just say a simple yes or no, so that you will not sin and be condemned for it.

The Power of Prayer

¹³Are any among you suffering? They should keep on praying about it. And those who have reason to be thankful should continually sing praises to the Lord.

¹⁴Are any among you sick? They should call for the elders of the church and have them pray over them, anointing them with oil in the name of the Lord. ¹⁵And their prayer offered in faith will heal the sick, and the Lord will make them well. And anyone who has committed sins will be forgiven.

¹⁶Confess your sins to each other and pray for each other so that you may be healed. The earnest prayer of a righteous person has great power and wonderful results. ¹⁷Elijah was as human as we are, and yet when he prayed earnestly that no rain would fall, none fell for the next three and a half years! ¹⁸Then he prayed for rain, and down it poured. The grass turned green, and the crops began to grow again.

Restore Wandering Believers

¹⁹My dear brothers and sisters, if anyone among you wanders away from the truth and is brought back again, ²⁰you can be sure that the one who brings that person back will save that sinner from death and bring about the forgiveness of many sins.

5:3 Or *will eat your flesh like fire.*   5:7 Greek *brothers;* also in 5:9, 10, 12, 19.

1 PETER

CHAPTER 1

Greetings from Peter

This letter is from Peter, an apostle of Jesus Christ.

I am writing to God's chosen people who are living as foreigners in the lands of Pontus, Galatia, Cappadocia, the province of Asia, and Bithynia. 2 God the Father chose you long ago, and the Spirit has made you holy. As a result, you have obeyed Jesus Christ and are cleansed by his blood.

May you have more and more of God's special favor and wonderful peace.

The Hope of Eternal Life

3 All honor to the God and Father of our Lord Jesus Christ, for it is by his boundless mercy that God has given us the privilege of being born again. Now we live with a wonderful expectation because Jesus Christ rose again from the dead. 4 For God has reserved a priceless inheritance for his children. It is kept in heaven for you, pure and undefiled, beyond the reach of change and decay. 5 And God, in his mighty power, will protect you until you receive this salvation, because you are trusting him. It will be revealed on the last day for all to see. 6 So be truly glad!* There is wonderful joy ahead, even though it is necessary for you to endure many trials for a while.

7 These trials are only to test your faith, to show that it is strong and pure. It is being tested as fire tests and purifies gold—and your faith is far more precious to God than mere gold. So if your faith remains strong after being tried by fiery trials, it will bring you much praise and glory and honor on the day when Jesus Christ is revealed to the whole world.

8 You love him even though you have never seen him. Though you do not see him, you trust him; and even now you are happy with a glorious, inexpressible joy. 9 Your reward for trusting him will be the salvation of your souls.

10 This salvation was something the prophets wanted to know more about. They prophesied about this gracious salvation prepared for you, even though they had many questions as to what it all could mean. 11 They wondered what the Spirit of Christ within them was talking about when he told them in advance about Christ's suffering and his great glory afterward. They wondered when and to whom all this would happen.

12 They were told that these things would not happen during their lifetime, but many years later, during yours. And now this Good News has been announced by those who preached to you in the power of the Holy Spirit sent from heaven. It is all so wonderful that even the angels are eagerly watching these things happen.

1:6 Or *So you are truly glad.*

A Call to Holy Living

13 So think clearly and exercise self-control. Look forward to the special blessings that will come to you at the return of Jesus Christ. 14 Obey God because you are his children. Don't slip back into your old ways of doing evil; you didn't know any better then. 15 But now you must be holy in everything you do, just as God—who chose you to be his children—is holy. 16 For he himself has said, "You must be holy because I am holy."*

17 And remember that the heavenly Father to whom you pray has no favorites when he judges. He will judge or reward you according to what you do. So you must live in reverent fear of him during your time as foreigners here on earth. 18 For you know that God paid a ransom to save you from the empty life you inherited from your ancestors. And the ransom he paid was not mere gold or silver. 19 He paid for you with the precious lifeblood of Christ, the sinless, spotless Lamb of God. 20 God chose him for this purpose long before the world began, but now in these final days, he was sent to the earth for all to see. And he did this for you.

21 Through Christ you have come to trust in God. And because God raised Christ from the dead and gave him great glory, your faith and hope can be placed confidently in God. 22 Now you can have sincere love for each other as brothers and sisters* because you were cleansed from your sins when you accepted the truth of the Good News. So see to it that you really do love each other intensely with all your hearts.*

23 For you have been born again. Your new life did not come from your earthly parents because the life they gave you will end in death. But this new life will last forever because it comes from the eternal, living word of God. 24 As the prophet says,

"People are like grass that dies away;
 their beauty fades as quickly as the beauty of wildflowers.
The grass withers,
 and the flowers fall away.
25 But the word of the Lord will last forever."*

And that word is the Good News that was preached to you.

CHAPTER 2

So get rid of all malicious behavior and deceit. Don't just pretend to be good! Be done with hypocrisy and jealousy and backstabbing. 2 You must crave pure spiritual milk so that you can grow into the fullness of your salvation. Cry out for this nourishment as a baby cries for milk, 3 now that you have had a taste of the Lord's kindness.

Living Stones for God's House

4 Come to Christ, who is the living cornerstone of God's temple. He was rejected by the people, but he is precious to God who chose him.

5 And now God is building you, as living stones, into his spiritual temple. What's more, you are God's holy priests, who offer the

1:16 Lev 11:44-45; 19:2; 20:7. **1:22a** Greek *can have brotherly love.* **1:22b** Some manuscripts read *with a pure heart.* **1:24-25** Isa 40:6-8.

spiritual sacrifices that please him because of Jesus Christ. 6As the Scriptures express it,

"I am placing a stone in Jerusalem,*
        a chosen cornerstone,
    and anyone who believes in him
        will never be disappointed.*"

7Yes, he is very precious to you who believe. But for those who reject him,

"The stone that was rejected by the builders
        has now become the cornerstone."*

8And the Scriptures also say,

"He is the stone that makes people stumble,
        the rock that will make them fall."*

They stumble because they do not listen to God's word or obey it, and so they meet the fate that has been planned for them.

9But you are not like that, for you are a chosen people. You are a kingdom of priests, God's holy nation, his very own possession. This is so you can show others the goodness of God, for he called you out of the darkness into his wonderful light.

10 "Once you were not a people;
        now you are the people of God.
    Once you received none of God's mercy;
        now you have received his mercy."*

11Dear brothers and sisters, you are foreigners and aliens here. So I warn you to keep away from evil desires because they fight against your very souls. 12Be careful how you live among your unbelieving neighbors. Even if they accuse you of doing wrong, they will see your honorable behavior, and they will believe and give honor to God when he comes to judge the world.*

Respecting People in Authority

13For the Lord's sake, accept all authority—the king as head of state, 14and the officials he has appointed. For the king has sent them to punish all who do wrong and to honor those who do right.

15It is God's will that your good lives should silence those who make foolish accusations against you. 16You are not slaves; you are free. But your freedom is not an excuse to do evil. You are free to live as God's slaves. 17Show respect for everyone. Love your Christian brothers and sisters.* Fear God. Show respect for the king.

Slaves

18You who are slaves must accept the authority of your masters. Do whatever they tell you—not only if they are kind and reasonable, but even if they are harsh. 19For God is pleased with you when, for the sake of your conscience, you patiently endure unfair treatment. 20Of course, you get no credit for being patient if you are beaten for doing wrong. But if you suffer for doing right and are patient beneath the blows, God is pleased with you.

2:6a Greek *in Zion.*   2:6b Or *will never be put to shame.* Isa 28:16.   2:7 Ps 118:22.
2:8 Isa 8:14.   2:10 Hos 1:6, 9; 2:23.   2:12 Or *on the day of visitation.*   2:17 Greek *Love the brotherhood.*

²¹This suffering is all part of what God has called you to. Christ, who suffered for you, is your example. Follow in his steps. ²²He never sinned, and he never deceived anyone. ²³He did not retaliate when he was insulted. When he suffered, he did not threaten to get even. He left his case in the hands of God, who always judges fairly. ²⁴He personally carried away our sins in his own body on the cross so we can be dead to sin and live for what is right. You have been healed by his wounds! ²⁵Once you were wandering like lost sheep. But now you have turned to your Shepherd, the Guardian of your souls.

CHAPTER 3

Wives

In the same way, you wives must accept the authority of your husbands, even those who refuse to accept the Good News. Your godly lives will speak to them better than any words. They will be won over ²by watching your pure, godly behavior.

³Don't be concerned about the outward beauty that depends on fancy hairstyles, expensive jewelry, or beautiful clothes. ⁴You should be known for the beauty that comes from within, the unfading beauty of a gentle and quiet spirit, which is so precious to God. ⁵That is the way the holy women of old made themselves beautiful. They trusted God and accepted the authority of their husbands. ⁶ For instance, Sarah obeyed her husband, Abraham, when she called him her master. You are her daughters when you do what is right without fear of what your husbands might do.

Husbands

⁷In the same way, you husbands must give honor to your wives. Treat her with understanding as you live together. She may be weaker than you are, but she is your equal partner in God's gift of new life. If you don't treat her as you should, your prayers will not be heard.

All Christians

⁸Finally, all of you should be of one mind, full of sympathy toward each other, loving one another with tender hearts and humble minds. ⁹Don't repay evil for evil. Don't retaliate when people say unkind things about you. Instead, pay them back with a blessing. That is what God wants you to do, and he will bless you for it. ¹⁰For the Scriptures say,

"If you want a happy life and good days,
  keep your tongue from speaking evil,
  and keep your lips from telling lies.
¹¹ Turn away from evil and do good.
  Work hard at living in peace with others.
¹² The eyes of the Lord watch over those who do right,
  and his ears are open to their prayers.
But the Lord turns his face
  against those who do evil."*

Suffering for Doing Good

¹³Now, who will want to harm you if you are eager to do good? ¹⁴But even if you suffer for doing what is right, God will reward you for it. So don't be afraid and don't worry. ¹⁵Instead, you must

3:10-12 Ps 34:12-16.

worship Christ as Lord of your life. And if you are asked about your Christian hope, always be ready to explain it. [16]But you must do this in a gentle and respectful way. Keep your conscience clear. Then if people speak evil against you, they will be ashamed when they see what a good life you live because you belong to Christ. [17]Remember, it is better to suffer for doing good, if that is what God wants, than to suffer for doing wrong!

[18]Christ also suffered when he died for our sins once for all time. He never sinned, but he died for sinners that he might bring us safely home to God. He suffered physical death, but he was raised to life in the Spirit.*

[19]So he went and preached to the spirits in prison—[20]those who disobeyed God long ago when God waited patiently while Noah was building his boat. Only eight people were saved from drowning in that terrible flood.* [21]And this is a picture of baptism, which now saves you by the power of Jesus Christ's resurrection. Baptism is not a removal of dirt from your body; it is an appeal to God from* a clean conscience.

[22]Now Christ has gone to heaven. He is seated in the place of honor next to God, and all the angels and authorities and powers are bowing before him.

CHAPTER 4

Living for God

So then, since Christ suffered physical pain, you must arm yourselves with the same attitude he had, and be ready to suffer, too. For if you are willing to suffer for Christ, you have decided to stop sinning. [2]And you won't spend the rest of your life chasing after evil desires, but you will be anxious to do the will of God. [3]You have had enough in the past of the evil things that godless people enjoy—their immorality and lust, their feasting and drunkenness and wild parties, and their terrible worship of idols.

[4]Of course, your former friends are very surprised when you no longer join them in the wicked things they do, and they say evil things about you. [5]But just remember that they will have to face God, who will judge everyone, both the living and the dead. [6]That is why the Good News was preached even to those who have died—so that although their bodies were punished with death, they could still live in the spirit as God does.

[7]The end of the world is coming soon. Therefore, be earnest and disciplined in your prayers. [8]Most important of all, continue to show deep love for each other, for love covers a multitude of sins. [9]Cheerfully share your home with those who need a meal or a place to stay.

[10]God has given gifts to each of you from his great variety of spiritual gifts. Manage them well so that God's generosity can flow through you. [11]Are you called to be a speaker? Then speak as though God himself were speaking through you. Are you called to help others? Do it with all the strength and energy that God supplies. Then God will be given glory in everything

3:18 Or *spirit.* **3:20** Greek *saved through water.* **3:21** Or *for.*

through Jesus Christ. All glory and power belong to him forever and ever. Amen.

Suffering for Being a Christian

12Dear friends, don't be surprised at the fiery trials you are going through, as if something strange were happening to you. 13Instead, be very glad—because these trials will make you partners with Christ in his suffering, and afterward you will have the wonderful joy of sharing his glory when it is displayed to all the world.

14Be happy if you are insulted for being a Christian, for then the glorious Spirit of God will come upon you. 15If you suffer, however, it must not be for murder, stealing, making trouble, or prying into other people's affairs. 16But it is no shame to suffer for being a Christian. Praise God for the privilege of being called by his wonderful name! 17For the time has come for judgment, and it must begin first among God's own children. And if even we Christians must be judged, what terrible fate awaits those who have never believed God's Good News? 18And

> "If the righteous are barely saved,
>   what chance will the godless and sinners have?" *

19So if you are suffering according to God's will, keep on doing what is right, and trust yourself to the God who made you, for he will never fail you.

CHAPTER 5

Advice for Elders and Young Men

And now, a word to you who are elders in the churches. I, too, am an elder and a witness to the sufferings of Christ. And I, too, will share his glory and his honor when he returns. As a fellow elder, this is my appeal to you: 2 Care for the flock of God entrusted to you. Watch over it willingly, not grudgingly—not for what you will get out of it, but because you are eager to serve God. 3Don't lord it over the people assigned to your care, but lead them by your good example. 4And when the head Shepherd comes, your reward will be a never-ending share in his glory and honor.

5You younger men, accept the authority of the elders. And all of you, serve each other in humility, for

> "God sets himself against the proud,
>   but he shows favor to the humble." *

6So humble yourselves under the mighty power of God, and in his good time he will honor you. 7Give all your worries and cares to God, for he cares about what happens to you.

8 Be careful! Watch out for attacks from the Devil, your great enemy. He prowls around like a roaring lion, looking for some victim to devour. 9Take a firm stand against him, and be strong in your faith. Remember that your Christian brothers and sisters* all over the world are going through the same kind of suffering you are.

10In his kindness God called you to his eternal glory by means of Jesus Christ. After you have suffered a little while, he will restore,

4:18 Prov 11:31. 5:5 Prov 3:34. 5:9 Greek *your brothers.*

support, and strengthen you, and he will place you on a firm foundation. ¹¹All power is his forever and ever. Amen.

Peter's Final Greetings

¹²I have written this short letter to you with the help of Silas,* whom I consider a faithful brother. My purpose in writing is to encourage you and assure you that the grace of God is with you no matter what happens.

¹³Your sister church here in Rome* sends you greetings, and so does my son Mark. ¹⁴Greet each other in Christian love.*

Peace be to all of you who are in Christ.

5:12 Greek *Silvanus.*   5:13 Greek *The elect one in Babylon.* Babylon was probably a code name for Rome.   5:14 Greek *with a kiss of love.*

2 PETER

CHAPTER 1

Greetings from Peter

This letter is from Simon* Peter, a slave and apostle of Jesus Christ.

I am writing to all of you who share the same precious faith we have, faith given to us by Jesus Christ, our God and Savior, who makes us right with God.

²May God bless you with his special favor and wonderful peace as you come to know Jesus, our God and Lord,* better and better.

Growing in the Knowledge of God

³As we know Jesus better, his divine power gives us everything we need for living a godly life. He has called us to receive his own glory and goodness! ⁴And by that same mighty power, he has given us all of his rich and wonderful promises. He has promised that you will escape the decadence all around you caused by evil desires and that you will share in his divine nature.

⁵So make every effort to apply the benefits of these promises to your life. Then your faith will produce a life of moral excellence. A life of moral excellence leads to knowing God better. ⁶Knowing God leads to self-control. Self-control leads to patient endurance, and patient endurance leads to godliness. ⁷Godliness leads to love for other Christians,* and finally you will grow to have genuine love for everyone. ⁸The more you grow like this, the more you will become productive and useful in your knowledge of our Lord Jesus Christ. ⁹But those who fail to develop these virtues are blind or, at least, very shortsighted. They have already forgotten that God has cleansed them from their old life of sin.

¹⁰So, dear brothers and sisters,* work hard to prove that you really are among those God has called and chosen. Doing this, you will never stumble or fall away. ¹¹And God will open wide the gates of heaven for you to enter into the eternal Kingdom of our Lord and Savior Jesus Christ.

1:1 Greek *Simeon.*   1:2 Or *come to know God and Jesus our Lord.*   1:7 Greek *brotherly love.*   1:10 Greek *brothers.*

Paying Attention to Scripture

¹²I plan to keep on reminding you of these things—even though you already know them and are standing firm in the truth. ¹³Yes, I believe I should keep on reminding you of these things as long as I live. ¹⁴But the Lord Jesus Christ has shown me that my days here on earth are numbered and I am soon to die.* ¹⁵So I will work hard to make these things clear to you. I want you to remember them long after I am gone.

¹⁶For we were not making up clever stories when we told you about the power of our Lord Jesus Christ and his coming again. We have seen his majestic splendor with our own eyes. ¹⁷And he received honor and glory from God the Father when God's glorious, majestic voice called down from heaven, "This is my beloved Son; I am fully pleased with him." ¹⁸We ourselves heard the voice when we were there with him on the holy mountain.

¹⁹Because of that, we have even greater confidence in the message proclaimed by the prophets. Pay close attention to what they wrote, for their words are like a light shining in a dark place—until the day Christ appears and his brilliant light shines in your hearts.* ²⁰Above all, you must understand that no prophecy in Scripture ever came from the prophets themselves* ²¹or because they wanted to prophesy. It was the Holy Spirit who moved the prophets to speak from God.

CHAPTER 2

The Danger of False Teachers

But there were also false prophets in Israel, just as there will be false teachers among you. They will cleverly teach their destructive heresies about God and even turn against their Master who bought them. Theirs will be a swift and terrible end. ²Many will follow their evil teaching and shameful immorality. And because of them, Christ and his true way will be slandered. ³In their greed they will make up clever lies to get hold of your money. But God condemned them long ago, and their destruction is on the way.

⁴For God did not spare even the angels when they sinned; he threw them into hell,* in gloomy caves* and darkness until the judgment day. ⁵And God did not spare the ancient world—except for Noah and his family of seven. Noah warned the world of God's righteous judgment. Then God destroyed the whole world of ungodly people with a vast flood. ⁶Later, he turned the cities of Sodom and Gomorrah into heaps of ashes and swept them off the face of the earth. He made them an example of what will happen to ungodly people. ⁷But at the same time, God rescued Lot out of Sodom because he was a good man who was sick of all the immorality and wickedness around him. ⁸Yes, he was a righteous man who was distressed by the wickedness he saw and heard day after day.

⁹So you see, the Lord knows how to rescue godly people from their trials, even while punishing the wicked right up until the day of judgment. ¹⁰He is especially hard on those who follow their own evil, lustful desires and who despise authority. These people are proud and arrogant, daring even to scoff at the glorious ones*

1:14 Greek *I must soon put off this earthly tent.* 1:19 Or *until the day dawns and the morning star rises in your hearts.* 1:20 Or *is a matter of one's own interpretation.* 2:4a Greek *Tartaros.* 2:4b Some manuscripts read *chains of gloom.* 2:10 *The glorious ones* are probably evil angels; also in 2:11.

without so much as trembling. [11] But the angels, even though they are far greater in power and strength than these false teachers, never speak out disrespectfully against* the glorious ones.

[12] These false teachers are like unthinking animals, creatures of instinct, who are born to be caught and killed. They laugh at the terrifying powers they know so little about, and they will be destroyed along with them. [13] Their destruction is their reward for the harm they have done. They love to indulge in evil pleasures in broad daylight. They are a disgrace and a stain among you. They revel in deceitfulness while they feast with you. [14] They commit adultery with their eyes, and their lust is never satisfied. They make a game of luring unstable people into sin. They train themselves to be greedy; they are doomed and cursed. [15] They have wandered off the right road and followed the way of Balaam son of Beor,* who loved to earn money by doing wrong. [16] But Balaam was stopped from his mad course when his donkey rebuked him with a human voice.

[17] These people are as useless as dried-up springs of water or as clouds blown away by the wind—promising much and delivering nothing. They are doomed to blackest darkness. [18] They brag about themselves with empty, foolish boasting. With lustful desire as their bait, they lure back into sin those who have just escaped from such wicked living. [19] They promise freedom, but they themselves are slaves to sin and corruption. For you are a slave to whatever controls you. [20] And when people escape from the wicked ways of the world by learning about our Lord and Savior Jesus Christ and then get tangled up with sin and become its slave again, they are worse off than before. [21] It would be better if they had never known the right way to live than to know it and then reject the holy commandments that were given to them. [22] They make these proverbs come true: "A dog returns to its vomit,"* and "A washed pig returns to the mud."

CHAPTER 3

The Day of the Lord Is Coming

This is my second letter to you, dear friends, and in both of them I have tried to stimulate your wholesome thinking and refresh your memory. [2] I want you to remember and understand what the holy prophets said long ago and what our Lord and Savior commanded through your apostles.

[3] First, I want to remind you that in the last days there will be scoffers who will laugh at the truth and do every evil thing they desire. [4] This will be their argument: "Jesus promised to come back, did he? Then where is he? Why, as far back as anyone can remember, everything has remained exactly the same since the world was first created."

[5] They deliberately forget that God made the heavens by the word of his command, and he brought the earth up from the water and surrounded it with water. [6] Then he used the water to destroy the world with a mighty flood. [7] And God has also commanded that the heavens and the earth will be consumed by fire on the day of judgment, when ungodly people will perish.

[8] But you must not forget, dear friends, that a day is like a

2:11 Greek *never bring blasphemous judgment from the Lord against.* 2:15 Other manuscripts read *Bosor.* 2:22 Prov 26:11.

thousand years to the Lord, and a thousand years is like a day. ⁹The Lord isn't really being slow about his promise to return, as some people think. No, he is being patient for your sake. He does not want anyone to perish, so he is giving more time for everyone to repent. ¹⁰But the day of the Lord will come as unexpectedly as a thief. Then the heavens will pass away with a terrible noise, and everything in them will disappear in fire, and the earth and everything on it will be exposed to judgment.*

¹¹Since everything around us is going to melt away, what holy, godly lives you should be living! ¹²You should look forward to that day and hurry it along—the day when God will set the heavens on fire and the elements will melt away in the flames. ¹³But we are looking forward to the new heavens and new earth he has promised, a world where everyone is right with God.

¹⁴And so, dear friends, while you are waiting for these things to happen, make every effort to live a pure and blameless life. And be at peace with God.

¹⁵And remember, the Lord is waiting so that people have time to be saved. This is just as our beloved brother Paul wrote to you with the wisdom God gave him—¹⁶speaking of these things in all of his letters. Some of his comments are hard to understand, and those who are ignorant and unstable have twisted his letters around to mean something quite different from what he meant, just as they do the other parts of Scripture—and the result is disaster for them.

Peter's Final Words

¹⁷I am warning you ahead of time, dear friends, so that you can watch out and not be carried away by the errors of these wicked people. I don't want you to lose your own secure footing. ¹⁸But grow in the special favor and knowledge of our Lord and Savior Jesus Christ.

To him be all glory and honor, both now and forevermore. Amen.

3:10 Some manuscripts read *will be burned up.*

1 JOHN

CHAPTER 1

Introduction

The one who existed from the beginning* is the one we have heard and seen. We saw him with our own eyes and touched him with our own hands. He is Jesus Christ, the Word of life. ²This one who is life from God was shown to us, and we have seen him. And now we testify and announce to you that he is the one who is eternal life. He was with the Father, and then he was shown to us. ³We are telling you about what we ourselves

1:1 Greek *What was from the beginning.*

have actually seen and heard, so that you may have fellowship with us. And our fellowship is with the Father and with his Son, Jesus Christ.

⁴We are writing these things so that our* joy will be complete.

Living in the Light

⁵This is the message he has given us to announce to you: God is light and there is no darkness in him at all. ⁶So we are lying if we say we have fellowship with God but go on living in spiritual darkness. We are not living in the truth. ⁷But if we are living in the light of God's presence, just as Christ is, then we have fellowship with each other, and the blood of Jesus, his Son, cleanses us from every sin.

⁸If we say we have no sin, we are only fooling ourselves and refusing to accept the truth. ⁹But if we confess our sins to him, he is faithful and just to forgive us and to cleanse us from every wrong. ¹⁰If we claim we have not sinned, we are calling God a liar and showing that his word has no place in our hearts.

CHAPTER 2

My dear children, I am writing this to you so that you will not sin. But if you do sin, there is someone to plead for you before the Father. He is Jesus Christ, the one who pleases God completely.* ²He is the sacrifice for our sins. He takes away not only our sins but the sins of all the world.

³And how can we be sure that we belong to him? By obeying his commandments. ⁴If someone says, "I belong to God," but doesn't obey God's commandments, that person is a liar and does not live in the truth. ⁵But those who obey God's word really do love him. That is the way to know whether or not we live in him. ⁶Those who say they live in God should live their lives as Christ did.

A New Commandment

⁷Dear friends, I am not writing a new commandment, for it is an old one you have always had, right from the beginning. This commandment—to love one another—is the same message you heard before. ⁸Yet it is also new. This commandment is true in Christ and is true among you, because the darkness is disappearing and the true light is already shining.

⁹If anyone says, "I am living in the light," but hates a Christian brother or sister,* that person is still living in darkness. ¹⁰Anyone who loves other Christians* is living in the light and does not cause anyone to stumble. ¹¹Anyone who hates a Christian brother or sister is living and walking in darkness. Such a person is lost, having been blinded by the darkness.

¹²I am writing to you, my dear children, because your sins have been forgiven because of Jesus.

¹³I am writing to you who are mature because you know Christ, the one who is from the beginning.

I am writing to you who are young because you have won your battle with Satan.

1:4 Some manuscripts read *your*.　2:1 Greek *Jesus Christ, the righteous*.　2:9 Greek *his brother; also in 2:11*.　2:10 Greek *his brother*.

¹⁴I have written to you, children, because you have known the Father.

I have written to you who are mature because you know Christ, the one who is from the beginning.

I have written to you who are young because you are strong with God's word living in your hearts, and you have won your battle with Satan.

¹⁵Stop loving this evil world and all that it offers you, for when you love the world, you show that you do not have the love of the Father in you. ¹⁶For the world offers only the lust for physical pleasure, the lust for everything we see, and pride in our possessions. These are not from the Father. They are from this evil world. ¹⁷And this world is fading away, along with everything it craves. But if you do the will of God, you will live forever.

¹⁸Dear children, the last hour is here. You have heard that the Antichrist is coming, and already many such antichrists have appeared. From this we know that the end of the world has come. ¹⁹These people left our churches because they never really belonged with us; otherwise they would have stayed with us. When they left us, it proved that they do not belong with us. ²⁰But you are not like that, for the Holy Spirit has come upon you,* and all of you know the truth. ²¹So I am writing to you not because you don't know the truth but because you know the difference between truth and falsehood. ²²And who is the great liar? The one who says that Jesus is not the Christ. Such people are antichrists, for they have denied the Father and the Son. ²³Anyone who denies the Son doesn't have the Father either. But anyone who confesses the Son has the Father also.

²⁴So you must remain faithful to what you have been taught from the beginning. If you do, you will continue to live in fellowship with the Son and with the Father. ²⁵And in this fellowship we enjoy the eternal life he promised us.

²⁶I have written these things to you because you need to be aware of those who want to lead you astray. ²⁷But you have received the Holy Spirit,* and he lives within you, so you don't need anyone to teach you what is true. For the Spirit teaches you all things, and what he teaches is true—it is not a lie. So continue in what he has taught you, and continue to live in Christ.

²⁸And now, dear children, continue to live in fellowship with Christ so that when he returns, you will be full of courage and not shrink back from him in shame. ²⁹Since we know that God is always right, we also know that all who do what is right are his children.

CHAPTER 3

Living as Children of God

See how very much our heavenly Father loves us, for he allows us to be called his children, and we really are! But the people who belong to this world don't know God, so they don't understand that we are his children. ²Yes, dear friends, we are already God's children, and we can't even imagine what we will be like when

2:20 Greek *But you have an anointing from the Holy One.*　**2:27** Greek *the anointing.*

Christ returns. But we do know that when he comes we will be like him, for we will see him as he really is. ³And all who believe this will keep themselves pure, just as Christ is pure.

⁴ Those who sin are opposed to the law of God, for all sin opposes the law of God. ⁵And you know that Jesus came to take away our sins, for there is no sin in him. ⁶So if we continue to live in him, we won't sin either. But those who keep on sinning have never known him or understood who he is.

⁷Dear children, don't let anyone deceive you about this: When people do what is right, it is because they are righteous, even as Christ is righteous. ⁸But when people keep on sinning, it shows they belong to the Devil, who has been sinning since the beginning. But the Son of God came to destroy the works of the Devil. ⁹Those who have been born into God's family do not sin, because God's life is in them. So they can't keep on sinning, because they have been born of God. ¹⁰So now we can tell who are children of God and who are children of the Devil. Anyone who does not obey God's commands and does not love other Christians* does not belong to God.

Love One Another

¹¹This is the message we have heard from the beginning: We should love one another. ¹²We must not be like Cain, who belonged to the evil one and killed his brother. And why did he kill him? Because Cain had been doing what was evil, and his brother had been doing what was right. ¹³So don't be surprised, dear brothers and sisters,* if the world hates you.

¹⁴If we love our Christian brothers and sisters, it proves that we have passed from death to eternal life. But a person who has no love is still dead. ¹⁵Anyone who hates another Christian* is really a murderer at heart. And you know that murderers don't have eternal life within them. ¹⁶ We know what real love is because Christ gave up his life for us. And so we also ought to give up our lives for our Christian brothers and sisters. ¹⁷But if anyone has enough money to live well and sees a brother or sister in need and refuses to help—how can God's love be in that person?

¹⁸Dear children, let us stop just saying we love each other; let us really show it by our actions. ¹⁹It is by our actions that we know we are living in the truth, so we will be confident when we stand before the Lord, ²⁰even if our hearts condemn us. For God is greater than our hearts, and he knows everything.

²¹ Dear friends, if our conscience is clear, we can come to God with bold confidence. ²²And we will receive whatever we request because we obey him and do the things that please him. ²³And this is his commandment: We must believe in the name of his Son, Jesus Christ, and love one another, just as he commanded us. ²⁴Those who obey God's commandments live in fellowship with him, and he will know he lives in us because the Holy Spirit lives in us.

CHAPTER 4

Discerning False Prophets

Dear friends, do not believe everyone who claims to speak by the Spirit. You must test them to see if the spirit they have comes from

3:10 Greek *his brother.*   **3:13** Greek *brothers;* also in 3:14, 16.   **3:15** Greek *his brother.*

God. For there are many false prophets in the world. ²This is the way to find out if they have the Spirit of God: If a prophet acknowledges that Jesus Christ became a human being, that person has the Spirit of God. ³If a prophet does not acknowledge Jesus, that person is not from God. Such a person has the spirit of the Antichrist. You have heard that he is going to come into the world, and he is already here.

⁴But you belong to God, my dear children. You have already won your fight with these false prophets, because the Spirit who lives in you is greater than the spirit who lives in the world. ⁵These people belong to this world, so they speak from the world's viewpoint, and the world listens to them. ⁶But we belong to God; that is why those who know God listen to us. If they do not belong to God, they do not listen to us. That is how we know if someone has the Spirit of truth or the spirit of deception.

Loving One Another

⁷Dear friends, let us continue to love one another, for love comes from God. Anyone who loves is born of God and knows God. ⁸But anyone who does not love does not know God—for God is love.

⁹God showed how much he loved us by sending his only Son into the world so that we might have eternal life through him. ¹⁰This is real love. It is not that we loved God, but that he loved us and sent his Son as a sacrifice to take away our sins.

¹¹Dear friends, since God loved us that much, we surely ought to love each other. ¹²No one has ever seen God. But if we love each other, God lives in us, and his love has been brought to full expression through us.

¹³And God has given us his Spirit as proof that we live in him and he in us. ¹⁴Furthermore, we have seen with our own eyes and now testify that the Father sent his Son to be the Savior of the world. ¹⁵All who proclaim that Jesus is the Son of God have God living in them, and they live in God. ¹⁶We know how much God loves us, and we have put our trust in him.

God is love, and all who live in love live in God, and God lives in them. ¹⁷And as we live in God, our love grows more perfect. So we will not be afraid on the day of judgment, but we can face him with confidence because we are like Christ here in this world.

¹⁸Such love has no fear because perfect love expels all fear. If we are afraid, it is for fear of judgment, and this shows that his love has not been perfected in us. ¹⁹We love each other* as a result of his loving us first.

²⁰If someone says, "I love God," but hates a Christian brother or sister,* that person is a liar; for if we don't love people we can see, how can we love God, whom we have not seen? ²¹And God himself has commanded that we must love not only him but our Christian brothers and sisters, too.

CHAPTER 5

Faith in the Son of God

Everyone who believes that Jesus is the Christ is a child of God. And everyone who loves the Father loves his children, too. ²We know we love God's children if we love God and obey his commandments. ³Loving God means keeping his commandments, and really, that isn't

4:19 Or *We love him;* Greek reads *We love.*   4:20 Greek *brother;* also in 4:21.

difficult. [4]For every child of God defeats this evil world by trusting Christ to give the victory. [5]And the ones who win this battle against the world are the ones who believe that Jesus is the Son of God.

[6]And Jesus Christ was revealed as God's Son by his baptism in water and by shedding his blood on the cross*—not by water only, but by water and blood. And the Spirit also gives us the testimony that this is true. [7]So we have these three witnesses*—[8]the Spirit, the water, and the blood—and all three agree. [9]Since we believe human testimony, surely we can believe the testimony that comes from God. And God has testified about his Son. [10]All who believe in the Son of God know that this is true. Those who don't believe this are actually calling God a liar because they don't believe what God has testified about his Son.

[11]And this is what God has testified: He has given us eternal life, and this life is in his Son. [12]So whoever has God's Son has life; whoever does not have his Son does not have life.

Conclusion

[13]I write this to you who believe in the Son of God, so that you may know you have eternal life. [14]And we can be confident that he will listen to us whenever we ask him for anything in line with his will. [15]And if we know he is listening when we make our requests, we can be sure that he will give us what we ask for.

[16]If you see a Christian brother or sister* sinning in a way that does not lead to death, you should pray, and God will give that person life. But there is a sin that leads to death, and I am not saying you should pray for those who commit it. [17]Every wrong is sin, but not all sin leads to death.

[18]We know that those who have become part of God's family do not make a practice of sinning, for God's Son holds them securely, and the evil one cannot get his hands on them. [19]We know that we are children of God and that the world around us is under the power and control of the evil one. [20]And we know that the Son of God has come, and he has given us understanding so that we can know the true God. And now we are in God because we are in his Son, Jesus Christ. He is the only true God, and he is eternal life.

[21]Dear children, keep away from anything that might take God's place in your hearts.*

5:6 Greek *This is he who came by water and blood.*   5:7 Some very late manuscripts add *in heaven—the Father, the Word, and the Holy Spirit, and these three are one. And we have three witnesses on earth.*   5:16 Greek *your brother.*   5:21 Greek *keep yourselves from idols.*

2 JOHN

Greetings

This letter is from John the Elder.*

It is written to the chosen lady and to her children,* whom I love in the truth, as does everyone else who knows God's

1a Greek *From the elder.*   1b Or *the church God has chosen and her members,* or *the chosen Kyria and her children.*

truth—2 the truth that lives in us and will be in our hearts forever.

3May grace, mercy, and peace, which come from God our Father and from Jesus Christ his Son, be with us who live in truth and love.

Live in the Truth

4How happy I was to meet some of your children and find them living in the truth, just as we have been commanded by the Father.

5And now I want to urge you, dear lady, that we should love one another. This is not a new commandment, but one we had from the beginning. 6Love means doing what God has commanded us, and he has commanded us to love one another, just as you heard from the beginning.

7 Many deceivers have gone out into the world. They do not believe that Jesus Christ came to earth in a real body. Such a person is a deceiver and an antichrist. 8Watch out, so that you do not lose the prize for which we* have been working so hard. Be diligent so that you will receive your full reward. 9For if you wander beyond the teaching of Christ, you will not have fellowship with God. But if you continue in the teaching of Christ, you will have fellowship with both the Father and the Son.

10If someone comes to your meeting and does not teach the truth about Christ, don't invite him into your house or encourage him in any way. 11Anyone who encourages him becomes a partner in his evil work.

Conclusion

12Well, I have much more to say to you, but I don't want to say it in a letter. For I hope to visit you soon and to talk with you face to face. Then our joy will be complete.

13Greetings from the children of your sister,* chosen by God.

8 Some manuscripts read *you.*   13 Or *from the members of your sister church.*

3 JOHN

Greetings

This letter is from John the Elder.*

It is written to Gaius, my dear friend, whom I love in the truth.

2Dear friend, I am praying that all is well with you and that your body is as healthy as I know your soul is. 3Some of the brothers recently returned and made me very happy by telling me about your faithfulness and that you are living in the truth. 4I could have no greater joy than to hear that my children live in the truth.

Caring for the Lord's Workers

5Dear friend, you are doing a good work for God when you take care of the traveling teachers* who are passing through, even though they are strangers to you. 6They have told the church here

1 Greek *From the elder.*   5 Greek *the brothers;* also in verse 10.

of your friendship and your loving deeds. You do well to send them on their way in a manner that pleases God. [7]For they are traveling for the Lord* and accept nothing from those who are not Christians.* [8]So we ourselves should support them so that we may become partners with them for the truth.

[9]I sent a brief letter to the church about this, but Diotrephes, who loves to be the leader, does not acknowledge our authority. [10]When I come, I will report some of the things he is doing and the wicked things he is saying about us. He not only refuses to welcome the traveling teachers, he also tells others not to help them. And when they do help, he puts them out of the church.

[11]Dear friend, don't let this bad example influence you. Follow only what is good. Remember that those who do good prove that they are God's children, and those who do evil prove that they do not know God. [12]But everyone speaks highly of Demetrius, even truth itself. We ourselves can say the same for him, and you know we speak the truth.

Conclusion

[13]I have much to tell you, but I don't want to do it in a letter. [14]I hope to see you soon, and then we will talk face to face.

[15]May God's peace be with you.

Your friends here send you their greetings. Please give my personal greetings to each of our friends there.

7a Greek *the Name.* 7b Greek *from Gentiles.*

JUDE

Greetings from Jude

This letter is from Jude, a slave of Jesus Christ and a brother of James.

I am writing to all who are called to live in the love of God the Father and the care of Jesus Christ.

[2]May you receive more and more of God's mercy, peace, and love.

The Danger of False Teachers

[3]Dearly loved friends, I had been eagerly planning to write to you about the salvation we all share. But now I find that I must write about something else, urging you to defend the truth of the Good News.* God gave this unchanging truth once for all time to his holy people. [4]I say this because some godless people have wormed their way in among you, saying that God's forgiveness allows us to live immoral lives. The fate of such people was determined long ago, for they have turned against our only Master and Lord, Jesus Christ.

[5]I must remind you—and you know it well—that even though the Lord* rescued the whole nation of Israel from Egypt, he later destroyed every one of those who did not remain faithful. [6]And I

3 Greek *to contend for the faith.* 5 Some manuscripts read *Jesus.*

remind you of the angels who did not stay within the limits of authority God gave them but left the place where they belonged. God has kept them chained in prisons of darkness, waiting for the day of judgment. 7 And don't forget the cities of Sodom and Gomorrah and their neighboring towns, which were filled with sexual immorality and every kind of sexual perversion. Those cities were destroyed by fire and are a warning of the eternal fire that will punish all who are evil.

8Yet these false teachers, who claim authority from their dreams, live immoral lives, defy authority, and scoff at the power of the glorious ones.* 9 But even Michael, one of the mightiest of the angels, did not dare accuse Satan of blasphemy, but simply said, "The Lord rebuke you." (This took place when Michael was arguing with Satan about Moses' body.) 10But these people mock and curse the things they do not understand. Like animals, they do whatever their instincts tell them, and they bring about their own destruction. 11How terrible it will be for them! For they follow the evil example of Cain, who killed his brother. Like Balaam, they will do anything for money. And like Korah, they will perish because of their rebellion.

12When these people join you in fellowship meals celebrating the love of the Lord, they are like dangerous reefs that can shipwreck you.* They are shameless in the way they care only about themselves. They are like clouds blowing over dry land without giving rain, promising much but producing nothing. They are like trees without fruit at harvesttime. They are not only dead but doubly dead, for they have been pulled out by the roots. 13They are like wild waves of the sea, churning up the dirty foam of their shameful deeds. They are wandering stars, heading for everlasting gloom and darkness.

14Now Enoch, who lived seven generations after Adam, prophesied about these people. He said,

> "Look, the Lord is coming
>   with thousands of his holy ones.
> 15 He will bring the people of the world
>   to judgment.
> He will convict the ungodly of all the evil things
>   they have done in rebellion
> and of all the insults that godless sinners
>   have spoken against him."*

16These people are grumblers and complainers, doing whatever evil they feel like. They are loudmouthed braggarts, and they flatter others to get favors in return.

A Call to Remain Faithful

17But you, my dear friends, must remember what the apostles of our Lord Jesus Christ told you, 18that in the last times there would be scoffers whose purpose in life is to enjoy themselves in every evil way imaginable. 19Now they are here, and they are the ones who are creating divisions among you. They live by natural instinct because they do not have God's Spirit living in them.

---

8 *The glorious ones* are probably evil angels.   12 Or *they are contaminants among you*, or *they are stains.*   14-15 The quotation comes from the Apocrypha: Enoch 1:9.

20But you, dear friends, must continue to build your lives on the foundation of your holy faith. And continue to pray as you are directed by the Holy Spirit.* 21Live in such a way that God's love can bless you as you wait for the eternal life that our Lord Jesus Christ in his mercy is going to give you. 22Show mercy to those whose faith is wavering. 23Rescue others by snatching them from the flames of judgment. There are still others to whom you need to show mercy, but be careful that you aren't contaminated by their sins.*

A Prayer of Praise

24 And now, all glory to God, who is able to keep you from stumbling, and who will bring you into his glorious presence innocent of sin and with great joy. 25All glory to him, who alone is God our Savior, through Jesus Christ our Lord. Yes, glory, majesty, power, and authority belong to him, in the beginning, now, and forevermore. Amen.

20 Greek *Pray in the Holy Spirit.* **23** Greek *mercy, hating even the clothing stained by the flesh.*

REVELATION

CHAPTER 1

Prologue

This is a revelation from* Jesus Christ, which God gave him concerning the events that will happen soon. An angel was sent to God's servant John so that John could share the revelation with God's other servants. 2John faithfully reported the word of God and the testimony of Jesus Christ—everything he saw.

3God blesses the one who reads this prophecy to the church, and he blesses all who listen to it and obey what it says. For the time is near when these things will happen.

John's Greeting to the Seven Churches

4This letter is from John to the seven churches in the province of Asia. Grace and peace from the one who is, who always was, and who is still to come; from the sevenfold Spirit* before his throne; 5and from Jesus Christ, who is the faithful witness to these things, the first to rise from the dead, and the commander of all the rulers of the world.

All praise to him who loves us and has freed us from our sins by shedding his blood for us. 6He has made us his kingdom and his priests who serve before God his Father. Give to him everlasting glory! He rules forever and ever! Amen!

7Look! He comes with the clouds of heaven. And everyone will see him—even those who pierced him. And all the nations of the earth will weep because of him. Yes! Amen!

8"I am the Alpha and the Omega—the beginning and the end,"

1:1 Or *of.* **1:4** Greek *the seven spirits.*

says the Lord God. "I am the one who is, who always was, and who is still to come, the Almighty One."

Vision of the Son of Man

⁹I am John, your brother. In Jesus we are partners in suffering and in the Kingdom and in patient endurance. I was exiled to the island of Patmos for preaching the word of God and speaking about Jesus. ¹⁰ It was the Lord's Day, and I was worshiping in the Spirit.* Suddenly, I heard a loud voice behind me, a voice that sounded like a trumpet blast. ¹¹It said, "Write down what you see, and send it to the seven churches: Ephesus, Smyrna, Pergamum, Thyatira, Sardis, Philadelphia, and Laodicea."

¹²When I turned to see who was speaking to me, I saw seven gold lampstands. ¹³And standing in the middle of the lampstands was the Son of Man.* He was wearing a long robe with a gold sash across his chest. ¹⁴His head and his hair were white like wool, as white as snow. And his eyes were bright like flames of fire. ¹⁵His feet were as bright as bronze refined in a furnace, and his voice thundered like mighty ocean waves. ¹⁶He held seven stars in his right hand, and a sharp two-edged sword came from his mouth. And his face was as bright as the sun in all its brilliance.

¹⁷When I saw him, I fell at his feet as dead. But he laid his right hand on me and said, "Don't be afraid! I am the First and the Last. ¹⁸I am the living one who died. Look, I am alive forever and ever! And I hold the keys of death and the grave.* ¹⁹Write down what you have seen—both the things that are now happening and the things that will happen later. ²⁰This is the meaning of the seven stars you saw in my right hand and the seven gold lampstands: The seven stars are the angels of* the seven churches, and the seven lampstands are the seven churches.

CHAPTER 2

The Message to the Church in Ephesus

"Write this letter to the angel of* the church in Ephesus. This is the message from the one who holds the seven stars in his right hand, the one who walks among the seven gold lampstands:

²"I know all the things you do. I have seen your hard work and your patient endurance. I know you don't tolerate evil people. You have examined the claims of those who say they are apostles but are not. You have discovered they are liars. ³You have patiently suffered for me without quitting. ⁴But I have this complaint against you. You don't love me or each other as you did at first! ⁵Look how far you have fallen from your first love! Turn back to me again and work as you did at first. If you don't, I will come and remove your lampstand from its place among the churches. ⁶But there is this about you that is good: You hate the deeds of the immoral Nicolaitans, just as I do.

⁷"Anyone who is willing to hear should listen to the Spirit and understand what the Spirit is saying to the churches.

1:10 Or *in spirit.* **1:13** Or *one who looked like a man;* Greek reads *one like a son of man.* See Dan 7:13. **1:18** Greek *and Hades.* **1:20** Or *the messengers for;* also in 2:8, 12, 18. **2:1** Or *The messenger for;* also in 2:8, 12, 18.

Everyone who is victorious will eat from the tree of life in the paradise of God.

The Message to the Church in Smyrna

8"Write this letter to the angel of the church in Smyrna. This is the message from the one who is the First and the Last, who died and is alive:

9"I know about your suffering and your poverty—but you are rich! I know the slander of those opposing you. They say they are Jews, but they really aren't because theirs is a synagogue of Satan. 10Don't be afraid of what you are about to suffer. The Devil will throw some of you into prison and put you to the test. You will be persecuted for 'ten days.' Remain faithful even when facing death, and I will give you the crown of life.

11"Anyone who is willing to hear should listen to the Spirit and understand what the Spirit is saying to the churches. Whoever is victorious will not be hurt by the second death.

The Message to the Church in Pergamum

12"Write this letter to the angel of the church in Pergamum. This is the message from the one who has a sharp two-edged sword:

13"I know that you live in the city where that great throne of Satan is located, and yet you have remained loyal to me. And you refused to deny me even when Antipas, my faithful witness, was martyred among you by Satan's followers. 14And yet I have a few complaints against you. You tolerate some among you who are like Balaam, who showed Balak how to trip up the people of Israel. He taught them to worship idols by eating food offered to idols and by committing sexual sin. 15In the same way, you have some Nicolaitans among you—people who follow the same teaching and commit the same sins. 16Repent, or I will come to you suddenly and fight against them with the sword of my mouth.

17"Anyone who is willing to hear should listen to the Spirit and understand what the Spirit is saying to the churches. Everyone who is victorious will eat of the manna that has been hidden away in heaven. And I will give to each one a white stone, and on the stone will be engraved a new name that no one knows except the one who receives it.

The Message to the Church in Thyatira

18"Write this letter to the angel of the church in Thyatira. This is the message from the Son of God, whose eyes are bright like flames of fire, whose feet are like polished bronze:

19"I know all the things you do—your love, your faith, your service, and your patient endurance. And I can see your constant improvement in all these things. 20But I have this complaint against you. You are permitting that woman—that Jezebel who calls herself a prophet—to lead my servants astray. She is encouraging them to worship idols, eat food offered to idols, and commit sexual sin. 21I gave her time to repent, but she would not turn away from her immorality. 22Therefore, I will throw her upon a sickbed, and she will suffer greatly with all who commit adultery with her, unless they turn away from all their evil deeds. 23I will strike her children dead. And all the churches will know that I am the one who searches out the thoughts and intentions of every person. And I will give to each of you whatever you deserve. 24But I also have a message for the rest of you in Thyatira who have not followed this false teaching ('deeper truths,' as they call them—depths of Satan, really). I will ask nothing more of you 25except that you hold tightly to what you have until I come.

26"To all who are victorious, who obey me to the very end, I will give authority over all the nations. 27They will rule the nations with an iron rod and smash them like clay pots. 28They will have the same authority I received from my Father, and I will also give them the morning star! 29Anyone who is willing to hear should listen to the Spirit and understand what the Spirit is saying to the churches.

CHAPTER 3

The Message to the Church in Sardis

"Write this letter to the angel of* the church in Sardis. This is the message from the one who has the sevenfold Spirit* of God and the seven stars:

"I know all the things you do, and that you have a reputation for being alive—but you are dead. 2Now wake up! Strengthen what little remains, for even what is left is at the point of death. Your deeds are far from right in the sight of God. 3Go back to what you heard and believed at first; hold to it firmly and turn to me again. Unless you do, I will come upon you suddenly, as unexpected as a thief.

4"Yet even in Sardis there are some who have not soiled their garments with evil deeds. They will walk with me in white, for they are worthy. 5All who are victorious will be clothed in white. I will never erase their names from the Book of Life, but I will announce before my Father and his angels that they are mine. 6Anyone who is willing to hear should listen to the Spirit and understand what the Spirit is saying to the churches.

The Message to the Church in Philadelphia

7"Write this letter to the angel of the church in Philadelphia. This is the message from the one who is holy and true. He is the one who has the key of David. He opens doors, and no one can shut them; he shuts doors, and no one can open them.

8"I know all the things you do, and I have opened a door for you that no one can shut. You have little strength, yet you obeyed my word and did not deny me. 9Look! I will force those who belong to Satan—those liars who say they are Jews but are not—to come and bow down at your feet. They will acknowledge that you are the ones I love.

10"Because you have obeyed my command to persevere, I will protect you from the great time of testing that will come

3:1a Or the messenger for; also in 3:7, 14.   3:1b Greek the seven spirits.

upon the whole world to test those who belong to this world.
11Look, I am coming quickly. Hold on to what you have, so
that no one will take away your crown. 12All who are
victorious will become pillars in the Temple of my God, and
they will never have to leave it. And I will write my God's
name on them, and they will be citizens in the city of my
God—the new Jerusalem that comes down from heaven from
my God. And they will have my new name inscribed upon
them. 13Anyone who is willing to hear should listen to the
Spirit and understand what the Spirit is saying to the churches.

The Message to the Church in Laodicea
14"Write this letter to the angel of the church in Laodicea. This is
the message from the one who is the Amen—the faithful and true
witness, the ruler* of God's creation:

15"I know all the things you do, that you are neither hot nor
cold. I wish you were one or the other! 16But since you are like
lukewarm water, I will spit you out of my mouth! 17You say, 'I
am rich. I have everything I want. I don't need a thing!' And
you don't realize that you are wretched and miserable and
poor and blind and naked. 18I advise you to buy gold from
me—gold that has been purified by fire. Then you will be
rich. And also buy white garments so you will not be shamed
by your nakedness. And buy ointment for your eyes so you
will be able to see. 19I am the one who corrects and disciplines
everyone I love. Be diligent and turn from your indifference.

20"Look! Here I stand at the door and knock. If you hear
me calling and open the door, I will come in, and we will
share a meal as friends. 21I will invite everyone who is
victorious to sit with me on my throne, just as I was victorious
and sat with my Father on his throne. 22Anyone who is willing
to hear should listen to the Spirit and understand what the
Spirit is saying to the churches."

CHAPTER 4
Worship in Heaven
Then as I looked, I saw a door standing open in heaven, and the
same voice I had heard before spoke to me with the sound of a
mighty trumpet blast. The voice said, "Come up here, and I will
show you what must happen after these things." 2And instantly I
was in the Spirit,* and I saw a throne in heaven and someone
sitting on it! 3The one sitting on the throne was as brilliant as
gemstones—jasper and carnelian. And the glow of an emerald
circled his throne like a rainbow. 4Twenty-four thrones surrounded
him, and twenty-four elders sat on them. They were all clothed in
white and had gold crowns on their heads. 5And from the center
came flashes of lightning and the rumble of thunder. And in front
of the throne were seven lampstands with burning flames. They are
the seven spirits* of God. 6In front of the throne was a shiny sea
of glass, sparkling like crystal.

In the center and around the throne were four living beings, each
covered with eyes, front and back. 7The first of these living beings

3:14 Or *the source.* 4:2 Or *in spirit.* 4:5 See 1:4 and 3:1, where the same expression is
translated *the sevenfold Spirit.*

had the form of a lion; the second looked like an ox; the third had a human face; and the fourth had the form of an eagle with wings spread out as though in flight. [8]Each of these living beings had six wings, and their wings were covered with eyes, inside and out. Day after day and night after night they keep on saying,

"Holy, holy, holy is the Lord God Almighty—
the one who always was, who is, and who is still to come."

[9]Whenever the living beings give glory and honor and thanks to the one sitting on the throne, the one who lives forever and ever, [10]the twenty-four elders fall down and worship the one who lives forever and ever. And they lay their crowns before the throne and say,

[11] "You are worthy, O Lord our God,
to receive glory and honor and power.
For you created everything,
and it is for your pleasure that they exist and were created."

CHAPTER 5

The Lamb Opens the Scroll

And I saw a scroll in the right hand of the one who was sitting on the throne. There was writing on the inside and the outside of the scroll, and it was sealed with seven seals. [2]And I saw a strong angel, who shouted with a loud voice: "Who is worthy to break the seals on this scroll and unroll it?" [3]But no one in heaven or on earth or under the earth was able to open the scroll and read it.

[4]Then I wept because no one could be found who was worthy to open the scroll and read it. [5]But one of the twenty-four elders said to me, "Stop weeping! Look, the Lion of the tribe of Judah, the heir to David's throne,* has conquered. He is worthy to open the scroll and break its seven seals."

[6]I looked and I saw a Lamb that had been killed but was now standing between the throne and the four living beings and among the twenty-four elders. He had seven horns and seven eyes, which are the seven spirits* of God that are sent out into every part of the earth. [7]He stepped forward and took the scroll from the right hand of the one sitting on the throne. [8]And as he took the scroll, the four living beings and the twenty-four elders fell down before the Lamb. Each one had a harp, and they held gold bowls filled with incense—the prayers of God's people!

[9]And they sang a new song with these words:

"You are worthy to take the scroll
and break its seals and open it.
For you were killed, and your blood has ransomed people for God
from every tribe and language and people and nation.
[10] And you have caused them to become God's kingdom and his priests.
And they will reign* on the earth."

[11]Then I looked again, and I heard the singing of thousands and

5:5 Greek *the root of David.* 5:6 See note on 4:5. 5:10 Some manuscripts read *they are reigning.*

millions of angels around the throne and the living beings and the elders. [12]And they sang in a mighty chorus:

> "The Lamb is worthy—the Lamb who was killed.
> He is worthy to receive power and riches
> and wisdom and strength
> and honor and glory and blessing."

[13]And then I heard every creature in heaven and on earth and under the earth and in the sea. They also sang:

> "Blessing and honor and glory and power
> belong to the one sitting on the throne
> and to the Lamb forever and ever."

[14]And the four living beings said, "Amen!" And the twenty-four elders fell down and worshiped God and the Lamb.

CHAPTER 6

The Lamb Breaks the First Six Seals

As I watched, the Lamb broke the first of the seven seals on the scroll. Then one of the four living beings called out with a voice that sounded like thunder, "Come!" [2]I looked up and saw a white horse. Its rider carried a bow, and a crown was placed on his head. He rode out to win many battles and gain the victory.

[3]When the Lamb broke the second seal, I heard the second living being say, "Come!" [4]And another horse appeared, a red one. Its rider was given a mighty sword and the authority to remove peace from the earth. And there was war and slaughter everywhere.

[5]When the Lamb broke the third seal, I heard the third living being say, "Come!" And I looked up and saw a black horse, and its rider was holding a pair of scales in his hand. [6]And a voice from among the four living beings said, "A loaf of wheat bread or three loaves of barley for a day's pay.* And don't waste* the olive oil and wine."

[7]And when the Lamb broke the fourth seal, I heard the fourth living being say, "Come!" [8]I looked up and saw a horse whose color was pale green like a corpse. And Death was the name of its rider, who was followed around by the Grave.* They were given authority over one-fourth of the earth, to kill with the sword and famine and disease* and wild animals.

[9]And when the Lamb broke the fifth seal, I saw under the altar the souls of all who had been martyred for the word of God and for being faithful in their witness. [10]They called loudly to the Lord and said, "O Sovereign Lord, holy and true, how long will it be before you judge the people who belong to this world for what they have done to us? When will you avenge our blood against these people?" [11]Then a white robe was given to each of them. And they were told to rest a little longer until the full number of their brothers and sisters*—their fellow servants of Jesus—had been martyred.

[12]I watched as the Lamb broke the sixth seal, and there was a great earthquake. The sun became as dark as black cloth, and the moon became as red as blood. [13]Then the stars of the sky fell to the earth like green figs falling from trees shaken by mighty winds.

6:6a Greek *A choinix of wheat for a denarius, and 3 choinix of barley for a denarius.* 6:6b Or *hurt.* 6:8a Greek *by Hades.* 6:8b Greek *death.* 6:11 Greek *their brothers.*

¹⁴And the sky was rolled up like a scroll and taken away. And all of the mountains and all of the islands disappeared. ¹⁵Then the kings of the earth, the rulers, the generals, the wealthy people, the people with great power, and every slave and every free person—all hid themselves in the caves and among the rocks of the mountains. ¹⁶And they cried to the mountains and the rocks, "Fall on us and hide us from the face of the one who sits on the throne and from the wrath of the Lamb. ¹⁷For the great day of their wrath has come, and who will be able to survive?"

CHAPTER 7

God's People Will Be Preserved

Then I saw four angels standing at the four corners of the earth, holding back the four winds from blowing upon the earth. Not a leaf rustled in the trees, and the sea became as smooth as glass. ²And I saw another angel coming from the east, carrying the seal of the living God. And he shouted out to those four angels who had been given power to injure land and sea, ³"Wait! Don't hurt the land or the sea or the trees until we have placed the seal of God on the foreheads of his servants."

⁴And I heard how many were marked with the seal of God. There were 144,000 who were sealed from all the tribes of Israel:

⁵ from Judah	12,000
from Reuben	12,000
from Gad	12,000
⁶ from Asher	12,000
from Naphtali	12,000
from Manasseh	12,000
⁷ from Simeon	12,000
from Levi	12,000
from Issachar	12,000
⁸ from Zebulun	12,000
from Joseph	12,000
from Benjamin	12,000

Praise from the Great Multitude

⁹After this I saw a vast crowd, too great to count, from every nation and tribe and people and language, standing in front of the throne and before the Lamb. They were clothed in white and held palm branches in their hands. ¹⁰And they were shouting with a mighty shout, "Salvation comes from our God on the throne and from the Lamb!"

¹¹ And all the angels were standing around the throne and around the elders and the four living beings. And they fell face down before the throne and worshiped God. ¹²They said,

"Amen! Blessing and glory and wisdom
    and thanksgiving and honor and power and strength
        belong to our God forever and forever. Amen!"

¹³Then one of the twenty-four elders asked me, "Who are these who are clothed in white? Where do they come from?"

¹⁴And I said to him, "Sir, you are the one who knows."

Then he said to me, "These are the ones coming out of the great tribulation. They washed their robes in the blood of the Lamb and made them white. 15That is why they are standing in front of the throne of God, serving him day and night in his Temple. And he who sits on the throne will live among them and shelter them. 16They will never again be hungry or thirsty, and they will be fully protected from the scorching noontime heat. 17For the Lamb who stands in front of the throne will be their Shepherd. He will lead them to the springs of life-giving water. And God will wipe away all their tears."

CHAPTER 8

The Lamb Breaks the Seventh Seal

When the Lamb broke the seventh seal, there was silence throughout heaven for about half an hour. 2And I saw the seven angels who stand before God, and they were given seven trumpets.

3Then another angel with a gold incense burner came and stood at the altar. And a great quantity of incense was given to him to mix with the prayers of God's people, to be offered on the gold altar before the throne. 4The smoke of the incense, mixed with the prayers of the saints, ascended up to God from the altar where the angel had poured them out. 5Then the angel filled the incense burner with fire from the altar and threw it down upon the earth; and thunder crashed, lightning flashed, and there was a terrible earthquake.

The First Four Trumpets

6Then the seven angels with the seven trumpets prepared to blow their mighty blasts.

7The first angel blew his trumpet, and hail and fire mixed with blood were thrown down upon the earth, and one-third of the earth was set on fire. One-third of the trees were burned, and all the grass was burned.

8Then the second angel blew his trumpet, and a great mountain of fire was thrown into the sea. And one-third of the water in the sea became blood. 9And one-third of all things living in the sea died. And one-third of all the ships on the sea were destroyed.

10Then the third angel blew his trumpet, and a great flaming star fell out of the sky, burning like a torch. It fell upon one-third of the rivers and on the springs of water. 11 The name of the star was Bitterness.* It made one-third of the water bitter, and many people died because the water was so bitter.

12Then the fourth angel blew his trumpet, and one-third of the sun was struck, and one-third of the moon, and one-third of the stars, and they became dark. And one-third of the day was dark and one-third of the night also.

13Then I looked up. And I heard a single eagle crying loudly as it flew through the air, "Terror, terror, terror to all who belong to this world because of what will happen when the last three angels blow their trumpets."

CHAPTER 9

The Fifth Trumpet Brings the First Terror

Then the fifth angel blew his trumpet, and I saw a star that had fallen to earth from the sky, and he was given the key to the shaft

8:11 Greek *Wormwood.*

of the bottomless pit. ²When he opened it, smoke poured out as though from a huge furnace, and the sunlight and air were darkened by the smoke.

³Then locusts came from the smoke and descended on the earth, and they were given power to sting like scorpions. ⁴They were told not to hurt the grass or plants or trees but to attack all the people who did not have the seal of God on their foreheads. ⁵They were told not to kill them but to torture them for five months with agony like the pain of scorpion stings. ⁶In those days people will seek death but will not find it. They will long to die, but death will flee away!

⁷The locusts looked like horses armed for battle. They had gold crowns on their heads, and they had human faces. ⁸Their hair was long like the hair of a woman, and their teeth were like the teeth of a lion. ⁹They wore armor made of iron, and their wings roared like an army of chariots rushing into battle. ¹⁰They had tails that stung like scorpions, with power to torture people. This power was given to them for five months. ¹¹Their king is the angel from the bottomless pit; his name in Hebrew is *Abaddon*, and in Greek, *Apollyon*—the Destroyer.

¹²The first terror is past, but look, two more terrors are coming!

The Sixth Trumpet Brings the Second Terror

¹³Then the sixth angel blew his trumpet, and I heard a voice speaking from the four horns of the gold altar that stands in the presence of God. ¹⁴And the voice spoke to the sixth angel who held the trumpet: "Release the four angels who are bound at the great Euphrates River." ¹⁵And the four angels who had been prepared for this hour and day and month and year were turned loose to kill one-third of all the people on earth. ¹⁶They led an army of 200 million mounted troops—I heard an announcement of how many there were.

¹⁷And in my vision, I saw the horses and the riders sitting on them. The riders wore armor that was fiery red and sky blue and yellow. The horses' heads were like the heads of lions, and fire and smoke and burning sulfur billowed from their mouths. ¹⁸One-third of all the people on earth were killed by these three plagues—by the fire and the smoke and burning sulfur that came from the mouths of the horses. ¹⁹Their power was in their mouths, but also in their tails. For their tails had heads like snakes, with the power to injure people.

²⁰But the people who did not die in these plagues still refused to turn from their evil deeds. They continued to worship demons and idols made of gold, silver, bronze, stone, and wood—idols that neither see nor hear nor walk! ²¹And they did not repent of their murders or their witchcraft or their immorality or their thefts.

CHAPTER 10

The Angel and the Small Scroll

Then I saw another mighty angel coming down from heaven, surrounded by a cloud, with a rainbow over his head. His face shone like the sun, and his feet were like pillars of fire. ²And in his hand was a small scroll, which he had unrolled. He stood with his right foot on the sea and his left foot on the land. ³And he gave a great shout, like the roar of a lion. And when he shouted, the seven thunders answered.

⁴When the seven thunders spoke, I was about to write. But a voice from heaven called to me: "Keep secret what the seven thunders said. Do not write it down."

⁵Then the mighty angel standing on the sea and on the land lifted his right hand to heaven. ⁶And he swore an oath in the name of the one who lives forever and ever, who created heaven and everything in it, the earth and everything in it, and the sea and everything in it. He said, "God will wait no longer. ⁷But when the seventh angel blows his trumpet, God's mysterious plan will be fulfilled. It will happen just as he announced it to his servants the prophets."

⁸Then the voice from heaven called to me again: "Go and take the unrolled scroll from the angel who is standing on the sea and on the land."

⁹So I approached him and asked him to give me the little scroll. "Yes, take it and eat it," he said. "At first it will taste like honey, but when you swallow it, it will make your stomach sour!" ¹⁰So I took the little scroll from the hands of the angel, and I ate it! It was sweet in my mouth, but it made my stomach sour. ¹¹Then he said to me, "You must prophesy again about many peoples, nations, languages, and kings."

CHAPTER 11

The Two Witnesses

Then I was given a measuring stick, and I was told, "Go and measure the Temple of God and the altar, and count the number of worshipers. ²But do not measure the outer courtyard, for it has been turned over to the nations. They will trample the holy city for 42 months. ³And I will give power to my two witnesses, and they will be clothed in sackcloth and will prophesy during those 1,260 days."

⁴ These two prophets are the two olive trees and the two lampstands that stand before the Lord of all the earth. ⁵If anyone tries to harm them, fire flashes from the mouths of the prophets and consumes their enemies. This is how anyone who tries to harm them must die. ⁶They have power to shut the skies so that no rain will fall for as long as they prophesy. And they have the power to turn the rivers and oceans into blood, and to send every kind of plague upon the earth as often as they wish.

⁷When they complete their testimony, the beast that comes up out of the bottomless pit will declare war against them. He will conquer them and kill them. ⁸And their bodies will lie in the main street of Jerusalem,* the city which is called "Sodom" and "Egypt," the city where their Lord was crucified. ⁹And for three and a half days, all peoples, tribes, languages, and nations will come to stare at their bodies. No one will be allowed to bury them. ¹⁰All the people who belong to this world will give presents to each other to celebrate the death of the two prophets who had tormented them.

¹¹ But after three and a half days, the spirit of life from God entered them, and they stood up! And terror struck all who were

11:8 Greek *the great city.*

staring at them. 12Then a loud voice shouted from heaven, "Come up here!" And they rose to heaven in a cloud as their enemies watched.

13And in the same hour there was a terrible earthquake that destroyed a tenth of the city. Seven thousand people died in that earthquake. And everyone who did not die was terrified and gave glory to the God of heaven.

14The second terror is past, but look, now the third terror is coming quickly.

The Seventh Trumpet Brings the Third Terror

15Then the seventh angel blew his trumpet, and there were loud voices shouting in heaven: "The whole world has now become the kingdom of our Lord and of his Christ, and he will reign forever and ever."

16And the twenty-four elders sitting on their thrones before God fell on their faces and worshiped him. 17And they said,

"We give thanks to you, Lord God Almighty,
    the one who is and who always was,
for now you have assumed your great power
    and have begun to reign.
18 The nations were angry with you,
    but now the time of your wrath has come.
It is time to judge the dead and reward your servants.
You will reward your prophets and your holy people,
    all who fear your name, from the least to the greatest.
And you will destroy all who have caused destruction on the
    earth."

19Then, in heaven, the Temple of God was opened and the Ark of his covenant could be seen inside the Temple. Lightning flashed, thunder crashed and roared; there was a great hailstorm, and the world was shaken by a mighty earthquake.

CHAPTER 12

The Woman and the Dragon

Then I witnessed in heaven an event of great significance. I saw a woman clothed with the sun, with the moon beneath her feet, and a crown of twelve stars on her head. 2She was pregnant, and she cried out in the pain of labor as she awaited her delivery.

3Suddenly, I witnessed in heaven another significant event. I saw a large red dragon with seven heads and ten horns, with seven crowns on his heads. 4His tail dragged down one-third of the stars, which he threw to the earth. He stood before the woman as she was about to give birth to her child, ready to devour the baby as soon as it was born.

5She gave birth to a boy who was to rule all nations with an iron rod. And the child was snatched away from the dragon and was caught up to God and to his throne. 6And the woman fled into the wilderness, where God had prepared a place to give her care for 1,260 days.

7Then there was war in heaven. Michael and the angels under his command fought the dragon and his angels. 8And the dragon lost the battle and was forced out of heaven. 9This great dragon—

the ancient serpent called the Devil, or Satan, the one deceiving the whole world—was thrown down to the earth with all his angels. ¹⁰Then I heard a loud voice shouting across the heavens,

"It has happened at last—the salvation and power and kingdom of our God, and the authority of his Christ! For the Accuser has been thrown down to earth—the one who accused our brothers and sisters* before our God day and night. ¹¹And they have defeated him because of the blood of the Lamb and because of their testimony. And they were not afraid to die. ¹²Rejoice, O heavens! And you who live in the heavens, rejoice! But terror will come on the earth and the sea. For the Devil has come down to you in great anger, and he knows that he has little time."

¹³And when the dragon realized that he had been thrown down to the earth, he pursued the woman who had given birth to the child. ¹⁴But she was given two wings like those of a great eagle. This allowed her to fly to a place prepared for her in the wilderness, where she would be cared for and protected from the dragon* for a time, times, and half a time.

¹⁵Then the dragon tried to drown the woman with a flood of water that flowed from its mouth. ¹⁶But the earth helped her by opening its mouth and swallowing the river that gushed out from the mouth of the dragon. ¹⁷Then the dragon became angry at the woman, and he declared war against the rest of her children—all who keep God's commandments and confess that they belong to Jesus.

The Beast out of the Sea
¹⁸Then he stood* waiting on the shore of the sea.

CHAPTER 13

And now in my vision I saw a beast rising up out of the sea. It had seven heads and ten horns, with ten crowns on its horns. And written on each head were names that blasphemed God. ²This beast looked like a leopard, but it had bear's feet and a lion's mouth! And the dragon gave him his own power and throne and great authority.

³I saw that one of the heads of the beast seemed wounded beyond recovery—but the fatal wound was healed! All the world marveled at this miracle and followed the beast in awe. ⁴They worshiped the dragon for giving the beast such power, and they worshiped the beast. "Is there anyone as great as the beast?" they exclaimed. "Who is able to fight against him?"

⁵Then the beast was allowed to speak great blasphemies against God. And he was given authority to do what he wanted for forty-two months. ⁶And he spoke terrible words of blasphemy against God, slandering his name and all who live in heaven, who are his temple. ⁷And the beast was allowed to wage war against God's holy people and to overcome them. And he was given authority to rule over every tribe and people and language and nation. ⁸And all the people who belong to this world worshiped the beast. They are the ones whose names were not written in the

---

12:10 Greek *brothers.* **12:14** Greek *the serpent;* also in 12:15. See 12:9. **12:18** Some manuscripts read *Then I stood,* and some translations put this entire sentence into 13:1.

Book of Life, which belongs to the Lamb who was killed before the world was made.

⁹Anyone who is willing to hear should listen and understand. ¹⁰The people who are destined for prison will be arrested and taken away. Those who are destined for death will be killed. But do not be dismayed, for here is your opportunity to have endurance and faith.

The Beast out of the Earth

¹¹Then I saw another beast come up out of the earth. He had two horns like those of a lamb, and he spoke with the voice of a dragon. ¹²He exercised all the authority of the first beast. And he required all the earth and those who belong to this world to worship the first beast, whose death-wound had been healed. ¹³He did astounding miracles, such as making fire flash down to earth from heaven while everyone was watching. ¹⁴And with all the miracles he was allowed to perform on behalf of the first beast, he deceived all the people who belong to this world. He ordered the people of the world to make a great statue of the first beast, who was fatally wounded and then came back to life. ¹⁵He was permitted to give life to this statue so that it could speak. Then the statue commanded that anyone refusing to worship it must die.

¹⁶He required everyone—great and small, rich and poor, slave and free—to be given a mark on the right hand or on the forehead. ¹⁷And no one could buy or sell anything without that mark, which was either the name of the beast or the number representing his name. ¹⁸Wisdom is needed to understand this. Let the one who has understanding solve the number of the beast, for it is the number of a man.* His number is 666.*

CHAPTER 14

The Lamb and the 144,000

Then I saw the Lamb standing on Mount Zion, and with him were 144,000 who had his name and his Father's name written on their foreheads. ²And I heard a sound from heaven like the roaring of a great waterfall or the rolling of mighty thunder. It was like the sound of many harpists playing together.

³This great choir sang a wonderful new song in front of the throne of God and before the four living beings and the twenty-four elders. And no one could learn this song except those 144,000 who had been redeemed from the earth. ⁴For they are spiritually undefiled, pure as virgins,* following the Lamb wherever he goes. They have been purchased from among the people on the earth as a special offering* to God and to the Lamb. ⁵No falsehood can be charged against them; they are blameless.

The Three Angels

⁶And I saw another angel flying through the heavens, carrying the everlasting Good News to preach to the people who belong to this world—to every nation, tribe, language, and people. ⁷"Fear God," he shouted. "Give glory to him. For the time has come when he will sit as judge. Worship him who made heaven and earth, the sea, and all the springs of water."

⁸Then another angel followed him through the skies, shouting,

13:18a Or *of humanity.*   13:18b Some manuscripts read *616.*   14:4a Greek *they are virgins who have not defiled themselves with women.*   14:4b Greek *as firstfruits.*

"Babylon is fallen—that great city is fallen—because she seduced the nations of the world and made them drink the wine of her passionate immorality."

9 Then a third angel followed them, shouting, "Anyone who worships the beast and his statue or who accepts his mark on the forehead or the hand 10 must drink the wine of God's wrath. It is poured out undiluted into God's cup of wrath. And they will be tormented with fire and burning sulfur in the presence of the holy angels and the Lamb. 11 The smoke of their torment rises forever and ever, and they will have no relief day or night, for they have worshiped the beast and his statue and have accepted the mark of his name. 12 Let this encourage God's holy people to endure persecution patiently and remain firm to the end, obeying his commands and trusting in Jesus."

13 And I heard a voice from heaven saying, "Write this down: Blessed are those who die in the Lord from now on. Yes, says the Spirit, they are blessed indeed, for they will rest from all their toils and trials; for their good deeds follow them!"

The Harvest of the Earth

14 Then I saw the Son of Man* sitting on a white cloud. He had a gold crown on his head and a sharp sickle in his hand.

15 Then an angel came from the Temple and called out in a loud voice to the one sitting on the cloud, "Use the sickle, for the time has come for you to harvest; the crop is ripe on the earth." 16 So the one sitting on the cloud swung his sickle over the earth, and the whole earth was harvested.

17 After that, another angel came from the Temple in heaven, and he also had a sharp sickle. 18 Then another angel, who has power to destroy the world with fire, shouted to the angel with the sickle, "Use your sickle now to gather the clusters of grapes from the vines of the earth, for they are fully ripe for judgment." 19 So the angel swung his sickle on the earth and loaded the grapes into the great winepress of God's wrath. 20 And the grapes were trodden in the winepress outside the city, and blood flowed from the winepress in a stream about 180 miles* long and as high as a horse's bridle.

CHAPTER 15

The Song of Moses and of the Lamb

Then I saw in heaven another significant event, and it was great and marvelous. Seven angels were holding the seven last plagues, which would bring God's wrath to completion. 2 I saw before me what seemed to be a crystal sea mixed with fire. And on it stood all the people who had been victorious over the beast and his statue and the number representing his name. They were all holding harps that God had given them. 3 And they were singing the song of Moses, the servant of God, and the song of the Lamb:

"Great and marvelous are your actions,
    Lord God Almighty.
Just and true are your ways,
    O King of the nations.*

14:14 Or *one who looked like a man;* Greek reads *one like a son of man.*   **14:20** Greek *1,600 stadia* [296 kilometers].   **15:3** Some manuscripts read *King of the ages;* other manuscripts read *King of the saints.*

⁴ Who will not fear, O Lord, and glorify your name?
    For you alone are holy.
  All nations will come and worship before you,
    for your righteous deeds have been revealed."

The Seven Bowls of the Seven Plagues

⁵Then I looked and saw that the Temple in heaven, God's Tabernacle, was thrown wide open! ⁶The seven angels who were holding the bowls of the seven plagues came from the Temple, clothed in spotless white linen* with gold belts across their chests. ⁷And one of the four living beings handed each of the seven angels a gold bowl filled with the terrible wrath of God, who lives forever and forever. ⁸The Temple was filled with smoke from God's glory and power. No one could enter the Temple until the seven angels had completed pouring out the seven plagues.

CHAPTER 16

Then I heard a mighty voice shouting from the Temple to the seven angels, "Now go your ways and empty out the seven bowls of God's wrath on the earth."

²So the first angel left the Temple and poured out his bowl over the earth, and horrible, malignant sores broke out on everyone who had the mark of the beast and who worshiped his statue.

³Then the second angel poured out his bowl on the sea, and it became like the blood of a corpse. And everything in the sea died.

⁴Then the third angel poured out his bowl on the rivers and springs, and they became blood. ⁵And I heard the angel who had authority over all water saying, "You are just in sending this judgment, O Holy One, who is and who always was. ⁶For your holy people and your prophets have been killed, and their blood was poured out on the earth. So you have given their murderers blood to drink. It is their just reward." ⁷And I heard a voice from the altar saying, "Yes, Lord God Almighty, your punishments are true and just."

⁸Then the fourth angel poured out his bowl on the sun, causing it to scorch everyone with its fire. ⁹Everyone was burned by this blast of heat, and they cursed the name of God, who sent all of these plagues. They did not repent and give him glory.

¹⁰Then the fifth angel poured out his bowl on the throne of the beast, and his kingdom was plunged into darkness. And his subjects ground their teeth in anguish, ¹¹and they cursed the God of heaven for their pains and sores. But they refused to repent of all their evil deeds.

¹²Then the sixth angel poured out his bowl on the great Euphrates River, and it dried up so that the kings from the east could march their armies westward without hindrance. ¹³And I saw three evil spirits that looked like frogs leap from the mouth of the dragon, the beast, and the false prophet. ¹⁴These miracle-working demons caused all the rulers of the world to gather for battle against the Lord on that great judgment day of God Almighty.

15:6 Some manuscripts read *in bright and sparkling stone.*

15 "Take note: I will come as unexpectedly as a thief! Blessed are all who are watching for me, who keep their robes ready so they will not need to walk naked and ashamed."

16 And they gathered all the rulers and their armies to a place called *Armageddon* in Hebrew.

17 Then the seventh angel poured out his bowl into the air. And a mighty shout came from the throne of the Temple in heaven, saying, "It is finished!" 18 Then the thunder crashed and rolled, and lightning flashed. And there was an earthquake greater than ever before in human history. 19 The great city of Babylon split into three pieces, and cities around the world fell into heaps of rubble. And so God remembered all of Babylon's sins, and he made her drink the cup that was filled with the wine of his fierce wrath. 20 And every island disappeared, and all the mountains were leveled. 21 There was a terrible hailstorm, and hailstones weighing seventy-five pounds* fell from the sky onto the people below. They cursed God because of the hailstorm, which was a very terrible plague.

CHAPTER 17

The Great Prostitute

One of the seven angels who had poured out the seven bowls came over and spoke to me. "Come with me," he said, "and I will show you the judgment that is going to come on the great prostitute, who sits on many waters. 2 The rulers of the world have had immoral relations with her, and the people who belong to this world have been made drunk by the wine of her immorality."

3 So the angel took me in spirit* into the wilderness. There I saw a woman sitting on a scarlet beast that had seven heads and ten horns, written all over with blasphemies against God. 4 The woman wore purple and scarlet clothing and beautiful jewelry made of gold and precious gems and pearls. She held in her hand a gold goblet full of obscenities and the impurities of her immorality. 5 A mysterious name was written on her forehead: "Babylon the Great, Mother of All Prostitutes and Obscenities in the World." 6 I could see that she was drunk—drunk with the blood of God's holy people who were witnesses for Jesus. I stared at her completely amazed.

7 "Why are you so amazed?" the angel asked. "I will tell you the mystery of this woman and of the beast with seven heads and ten horns. 8 The beast you saw was alive but isn't now. And yet he will soon come up out of the bottomless pit and go to eternal destruction. And the people who belong to this world, whose names were not written in the Book of Life from before the world began, will be amazed at the reappearance of this beast who had died.

9 "And now understand this: The seven heads of the beast represent the seven hills of the city where this woman rules. They also represent seven kings. 10 Five kings have already fallen, the sixth now reigns, and the seventh is yet to come; but his reign will be brief. 11 The scarlet beast that was alive and then died is the eighth king. He is like the other seven, and he, too, will go to his doom. 12 His ten horns are ten kings who have not yet risen to

16:21 Greek *1 talent* [34 kilograms].   17:3 Or *in the Spirit.*

power; they will be appointed to their kingdoms for one brief moment to reign with the beast. [13]They will all agree to give their power and authority to him. [14]Together they will wage war against the Lamb, but the Lamb will defeat them because he is Lord over all lords and King over all kings, and his people are the called and chosen and faithful ones."

[15]And the angel said to me, "The waters where the prostitute is sitting represent masses of people of every nation and language. [16]The scarlet beast and his ten horns—which represent ten kings who will reign with him—all hate the prostitute. They will strip her naked, eat her flesh, and burn her remains with fire. [17]For God has put a plan into their minds, a plan that will carry out his purposes. They will mutually agree to give their authority to the scarlet beast, and so the words of God will be fulfilled. [18]And this woman you saw in your vision represents the great city that rules over the kings of the earth."

CHAPTER 18

The Fall of Babylon

After all this I saw another angel come down from heaven with great authority, and the earth grew bright with his splendor. [2]He gave a mighty shout, "Babylon is fallen—that great city is fallen! She has become the hideout of demons and evil spirits, a nest for filthy buzzards, and a den for dreadful beasts. [3]For all the nations have drunk the wine of her passionate immorality. The rulers of the world have committed adultery with her, and merchants throughout the world have grown rich as a result of her luxurious living."

[4]Then I heard another voice calling from heaven, "Come away from her, my people. Do not take part in her sins, or you will be punished with her. [5]For her sins are piled as high as heaven, and God is ready to judge her for her evil deeds. [6]Do to her as she has done to your people. Give her a double penalty for all her evil deeds. She brewed a cup of terror for others, so give her twice as much as she gave out. [7]She has lived in luxury and pleasure, so match it now with torments and sorrows. She boasts, 'I am queen on my throne. I am no helpless widow. I will not experience sorrow.' [8]Therefore, the sorrows of death and mourning and famine will overtake her in a single day. She will be utterly consumed by fire, for the Lord God who judges her is mighty.

[9]And the rulers of the world who took part in her immoral acts and enjoyed her great luxury will mourn for her as they see the smoke rising from her charred remains. [10]They will stand at a distance, terrified by her great torment. They will cry out, "How terrible, how terrible for Babylon, that great city! In one single moment God's judgment came on her."

[11]The merchants of the world will weep and mourn for her, for there is no one left to buy their goods. [12]She bought great quantities of gold, silver, jewels, pearls, fine linen, purple dye, silk, scarlet cloth, every kind of perfumed wood, ivory goods, objects made of expensive wood, bronze, iron, and marble. [13] She also bought cinnamon, spice, incense, myrrh, frankincense, wine, olive oil, fine

flour, wheat, cattle, sheep, horses, chariots, and slaves—yes, she even traded in human lives.

¹⁴"All the fancy things you loved so much are gone," they cry. "The luxuries and splendor that you prized so much will never be yours again. They are gone forever."

¹⁵The merchants who became wealthy by selling her these things will stand at a distance, terrified by her great torment. They will weep and cry. ¹⁶"How terrible, how terrible for that great city! She was so beautiful—like a woman clothed in finest purple and scarlet linens, decked out with gold and precious stones and pearls! ¹⁷And in one single moment all the wealth of the city is gone!"

And all the shipowners and captains of the merchant ships and their crews will stand at a distance. ¹⁸And they watch the smoke ascend, and they will say, "Where in all the world is there another city like this?" ¹⁹And they will throw dust on their heads to show their great sorrow. And they will say, "How terrible, how terrible for the great city! She made us all rich from her great wealth. And now in a single hour it is all gone."

²⁰But you, O heaven, rejoice over her fate. And you also rejoice, O holy people of God and apostles and prophets! For at last God has judged her on your behalf.

²¹Then a mighty angel picked up a boulder as large as a great millstone. He threw it into the ocean and shouted, "Babylon, the great city, will be thrown down as violently as I have thrown away this stone, and she will disappear forever. ²²Never again will the sound of music be heard there—no more harps, songs, flutes, or trumpets. There will be no industry of any kind, and no more milling of grain. ²³Her nights will be dark, without a single lamp. There will be no happy voices of brides and grooms. This will happen because her merchants, who were the greatest in the world, deceived the nations with her sorceries. ²⁴In her streets the blood of the prophets was spilled. She was the one who slaughtered God's people all over the world."

CHAPTER 19

Songs of Victory in Heaven

After this, I heard the sound of a vast crowd in heaven shouting, "Hallelujah! Salvation is from our God. Glory and power belong to him alone. ²His judgments are just and true. He has punished the great prostitute who corrupted the earth with her immorality, and he has avenged the murder of his servants." ³Again and again their voices rang, "Hallelujah! The smoke from that city ascends forever and forever!"

⁴Then the twenty-four elders and the four living beings fell down and worshiped God, who was sitting on the throne. They cried out, "Amen! Hallelujah!"

⁵And from the throne came a voice that said, "Praise our God, all his servants, from the least to the greatest, all who fear him."

⁶Then I heard again what sounded like the shout of a huge crowd, or the roar of mighty ocean waves, or the crash of loud thunder: "Hallelujah! For the Lord our God, the Almighty, reigns. ⁷Let us be glad and rejoice and honor him. For the time

has come for the wedding feast of the Lamb, and his bride has prepared herself. 8 She is permitted to wear the finest white linen." (Fine linen represents the good deeds done by the people of God.)

9 And the angel said, "Write this: Blessed are those who are invited to the wedding feast of the Lamb." And he added, "These are true words that come from God."

10 Then I fell down at his feet to worship him, but he said, "No, don't worship me. For I am a servant of God, just like you and other brothers and sisters* who testify of their faith in Jesus. Worship God. For the essence of prophecy is to give a clear witness for Jesus.*"

The Rider on the White Horse

11 Then I saw heaven opened, and a white horse was standing there. And the one sitting on the horse was named Faithful and True. For he judges fairly and then goes to war. 12 His eyes were bright like flames of fire, and on his head were many crowns. A name was written on him, and only he knew what it meant. 13 He was clothed with a robe dipped in blood, and his title was the Word of God. 14 The armies of heaven, dressed in pure white linen, followed him on white horses. 15 From his mouth came a sharp sword, and with it he struck down the nations. He ruled them with an iron rod, and he trod the winepress of the fierce wrath of almighty God. 16 On his robe and thigh was written this title: King of kings and Lord of lords.

17 Then I saw an angel standing in the sun, shouting to the vultures flying high in the sky: "Come! Gather together for the great banquet God has prepared. 18 Come and eat the flesh of kings, captains, and strong warriors; of horses and their riders; and of all humanity, both free and slave, small and great."

19 Then I saw the beast gathering the kings of the earth and their armies in order to fight against the one sitting on the horse and his army. 20 And the beast was captured, and with him the false prophet who did mighty miracles on behalf of the beast—miracles that deceived all who had accepted the mark of the beast and who worshiped his statue. Both the beast and his false prophet were thrown alive into the lake of fire that burns with sulfur. 21 Their entire army was killed by the sharp sword that came out of the mouth of the one riding the white horse. And all the vultures of the sky gorged themselves on the dead bodies.

CHAPTER 20

The Thousand Years

Then I saw an angel come down from heaven with the key to the bottomless pit and a heavy chain in his hand. 2 He seized the dragon—that old serpent, the Devil, Satan—and bound him in chains for a thousand years. 3 The angel threw him into the bottomless pit, which he then shut and locked so Satan could not deceive the nations anymore until the thousand years were finished. Afterward he would be released again for a little while.

4 Then I saw thrones, and the people sitting on them had been given the authority to judge. And I saw the souls of those who had been beheaded for their testimony about Jesus, for pro-

19:10a Greek *brothers.*   19:10b Or *is the message confirmed by Jesus.*

claiming the word of God. And I saw the souls of those who had not worshiped the beast or his statue, nor accepted his mark on their forehead or their hands. They came to life again, and they reigned with Christ for a thousand years. 5 This is the first resurrection. (The rest of the dead did not come back to life until the thousand years had ended.) 6Blessed and holy are those who share in the first resurrection. For them the second death holds no power, but they will be priests of God and of Christ and will reign with him a thousand years.

The Defeat of Satan

7When the thousand years end, Satan will be let out of his prison. 8 He will go out to deceive the nations from every corner of the earth, which are called Gog and Magog. He will gather them together for battle—a mighty host, as numberless as sand along the shore. 9And I saw them as they went up on the broad plain of the earth and surrounded God's people and the beloved city. But fire from heaven came down on the attacking armies and consumed them.

10Then the Devil, who betrayed them, was thrown into the lake of fire that burns with sulfur, joining the beast and the false prophet. There they will be tormented day and night forever and ever.

The Final Judgment

11 And I saw a great white throne, and I saw the one who was sitting on it. The earth and sky fled from his presence, but they found no place to hide. 12I saw the dead, both great and small, standing before God's throne. And the books were opened, including the Book of Life. And the dead were judged according to the things written in the books, according to what they had done. 13The sea gave up the dead in it, and death and the grave* gave up the dead in them. They were all judged according to their deeds. 14And death and the grave were thrown into the lake of fire. This is the second death—the lake of fire. 15 And anyone whose name was not found recorded in the Book of Life was thrown into the lake of fire.

CHAPTER 21

The New Jerusalem

Then I saw a new heaven and a new earth, for the old heaven and the old earth had disappeared. And the sea was also gone. 2And I saw the holy city, the new Jerusalem, coming down from God out of heaven like a beautiful bride prepared for her husband.

3I heard a loud shout from the throne, saying, "Look, the home of God is now among his people! He will live with them, and they will be his people. God himself will be with them.* 4 He will remove all of their sorrows, and there will be no more death or sorrow or crying or pain. For the old world and its evils are gone forever."

5And the one sitting on the throne said, "Look, I am making all things new!" And then he said to me, "Write this down, for what I tell you is trustworthy and true." 6And he also said, "It is finished!

20:13 Greek *and Hades;* also in 20:14.   21:3 Some manuscripts read *God himself will be with them, their God.*

I am the Alpha and the Omega—the Beginning and the End. To all who are thirsty I will give the springs of the water of life without charge! ⁷All who are victorious will inherit all these blessings, and I will be their God, and they will be my children. ⁸But cowards who turn away from me, and unbelievers, and the corrupt, and murderers, and the immoral, and those who practice witchcraft, and idol worshipers, and all liars—their doom is in the lake that burns with fire and sulfur. This is the second death."

⁹ Then one of the seven angels who held the seven bowls containing the seven last plagues came and said to me, "Come with me! I will show you the bride, the wife of the Lamb."

¹⁰So he took me in spirit* to a great, high mountain, and he showed me the holy city, Jerusalem, descending out of heaven from God. ¹¹It was filled with the glory of God and sparkled like a precious gem, crystal clear like jasper. ¹²Its walls were broad and high, with twelve gates guarded by twelve angels. And the names of the twelve tribes of Israel were written on the gates. ¹³There were three gates on each side—east, north, south, and west. ¹⁴The wall of the city had twelve foundation stones, and on them were written the names of the twelve apostles of the Lamb.

¹⁵The angel who talked to me held in his hand a gold measuring stick to measure the city, its gates, and its wall. ¹⁶When he measured it, he found it was a square, as wide as it was long. In fact, it was in the form of a cube, for its length and width and height were each 1,400 miles.* ¹⁷Then he measured the walls and found them to be 216 feet thick* (the angel used a standard human measure).

¹⁸The wall was made of jasper, and the city was pure gold, as clear as glass. ¹⁹The wall of the city was built on foundation stones inlaid with twelve gems: the first was jasper, the second sapphire, the third agate, the fourth emerald, ²⁰the fifth onyx, the sixth carnelian, the seventh chrysolite, the eighth beryl, the ninth topaz, the tenth chrysoprase, the eleventh jacinth, the twelfth amethyst.

²¹The twelve gates were made of pearls—each gate from a single pearl! And the main street was pure gold, as clear as glass.

²²No temple could be seen in the city, for the Lord God Almighty and the Lamb are its temple. ²³And the city has no need of sun or moon, for the glory of God illuminates the city, and the Lamb is its light. ²⁴The nations of the earth will walk in its light, and the rulers of the world will come and bring their glory to it. ²⁵Its gates never close at the end of day because there is no night. ²⁶And all the nations will bring their glory and honor into the city. ²⁷Nothing evil will be allowed to enter—no one who practices shameful idolatry and dishonesty—but only those whose names are written in the Lamb's Book of Life.

CHAPTER 22

And the angel showed me a pure river with the water of life, clear as crystal, flowing from the throne of God and of the Lamb, ²coursing down the center of the main street. On each side of the river grew a tree of life, bearing twelve crops of fruit,* with a fresh

21:10 Or *in the Spirit.*   21:16 Greek *12,000 stadia* [2,220 kilometers].   21:17 Greek *144 cubits* [65 meters].   22:2 Or *12 kinds of fruit.*

crop each month. The leaves were used for medicine to heal the nations.

³No longer will anything be cursed. For the throne of God and of the Lamb will be there, and his servants will worship him. ⁴And they will see his face, and his name will be written on their foreheads. ⁵And there will be no night there—no need for lamps or sun—for the Lord God will shine on them. And they will reign forever and ever.

⁶Then the angel said to me, "These words are trustworthy and true: 'The Lord God, who tells his prophets what the future holds, has sent his angel to tell you what will happen soon.'"

Jesus Is Coming

⁷"Look, I am coming soon! Blessed are those who obey the prophecy written in this scroll."

⁸I, John, am the one who saw and heard all these things. And when I saw and heard these things, I fell down to worship the angel who showed them to me. ⁹But again he said, "No, don't worship me. I am a servant of God, just like you and your brothers the prophets, as well as all who obey what is written in this scroll. Worship God!"

¹⁰Then he instructed me, "Do not seal up the prophetic words you have written, for the time is near. ¹¹Let the one who is doing wrong continue to do wrong; the one who is vile, continue to be vile; the one who is good, continue to do good; and the one who is holy, continue in holiness."

¹²"See, I am coming soon, and my reward is with me, to repay all according to their deeds. ¹³I am the Alpha and the Omega, the First and the Last, the Beginning and the End."

¹⁴ Blessed are those who wash their robes so they can enter through the gates of the city and eat the fruit from the tree of life. ¹⁵Outside the city are the dogs—the sorcerers, the sexually immoral, the murderers, the idol worshipers, and all who love to live a lie.

¹⁶"I, Jesus, have sent my angel to give you this message for the churches. I am both the source of David and the heir to his throne.* I am the bright morning star."

¹⁷The Spirit and the bride say, "Come." Let each one who hears them say, "Come." Let the thirsty ones come—anyone who wants to. Let them come and drink the water of life without charge. ¹⁸And I solemnly declare to everyone who hears the prophetic words of this book: If anyone adds anything to what is written here, God will add to that person the plagues described in this book. ¹⁹And if anyone removes any of the words of this prophetic book, God will remove that person's share in the tree of life and in the holy city that are described in this book.

²⁰He who is the faithful witness to all these things says, "Yes, I am coming soon!"

Amen! Come, Lord Jesus!

²¹The grace of the Lord Jesus be with you all.

22:16 Greek *I am the root and offspring of David.*

PSALMS

BOOK ONE (Psalms 1–41)

PSALM 1

¹ Oh, the joys of those
    who do not follow the advice of the wicked,
    or stand around with sinners,
    or join in with scoffers.
² But they delight in doing everything the LORD wants;
    day and night they think about his law.
³ They are like trees planted along the riverbank,
    bearing fruit each season without fail.
Their leaves never wither,
    and in all they do, they prosper.

⁴ But this is not true of the wicked.
    They are like worthless chaff, scattered by the wind.
⁵ They will be condemned at the time of judgment.
    Sinners will have no place among the godly.

⁶ For the LORD watches over the path of the godly,
    but the path of the wicked leads to destruction.

PSALM 2

¹ Why do the nations rage?
    Why do the people waste their time with futile plans?
² The kings of the earth prepare for battle;
    the rulers plot together
against the LORD
    and against his anointed one.
³ "Let us break their chains," they cry,
    "and free ourselves from this slavery."

⁴ But the one who rules in heaven laughs.
    The Lord scoffs at them.
⁵ Then in anger he rebukes them,
    terrifying them with his fierce fury.
⁶ For the LORD declares, "I have placed my chosen king on the
        throne
    in Jerusalem, my holy city.*"

⁷ The king proclaims the LORD's decree:
    "The LORD said to me, 'You are my son.*
    Today I have become your Father.*
⁸ Only ask, and I will give you the nations as your
        inheritance,
    the ends of the earth as your possession.

2:6 Hebrew on Zion, my holy mountain.   2:7a Or Son; also in 2:12.   2:7b Or Today I
reveal you as my son.

⁹ You will break them with an iron rod
  and smash them like clay pots.'"

¹⁰ Now then, you kings, act wisely!
  Be warned, you rulers of the earth!

¹¹ Serve the LORD with reverent fear,
  and rejoice with trembling.

¹² Submit to God's royal son, or he will become angry,
  and you will be destroyed in the midst of your pursuits—
  for his anger can flare up in an instant.

  But what joy for all who find protection in him!

PSALM 3

A psalm of David, regarding the time David fled from his son Absalom.

¹ O LORD, I have so many enemies;
  so many are against me.

² So many are saying,
  "God will never rescue him!"   *Interlude**

³ But you, O LORD, are a shield around me,
  my glory, and the one who lifts my head high.

⁴ I cried out to the LORD,
  and he answered me from his holy mountain.   *Interlude*

⁵ I lay down and slept.
  I woke up in safety,
  for the LORD was watching over me.

⁶ I am not afraid of ten thousand enemies
  who surround me on every side.

⁷ Arise, O LORD!
  Rescue me, my God!
  Slap all my enemies in the face!
  Shatter the teeth of the wicked!

⁸ Victory comes from you, O LORD.
  May your blessings rest on your people.   *Interlude*

PSALM 4

For the choir director: A psalm of David, to be accompanied by stringed instruments.

¹ Answer me when I call,
  O God who declares me innocent.
  Take away my distress.
  Have mercy on me and hear my prayer.

² How long will you people ruin my reputation?
  How long will you make these groundless accusations?
  How long will you pursue lies?   *Interlude*

³ You can be sure of this:
  The LORD has set apart the godly for himself.
  The LORD will answer when I call to him.

⁴ Don't sin by letting anger gain control over you.
  Think about it overnight and remain silent.   *Interlude*

3:2 Hebrew *Selah.* The meaning of this word is uncertain, though it is probably a musical or literary term. It is rendered *Interlude* throughout the Psalms.

⁵ Offer proper sacrifices,
and trust in the LORD.

⁶ Many people say, "Who will show us better times?"
Let the smile of your face shine on us, LORD.

⁷ You have given me greater joy
than those who have abundant harvests of grain and wine.

⁸ I will lie down in peace and sleep,
for you alone, O LORD, will keep me safe.

PSALM 5

For the choir director: A psalm of David, to be accompanied by the flute.

¹ O LORD, hear me as I pray;
pay attention to my groaning.
² Listen to my cry for help, my King and my God,
for I will never pray to anyone but you.
³ Listen to my voice in the morning, LORD.
Each morning I bring my requests to you and wait expectantly.

⁴ O God, you take no pleasure in wickedness;
you cannot tolerate the slightest sin.
⁵ Therefore, the proud will not be allowed to stand in your presence,
for you hate all who do evil.
⁶ You will destroy those who tell lies.
The LORD detests murderers and deceivers.

⁷ Because of your unfailing love, I can enter your house;
with deepest awe I will worship at your Temple.
⁸ Lead me in the right path, O LORD,
or my enemies will conquer me.
Tell me clearly what to do,
and show me which way to turn.

⁹ My enemies cannot speak one truthful word.
Their deepest desire is to destroy others.
Their talk is foul, like the stench from an open grave.
Their speech is filled with flattery.
¹⁰ O God, declare them guilty.
Let them be caught in their own traps.
Drive them away because of their many sins,
for they rebel against you.

¹¹ But let all who take refuge in you rejoice;
let them sing joyful praises forever.
Protect them,
so all who love your name may be filled with joy.
¹² For you bless the godly, O LORD,
surrounding them with your shield of love.

PSALM 6

For the choir director: A psalm of David, to be accompanied by an eight-stringed instrument. *

¹ O LORD, do not rebuke me in your anger
or discipline me in your rage.

6:TITLE Hebrew *with stringed instruments; according to the sheminith.*

2 Have compassion on me, LORD, for I am weak.
　　Heal me, LORD, for my body is in agony.
3 I am sick at heart.
　　How long, O LORD, until you restore me?

4 Return, O LORD, and rescue me.
　　Save me because of your unfailing love.
5 For in death, who remembers you?
　　Who can praise you from the grave?

6 I am worn out from sobbing.
　　Every night tears drench my bed;
　　my pillow is wet from weeping.
7 My vision is blurred by grief;
　　my eyes are worn out because of all my enemies.

8 Go away, all you who do evil,
　　for the LORD has heard my crying.
9 The LORD has heard my plea;
　　the LORD will answer my prayer.
10 May all my enemies be disgraced and terrified.
　　May they suddenly turn back in shame.

PSALM 7

A psalm of David, which he sang to the LORD concerning Cush of the tribe of Benjamin.

1 I come to you for protection, O LORD my God.
　　Save me from my persecutors—rescue me!
2 If you don't, they will maul me like a lion,
　　tearing me to pieces with no one to rescue me.

3 O LORD my God, if I have done wrong
　　or am guilty of injustice,
4 if I have betrayed a friend
　　or plundered my enemy without cause,
5 then let my enemies capture me.
　　Let them trample me into the ground.
　　Let my honor be left in the dust.　　　　　　　*Interlude*

6 Arise, O LORD, in anger!
　　Stand up against the fury of my enemies!
　　Wake up, my God, and bring justice!
7 Gather the nations before you.
　　Sit on your throne high above them.
8 The LORD passes judgment on the nations.
　　Declare me righteous, O LORD,
　　for I am innocent, O Most High!
9 End the wickedness of the ungodly,
　　but help all those who obey you.
　For you look deep within the mind and heart,
　　O righteous God.

10 God is my shield,
　　saving those whose hearts are true and right.
11 God is a judge who is perfectly fair.
　　He is angry with the wicked every day.

12 If a person does not repent,
     God* will sharpen his sword;
  he will bend and string his bow.
13 He will prepare his deadly weapons
     and ignite his flaming arrows.

14 The wicked conceive evil;
     they are pregnant with trouble
     and give birth to lies.
15 They dig a pit to trap others
     and then fall into it themselves.
16 They make trouble,
     but it backfires on them.
  They plan violence for others,
     but it falls on their own heads.

17 I will thank the LORD because he is just;
     I will sing praise to the name of the LORD Most High.

PSALM 8

For the choir director: A psalm of David, to be accompanied by a stringed instrument. *

1 O LORD, our Lord, the majesty of your name fills the earth!
     Your glory is higher than the heavens.

2 You have taught children and nursing infants
     to give you praise. *
  They silence your enemies
     who were seeking revenge.

3 When I look at the night sky and see the work of your
           fingers—
     the moon and the stars you have set in place—
4 what are mortals that you should think of us,
     mere humans that you should care for us?
5 For you made us only a little lower than God,*
     and you crowned us with glory and honor.
6 You put us in charge of everything you made,
     giving us authority over all things—
7 the sheep and the cattle
     and all the wild animals,
8 the birds in the sky, the fish in the sea,
     and everything that swims the ocean currents.

9 O LORD, our Lord, the majesty of your name fills the earth!

PSALM 9

For the choir director: A psalm of David, to be sung to the tune "Death of the Son."

1 I will thank you, LORD, with all my heart;
     I will tell of all the marvelous things you have done.
2 I will be filled with joy because of you.
     I will sing praises to your name, O Most High.

7:12 Hebrew *he.*   **8:TITLE** Hebrew *according to the gittith.*   **8:2** As in Greek version; Hebrew reads *to show strength.*   **8:4** Hebrew *what is man that you should think of him, the son of man that you should care for him?*   **8:5** Or *a little lower than the angels;* Hebrew reads *Elohim.*

³ My enemies turn away in retreat;
　　they are overthrown and destroyed before you.
⁴ For you have judged in my favor;
　　from your throne, you have judged with fairness.

⁵ You have rebuked the nations and destroyed the wicked;
　　you have wiped out their names forever.
⁶ My enemies have met their doom;
　　their cities are perpetual ruins.
　　Even the memory of their uprooted cities is lost.

⁷ But the Lord reigns forever,
　　executing judgment from his throne.
⁸ He will judge the world with justice
　　and rule the nations with fairness.

⁹ The Lord is a shelter for the oppressed,
　　a refuge in times of trouble.
¹⁰ Those who know your name trust in you,
　　for you, O Lord, have never abandoned anyone who
　　　searches for you.

¹¹ Sing praises to the Lord who reigns in Jerusalem.*
　　Tell the world about his unforgettable deeds.
¹² For he who avenges murder cares for the helpless.
　　He does not ignore those who cry to him for help.

¹³ Lord, have mercy on me.
　　See how I suffer at the hands of those who hate me.
　　Snatch me back from the jaws of death.
¹⁴ Save me, so I can praise you publicly at Jerusalem's gates,
　　so I can rejoice that you have rescued me.

¹⁵ The nations have fallen into the pit they dug for others.
　　They have been caught in their own trap.
¹⁶ The Lord is known for his justice.
　　The wicked have trapped themselves in their own snares.
　　　　　　　　　　　　　　　　　　　　　*Quiet Interlude**

¹⁷ The wicked will go down to the grave.*
　　This is the fate of all the nations who ignore God.
¹⁸ For the needy will not be forgotten forever;
　　the hopes of the poor will not always be crushed.

¹⁹ Arise, O Lord!
　　Do not let mere mortals defy you!
　　Let the nations be judged in your presence!
²⁰ Make them tremble in fear, O Lord.
　　Let them know they are merely human.　　　　　*Interlude*

PSALM 10
¹ O Lord, why do you stand so far away?
　　Why do you hide when I need you the most?
² Proud and wicked people viciously oppress the poor.
　　Let them be caught in the evil they plan for others.
³ For they brag about their evil desires;

9:11 Hebrew *Zion*; also in 9:14.　　**9:16** Hebrew *Higgaion Selah.* The meaning of this phrase is uncertain.　　**9:17** Hebrew to *Sheol.*

they praise the greedy and curse the LORD.

4 These wicked people are too proud to seek God.
  They seem to think that God is dead.
5 Yet they succeed in everything they do.
  They do not see your punishment awaiting them.
  They pour scorn on all their enemies.
6 They say to themselves, "Nothing bad will ever happen to us!
  We will be free of trouble forever!"

7 Their mouths are full of cursing, lies, and threats.
  Trouble and evil are on the tips of their tongues.
8 They lurk in dark alleys,
  murdering the innocent who pass by.

  They are always searching
  for some helpless victim.
9 Like lions they crouch silently,
  waiting to pounce on the helpless.
  Like hunters they capture their victims
  and drag them away in nets.
10 The helpless are overwhelmed and collapse;
  they fall beneath the strength of the wicked.
11 The wicked say to themselves, "God isn't watching!
  He will never notice!"

12 Arise, O LORD!
  Punish the wicked, O God!
  Do not forget the helpless!
13 Why do the wicked get away with cursing God?
  How can they think, "God will never call us to account"?

14 But you do see the trouble and grief they cause.
  You take note of it and punish them.
  The helpless put their trust in you.
  You are the defender of orphans.

15 Break the arms of these wicked, evil people!
  Go after them until the last one is destroyed!
16 The LORD is king forever and ever!
  Let those who worship other gods be swept from the land.

17 LORD, you know the hopes of the helpless.
  Surely you will listen to their cries and comfort them.
18 You will bring justice to the orphans and the oppressed,
  so people can no longer terrify them.

PSALM 11
For the choir director: A psalm of David.

1 I trust in the LORD for protection.
  So why do you say to me,
  "Fly to the mountains for safety!
2   The wicked are stringing their bows
  and setting their arrows in the bowstrings.
  They shoot from the shadows at those who do right.
3 The foundations of law and order have collapsed.
  What can the righteous do?"

⁴ But the LORD is in his holy Temple;
  the LORD still rules from heaven.
 He watches everything closely,
  examining everyone on earth.
⁵ The LORD examines both the righteous and the wicked.
  He hates everyone who loves violence.
⁶ He rains down blazing coals on the wicked,
  punishing them with burning sulfur and scorching winds.
⁷ For the LORD is righteous, and he loves justice.
  Those who do what is right will see his face.

P S A L M   1 2
For the choir director: A psalm of David, to be accompanied by an eight-stringed instrument. *

¹ Help, O LORD, for the godly are fast disappearing!
  The faithful have vanished from the earth!
² Neighbors lie to each other,
  speaking with flattering lips and insincere hearts.
³ May the LORD bring their flattery to an end
  and silence their proud tongues.
⁴ They say, "We will lie to our hearts' content.
  Our lips are our own—who can stop us?"

⁵ The LORD replies, "I have seen violence done to the helpless,
  and I have heard the groans of the poor.
 Now I will rise up to rescue them,
  as they have longed for me to do."
⁶ The LORD's promises are pure,
  like silver refined in a furnace,
  purified seven times over.

⁷ Therefore, LORD, we know you will protect the oppressed,
  preserving them forever from this lying generation,
⁸ even though the wicked strut about,
  and evil is praised throughout the land.

P S A L M   1 3
For the choir director: A psalm of David.

¹ O LORD, how long will you forget me? Forever?
  How long will you look the other way?
² How long must I struggle with anguish in my soul,
  with sorrow in my heart every day?
  How long will my enemy have the upper hand?

³ Turn and answer me, O LORD my God!
  Restore the light to my eyes, or I will die.
⁴ Don't let my enemies gloat, saying, "We have defeated him!"
  Don't let them rejoice at my downfall.

⁵ But I trust in your unfailing love.
  I will rejoice because you have rescued me.
⁶ I will sing to the LORD
  because he has been so good to me.

12:TITLE Hebrew *according to the sheminith.*

PSALM 14

For the choir director: A psalm of David.

1 Only fools say in their hearts,
    "There is no God."
  They are corrupt, and their actions are evil;
    no one does good!

2 The LORD looks down from heaven
    on the entire human race;
  he looks to see if there is even one with real understanding,
    one who seeks for God.

3 But no, all have turned away from God;
    all have become corrupt.
  No one does good,
    not even one!

4 Will those who do evil never learn?
    They eat up my people like bread;
    they wouldn't think of praying to the LORD.

5 Terror will grip them,
    for God is with those who obey him.

6 The wicked frustrate the plans of the oppressed,
    but the LORD will protect his people.

7 Oh, that salvation would come from Mount Zion to rescue
        Israel!
  For when the LORD restores his people,
    Jacob will shout with joy, and Israel will rejoice.

PSALM 15

A psalm of David.

1 Who may worship in your sanctuary, LORD?
    Who may enter your presence on your holy hill?

2 Those who lead blameless lives
    and do what is right,
    speaking the truth from sincere hearts.

3 Those who refuse to slander others
    or harm their neighbors
    or speak evil of their friends.

4 Those who despise persistent sinners,
    and honor the faithful followers of the LORD
    and keep their promises even when it hurts.

5 Those who do not charge interest on the money they lend,
    and who refuse to accept bribes to testify against the
        innocent.

  Such people will stand firm forever.

PSALM 16

A psalm of David.

1 Keep me safe, O God,
    for I have come to you for refuge.

2 I said to the LORD, "You are my Master!
    All the good things I have are from you."

³ The godly people in the land
  are my true heroes!
  I take pleasure in them!
⁴ Those who chase after other gods will be filled with sorrow.
  I will not take part in their sacrifices
  or even speak the names of their gods.

⁵ LORD, you alone are my inheritance, my cup of blessing.
  You guard all that is mine.
⁶ The land you have given me is a pleasant land.
  What a wonderful inheritance!

⁷ I will bless the LORD who guides me;
  even at night my heart instructs me.
⁸ I know the LORD is always with me.
  I will not be shaken, for he is right beside me.

⁹ No wonder my heart is filled with joy,
  and my mouth* shouts his praises!
  My body rests in safety.
¹⁰ For you will not leave my soul among the dead*
  or allow your godly one* to rot in the grave.
¹¹ You will show me the way of life,
  granting me the joy of your presence
  and the pleasures of living with you forever.

PSALM 17

A prayer of David.

¹ O LORD, hear my plea for justice.
  Listen to my cry for help.
  Pay attention to my prayer,
  for it comes from an honest heart.
² Declare me innocent,
  for you know those who do right.

³ You have tested my thoughts and examined my heart in the
  night.
  You have scrutinized me and found nothing amiss,
  for I am determined not to sin in what I say.
⁴ I have followed your commands,
  which have kept me from going along with cruel and evil
  people.
⁵ My steps have stayed on your path;
  I have not wavered from following you.

⁶ I am praying to you because I know you will answer, O God.
  Bend down and listen as I pray.
⁷ Show me your unfailing love in wonderful ways.
  You save with your strength
  those who seek refuge from their enemies.
⁸ Guard me as the apple of your eye.
  Hide me in the shadow of your wings.
⁹ Protect me from wicked people who attack me,
  from murderous enemies who surround me.

16:9 As in Greek version; Hebrew reads *glory.* **16:10a** Hebrew *in Sheol.* **16:10b** Or *your Holy One.*

10 They are without pity.
   Listen to their boasting.
11 They track me down, surround me,
   and throw me to the ground.
12 They are like hungry lions, eager to tear me apart—
   like young lions in hiding, waiting for their chance.

13 Arise, O LORD!
   Stand against them and bring them to their knees!
   Rescue me from the wicked with your sword!
14 Save me by your mighty hand, O LORD,
   from those whose only concern is earthly gain.
   May they have their punishment in full.
      May their children inherit more of the same,
      and may the judgment continue to their children's children.

15 But because I have done what is right, I will see you.
   When I awake, I will be fully satisfied,
   for I will see you face to face.

PSALM 18

For the choir director: A psalm of David, the servant of the LORD. He sang this song to the LORD on the day the LORD rescued him from all his enemies and from Saul.

1 I love you, LORD; you are my strength.
2 The LORD is my rock, my fortress, and my savior;
   my God is my rock, in whom I find protection.
   He is my shield, the strength of my salvation, and my
      stronghold.
3 I will call on the LORD, who is worthy of praise,
   for he saves me from my enemies.

4 The ropes of death surrounded me;
   the floods of destruction swept over me.
5 The grave* wrapped its ropes around me;
   death itself stared me in the face.
6 But in my distress I cried out to the LORD;
   yes, I prayed to my God for help.
   He heard me from his sanctuary;
   my cry reached his ears.

7 Then the earth quaked and trembled;
   the foundations of the mountains shook;
   they quaked because of his anger.
8 Smoke poured from his nostrils;
   fierce flames leaped from his mouth;
   glowing coals flamed forth from him.
9 He opened the heavens and came down;
   dark storm clouds were beneath his feet.
10 Mounted on a mighty angel,* he flew,
   soaring on the wings of the wind.
11 He shrouded himself in darkness,
   veiling his approach with dense rain clouds.
12 The brilliance of his presence broke through the clouds,
   raining down hail and burning coals.

18:5 Hebrew *Sheol*.   **18:10** Hebrew *a cherub*.

¹³ The LORD thundered from heaven;
the Most High gave a mighty shout.*

¹⁴ He shot his arrows and scattered his enemies;
his lightning flashed, and they were greatly confused.

¹⁵ Then at your command, O LORD,
at the blast of your breath,
the bottom of the sea could be seen,
and the foundations of the earth were laid bare.

¹⁶ He reached down from heaven and rescued me;
he drew me out of deep waters.

¹⁷ He delivered me from my powerful enemies,
from those who hated me and were too strong for me.

¹⁸ They attacked me at a moment when I was weakest,
but the LORD upheld me.

¹⁹ He led me to a place of safety;
he rescued me because he delights in me.

²⁰ The LORD rewarded me for doing right;
he compensated me because of my innocence.

²¹ For I have kept the ways of the LORD;
I have not turned from my God to follow evil.

²² For all his laws are constantly before me;
I have never abandoned his principles.

²³ I am blameless before God;
I have kept myself from sin.

²⁴ The LORD rewarded me for doing right,
because of the innocence of my hands in his sight.

²⁵ To the faithful you show yourself faithful;
to those with integrity you show integrity.

²⁶ To the pure you show yourself pure,
but to the wicked you show yourself hostile.

²⁷ You rescue those who are humble,
but you humiliate the proud.

²⁸ LORD, you have brought light to my life;
my God, you light up my darkness.

²⁹ In your strength I can crush an army;
with my God I can scale any wall.

³⁰ As for God, his way is perfect.
All the LORD's promises prove true.
He is a shield for all who look to him for protection.

³¹ For who is God except the LORD?
Who but our God is a solid rock?

³² God arms me with strength;
he has made my way safe.

³³ He makes me as surefooted as a deer,
leading me safely along the mountain heights.

³⁴ He prepares me for battle;
he strengthens me to draw a bow of bronze.

³⁵ You have given me the shield of your salvation.
Your right hand supports me;
your gentleness has made me great.

18:13 As in Greek version (see also 2 Sam 22:14); Hebrew adds *raining down hail and burning coals.*

³⁶ You have made a wide path for my feet
   to keep them from slipping.

³⁷ I chased my enemies and caught them;
   I did not stop until they were conquered.
³⁸ I struck them down so they could not get up;
   they fell beneath my feet.
³⁹ You have armed me with strength for the battle;
   you have subdued my enemies under my feet.
⁴⁰ You made them turn and run;
   I have destroyed all who hated me.
⁴¹ They called for help, but no one came to rescue them.
   They cried to the Lᴏʀᴅ, but he refused to answer them.
⁴² I ground them as fine as dust carried by the wind.
   I swept them into the gutter like dirt.

⁴³ You gave me victory over my accusers.
   You appointed me as the ruler over nations;
   people I don't even know now serve me.
⁴⁴ As soon as they hear of me, they submit;
   foreigners cringe before me.
⁴⁵ They all lose their courage
   and come trembling from their strongholds.

⁴⁶ The Lᴏʀᴅ lives! Blessed be my rock!
   May the God of my salvation be exalted!
⁴⁷ He is the God who pays back those who harm me;
   he subdues the nations under me
⁴⁸ and rescues me from my enemies.
   You hold me safe beyond the reach of my enemies;
   you save me from violent opponents.
⁴⁹ For this, O Lᴏʀᴅ, I will praise you among the nations;
   I will sing joyfully to your name.
⁵⁰ You give great victories to your king;
   you show unfailing love to your anointed,
   to David and all his descendants forever.

PSALM 19

For the choir director: A psalm of David.

¹ The heavens tell of the glory of God.
   The skies display his marvelous craftsmanship.
² Day after day they continue to speak;
   night after night they make him known.
³ They speak without a sound or a word;
   their voice is silent in the skies;*
⁴ yet their message has gone out to all the earth,
   and their words to all the world.

The sun lives in the heavens
   where God placed it.
⁵ It bursts forth like a radiant bridegroom
   after his wedding.
It rejoices like a great athlete
   eager to run the race.

19:3 Or *There is no speech or language where their voice is not heard.*

⁶ The sun rises at one end of the heavens
  and follows its course to the other end.
  Nothing can hide from its heat.

⁷ The law of the LORD is perfect,
  reviving the soul.
The decrees of the LORD are trustworthy,
  making wise the simple.
⁸ The commandments of the LORD are right,
  bringing joy to the heart.
The commands of the LORD are clear,
  giving insight to life.
⁹ Reverence for the LORD is pure,
  lasting forever.
The laws of the LORD are true;
  each one is fair.
¹⁰ They are more desirable than gold,
  even the finest gold.
They are sweeter than honey,
  even honey dripping from the comb.
¹¹ They are a warning to those who hear them;
  there is great reward for those who obey them.

¹² How can I know all the sins lurking in my heart?
  Cleanse me from these hidden faults.
¹³ Keep me from deliberate sins!
  Don't let them control me.
Then I will be free of guilt
  and innocent of great sin.

¹⁴ May the words of my mouth and the thoughts of my heart
  be pleasing to you,
O LORD, my rock and my redeemer.

PSALM 20
For the choir director: A psalm of David.

¹ In times of trouble, may the LORD respond to your cry.
  May the God of Israel* keep you safe from all harm.
² May he send you help from his sanctuary
  and strengthen you from Jerusalem.*
³ May he remember all your gifts
  and look favorably on your burnt offerings.   *Interlude*

⁴ May he grant your heart's desire
  and fulfill all your plans.
⁵ May we shout for joy when we hear of your victory,
  flying banners to honor our God.
May the LORD answer all your prayers.

⁶ Now I know that the LORD saves his anointed king.
  He will answer him from his holy heaven
  and rescue him by his great power.
⁷ Some nations boast of their armies and weapons,*
  but we boast in the LORD our God.

20:1 Hebrew *of Jacob.*   20:2 Hebrew *Zion.*   20:7 Hebrew *chariots and horses.*

8 Those nations will fall down and collapse,
but we will rise up and stand firm.

9 Give victory to our king, O LORD!
Respond to our cry for help.

PSALM 21
For the choir director: A psalm of David.

1 How the king rejoices in your strength, O LORD!
He shouts with joy because of your victory.

2 For you have given him his heart's desire;
you have held back nothing that he requested.   *Interlude*

3 You welcomed him back with success and prosperity.
You placed a crown of finest gold on his head.

4 He asked you to preserve his life,
and you have granted his request.
The days of his life stretch on forever.

5 Your victory brings him great honor,
and you have clothed him with splendor and majesty.

6 You have endowed him with eternal blessings.
You have given him the joy of being in your presence.

7 For the king trusts in the LORD.
The unfailing love of the Most High will keep him from
stumbling.

8 You will capture all your enemies.
Your strong right hand will seize all those who hate you.

9 You will destroy them as in a flaming furnace
when you appear.
The LORD will consume them in his anger;
fire will devour them.

10 You will wipe their children from the face of the earth;
they will never have descendants.

11 Although they plot against you,
their evil schemes will never succeed.

12 For they will turn and run
when they see your arrows aimed at them.

13 We praise you, LORD, for all your glorious power.
With music and singing we celebrate your mighty acts.

PSALM 22
For the choir director: A psalm of David, to be sung to the tune "Doe of the Dawn."

1 My God, my God! Why have you forsaken me?
Why do you remain so distant?
Why do you ignore my cries for help?

2 Every day I call to you, my God, but you do not answer.
Every night you hear my voice, but I find no relief.

3 Yet you are holy.
The praises of Israel surround your throne.

4 Our ancestors trusted in you,
and you rescued them.

5 You heard their cries for help and saved them.
They put their trust in you and were never disappointed.

⁶ But I am a worm and not a man.
  I am scorned and despised by all!
⁷ Everyone who sees me mocks me.
  They sneer and shake their heads, saying,
⁸ "Is this the one who relies on the LORD?
  Then let the LORD save him!
  If the LORD loves him so much,
    let the LORD rescue him!"

⁹ Yet you brought me safely from my mother's womb
    and led me to trust you when I was a nursing infant.
¹⁰ I was thrust upon you at my birth.
  You have been my God from the moment I was
    born.

¹¹ Do not stay so far from me,
    for trouble is near,
    and no one else can help me.
¹² My enemies surround me like a herd of bulls;
    fierce bulls of Bashan have hemmed me in!
¹³ Like roaring lions attacking their prey,
    they come at me with open mouths.
¹⁴ My life is poured out like water,
    and all my bones are out of joint.
  My heart is like wax,
    melting within me.
¹⁵ My strength has dried up like sunbaked clay.
  My tongue sticks to the roof of my mouth.
  You have laid me in the dust and left me for dead.

¹⁶ My enemies surround me like a pack of dogs;
    an evil gang closes in on me.
  They have pierced my hands and feet.
¹⁷ I can count every bone in my body.
  My enemies stare at me and gloat.
¹⁸ They divide my clothes among themselves
    and throw dice* for my garments.

¹⁹ O LORD, do not stay away!
  You are my strength; come quickly to my aid!
²⁰ Rescue me from a violent death;
    spare my precious life from these dogs.
²¹ Snatch me from the lions' jaws,
    and from the horns of these wild oxen.

²² Then I will declare the wonder of your name to my brothers
    and sisters.
  I will praise you among all your people.
²³ Praise the LORD, all you who fear him!
  Honor him, all you descendants of Jacob!
  Show him reverence, all you descendants of Israel!
²⁴ For he has not ignored the suffering of the needy.
  He has not turned and walked away.
  He has listened to their cries for help.

22:18 Hebrew *cast lots.*

²⁵ I will praise you among all the people;
   I will fulfill my vows in the presence of those who worship
      you.
²⁶ The poor will eat and be satisfied.
   All who seek the LORD will praise him.
   Their hearts will rejoice with everlasting joy.
²⁷ The whole earth will acknowledge the LORD and return to
      him.
   People from every nation will bow down before him.
²⁸ For the LORD is king!
   He rules all the nations.

²⁹ Let the rich of the earth feast and worship.
   Let all mortals—those born to die—bow down in his
      presence.
³⁰ Future generations will also serve him.
   Our children will hear about the wonders of the Lord.
³¹ His righteous acts will be told to those yet unborn.
   They will hear about everything he has done.

PSALM 23
A psalm of David.

¹ The LORD is my shepherd;
   I have everything I need.
² He lets me rest in green meadows;
   he leads me beside peaceful streams.
³   He renews my strength.
   He guides me along right paths,
      bringing honor to his name.

⁴ Even when I walk
      through the dark valley of death,*
   I will not be afraid,
      for you are close beside me.
   Your rod and your staff
      protect and comfort me.

⁵ You prepare a feast for me
      in the presence of my enemies.
   You welcome me as a guest,
      anointing my head with oil.
   My cup overflows with blessings.
⁶ Surely your goodness and unfailing love will pursue me
      all the days of my life,
   and I will live in the house of the LORD
      forever.

PSALM 24
A psalm of David.

¹ The earth is the LORD's, and everything in it.
   The world and all its people belong to him.
² For he laid the earth's foundation on the seas
      and built it on the ocean depths.

23:4 Or *the darkest valley.*

³ Who may climb the mountain of the LORD?
  Who may stand in his holy place?
⁴ Only those whose hands and hearts are pure,
  who do not worship idols
  and never tell lies.
⁵ They will receive the LORD's blessing
  and have right standing with God their savior.
⁶ They alone may enter God's presence
  and worship the God of Israel.*   *Interlude*

⁷ Open up, ancient gates!
  Open up, ancient doors,
  and let the King of glory enter.
⁸ Who is the King of glory?
  The LORD, strong and mighty,
  the LORD, invincible in battle.
⁹ Open up, ancient gates!
  Open up, ancient doors,
  and let the King of glory enter.
¹⁰ Who is the King of glory?
  The LORD Almighty—
  he is the King of glory.   *Interlude*

PSALM 25
A psalm of David.

¹ To you, O LORD, I lift up my soul.
²   I trust in you, my God!
  Do not let me be disgraced,
  or let my enemies rejoice in my defeat.
³ No one who trusts in you will ever be disgraced,
  but disgrace comes to those who try to deceive others.

⁴ Show me the path where I should walk, O LORD;
  point out the right road for me to follow.
⁵ Lead me by your truth and teach me,
  for you are the God who saves me.
  All day long I put my hope in you.

⁶ Remember, O LORD, your unfailing love and compassion,
  which you have shown from long ages past.
⁷ Forgive the rebellious sins of my youth;
  look instead through the eyes of your unfailing love,
  for you are merciful, O LORD.

⁸ The LORD is good and does what is right;
  he shows the proper path to those who go astray.
⁹ He leads the humble in what is right,
  teaching them his way.
¹⁰ The LORD leads with unfailing love and faithfulness
  all those who keep his covenant and obey his decrees.

¹¹ For the honor of your name, O LORD,
  forgive my many, many sins.
¹² Who are those who fear the LORD?

24:6 Hebrew *of Jacob.*

He will show them the path they should choose.
¹³ They will live in prosperity,
    and their children will inherit the Promised Land.
¹⁴ Friendship with the LORD is reserved for those who fear him.
    With them he shares the secrets of his covenant.
¹⁵ My eyes are always looking to the LORD for help,
    for he alone can rescue me from the traps of my enemies.

¹⁶ Turn to me and have mercy on me,
    for I am alone and in deep distress.
¹⁷ My problems go from bad to worse.
    Oh, save me from them all!
¹⁸ Feel my pain and see my trouble.
    Forgive all my sins.
¹⁹ See how many enemies I have,
    and how viciously they hate me!
²⁰ Protect me! Rescue my life from them!
    Do not let me be disgraced, for I trust in you.
²¹ May integrity and honesty protect me,
    for I put my hope in you.

²² O God, ransom Israel
    from all its troubles.

PSALM 26

A psalm of David.

¹ Declare me innocent, O LORD,
    for I have acted with integrity;
    I have trusted in the LORD without wavering.
² Put me on trial, LORD, and cross-examine me.
    Test my motives and affections.
³ For I am constantly aware of your unfailing love,
    and I have lived according to your truth.

⁴ I do not spend time with liars
    or go along with hypocrites.
⁵ I hate the gatherings of those who do evil,
    and I refuse to join in with the wicked.

⁶ I wash my hands to declare my innocence.
    I come to your altar, O LORD,
⁷ singing a song of thanksgiving
    and telling of all your miracles.
⁸ I love your sanctuary, LORD,
    the place where your glory shines.

⁹ Don't let me suffer the fate of sinners.
    Don't condemn me along with murderers.
¹⁰ Their hands are dirty with wicked schemes,
    and they constantly take bribes.

¹¹ But I am not like that; I do what is right.
    So in your mercy, save me.
¹² I have taken a stand,
    and I will publicly praise the LORD.

PSALM 27

A psalm of David.

¹ The LORD is my light and my salvation—
   so why should I be afraid?
 The LORD protects me from danger—
   so why should I tremble?

² When evil people come to destroy me,
   when my enemies and foes attack me,
   they will stumble and fall.
³ Though a mighty army surrounds me,
   my heart will know no fear.
 Even if they attack me,
   I remain confident.

⁴ The one thing I ask of the LORD—
   the thing I seek most—
 is to live in the house of the LORD all the days of my
     life,
   delighting in the LORD's perfections
   and meditating in his Temple.
⁵ For he will conceal me there when troubles come;
   he will hide me in his sanctuary.
 He will place me out of reach on a high rock.
⁶ Then I will hold my head high,
   above my enemies who surround me.
 At his Tabernacle I will offer sacrifices with shouts of
     joy,
   singing and praising the LORD with music.

⁷ Listen to my pleading, O LORD.
   Be merciful and answer me!
⁸ My heart has heard you say, "Come and talk with me."
   And my heart responds, "LORD, I am coming."
⁹ Do not hide yourself from me.
   Do not reject your servant in anger.
 You have always been my helper.
 Don't leave me now; don't abandon me,
   O God of my salvation!
¹⁰ Even if my father and mother abandon me,
   the LORD will hold me close.

¹¹ Teach me how to live, O LORD.
   Lead me along the path of honesty,
   for my enemies are waiting for me to fall.
¹² Do not let me fall into their hands.
   For they accuse me of things I've never done
   and breathe out violence against me.
¹³ Yet I am confident that I will see the LORD's goodness
   while I am here in the land of the living.

¹⁴ Wait patiently for the LORD.
   Be brave and courageous.
   Yes, wait patiently for the LORD.

PSALM 28

A psalm of David.

1 O LORD, you are my rock of safety.
　　Please help me; don't refuse to answer me.
　For if you are silent,
　　I might as well give up and die.
2 Listen to my prayer for mercy
　　as I cry out to you for help,
　　as I lift my hands toward your holy sanctuary.

3 Don't drag me away with the wicked—
　　with those who do evil—
　those who speak friendly words to their neighbors
　　while planning evil in their hearts.
4 Give them the punishment they so richly deserve!
　　Measure it out in proportion to their wickedness.
　Pay them back for all their evil deeds!
　　Give them a taste of what they have done to others.
5 They care nothing for what the LORD has done
　　or for what his hands have made.
　So he will tear them down like old buildings,
　　and they will never be rebuilt!

6 Praise the LORD!
　　For he has heard my cry for mercy.
7 The LORD is my strength, my shield from every danger.
　　I trust in him with all my heart.
　He helps me, and my heart is filled with joy.
　　I burst out in songs of thanksgiving.

8 The LORD protects his people
　　and gives victory to his anointed king.
9 Save your people!
　　Bless Israel, your special possession!
　Lead them like a shepherd,
　　and carry them forever in your arms.

PSALM 29

A psalm of David.

1 Give honor to the LORD, you angels;
　　give honor to the LORD for his glory and strength.
2 Give honor to the LORD for the glory of his name.
　　Worship the LORD in the splendor of his holiness.

3 The voice of the LORD echoes above the sea.
　　The God of glory thunders.
　The LORD thunders over the mighty sea.
4 The voice of the LORD is powerful;
　　the voice of the LORD is full of majesty.
5 The voice of the LORD splits the mighty cedars;
　　the LORD shatters the cedars of Lebanon.
6 He makes Lebanon's mountains skip like a calf
　　and Mount Hermon* to leap like a young bull.

29:6 Hebrew *Sirion,* another name for Mount Hermon.

7 The voice of the LORD strikes with lightning bolts.
8 The voice of the LORD makes the desert quake;
  the LORD shakes the desert of Kadesh.
9 The voice of the LORD twists mighty oaks*
  and strips the forests bare.
In his Temple everyone shouts, "Glory!"

10 The LORD rules over the floodwaters.
  The LORD reigns as king forever.
11 The LORD gives his people strength.
  The LORD blesses them with peace.

PSALM 30

A psalm of David, sung at the dedication of the Temple.

1 I will praise you, LORD, for you have rescued me.
  You refused to let my enemies triumph over me.
2 O LORD my God, I cried out to you for help,
  and you restored my health.
3 You brought me up from the grave, O LORD.
  You kept me from falling into the pit of death.

4 Sing to the LORD, all you godly ones!
  Praise his holy name.
5 His anger lasts for a moment,
  but his favor lasts a lifetime!
Weeping may go on all night,
  but joy comes with the morning.

6 When I was prosperous I said,
  "Nothing can stop me now!"
7 Your favor, O LORD, made me as secure as a mountain.
  Then you turned away from me, and I was shattered.

8 I cried out to you, O LORD.
  I begged the Lord for mercy, saying,
9 "What will you gain if I die,
  if I sink down into the grave?
Can my dust praise you from the grave?
  Can it tell the world of your faithfulness?
10 Hear me, LORD, and have mercy on me.
  Help me, O LORD."

11 You have turned my mourning into joyful dancing.
  You have taken away my clothes of mourning and clothed
  me with joy,
12 that I might sing praises to you and not be silent.
  O LORD my God, I will give you thanks forever!

PSALM 31

For the choir director: A psalm of David.

1 O LORD, I have come to you for protection;
  don't let me be put to shame.
  Rescue me, for you always do what is right.
2 Bend down and listen to me;

29:9 Or *causes the deer to writhe in labor.*

rescue me quickly.
Be for me a great rock of safety,
    a fortress where my enemies cannot reach me.

³ You are my rock and my fortress.
    For the honor of your name, lead me out of this peril.
⁴ Pull me from the trap my enemies set for me,
    for I find protection in you alone.
⁵ I entrust my spirit into your hand.
    Rescue me, LORD, for you are a faithful God.

⁶ I hate those who worship worthless idols.
    I trust in the LORD.
⁷ I am overcome with joy because of your unfailing love,
    for you have seen my troubles,
    and you care about the anguish of my soul.
⁸ You have not handed me over to my enemy
    but have set me in a safe place.

⁹ Have mercy on me, LORD, for I am in distress.
    My sight is blurred because of my tears.
    My body and soul are withering away.
¹⁰ I am dying from grief;
    my years are shortened by sadness.
   Misery* has drained my strength;
    I am wasting away from within.
¹¹ I am scorned by all my enemies
    and despised by my neighbors—
    even my friends are afraid to come near me.
   When they see me on the street,
    they turn the other way.
¹² I have been ignored as if I were dead,
    as if I were a broken pot.
¹³ I have heard the many rumors about me,
    and I am surrounded by terror.
   My enemies conspire against me,
    plotting to take my life.

¹⁴ But I am trusting you, O LORD,
    saying, "You are my God!"
¹⁵ My future is in your hands.
    Rescue me from those who hunt me down relentlessly.
¹⁶ Let your favor shine on your servant.
    In your unfailing love, save me.
¹⁷ Don't let me be disgraced, O LORD,
    for I call out to you for help.
   Let the wicked be disgraced;
    let them lie silent in the grave.
¹⁸ May their lying lips be silenced—
    those proud and arrogant lips that accuse the godly.

¹⁹ Your goodness is so great!
    You have stored up great blessings for those who honor you.

31:10 Or *Sin.*

You have done so much for those who come to you for
protection,
    blessing them before the watching world.
²⁰ You hide them in the shelter of your presence,
    safe from those who conspire against them.
You shelter them in your presence,
    far from accusing tongues.

²¹ Praise the LORD,
    for he has shown me his unfailing love.
    He kept me safe when my city was under attack.
²² In sudden fear I had cried out,
    "I have been cut off from the LORD!"
But you heard my cry for mercy
    and answered my call for help.

²³ Love the LORD, all you faithful ones!
    For the LORD protects those who are loyal to him,
    but he harshly punishes all who are arrogant.
²⁴ So be strong and take courage,
    all you who put your hope in the LORD!

PSALM 32
A psalm of David.

¹ Oh, what joy for those
    whose rebellion is forgiven,
    whose sin is put out of sight!
² Yes, what joy for those
    whose record the LORD has cleared of sin,
    whose lives are lived in complete honesty!

³ When I refused to confess my sin,
    I was weak and miserable,
    and I groaned all day long.
⁴ Day and night your hand of discipline was heavy on
me.
    My strength evaporated like water in the summer heat.
                              Interlude

⁵ Finally, I confessed all my sins to you
    and stopped trying to hide them.
I said to myself, "I will confess my rebellion to the LORD."
    And you forgave me! All my guilt is gone.   *Interlude*

⁶ Therefore, let all the godly confess their rebellion to you while
there is time,
    that they may not drown in the floodwaters of judgment.
⁷ For you are my hiding place;
    you protect me from trouble.
    You surround me with songs of victory.   *Interlude*

⁸ The LORD says, "I will guide you along the best pathway for
your life.
    I will advise you and watch over you.
⁹ Do not be like a senseless horse or mule
    that needs a bit and bridle to keep it under control."

¹⁰ Many sorrows come to the wicked,
  but unfailing love surrounds those who trust the LORD.
¹¹ So rejoice in the LORD and be glad, all you who obey him!
  Shout for joy, all you whose hearts are pure!

PSALM 33

¹ Let the godly sing with joy to the LORD,
  for it is fitting to praise him.
² Praise the LORD with melodies on the lyre;
  make music for him on the ten-stringed harp.
³ Sing new songs of praise to him;
  play skillfully on the harp and sing with joy.

⁴ For the word of the LORD holds true,
  and everything he does is worthy of our trust.
⁵ He loves whatever is just and good,
  and his unfailing love fills the earth.

⁶ The LORD merely spoke,
  and the heavens were created.
 He breathed the word,
  and all the stars were born.
⁷ He gave the sea its boundaries
  and locked the oceans in vast reservoirs.

⁸ Let everyone in the world fear the LORD,
  and let everyone stand in awe of him.
⁹ For when he spoke, the world began!
  It appeared at his command.

¹⁰ The LORD shatters the plans of the nations
  and thwarts all their schemes.
¹¹ But the LORD's plans stand firm forever;
  his intentions can never be shaken.

¹² What joy for the nation whose God is the LORD,
  whose people he has chosen for his own.

¹³ The LORD looks down from heaven
  and sees the whole human race.
¹⁴ From his throne he observes
  all who live on the earth.
¹⁵ He made their hearts,
  so he understands everything they do.
¹⁶ The best-equipped army cannot save a king,
  nor is great strength enough to save a warrior.
¹⁷ Don't count on your warhorse to give you victory—
  for all its strength, it cannot save you.

¹⁸ But the LORD watches over those who fear him,
  those who rely on his unfailing love.
¹⁹ He rescues them from death
  and keeps them alive in times of famine.

²⁰ We depend on the LORD alone to save us.
  Only he can help us, protecting us like a shield.
²¹ In him our hearts rejoice,

for we are trusting in his holy name.
²² Let your unfailing love surround us, LORD,
for our hope is in you alone.

PSALM 34

A psalm of David, regarding the time he pretended to be insane in front of Abimelech, who sent him away.

¹ I will praise the LORD at all times.
I will constantly speak his praises.
² I will boast only in the LORD;
let all who are discouraged take heart.
³ Come, let us tell of the LORD's greatness;
let us exalt his name together.

⁴ I prayed to the LORD, and he answered me,
freeing me from all my fears.
⁵ Those who look to him for help will be radiant with joy;
no shadow of shame will darken their faces.
⁶ I cried out to the LORD in my suffering, and he heard me.
He set me free from all my fears.
⁷ For the angel of the LORD guards all who fear him,
and he rescues them.

⁸ Taste and see that the LORD is good.
Oh, the joys of those who trust in him!
⁹ Let the LORD's people show him reverence,
for those who honor him will have all they need.
¹⁰ Even strong young lions sometimes go hungry,
but those who trust in the LORD will never lack any good thing.

¹¹ Come, my children, and listen to me,
and I will teach you to fear the LORD.
¹² Do any of you want to live
a life that is long and good?
¹³ Then watch your tongue!
Keep your lips from telling lies!
¹⁴ Turn away from evil and do good.
Work hard at living in peace with others.

¹⁵ The eyes of the LORD watch over those who do right;
his ears are open to their cries for help.
¹⁶ But the LORD turns his face against those who do evil;
he will erase their memory from the earth.

¹⁷ The LORD hears his people when they call to him for help.
He rescues them from all their troubles.
¹⁸ The LORD is close to the brokenhearted;
he rescues those who are crushed in spirit.

¹⁹ The righteous face many troubles,
but the LORD rescues them from each and every one.
²⁰ For the LORD protects them from harm—
not one of their bones* will be broken!

²¹ Calamity will surely overtake the wicked,
and those who hate the righteous will be punished.

34:20 Hebrew *protects him from harm—not one of his bones.*

²² But the LORD will redeem those who serve him.
　　Everyone who trusts in him will be freely pardoned.

PSALM 35
A psalm of David.

¹ O LORD, oppose those who oppose me.
　　Declare war on those who are attacking me.
² Put on your armor, and take up your shield.
　　Prepare for battle, and come to my aid.
³ Lift up your spear and javelin
　　and block the way of my enemies.
　Let me hear you say,
　　"I am your salvation!"

⁴ Humiliate and disgrace those trying to kill me;
　　turn them back in confusion.
⁵ Blow them away like chaff in the wind—
　　a wind sent by the angel of the LORD.
⁶ Make their path dark and slippery,
　　with the angel of the LORD pursuing them.
⁷ Although I did them no wrong,
　　they laid a trap for me.
　Although I did them no wrong,
　　they dug a pit for me.
⁸ So let sudden ruin overtake them!
　　Let them be caught in the snare they set for me!
　　Let them fall to destruction in the pit they dug for me.

⁹ Then I will rejoice in the LORD.
　　I will be glad because he rescues me.
¹⁰ I will praise him from the bottom of my heart:
　　"LORD, who can compare with you?
　Who else rescues the weak and helpless from the strong?
　　Who else protects the poor and needy from those who want
　　　to rob them?"

¹¹ Malicious witnesses testify against me.
　　They accuse me of things I don't even know about.
¹² They repay me with evil for the good I do.
　　I am sick with despair.
¹³ Yet when they were ill,
　　I grieved for them.
　I even fasted and prayed for them,
　　but my prayers returned unanswered.
¹⁴ I was sad, as though they were my friends or family,
　　as if I were grieving for my own mother.

¹⁵ But they are glad now that I am in trouble;
　　they gleefully join together against me.
　I am attacked by people I don't even know;
　　they hurl slander at me continually.
¹⁶ They mock me with the worst kind of profanity,
　　and they snarl at me.

¹⁷ How long, O Lord, will you look on and do nothing?
　　Rescue me from their fierce attacks.

Protect my life from these lions!
¹⁸ Then I will thank you in front of the entire congregation.
I will praise you before all the people.

¹⁹ Don't let my treacherous enemies
rejoice over my defeat.
Don't let those who hate me without cause
gloat over my sorrow.
²⁰ They don't talk of peace;
they plot against innocent people
who are minding their own business.
²¹ They shout that they have seen me doing wrong.
"Aha," they say. "Aha!
With our own eyes we saw him do it!"

²² O Lᴏʀᴅ, you know all about this.
Do not stay silent.
Don't abandon me now, O Lord.
²³ Wake up! Rise to my defense!
Take up my case, my God and my Lord.
²⁴ Declare me "not guilty," O Lᴏʀᴅ my God, for you give justice.
Don't let my enemies laugh about me in my troubles.
²⁵ Don't let them say, "Look! We have what we wanted!
Now we will eat him alive!"

²⁶ May those who rejoice at my troubles
be humiliated and disgraced.
May those who triumph over me
be covered with shame and dishonor.

²⁷ But give great joy to those
who have stood with me in my defense.
Let them continually say, "Great is the Lᴏʀᴅ,
who enjoys helping his servant."
²⁸ Then I will tell everyone of your justice and goodness,
and I will praise you all day long.

PSALM 36
For the choir director: A psalm of David, the servant of the Lᴏʀᴅ.

¹ Sin whispers to the wicked, deep within their hearts.
They have no fear of God to restrain them.
² In their blind conceit,
they cannot see how wicked they really are.
³ Everything they say is crooked and deceitful.
They refuse to act wisely or do what is good.
⁴ They lie awake at night, hatching sinful plots.
Their course of action is never good.
They make no attempt to turn from evil.

⁵ Your unfailing love, O Lᴏʀᴅ, is as vast as the heavens;
your faithfulness reaches beyond the clouds.
⁶ Your righteousness is like the mighty mountains,
your justice like the ocean depths.
You care for people and animals alike, O Lᴏʀᴅ.
⁷ How precious is your unfailing love, O God!
All humanity finds shelter

in the shadow of your wings.
⁸ You feed them from the abundance of your own house,
letting them drink from your rivers of delight.
⁹ For you are the fountain of life,
the light by which we see.

¹⁰ Pour out your unfailing love on those who love you;
give justice to those with honest hearts.
¹¹ Don't let the proud trample me;
don't let the wicked push me around.
¹² Look! They have fallen!
They have been thrown down, never to rise again.

PSALM 3 7

A psalm of David.

¹ Don't worry about the wicked.
Don't envy those who do wrong.
² For like grass, they soon fade away.
Like springtime flowers, they soon wither.

³ Trust in the LORD and do good.
Then you will live safely in the land and prosper.
⁴ Take delight in the LORD,
and he will give you your heart's desires.

⁵ Commit everything you do to the LORD.
Trust him, and he will help you.
⁶ He will make your innocence as clear as the dawn,
and the justice of your cause will shine like the noonday
sun.

⁷ Be still in the presence of the LORD,
and wait patiently for him to act.
Don't worry about evil people who prosper
or fret about their wicked schemes.

⁸ Stop your anger!
Turn from your rage!
Do not envy others—
it only leads to harm.
⁹ For the wicked will be destroyed,
but those who trust in the LORD will possess the land.

¹⁰ In a little while, the wicked will disappear.
Though you look for them, they will be gone.
¹¹ Those who are gentle and lowly will possess the land;
they will live in prosperous security.

¹² The wicked plot against the godly;
they snarl at them in defiance.
¹³ But the Lord just laughs,
for he sees their day of judgment coming.

¹⁴ The wicked draw their swords
and string their bows
to kill the poor and the oppressed,
to slaughter those who do right.

¹⁵ But they will be stabbed through the heart with their own
swords,
and their bows will be broken.

¹⁶ It is better to be godly and have little
than to be evil and possess much.
¹⁷ For the strength of the wicked will be shattered,
but the LORD takes care of the godly.

¹⁸ Day by day the LORD takes care of the innocent,
and they will receive a reward that lasts forever.
¹⁹ They will survive through hard times;
even in famine they will have more than enough.

²⁰ But the wicked will perish.
The LORD's enemies are like flowers in a field—
they will disappear like smoke.

²¹ The wicked borrow and never repay,
but the godly are generous givers.
²² Those blessed by the LORD will inherit the land,
but those cursed by him will die.

²³ The steps of the godly are directed by the LORD.
He delights in every detail of their lives.
²⁴ Though they stumble, they will not fall,
for the LORD holds them by the hand.

²⁵ Once I was young, and now I am old.
Yet I have never seen the godly forsaken,
nor seen their children begging for bread.
²⁶ The godly always give generous loans to others,
and their children are a blessing.

²⁷ Turn from evil and do good,
and you will live in the land forever.
²⁸ For the LORD loves justice,
and he will never abandon the godly.

He will keep them safe forever,
but the children of the wicked will perish.
²⁹ The godly will inherit the land
and will live there forever.

³⁰ The godly offer good counsel;
they know what is right from wrong.
³¹ They fill their hearts with God's law,
so they will never slip from his path.

³² Those who are evil spy on the godly,
waiting for an excuse to kill them.
³³ But the LORD will not let the wicked succeed
or let the godly be condemned when they are brought
before the judge.

³⁴ Don't be impatient for the LORD to act!
Travel steadily along his path.
He will honor you, giving you the land.
You will see the wicked destroyed.

³⁵ I myself have seen it happen—
   proud and evil people thriving like mighty trees.
³⁶ But when I looked again, they were gone!
   Though I searched for them, I could not find them!

³⁷ Look at those who are honest and good,
   for a wonderful future lies before those who love peace.
³⁸ But the wicked will be destroyed;
   they have no future.

³⁹ The LORD saves the godly;
   he is their fortress in times of trouble.
⁴⁰ The LORD helps them,
   rescuing them from the wicked.
He saves them,
   and they find shelter in him.

PSALM 38

A psalm of David, to bring us to the LORD's remembrance.

¹ O LORD, don't rebuke me in your anger!
   Don't discipline me in your rage!
² Your arrows have struck deep,
   and your blows are crushing me.

³ Because of your anger, my whole body is sick;
   my health is broken because of my sins.
⁴ My guilt overwhelms me—
   it is a burden too heavy to bear.
⁵ My wounds fester and stink
   because of my foolish sins.
⁶ I am bent over and racked with pain.
   My days are filled with grief.
⁷ A raging fever burns within me,
   and my health is broken.
⁸ I am exhausted and completely crushed.
   My groans come from an anguished heart.

⁹ You know what I long for, Lord;
   you hear my every sigh.
¹⁰ My heart beats wildly, my strength fails,
   and I am going blind.
¹¹ My loved ones and friends stay away, fearing my disease.
   Even my own family stands at a distance.
¹² Meanwhile, my enemies lay traps for me;
   they make plans to ruin me.
   They think up treacherous deeds all day long.
¹³ But I am deaf to all their threats.
   I am silent before them as one who cannot speak.
¹⁴ I choose to hear nothing,
   and I make no reply.

¹⁵ For I am waiting for you, O LORD.
   You must answer for me, O Lord my God.
¹⁶ I prayed, "Don't let my enemies gloat over me
   or rejoice at my downfall."
¹⁷ I am on the verge of collapse,

facing constant pain.
18 But I confess my sins;
    I am deeply sorry for what I have done.
19 My enemies are many;
    they hate me though I have done nothing against them.
20 They repay me evil for good
    and oppose me because I stand for the right.

21 Do not abandon me, LORD.
    Do not stand at a distance, my God.
22 Come quickly to help me, O Lord my savior.

PSALM 39

For Jeduthun, the choir director: A psalm of David.

1 I said to myself, "I will watch what I do
    and not sin in what I say.
  I will curb my tongue
    when the ungodly are around me."
2 But as I stood there in silence—
    not even speaking of good things—
    the turmoil within me grew to the bursting point.
3 My thoughts grew hot within me
    and began to burn,
    igniting a fire of words:
4 "LORD, remind me how brief my time on earth will be.
    Remind me that my days are numbered,
    and that my life is fleeing away.
5 My life is no longer than the width of my hand.
    An entire lifetime is just a moment to you;
    human existence is but a breath."   *Interlude*

6 We are merely moving shadows,
    and all our busy rushing ends in nothing.
    We heap up wealth for someone else to spend.

7 And so, Lord, where do I put my hope?
    My only hope is in you.
8 Rescue me from my rebellion,
    for even fools mock me when I rebel.
9 I am silent before you; I won't say a word.
    For my punishment is from you.
10 Please, don't punish me anymore!
    I am exhausted by the blows from your hand.
11 When you discipline people for their sins,
    their lives can be crushed like the life of a moth.
    Human existence is as frail as breath.   *Interlude*

12 Hear my prayer, O LORD!
    Listen to my cries for help!
    Don't ignore my tears.
  For I am your guest—
    a traveler passing through,
    as my ancestors were before me.
13 Spare me so I can smile again
    before I am gone and exist no more.

PSALM 40

For the choir director: A psalm of David.

1 I waited patiently for the LORD to help me,
   and he turned to me and heard my cry.
2 He lifted me out of the pit of despair,
   out of the mud and the mire.
 He set my feet on solid ground
   and steadied me as I walked along.
3 He has given me a new song to sing,
   a hymn of praise to our God.
 Many will see what he has done and be astounded.
   They will put their trust in the LORD.

4 Oh, the joys of those who trust the LORD,
   who have no confidence in the proud,
   or in those who worship idols.
5 O LORD my God, you have done many miracles for us.
   Your plans for us are too numerous to list.
 If I tried to recite all your wonderful deeds,
   I would never come to the end of them.

6 You take no delight in sacrifices or offerings.
   Now that you have made me listen, I finally
      understand—
   you don't require burnt offerings or sin offerings.
7 Then I said, "Look, I have come.
   And this has been written about me in your scroll:
8 I take joy in doing your will, my God,
   for your law is written on my heart."

9 I have told all your people about your justice.
   I have not been afraid to speak out,
   as you, O LORD, well know.
10 I have not kept this good news hidden in my heart;
    I have talked about your faithfulness and saving power.
 I have told everyone in the great assembly
    of your unfailing love and faithfulness.

11 LORD, don't hold back your tender mercies from me.
    My only hope is in your unfailing love and faithfulness.
12 For troubles surround me—
    too many to count!
 They pile up so high
    I can't see my way out.
 They are more numerous than the hairs on my head.
    I have lost all my courage.

13 Please, LORD, rescue me!
    Come quickly, LORD, and help me.
14 May those who try to destroy me
    be humiliated and put to shame.
 May those who take delight in my trouble
    be turned back in disgrace.
15 Let them be horrified by their shame,
    for they said, "Aha! We've got him now!"

¹⁶ But may all who search for you
    be filled with joy and gladness.
  May those who love your salvation
    repeatedly shout, "The LORD is great!"

¹⁷ As for me, I am poor and needy,
    but the Lord is thinking about me right now.
  You are my helper and my savior.
    Do not delay, O my God.

PSALM 41

For the choir director: A psalm of David.

¹ Oh, the joys of those who are kind to the poor.
    The LORD rescues them in times of trouble.
² The LORD protects them
    and keeps them alive.
  He gives them prosperity
    and rescues them from their enemies.
³ The LORD nurses them when they are sick
    and eases their pain and discomfort.

⁴ "O LORD," I prayed, "have mercy on me.
    Heal me, for I have sinned against you."
⁵ But my enemies say nothing but evil about me.
    "How soon will he die and be forgotten?" they ask.
⁶ They visit me as if they are my friends,
    but all the while they gather gossip,
    and when they leave, they spread it everywhere.
⁷ All who hate me whisper about me,
    imagining the worst for me.
⁸ "Whatever he has, it is fatal," they say.
    "He will never get out of that bed!"
⁹ Even my best friend, the one I trusted completely,
    the one who shared my food,
    has turned against me.

¹⁰ LORD, have mercy on me.
    Make me well again, so I can pay them back!
¹¹ I know that you are pleased with me,
    for you have not let my enemy triumph over me.
¹² You have preserved my life because I am innocent;
    you have brought me into your presence forever.

¹³ Bless the LORD, the God of Israel,
    who lives forever from eternal ages past.
  Amen and amen!

BOOK TWO (Psalms 42–72)

PSALM 42

For the choir director: A psalm of the descendants of Korah.

¹ As the deer pants for streams of water,
    so I long for you, O God.
² I thirst for God, the living God.
    When can I come and stand before him?

3 Day and night, I have only tears for food,
    while my enemies continually taunt me, saying,
    "Where is this God of yours?"

4 My heart is breaking
    as I remember how it used to be:
  I walked among the crowds of worshipers,
    leading a great procession to the house of God,
  singing for joy and giving thanks—
    it was the sound of a great celebration!

5 Why am I discouraged?
    Why so sad?
  I will put my hope in God!
    I will praise him again—
    my Savior and 6my God!

  Now I am deeply discouraged,
    but I will remember your kindness—
  from Mount Hermon, the source of the Jordan,
    from the land of Mount Mizar.
7 I hear the tumult of the raging seas
    as your waves and surging tides sweep over me.

8 Through each day the LORD pours his unfailing love upon
        me,
    and through each night I sing his songs,
    praying to God who gives me life.

9 "O God my rock," I cry,
    "Why have you forsaken me?
  Why must I wander in darkness,
    oppressed by my enemies?"
10 Their taunts pierce me like a fatal wound.
    They scoff, "Where is this God of yours?"

11 Why am I discouraged?
    Why so sad?
  I will put my hope in God!
    I will praise him again—
    my Savior and my God!

P S A L M 4 3
1 O God, take up my cause!
    Defend me against these ungodly people.
    Rescue me from these unjust liars.
2 For you are God, my only safe haven.
    Why have you tossed me aside?
  Why must I wander around in darkness,
    oppressed by my enemies?

3 Send out your light and your truth;
    let them guide me.
  Let them lead me to your holy mountain,
    to the place where you live.
4 There I will go to the altar of God,
    to God—the source of all my joy.

I will praise you with my harp,
O God, my God!

5 Why am I discouraged?
Why so sad?
I will put my hope in God!
I will praise him again—
my Savior and my God!

PSALM 44

For the choir director: A psalm of the descendants of Korah.

1 O God, we have heard it with our own ears—
our ancestors have told us
of all you did in other days,
in days long ago:
2 You drove out the pagan nations
and gave all the land to our ancestors;
you crushed their enemies,
setting our ancestors free.
3 They did not conquer the land with their swords;
it was not their own strength that gave them victory.
It was by your mighty power that they succeeded;
it was because you favored them and smiled on them.

4 You are my King and my God.
You command victories for your people.*
5 Only by your power can we push back our enemies;
only in your name can we trample our foes.
6 I do not trust my bow;
I do not count on my sword to save me.
7 It is you who gives us victory over our enemies;
it is you who humbles those who hate us.
8 O God, we give glory to you all day long
and constantly praise your name.   *Interlude*

9 But now you have tossed us aside in dishonor.
You no longer lead our armies to battle.
10 You make us retreat from our enemies
and allow them to plunder our land.
11 You have treated us like sheep waiting to be slaughtered;
you have scattered us among the nations.
12 You sold us—your precious people—for a pittance.
You valued us at nothing at all.

13 You have caused all our neighbors to mock us.
We are an object of scorn and derision to the nations
around us.
14 You have made us the butt of their jokes;
we are scorned by the whole world.
15 We can't escape the constant humiliation;
shame is written across our faces.
16 All we hear are the taunts of our mockers.
All we see are our vengeful enemies.

44:4 Hebrew *for Jacob.*

¹⁷ All this has happened despite our loyalty to you.
    We have not violated your covenant.
¹⁸ Our hearts have not deserted you.
    We have not strayed from your path.
¹⁹ Yet you have crushed us in the desert.
    You have covered us with darkness and death.

²⁰ If we had turned away from worshiping our God
    or spread our hands in prayer to foreign gods,
²¹ God would surely have known it,
    for he knows the secrets of every heart.
²² For your sake we are killed every day;
    we are being slaughtered like sheep.

²³ Wake up, O Lord! Why do you sleep?
    Get up! Do not reject us forever.
²⁴ Why do you look the other way?
    Why do you ignore our suffering and oppression?
²⁵ We collapse in the dust,
    lying face down in the dirt.
²⁶ Rise up! Come and help us!
    Save us because of your unfailing love.

PSALM 45

For the choir director: A psalm of the descendants of Korah, to be sung to the tune "Lilies." A love song.

¹ My heart overflows with a beautiful thought!
    I will recite a lovely poem to the king,
    for my tongue is like the pen of a skillful poet.

² You are the most handsome of all.
    Gracious words stream from your lips.
    God himself has blessed you forever.
³ Put on your sword, O mighty warrior!
    You are so glorious, so majestic!
⁴ In your majesty, ride out to victory,
    defending truth, humility, and justice.
    Go forth to perform awe-inspiring deeds!
⁵ Your arrows are sharp,
    piercing your enemies' hearts.
  The nations fall before you,
    lying down beneath your feet.

⁶ Your throne, O God,* endures forever and ever.
    Your royal power is expressed in justice.
⁷ You love what is right and hate what is wrong.
    Therefore God, your God, has anointed you,
    pouring out the oil of joy on you more than on anyone else.
⁸ Your robes are perfumed with myrrh, aloes, and cassia.
    In palaces decorated with ivory,
    you are entertained by the music of harps.
⁹ Kings' daughters are among your concubines.
    At your right side stands the queen,
    wearing jewelry of finest gold from Ophir!

45:6 Or *Your divine throne.*

10 Listen to me, O royal daughter; take to heart what I say.
　　Forget your people and your homeland far away.
11 For your royal husband delights in your beauty;
　　honor him, for he is your lord.
12 The princes of Tyre* will shower you with gifts.
　　People of great wealth will entreat your favor.

13 The bride, a princess, waits within her chamber,
　　dressed in a gown woven with gold.
14 In her beautiful robes, she is led to the king,
　　accompanied by her bridesmaids.
15 What a joyful, enthusiastic procession
　　as they enter the king's palace!

16 Your sons will become kings like their father.
　　You will make them rulers over many lands.

17 I will bring honor to your name in every generation.
　　Therefore, the nations will praise you forever and ever.

PSALM 46

For the choir director: A psalm of the descendants of Korah, to be sung by soprano voices.* A song.

1 God is our refuge and strength,
　　always ready to help in times of trouble.
2 So we will not fear, even if earthquakes come
　　and the mountains crumble into the sea.
3 Let the oceans roar and foam.
　　Let the mountains tremble as the waters surge!　　*Interlude*

4 A river brings joy to the city of our God,
　　the sacred home of the Most High.
5 God himself lives in that city; it cannot be destroyed.
　　God will protect it at the break of day.
6 The nations are in an uproar,
　　and kingdoms crumble!
　God thunders,
　　and the earth melts!

7 The LORD Almighty is here among us;
　　the God of Israel* is our fortress.　　*Interlude*

8 Come, see the glorious works of the LORD:
　　See how he brings destruction upon the world
9 and causes wars to end throughout the earth.
　　He breaks the bow and snaps the spear in two;
　　he burns the shields with fire.

10 "Be silent, and know that I am God!
　　I will be honored by every nation.
　　I will be honored throughout the world."

11 The LORD Almighty is here among us;
　　the God of Israel is our fortress.　　*Interlude*

45:12 Hebrew *The daughter of Tyre.*　　46:TITLE Hebrew *according to alamoth.*
46:7 Hebrew *of Jacob;* also in 46:11.

P S A L M   4 7
For the choir director: A psalm of the descendants of Korah.

1 Come, everyone, and clap your hands for joy!
    Shout to God with joyful praise!
2 For the LORD Most High is awesome.
    He is the great King of all the earth.
3 He subdues the nations before us,
    putting our enemies beneath our feet.
4 He chose the Promised Land as our inheritance,
    the proud possession of Jacob's descendants, whom he
        loves.   *Interlude*

5 God has ascended with a mighty shout.
    The LORD has ascended with trumpets blaring.
6 Sing praise to God, sing praises;
    sing praise to our King, sing praises!

7 For God is the King over all the earth.
    Praise him with a psalm!
8 God reigns above the nations,
    sitting on his holy throne.
9 The rulers of the world have gathered together.
    They join us in praising the God of Abraham.
For all the kings of the earth belong to God.
    He is highly honored everywhere.

P S A L M   4 8
A psalm of the descendants of Korah. A song.

1 How great is the LORD,
    and how much we should praise him
in the city of our God,
    which is on his holy mountain!
2 It is magnificent in elevation—
    the whole earth rejoices to see it!
Mount Zion, the holy mountain,*
    is the city of the great King!
3 God himself is in Jerusalem's towers.
    He reveals himself as her defender.

4 The kings of the earth joined forces
    and advanced against the city.
5 But when they saw it, they were stunned;
    they were terrified and ran away.
6 They were gripped with terror,
    like a woman writhing in the pain of childbirth
7 or like the mighty ships of Tarshish
    being shattered by a powerful east wind.

8 We had heard of the city's glory,
    but now we have seen it ourselves—
    the city of the LORD Almighty.
It is the city of our God;
    he will make it safe forever.   *Interlude*

48:2 Or *Mount Zion, in the far north*; Hebrew reads *Mount Zion, the heights of Zaphon.*

⁹ O God, we meditate on your unfailing love
    as we worship in your Temple.
¹⁰ As your name deserves, O God,
    you will be praised to the ends of the earth.
    Your strong right hand is filled with victory.
¹¹ Let the people on Mount Zion rejoice.
    Let the towns of Judah be glad,
    for your judgments are just.

¹² Go, inspect the city of Jerusalem.*
    Walk around and count the many towers.
¹³ Take note of the fortified walls,
    and tour all the citadels,
that you may describe them
    to future generations.
¹⁴ For that is what God is like.
    He is our God forever and ever,
    and he will be our guide until we die.

PSALM 49

For the choir director: A psalm of the descendants of Korah.

¹ Listen to this, all you people!
    Pay attention, everyone in the world!
² High and low,
    rich and poor—listen!
³ For my words are wise,
    and my thoughts are filled with insight.
⁴ I listen carefully to many proverbs
    and solve riddles with inspiration from a harp.

⁵ There is no need to fear when times of trouble come,
    when enemies are surrounding me.
⁶ They trust in their wealth
    and boast of great riches.
⁷ Yet they cannot redeem themselves from death*
    by paying a ransom to God.
⁸ Redemption does not come so easily,
    for no one can ever pay enough
⁹ to live forever
    and never see the grave.

¹⁰ Those who are wise must finally die,
    just like the foolish and senseless,
    leaving all their wealth behind.
¹¹ The grave is their eternal home,
    where they will stay forever.
They may name their estates after themselves,
    but they leave their wealth to others.
¹² They will not last long despite their riches—
    they will die like the animals.
¹³ This is the fate of fools,
    though they will be remembered as being so wise.

Interlude

48:12 Hebrew *Zion*.   **49:7** Or *no one can redeem the life of another.*

¹⁴ Like sheep, they are led to the grave,
    where death will be their shepherd.
  In the morning the godly will rule over them.
    Their bodies will rot in the grave,
    far from their grand estates.
¹⁵ But as for me, God will redeem my life.
    He will snatch me from the power of death.   *Interlude*

¹⁶ So don't be dismayed when the wicked grow rich,
    and their homes become ever more splendid.
¹⁷ For when they die, they carry nothing with them.
    Their wealth will not follow them into the grave.
¹⁸ In this life they consider themselves fortunate,
    and the world loudly applauds their success.
¹⁹ But they will die like all others before them
    and never again see the light of day.
²⁰ People who boast of their wealth don't understand
    that they will die like the animals.

PSALM 50

A psalm of Asaph.

¹ The mighty God, the LORD, has spoken;
    he has summoned all humanity from east to west!
² From Mount Zion, the perfection of beauty,
    God shines in glorious radiance.
³ Our God approaches with the noise of thunder.
    Fire devours everything in his way,
    and a great storm rages around him.
⁴ Heaven and earth will be his witnesses
    as he judges his people:
⁵ "Bring my faithful people to me—
    those who made a covenant with me by giving
        sacrifices."
⁶ Then let the heavens proclaim his justice,
    for God himself will be the judge.   *Interlude*

⁷ "O my people, listen as I speak.
    Here are my charges against you, O Israel:
    I am God, your God!
⁸ I have no complaint about your sacrifices
    or the burnt offerings you constantly bring to my altar.
⁹ But I want no more bulls from your barns;
    I want no more goats from your pens.
¹⁰ For all the animals of the forest are mine,
    and I own the cattle on a thousand hills.
¹¹ Every bird of the mountains
    and all the animals of the field belong to me.
¹² If I were hungry, I would not mention it to you,
    for all the world is mine and everything in it.
¹³ I don't need the bulls you sacrifice;
    I don't need the blood of goats.
¹⁴ What I want instead is your true thanks to God;
    I want you to fulfill your vows to the Most High.
¹⁵ Trust me in your times of trouble,

and I will rescue you,
and you will give me glory."

16 But God says to the wicked:
"Recite my laws no longer,
and don't pretend that you obey me.
17 For you refuse my discipline
and treat my laws like trash.
18 When you see a thief, you help him,
and you spend your time with adulterers.
19 Your mouths are filled with wickedness,
and your tongues are full of lies.
20 You sit around and slander a brother—
your own mother's son.
21 While you did all this, I remained silent,
and you thought I didn't care.
But now I will rebuke you,
listing all my charges against you.
22 Repent, all of you who ignore me,
or I will tear you apart,
and no one will help you.
23 But giving thanks is a sacrifice that truly honors me.
If you keep to my path,
I will reveal to you the salvation of God."

P S A L M   5 1
*For the choir director: A psalm of David, regarding the time Nathan the prophet
came to him after David had committed adultery with Bathsheba.*

1 Have mercy on me, O God,
because of your unfailing love.
Because of your great compassion,
blot out the stain of my sins.
2 Wash me clean from my guilt.
Purify me from my sin.

3 For I recognize my shameful deeds—
they haunt me day and night.
4 Against you, and you alone, have I sinned;
I have done what is evil in your sight.
You will be proved right in what you say,
and your judgment against me is just.

5 For I was born a sinner—
yes, from the moment my mother conceived me.
6 But you desire honesty from the heart,
so you can teach me to be wise in my inmost being.

7 Purify me from my sins,* and I will be clean;
wash me, and I will be whiter than snow.
8 Oh, give me back my joy again;
you have broken me—
now let me rejoice.
9 Don't keep looking at my sins.
Remove the stain of my guilt.

51:7 Hebrew *Purify me with the hyssop branch.*

¹⁰ Create in me a clean heart, O God.
    Renew a right spirit within me.
¹¹ Do not banish me from your presence,
    and don't take your Holy Spirit from me.
¹² Restore to me again the joy of your salvation,
    and make me willing to obey you.
¹³ Then I will teach your ways to sinners,
    and they will return to you.
¹⁴ Forgive me for shedding blood, O God who saves;
    then I will joyfully sing of your forgiveness.
¹⁵ Unseal my lips, O Lord,
    that I may praise you.

¹⁶ You would not be pleased with sacrifices,
    or I would bring them.
  If I brought you a burnt offering,
    you would not accept it.
¹⁷ The sacrifice you want is a broken spirit.
    A broken and repentant heart, O God,
    you will not despise.

¹⁸ Look with favor on Zion and help her;
    rebuild the walls of Jerusalem.
¹⁹ Then you will be pleased with worthy sacrifices
    and with our whole burnt offerings;
    and bulls will again be sacrificed on your altar.

PSALM 52

For the choir director: A psalm of David, regarding the time Doeg the Edomite
told Saul that Ahimelech had given refuge to David.

¹ You call yourself a hero, do you?
    Why boast about this crime of yours,
    you who have disgraced God's people?
² All day long you plot destruction.
    Your tongue cuts like a sharp razor;
    you're an expert at telling lies.
³ You love evil more than good
    and lies more than truth.   *Interlude*

⁴ You love to say things that harm others,
    you liar!
⁵ But God will strike you down once and for all.
    He will pull you from your home
    and drag you from the land of the living.   *Interlude*

⁶ The righteous will see it and be amazed.
    They will laugh and say,
⁷ "Look what happens to mighty warriors
    who do not trust in God.
  They trust their wealth instead
    and grow more and more bold in their wickedness."

⁸ But I am like an olive tree,
    thriving in the house of God.
  I trust in God's unfailing love
    forever and ever.

⁹ I will praise you forever, O God,
  for what you have done.
I will wait for your mercies
  in the presence of your people.

PSALM 53

For the choir director: A meditation of David.

¹ Only fools say in their hearts,
  "There is no God."
They are corrupt, and their actions are evil;
  no one does good!

² God looks down from heaven
  on the entire human race;
he looks to see if there is even one with real
    understanding,
  one who seeks for God.
³ But no, all have turned away from God;
  all have become corrupt.
No one does good,
  not even one!

⁴ Will those who do evil never learn?
  They eat up my people like bread;
  they wouldn't think of praying to God.
⁵ But then terror will grip them,
  terror like they have never known before.
God will scatter the bones of your enemies.
  You will put them to shame, for God has rejected them.

⁶ Oh, that salvation would come from Mount Zion to rescue
    Israel!
For when God restores his people,
  Jacob will shout with joy, and Israel will rejoice.

PSALM 54

For the choir director: A meditation of David, regarding the time the Ziphites came and said to Saul, "We know where David is hiding." To be accompanied by stringed instruments.

¹ Come with great power, O God, and rescue me!
  Defend me with your might.
² O God, listen to my prayer.
  Pay attention to my plea.

³ For strangers are attacking me;
  violent men are trying to kill me.
  They care nothing for God.   *Interlude*

⁴ But God is my helper.
  The Lord is the one who keeps me alive!
⁵ May my enemies' plans for evil be turned against them.
  Do as you promised and put an end to them.

⁶ I will sacrifice a voluntary offering to you;
  I will praise your name, O LORD,
  for it is good.

7 For you will rescue me from my troubles
  and help me to triumph over my enemies.

PSALM 55

For the choir director: A psalm of David, to be accompanied by stringed instruments.

1 Listen to my prayer, O God.
  Do not ignore my cry for help!
2 Please listen and answer me,
  for I am overwhelmed by my troubles.
3 My enemies shout at me,
  making loud and wicked threats.
They bring trouble on me,
  hunting me down in their anger.

4 My heart is in anguish.
  The terror of death overpowers me.
5 Fear and trembling overwhelm me.
  I can't stop shaking.
6 Oh, how I wish I had wings like a dove;
  then I would fly away and rest!
7 I would fly far away
  to the quiet of the wilderness.   *Interlude*
8 How quickly I would escape—
  far away from this wild storm of hatred.

9 Destroy them, Lord, and confuse their speech,
  for I see violence and strife in the city.
10 Its walls are patrolled day and night against invaders,
  but the real danger is wickedness within the city.
11 Murder and robbery are everywhere there;
  threats and cheating are rampant in the streets.

12 It is not an enemy who taunts me—
  I could bear that.
It is not my foes who so arrogantly insult me—
  I could have hidden from them.
13 Instead, it is you—my equal,
  my companion and close friend.
14 What good fellowship we enjoyed
  as we walked together to the house of God.

15 Let death seize my enemies by surprise;
  let the grave* swallow them alive,
  for evil makes its home within them.

16 But I will call on God,
  and the LORD will rescue me.
17 Morning, noon, and night
  I plead aloud in my distress,
  and the LORD hears my voice.
18 He rescues me and keeps me safe
  from the battle waged against me,
  even though many still oppose me.
19 God, who is king forever,

55:15 Hebrew *let Sheol.*

will hear me and will humble them.   *Interlude*
  For my enemies refuse to change their ways;
    they do not fear God.

20 As for this friend of mine, he betrayed me;
    he broke his promises.
21 His words are as smooth as cream,
    but in his heart is war.
  His words are as soothing as lotion,
    but underneath are daggers!

22 Give your burdens to the LORD,
    and he will take care of you.
  He will not permit the godly to slip and fall.

23 But you, O God, will send the wicked
    down to the pit of destruction.
  Murderers and liars will die young,
    but I am trusting you to save me.

PSALM 56

For the choir director: A psalm of David, regarding the time the Philistines seized him in Gath. To be sung to the tune "Dove on Distant Oaks."

1 O God, have mercy on me.
    The enemy troops press in on me.
    My foes attack me all day long.
2 My slanderers hound me constantly,
    and many are boldly attacking me.
3 But when I am afraid,
    I put my trust in you.
4 O God, I praise your word.
    I trust in God, so why should I be afraid?
    What can mere mortals do to me?

5 They are always twisting what I say;
    they spend their days plotting ways to harm me.
6 They come together to spy on me—
    watching my every step, eager to kill me.
7 Don't let them get away with their wickedness;
    in your anger, O God, throw them to the ground.

8 You keep track of all my sorrows.
    You have collected all my tears in your bottle.
    You have recorded each one in your book.

9 On the very day I call to you for help,
    my enemies will retreat.
    This I know: God is on my side.*
10 O God, I praise your word.
    Yes, LORD, I praise your word.
11 I trust in God, so why should I be afraid?
    What can mere mortals do to me?

12 I will fulfill my vows to you, O God,
    and offer a sacrifice of thanks for your help.
13 For you have rescued me from death;

56:9 Or *By this I will know that God is on my side.*

you have kept my feet from slipping.
So now I can walk in your presence, O God,
in your life-giving light.

PSALM 57

For the choir director: A psalm of David, regarding the time he fled from Saul and went into the cave. To be sung to the tune "Do Not Destroy!"

1 Have mercy on me, O God, have mercy!
I look to you for protection.
I will hide beneath the shadow of your wings
until this violent storm is past.

2 I cry out to God Most High,
to God who will fulfill his purpose for me.
3 He will send help from heaven to save me,
rescuing me from those who are out to get me.   *Interlude*
My God will send forth his unfailing love and faithfulness.

4 I am surrounded by fierce lions
who greedily devour human prey—
whose teeth pierce like spears and arrows,
and whose tongues cut like swords.

5 Be exalted, O God, above the highest heavens!
May your glory shine over all the earth.

6 My enemies have set a trap for me.
I am weary from distress.
They have dug a deep pit in my path,
but they themselves have fallen into it.   *Interlude*

7 My heart is confident in you, O God;
no wonder I can sing your praises!
8 Wake up, my soul!
Wake up, O harp and lyre!
I will waken the dawn with my song.
9 I will thank you, Lord, in front of all the people.
I will sing your praises among the nations.
10 For your unfailing love is as high as the heavens.
Your faithfulness reaches to the clouds.

11 Be exalted, O God, above the highest heavens.
May your glory shine over all the earth.

PSALM 58

For the choir director: A psalm of David, to be sung to the tune "Do Not Destroy!"

1 Justice—do you rulers know the meaning of the word?
Do you judge the people fairly?
2 No, all your dealings are crooked;
you hand out violence instead of justice.
3 These wicked people are born sinners;
even from birth they have lied and gone their own way.
4 They spit poison like deadly snakes;
they are like cobras that refuse to listen,
5 ignoring the tunes of the snake charmers,
no matter how skillfully they play.

6 Break off their fangs, O God!
    Smash the jaws of these lions, O LORD!
7 May they disappear like water into thirsty ground.
    Make their weapons useless in their hands.*
8 May they be like snails that dissolve into slime,
    like a stillborn child who will never see the sun.
9 God will sweep them away, both young and old,
    faster than a pot heats on an open flame.

10 The godly will rejoice when they see injustice avenged.
    They will wash their feet in the blood of the wicked.
11 Then at last everyone will say,
    "There truly is a reward for those who live for God;
    surely there is a God who judges justly here on earth."

PSALM 59

For the choir director: A psalm of David, regarding the time Saul sent soldiers to watch David's house in order to kill him. To be sung to the tune "Do Not Destroy!"

1 Rescue me from my enemies, O God.
    Protect me from those who have come to destroy me.
2 Rescue me from these criminals;
    save me from these murderers.

3 They have set an ambush for me.
    Fierce enemies are out there waiting,
    though I have done them no wrong, O LORD.
4 Despite my innocence, they prepare to kill me.
    Rise up and help me! Look on my plight!
5 O LORD God Almighty, the God of Israel,
    rise up to punish hostile nations.
    Show no mercy to wicked traitors.   *Interlude*

6 They come at night,
    snarling like vicious dogs
    as they prowl the streets.
7 Listen to the filth that comes from their mouths,
    the piercing swords that fly from their lips.
    "Who can hurt us?" they sneer.

8 But LORD, you laugh at them.
    You scoff at all the hostile nations.
9 You are my strength; I wait for you to rescue me,
    for you, O God, are my place of safety.

10 In his unfailing love, my God will come and help me.
    He will let me look down in triumph on all my enemies.

11 Don't kill them, for my people soon forget such lessons;
    stagger them with your power, and bring them to their
        knees,
    O Lord our shield.
12 Because of the sinful things they say,
    because of the evil that is on their lips,
    let them be captured by their pride,
        their curses, and their lies.

58:7 Or *Let them be trodden down and wither like grass.* The meaning of the Hebrew is uncertain.

13 Destroy them in your anger!
Wipe them out completely!
Then the whole world will know
that God reigns in Israel.*   *Interlude*

14 My enemies come out at night,
snarling like vicious dogs
as they prowl the streets.
15 They scavenge for food
but go to sleep unsatisfied.*

16 But as for me, I will sing about your power.
I will shout with joy each morning because of your
unfailing love.
For you have been my refuge,
a place of safety in the day of distress.

17 O my Strength, to you I sing praises,
for you, O God, are my refuge,
the God who shows me unfailing love.

PSALM 60

For the choir director: A psalm of David useful for teaching, regarding the time David fought Aram-naharaim and Aram-zobah, and Joab returned and killed twelve thousand Edomites in the Valley of Salt. To be sung to the tune "Lily of the Testimony."

1 You have rejected us, O God, and broken our defenses.
You have been angry with us; now restore us to your favor.
2 You have shaken our land and split it open.
Seal the cracks before it completely collapses.
3 You have been very hard on us,
making us drink wine that sent us reeling.
4 But you have raised a banner for those who honor you—
a rallying point in the face of attack.   *Interlude*

5 Use your strong right arm to save us,
and rescue your beloved people.
6 God has promised this by his holiness*:
"I will divide up Shechem with joy.
I will measure out the valley of Succoth.
7 Gilead is mine,
and Manasseh is mine.
Ephraim will produce my warriors,
and Judah will produce my kings.
8 Moab will become my lowly servant,
and Edom will be my slave.
I will shout in triumph over the Philistines."

9 But who will bring me into the fortified city?
Who will bring me victory over Edom?
10 Have you rejected us, O God?
Will you no longer march with our armies?
11 Oh, please help us against our enemies,
for all human help is useless.

59:13 Hebrew *in Jacob.*   59:15 Or *and growl if they don't get enough.*   60:6 Or *in his sanctuary.*

¹² With God's help we will do mighty things,
    for he will trample down our foes.

PSALM 61

For the choir director: A psalm of David, to be accompanied by stringed instruments.

¹ O God, listen to my cry!
    Hear my prayer!
² From the ends of the earth,
    I will cry to you for help,
    for my heart is overwhelmed.
  Lead me to the towering rock of safety,
³   for you are my safe refuge,
    a fortress where my enemies cannot reach me.
⁴ Let me live forever in your sanctuary,
    safe beneath the shelter of your wings!   *Interlude*
⁵ For you have heard my vows, O God.
    You have given me an inheritance reserved for those who
      fear your name.

⁶ Add many years to the life of the king!
    May his years span the generations!
⁷ May he reign under God's protection forever.
    Appoint your unfailing love and faithfulness to watch over
      him.

⁸ Then I will always sing praises to your name
    as I fulfill my vows day after day.

PSALM 62

For Jeduthun, the choir director: A psalm of David.

¹ I wait quietly before God,
    for my salvation comes from him.
² He alone is my rock and my salvation,
    my fortress where I will never be shaken.

³ So many enemies against one man—
    all of them trying to kill me.
  To them I'm just a broken-down wall
    or a tottering fence.
⁴ They plan to topple me from my high position.
    They delight in telling lies about me.
  They are friendly to my face,
    but they curse me in their hearts.   *Interlude*

⁵ I wait quietly before God,
    for my hope is in him.
⁶ He alone is my rock and my salvation,
    my fortress where I will not be shaken.
⁷ My salvation and my honor come from God alone.
    He is my refuge, a rock where no enemy can reach me.

⁸ O my people, trust in him at all times.
    Pour out your heart to him,
    for God is our refuge.   *Interlude*

9 From the greatest to the lowliest—
all are nothing in his sight.
If you weigh them on the scales,
they are lighter than a puff of air.
10 Don't try to get rich
by extortion or robbery.
And if your wealth increases,
don't make it the center of your life.

11 God has spoken plainly,
and I have heard it many times:
Power, O God, belongs to you;
12 unfailing love, O Lord, is yours.
Surely you judge all people
according to what they have done.

PSALM 63

A psalm of David, regarding a time when David was in the wilderness of Judah.

1 O God, you are my God;
I earnestly search for you.
My soul thirsts for you;
my whole body longs for you
in this parched and weary land
where there is no water.

2 I have seen you in your sanctuary
and gazed upon your power and glory.
3 Your unfailing love is better to me than life itself;
how I praise you!
4 I will honor you as long as I live,
lifting up my hands to you in prayer.
5 You satisfy me more than the richest of foods.
I will praise you with songs of joy.

6 I lie awake thinking of you,
meditating on you through the night.
7 I think how much you have helped me;
I sing for joy in the shadow of your protecting wings.
8 I follow close behind you;
your strong right hand holds me securely.

9 But those plotting to destroy me will come to ruin.
They will go down into the depths of the earth.
10 They will die by the sword
and become the food of jackals.

11 But the king will rejoice in God.
All who trust in him will praise him,
while liars will be silenced.

PSALM 64

For the choir director: A psalm of David.

1 O God, listen to my complaint.
Do not let my enemies' threats overwhelm me.
2 Protect me from the plots of the wicked,
from the scheming of those who do evil.

3 Sharp tongues are the swords they wield;
   bitter words are the arrows they aim.
4 They shoot from ambush at the innocent,
   attacking suddenly and fearlessly.
5 They encourage each other to do evil
   and plan how to set their traps.
   "Who will ever notice?" they ask.
6 As they plot their crimes, they say,
   "We have devised the perfect plan!"
   Yes, the human heart and mind are cunning.

7 But God himself will shoot them down.
   Suddenly, his arrows will pierce them.
8 Their own words will be turned against them, destroying them.
   All who see it happening will shake their heads in scorn.
9 Then everyone will stand in awe,
   proclaiming the mighty acts of God,
   realizing all the amazing things he does.

10 The godly will rejoice in the LORD
   and find shelter in him.
   And those who do what is right
   will praise him.

PSALM 65
For the choir director: A psalm of David. A song.

1 What mighty praise, O God,
   belongs to you in Zion.
   We will fulfill our vows to you,
2   for you answer our prayers,
   and to you all people will come.
3 Though our hearts are filled with sins,
   you forgive them all.
4 What joy for those you choose to bring near,
   those who live in your holy courts.
   What joys await us
   inside your holy Temple.

5 You faithfully answer our prayers with awesome deeds,
   O God our savior.
   You are the hope of everyone on earth,
   even those who sail on distant seas.
6 You formed the mountains by your power
   and armed yourself with mighty strength.
7 You quieted the raging oceans
   with their pounding waves
   and silenced the shouting of the nations.
8 Those who live at the ends of the earth
   stand in awe of your wonders.
   From where the sun rises to where it sets,
   you inspire shouts of joy.

9 You take care of the earth and water it,
   making it rich and fertile.
   The rivers of God will not run dry;

they provide a bountiful harvest of grain,
for you have ordered it so.
10 You drench the plowed ground with rain,
melting the clods and leveling the ridges.
You soften the earth with showers
and bless its abundant crops.
11 You crown the year with a bountiful harvest;
even the hard pathways overflow with abundance.
12 The wilderness becomes a lush pasture,
and the hillsides blossom with joy.
13 The meadows are clothed with flocks of sheep,
and the valleys are carpeted with grain.
They all shout and sing for joy!

P S A L M   6 6

For the choir director: A psalm. A song.

1 Shout joyful praises to God, all the earth!
2 Sing about the glory of his name!
Tell the world how glorious he is.
3 Say to God, "How awesome are your deeds!
Your enemies cringe before your mighty power.
4 Everything on earth will worship you;
they will sing your praises,
shouting your name in glorious songs." *Interlude*

5 Come and see what our God has done,
what awesome miracles he does for his people!
6 He made a dry path through the Red Sea, *
and his people went across on foot.
Come, let us rejoice in who he is.
7 For by his great power he rules forever.
He watches every movement of the nations;
let no rebel rise in defiance. *Interlude*

8 Let the whole world bless our God
and sing aloud his praises.
9 Our lives are in his hands,
and he keeps our feet from stumbling.
10 You have tested us, O God;
you have purified us like silver melted in a crucible.
11 You captured us in your net
and laid the burden of slavery on our backs.
12 You sent troops to ride across our broken bodies.
We went through fire and flood.
But you brought us to a place of great abundance.

13 Now I come to your Temple with burnt offerings
to fulfill the vows I made to you—
14 yes, the sacred vows you heard me make
when I was in deep trouble.
15 That is why I am sacrificing burnt offerings to you—
the best of my rams as a pleasing aroma.
And I will sacrifice bulls and goats. *Interlude*

66:6 Hebrew *the sea.*

¹⁶ Come and listen, all you who fear God,
   and I will tell you what he did for me.
¹⁷ For I cried out to him for help,
   praising him as I spoke.
¹⁸ If I had not confessed the sin in my heart,
   my Lord would not have listened.
¹⁹ But God did listen!
   He paid attention to my prayer.

²⁰ Praise God, who did not ignore my prayer
   and did not withdraw his unfailing love from me.

P S A L M   6 7
For the choir director: A psalm, to be accompanied by stringed instruments. A song.

¹ May God be merciful and bless us.
   May his face shine with favor upon us.   *Interlude*
² May your ways be known throughout the earth,
   your saving power among people everywhere.
³ May the nations praise you, O God.
   Yes, may all the nations praise you.

⁴ How glad the nations will be, singing for joy,
   because you govern them with justice
   and direct the actions of the whole world.   *Interlude*
⁵ May the nations praise you, O God.
   Yes, may all the nations praise you.

⁶ Then the earth will yield its harvests,
   and God, our God, will richly bless us.
⁷ Yes, God will bless us,
   and people all over the world will fear him.

P S A L M   6 8
For the choir director: A psalm of David. A song.

¹ Arise, O God, and scatter your enemies.
   Let those who hate God run for their lives.
² Drive them off like smoke blown by the wind.
   Melt them like wax in fire.
   Let the wicked perish in the presence of God.
³ But let the godly rejoice.
   Let them be glad in God's presence.
   Let them be filled with joy.

⁴ Sing praises to God and to his name!
   Sing loud praises to him who rides the clouds.
His name is the LORD—
   rejoice in his presence!

⁵ Father to the fatherless, defender of widows—
   this is God, whose dwelling is holy.
⁶ God places the lonely in families;
   he sets the prisoners free and gives them joy.
   But for rebels, there is only famine and distress.

⁷ O God, when you led your people from Egypt,
   when you marched through the wilderness,   *Interlude*

8 the earth trembled, and the heavens poured rain
  before you, the God of Sinai,
  before God, the God of Israel.
9 You sent abundant rain, O God,
  to refresh the weary Promised Land.
10 There your people finally settled,
  and with a bountiful harvest, O God,
  you provided for your needy people.

11 The Lord announces victory,
  and throngs of women shout the happy news.
12 Enemy kings and their armies flee,
  while the women of Israel divide the plunder.
13 Though they lived among the sheepfolds,
  now they are covered with silver and gold,
  as a dove is covered by its wings.
14 The Almighty scattered the enemy kings
  like a blowing snowstorm on Mount Zalmon.

15 The majestic mountains of Bashan
  stretch high into the sky.
16 Why do you look with envy, O rugged mountains,
  at Mount Zion, where God has chosen to live,
  where the LORD himself will live forever?

17 Surrounded by unnumbered thousands of chariots,
  the Lord came from Mount Sinai into his sanctuary.
18 When you ascended to the heights,
  you led a crowd of captives.
  You received gifts from the people,
  even from those who rebelled against you.
  Now the LORD God will live among us here.

19 Praise the Lord; praise God our savior!
  For each day he carries us in his arms.   *Interlude*
20 Our God is a God who saves!
  The Sovereign LORD rescues us from death.

21 But God will smash the heads of his enemies,
  crushing the skulls of those who love their guilty ways.
22 The Lord says, " I will bring my enemies down from
        Bashan;
  I will bring them up from the depths of the sea.
23 You, my people, will wash your feet in their blood,
  and even your dogs will get their share!"

24 Your procession has come into view, O God—
  the procession of my God and King
  as he goes into the sanctuary.
25 Singers are in front, musicians are behind;
  with them are young women playing tambourines.
26 Praise God, all you people of Israel;
  praise the LORD, the source of Israel's life.
27 Look, the little tribe of Benjamin leads the way.
  Then comes a great throng of rulers from Judah
  and all the rulers of Zebulun and Naphtali.

²⁸ Summon your might, O God.
Display your power, O God, as you have in the past.
²⁹ The kings of the earth are bringing tribute
to your Temple in Jerusalem.
³⁰ Rebuke these enemy nations—
these wild animals lurking in the reeds,
this herd of bulls among the weaker calves.
Humble those who demand tribute from us.*
Scatter the nations that delight in war.
³¹ Let Egypt come with gifts of precious metals;
let Ethiopia* bow in submission to God.
³² Sing to God, you kingdoms of the earth.
Sing praises to the Lord. *Interlude*

³³ Sing to the one who rides across the ancient heavens,
his mighty voice thundering from the sky.
³⁴ Tell everyone about God's power.
His majesty shines down on Israel;
his strength is mighty in the heavens.
³⁵ God is awesome in his sanctuary.
The God of Israel gives power and strength to his people.

Praise be to God!

PSALM 69
For the choir director: A psalm of David, to be sung to the tune "Lilies."

¹ Save me, O God,
for the floodwaters are up to my neck.
² Deeper and deeper I sink into the mire;
I can't find a foothold to stand on.
I am in deep water,
and the floods overwhelm me.
³ I am exhausted from crying for help;
my throat is parched and dry.
My eyes are swollen with weeping,
waiting for my God to help me.

⁴ Those who hate me without cause
are more numerous than the hairs on my head.
These enemies who seek to destroy me
are doing so without cause.
They attack me with lies,
demanding that I give back what I didn't steal.

⁵ O God, you know how foolish I am;
my sins cannot be hidden from you.
⁶ Don't let those who trust in you stumble because of
me,
O Sovereign Lord Almighty.
Don't let me cause them to be humiliated,
O God of Israel.
⁷ For I am mocked and shamed for your sake;
humiliation is written all over my face.

⁸ Even my own brothers pretend they don't know me;
　　they treat me like a stranger.

⁹ Passion for your house burns within me,
　　so those who insult you are also insulting me.
¹⁰ When I weep and fast before the Lᴏʀᴅ,
　　they scoff at me.
¹¹ When I dress in sackcloth to show sorrow,
　　they make fun of me.
¹² I am the favorite topic of town gossip,
　　and all the drunkards sing about me.

¹³ But I keep right on praying to you, Lᴏʀᴅ,
　　hoping this is the time you will show me favor.
In your unfailing love, O God,
　　answer my prayer with your sure salvation.
¹⁴ Pull me out of the mud;
　　don't let me sink any deeper!
Rescue me from those who hate me,
　　and pull me from these deep waters.
¹⁵ Don't let the floods overwhelm me,
　　or the deep waters swallow me,
　　or the pit of death devour me.

¹⁶ Answer my prayers, O Lᴏʀᴅ,
　　for your unfailing love is wonderful.
Turn and take care of me,
　　for your mercy is so plentiful.
¹⁷ Don't hide from your servant;
　　answer me quickly, for I am in deep trouble!
¹⁸ Come and rescue me;
　　free me from all my enemies.

¹⁹ You know the insults I endure—
　　the humiliation and disgrace.
You have seen all my enemies
　　and know what they have said.
²⁰ Their insults have broken my heart,
　　and I am in despair.
If only one person would show some pity;
　　if only one would turn and comfort me.
²¹ But instead, they give me poison for food;
　　they offer me sour wine to satisfy my thirst.

²² Let the bountiful table set before them become a snare,
　　and let their security become a trap.
²³ Let their eyes go blind so they cannot see,
　　and let their bodies grow weaker and weaker.
²⁴ Pour out your fury on them;
　　consume them with your burning anger.
²⁵ May their homes become desolate
　　and their tents be deserted.
²⁶ To those you have punished, they add insult to injury;
　　they scoff at the pain of those you have hurt.
²⁷ Pile their sins up high,
　　and don't let them go free.

²⁸ Erase their names from the Book of Life;
    don't let them be counted among the righteous.

²⁹ I am suffering and in pain.
    Rescue me, O God, by your saving power.

³⁰ Then I will praise God's name with singing,
    and I will honor him with thanksgiving.
³¹ For this will please the LORD more than sacrificing an ox
    or presenting a bull with its horns and hooves.
³² The humble will see their God at work and be glad.
    Let all who seek God's help live in joy.
³³ For the LORD hears the cries of his needy ones;
    he does not despise his people who are oppressed.

³⁴ Praise him, O heaven and earth,
    the seas and all that move in them.
³⁵ For God will save Jerusalem*
    and rebuild the towns of Judah.
  His people will live there
    and take possession of the land.
³⁶ The descendants of those who obey him will inherit the
      land,
    and those who love him will live there in safety.

PSALM 70

For the choir director: A psalm of David, to bring us to the LORD's remembrance.

¹ Please, God, rescue me!
    Come quickly, LORD, and help me.
² May those who try to destroy me
    be humiliated and put to shame.
  May those who take delight in my trouble
    be turned back in disgrace.
³ Let them be horrified by their shame,
    for they said, "Aha! We've got him now!"
⁴ But may all who search for you
    be filled with joy and gladness.
  May those who love your salvation
    repeatedly shout, "God is great!"
⁵ But I am poor and needy;
    please hurry to my aid, O God.
  You are my helper and my savior;
    O LORD, do not delay!

PSALM 71

¹ O LORD, you are my refuge;
    never let me be disgraced.
² Rescue me! Save me from my enemies, for you are just.
    Turn your ear to listen and set me free.
³ Be to me a protecting rock of safety,
    where I am always welcome.
  Give the order to save me,
    for you are my rock and my fortress.

69:35 Hebrew *Zion.*

⁴ My God, rescue me from the power of the wicked,
    from the clutches of cruel oppressors.
⁵ O Lord, you alone are my hope.
    I've trusted you, O LORD, from childhood.
⁶ Yes, you have been with me from birth;
    from my mother's womb you have cared for me.
  No wonder I am always praising you!

⁷ My life is an example to many,
    because you have been my strength and protection.
⁸ That is why I can never stop praising you;
    I declare your glory all day long.

⁹ And now, in my old age, don't set me aside.
    Don't abandon me when my strength is failing.
¹⁰ For my enemies are whispering against me.
    They are plotting together to kill me.
¹¹ They say, "God has abandoned him.
    Let's go and get him,
    for there is no one to help him now."

¹² O God, don't stay away.
    My God, please hurry to help me.
¹³ Bring disgrace and destruction on those who accuse me.
    May humiliation and shame cover
    those who want to harm me.

¹⁴ But I will keep on hoping for you to help me;
    I will praise you more and more.
¹⁵ I will tell everyone about your righteousness.
    All day long I will proclaim your saving power,
    for I am overwhelmed by how much you have done for
    me.
¹⁶ I will praise your mighty deeds, O Sovereign LORD.
    I will tell everyone that you alone are just and good.

¹⁷ O God, you have taught me from my earliest childhood,
    and I have constantly told others about the wonderful
      things you do.
¹⁸ Now that I am old and gray,
    do not abandon me, O God.
  Let me proclaim your power to this new generation,
    your mighty miracles to all who come after me.

¹⁹ Your righteousness, O God, reaches to the highest heavens.
    You have done such wonderful things.
    Who can compare with you, O God?
²⁰ You have allowed me to suffer much hardship,
    but you will restore me to life again
    and lift me up from the depths of the earth.
²¹ You will restore me to even greater honor
    and comfort me once again.

²² Then I will praise you with music on the harp,
    because you are faithful to your promises, O God.
  I will sing for you with a lyre,
    O Holy One of Israel.

23 I will shout for joy and sing your praises,
   for you have redeemed me.
24 I will tell about your righteous deeds
   all day long,
for everyone who tried to hurt me
   has been shamed and humiliated.

PSALM 72

A psalm of Solomon.

1 Give justice to the king, O God,
   and righteousness to the king's son.
2 Help him judge your people in the right way;
   let the poor always be treated fairly.
3 May the mountains yield prosperity for all,
   and may the hills be fruitful,
   because the king does what is right.
4 Help him to defend the poor,
   to rescue the children of the needy,
   and to crush their oppressors.
5 May he live* as long as the sun shines,
   as long as the moon continues in the skies.
   Yes, forever!
6 May his reign be as refreshing as the springtime rains—
   like the showers that water the earth.
7 May all the godly flourish during his reign.
   May there be abundant prosperity until the end of time.

8 May he reign from sea to sea,
   and from the Euphrates River* to the ends of the earth.
9 Desert nomads will bow before him;
   his enemies will fall before him in the dust.
10 The western kings of Tarshish and the islands
   will bring him tribute.
The eastern kings of Sheba and Seba
   will bring him gifts.
11 All kings will bow before him,
   and all nations will serve him.

12 He will rescue the poor when they cry to him;
   he will help the oppressed, who have no one to defend
   them.
13 He feels pity for the weak and the needy,
   and he will rescue them.
14 He will save them from oppression and from violence,
   for their lives are precious to him.

15 Long live the king!
   May the gold of Sheba be given to him.
May the people always pray for him
   and bless him all day long.
16 May there be abundant crops throughout the land,
   flourishing even on the mountaintops.
   May the fruit trees flourish as they do in Lebanon,

72:5 As in Greek version; Hebrew reads *May they fear you.*   **72:8** Hebrew *the river.*

sprouting up like grass in a field.
17 May the king's name endure forever;
    may it continue as long as the sun shines.
   May all nations be blessed through him
    and bring him praise.

18 Bless the LORD God, the God of Israel,
    who alone does such wonderful things.
19 Bless his glorious name forever!
    Let the whole earth be filled with his glory.
    Amen and amen!

20 (This ends the prayers of David son of Jesse.)

BOOK THREE (Psalms 73–89)

P S A L M   7 3
A psalm of Asaph.

1 Truly God is good to Israel,
    to those whose hearts are pure.

2 But as for me, I came so close to the edge of the cliff!
    My feet were slipping, and I was almost gone.
3 For I envied the proud
    when I saw them prosper despite their wickedness.
4 They seem to live such a painless life;
    their bodies are so healthy and strong.
5 They aren't troubled like other people
    or plagued with problems like everyone else.
6 They wear pride like a jeweled necklace,
    and their clothing is woven of cruelty.
7 These fat cats have everything
    their hearts could ever wish for!
8 They scoff and speak only evil;
    in their pride they seek to crush others.
9 They boast against the very heavens,
    and their words strut throughout the earth.
10 And so the people are dismayed and confused,
    drinking in all their words.
11 "Does God realize what is going on?" they ask.
    "Is the Most High even aware of what is happening?"
12 Look at these arrogant people—
    enjoying a life of ease while their riches multiply.

13 Was it for nothing that I kept my heart pure
    and kept myself from doing wrong?
14 All I get is trouble all day long;
    every morning brings me pain.

15 If I had really spoken this way,
    I would have been a traitor to your people.
16 So I tried to understand why the wicked prosper.
    But what a difficult task it is!
17 Then one day I went into your sanctuary, O God,
    and I thought about the destiny of the wicked.

¹⁸ Truly, you put them on a slippery path
    and send them sliding over the cliff to destruction.
¹⁹ In an instant they are destroyed,
    swept away by terrors.
²⁰ Their present life is only a dream
    that is gone when they awake.
  When you arise, O Lord,
    you will make them vanish from this life.

²¹ Then I realized how bitter I had become,
    how pained I had been by all I had seen.
²² I was so foolish and ignorant—
    I must have seemed like a senseless animal to you.
²³ Yet I still belong to you;
    you are holding my right hand.
²⁴ You will keep on guiding me with your counsel,
    leading me to a glorious destiny.
²⁵ Whom have I in heaven but you?
    I desire you more than anything on earth.
²⁶ My health may fail, and my spirit may grow weak,
    but God remains the strength of my heart;
    he is mine forever.

²⁷ But those who desert him will perish,
    for you destroy those who abandon you.
²⁸ But as for me, how good it is to be near God!
    I have made the Sovereign LORD my shelter,
    and I will tell everyone about the wonderful things you do.

PSALM 74

A psalm of Asaph.

¹ O God, why have you rejected us forever?
    Why is your anger so intense against the sheep of your own
        pasture?
² Remember that we are the people you chose in ancient times,
    the tribe you redeemed as your own special possession!
  And remember Jerusalem,* your home here on earth.
³ Walk through the awful ruins of the city;
    see how the enemy has destroyed your sanctuary.
⁴ There your enemies shouted their victorious battle cries;
    there they set up their battle standards.
⁵ They chopped down the entrance
    like woodcutters in a forest.
⁶ With axes and picks,
    they smashed the carved paneling.
⁷ They set the sanctuary on fire, burning it to the ground.
    They utterly defiled the place that bears your holy name.
⁸ Then they thought, "Let's destroy everything!"
    So they burned down all the places where God was
        worshiped.

⁹ We see no miraculous signs
    as evidence that you will save us.

74:2 Hebrew *Mount Zion.*

All the prophets are gone;
no one can tell us when it will end.
¹⁰ How long, O God, will you allow our enemies to mock you?
Will you let them dishonor your name forever?
¹¹ Why do you hold back your strong right hand?
Unleash your powerful fist and deliver a deathblow.

¹² You, O God, are my king from ages past,
bringing salvation to the earth.
¹³ You split the sea by your strength
and smashed the sea monster's heads.
¹⁴ You crushed the heads of Leviathan
and let the desert animals eat him.
¹⁵ You caused the springs and streams to gush forth,
and you dried up rivers that never run dry.
¹⁶ Both day and night belong to you;
you made the starlight* and the sun.
¹⁷ You set the boundaries of the earth,
and you make both summer and winter.

¹⁸ See how these enemies scoff at you, LORD.
A foolish nation has dishonored your name.
¹⁹ Don't let these wild beasts destroy your doves.
Don't forget your afflicted people forever.

²⁰ Remember your covenant promises,
for the land is full of darkness and violence!
²¹ Don't let the downtrodden be constantly disgraced!
Instead, let these poor and needy ones give praise to your
name.

²² Arise, O God, and defend your cause.
Remember how these fools insult you all day long.
²³ Don't overlook these things your enemies have said.
Their uproar of rebellion grows ever louder.

PSALM 75

*For the choir director: A psalm of Asaph, to be sung to the tune "Do Not
Destroy!" A song.*

¹ We thank you, O God!
We give thanks because you are near.
People everywhere tell of your mighty miracles.

² God says, "At the time I have planned,
I will bring justice against the wicked.
³ When the earth quakes and its people live in turmoil,
I am the one who keeps its foundations firm.   *Interlude*

⁴ "I warned the proud, 'Stop your boasting!'
I told the wicked, 'Don't raise your fists!'
⁵ Don't lift your fists in defiance at the heavens
or speak with rebellious arrogance.'"

⁶ For no one on earth—from east or west,
or even from the wilderness—
can raise another person up.

74:16 Or *moon;* Hebrew reads *light.*

⁷ It is God alone who judges;
  he decides who will rise and who will fall.
⁸ For the LORD holds a cup in his hand;
  it is full of foaming wine mixed with spices.
  He pours the wine out in judgment,
    and all the wicked must drink it,
    draining it to the dregs.

⁹ But as for me, I will always proclaim what God has done;
  I will sing praises to the God of Israel.*

¹⁰ For God says, "I will cut off the strength of the wicked,
  but I will increase the power of the godly."

PSALM 76

For the choir director: A psalm of Asaph, to be accompanied by stringed instruments. A song.

¹ God is well known in Judah;
  his name is great in Israel.
² Jerusalem* is where he lives;
  Mount Zion is his home.
³ There he breaks the arrows of the enemy,
  the shields and swords and weapons of his foes.   *Interlude*

⁴ You are glorious and more majestic
  than the everlasting mountains.*
⁵ The mightiest of our enemies have been plundered.
  They lie before us in the sleep of death.
  No warrior could lift a hand against us.
⁶ When you rebuked them, O God of Jacob,
  their horses and chariots stood still.

⁷ No wonder you are greatly feared!
  Who can stand before you when your anger explodes?
⁸ From heaven you sentenced your enemies;
  the earth trembled and stood silent before you.
⁹ You stand up to judge those who do evil, O God,
  and to rescue the oppressed of the earth.   *Interlude*

¹⁰ Human opposition only enhances your glory,
  for you use it as a sword of judgment.*

¹¹ Make vows to the LORD your God, and fulfill them.
  Let everyone bring tribute to the Awesome One.
¹² For he breaks the spirit of princes
  and is feared by the kings of the earth.

PSALM 77

For Jeduthun, the choir director: A psalm of Asaph.

¹ I cry out to God without holding back.
  Oh, that God would listen to me!
² When I was in deep trouble,
  I searched for the Lord.

75:9 Hebrew *of Jacob.*   76:2 Hebrew *Salem,* another name for Jerusalem.   76:4 As in Greek version; Hebrew reads *than mountains filled with beasts of prey.*   76:10 The meaning of the Hebrew is uncertain.

All night long I pray, with hands lifted toward heaven,
pleading.
There can be no joy for me until he acts.
3 I think of God, and I moan,
overwhelmed with longing for his help.   *Interlude*

4 You don't let me sleep.
I am too distressed even to pray!
5 I think of the good old days, long since ended,
6   when my nights were filled with joyful songs.
I search my soul and think about the difference now.
7 Has the Lord rejected me forever?
Will he never again show me favor?
8 Is his unfailing love gone forever?
Have his promises permanently failed?
9 Has God forgotten to be kind?
Has he slammed the door on his compassion?   *Interlude*

10 And I said, "This is my fate,
that the blessings of the Most High have changed to hatred."
11 I recall all you have done, O LORD;
I remember your wonderful deeds of long ago.
12 They are constantly in my thoughts.
I cannot stop thinking about them.

13 O God, your ways are holy.
Is there any god as mighty as you?
14 You are the God of miracles and wonders!
You demonstrate your awesome power among the nations.
15 You have redeemed your people by your strength,
the descendants of Jacob and of Joseph by your might.
Interlude

16 When the Red Sea* saw you, O God,
its waters looked and trembled!
The sea quaked to its very depths.
17 The clouds poured down their rain;
the thunder rolled and crackled in the sky.
Your arrows of lightning flashed.
18 Your thunder roared from the whirlwind;
the lightning lit up the world!
The earth trembled and shook.
19 Your road led through the sea,
your pathway through the mighty waters—
a pathway no one knew was there!
20 You led your people along that road like a flock of sheep,
with Moses and Aaron as their shepherds.

PSALM   7 8
A psalm of Asaph.

1 O my people, listen to my teaching.
Open your ears to what I am saying,
2   for I will speak to you in a parable.
I will teach you hidden lessons from our past—

77:16 Hebrew *the waters.*

3   stories we have heard and know,
        stories our ancestors handed down to us.
4 We will not hide these truths from our children
        but will tell the next generation about the glorious deeds of
            the LORD.
        We will tell of his power and the mighty miracles he did.
5 For he issued his decree to Jacob;
        he gave his law to Israel.
    He commanded our ancestors
        to teach them to their children,
6 so the next generation might know them—
        even the children not yet born—
        that they in turn might teach their children.
7 So each generation can set its hope anew on God,
        remembering his glorious miracles
        and obeying his commands.
8 Then they will not be like their ancestors—
        stubborn, rebellious, and unfaithful,
        refusing to give their hearts to God.

9 The warriors of Ephraim, though fully armed,
        turned their backs and fled when the day of battle came.
10 They did not keep God's covenant,
        and they refused to live by his law.
11 They forgot what he had done—
        the wonderful miracles he had shown them,
12   the miracles he did for their ancestors in Egypt, on the plain
            of Zoan.
13 For he divided the sea before them and led them through!
        The water stood up like walls beside them!
14 In the daytime he led them by a cloud,
        and at night by a pillar of fire.
15 He split open the rocks in the wilderness
        to give them plenty of water, as from a gushing spring.
16 He made streams pour from the rock,
        making the waters flow down like a river!

17 Yet they kept on with their sin,
        rebelling against the Most High in the desert.
18 They willfully tested God in their hearts,
        demanding the foods they craved.
19 They even spoke against God himself, saying,
        "God can't give us food in the desert.
20 Yes, he can strike a rock so water gushes out,
        but he can't give his people bread and meat."
21 When the LORD heard them, he was angry.
        The fire of his wrath burned against Jacob.
    Yes, his anger rose against Israel,
22   for they did not believe God
        or trust him to care for them.
23 But he commanded the skies to open—
        he opened the doors of heaven—
24   and rained down manna for them to eat.
        He gave them bread from heaven.

25 They ate the food of angels!
   God gave them all they could hold.
26 He released the east wind in the heavens
   and guided the south wind by his mighty power.
27 He rained down meat as thick as dust—
   birds as plentiful as the sands along the seashore!
28 He caused the birds to fall within their camp
   and all around their tents.
29 The people ate their fill.
   He gave them what they wanted.
30 But before they finished eating this food they had craved,
   while the meat was yet in their mouths,
31 the anger of God rose against them,
   and he killed their strongest men;
   he struck down the finest of Israel's young men.
32 But in spite of this, the people kept on sinning.
   They refused to believe in his miracles.
33 So he ended their lives in failure
   and gave them years of terror.

34 When God killed some of them, the rest finally sought him.
   They repented and turned to God.
35 Then they remembered that God was their rock,
   that their redeemer was the Most High.
36 But they followed him only with their words;
   they lied to him with their tongues.
37 Their hearts were not loyal to him.
   They did not keep his covenant.
38 Yet he was merciful and forgave their sins
   and didn't destroy them all.
   Many a time he held back his anger
   and did not unleash his fury!
39 For he remembered that they were merely mortal,
   gone in a moment like a breath of wind, never to return.

40 Oh, how often they rebelled against him in the desert
   and grieved his heart in the wilderness.
41 Again and again they tested God's patience
   and frustrated the Holy One of Israel.
42 They forgot about his power
   and how he rescued them from their enemies.
43 They forgot his miraculous signs in Egypt,
   his wonders on the plain of Zoan.
44 For he turned their rivers into blood,
   so no one could drink from the streams.
45 He sent vast swarms of flies to consume them
   and hordes of frogs to ruin them.
46 He gave their crops to caterpillars;
   their harvest was consumed by locusts.
47 He destroyed their grapevines with hail
   and shattered their sycamores with sleet.
48 He abandoned their cattle to the hail,
   their livestock to bolts of lightning.
49 He loosed on them his fierce anger—

all his fury, rage, and hostility.
He dispatched against them
a band of destroying angels.
50 He turned his anger against them;
he did not spare the Egyptians' lives
but handed them over to the plague.
51 He killed the oldest son in each Egyptian family,
the flower of youth throughout the land of Egypt.*
52 But he led his own people like a flock of sheep,
guiding them safely through the wilderness.
53 He kept them safe so they were not afraid;
but the sea closed in upon their enemies.
54 He brought them to the border of his holy land,
to this land of hills he had won for them.
55 He drove out the nations before them;
he gave them their inheritance by lot.
He settled the tribes of Israel into their homes.

56 Yet though he did all this for them,
they continued to test his patience.
They rebelled against the Most High
and refused to follow his decrees.
57 They turned back and were as faithless as their parents had
been.
They were as useless as a crooked bow.
58 They made God angry by building altars to other gods;
they made him jealous with their idols.
59 When God heard them, he was very angry,
and he rejected Israel completely.
60 Then he abandoned his dwelling at Shiloh,
the Tabernacle where he had lived among the people.
61 He allowed the Ark of his might to be captured;
he surrendered his glory into enemy hands.
62 He gave his people over to be butchered by the sword,
because he was so angry with his own people—his special
possession.
63 Their young men were killed by fire;
their young women died before singing their wedding songs.
64 Their priests were slaughtered,
and their widows could not mourn their deaths.
65 Then the Lord rose up as though waking from sleep,
like a mighty man aroused from a drunken stupor.
66 He routed his enemies
and sent them to eternal shame.
67 But he rejected Joseph's descendants;
he did not choose the tribe of Ephraim.
68 He chose instead the tribe of Judah,
Mount Zion, which he loved.
69 There he built his towering sanctuary,
as solid and enduring as the earth itself.
70 He chose his servant David,
calling him from the sheep pens.

78:51 Hebrew *in the tents of Ham.*

71 He took David from tending the ewes and lambs
　　and made him the shepherd of Jacob's descendants—
　　　　God's own people, Israel.
72 He cared for them with a true heart
　　and led them with skillful hands.

PSALM 79

A psalm of Asaph.

1 O God, pagan nations have conquered your land, your special
　　possession.
　　They have defiled your holy Temple
　　and made Jerusalem a heap of ruins.
2 They have left the bodies of your servants
　　as food for the birds of heaven.
　　The flesh of your godly ones
　　has become food for the wild animals.
3 Blood has flowed like water all around Jerusalem;
　　no one is left to bury the dead.
4 We are mocked by our neighbors,
　　an object of scorn and derision to those around us.

5 O LORD, how long will you be angry with us? Forever?
　　How long will your jealousy burn like fire?
6 Pour out your wrath on the nations that refuse to recognize you—
　　on kingdoms that do not call upon your name.
7 For they have devoured your people Israel,*
　　making the land a desolate wilderness.
8 Oh, do not hold us guilty for our former sins!
　　Let your tenderhearted mercies quickly meet our needs,
　　for we are brought low to the dust.
9 Help us, O God of our salvation!
　　Help us for the honor of your name.
　　Oh, save us and forgive our sins
　　for the sake of your name.
10 Why should pagan nations be allowed to scoff,
　　asking, "Where is their God?"
　　Show us your vengeance against the nations,
　　for they have spilled the blood of your servants.
11 Listen to the moaning of the prisoners.
　　Demonstrate your great power by saving those condemned
　　　　to die.

12 O Lord, take sevenfold vengeance on our neighbors
　　for the scorn they have hurled at you.
13 Then we your people, the sheep of your pasture,
　　will thank you forever and ever,
　　praising your greatness from generation to generation.

PSALM 80

For the choir director: A psalm of Asaph, to be sung to the tune "Lilies of the Covenant."

1 Please listen, O Shepherd of Israel,
　　you who lead Israel* like a flock.

79:7 Hebrew *Jacob.*　80:1 Hebrew *Joseph.*

O God, enthroned above the cherubim,
   display your radiant glory
2   to Ephraim, Benjamin, and Manasseh.
Show us your mighty power.
   Come to rescue us!

3 Turn us again to yourself, O God.
   Make your face shine down upon us.
   Only then will we be saved.

4 O Lord God Almighty,
   how long will you be angry and reject our prayers?
5 You have fed us with sorrow
   and made us drink tears by the bucketful.
6 You have made us the scorn of neighboring nations.
   Our enemies treat us as a joke.

7 Turn us again to yourself, O God Almighty.
   Make your face shine down upon us.
   Only then will we be saved.

8 You brought us from Egypt as though we were a tender vine;
   you drove away the pagan nations and transplanted us into
      your land.
9 You cleared the ground for us,
   and we took root and filled the land.
10 The mountains were covered with our shade;
   the mighty cedars were covered with our branches.
11 We spread our branches west to the Mediterranean Sea,
   our limbs east to the Euphrates River.*
12 But now, why have you broken down our walls
   so that all who pass may steal our fruit?
13 The boar from the forest devours us,
   and the wild animals feed on us.

14 Come back, we beg you, O God Almighty.
   Look down from heaven and see our plight.
Watch over and care for this vine
15   that you yourself have planted,
   this son you have raised for yourself.
16 For we are chopped up and burned by our enemies.
   May they perish at the sight of your frown.
17 Strengthen the man you love,
   the son of your choice.
18 Then we will never forsake you again.
   Revive us so we can call on your name once more.

19 Turn us again to yourself, O Lord God Almighty.
   Make your face shine down upon us.
   Only then will we be saved.

P S A L M   8 1
For the choir director: A psalm of Asaph, to be accompanied by a stringed instrument. *

1 Sing praises to God, our strength.
   Sing to the God of Israel.*

80:11 Hebrew *west to the sea, . . . east to the river.* 81:TITLE Hebrew *according to the gittith.*
81:1 Hebrew *of Jacob.*

² Sing! Beat the tambourine.
　　Play the sweet lyre and the harp.
³ Sound the trumpet for a sacred feast
　　when the moon is new,
　　when the moon is full.
⁴ For this is required by the laws of Israel;
　　it is a law of the God of Jacob.
⁵ He made it a decree for Israel*
　　when he attacked Egypt to set us free.

I heard an unknown voice that said,
⁶ "Now I will relieve your shoulder of its burden;
　　I will free your hands from their heavy tasks.
⁷ You cried to me in trouble, and I saved you;
　　I answered out of the thundercloud.
　I tested your faith at Meribah,
　　when you complained that there was no water.　*Interlude*

⁸ "Listen to me, O my people, while I give you stern warnings.
　　O Israel, if you would only listen!
⁹ You must never have a foreign god;
　　you must not bow down before a false god.
¹⁰ For it was I, the LORD your God,
　　who rescued you from the land of Egypt.
　　Open your mouth wide, and I will fill it with good things.

¹¹ "But no, my people wouldn't listen.
　　Israel did not want me around.
¹² So I let them follow their blind and stubborn way,
　　living according to their own desires.
¹³ But oh, that my people would listen to me!
　　Oh, that Israel would follow me, walking in my paths!
¹⁴ How quickly I would then subdue their enemies!
　　How soon my hands would be upon their foes!
¹⁵ Those who hate the LORD would cringe before him;
　　their desolation would last forever.
¹⁶ But I would feed you with the best of foods.
　　I would satisfy you with wild honey from the rock."

PSALM 82

A psalm of Asaph.

¹ God presides over heaven's court;
　　he pronounces judgment on the judges:
² "How long will you judges hand down unjust decisions?
　　How long will you shower special favors on the wicked?
　　　　　　　　　　　　　　　　　　　　　　Interlude

³ "Give fair judgment to the poor and the orphan;
　　uphold the rights of the oppressed and the destitute.
⁴ Rescue the poor and helpless;
　　deliver them from the grasp of evil people.
⁵ But these oppressors know nothing;
　　they are so ignorant!

81:5 Hebrew for *Joseph.*

And because they are in darkness,
the whole world is shaken to the core.
6 I say, 'You are gods
and children of the Most High.
7 But in death you are mere men.
You will fall as any prince,
for all must die.'"

8 Rise up, O God, and judge the earth,
for all the nations belong to you.

PSALM 83

A psalm of Asaph. A song.

1 O God, don't sit idly by,
silent and inactive!
2 Don't you hear the tumult of your enemies?
Don't you see what your arrogant enemies are doing?
3 They devise crafty schemes against your people,
laying plans against your precious ones.
4 "Come," they say, "let us wipe out Israel as a nation.
We will destroy the very memory of its existence."
5   This was their unanimous decision.
They signed a treaty as allies against you—
6   these Edomites and Ishmaelites,
Moabites and Hagrites,
7   Gebalites, Ammonites, and Amalekites,
and people from Philistia and Tyre.
8 Assyria has joined them, too,
and is allied with the descendants of Lot.   *Interlude*

9 Do to them as you did to the Midianites
or as you did to Sisera and Jabin at the Kishon River.
10 They were destroyed at Endor,
and their decaying corpses fertilized the soil.
11 Let their mighty nobles die as Oreb and Zeeb did.
Let all their princes die like Zebah and Zalmunna,
12 for they said, "Let us seize for our own use
these pasturelands of God!"

13 O my God, blow them away like whirling dust,
like chaff before the wind!
14 As a fire roars through a forest
and as a flame sets mountains ablaze,
15 chase them with your fierce storms;
terrify them with your tempests.
16 Utterly disgrace them
until they submit to your name, O Lord.
17 Let them be ashamed and terrified forever.
Make them failures in everything they do,
18 until they learn that you alone are called the Lord,
that you alone are the Most High, supreme over all the
earth.

PSALM 84

For the choir director: A psalm of the descendants of Korah, to be accompanied by a stringed instrument. *

1 How lovely is your dwelling place,
　　O LORD Almighty.
2 I long, yes, I faint with longing
　　to enter the courts of the LORD.
　With my whole being, body and soul,
　　I will shout joyfully to the living God.
3 Even the sparrow finds a home there,
　　and the swallow builds her nest
　　and raises her young—
　　at a place near your altar,
　　O LORD Almighty, my King and my God!
4 How happy are those who can live in your house,
　　always singing your praises. 　　　　　　　*Interlude*

5 Happy are those who are strong in the LORD,
　　who set their minds on a pilgrimage to Jerusalem.
6 When they walk through the Valley of Weeping, *
　　it will become a place of refreshing springs,
　　where pools of blessing collect after the rains!
7 They will continue to grow stronger,
　　and each of them will appear before God in Jerusalem. *

8 O LORD God Almighty, hear my prayer.
　　Listen, O God of Israel. * 　　　　　　　*Interlude*

9 O God, look with favor on the king, our protector!
　　Have mercy on the one you have anointed.

10 A single day in your courts
　　is better than a thousand anywhere else!
　I would rather be a gatekeeper in the house of my God
　　than live the good life in the homes of the wicked.
11 For the LORD God is our light and protector.
　　He gives us grace and glory.
　No good thing will the LORD withhold
　　from those who do what is right.
12 O LORD Almighty,
　　happy are those who trust in you.

PSALM 85

For the choir director: A psalm of the descendants of Korah.

1 LORD, you have poured out amazing blessings on your land!
　　You have restored the fortunes of Israel. *
2 You have forgiven the guilt of your people—
　　yes, you have covered all their sins. 　　　　*Interlude*

3 You have withdrawn your fury.
　　You have ended your blazing anger.
4 Now turn to us again, O God of our salvation.
　　Put aside your anger against us.

84:TITLE Hebrew *according to the gittith.* 　84:6 Hebrew *valley of Baca.* 　84:7 Hebrew *Zion.* 　84:8 Hebrew *of Jacob.* 　85:1 Hebrew *of Jacob.*

⁵ Will you be angry with us always?
   Will you prolong your wrath to distant generations?
⁶ Won't you revive us again,
   so your people can rejoice in you?
⁷ Show us your unfailing love, O LORD,
   and grant us your salvation.

⁸ I listen carefully to what God the LORD is saying,
   for he speaks peace to his people, his faithful ones.
   But let them not return to their foolish ways.
⁹ Surely his salvation is near to those who honor him;
   our land will be filled with his glory.

¹⁰ Unfailing love and truth have met together.
   Righteousness and peace have kissed!
¹¹ Truth springs up from the earth,
   and righteousness smiles down from heaven.
¹² Yes, the LORD pours down his blessings.
   Our land will yield its bountiful crops.
¹³ Righteousness goes as a herald before him,
   preparing the way for his steps.

PSALM 86

A prayer of David.

¹ Bend down, O LORD, and hear my prayer;
   answer me, for I need your help.
² Protect me, for I am devoted to you.
   Save me, for I serve you and trust you.
   You are my God.
³ Be merciful, O Lord,
   for I am calling on you constantly.
⁴ Give me happiness, O Lord,
   for my life depends on you.
⁵ O Lord, you are so good, so ready to forgive,
   so full of unfailing love for all who ask your aid.
⁶ Listen closely to my prayer, O LORD;
   hear my urgent cry.
⁷ I will call to you whenever trouble strikes,
   and you will answer me.

⁸ Nowhere among the pagan gods is there a god like you,
      O Lord.
   There are no other miracles like yours.
⁹ All the nations—and you made each one—
   will come and bow before you, Lord;
   they will praise your great and holy name.
¹⁰ For you are great and perform great miracles.
   You alone are God.

¹¹ Teach me your ways, O LORD,
   that I may live according to your truth!
   Grant me purity of heart,
      that I may honor you.
¹² With all my heart I will praise you, O Lord my God.
   I will give glory to your name forever,

¹³ for your love for me is very great.
You have rescued me from the depths of death*!

¹⁴ O God, insolent people rise up against me;
violent people are trying to kill me.
And you mean nothing to them.

¹⁵ But you, O Lord, are a merciful and gracious God,
slow to get angry,
full of unfailing love and truth.

¹⁶ Look down and have mercy on me.
Give strength to your servant;
yes, save me, for I am your servant.

¹⁷ Send me a sign of your favor.
Then those who hate me will be put to shame,
for you, O Lord, help and comfort me.

PSALM 87

A psalm of the descendants of Korah. A song.

¹ On the holy mountain stands the city founded by the Lord.
²   He loves the city of Jerusalem
more than any other city in Israel.*

³ O city of God,
what glorious things are said of you!   *Interlude*

⁴ I will record Egypt* and Babylon among those who know
me—
also Philistia and Tyre, and even distant Ethiopia.*
They have all become citizens of Jerusalem!

⁵ And it will be said of Jerusalem,*
"Everyone has become a citizen here."
And the Most High will personally bless this city.

⁶ When the Lord registers the nations,
he will say, "This one has become a citizen of Jerusalem."
Interlude

⁷ At all the festivals, the people will sing,
"The source of my life is in Jerusalem!"

PSALM 88

For the choir director: A psalm of the descendants of Korah, to be sung to the tune "The Suffering of Affliction." A psalm of Heman the Ezrahite. A song.

¹ O Lord, God of my salvation,
I have cried out to you day and night.

² Now hear my prayer;
listen to my cry.

³ For my life is full of troubles,
and death draws near.

⁴ I have been dismissed as one who is dead,
like a strong man with no strength left.

⁵ They have abandoned me to death,
and I am as good as dead.

86:13 Hebrew *of Sheol.*   **87:2** Hebrew *He loves the gates of Zion more than all the dwellings of Jacob.*   **87:4a** Hebrew *Rahab,* the name of a mythical sea monster that represents chaos in ancient literature. The name is used here as a poetic name for Egypt. **87:4b** Hebrew *Cush.*   **87:5** Hebrew *Zion.*

I am forgotten,
cut off from your care.
6 You have thrust me down to the lowest pit,
into the darkest depths.
7 Your anger lies heavy on me;
wave after wave engulfs me.   *Interlude*

8 You have caused my friends to loathe me;
you have sent them all away.
I am in a trap with no way of escape.
9   My eyes are blinded by my tears.
Each day I beg for your help, O LORD;
I lift my pleading hands to you for mercy.
10 Of what use to the dead are your miracles?
Do the dead get up and praise you?   *Interlude*

11 Can those in the grave declare your unfailing love?
In the place of destruction, can they proclaim your
faithfulness?
12 Can the darkness speak of your miracles?
Can anyone in the land of forgetfulness talk about your
righteousness?

13 O LORD, I cry out to you.
I will keep on pleading day by day.
14 O LORD, why do you reject me?
Why do you turn your face away from me?
15 I have been sickly and close to death since my youth.
I stand helpless and desperate before your terrors.
16 Your fierce anger has overwhelmed me.
Your terrors have cut me off.
17 They swirl around me like floodwaters all day long.
They have encircled me completely.
18 You have taken away my companions and loved ones;
only darkness remains.

PSALM 89
A psalm of Ethan the Ezrahite.

1 I will sing of the tender mercies of the LORD forever!
Young and old will hear of your faithfulness.
2 Your unfailing love will last forever.
Your faithfulness is as enduring as the heavens.

3 The LORD said, "I have made a solemn agreement with David,
my chosen servant.
I have sworn this oath to him:
4 'I will establish your descendants as kings forever;
they will sit on your throne from now until eternity.'"   *Interlude*

5 All heaven will praise your miracles, LORD;
myriads of angels will praise you for your faithfulness.
6 For who in all of heaven can compare with the LORD?
What mightiest angel is anything like the LORD?
7 The highest angelic powers stand in awe of God.

He is far more awesome than those who surround his
throne.
⁸ O LORD God Almighty!
Where is there anyone as mighty as you, LORD?
Faithfulness is your very character.

⁹ You are the one who rules the oceans.
When their waves rise in fearful storms, you subdue
them.
¹⁰ You are the one who crushed the great sea monster.*
You scattered your enemies with your mighty arm.
¹¹ The heavens are yours, and the earth is yours;
everything in the world is yours—you created it all.
¹² You created north and south.
Mount Tabor and Mount Hermon praise your name.
¹³ Powerful is your arm!
Strong is your hand!
Your right hand is lifted high in glorious strength.
¹⁴ Your throne is founded on two strong pillars—righteousness
and justice.
Unfailing love and truth walk before you as attendants.
¹⁵ Happy are those who hear the joyful call to worship,
for they will walk in the light of your presence, LORD.
¹⁶ They rejoice all day long in your wonderful reputation.
They exult in your righteousness.
¹⁷ You are their glorious strength.
Our power is based on your favor.
¹⁸ Yes, our protection comes from the LORD,
and he, the Holy One of Israel, has given us our king.

¹⁹ You once spoke in a vision to your prophet and said,
"I have given help to a warrior.
I have selected him from the common people to be king.
²⁰ I have found my servant David.
I have anointed him with my holy oil.
²¹ I will steady him,
and I will make him strong.
²² His enemies will not get the best of him,
nor will the wicked overpower him.
²³ I will beat down his adversaries before him
and destroy those who hate him.
²⁴ My faithfulness and unfailing love will be with him,
and he will rise to power because of me.
²⁵ I will extend his rule from the Mediterranean Sea in the
west
to the Tigris and Euphrates rivers in the east.*
²⁶ And he will say to me, 'You are my Father,
my God, and the Rock of my salvation.'
²⁷ I will make him my firstborn son,
the mightiest king on earth.
²⁸ I will love him and be kind to him forever;
my covenant with him will never end.

89:10 Hebrew *Rahab,* the name of a mythical sea monster that represents chaos in
ancient literature.   89:25 Hebrew *I will set his hand on the sea, his right hand on the rivers.*

29 I will preserve an heir for him;
   his throne will be as endless as the days of heaven.
30 But if his sons forsake my law
   and fail to walk in my ways,
31 if they do not obey my decrees
   and fail to keep my commands,
32 then I will punish their sin with the rod,
   and their disobedience with beating.
33 But I will never stop loving him,
   nor let my promise to him fail.
34 No, I will not break my covenant;
   I will not take back a single word I said.
35 I have sworn an oath to David,
   and in my holiness I cannot lie:
36 His dynasty will go on forever;
   his throne is as secure as the sun,
37   as eternal as the moon,
   my faithful witness in the sky!"   *Interlude*

38 But now you have rejected him.
   Why are you so angry with the one you chose as
      king?
39 You have renounced your covenant with him,
   for you have thrown his crown in the dust.
40 You have broken down the walls protecting him
   and laid in ruins every fort defending him.
41 Everyone who comes along has robbed him
   while his neighbors mock.
42 You have strengthened his enemies against him
   and made them all rejoice.
43 You have made his sword useless
   and have refused to help him in battle.
44 You have ended his splendor
   and overturned his throne.
45 You have made him old before his time
   and publicly disgraced him.   *Interlude*

46 O LORD, how long will this go on?
   Will you hide yourself forever?
   How long will your anger burn like fire?
47 Remember how short my life is,
   how empty and futile this human existence!
48 No one can live forever; all will die.
   No one can escape the power of the grave.   *Interlude*

49 Lord, where is your unfailing love?
   You promised it to David with a faithful pledge.
50 Consider, Lord, how your servants are disgraced!
   I carry in my heart the insults of so many people.
51 Your enemies have mocked me, O LORD;
   they mock the one you anointed as king.

52 Blessed be the LORD forever!
   Amen and amen!

BOOK FOUR (Psalms 90–106)

P S A L M   9 0

A prayer of Moses, the man of God.

1 Lord, through all the generations
   you have been our home!
2 Before the mountains were created,
   before you made the earth and the world,
   you are God, without beginning or end.

3 You turn people back to dust, saying,
   "Return to dust!"
4 For you, a thousand years are as yesterday!
   They are like a few hours!
5 You sweep people away like dreams that disappear
   or like grass that springs up in the morning.
6 In the morning it blooms and flourishes,
   but by evening it is dry and withered.

7 We wither beneath your anger;
   we are overwhelmed by your fury.
8 You spread out our sins before you—
   our secret sins—and you see them all.
9 We live our lives beneath your wrath.
   We end our lives with a groan.

10 Seventy years are given to us!
    Some may even reach eighty.
   But even the best of these years are filled with pain and trouble;
    soon they disappear, and we are gone.
11 Who can comprehend the power of your anger?
    Your wrath is as awesome as the fear you deserve.
12 Teach us to make the most of our time,
    so that we may grow in wisdom.

13 O Lord, come back to us!
    How long will you delay?
    Take pity on your servants!
14 Satisfy us in the morning with your unfailing love,
    so we may sing for joy to the end of our lives.
15 Give us gladness in proportion to our former misery!
    Replace the evil years with good.
16 Let us see your miracles again;
    let our children see your glory at work.
17 And may the Lord our God show us his approval
    and make our efforts successful.
    Yes, make our efforts successful!

P S A L M   9 1

1 Those who live in the shelter of the Most High
   will find rest in the shadow of the Almighty.
2 This I declare of the LORD:
   He alone is my refuge, my place of safety;
   he is my God, and I am trusting him.
3 For he will rescue you from every trap
   and protect you from the fatal plague.

4 He will shield you with his wings.
   He will shelter you with his feathers.
   His faithful promises are your armor and protection.
5 Do not be afraid of the terrors of the night,
   nor fear the dangers of the day,
6 nor dread the plague that stalks in darkness,
   nor the disaster that strikes at midday.
7 Though a thousand fall at your side,
   though ten thousand are dying around you,
   these evils will not touch you.
8 But you will see it with your eyes;
   you will see how the wicked are punished.

9 If you make the LORD your refuge,
   if you make the Most High your shelter,
10 no evil will conquer you;
   no plague will come near your dwelling.
11 For he orders his angels
   to protect you wherever you go.
12 They will hold you with their hands
   to keep you from striking your foot on a stone.
13 You will trample down lions and poisonous snakes;
   you will crush fierce lions and serpents under your feet!

14 The LORD says, "I will rescue those who love me.
   I will protect those who trust in my name.
15 When they call on me, I will answer;
   I will be with them in trouble.
   I will rescue them and honor them.
16 I will satisfy them with a long life
   and give them my salvation."

PSALM 92

A psalm to be sung on the LORD's Day. A song.

1 It is good to give thanks to the LORD,
   to sing praises to the Most High.
2 It is good to proclaim your unfailing love in the morning,
   your faithfulness in the evening,
3 accompanied by the harp and lute
   and the harmony of the lyre.
4 You thrill me, LORD, with all you have done for me!
   I sing for joy because of what you have done.

5 O LORD, what great miracles you do!
   And how deep are your thoughts.
6 Only an ignorant person would not know this!
   Only a fool would not understand it.
7 Although the wicked flourish like weeds,
   and evildoers blossom with success,
   there is only eternal destruction ahead of them.
8 But you are exalted in the heavens.
   You, O LORD, continue forever.
9 Your enemies, LORD, will surely perish;
   all evildoers will be scattered.

¹⁰ But you have made me as strong as a wild bull.
    How refreshed I am by your power!
¹¹ With my own eyes I have seen the downfall of my enemies;
    with my own ears I have heard the defeat of my wicked
        opponents.
¹² But the godly will flourish like palm trees
    and grow strong like the cedars of Lebanon.
¹³ For they are transplanted into the LORD's own house.
    They flourish in the courts of our God.
¹⁴ Even in old age they will still produce fruit;
    they will remain vital and green.
¹⁵ They will declare, "The LORD is just!
    He is my rock!
    There is nothing but goodness in him!"

PSALM 93

¹ The LORD is king! He is robed in majesty.
    Indeed, the LORD is robed in majesty and armed with
        strength.
  The world is firmly established;
    it cannot be shaken.

² Your throne, O LORD, has been established from time
        immemorial.
    You yourself are from the everlasting past.

³ The mighty oceans have roared, O LORD.
    The mighty oceans roar like thunder;
    the mighty oceans roar as they pound the shore.

⁴ But mightier than the violent raging of the seas,
    mightier than the breakers on the shore—
    the LORD above is mightier than these!

⁵ Your royal decrees cannot be changed.
    The nature of your reign, O LORD, is holiness forever.

PSALM 94

¹ O LORD, the God to whom vengeance belongs,
    O God of vengeance, let your glorious justice be seen!
² Arise, O judge of the earth.
    Sentence the proud to the penalties they deserve.
³ How long, O LORD?
    How long will the wicked be allowed to gloat?
⁴ Hear their arrogance!
    How these evildoers boast!
⁵ They oppress your people, LORD,
    hurting those you love.
⁶ They kill widows and foreigners
    and murder orphans.
⁷ "The LORD isn't looking," they say,
    "and besides, the God of Israel* doesn't care."

⁸ Think again, you fools!
    When will you finally catch on?
⁹ Is the one who made your ears deaf?
    Is the one who formed your eyes blind?

94:7 Hebrew *of Jacob.*

10 He punishes the nations—won't he also punish you?
    He knows everything—doesn't he also know what you are
        doing?
11 The LORD knows people's thoughts,
    that they are worthless!

12 Happy are those whom you discipline, LORD,
    and those whom you teach from your law.
13 You give them relief from troubled times
    until a pit is dug for the wicked.
14 The LORD will not reject his people;
    he will not abandon his own special possession.
15 Judgment will come again for the righteous,
    and those who are upright will have a reward.

16 Who will protect me from the wicked?
    Who will stand up for me against evildoers?
17 Unless the LORD had helped me,
    I would soon have died.
18 I cried out, "I'm slipping!"
    and your unfailing love, O LORD, supported me.
19 When doubts filled my mind,
    your comfort gave me renewed hope and cheer.

20 Can unjust leaders claim that God is on their side—
    leaders who permit injustice by their laws?
21 They attack the righteous
    and condemn the innocent to death.
22 But the LORD is my fortress;
    my God is a mighty rock where I can hide.
23 God will make the sins of evil people fall back upon them.
    He will destroy them for their sins.
    The LORD our God will destroy them.

PSALM 95

1 Come, let us sing to the LORD!
    Let us give a joyous shout to the rock of our salvation!
2 Let us come before him with thanksgiving.
    Let us sing him psalms of praise.
3 For the LORD is a great God,
    the great King above all gods.
4 He owns the depths of the earth,
    and even the mightiest mountains are his.
5 The sea belongs to him, for he made it.
    His hands formed the dry land, too.

6 Come, let us worship and bow down.
    Let us kneel before the LORD our maker,
7   for he is our God.
    We are the people he watches over,
        the sheep under his care.

    Oh, that you would listen to his voice today!
8 The LORD says, "Don't harden your hearts as Israel did at
        Meribah,
    as they did at Massah in the wilderness.

⁹ For there your ancestors tried my patience;
   they courted my wrath though they had seen my many miracles.
¹⁰ For forty years I was angry with them, and I said,
   'They are a people whose hearts turn away from me.
   They refuse to do what I tell them.'
¹¹ So in my anger I made a vow:
   'They will never enter my place of rest.'"

PSALM 96

¹ Sing a new song to the LORD!
   Let the whole earth sing to the LORD!
² Sing to the LORD; bless his name.
   Each day proclaim the good news that he saves.
³ Publish his glorious deeds among the nations.
   Tell everyone about the amazing things he does.
⁴ Great is the LORD! He is most worthy of praise!
   He is to be revered above all the gods.
⁵ The gods of other nations are merely idols,
   but the LORD made the heavens!
⁶ Honor and majesty surround him;
   strength and beauty are in his sanctuary.

⁷ O nations of the world, recognize the LORD;
   recognize that the LORD is glorious and strong.
⁸ Give to the LORD the glory he deserves!
   Bring your offering and come to worship him.
⁹ Worship the LORD in all his holy splendor.
   Let all the earth tremble before him.
¹⁰ Tell all the nations that the LORD is king.
   The world is firmly established and cannot be shaken.
   He will judge all peoples fairly.

¹¹ Let the heavens be glad, and let the earth rejoice!
   Let the sea and everything in it shout his praise!
¹² Let the fields and their crops burst forth with joy!
   Let the trees of the forest rustle with praise
¹³   before the LORD!
   For the LORD is coming!
   He is coming to judge the earth.
   He will judge the world with righteousness
   and all the nations with his truth.

PSALM 97

¹ The LORD is king! Let the earth rejoice!
   Let the farthest islands be glad.
² Clouds and darkness surround him.
   Righteousness and justice are the foundation of his throne.
³ Fire goes forth before him
   and burns up all his foes.
⁴ His lightning flashes out across the world.
   The earth sees and trembles.
⁵ The mountains melt like wax before the LORD,
   before the Lord of all the earth.
⁶ The heavens declare his righteousness;
   every nation sees his glory.

⁷ Those who worship idols are disgraced—
    all who brag about their worthless gods—
    for every god must bow to him.
⁸ Jerusalem* has heard and rejoiced,
    and all the cities of Judah are glad
    because of your justice, LORD!
⁹ For you, O LORD, are most high over all the earth;
    you are exalted far above all gods.

¹⁰ You who love the LORD, hate evil!
    He protects the lives of his godly people
    and rescues them from the power of the wicked.
¹¹ Light shines on the godly,
    and joy on those who do right.
¹² May all who are godly be happy in the LORD
    and praise his holy name!

PSALM 98

A psalm.

¹ Sing a new song to the LORD,
    for he has done wonderful deeds.
He has won a mighty victory
    by his power and holiness.
² The LORD has announced his victory
    and has revealed his righteousness to every nation!
³ He has remembered his promise to love and be faithful to
    Israel.
The whole earth has seen the salvation of our God.

⁴ Shout to the LORD, all the earth;
    break out in praise and sing for joy!
⁵ Sing your praise to the LORD with the harp,
    with the harp and melodious song,
⁶   with trumpets and the sound of the ram's horn.
Make a joyful symphony before the LORD, the King!

⁷ Let the sea and everything in it shout his praise!
    Let the earth and all living things join in.
⁸ Let the rivers clap their hands in glee!
    Let the hills sing out their songs of joy
⁹   before the LORD.
For the LORD is coming to judge the earth.
    He will judge the world with justice,
    and the nations with fairness.

PSALM 99

¹ The LORD is king!
    Let the nations tremble!
He sits on his throne between the cherubim.
    Let the whole earth quake!
² The LORD sits in majesty in Jerusalem,*
    supreme above all the nations.
³ Let them praise your great and awesome name.
    Your name is holy!

97:8 Hebrew *Zion.*   99:2 Hebrew *Zion.*

⁴ Mighty king, lover of justice,
   you have established fairness.
You have acted with justice
   and righteousness throughout Israel.*
⁵ Exalt the LORD our God!
   Bow low before his feet, for he is holy!

⁶ Moses and Aaron were among his priests;
   Samuel also called on his name.
They cried to the LORD for help,
   and he answered them.
⁷ He spoke to them from the pillar of cloud,
   and they followed the decrees and principles he gave them.
⁸ O LORD our God, you answered them.
   You were a forgiving God,
   but you punished them when they went wrong.

⁹ Exalt the LORD our God
   and worship at his holy mountain in Jerusalem,
   for the LORD our God is holy!

PSALM 100

A psalm of thanksgiving.

¹ Shout with joy to the LORD, O earth!
²   Worship the LORD with gladness.
   Come before him, singing with joy.
³ Acknowledge that the LORD is God!
   He made us, and we are his.
   We are his people, the sheep of his pasture.

⁴ Enter his gates with thanksgiving;
   go into his courts with praise.
   Give thanks to him and bless his name.
⁵ For the LORD is good.
   His unfailing love continues forever,
   and his faithfulness continues to each generation.

PSALM 101

A psalm of David.

¹ I will sing of your love and justice.
   I will praise you, LORD, with songs.
² I will be careful to live a blameless life—
   when will you come to my aid?
   I will lead a life of integrity
   in my own home.
³ I will refuse to look at
   anything vile and vulgar.
   I hate all crooked dealings;
   I will have nothing to do with them.
⁴ I will reject perverse ideas
   and stay away from every evil.
⁵ I will not tolerate people who slander their neighbors.
   I will not endure conceit and pride.

99:4 Hebrew *Jacob.*

⁶ I will keep a protective eye on the godly,
    so they may dwell with me in safety.
Only those who are above reproach
    will be allowed to serve me.
⁷ I will not allow deceivers to serve me,
    and liars will not be allowed to enter my presence.
⁸ My daily task will be to ferret out criminals
    and free the city of the LORD from their grip.

PSALM 102

A prayer of one overwhelmed with trouble, pouring out problems before the LORD.

¹ LORD, hear my prayer!
    Listen to my plea!
² Don't turn away from me
    in my time of distress.
Bend down your ear
    and answer me quickly when I call to you,
³   for my days disappear like smoke,
    and my bones burn like red-hot coals.
⁴ My heart is sick, withered like grass,
    and I have lost my appetite.
⁵ Because of my groaning,
    I am reduced to skin and bones.
⁶ I am like an owl in the desert,
    like a lonely owl in a far-off wilderness.
⁷ I lie awake,
    lonely as a solitary bird on the roof.
⁸ My enemies taunt me day after day.
    They mock and curse me.
⁹ I eat ashes instead of my food.
    My tears run down into my drink
¹⁰ because of your anger and wrath.
    For you have picked me up and thrown me out.
¹¹ My life passes as swiftly as the evening shadows.
    I am withering like grass.

¹² But you, O LORD, will rule forever.
    Your fame will endure to every generation.
¹³ You will arise and have mercy on Jerusalem*—
    and now is the time to pity her,
    now is the time you promised to help.
¹⁴ For your people love every stone in her walls
    and show favor even to the dust in her streets.
¹⁵ And the nations will tremble before the LORD.
    The kings of the earth will tremble before his glory.
¹⁶ For the LORD will rebuild Jerusalem.
    He will appear in his glory.
¹⁷ He will listen to the prayers of the destitute.
    He will not reject their pleas.

¹⁸ Let this be recorded for future generations,
    so that a nation yet to be created will praise the LORD.
¹⁹ Tell them the LORD looked down

102:13 Hebrew *Zion;* also in 102:16.

from his heavenly sanctuary.
He looked to the earth from heaven
20 to hear the groans of the prisoners,
to release those condemned to die.
21 And so the LORD's fame will be celebrated in Zion,
his praises in Jerusalem,
22 when multitudes gather together
and kingdoms come to worship the LORD.

23 He has cut me down in midlife,
shortening my days.
24 But I cried to him, "My God, who lives forever,
don't take my life while I am still so young!
25 In ages past you laid the foundation of the earth,
and the heavens are the work of your hands.
26 Even they will perish, but you remain forever;
they will wear out like old clothing.
You will change them like a garment,
and they will fade away.
27 But you are always the same;
your years never end.
28 The children of your people
will live in security.
Their children's children
will thrive in your presence."

PSALM 103

A psalm of David.

1 Praise the LORD, I tell myself;
with my whole heart, I will praise his holy name.
2 Praise the LORD, I tell myself,
and never forget the good things he does for me.
3 He forgives all my sins
and heals all my diseases.
4 He ransoms me from death
and surrounds me with love and tender mercies.
5 He fills my life with good things.
My youth is renewed like the eagle's!
6 The LORD gives righteousness
and justice to all who are treated unfairly.
7 He revealed his character to Moses
and his deeds to the people of Israel.
8 The LORD is merciful and gracious;
he is slow to get angry and full of unfailing love.
9 He will not constantly accuse us,
nor remain angry forever.
10 He has not punished us for all our sins,
nor does he deal with us as we deserve.
11 For his unfailing love toward those who fear him
is as great as the height of the heavens above the earth.
12 He has removed our rebellious acts
as far away from us as the east is from the west.
13 The LORD is like a father to his children,
tender and compassionate to those who fear him.

¹⁴ For he understands how weak we are;
    he knows we are only dust.
¹⁵ Our days on earth are like grass;
    like wildflowers, we bloom and die.
¹⁶ The wind blows, and we are gone—
    as though we had never been here.
¹⁷ But the love of the LORD remains forever
    with those who fear him.
His salvation extends to the children's children
¹⁸   of those who are faithful to his covenant,
    of those who obey his commandments!

¹⁹ The LORD has made the heavens his throne;
    from there he rules over everything.
²⁰ Praise the LORD, you angels of his,
    you mighty creatures who carry out his plans,
    listening for each of his commands.
²¹ Yes, praise the LORD, you armies of angels
    who serve him and do his will!
²² Praise the LORD, everything he has created,
    everywhere in his kingdom.
    As for me—I, too, will praise the LORD.

PSALM 104

¹ Praise the LORD, I tell myself;
    O LORD my God, how great you are!
You are robed with honor and with majesty;
²   you are dressed in a robe of light.
You stretch out the starry curtain of the heavens;
³   you lay out the rafters of your home in the rain clouds.
You make the clouds your chariots;
    you ride upon the wings of the wind.
⁴ The winds are your messengers;
    flames of fire are your servants.

⁵ You placed the world on its foundation
    so it would never be moved.
⁶ You clothed the earth with floods of water,
    water that covered even the mountains.
⁷ At the sound of your rebuke, the water fled;
    at the sound of your thunder, it fled away.
⁸ Mountains rose and valleys sank
    to the levels you decreed.
⁹ Then you set a firm boundary for the seas,
    so they would never again cover the earth.

¹⁰ You make the springs pour water into ravines,
    so streams gush down from the mountains.
¹¹ They provide water for all the animals,
    and the wild donkeys quench their thirst.
¹² The birds nest beside the streams
    and sing among the branches of the trees.
¹³ You send rain on the mountains from your heavenly home,
    and you fill the earth with the fruit of your labor.
¹⁴ You cause grass to grow for the cattle.

You cause plants to grow for people to use.
You allow them to produce food from the earth—
¹⁵ wine to make them glad,
olive oil as lotion for their skin,
and bread to give them strength.
¹⁶ The trees of the LORD are well cared for—
the cedars of Lebanon that he planted.
¹⁷ There the birds make their nests,
and the storks make their homes in the firs.
¹⁸ High in the mountains are pastures for the wild goats,
and the rocks form a refuge for rock badgers.*
¹⁹ You made the moon to mark the seasons
and the sun that knows when to set.
²⁰ You send the darkness, and it becomes night,
when all the forest animals prowl about.
²¹ Then the young lions roar for their food,
but they are dependent on God.
²² At dawn they slink back
into their dens to rest.
²³ Then people go off to their work;
they labor until the evening shadows fall again.

²⁴ O LORD, what a variety of things you have made!
In wisdom you have made them all.
The earth is full of your creatures.
²⁵ Here is the ocean, vast and wide,
teeming with life of every kind,
both great and small.
²⁶ See the ships sailing along,
and Leviathan, which you made to play in the sea.
²⁷ Every one of these depends on you
to give them their food as they need it.
²⁸ When you supply it, they gather it.
You open your hand to feed them, and they are satisfied.
²⁹ But if you turn away from them, they panic.
When you take away their breath, they die
and turn again to dust.
³⁰ When you send your Spirit, new life is born
to replenish all the living of the earth.

³¹ May the glory of the LORD last forever!
The LORD rejoices in all he has made!
³² The earth trembles at his glance;
the mountains burst into flame at his touch.
³³ I will sing to the LORD as long as I live.
I will praise my God to my last breath!
³⁴ May he be pleased by all these thoughts about him,
for I rejoice in the LORD.
³⁵ Let all sinners vanish from the face of the earth;
let the wicked disappear forever.
As for me—I will praise the LORD!

Praise the LORD!

104:18 Or *coneys*, or *hyraxes*.

PSALM 105

1 Give thanks to the LORD and proclaim his greatness.
   Let the whole world know what he has done.
2 Sing to him; yes, sing his praises.
   Tell everyone about his miracles.
3 Exult in his holy name;
   O worshipers of the LORD, rejoice!
4 Search for the LORD and for his strength,
   and keep on searching.
5 Think of the wonderful works he has done,
   the miracles and the judgments he handed down,
6 O children of Abraham, God's servant,
   O descendants of Jacob, God's chosen one.
7 He is the LORD our God.
   His rule is seen throughout the land.
8 He always stands by his covenant—
   the commitment he made to a thousand generations.
9 This is the covenant he made with Abraham
   and the oath he swore to Isaac.
10 He confirmed it to Jacob as a decree,
   to the people of Israel as a never-ending treaty:
11 "I will give you the land of Canaan
   as your special possession."

12 He said this when they were few in number,
   a tiny group of strangers in Canaan.
13 They wandered back and forth between nations,
   from one kingdom to another.
14 Yet he did not let anyone oppress them.
   He warned kings on their behalf:
15 "Do not touch these people I have chosen,
   and do not hurt my prophets."
16 He called for a famine on the land of Canaan,
   cutting off its food supply.
17 Then he sent someone to Egypt ahead of them—
   Joseph, who was sold as a slave.
18 There in prison, they bruised his feet with fetters
   and placed his neck in an iron collar.
19 Until the time came to fulfill his word,
   the LORD tested Joseph's character.
20 Then Pharaoh sent for him and set him free;
   the ruler of the nation opened his prison door.
21 Joseph was put in charge of all the king's household;
   he became ruler over all the king's possessions.
22 He could instruct the king's aides as he pleased
   and teach the king's advisers.

23 Then Israel arrived in Egypt;
   Jacob lived as a foreigner in the land of Ham.
24 And the LORD multiplied the people of Israel
   until they became too mighty for their enemies.
25 Then he turned the Egyptians against the Israelites,
   and they plotted against the LORD's servants.

²⁶ But the LORD sent Moses his servant,
along with Aaron, whom he had chosen.
²⁷ They performed miraculous signs among the Egyptians,
and miracles in the land of Ham.
²⁸ The LORD blanketed Egypt in darkness,
for they had defied his commands to let his people go.
²⁹ He turned the nation's water into blood,
poisoning all the fish.
³⁰ Then frogs overran the land;
they were found even in the king's private rooms.
³¹ When he spoke, flies descended on the Egyptians,
and gnats swarmed across Egypt.
³² Instead of rain, he sent murderous hail,
and flashes of lightning overwhelmed the land.
³³ He ruined their grapevines and fig trees
and shattered all the trees.
³⁴ He spoke, and hordes of locusts came—
locusts beyond number.
³⁵ They ate up everything green in the land,
destroying all the crops.
³⁶ Then he killed the oldest child in each Egyptian home,
the pride and joy of each family.

³⁷ But he brought his people safely out of Egypt, loaded with
silver and gold;
there were no sick or feeble people among them.
³⁸ Egypt was glad when they were gone,
for the dread of them was great.
³⁹ The LORD spread out a cloud above them as a covering
and gave them a great fire to light the darkness.
⁴⁰ They asked for meat, and he sent them quail;
he gave them manna—bread from heaven.
⁴¹ He opened up a rock, and water gushed out
to form a river through the dry and barren land.
⁴² For he remembered his sacred promise
to Abraham his servant.
⁴³ So he brought his people out of Egypt with joy,
his chosen ones with rejoicing.
⁴⁴ He gave his people the lands of pagan nations,
and they harvested crops that others had planted.
⁴⁵ All this happened so they would follow his principles
and obey his laws.

Praise the LORD!

PSALM 106
¹ Praise the LORD!

Give thanks to the LORD, for he is good!
His faithful love endures forever.
² Who can list the glorious miracles of the LORD?
Who can ever praise him half enough?
³ Happy are those who deal justly with others
and always do what is right.

⁴ Remember me, too, LORD, when you show favor to your
people;
come to me with your salvation.
⁵ Let me share in the prosperity of your chosen ones.
Let me rejoice in the joy of your people;
let me praise you with those who are your heritage.

⁶ Both we and our ancestors have sinned.
We have done wrong! We have acted wickedly!
⁷ Our ancestors in Egypt
were not impressed by the LORD's miracles.
They soon forgot his many acts of kindness to them.
Instead, they rebelled against him at the Red Sea.*
⁸ Even so, he saved them—
to defend the honor of his name
and to demonstrate his mighty power.
⁹ He commanded the Red Sea* to divide, and a dry path appeared.
He led Israel across the sea bottom that was as dry as a
desert.
¹⁰ So he rescued them from their enemies
and redeemed them from their foes.
¹¹ Then the water returned and covered their enemies;
not one of them survived.
¹² Then at last his people believed his promises.
Then they finally sang his praise.

¹³ Yet how quickly they forgot what he had done!
They wouldn't wait for his counsel!
¹⁴ In the wilderness, their desires ran wild,
testing God's patience in that dry land.
¹⁵ So he gave them what they asked for,
but he sent a plague along with it.
¹⁶ The people in the camp were jealous of Moses
and envious of Aaron, the LORD's holy priest.
¹⁷ Because of this, the earth opened up;
it swallowed Dathan
and buried Abiram and the other rebels.
¹⁸ Fire fell upon their followers;
a flame consumed the wicked.

¹⁹ The people made a calf at Mount Sinai*;
they bowed before an image made of gold.
²⁰ They traded their glorious God
for a statue of a grass-eating ox!
²¹ They forgot God, their savior,
who had done such great things in Egypt—
²² such wonderful things in that land,
such awesome deeds at the Red Sea.
²³ So he declared he would destroy them.
But Moses, his chosen one, stepped between the LORD and
the people.
He begged him to turn from his anger and not destroy
them.

106:7 Hebrew *at the sea, the sea of reeds.*   **106:9** Hebrew *sea of reeds*; also in 106:22.
106:19 Hebrew *at Horeb,* another name for Sinai.

²⁴ The people refused to enter the pleasant land,
for they wouldn't believe his promise to care for them.
²⁵ Instead, they grumbled in their tents
and refused to obey the LORD.
²⁶ Therefore, he swore
that he would kill them in the wilderness,
²⁷ that he would scatter their descendants among the nations,
exiling them to distant lands.

²⁸ Then our ancestors joined in the worship of Baal at Peor;
they even ate sacrifices offered to the dead!
²⁹ They angered the LORD with all these things,
so a plague broke out among them.
³⁰ But Phinehas had the courage to step in,
and the plague was stopped.
³¹ So he has been regarded as a righteous man
ever since that time.

³² At Meribah, too, they angered the LORD,
causing Moses serious trouble.
³³ They made Moses angry, *
and he spoke foolishly.

³⁴ Israel failed to destroy the nations in the land,
as the LORD had told them to.
³⁵ Instead, they mingled among the pagans
and adopted their evil customs.
³⁶ They worshiped their idols,
and this led to their downfall.
³⁷ They even sacrificed their sons
and their daughters to the demons.
³⁸ They shed innocent blood,
the blood of their sons and daughters.
By sacrificing them to the idols of Canaan,
they polluted the land with murder.
³⁹ They defiled themselves by their evil deeds,
and their love of idols was adultery in the LORD's sight.

⁴⁰ That is why the LORD's anger burned against his people,
and he abhorred his own special possession.
⁴¹ He handed them over to pagan nations,
and those who hated them ruled over them.
⁴² Their enemies crushed them
and brought them under their cruel power.
⁴³ Again and again he delivered them,
but they continued to rebel against him,
and they were finally destroyed by their sin.
⁴⁴ Even so, he pitied them in their distress
and listened to their cries.
⁴⁵ He remembered his covenant with them
and relented because of his unfailing love.
⁴⁶ He even caused their captors
to treat them with kindness.

106:33 Hebrew *They embittered his spirit.*

⁴⁷ O LORD our God, save us!
  Gather us back from among the nations,
  so we can thank your holy name
    and rejoice and praise you.

⁴⁸ Blessed be the LORD, the God of Israel,
    from everlasting to everlasting!
  Let all the people say, "Amen!"

  Praise the LORD!

BOOK FIVE (Psalms 107–150)

P S A L M   1 0 7
¹ Give thanks to the LORD, for he is good!
    His faithful love endures forever.
² Has the LORD redeemed you? Then speak out!
    Tell others he has saved you from your enemies.
³ For he has gathered the exiles from many lands,
    from east and west, from north and south.

⁴ Some wandered in the desert,
    lost and homeless.
⁵ Hungry and thirsty,
    they nearly died.
⁶ "LORD, help!" they cried in their trouble,
    and he rescued them from their distress.
⁷ He led them straight to safety,
    to a city where they could live.
⁸ Let them praise the LORD for his great love
    and for all his wonderful deeds to them.
⁹ For he satisfies the thirsty
    and fills the hungry with good things.

¹⁰ Some sat in darkness and deepest gloom,
    miserable prisoners in chains.
¹¹ They rebelled against the words of God,
    scorning the counsel of the Most High.
¹² That is why he broke them with hard labor;
    they fell, and no one helped them rise again.
¹³ "LORD, help!" they cried in their trouble,
    and he saved them from their distress.
¹⁴ He led them from the darkness and deepest gloom;
    he snapped their chains.
¹⁵ Let them praise the LORD for his great love
    and for all his wonderful deeds to them.
¹⁶ For he broke down their prison gates of bronze;
    he cut apart their bars of iron.

¹⁷ Some were fools in their rebellion;
    they suffered for their sins.
¹⁸ Their appetites were gone,
    and death was near.
¹⁹ "LORD, help!" they cried in their trouble,
    and he saved them from their distress.

²⁰ He spoke, and they were healed—
    snatched from the door of death.
²¹ Let them praise the Lord for his great love
    and for all his wonderful deeds to them.
²² Let them offer sacrifices of thanksgiving
    and sing joyfully about his glorious acts.

²³ Some went off in ships,
    plying the trade routes of the world.
²⁴ They, too, observed the Lord's power in action,
    his impressive works on the deepest seas.
²⁵ He spoke, and the winds rose,
    stirring up the waves.
²⁶ Their ships were tossed to the heavens
    and sank again to the depths;
    the sailors cringed in terror.
²⁷ They reeled and staggered like drunkards
    and were at their wits' end.
²⁸ "Lord, help!" they cried in their trouble,
    and he saved them from their distress.
²⁹ He calmed the storm to a whisper
    and stilled the waves.
³⁰ What a blessing was that stillness
    as he brought them safely into harbor!
³¹ Let them praise the Lord for his great love
    and for all his wonderful deeds to them.
³² Let them exalt him publicly before the congregation
    and before the leaders of the nation.

³³ He changes rivers into deserts,
    and springs of water into dry land.
³⁴ He turns the fruitful land into salty wastelands,
    because of the wickedness of those who live there.
³⁵ But he also turns deserts into pools of water,
    the dry land into flowing springs.
³⁶ He brings the hungry to settle there
    and build their cities.
³⁷ They sow their fields, plant their vineyards,
    and harvest their bumper crops.
³⁸ How he blesses them!
    They raise large families there,
    and their herds of cattle increase.

³⁹ When they decrease in number and become impoverished
    through oppression, trouble, and sorrow,
⁴⁰ the Lord pours contempt on their princes,
    causing them to wander in trackless wastelands.
⁴¹ But he rescues the poor from their distress
    and increases their families like vast flocks of sheep.
⁴² The godly will see these things and be glad,
    while the wicked are stricken silent.
⁴³ Those who are wise will take all this to heart;
    they will see in our history the faithful love of the Lord.

PSALM 108

A psalm of David. A song.

1 My heart is confident in you, O God;
　no wonder I can sing your praises!
Wake up, my soul!
2 　Wake up, O harp and lyre!
　I will waken the dawn with my song.
3 I will thank you, LORD, in front of all the people.
　I will sing your praises among the nations.
4 For your unfailing love is higher than the heavens.
　Your faithfulness reaches to the clouds.
5 Be exalted, O God, above the highest heavens.
　May your glory shine over all the earth.

6 Use your strong right arm to save me,
　and rescue your beloved people.
7 God has promised this by his holiness*:
　"I will divide up Shechem with joy.
　I will measure out the valley of Succoth.
8 Gilead is mine,
　and Manasseh is mine.
Ephraim will produce my warriors,
　and Judah will produce my kings.
9 Moab will become my lowly servant,
　and Edom will be my slave.
　I will shout in triumph over the Philistines."

10 But who will bring me into the fortified city?
　Who will bring me victory over Edom?
11 Have you rejected us, O God?
　Will you no longer march with our armies?
12 Oh, please help us against our enemies,
　for all human help is useless.
13 With God's help we will do mighty things,
　for he will trample down our foes.

PSALM 109

For the choir director: A psalm of David.

1 O God, whom I praise,
　don't stand silent and aloof
2 while the wicked slander me
　and tell lies about me.
3 They are all around me with their hateful words,
　and they fight against me for no reason.
4 I love them, but they try to destroy me—
　even as I am praying for them!
5 They return evil for good,
　and hatred for my love.

6 Arrange for an evil person to turn on him.
　Send an accuser to bring him to trial.
7 When his case is called for judgment,
　let him be pronounced guilty.

108:7 Or *in his sanctuary.*

Count his prayers as sins.
⁸ Let his years be few;
    let his position be given to someone else.
⁹ May his children become fatherless,
    and may his wife become a widow.
¹⁰ May his children wander as beggars;
    may they be evicted from their ruined homes.
¹¹ May creditors seize his entire estate,
    and strangers take all he has earned.
¹² Let no one be kind to him;
    let no one pity his fatherless children.
¹³ May all his offspring die.
    May his family name be blotted out in a single generation.
¹⁴ May the LORD never forget the sins of his ancestors;
    may his mother's sins never be erased from the record.
¹⁵ May these sins always remain before the LORD,
    but may his name be cut off from human memory.
¹⁶ For he refused all kindness to others;
    he persecuted the poor and needy,
    and he hounded the brokenhearted to death.
¹⁷ He loved to curse others;
    now you curse him.
  He never blessed others;
    now don't you bless him.
¹⁸ Cursing is as much a part of him as his clothing,
    or as the water he drinks,
    or the rich food he eats.
¹⁹ Now may his curses return and cling to him like clothing;
    may they be tied around him like a belt.

²⁰ May those curses become the LORD's punishment for my accusers
    who are plotting against my life.
²¹ But deal well with me, O Sovereign LORD,
    for the sake of your own reputation!
  Rescue me because you are so faithful and good.
²²   For I am poor and needy,
    and my heart is full of pain.
²³ I am fading like a shadow at dusk;
    I am falling like a grasshopper that is brushed aside.
²⁴ My knees are weak from fasting,
    and I am skin and bones.
²⁵ I am an object of mockery to people everywhere;
    when they see me, they shake their heads.

²⁶ Help me, O LORD my God!
    Save me because of your unfailing love.
²⁷ Let them see that this is your doing,
    that you yourself have done it, LORD.
²⁸ Then let them curse me if they like,
    but you will bless me!
  When they attack me, they will be disgraced!
    But I, your servant, will go right on rejoicing!
²⁹ Make their humiliation obvious to all;
    clothe my accusers with disgrace.

30 But I will give repeated thanks to the LORD,
   praising him to everyone.
31 For he stands beside the needy,
   ready to save them from those who condemn them.

PSALM 110
A psalm of David.

1 The LORD said to my Lord,
   "Sit in honor at my right hand
until I humble your enemies,
   making them a footstool under your feet."

2 The LORD will extend your powerful dominion from
      Jerusalem*;
   you will rule over your enemies.
3 In that day of battle,
   your people will serve you willingly.
Arrayed in holy garments,
   your vigor will be renewed each day like the morning
      dew.
4 The LORD has taken an oath and will not break his vow:
   "You are a priest forever in the line of Melchizedek."
5 The Lord stands at your right hand to protect you.
   He will strike down many kings in the day of his anger.
6 He will punish the nations
   and fill them with their dead;
he will shatter heads
   over the whole earth.
7 But he himself will be refreshed from brooks along the way.
   He will be victorious.

PSALM 111
1 Praise the LORD!

I will thank the LORD with all my heart
   as I meet with his godly people.
2 How amazing are the deeds of the LORD!
   All who delight in him should ponder them.
3 Everything he does reveals his glory and majesty.
   His righteousness never fails.
4 Who can forget the wonders he performs?
   How gracious and merciful is our LORD!
5 He gives food to those who trust him;
   he always remembers his covenant.
6 He has shown his great power to his people
   by giving them the lands of other nations.
7 All he does is just and good,
   and all his commandments are trustworthy.
8 They are forever true,
   to be obeyed faithfully and with integrity.
9 He has paid a full ransom for his people.
   He has guaranteed his covenant with them forever.
   What a holy, awe-inspiring name he has!

110:2 Hebrew *Zion.*

¹⁰ Reverence for the LORD is the foundation of true wisdom.
    The rewards of wisdom come to all who obey him.

Praise his name forever!

PSALM 112

¹ Praise the LORD!

Happy are those who fear the LORD.
    Yes, happy are those who delight in doing what he commands.
² Their children will be successful everywhere;
    an entire generation of godly people will be blessed.
³ They themselves will be wealthy,
    and their good deeds will never be forgotten.
⁴ When darkness overtakes the godly, light will come bursting in.
    They are* generous, compassionate, and righteous.
⁵ All goes well for those who are generous,
    who lend freely and conduct their business fairly.
⁶ Such people will not be overcome by evil circumstances.
    Those who are righteous will be long remembered.
⁷ They do not fear bad news;
    they confidently trust the LORD to care for them.
⁸ They are confident and fearless
    and can face their foes triumphantly.
⁹ They give generously to those in need.
    Their good deeds will never be forgotten.
    They will have influence and honor.
¹⁰ The wicked will be infuriated when they see this.
    They will grind their teeth in anger;
    they will slink away, their hopes thwarted.

PSALM 113

¹ Praise the LORD!

Yes, give praise, O servants of the LORD.
    Praise the name of the LORD!
² Blessed be the name of the LORD
    forever and ever.
³ Everywhere—from east to west—
    praise the name of the LORD.
⁴ For the LORD is high above the nations;
    his glory is far greater than the heavens.

⁵ Who can be compared with the LORD our God,
    who is enthroned on high?
⁶ Far below him are the heavens and the earth.
    He stoops to look,
⁷ and he lifts the poor from the dirt
    and the needy from the garbage dump.
⁸ He sets them among princes,
    even the princes of his own people!
⁹ He gives the barren woman a home,
    so that she becomes a happy mother.

Praise the LORD!

112:4 Greek version reads *The LORD is.*

PSALM 114

1 When the Israelites escaped from Egypt—
    when the family of Jacob left that foreign land—
2 the land of Judah became God's sanctuary,
    and Israel became his kingdom.

3 The Red Sea* saw them coming and hurried out of their way!
    The water of the Jordan River turned away.
4 The mountains skipped like rams,
    the little hills like lambs!
5 What's wrong, Red Sea, that made you hurry out of their way?
    What happened, Jordan River, that you turned away?
6 Why, mountains, did you skip like rams?
    Why, little hills, like lambs?

7 Tremble, O earth, at the presence of the Lord,
    at the presence of the God of Israel.*
8 He turned the rock into pools of water;
    yes, springs of water came from solid rock.

PSALM 115

1 Not to us, O LORD, but to you goes all the glory
    for your unfailing love and faithfulness.
2 Why let the nations say,
    "Where is their God?"
3 For our God is in the heavens,
    and he does as he wishes.
4 Their idols are merely things of silver and gold,
    shaped by human hands.
5 They cannot talk, though they have mouths,
    or see, though they have eyes!
6 They cannot hear with their ears,
    or smell with their noses,
7   or feel with their hands,
    or walk with their feet,
    or utter sounds with their throats!
8 And those who make them are just like them,
    as are all who trust in them.

9 O Israel, trust the LORD!
    He is your helper; he is your shield.
10 O priests of Aaron, trust the LORD!
    He is your helper; he is your shield.
11 All you who fear the LORD, trust the LORD!
    He is your helper; he is your shield.

12 The LORD remembers us,
    and he will surely bless us.
    He will bless the people of Israel
    and the family of Aaron, the priests.
13 He will bless those who fear the LORD,
    both great and small.

14 May the LORD richly bless
    both you and your children.

114:3 Hebrew *the sea;* also in 114:5.   **114:7** Hebrew *of Jacob.*

15 May you be blessed by the LORD,
  who made heaven and earth.
16 The heavens belong to the LORD,
  but he has given the earth to all humanity.

17 The dead cannot sing praises to the LORD,
  for they have gone into the silence of the grave.
18 But we can praise the LORD
  both now and forever!

  Praise the LORD!

PSALM 116

1 I love the LORD because he hears
  and answers my prayers.
2 Because he bends down and listens,
  I will pray as long as I have breath!
3 Death had its hands around my throat;
  the terrors of the grave* overtook me.
  I saw only trouble and sorrow.
4 Then I called on the name of the LORD:
  "Please, LORD, save me!"
5 How kind the LORD is! How good he is!
  So merciful, this God of ours!
6 The LORD protects those of childlike faith;
  I was facing death, and then he saved me.
7 Now I can rest again,
  for the LORD has been so good to me.
8 He has saved me from death,
  my eyes from tears,
  my feet from stumbling.
9 And so I walk in the LORD's presence
  as I live here on earth!
10 I believed in you, so I prayed,
  "I am deeply troubled, LORD."
11 In my anxiety I cried out to you,
  "These people are all liars!"
12 What can I offer the LORD
  for all he has done for me?
13 I will lift up a cup symbolizing his salvation;
  I will praise the LORD's name for saving me.
14 I will keep my promises to the LORD
  in the presence of all his people.

15 The LORD's loved ones are precious to him;
  it grieves him when they die.
16 O LORD, I am your servant;
  yes, I am your servant, the son of your handmaid,
  and you have freed me from my bonds!
17 I will offer you a sacrifice of thanksgiving
  and call on the name of the LORD.
18 I will keep my promises to the LORD
  in the presence of all his people,

116:3 Hebrew *of Sheol*.

¹⁹ in the house of the LORD,
    in the heart of Jerusalem.

Praise the LORD!

PSALM 117

¹ Praise the LORD, all you nations.
    Praise him, all you people of the earth.
² For he loves us with unfailing love;
    the faithfulness of the LORD endures forever.

Praise the LORD!

PSALM 118

¹ Give thanks to the LORD, for he is good!
    His faithful love endures forever.

² Let the congregation of Israel repeat:
    "His faithful love endures forever."
³ Let Aaron's descendants, the priests, repeat:
    "His faithful love endures forever."
⁴ Let all who fear the LORD repeat:
    "His faithful love endures forever."

⁵ In my distress I prayed to the LORD,
    and the LORD answered me and rescued me.
⁶ The LORD is for me, so I will not be afraid.
    What can mere mortals do to me?
⁷ Yes, the LORD is for me; he will help me.
    I will look in triumph at those who hate me.
⁸ It is better to trust the LORD
    than to put confidence in people.
⁹ It is better to trust the LORD
    than to put confidence in princes.

¹⁰ Though hostile nations surrounded me,
    I destroyed them all in the name of the LORD.
¹¹ Yes, they surrounded and attacked me,
    but I destroyed them all in the name of the LORD.
¹² They swarmed around me like bees;
    they blazed against me like a roaring flame.
    But I destroyed them all in the name of the LORD.
¹³ You did your best to kill me, O my enemy,
    but the LORD helped me.
¹⁴ The LORD is my strength and my song;
    he has become my victory.
¹⁵ Songs of joy and victory are sung in the camp of the godly.
    The strong right arm of the LORD has done glorious
        things!
¹⁶ The strong right arm of the LORD is raised in triumph.
    The strong right arm of the LORD has done glorious things!
¹⁷ I will not die, but I will live
    to tell what the LORD has done.
¹⁸ The LORD has punished me severely,
    but he has not handed me over to death.

¹⁹ Open for me the gates where the righteous enter,
and I will go in and thank the LORD.
²⁰ Those gates lead to the presence of the LORD,
and the godly enter there.
²¹ I thank you for answering my prayer
and saving me!

²² The stone rejected by the builders
has now become the cornerstone.
²³ This is the LORD's doing,
and it is marvelous to see.
²⁴ This is the day the LORD has made.
We will rejoice and be glad in it.
²⁵ Please, LORD, please save us.
Please, LORD, please give us success.
²⁶ Bless the one who comes in the name of the LORD.
We bless you from the house of the LORD.
²⁷ The LORD is God, shining upon us.
Bring forward the sacrifice and put it on the altar.
²⁸ You are my God, and I will praise you!
You are my God, and I will exalt you!

²⁹ Give thanks to the LORD, for he is good!
His faithful love endures forever.

PSALM 119

¹ Happy are people of integrity,
who follow the law of the LORD.
² Happy are those who obey his decrees
and search for him with all their hearts.
³ They do not compromise with evil,
and they walk only in his paths.
⁴ You have charged us
to keep your commandments carefully.
⁵ Oh, that my actions would consistently
reflect your principles!
⁶ Then I will not be disgraced
when I compare my life with your commands.
⁷ When I learn your righteous laws,
I will thank you by living as I should!
⁸ I will obey your principles.
Please don't give up on me!

⁹ How can a young person stay pure?
By obeying your word and following its rules.
¹⁰ I have tried my best to find you—
don't let me wander from your commands.
¹¹ I have hidden your word in my heart,
that I might not sin against you.
¹² Blessed are you, O LORD;
teach me your principles.
¹³ I have recited aloud

119 This psalm is a Hebrew acrostic poem; there are 22 stanzas, one for each letter of the Hebrew alphabet. The 8 verses within each stanza begin with the Hebrew letter of its section.

all the laws you have given us.
¹⁴ I have rejoiced in your decrees
as much as in riches.
¹⁵ I will study your commandments
and reflect on your ways.
¹⁶ I will delight in your principles
and not forget your word.

¹⁷ Be good to your servant,
that I may live and obey your word.
¹⁸ Open my eyes to see
the wonderful truths in your law.
¹⁹ I am but a foreigner here on earth;
I need the guidance of your commands.
Don't hide them from me!
²⁰ I am overwhelmed continually
with a desire for your laws.
²¹ You rebuke those cursed proud ones
who wander from your commands.
²² Don't let them scorn and insult me,
for I have obeyed your decrees.
²³ Even princes sit and speak against me,
but I will meditate on your principles.
²⁴ Your decrees please me;
they give me wise advice.

²⁵ I lie in the dust, completely discouraged;
revive me by your word.
²⁶ I told you my plans, and you answered.
Now teach me your principles.
²⁷ Help me understand the meaning of your commandments,
and I will meditate on your wonderful miracles.
²⁸ I weep with grief;
encourage me by your word.
²⁹ Keep me from lying to myself;
give me the privilege of knowing your law.
³⁰ I have chosen to be faithful;
I have determined to live by your laws.
³¹ I cling to your decrees.
LORD, don't let me be put to shame!
³² If you will help me,
I will run to follow your commands.

³³ Teach me, O LORD,
to follow every one of your principles.
³⁴ Give me understanding and I will obey your law;
I will put it into practice with all my heart.
³⁵ Make me walk along the path of your commands,
for that is where my happiness is found.
³⁶ Give me an eagerness for your decrees;
do not inflict me with love for money!
³⁷ Turn my eyes from worthless things,
and give me life through your word. *

119:37 Some manuscripts read *in your ways.*

38 Reassure me of your promise,
    which is for those who honor you.
39 Help me abandon my shameful ways;
    your laws are all I want in life.
40 I long to obey your commandments!
    Renew my life with your goodness.

41 LORD, give to me your unfailing love,
    the salvation that you promised me.
42 Then I will have an answer for those who taunt me,
    for I trust in your word.
43 Do not snatch your word of truth from me,
    for my only hope is in your laws.
44 I will keep on obeying your law
    forever and forever.
45 I will walk in freedom,
    for I have devoted myself to your commandments.
46 I will speak to kings about your decrees,
    and I will not be ashamed.
47 How I delight in your commands!
    How I love them!
48 I honor and love your commands.
    I meditate on your principles.

49 Remember your promise to me,
    for it is my only hope.
50 Your promise revives me;
    it comforts me in all my troubles.
51 The proud hold me in utter contempt,
    but I do not turn away from your law.
52 I meditate on your age-old laws;
    O LORD, they comfort me.
53 I am furious with the wicked,
    those who reject your law.
54 Your principles have been the music of my life
    throughout the years of my pilgrimage.
55 I reflect at night on who you are, O LORD,
    and I obey your law because of this.
56 This is my happy way of life:
    obeying your commandments.

57 LORD, you are mine!
    I promise to obey your words!
58 With all my heart I want your blessings.
    Be merciful just as you promised.
59 I pondered the direction of my life,
    and I turned to follow your statutes.
60 I will hurry, without lingering,
    to obey your commands.
61 Evil people try to drag me into sin,
    but I am firmly anchored to your law.
62 At midnight I rise to thank you
    for your just laws.
63 Anyone who fears you is my friend—
    anyone who obeys your commandments.

⁶⁴ O LORD, the earth is full of your unfailing love;
   teach me your principles.

⁶⁵ You have done many good things for me, LORD,
   just as you promised.
⁶⁶ I believe in your commands;
   now teach me good judgment and knowledge.
⁶⁷ I used to wander off until you disciplined me;
   but now I closely follow your word.
⁶⁸ You are good and do only good;
   teach me your principles.
⁶⁹ Arrogant people have made up lies about me,
   but in truth I obey your commandments with all my heart.
⁷⁰ Their hearts are dull and stupid,
   but I delight in your law.
⁷¹ The suffering you sent was good for me,
   for it taught me to pay attention to your principles.
⁷² Your law is more valuable to me
   than millions in gold and silver!

⁷³ You made me; you created me.
   Now give me the sense to follow your commands.
⁷⁴ May all who fear you find in me a cause for joy,
   for I have put my hope in your word.
⁷⁵ I know, O LORD, that your decisions are fair;
   you disciplined me because I needed it.
⁷⁶ Now let your unfailing love comfort me,
   just as you promised me, your servant.
⁷⁷ Surround me with your tender mercies so I may live,
   for your law is my delight.
⁷⁸ Bring disgrace upon the arrogant people who lied about me;
   meanwhile, I will concentrate on your commandments.
⁷⁹ Let me be reconciled
   with all who fear you and know your decrees.
⁸⁰ May I be blameless in keeping your principles;
   then I will never have to be ashamed.

⁸¹ I faint with longing for your salvation;
   but I have put my hope in your word.
⁸² My eyes are straining to see your promises come true.
   When will you comfort me?
⁸³ I am shriveled like a wineskin in the smoke, exhausted with
      waiting.
   But I cling to your principles and obey them.
⁸⁴ How long must I wait?
   When will you punish those who persecute me?
⁸⁵ These arrogant people who hate your law
   have dug deep pits for me to fall into.
⁸⁶ All your commands are trustworthy.
   Protect me from those who hunt me down without cause.
⁸⁷ They almost finished me off,
   but I refused to abandon your commandments.
⁸⁸ In your unfailing love, spare my life;
   then I can continue to obey your decrees.

89 Forever, O LORD,
     your word stands firm in heaven.
90 Your faithfulness extends to every generation,
     as enduring as the earth you created.
91 Your laws remain true today,
     for everything serves your plans.
92 If your law hadn't sustained me with joy,
     I would have died in my misery.
93 I will never forget your commandments,
     for you have used them to restore my joy and health.
94 I am yours; save me!
     For I have applied myself to obey your
        commandments.
95 Though the wicked hide along the way to kill me,
     I will quietly keep my mind on your decrees.
96 Even perfection has its limits,
     but your commands have no limit.

97 Oh, how I love your law!
     I think about it all day long.
98 Your commands make me wiser than my enemies,
     for your commands are my constant guide.
99 Yes, I have more insight than my teachers,
     for I am always thinking of your decrees.
100 I am even wiser than my elders,
     for I have kept your commandments.
101 I have refused to walk on any path of evil,
     that I may remain obedient to your word.
102 I haven't turned away from your laws,
     for you have taught me well.
103 How sweet are your words to my taste;
     they are sweeter than honey.
104 Your commandments give me understanding;
     no wonder I hate every false way of life.

105 Your word is a lamp for my feet
     and a light for my path.
106 I've promised it once, and I'll promise again:
     I will obey your wonderful laws.
107 I have suffered much, O LORD;
     restore my life again, just as you promised.
108 LORD, accept my grateful thanks
     and teach me your laws.
109 My life constantly hangs in the balance,
     but I will not stop obeying your law.
110 The wicked have set their traps for me along your path,
     but I will not turn from your commandments.
111 Your decrees are my treasure;
     they are truly my heart's delight.
112 I am determined to keep your principles,
     even forever, to the very end.

113 I hate those who are undecided about you,
     but my choice is clear—I love your law.
114 You are my refuge and my shield;

your word is my only source of hope.

115 Get out of my life, you evil-minded people,
for I intend to obey the commands of my God.
116 LORD, sustain me as you promised, that I may live!
Do not let my hope be crushed.
117 Sustain me, and I will be saved;
then I will meditate on your principles continually.
118 But you have rejected all who stray from your principles.
They are only fooling themselves.
119 All the wicked of the earth are the scum you skim off;
no wonder I love to obey your decrees!
120 I tremble in fear of you;
I fear your judgments.

121 Don't leave me to the mercy of my enemies,
for I have done what is just and right.
122 Please guarantee a blessing for me.
Don't let those who are arrogant oppress me!
123 My eyes strain to see your deliverance,
to see the truth of your promise fulfilled.
124 I am your servant;
deal with me in unfailing love,
and teach me your principles.
125 Give discernment to me, your servant;
then I will understand your decrees.
126 LORD, it is time for you to act,
for these evil people have broken your law.
127 Truly, I love your commands
more than gold, even the finest gold.
128 Truly, each of your commandments is right.
That is why I hate every false way.

129 Your decrees are wonderful.
No wonder I obey them!
130 As your words are taught, they give light;
even the simple can understand them.
131 I open my mouth, panting expectantly,
longing for your commands.
132 Come and show me your mercy,
as you do for all who love your name.
133 Guide my steps by your word,
so I will not be overcome by any evil.
134 Rescue me from the oppression of evil people;
then I can obey your commandments.
135 Look down on me with love;
teach me all your principles.
136 Rivers of tears gush from my eyes
because people disobey your law.

137 O LORD, you are righteous,
and your decisions are fair.
138 Your decrees are perfect;
they are entirely worthy of our trust.
139 I am overwhelmed with rage,
for my enemies have disregarded your words.

140 Your promises have been thoroughly tested;
     that is why I love them so much.
141 I am insignificant and despised,
     but I don't forget your commandments.
142 Your justice is eternal,
     and your law is perfectly true.
143 As pressure and stress bear down on me,
     I find joy in your commands.
144 Your decrees are always fair;
     help me to understand them, that I may live.

145 I pray with all my heart; answer me, LORD!
     I will obey your principles.
146 I cry out to you; save me,
     that I may obey your decrees.
147 I rise early, before the sun is up;
     I cry out for help and put my hope in your words.
148 I stay awake through the night,
     thinking about your promise.
149 In your faithful love, O LORD, hear my cry;
     in your justice, save my life.
150 Those lawless people are coming near to attack me;
     they live far from your law.
151 But you are near, O LORD,
     and all your commands are true.
152 I have known from my earliest days
     that your decrees never change.

153 Look down upon my sorrows and rescue me,
     for I have not forgotten your law.
154 Argue my case; take my side!
     Protect my life as you promised.
155 The wicked are far from salvation,
     for they do not bother with your principles.
156 LORD, how great is your mercy;
     in your justice, give me back my life.
157 Many persecute and trouble me,
     yet I have not swerved from your decrees.
158 I hate these traitors
     because they care nothing for your word.
159 See how I love your commandments, LORD.
     Give back my life because of your unfailing love.
160 All your words are true;
     all your just laws will stand forever.

161 Powerful people harass me without cause,
     but my heart trembles only at your word.
162 I rejoice in your word
     like one who finds a great treasure.
163 I hate and abhor all falsehood,
     but I love your law.
164 I will praise you seven times a day
     because all your laws are just.
165 Those who love your law have great peace
     and do not stumble.

166 I long for your salvation, LORD,
    so I have obeyed your commands.
167 I have obeyed your decrees,
    and I love them very much.
168 Yes, I obey your commandments and decrees,
    because you know everything I do.

169 O LORD, listen to my cry;
    give me the discerning mind you promised.
170 Listen to my prayer;
    rescue me as you promised.
171 Let my lips burst forth with praise,
    for you have taught me your principles.
172 Let my tongue sing about your word,
    for all your commands are right.
173 Stand ready to help me,
    for I have chosen to follow your commandments.
174 O LORD, I have longed for your salvation,
    and your law is my delight.
175 Let me live so I can praise you,
    and may your laws sustain me.
176 I have wandered away like a lost sheep;
    come and find me,
    for I have not forgotten your commands.

PSALM 120

A song for the ascent to Jerusalem.

1 I took my troubles to the LORD;
    I cried out to him, and he answered my prayer.
2 Rescue me, O LORD, from liars
    and from all deceitful people.
3 O deceptive tongue, what will God do to you?
    How will he increase your punishment?
4 You will be pierced with sharp arrows
    and burned with glowing coals.

5 How I suffer among these scoundrels of Meshech!
    It pains me to live with these people from Kedar!
6 I am tired of living here
    among people who hate peace.
7 As for me, I am for peace;
    but when I speak, they are for war!

PSALM 121

A song for the ascent to Jerusalem.

1 I look up to the mountains—
    does my help come from there?
2 My help comes from the LORD,
    who made the heavens and the earth!

3 He will not let you stumble and fall;
    the one who watches over you will not sleep.
4 Indeed, he who watches over Israel
    never tires and never sleeps.

5 The LORD himself watches over you!
  The LORD stands beside you as your protective shade.
6 The sun will not hurt you by day,
  nor the moon at night.
7 The LORD keeps you from all evil
  and preserves your life.
8 The LORD keeps watch over you as you come and go,
  both now and forever.

PSALM 122

A song for the ascent to Jerusalem. A psalm of David.

1 I was glad when they said to me,
  "Let us go to the house of the LORD."
2 And now we are standing here
  inside your gates, O Jerusalem.
3 Jerusalem is a well-built city,
  knit together as a single unit.
4 All the people of Israel—the LORD's people—
  make their pilgrimage here.
  They come to give thanks to the name of the LORD
  as the law requires.
5 Here stand the thrones where judgment is given,
  the thrones of the dynasty of David.

6 Pray for the peace of Jerusalem.
  May all who love this city prosper.
7 O Jerusalem, may there be peace within your walls
  and prosperity in your palaces.
8 For the sake of my family and friends, I will say,
  "Peace be with you."
9 For the sake of the house of the LORD our God,
  I will seek what is best for you, O Jerusalem.

PSALM 123

A song for the ascent to Jerusalem.

1 I lift my eyes to you,
  O God, enthroned in heaven.
2 We look to the LORD our God for his mercy,
  just as servants keep their eyes on their master,
  as a slave girl watches her mistress for the slightest signal.

3 Have mercy on us, LORD, have mercy,
  for we have had our fill of contempt.
4 We have had our fill of the scoffing of the proud
  and the contempt of the arrogant.

PSALM 124

A song for the ascent to Jerusalem. A psalm of David.

1 If the LORD had not been on our side—
  let Israel now say—
2 if the LORD had not been on our side
  when people rose up against us,
3 they would have swallowed us alive
  because of their burning anger against us.

⁴ The waters would have engulfed us;
     a torrent would have overwhelmed us.
⁵ Yes, the raging waters of their fury
     would have overwhelmed our very lives.

⁶ Blessed be the LORD,
     who did not let their teeth tear us apart!
⁷ We escaped like a bird from a hunter's trap.
     The trap is broken, and we are free!
⁸ Our help is from the LORD,
     who made the heavens and the earth.

PSALM 125
A song for the ascent to Jerusalem.

¹ Those who trust in the LORD are as secure as Mount Zion;
     they will not be defeated but will endure forever.
² Just as the mountains surround and protect Jerusalem,
     so the LORD surrounds and protects his people, both now
        and forever.
³ The wicked will not rule the godly,
     for then the godly might be forced to do wrong.
⁴ O LORD, do good to those who are good,
     whose hearts are in tune with you.
⁵ But banish those who turn to crooked ways, O LORD.
     Take them away with those who do evil.
     And let Israel have quietness and peace.

PSALM 126
A song for the ascent to Jerusalem.

¹ When the LORD restored his exiles to Jerusalem,*
     it was like a dream!
² We were filled with laughter,
     and we sang for joy.
   And the other nations said,
     "What amazing things the LORD has done for them."
³ Yes, the LORD has done amazing things for us!
     What joy!

⁴ Restore our fortunes, LORD,
     as streams renew the desert.
⁵ Those who plant in tears
     will harvest with shouts of joy.
⁶ They weep as they go to plant their seed,
     but they sing as they return with the harvest.

PSALM 127
A song for the ascent to Jerusalem. A psalm of Solomon.

¹ Unless the LORD builds a house,
     the work of the builders is useless.
   Unless the LORD protects a city,
     guarding it with sentries will do no good.
² It is useless for you to work so hard
     from early morning until late at night,

126:1 Hebrew *Zion.*

anxiously working for food to eat;
for God gives rest to his loved ones.

3 Children are a gift from the LORD;
they are a reward from him.
4 Children born to a young man
are like sharp arrows in a warrior's hands.
5 How happy is the man whose quiver is full of them!
He will not be put to shame when he confronts his accusers
at the city gates.

PSALM 128

A song for the ascent to Jerusalem.

1 How happy are those who fear the LORD—
all who follow his ways!
2 You will enjoy the fruit of your labor.
How happy you will be! How rich your life!
3 Your wife will be like a fruitful vine,
flourishing within your home.
And look at all those children!
There they sit around your table
as vigorous and healthy as young olive trees.
4 That is the LORD's reward
for those who fear him.

5 May the LORD continually bless you from Zion.
May you see Jerusalem prosper as long as you live.
6 May you live to enjoy your grandchildren.
And may Israel have quietness and peace.

PSALM 129

A song for the ascent to Jerusalem.

1 From my earliest youth my enemies have persecuted me—
let Israel now say—
2 from my earliest youth my enemies have persecuted me,
but they have never been able to finish me off.
3 My back is covered with cuts,
as if a farmer had plowed long furrows.
4 But the LORD is good;
he has cut the cords used by the ungodly to bind me.
5 May all who hate Jerusalem*
be turned back in shameful defeat.
6 May they be as useless as grass on a rooftop,
turning yellow when only half grown,
7 ignored by the harvester,
despised by the binder.
8 And may those who pass by refuse to give them this
blessing:
"The LORD's blessings be upon you;
we bless you in the LORD's name."

129:5 Hebrew *Zion.*

PSALM 130
A song for the ascent to Jerusalem.

¹ From the depths of despair, O LORD,
    I call for your help.
² Hear my cry, O Lord.
    Pay attention to my prayer.

³ LORD, if you kept a record of our sins,
    who, O Lord, could ever survive?
⁴ But you offer forgiveness,
    that we might learn to fear you.

⁵ I am counting on the LORD;
    yes, I am counting on him.
    I have put my hope in his word.
⁶ I long for the Lord
    more than sentries long for the dawn,
    yes, more than sentries long for the dawn.

⁷ O Israel, hope in the LORD;
    for with the LORD there is unfailing love
    and an overflowing supply of salvation.
⁸ He himself will free Israel
    from every kind of sin.

PSALM 131
A song for the ascent to Jerusalem. A psalm of David.

¹ LORD, my heart is not proud;
    my eyes are not haughty.
I don't concern myself with matters too great
    or awesome for me.
² But I have stilled and quieted myself,
    just as a small child is quiet with its mother.
    Yes, like a small child is my soul within me.

³ O Israel, put your hope in the LORD—
    now and always.

PSALM 132
A song for the ascent to Jerusalem.

¹ LORD, remember David
    and all that he suffered.
² He took an oath before the LORD.
    He vowed to the Mighty One of Israel,*
³ "I will not go home;
    I will not let myself rest.
⁴ I will not let my eyes sleep
    nor close my eyelids in slumber
⁵   until I find a place to build a house for the LORD,
    a sanctuary for the Mighty One of Israel."
⁶ We heard that the Ark was in Ephrathah;
    then we found it in the distant countryside of Jaar.

132:2 Hebrew *of Jacob;* also in 132:5.

7 Let us go to the dwelling place of the LORD;
　　let us bow low before him.
8 Arise, O LORD, and enter your sanctuary,
　　along with the Ark, the symbol of your power.
9 Your priests will be agents of salvation;
　　may your loyal servants sing for joy.

10 For the sake of your servant David,
　　do not reject the king you chose for your people.
11 The LORD swore to David
　　a promise he will never take back:
　"I will place one of your descendants on your throne.
12 If your descendants obey the terms of my covenant
　　and follow the decrees that I teach them,
　then your royal line will never end."

13 For the LORD has chosen Jerusalem*;
　　he has desired it as his home.
14 "This is my home where I will live forever," he said.
　　"I will live here, for this is the place I desired.
15 I will make this city prosperous
　　and satisfy its poor with food.
16 I will make its priests the agents of salvation;
　　its godly people will sing for joy.
17 Here I will increase the power of David;
　　my anointed one will be a light for my people.
18 I will clothe his enemies with shame,
　　but he will be a glorious king."

PSALM　133

A song for the ascent to Jerusalem. A psalm of David.

1 How wonderful it is, how pleasant,
　　when brothers live together in harmony!
2 For harmony is as precious as the fragrant anointing
　　　oil
　　that was poured over Aaron's head,
　　that ran down his beard
　　and onto the border of his robe.
3 Harmony is as refreshing as the dew from Mount Hermon
　　that falls on the mountains of Zion.
　And the LORD has pronounced his blessing,
　　even life forevermore.

PSALM　134

A song for the ascent to Jerusalem.

1 Oh, bless the LORD, all you servants of the LORD,
　　you who serve as night watchmen in the house of the
　　　LORD.
2 Lift your hands in holiness,
　　and bless the LORD.

3 May the LORD, who made heaven and earth,
　　bless you from Jerusalem.*

132:13 Hebrew *Zion.*　**134:3** Hebrew *Zion.*

PSALM 135

1 Praise the LORD!

Praise the name of the LORD!
Praise him, you who serve the LORD,
2   you who serve in the house of the LORD,
   in the courts of the house of our God.
3 Praise the LORD, for the LORD is good;
   celebrate his wonderful name with music.
4 For the LORD has chosen Jacob for himself,
   Israel for his own special treasure.

5 I know the greatness of the LORD—
   that our Lord is greater than any other god.
6 The LORD does whatever pleases him
   throughout all heaven and earth,
   and on the seas and in their depths.
7 He causes the clouds to rise over the earth.
   He sends the lightning with the rain
   and releases the wind from his storehouses.
8 He destroyed the firstborn in each Egyptian home,
   both people and animals.
9 He performed miraculous signs and wonders in
      Egypt;
   Pharaoh and all his people watched.
10 He struck down great nations
   and slaughtered mighty kings—
11   Sihon king of the Amorites,
   Og king of Bashan,
   and all the kings of Canaan.
12 He gave their land as an inheritance,
   a special possession to his people Israel.
13 Your name, O LORD, endures forever;
   your fame, O LORD, is known to every generation.
14 For the LORD will vindicate his people
   and have compassion on his servants.

15 Their idols are merely things of silver and gold,
   shaped by human hands.
16 They cannot talk, though they have mouths,
   or see, though they have eyes!
17 They cannot hear with their ears
   or smell with their noses.
18 And those who make them are just like them,
   as are all who trust in them.

19 O Israel, praise the LORD!
   O priests of Aaron, praise the LORD!
20 O Levites, praise the LORD!
   All you who fear the LORD, praise the LORD!
21 The LORD be praised from Zion,
   for he lives here in Jerusalem.

Praise the LORD!

PSALM 136

1 Give thanks to the LORD, for he is good!
His faithful love endures forever.

2 Give thanks to the God of gods.
His faithful love endures forever.

3 Give thanks to the Lord of lords.
His faithful love endures forever.

4 Give thanks to him who alone does mighty miracles.
His faithful love endures forever.

5 Give thanks to him who made the heavens so skillfully.
His faithful love endures forever.

6 Give thanks to him who placed the earth on the water.
His faithful love endures forever.

7 Give thanks to him who made the heavenly lights—
His faithful love endures forever.

8   the sun to rule the day,
His faithful love endures forever.

9   and the moon and stars to rule the night.
His faithful love endures forever.

10 Give thanks to him who killed the firstborn of Egypt.
His faithful love endures forever.

11 He brought Israel out of Egypt.
His faithful love endures forever.

12 He acted with a strong hand and powerful arm.
His faithful love endures forever.

13 Give thanks to him who parted the Red Sea.*
His faithful love endures forever.

14 He led Israel safely through,
His faithful love endures forever.

15   but he hurled Pharaoh and his army into the sea.
His faithful love endures forever.

16 Give thanks to him who led his people through the
wilderness.
His faithful love endures forever.

17 Give thanks to him who struck down mighty kings.
His faithful love endures forever.

18 He killed powerful kings—
His faithful love endures forever.

19   Sihon king of the Amorites,
His faithful love endures forever.

20   and Og king of Bashan.
His faithful love endures forever.

21 God gave the land of these kings as an inheritance—
His faithful love endures forever.

22   a special possession to his servant Israel.
His faithful love endures forever.

23 He remembered our utter weakness.
His faithful love endures forever.

24 He saved us from our enemies.
His faithful love endures forever.

136:13 Hebrew *sea of reeds*; also in 136:15.

²⁵ He gives food to every living thing.
> *His faithful love endures forever.*

²⁶ Give thanks to the God of heaven.
> *His faithful love endures forever.*

PSALM 137

¹ Beside the rivers of Babylon, we sat and wept
  as we thought of Jerusalem.*
² We put away our lyres,
  hanging them on the branches of the willow trees.
³ For there our captors demanded a song of us.
  Our tormentors requested a joyful hymn:
  "Sing us one of those songs of Jerusalem!"
⁴ But how can we sing the songs of the LORD
  while in a foreign land?

⁵ If I forget you, O Jerusalem,
  let my right hand forget its skill upon the harp.
⁶ May my tongue stick to the roof of my mouth
  if I fail to remember you,
  if I don't make Jerusalem my highest joy.

⁷ O LORD, remember what the Edomites did
  on the day the armies of Babylon captured Jerusalem.
  "Destroy it!" they yelled.
  "Level it to the ground!"
⁸ O Babylon, you will be destroyed.
  Happy is the one who pays you back
  for what you have done to us.
⁹ Happy is the one who takes your babies
  and smashes them against the rocks!

PSALM 138

A psalm of David.

¹ I give you thanks, O LORD, with all my heart;
  I will sing your praises before the gods.
² I bow before your holy Temple as I worship.
  I will give thanks to your name
  for your unfailing love and faithfulness,
because your promises are backed
  by all the honor of your name.
³ When I pray, you answer me;
  you encourage me by giving me the strength I need.

⁴ Every king in all the earth will give you thanks,
    O LORD,
  for all of them will hear your words.
⁵ Yes, they will sing about the LORD's ways,
  for the glory of the LORD is very great.
⁶ Though the LORD is great, he cares for the humble,
  but he keeps his distance from the proud.
⁷ Though I am surrounded by troubles,
  you will preserve me against the anger of my enemies.

137:1 Hebrew *Zion;* also in 137:3.

You will clench your fist against my angry enemies!
　Your power will save me.
8 The LORD will work out his plans for my life—
　for your faithful love, O LORD, endures forever.
　Don't abandon me, for you made me.

PSALM 139

For the choir director: A psalm of David.

1 O LORD, you have examined my heart
　and know everything about me.
2 You know when I sit down or stand up.
　You know my every thought when far away.
3 You chart the path ahead of me
　and tell me where to stop and rest.
　Every moment you know where I am.
4 You know what I am going to say
　even before I say it, LORD.
5 You both precede and follow me.
　You place your hand of blessing on my head.
6 Such knowledge is too wonderful for me,
　too great for me to know!

7 I can never escape from your spirit!
　I can never get away from your presence!
8 If I go up to heaven, you are there;
　if I go down to the place of the dead,* you are there.
9 If I ride the wings of the morning,
　if I dwell by the farthest oceans,
10 even there your hand will guide me,
　and your strength will support me.
11 I could ask the darkness to hide me
　and the light around me to become night—
12 but even in darkness I cannot hide from you.
To you the night shines as bright as day.
　Darkness and light are both alike to you.

13 You made all the delicate, inner parts of my body
　and knit me together in my mother's womb.
14 Thank you for making me so wonderfully complex!
　Your workmanship is marvelous—and how well I know it.
15 You watched me as I was being formed in utter seclusion,
　as I was woven together in the dark of the womb.
16 You saw me before I was born.
　Every day of my life was recorded in your book.
　Every moment was laid out
　before a single day had passed.

17 How precious are your thoughts about me,* O God!
　They are innumerable!
18 I can't even count them;
　they outnumber the grains of sand!
And when I wake up in the morning,
　you are still with me!

139:8 Hebrew *to Sheol.*　**139:17** Or *How precious to me are your thoughts.*

¹⁹ O God, if only you would destroy the wicked!
  Get out of my life, you murderers!
²⁰ They blaspheme you;
  your enemies take your name in vain.
²¹ O LORD, shouldn't I hate those who hate you?
  Shouldn't I despise those who resist you?
²² Yes, I hate them with complete hatred,
  for your enemies are my enemies.

²³ Search me, O God, and know my heart;
  test me and know my thoughts.
²⁴ Point out anything in me that offends you,
  and lead me along the path of everlasting life.

PSALM 140
For the choir director: A psalm of David.

¹ O LORD, rescue me from evil people.
  Preserve me from those who are violent,
² those who plot evil in their hearts
  and stir up trouble all day long.
³ Their tongues sting like a snake;
  the poison of a viper drips from their lips.   *Interlude*

⁴ O LORD, keep me out of the hands of the wicked.
  Preserve me from those who are violent,
  for they are plotting against me.
⁵ The proud have set a trap to catch me;
  they have stretched out a net;
  they have placed traps all along the way.   *Interlude*

⁶ I said to the LORD, "You are my God!"
  Listen, O LORD, to my cries for mercy!
⁷ O Sovereign LORD, my strong savior,
  you protected me on the day of battle.
⁸ LORD, do not give in to their evil desires.
  Do not let their evil schemes succeed, O God.   *Interlude*

⁹ Let my enemies be destroyed
  by the very evil they have planned for me.
¹⁰ Let burning coals fall down on their heads,
  or throw them into the fire,
  or into deep pits from which they can't escape.
¹¹ Don't let liars prosper here in our land.
  Cause disaster to fall with great force on the violent.

¹² But I know the LORD will surely help those they persecute;
  he will maintain the rights of the poor.
¹³ Surely the godly are praising your name,
  for they will live in your presence.

PSALM 141
A psalm of David.

¹ O LORD, I am calling to you. Please hurry!
  Listen when I cry to you for help!
² Accept my prayer as incense offered to you,
  and my upraised hands as an evening offering.

³ Take control of what I say, O Lord,
    and keep my lips sealed.
⁴ Don't let me lust for evil things;
    don't let me participate in acts of wickedness.
    Don't let me share in the delicacies
      of those who do evil.

⁵ Let the godly strike me!
    It will be a kindness!
If they reprove me, it is soothing medicine.
    Don't let me refuse it.

But I am in constant prayer
    against the wicked and their deeds.
⁶ When their leaders are thrown down from a cliff,
    they will listen to my words and find them pleasing.
⁷ Even as a farmer breaks up the soil and brings up rocks,
    so the bones of the wicked will be scattered without a
      decent burial.

⁸ I look to you for help, O Sovereign Lord.
    You are my refuge; don't let them kill me.
⁹ Keep me out of the traps they have set for me,
    out of the snares of those who do evil.
¹⁰ Let the wicked fall into their own snares,
    but let me escape.

PSALM 142

A psalm of David, regarding his experience in the cave. A prayer.

¹ I cry out to the Lord;
    I plead for the Lord's mercy.
² I pour out my complaints before him
    and tell him all my troubles.
³ For I am overwhelmed,
    and you alone know the way I should turn.
Wherever I go,
    my enemies have set traps for me.
⁴ I look for someone to come and help me,
    but no one gives me a passing thought!
No one will help me;
    no one cares a bit what happens to me.
⁵ Then I pray to you, O Lord.
    I say, "You are my place of refuge.
    You are all I really want in life.
⁶ Hear my cry,
    for I am very low.
Rescue me from my persecutors,
    for they are too strong for me.
⁷ Bring me out of prison
    so I can thank you.
The godly will crowd around me,
    for you treat me kindly."

PSALM 143

A psalm of David.

¹ Hear my prayer, O LORD;
   listen to my plea!
   Answer me because you are faithful and righteous.
² Don't bring your servant to trial!
   Compared to you, no one is perfect.
³ My enemy has chased me.
   He has knocked me to the ground.
   He forces me to live in darkness like those in the grave.
⁴ I am losing all hope;
   I am paralyzed with fear.
⁵ I remember the days of old.
   I ponder all your great works.
   I think about what you have done.
⁶ I reach out for you.
   I thirst for you as parched land thirsts for rain.   *Interlude*

⁷ Come quickly, LORD, and answer me,
   for my depression deepens.
Don't turn away from me,
   or I will die.
⁸ Let me hear of your unfailing love to me in the morning,
   for I am trusting you.
Show me where to walk,
   for I have come to you in prayer.
⁹ Save me from my enemies, LORD;
   I run to you to hide me.
¹⁰ Teach me to do your will,
   for you are my God.
May your gracious Spirit lead me forward
   on a firm footing.
¹¹ For the glory of your name, O LORD, save me.
   In your righteousness, bring me out of this distress.
¹² In your unfailing love, cut off all my enemies
   and destroy all my foes,
   for I am your servant.

PSALM 144

A psalm of David.

¹ Bless the LORD, who is my rock.
   He gives me strength for war
   and skill for battle.
² He is my loving ally and my fortress,
   my tower of safety, my deliverer.
   He stands before me as a shield, and I take refuge in him.
   He subdues the nations* under me.

³ O LORD, what are mortals that you should notice us,
   mere humans that you should care for us?
⁴ For we are like a breath of air;
   our days are like a passing shadow.

144:2 Some manuscripts read *my people.*

5 Bend down the heavens, LORD, and come down.
Touch the mountains so they billow smoke.
6 Release your lightning bolts and scatter your enemies!
Release your arrows and confuse them!
7 Reach down from heaven and rescue me;
deliver me from deep waters,
from the power of my enemies.
8 Their mouths are full of lies;
they swear to tell the truth, but they lie.

9 I will sing a new song to you, O God!
I will sing your praises with a ten-stringed harp.
10 For you grant victory to kings!
You are the one who rescued your servant David.
11 Save me from the fatal sword!
Rescue me from the power of my enemies.
Their mouths are full of lies;
they swear to tell the truth, but they lie.

12 May our sons flourish in their youth
like well-nurtured plants.
May our daughters be like graceful pillars,
carved to beautify a palace.
13 May our farms be filled
with crops of every kind.
May the flocks in our fields multiply by the thousands,
even tens of thousands,
14 and may our oxen be loaded down with produce.
May there be no breached walls, no forced exile,
no cries of distress in our squares.
15 Yes, happy are those who have it like this!
Happy indeed are those whose God is the LORD.

PSALM 145

A psalm of praise of David.

1 I will praise you, my God and King,
and bless your name forever and ever.
2 I will bless you every day,
and I will praise you forever.
3 Great is the LORD! He is most worthy of praise!
His greatness is beyond discovery!

4 Let each generation tell its children
of your mighty acts.
5 I will meditate* on your majestic, glorious splendor
and your wonderful miracles.
6 Your awe-inspiring deeds will be on every tongue;
I will proclaim your greatness.
7 Everyone will share the story of your wonderful goodness;
they will sing with joy of your righteousness.

8 The LORD is kind and merciful,
slow to get angry, full of unfailing love.
9 The LORD is good to everyone.

145:5 Some manuscripts read *They will speak.*

He showers compassion on all his creation.
¹⁰ All of your works will thank you, LORD,
and your faithful followers will bless you.
¹¹ They will talk together about the glory of your kingdom;
they will celebrate examples of your power.
¹² They will tell about your mighty deeds
and about the majesty and glory of your reign.
¹³ For your kingdom is an everlasting kingdom.
You rule generation after generation.

The LORD is faithful in all he says;
he is gracious in all he does.*
¹⁴ The LORD helps the fallen
and lifts up those bent beneath their loads.
¹⁵ All eyes look to you for help;
you give them their food as they need it.
¹⁶ When you open your hand,
you satisfy the hunger and thirst of every living thing.

¹⁷ The LORD is righteous in everything he does;
he is filled with kindness.
¹⁸ The LORD is close to all who call on him,
yes, to all who call on him sincerely.
¹⁹ He fulfills the desires of those who fear him;
he hears their cries for help and rescues them.
²⁰ The LORD protects all those who love him,
but he destroys the wicked.

²¹ I will praise the LORD,
and everyone on earth will bless his holy name
forever and forever.

PSALM 146

¹ Praise the LORD!

Praise the LORD, I tell myself.
² I will praise the LORD as long as I live.
I will sing praises to my God even with my dying breath.

³ Don't put your confidence in powerful people;
there is no help for you there.
⁴ When their breathing stops, they return to the earth,
and in a moment all their plans come to an end.
⁵ But happy are those who have the God of Israel* as their helper,
whose hope is in the LORD their God.
⁶ He is the one who made heaven and earth,
the sea, and everything in them.
He is the one who keeps every promise forever,
⁷ who gives justice to the oppressed
and food to the hungry.
The LORD frees the prisoners.
⁸ The LORD opens the eyes of the blind.
The LORD lifts the burdens of those bent beneath their loads.
The LORD loves the righteous.

145:13 The last two lines of 145:13 are not found in many of the ancient manuscripts.
146:5 Hebrew *of Jacob.*

9 The LORD protects the foreigners among us.
   He cares for the orphans and widows,
   but he frustrates the plans of the wicked.

10 The LORD will reign forever.
   O Jerusalem,* your God is King in every generation!

Praise the LORD!

PSALM 147

1 Praise the LORD!

How good it is to sing praises to our God!
   How delightful and how right!
2 The LORD is rebuilding Jerusalem
   and bringing the exiles back to Israel.
3 He heals the brokenhearted,
   binding up their wounds.
4 He counts the stars
   and calls them all by name.
5 How great is our Lord! His power is absolute!
   His understanding is beyond comprehension!
6 The LORD supports the humble,
   but he brings the wicked down into the dust.

7 Sing out your thanks to the LORD;
   sing praises to our God, accompanied by harps.
8 He covers the heavens with clouds,
   provides rain for the earth,
   and makes the green grass grow in mountain
      pastures.
9 He feeds the wild animals,
   and the young ravens cry to him for food.
10 The strength of a horse does not impress him;
   how puny in his sight is the strength of a man.
11 Rather, the LORD's delight is in those who honor him,
   those who put their hope in his unfailing love.

12 Praise the LORD, O Jerusalem!
   Praise your God, O Zion!
13 For he has fortified the bars of your gates
   and blessed your children within you.
14 He sends peace across your nation
   and satisfies you with plenty of the finest wheat.
15 He sends his orders to the world—
   how swiftly his word flies!
16 He sends the snow like white wool;
   he scatters frost upon the ground like ashes.
17 He hurls the hail like stones.
   Who can stand against his freezing cold?
18 Then, at his command, it all melts.
   He sends his winds, and the ice thaws.

19 He has revealed his words to Jacob,
   his principles and laws to Israel.

146:10 Hebrew *Zion.*

²⁰ He has not done this with any other nation;
   they do not know his laws.

   Praise the LORD!

P S A L M 1 4 8

¹ Praise the LORD!

   Praise the LORD from the heavens!
      Praise him from the skies!
² Praise him, all his angels!
      Praise him, all the armies of heaven!
³ Praise him, sun and moon!
      Praise him, all you twinkling stars!
⁴ Praise him, skies above!
      Praise him, vapors high above the clouds!
⁵ Let every created thing give praise to the LORD,
      for he issued his command, and they came into being.
⁶ He established them forever and forever.
      His orders will never be revoked.

⁷ Praise the LORD from the earth,
      you creatures of the ocean depths,
⁸ fire and hail, snow and storm,
      wind and weather that obey him,
⁹ mountains and all hills,
      fruit trees and all cedars,
¹⁰ wild animals and all livestock,
      reptiles and birds,
¹¹ kings of the earth and all people,
      rulers and judges of the earth,
¹² young men and maidens,
      old men and children.
¹³ Let them all praise the name of the LORD.
      For his name is very great;
      his glory towers over the earth and heaven!
¹⁴ He has made his people strong,
      honoring his godly ones—
      the people of Israel who are close to him.

   Praise the LORD!

P S A L M 1 4 9

¹ Praise the LORD!

   Sing to the LORD a new song.
      Sing his praises in the assembly of the faithful.
² O Israel, rejoice in your Maker.
      O people of Jerusalem,* exult in your King.
³ Praise his name with dancing,
      accompanied by tambourine and harp.
⁴ For the LORD delights in his people;
      he crowns the humble with salvation.
⁵ Let the faithful rejoice in this honor.
      Let them sing for joy as they lie on their beds.

149:2 Hebrew *Zion.*

⁶ Let the praises of God be in their mouths,
and a sharp sword in their hands—
⁷ to execute vengeance on the nations
and punishment on the peoples,
⁸ to bind their kings with shackles
and their leaders with iron chains,
⁹ to execute the judgment written against them.
This is the glory of his faithful ones.

Praise the LORD!

PSALM 150
¹ Praise the LORD!

Praise God in his heavenly dwelling;
praise him in his mighty heaven!
² Praise him for his mighty works;
praise his unequaled greatness!
³ Praise him with a blast of the trumpet;
praise him with the lyre and harp!
⁴ Praise him with the tambourine and dancing;
praise him with stringed instruments and flutes!
⁵ Praise him with a clash of cymbals;
praise him with loud clanging cymbals.
⁶ Let everything that lives sing praises to the LORD!

Praise the LORD!

PROVERBS

CHAPTER 1
The Purpose of Proverbs
These are the proverbs of Solomon, David's son, king of Israel.

²The purpose of these proverbs is to teach people wisdom and discipline, and to help them understand wise sayings. ³Through these proverbs, people will receive instruction in discipline, good conduct, and doing what is right, just, and fair. ⁴These proverbs will make the simpleminded clever. They will give knowledge and purpose to young people.

⁵Let those who are wise listen to these proverbs and become even wiser. And let those who understand receive guidance ⁶by exploring the depth of meaning in these proverbs, parables, wise sayings, and riddles.

⁷Fear of the LORD is the beginning of knowledge. Only fools despise wisdom and discipline.

A Father's Exhortation: Acquire Wisdom
⁸Listen, my child,* to what your father teaches you. Don't neglect

1:8 Hebrew *my son;* also in 1:10, 15.

your mother's teaching. ⁹What you learn from them will crown you with grace and clothe you with honor.

¹⁰My child, if sinners entice you, turn your back on them! ¹¹They may say, "Come and join us. Let's hide and kill someone! Let's ambush the innocent! ¹²Let's swallow them alive as the grave swallows its victims. Though they are in the prime of life, they will go down into the pit of death. ¹³And the loot we'll get! We'll fill our houses with all kinds of things! ¹⁴Come on, throw in your lot with us; we'll split our loot with you."

¹⁵Don't go along with them, my child! Stay far away from their paths. ¹⁶They rush to commit crimes. They hurry to commit murder. ¹⁷When a bird sees a trap being set, it stays away. ¹⁸But not these people! They set an ambush for themselves; they booby-trap their own lives! ¹⁹Such is the fate of all who are greedy for gain. It ends up robbing them of life.

Wisdom Shouts in the Streets

²⁰Wisdom shouts in the streets. She cries out in the public square. ²¹She calls out to the crowds along the main street, and to those in front of city hall. ²²"You simpletons!" she cries. "How long will you go on being simpleminded? How long will you mockers relish your mocking? How long will you fools fight the facts? ²³Come here and listen to me! I'll pour out the spirit of wisdom upon you and make you wise.

²⁴"I called you so often, but you didn't come. I reached out to you, but you paid no attention. ²⁵You ignored my advice and rejected the correction I offered. ²⁶So I will laugh when you are in trouble! I will mock you when disaster overtakes you—²⁷when calamity overcomes you like a storm, when you are engulfed by trouble, and when anguish and distress overwhelm you.

²⁸"I will not answer when they cry for help. Even though they anxiously search for me, they will not find me. ²⁹For they hated knowledge and chose not to fear the LORD. ³⁰They rejected my advice and paid no attention when I corrected them. ³¹That is why they must eat the bitter fruit of living their own way. They must experience the full terror of the path they have chosen. ³²For they are simpletons who turn away from me—to death. They are fools, and their own complacency will destroy them. ³³But all who listen to me will live in peace and safety, unafraid of harm."

CHAPTER 2

The Benefits of Wisdom

My child,* listen to me and treasure my instructions. ²Tune your ears to wisdom, and concentrate on understanding. ³Cry out for insight and understanding. ⁴Search for them as you would for lost money or hidden treasure. ⁵Then you will understand what it means to fear the LORD, and you will gain knowledge of God. ⁶For the LORD grants wisdom! From his mouth come knowledge and understanding. ⁷He grants a treasure of good sense to the godly. He is their shield, protecting those who walk with integrity. ⁸He guards the paths of justice and protects those who are faithful to him.

⁹Then you will understand what is right, just, and fair, and you will know how to find the right course of action every time. ¹⁰For wisdom

2:1 Hebrew *My son.*

will enter your heart, and knowledge will fill you with joy. ¹¹Wise planning will watch over you. Understanding will keep you safe.

¹²Wisdom will save you from evil people, from those whose speech is corrupt. ¹³These people turn from right ways to walk down dark and evil paths. ¹⁴They rejoice in doing wrong, and they enjoy evil as it turns things upside down. ¹⁵What they do is crooked, and their ways are wrong.

¹⁶Wisdom will save you from the immoral woman, from the flattery of the adulterous woman. ¹⁷She has abandoned her husband and ignores the covenant she made before God. ¹⁸Entering her house leads to death; it is the road to hell.* ¹⁹The man who visits her is doomed. He will never reach the paths of life.

²⁰Follow the steps of good men instead, and stay on the paths of the righteous. ²¹For only the upright will live in the land, and those who have integrity will remain in it. ²²But the wicked will be removed from the land, and the treacherous will be destroyed.

CHAPTER 3

Trusting in the LORD

My child,* never forget the things I have taught you. Store my commands in your heart, ²for they will give you a long and satisfying life. ³Never let loyalty and kindness get away from you! Wear them like a necklace; write them deep within your heart. ⁴Then you will find favor with both God and people, and you will gain a good reputation.

⁵Trust in the LORD with all your heart; do not depend on your own understanding. ⁶Seek his will in all you do, and he will direct your paths.

⁷Don't be impressed with your own wisdom. Instead, fear the LORD and turn your back on evil. ⁸Then you will gain renewed health and vitality.

⁹Honor the LORD with your wealth and with the best part of everything your land produces. ¹⁰Then he will fill your barns with grain, and your vats will overflow with the finest wine.

¹¹My child, don't ignore it when the LORD disciplines you, and don't be discouraged when he corrects you. ¹²For the LORD corrects those he loves, just as a father corrects a child* in whom he delights.

¹³Happy is the person who finds wisdom and gains understanding. ¹⁴For the profit of wisdom is better than silver, and her wages are better than gold. ¹⁵Wisdom is more precious than rubies; nothing you desire can compare with her. ¹⁶She offers you life in her right hand, and riches and honor in her left. ¹⁷She will guide you down delightful paths; all her ways are satisfying. ¹⁸Wisdom is a tree of life to those who embrace her; happy are those who hold her tightly.

¹⁹By wisdom the LORD founded the earth; by understanding he established the heavens. ²⁰By his knowledge the deep fountains of the earth burst forth, and the clouds poured down rain.

²¹My child, don't lose sight of good planning and insight. Hang on to them, ²²for they fill you with life and bring you honor and respect. ²³They keep you safe on your way and keep your feet from

2:18 Hebrew *to the spirits of the dead.*   3:1 Hebrew *My son;* also in 3:11, 21.
3:12 Hebrew *a son.*

stumbling. 24You can lie down without fear and enjoy pleasant dreams. 25You need not be afraid of disaster or the destruction that comes upon the wicked, 26for the LORD is your security. He will keep your foot from being caught in a trap.

27Do not withhold good from those who deserve it when it's in your power to help them. 28If you can help your neighbor now, don't say, "Come back tomorrow, and then I'll help you."

29Do not plot against your neighbors, for they trust you. 30Don't make accusations against someone who hasn't wronged you.

31Do not envy violent people; don't copy their ways. 32Such wicked people are an abomination to the LORD, but he offers his friendship to the godly.

33The curse of the LORD is on the house of the wicked, but his blessing is on the home of the upright.

34The LORD mocks at mockers, but he shows favor to the humble.

35The wise inherit honor, but fools are put to shame!

CHAPTER 4

A Father's Wise Advice

My children,* listen to me. Listen to your father's instruction. Pay attention and grow wise, 2for I am giving you good guidance. Don't turn away from my teaching. 3For I, too, was once my father's son, tenderly loved by my mother as an only child.

4My father told me, "Take my words to heart. Follow my instructions and you will live. 5Learn to be wise, and develop good judgment. Don't forget or turn away from my words. 6Don't turn your back on wisdom, for she will protect you. Love her, and she will guard you. 7Getting wisdom is the most important thing you can do! And whatever else you do, get good judgment. 8If you prize wisdom, she will exalt you. Embrace her and she will honor you. 9She will place a lovely wreath on your head; she will present you with a beautiful crown."

10My child,* listen to me and do as I say, and you will have a long, good life. 11I will teach you wisdom's ways and lead you in straight paths. 12If you live a life guided by wisdom, you won't limp or stumble as you run. 13Carry out my instructions; don't forsake them. Guard them, for they will lead you to a fulfilled life.

14Do not do as the wicked do or follow the path of evildoers. 15Avoid their haunts. Turn away and go somewhere else, 16for evil people cannot sleep until they have done their evil deed for the day. They cannot rest unless they have caused someone to stumble. 17They eat wickedness and drink violence!

18The way of the righteous is like the first gleam of dawn, which shines ever brighter until the full light of day. 19But the way of the wicked is like complete darkness. Those who follow it have no idea what they are stumbling over.

20Pay attention, my child, to what I say. Listen carefully. 21Don't lose sight of my words. Let them penetrate deep within your heart, 22for they bring life and radiant health to anyone who discovers their meaning.

23Above all else, guard your heart, for it affects everything you do.*

24Avoid all perverse talk; stay far from corrupt speech.

4:1 Hebrew *My sons.*   4:10 Hebrew *My son;* also in 4:20.   4:23 Hebrew *for from it flow the springs of life.*

²⁵Look straight ahead, and fix your eyes on what lies before you. ²⁶Mark out a straight path for your feet; then stick to the path and stay safe. ²⁷Don't get sidetracked; keep your feet from following evil.

CHAPTER 5
Avoid Immoral Women

My son, pay attention to my wisdom; listen carefully to my wise counsel. ²Then you will learn to be discreet and will store up knowledge.

³The lips of an immoral woman are as sweet as honey, and her mouth is smoother than oil. ⁴But the result is as bitter as poison, sharp as a double-edged sword. ⁵Her feet go down to death; her steps lead straight to the grave.* ⁶For she does not care about the path to life. She staggers down a crooked trail and doesn't even realize where it leads.

⁷So now, my sons, listen to me. Never stray from what I am about to say: ⁸Run from her! Don't go near the door of her house! ⁹If you do, you will lose your honor and hand over to merciless people everything you have achieved in life. ¹⁰Strangers will obtain your wealth, and someone else will enjoy the fruit of your labor. ¹¹Afterward you will groan in anguish when disease consumes your body, ¹²and you will say, "How I hated discipline! If only I had not demanded my own way! ¹³Oh, why didn't I listen to my teachers? Why didn't I pay attention to those who gave me instruction? ¹⁴I have come to the brink of utter ruin, and now I must face public disgrace."

¹⁵Drink water from your own well—share your love only with your wife.* ¹⁶Why spill the water of your springs in public, having sex with just anyone?* ¹⁷You should reserve it for yourselves. Don't share it with strangers.

¹⁸Let your wife be a fountain of blessing for you. Rejoice in the wife of your youth. ¹⁹She is a loving doe, a graceful deer. Let her breasts satisfy you always. May you always be captivated by her love. ²⁰Why be captivated, my son, with an immoral woman, or embrace the breasts of an adulterous woman?

²¹For the LORD sees clearly what a man does, examining every path he takes. ²²An evil man is held captive by his own sins; they are ropes that catch and hold him. ²³He will die for lack of self-control; he will be lost because of his incredible folly.

CHAPTER 6
Lessons for Daily Life

My child,* if you co-sign a loan for a friend or guarantee the debt of someone you hardly know—²if you have trapped yourself by your agreement and are caught by what you said—³quick, get out of it if you possibly can! You have placed yourself at your friend's mercy. Now swallow your pride, and beg to have your name erased. ⁴Don't put it off. Do it now! Don't rest until you do. ⁵Save yourself like a deer escaping from a hunter, like a bird fleeing from a net.

⁶Take a lesson from the ants, you lazybones. Learn from their ways and be wise! ⁷Even though they have no prince, governor, or

5:5 Hebrew *to Sheol.*   5:15 Hebrew *Drink water from your own cistern, flowing water from your own well.*   5:16 Hebrew *Why spill your springs in public, your streams in the streets?*
6:1 Hebrew *My son.*

ruler to make them work, [8]they labor hard all summer, gathering food for the winter. [9]But you, lazybones, how long will you sleep? When will you wake up? I want you to learn this lesson: [10]A little extra sleep, a little more slumber, a little folding of the hands to rest—[11]and poverty will pounce on you like a bandit; scarcity will attack you like an armed robber.

[12]Here is a description of worthless and wicked people: They are constant liars, [13]signaling their true intentions to their friends by making signs with their eyes and feet and fingers. [14]Their perverted hearts plot evil. They stir up trouble constantly. [15]But they will be destroyed suddenly, broken beyond all hope of healing.

[16]There are six things the LORD hates—no, seven things he detests:

[17] haughty eyes,
   a lying tongue,
   hands that kill the innocent,
[18] a heart that plots evil,
   feet that race to do wrong,
[19] a false witness who pours out lies,
   a person who sows discord among brothers.

[20]My son, obey your father's commands, and don't neglect your mother's teaching. [21]Keep their words always in your heart. Tie them around your neck. [22]Wherever you walk, their counsel can lead you. When you sleep, they will protect you. When you wake up in the morning, they will advise you. [23]For these commands and this teaching are a lamp to light the way ahead of you. The correction of discipline is the way to life.

[24]These commands and this teaching will keep you from the immoral woman, from the smooth tongue of an adulterous woman. [25]Don't lust for her beauty. Don't let her coyness seduce you. [26]For a prostitute will bring you to poverty, and sleeping with another man's wife may cost you your very life. [27]Can a man scoop fire into his lap and not be burned? [28]Can he walk on hot coals and not blister his feet? [29]So it is with the man who sleeps with another man's wife. He who embraces her will not go unpunished.

[30]Excuses might be found for a thief who steals because he is starving. [31]But if he is caught, he will be fined seven times as much as he stole, even if it means selling everything in his house to pay it back.

[32]But the man who commits adultery is an utter fool, for he destroys his own soul. [33]Wounds and constant disgrace are his lot. His shame will never be erased. [34]For the woman's husband will be furious in his jealousy, and he will have no mercy in his day of vengeance. [35]There is no compensation or bribe that will satisfy him.

CHAPTER 7

Another Warning about Immoral Women

Follow my advice, my son; always treasure my commands. [2]Obey them and live! Guard my teachings as your most precious posses-sion.* [3]Tie them on your fingers as a reminder. Write them deep within your heart.

7:2 Hebrew *as the apple of your eye.*

⁴Love wisdom like a sister; make insight a beloved member of your family. ⁵Let them hold you back from an affair with an immoral woman, from listening to the flattery of an adulterous woman.

⁶I was looking out the window of my house one day ⁷and saw a simpleminded young man who lacked common sense. ⁸He was crossing the street near the house of an immoral woman. He was strolling down the path by her house ⁹at twilight, as the day was fading, as the dark of night set in. ¹⁰The woman approached him, dressed seductively and sly of heart. ¹¹She was the brash, rebellious type who never stays at home. ¹²She is often seen in the streets and markets, soliciting at every corner.

¹³She threw her arms around him and kissed him, and with a brazen look she said, ¹⁴"I've offered my sacrifices and just finished my vows. ¹⁵It's you I was looking for! I came out to find you, and here you are! ¹⁶My bed is spread with colored sheets of finest linen imported from Egypt. ¹⁷I've perfumed my bed with myrrh, aloes, and cinnamon. ¹⁸Come, let's drink our fill of love until morning. Let's enjoy each other's caresses, ¹⁹for my husband is not home. He's away on a long trip. ²⁰He has taken a wallet full of money with him, and he won't return until later in the month."

²¹So she seduced him with her pretty speech. With her flattery she enticed him. ²²He followed her at once, like an ox going to the slaughter or like a trapped stag, ²³awaiting the arrow that would pierce its heart. He was like a bird flying into a snare, little knowing it would cost him his life.

²⁴Listen to me, my sons, and pay attention to my words. ²⁵Don't let your hearts stray away toward her. Don't wander down her wayward path. ²⁶For she has been the ruin of many; numerous men have been her victims. ²⁷Her house is the road to the grave.* Her bedroom is the den of death.

CHAPTER 8

Wisdom Calls for a Hearing

Listen as wisdom calls out! Hear as understanding raises her voice! ²She stands on the hilltop and at the crossroads. ³At the entrance to the city, at the city gates, she cries aloud, ⁴"I call to you, to all of you! I am raising my voice to all people. ⁵How naive you are! Let me give you common sense. O foolish ones, let me give you understanding. ⁶Listen to me! For I have excellent things to tell you. Everything I say is right, ⁷for I speak the truth and hate every kind of deception. ⁸My advice is wholesome and good. There is nothing crooked or twisted in it. ⁹My words are plain to anyone with understanding, clear to those who want to learn.

¹⁰"Choose my instruction rather than silver, and knowledge over pure gold. ¹¹For wisdom is far more valuable than rubies. Nothing you desire can be compared with it.

¹²"I, Wisdom, live together with good judgment. I know where to discover knowledge and discernment. ¹³All who fear the LORD will hate evil. That is why I hate pride, arrogance, corruption, and perverted speech. ¹⁴Good advice and success belong to me. Insight and strength are mine. ¹⁵Because of me, kings reign, and rulers

7:27 Hebrew *to Sheol.*

make just laws. [16]Rulers lead with my help, and nobles make righteous judgments.

[17]"I love all who love me. Those who search for me will surely find me. [18]Unending riches, honor, wealth, and justice are mine to distribute. [19]My gifts are better than the purest gold, my wages better than sterling silver! [20]I walk in righteousness, in paths of justice. [21]Those who love me inherit wealth, for I fill their treasuries.

[22]"The LORD formed me from the beginning, before he created anything else. [23]I was appointed in ages past, at the very first, before the earth began. [24]I was born before the oceans were created, before the springs bubbled forth their waters. [25]Before the mountains and the hills were formed, I was born—[26]before he had made the earth and fields and the first handfuls of soil.

[27]"I was there when he established the heavens, when he drew the horizon on the oceans. [28]I was there when he set the clouds above, when he established the deep fountains of the earth. [29]I was there when he set the limits of the seas, so they would not spread beyond their boundaries. And when he marked off the earth's foundations, [30]I was the architect at his side. I was his constant delight, rejoicing always in his presence. [31]And how happy I was with what he created—his wide world and all the human family!

[32]"And so, my children,* listen to me, for happy are all who follow my ways. [33]Listen to my counsel and be wise. Don't ignore it.

[34]"Happy are those who listen to me, watching for me daily at my gates, waiting for me outside my home! [35]For whoever finds me finds life and wins approval from the LORD. [36]But those who miss me have injured themselves. All who hate me love death."

CHAPTER 9

Wisdom has built her spacious house with seven pillars. [2]She has prepared a great banquet, mixed the wines, and set the table. [3]She has sent her servants to invite everyone to come. She calls out from the heights overlooking the city. [4]"Come home with me," she urges the simple. To those without good judgment, she says, [5]"Come, eat my food, and drink the wine I have mixed. [6]Leave your foolish ways behind, and begin to live; learn how to be wise."

[7]Anyone who rebukes a mocker will get a smart retort. Anyone who rebukes the wicked will get hurt. [8]So don't bother rebuking mockers; they will only hate you. But the wise, when rebuked, will love you all the more. [9]Teach the wise, and they will be wiser. Teach the righteous, and they will learn more.

[10]Fear of the LORD is the beginning of wisdom. Knowledge of the Holy One results in understanding.

[11]Wisdom will multiply your days and add years to your life. [12]If you become wise, you will be the one to benefit. If you scorn wisdom, you will be the one to suffer.

Folly Calls for a Hearing

[13]The woman named Folly is loud and brash. She is ignorant and doesn't even know it. [14]She sits in her doorway on the heights overlooking the city. [15]She calls out to men going by who are minding their own business. [16]"Come home with me," she urges

8:32 Hebrew *my sons.*

the simple. To those without good judgment, she says, [17]"Stolen water is refreshing; food eaten in secret tastes the best!" [18]But the men don't realize that her former guests are now in the grave.*

CHAPTER 10

The Proverbs of Solomon

The proverbs of Solomon:

A wise child* brings joy to a father; a foolish child brings grief to a mother.

[2]Ill-gotten gain has no lasting value, but right living can save your life.

[3]The LORD will not let the godly starve to death, but he refuses to satisfy the craving of the wicked.

[4]Lazy people are soon poor; hard workers get rich.

[5]A wise youth works hard all summer; a youth who sleeps away the hour of opportunity brings shame.

[6]The godly are showered with blessings; evil people cover up their harmful intentions.

[7]We all have happy memories of the godly, but the name of a wicked person rots away.

[8]The wise are glad to be instructed, but babbling fools fall flat on their faces.

[9]People with integrity have firm footing, but those who follow crooked paths will slip and fall.

[10]People who wink at wrong cause trouble, but a bold reproof promotes peace.*

[11]The words of the godly lead to life; evil people cover up their harmful intentions.

[12]Hatred stirs up quarrels, but love covers all offenses.

[13]Wise words come from the lips of people with understanding, but fools will be punished with a rod.

[14]Wise people treasure knowledge, but the babbling of a fool invites trouble.

[15]The wealth of the rich is their fortress; the poverty of the poor is their calamity.

[16]The earnings of the godly enhance their lives, but evil people squander their money on sin.

[17]People who accept correction are on the pathway to life, but those who ignore it will lead others astray.

[18]To hide hatred is to be a liar; to slander is to be a fool.

[19]Don't talk too much, for it fosters sin. Be sensible and turn off the flow!

[20]The words of the godly are like sterling silver; the heart of a fool is worthless.

[21]The godly give good advice, but fools are destroyed by their lack of common sense.

[22]The blessing of the LORD makes a person rich, and he adds no sorrow with it.

[23]Doing wrong is fun for a fool, while wise conduct is a pleasure to the wise.

[24]The fears of the wicked will all come true; so will the hopes of the godly.

9:18 Hebrew in *Sheol.*   **10:1** Hebrew *son;* also in 10:1b.   **10:10** As in Greek version; Hebrew reads *but babbling fools fall flat on their faces.*

²⁵Disaster strikes like a cyclone, whirling the wicked away, but the godly have a lasting foundation.

²⁶Lazy people are a pain to their employer. They are like smoke in the eyes or vinegar that sets the teeth on edge.

²⁷Fear of the LORD lengthens one's life, but the years of the wicked are cut short.

²⁸The hopes of the godly result in happiness, but the expectations of the wicked are all in vain.

²⁹The LORD protects the upright but destroys the wicked.

³⁰The godly will never be disturbed, but the wicked will be removed from the land.

³¹The godly person gives wise advice, but the tongue that deceives will be cut off.

³²The godly speak words that are helpful, but the wicked speak only what is corrupt.

CHAPTER 11

The LORD hates cheating, but he delights in honesty.

²Pride leads to disgrace, but with humility comes wisdom.

³Good people are guided by their honesty; treacherous people are destroyed by their dishonesty.

⁴Riches won't help on the day of judgment, but right living is a safeguard against death.

⁵The godly are directed by their honesty; the wicked fall beneath their load of sin.

⁶The godliness of good people rescues them; the ambition of treacherous people traps them.

⁷When the wicked die, their hopes all perish, for they rely on their own feeble strength.

⁸God rescues the godly from danger, but he lets the wicked fall into trouble.

⁹Evil words destroy one's friends; wise discernment rescues the godly.

¹⁰The whole city celebrates when the godly succeed; they shout for joy when the godless die.

¹¹Upright citizens bless a city and make it prosper, but the talk of the wicked tears it apart.

¹²It is foolish to belittle a neighbor; a person with good sense remains silent.

¹³A gossip goes around revealing secrets, but those who are trustworthy can keep a confidence.

¹⁴Without wise leadership, a nation falls; with many counselors, there is safety.

¹⁵Guaranteeing a loan for a stranger is dangerous; it is better to refuse than to suffer later.

¹⁶Beautiful women obtain wealth, and violent men get rich.

¹⁷Your own soul is nourished when you are kind, but you destroy yourself when you are cruel.

¹⁸Evil people get rich for the moment, but the reward of the godly will last.

¹⁹Godly people find life; evil people find death.

²⁰The LORD hates people with twisted hearts, but he delights in those who have integrity.

²¹You can be sure that evil people will be punished, but the children of the godly will go free.

²²A woman who is beautiful but lacks discretion is like a gold ring in a pig's snout.

²³The godly can look forward to happiness, while the wicked can expect only wrath.

²⁴It is possible to give freely and become more wealthy, but those who are stingy will lose everything.

²⁵The generous prosper and are satisfied; those who refresh others will themselves be refreshed.

²⁶People curse those who hold their grain for higher prices, but they bless the one who sells to them in their time of need.

²⁷If you search for good, you will find favor; but if you search for evil, it will find you!

²⁸Trust in your money and down you go! But the godly flourish like leaves in spring.

²⁹Those who bring trouble on their families inherit only the wind. The fool will be a servant to the wise.

³⁰The godly are like trees that bear life-giving fruit, and those who save lives are wise.

³¹If the righteous are rewarded here on earth, how much more true that the wicked and the sinner will get what they deserve!

CHAPTER 12

To learn, you must love discipline; it is stupid to hate correction.

²The LORD approves of those who are good, but he condemns those who plan wickedness.

³Wickedness never brings stability; only the godly have deep roots.

⁴A worthy wife is her husband's joy and crown; a shameful wife saps his strength.

⁵The plans of the godly are just; the advice of the wicked is treacherous.

⁶The words of the wicked are like a murderous ambush, but the words of the godly save lives.

⁷The wicked perish and are gone, but the children of the godly stand firm.

⁸Everyone admires a person with good sense, but a warped mind is despised.

⁹It is better to be a nobody with a servant than to be self-important but have no food.

¹⁰The godly are concerned for the welfare of their animals, but even the kindness of the wicked is cruel.

¹¹Hard work means prosperity; only fools idle away their time.

¹²Thieves are jealous of each other's loot, while the godly bear their own fruit.

¹³The wicked are trapped by their own words, but the godly escape such trouble.

¹⁴People can get many good things by the words they say; the work of their hands also gives them many benefits.

¹⁵Fools think they need no advice, but the wise listen to others.

16A fool is quick-tempered, but a wise person stays calm when insulted.

17An honest witness tells the truth; a false witness tells lies.

18Some people make cutting remarks, but the words of the wise bring healing.

19Truth stands the test of time; lies are soon exposed.

20Deceit fills hearts that are plotting evil; joy fills hearts that are planning peace!

21No real harm befalls the godly, but the wicked have their fill of trouble.

22The LORD hates those who don't keep their word, but he delights in those who do.

23Wise people don't make a show of their knowledge, but fools broadcast their folly.

24Work hard and become a leader; be lazy and become a slave.

25Worry weighs a person down; an encouraging word cheers a person up.

26The godly give good advice to their friends;* the wicked lead them astray.

27Lazy people don't even cook the game they catch, but the diligent make use of everything they find.

28The way of the godly leads to life; their path does not lead to death.

CHAPTER 13

A wise child* accepts a parent's discipline; a young mocker refuses to listen.

2Good people enjoy the positive results of their words, but those who are treacherous crave violence.

3Those who control their tongue will have a long life; a quick retort can ruin everything.

4Lazy people want much but get little, but those who work hard will prosper and be satisfied.

5Those who are godly hate lies; the wicked come to shame and disgrace.

6Godliness helps people all through life, while the evil are destroyed by their wickedness.

7Some who are poor pretend to be rich; others who are rich pretend to be poor.

8The rich can pay a ransom, but the poor won't even get threatened.

9The life of the godly is full of light and joy, but the sinner's light is snuffed out.

10Pride leads to arguments; those who take advice are wise.

11Wealth from get-rich-quick schemes quickly disappears; wealth from hard work grows.

12Hope deferred makes the heart sick, but when dreams come true, there is life and joy.

13People who despise advice will find themselves in trouble; those who respect it will succeed.

14The advice of the wise is like a life-giving fountain; those who accept it avoid the snares of death.

12:26 Or *The godly are cautious in friendship,* or *the godly are freed from evil.* The meaning of the Hebrew is uncertain. **13:1** Hebrew *son.*

¹⁵A person with good sense is respected; a treacherous person walks a rocky road.

¹⁶Wise people think before they act; fools don't and even brag about it!

¹⁷An unreliable messenger stumbles into trouble, but a reliable messenger brings healing.

¹⁸If you ignore criticism, you will end in poverty and disgrace; if you accept criticism, you will be honored.

¹⁹It is pleasant to see dreams come true, but fools will not turn from evil to attain them.

²⁰Whoever walks with the wise will become wise; whoever walks with fools will suffer harm.

²¹Trouble chases sinners, while blessings chase the righteous!

²²Good people leave an inheritance to their grandchildren, but the sinner's wealth passes to the godly.

²³A poor person's farm may produce much food, but injustice sweeps it all away.

²⁴If you refuse to discipline your children, it proves you don't love them; if you love your children, you will be prompt to discipline them.

²⁵The godly eat to their hearts' content, but the belly of the wicked goes hungry.

CHAPTER 14

A wise woman builds her house; a foolish woman tears hers down with her own hands.

²Those who follow the right path fear the LORD; those who take the wrong path despise him.

³The talk of fools is a rod for their backs,* but the words of the wise keep them out of trouble.

⁴An empty stable stays clean, but no income comes from an empty stable.

⁵A truthful witness does not lie; a false witness breathes lies.

⁶A mocker seeks wisdom and never finds it, but knowledge comes easily to those with understanding.

⁷Stay away from fools, for you won't find knowledge there.

⁸The wise look ahead to see what is coming, but fools deceive themselves.

⁹Fools make fun of guilt, but the godly acknowledge it and seek reconciliation.

¹⁰Each heart knows its own bitterness, and no one else can fully share its joy.

¹¹The house of the wicked will perish, but the tent of the godly will flourish.

¹²There is a path before each person that seems right, but it ends in death.

¹³Laughter can conceal a heavy heart; when the laughter ends, the grief remains.

¹⁴Backsliders get what they deserve; good people receive their reward.

¹⁵Only simpletons believe everything they are told! The prudent carefully consider their steps.

14:3 Hebrew *a rod of pride.*

16The wise are cautious* and avoid danger; fools plunge ahead with great confidence.

17Those who are short-tempered do foolish things, and schemers are hated.

18The simpleton is clothed with folly, but the wise person is crowned with knowledge.

19Evil people will bow before good people; the wicked will bow at the gates of the godly.

20The poor are despised even by their neighbors, while the rich have many "friends."

21It is sin to despise one's neighbors; blessed are those who help the poor.

22If you plot evil, you will be lost; but if you plan good, you will be granted unfailing love and faithfulness.

23Work brings profit, but mere talk leads to poverty!

24Wealth is a crown for the wise; the effort of fools yields only folly.

25A truthful witness saves lives, but a false witness is a traitor.

26Those who fear the LORD are secure; he will be a place of refuge for their children.

27Fear of the LORD is a life-giving fountain; it offers escape from the snares of death.

28A growing population is a king's glory; a dwindling nation is his doom.

29Those who control their anger have great understanding; those with a hasty temper will make mistakes.

30A relaxed attitude lengthens life; jealousy rots it away.

31Those who oppress the poor insult their Maker, but those who help the poor honor him.

32The wicked are crushed by their sins, but the godly have a refuge when they die.

33Wisdom is enshrined in an understanding heart; wisdom is not* found among fools.

34Godliness exalts a nation, but sin is a disgrace to any people.

35A king rejoices in servants who know what they are doing; he is angry with those who cause trouble.

CHAPTER 15

A gentle answer turns away wrath, but harsh words stir up anger.

2The wise person makes learning a joy; fools spout only foolishness.

3The LORD is watching everywhere, keeping his eye on both the evil and the good.

4Gentle words bring life and health; a deceitful tongue crushes the spirit.

5Only a fool despises a parent's discipline; whoever learns from correction is wise.

6There is treasure in the house of the godly, but the earnings of the wicked bring trouble.

7Only the wise can give good advice; fools cannot do so.

8The LORD hates the sacrifice of the wicked, but he delights in the prayers of the upright.

14:16 Hebrew *The wise fear.*   **14:33** As in Greek version; Hebrew lacks *not.*

⁹The LORD despises the way of the wicked, but he loves those who pursue godliness.

¹⁰Whoever abandons the right path will be severely punished; whoever hates correction will die.

¹¹Even the depths of Death and Destruction* are known by the LORD. How much more does he know the human heart!

¹²Mockers don't love those who rebuke them, so they stay away from the wise.

¹³A glad heart makes a happy face; a broken heart crushes the spirit.

¹⁴A wise person is hungry for truth, while the fool feeds on trash.

¹⁵For the poor, every day brings trouble; for the happy heart, life is a continual feast.

¹⁶It is better to have little with fear for the LORD than to have great treasure with turmoil.

¹⁷A bowl of soup with someone you love is better than steak with someone you hate.

¹⁸A hothead starts fights; a cool-tempered person tries to stop them.

¹⁹A lazy person has trouble all through life; the path of the upright is easy!

²⁰Sensible children bring joy to their father; foolish children despise their mother.

²¹Foolishness brings joy to those who have no sense; a sensible person stays on the right path.

²²Plans go wrong for lack of advice; many counselors bring success.

²³Everyone enjoys a fitting reply; it is wonderful to say the right thing at the right time!

²⁴The path of the wise leads to life above; they leave the grave* behind.

²⁵The LORD destroys the house of the proud, but he protects the property of widows.

²⁶The LORD despises the thoughts of the wicked, but he delights in pure words.

²⁷Dishonest money brings grief to the whole family, but those who hate bribes will live.

²⁸The godly think before speaking; the wicked spout evil words.

²⁹The LORD is far from the wicked, but he hears the prayers of the righteous.

³⁰A cheerful look brings joy to the heart; good news makes for good health.

³¹If you listen to constructive criticism, you will be at home among the wise.

³²If you reject criticism, you only harm yourself; but if you listen to correction, you grow in understanding.

³³Fear of the LORD teaches a person to be wise; humility precedes honor.

CHAPTER 16

We can gather our thoughts, but the LORD gives the right answer.

²People may be pure in their own eyes, but the LORD examines their motives.

15:11 Hebrew *Sheol and Abaddon.*   **15:24** Hebrew *Sheol.*

³Commit your work to the LORD, and then your plans will succeed.

⁴The LORD has made everything for his own purposes, even the wicked for punishment.

⁵The LORD despises pride; be assured that the proud will be punished.

⁶Unfailing love and faithfulness cover sin; evil is avoided by fear of the LORD.

⁷When the ways of people please the LORD, he makes even their enemies live at peace with them.

⁸It is better to be poor and godly than rich and dishonest.

⁹We can make our plans, but the LORD determines our steps.

¹⁰The king speaks with divine wisdom; he must never judge unfairly.

¹¹The LORD demands fairness in every business deal; he sets the standard.

¹²A king despises wrongdoing, for his rule depends on his justice.

¹³The king is pleased with righteous lips; he loves those who speak honestly.

¹⁴The anger of the king is a deadly threat; the wise do what they can to appease it.

¹⁵When the king smiles, there is life; his favor refreshes like a gentle rain.

¹⁶How much better to get wisdom than gold, and understanding than silver!

¹⁷The path of the upright leads away from evil; whoever follows that path is safe.

¹⁸Pride goes before destruction, and haughtiness before a fall.

¹⁹It is better to live humbly with the poor than to share plunder with the proud.

²⁰Those who listen to instruction will prosper; those who trust the LORD will be happy.

²¹The wise are known for their understanding, and instruction is appreciated if it's well presented.

²²Discretion is a life-giving fountain to those who possess it, but discipline is wasted on fools.

²³From a wise mind comes wise speech; the words of the wise are persuasive.

²⁴Kind words are like honey—sweet to the soul and healthy for the body.

²⁵There is a path before each person that seems right, but it ends in death.

²⁶It is good for workers to have an appetite; an empty stomach drives them on.

²⁷Scoundrels hunt for scandal; their words are a destructive blaze.

²⁸A troublemaker plants seeds of strife; gossip separates the best of friends.

²⁹Violent people deceive their companions, leading them down a harmful path.

³⁰With narrowed eyes, they plot evil; without a word, they plan their mischief.

³¹Gray hair is a crown of glory; it is gained by living a godly life.

³²It is better to be patient than powerful; it is better to have self-control than to conquer a city.

³³We may throw the dice, but the LORD determines how they fall.

CHAPTER 17

A dry crust eaten in peace is better than a great feast with strife.

²A wise slave will rule over the master's shameful sons and will share their inheritance.

³Fire tests the purity of silver and gold, but the LORD tests the heart.

⁴Wrongdoers listen to wicked talk; liars pay attention to destructive words.

⁵Those who mock the poor insult their Maker; those who rejoice at the misfortune of others will be punished.

⁶Grandchildren are the crowning glory of the aged; parents are the pride of their children.

⁷Eloquent speech is not fitting for a fool; even less are lies fitting for a ruler.

⁸A bribe seems to work like magic for those who give it; they succeed in all they do.

⁹Disregarding another person's faults preserves love; telling about them separates close friends.

¹⁰A single rebuke does more for a person of understanding than a hundred lashes on the back of a fool.

¹¹Evil people seek rebellion, but they will be severely punished.

¹²It is safer to meet a bear robbed of her cubs than to confront a fool caught in folly.

¹³If you repay evil for good, evil will never leave your house.

¹⁴Beginning a quarrel is like opening a floodgate, so drop the matter before a dispute breaks out.

¹⁵The LORD despises those who acquit the guilty and condemn the innocent.

¹⁶It is senseless to pay tuition to educate a fool who has no heart for wisdom.

¹⁷A friend is always loyal, and a brother is born to help in time of need.

¹⁸It is poor judgment to co-sign a friend's note, to become responsible for a neighbor's debts.

¹⁹Anyone who loves to quarrel loves sin; anyone who speaks boastfully* invites disaster.

²⁰The crooked heart will not prosper; the twisted tongue tumbles into trouble.

²¹It is painful to be the parent of a fool; there is no joy for the father of a rebel.

²²A cheerful heart is good medicine, but a broken spirit saps a person's strength.

²³The wicked accept secret bribes to pervert justice.

²⁴Sensible people keep their eyes glued on wisdom, but a fool's eyes wander to the ends of the earth.

²⁵A foolish child* brings grief to a father and bitterness to a mother.

17:19 Or *who builds up defenses;* Hebrew reads *who makes a high gate.*   17:25 Hebrew *son.*

²⁶It is wrong to fine the godly for being good or to punish nobles for being honest!

²⁷A truly wise person uses few words; a person with understanding is even-tempered.

²⁸Even fools are thought to be wise when they keep silent; when they keep their mouths shut, they seem intelligent.

CHAPTER 18

A recluse is self-indulgent, snarling at every sound principle of conduct.

²Fools have no interest in understanding; they only want to air their own opinions.

³When the wicked arrive, contempt, shame, and disgrace are sure to follow.

⁴A person's words can be life-giving water; words of true wisdom are as refreshing as a bubbling brook.

⁵It is wrong for a judge to favor the guilty or condemn the innocent.

⁶Fools get into constant quarrels; they are asking for a beating.

⁷The mouths of fools are their ruin; their lips get them into trouble.

⁸What dainty morsels rumors are—but they sink deep into one's heart.

⁹A lazy person is as bad as someone who destroys things.

¹⁰The name of the LORD is a strong fortress; the godly run to him and are safe.

¹¹The rich think of their wealth as an impregnable defense; they imagine it is a high wall of safety.

¹²Haughtiness goes before destruction; humility precedes honor.

¹³What a shame, what folly, to give advice before listening to the facts!

¹⁴The human spirit can endure a sick body, but who can bear it if the spirit is crushed?

¹⁵Intelligent people are always open to new ideas. In fact, they look for them.

¹⁶Giving a gift works wonders; it may bring you before important people!

¹⁷Any story sounds true until someone sets the record straight.

¹⁸Casting lots can end arguments and settle disputes between powerful opponents.

¹⁹It's harder to make amends with an offended friend than to capture a fortified city. Arguments separate friends like a gate locked with iron bars.

²⁰Words satisfy the soul as food satisfies the stomach; the right words on a person's lips bring satisfaction.

²¹Those who love to talk will experience the consequences, for the tongue can kill or nourish life.

²²The man who finds a wife finds a treasure and receives favor from the LORD.

²³The poor plead for mercy; the rich answer with insults.

²⁴There are "friends" who destroy each other, but a real friend sticks closer than a brother.

CHAPTER 19

It is better to be poor and honest than to be a fool and dishonest.

²Zeal without knowledge is not good; a person who moves too quickly may go the wrong way.

³People ruin their lives by their own foolishness and then are angry at the LORD.

⁴Wealth makes many "friends"; poverty drives them away.

⁵A false witness will not go unpunished, nor will a liar escape.

⁶Many beg favors from a prince; everyone is the friend of a person who gives gifts!

⁷If the relatives of the poor despise them, how much more will their friends avoid them. The poor call after them, but they are gone.

⁸To acquire wisdom is to love oneself; people who cherish understanding will prosper.

⁹A false witness will not go unpunished, and a liar will be destroyed.

¹⁰It isn't right for a fool to live in luxury or for a slave to rule over princes!

¹¹People with good sense restrain their anger; they earn esteem by overlooking wrongs.

¹²The king's anger is like a lion's roar, but his favor is like dew on the grass.

¹³A foolish child* is a calamity to a father; a nagging wife annoys like a constant dripping.

¹⁴Parents can provide their sons with an inheritance of houses and wealth, but only the LORD can give an understanding wife.

¹⁵A lazy person sleeps soundly—and goes hungry.

¹⁶Keep the commandments and keep your life; despising them leads to death.

¹⁷If you help the poor, you are lending to the LORD—and he will repay you!

¹⁸Discipline your children while there is hope. If you don't, you will ruin their lives.

¹⁹Short-tempered people must pay their own penalty. If you rescue them once, you will have to do it again.

²⁰Get all the advice and instruction you can, and be wise the rest of your life.

²¹You can make many plans, but the LORD's purpose will prevail.

²²Loyalty makes a person attractive. And it is better to be poor than dishonest.

²³Fear of the LORD gives life, security, and protection from harm.

²⁴Some people are so lazy that they won't even lift a finger to feed themselves.

²⁵If you punish a mocker, the simpleminded will learn a lesson; if you reprove the wise, they will be all the wiser.

²⁶Children who mistreat their father or chase away their mother are a public disgrace and an embarrassment.

²⁷If you stop listening to instruction, my child, you have turned your back on knowledge.

²⁸A corrupt witness makes a mockery of justice; the mouth of the wicked gulps down evil.

19:13 Hebrew *son;* also in 19:27.

²⁹Mockers will be punished, and the backs of fools will be beaten.

CHAPTER 20

Wine produces mockers; liquor leads to brawls. Whoever is led astray by drink cannot be wise.

²The king's fury is like a lion's roar; to rouse his anger is to risk your life.

³Avoiding a fight is a mark of honor; only fools insist on quarreling.

⁴If you are too lazy to plow in the right season, you will have no food at the harvest.

⁵Though good advice lies deep within a person's heart, the wise will draw it out.

⁶Many will say they are loyal friends, but who can find one who is really faithful?

⁷The godly walk with integrity; blessed are their children after them.

⁸When a king judges, he carefully weighs all the evidence, distinguishing the bad from the good.

⁹Who can say, "I have cleansed my heart; I am pure and free from sin"?

¹⁰The LORD despises double standards of every kind.

¹¹Even children are known by the way they act, whether their conduct is pure and right.

¹²Ears to hear and eyes to see—both are gifts from the LORD.

¹³If you love sleep, you will end in poverty. Keep your eyes open, and there will be plenty to eat!

¹⁴The buyer haggles over the price, saying, "It's worthless," then brags about getting a bargain!

¹⁵Wise speech is rarer and more valuable than gold and rubies.

¹⁶Be sure to get collateral from anyone who guarantees the debt of a stranger. Get a deposit if someone guarantees the debt of a foreigner.*

¹⁷Stolen bread tastes sweet, but it turns to gravel in the mouth.

¹⁸Plans succeed through good counsel; don't go to war without the advice of others.

¹⁹A gossip tells secrets, so don't hang around with someone who talks too much.

²⁰If you curse your father or mother, the lamp of your life will be snuffed out.

²¹An inheritance obtained early in life is not a blessing in the end.

²²Don't say, "I will get even for this wrong." Wait for the LORD to handle the matter.

²³The LORD despises double standards; he is not pleased by dishonest scales.

²⁴How can we understand the road we travel? It is the LORD who directs our steps.

²⁵It is dangerous to make a rash promise to God before counting the cost.

20:16 An alternate reading in the Hebrew text is *the debt of an adulterous woman;* compare 27:13.

²⁶A wise king finds the wicked, lays them out like wheat, then runs the crushing wheel over them.

²⁷The Lord's searchlight penetrates the human spirit,* exposing every hidden motive.

²⁸Unfailing love and faithfulness protect the king; his throne is made secure through love.

²⁹The glory of the young is their strength; the gray hair of experience is the splendor of the old.

³⁰Physical punishment cleanses away evil;* such discipline purifies the heart.

CHAPTER 21

The king's heart is like a stream of water directed by the Lord; he turns it wherever he pleases.

²People may think they are doing what is right, but the Lord examines the heart.

³The Lord is more pleased when we do what is just and right than when we give him sacrifices.

⁴Haughty eyes, a proud heart, and evil actions are all sin.

⁵Good planning and hard work lead to prosperity, but hasty shortcuts lead to poverty.

⁶Wealth created by lying is a vanishing mist and a deadly trap.*

⁷Because the wicked refuse to do what is just, their violence boomerangs and destroys them.

⁸The guilty walk a crooked path; the innocent travel a straight road.

⁹It is better to live alone in the corner of an attic than with a contentious wife in a lovely home.

¹⁰Evil people love to harm others; their neighbors get no mercy from them.

¹¹A simpleton can learn only by seeing mockers punished; a wise person learns from instruction.

¹²The Righteous One* knows what is going on in the homes of the wicked; he will bring the wicked to disaster.

¹³Those who shut their ears to the cries of the poor will be ignored in their own time of need.

¹⁴A secret gift calms anger; a secret bribe pacifies fury.

¹⁵Justice is a joy to the godly, but it causes dismay among evildoers.

¹⁶The person who strays from common sense will end up in the company of the dead.

¹⁷Those who love pleasure become poor; wine and luxury are not the way to riches.

¹⁸Sometimes the wicked are punished to save the godly, and the treacherous for the upright.

¹⁹It is better to live alone in the desert than with a crabby, complaining wife.

²⁰The wise have wealth and luxury, but fools spend whatever they get.

²¹Whoever pursues godliness and unfailing love will find life, godliness, and honor.

20:27 Or *The human spirit is the LORD's searchlight.*   **20:30** The meaning of the Hebrew is uncertain.   **21:6** As in Greek version; Hebrew reads *mist for those who seek death.*
21:12 Or *The righteous man.*

²²The wise conquer the city of the strong and level the fortress in which they trust.

²³If you keep your mouth shut, you will stay out of trouble.

²⁴Mockers are proud and haughty; they act with boundless arrogance.

²⁵The desires of lazy people will be their ruin, for their hands refuse to work. ²⁶They are always greedy for more, while the godly love to give!

²⁷God loathes the sacrifice of an evil person, especially when it is brought with ulterior motives.

²⁸A false witness will be cut off, but an attentive witness will be allowed to speak.

²⁹The wicked put up a bold front, but the upright proceed with care.

³⁰Human plans, no matter how wise or well advised, cannot stand against the LORD.

³¹The horses are prepared for battle, but the victory belongs to the LORD.

CHAPTER 22

Choose a good reputation over great riches, for being held in high esteem is better than having silver or gold.

²The rich and the poor have this in common: The LORD made them both.

³A prudent person foresees the danger ahead and takes precautions; the simpleton goes blindly on and suffers the consequences.

⁴True humility and fear of the LORD lead to riches, honor, and long life.

⁵The deceitful walk a thorny, treacherous road; whoever values life will stay away.

⁶Teach your children to choose the right path, and when they are older, they will remain upon it.

⁷Just as the rich rule the poor, so the borrower is servant to the lender.

⁸Those who plant seeds of injustice will harvest disaster, and their reign of terror will end.

⁹Blessed are those who are generous, because they feed the poor.

¹⁰Throw out the mocker, and fighting, quarrels, and insults will disappear.

¹¹Anyone who loves a pure heart and gracious speech is the king's friend.

¹²The LORD preserves knowledge, but he ruins the plans of the deceitful.

¹³The lazy person is full of excuses, saying, "If I go outside, I might meet a lion in the street and be killed!"

¹⁴The mouth of an immoral woman is a deep pit; those living under the LORD's displeasure will fall into it.

¹⁵A youngster's heart is filled with foolishness, but discipline will drive it away.

¹⁶A person who gets ahead by oppressing the poor or by showering gifts on the rich will end in poverty.

Thirty Sayings of the Wise

¹⁷Listen to the words of the wise; apply your heart to my instruction. ¹⁸For it is good to keep these sayings deep within yourself, always ready on your lips. ¹⁹I am teaching you today—yes, you— so you will trust in the LORD. ²⁰I have written thirty sayings for you, filled with advice and knowledge. ²¹In this way, you may know the truth and bring an accurate report to those who sent you.

²²Do not rob the poor because they are poor or exploit the needy in court. ²³For the LORD is their defender. He will injure anyone who injures them.

²⁴Keep away from angry, short-tempered people, ²⁵or you will learn to be like them and endanger your soul.

²⁶Do not co-sign another person's note or put up a guarantee for someone else's loan. ²⁷If you can't pay it, even your bed will be snatched from under you.

²⁸Do not steal your neighbor's property by moving the ancient boundary markers set up by your ancestors.

²⁹Do you see any truly competent workers? They will serve kings rather than ordinary people.

C H A P T E R   2 3

When dining with a ruler, pay attention to what is put before you. ²If you are a big eater, put a knife to your throat, ³and don't desire all the delicacies—deception may be involved.

⁴Don't weary yourself trying to get rich. Why waste your time? ⁵For riches can disappear as though they had the wings of a bird!

⁶Don't eat with people who are stingy; don't desire their delicacies. ⁷"Eat and drink," they say, but they don't mean it. They are always thinking about how much it costs. ⁸You will vomit up the delicious food they serve, and you will have to take back your words of appreciation for their "kindness."

⁹Don't waste your breath on fools, for they will despise the wisest advice.

¹⁰Don't steal the land of defenseless orphans by moving the ancient boundary markers, ¹¹for their Redeemer is strong. He himself will bring their charges against you.

¹²Commit yourself to instruction; attune your ears to hear words of knowledge.

¹³Don't fail to correct your children. They won't die if you spank them. ¹⁴Physical discipline may well save them from death.*

¹⁵My child,* how I will rejoice if you become wise. ¹⁶Yes, my heart will thrill when you speak what is right and just.

¹⁷Don't envy sinners, but always continue to fear the LORD. ¹⁸For surely you have a future ahead of you; your hope will not be disappointed.

¹⁹My child, listen and be wise. Keep your heart on the right course. ²⁰Do not carouse with drunkards and gluttons, ²¹for they are on their way to poverty. Too much sleep clothes a person with rags.

²²Listen to your father, who gave you life, and don't despise your mother's experience when she is old. ²³Get the truth and don't ever sell it; also get wisdom, discipline, and discernment. ²⁴The father

23:14 Hebrew *from Sheol.*   23:15 Hebrew *My son;* also in 23:19.

of godly children has cause for joy. What a pleasure it is to have wise children.* ²⁵So give your parents joy! May she who gave you birth be happy.

²⁶O my son, give me your heart. May your eyes delight in my ways of wisdom. ²⁷A prostitute is a deep pit; an adulterous woman is treacherous.* ²⁸She hides and waits like a robber, looking for another victim who will be unfaithful to his wife.

²⁹Who has anguish? Who has sorrow? Who is always fighting? Who is always complaining? Who has unnecessary bruises? Who has bloodshot eyes? ³⁰It is the one who spends long hours in the taverns, trying out new drinks. ³¹Don't let the sparkle and smooth taste of wine deceive you. ³²For in the end it bites like a poisonous serpent; it stings like a viper. ³³You will see hallucinations, and you will say crazy things. ³⁴You will stagger like a sailor tossed at sea, clinging to a swaying mast. ³⁵And you will say, "They hit me, but I didn't feel it. I didn't even know it when they beat me up. When will I wake up so I can have another drink?"

CHAPTER 24

Don't envy evil people; don't desire their company. ²For they spend their days plotting violence, and their words are always stirring up trouble.

³A house is built by wisdom and becomes strong through good sense. ⁴Through knowledge its rooms are filled with all sorts of precious riches and valuables.

⁵A wise man is mightier than a strong man,* and a man of knowledge is more powerful than a strong man. ⁶So don't go to war without wise guidance; victory depends on having many counselors.

⁷Wisdom is too much for a fool. When the leaders gather, the fool has nothing to say.

⁸A person who plans evil will get a reputation as a troublemaker. ⁹The schemes of a fool are sinful; everyone despises a mocker.

¹⁰If you fail under pressure, your strength is not very great.

¹¹Rescue those who are unjustly sentenced to death; don't stand back and let them die. ¹²Don't try to avoid responsibility by saying you didn't know about it. For God knows all hearts, and he sees you. He keeps watch over your soul, and he knows you knew! And he will judge all people according to what they have done.

¹³My child,* eat honey, for it is good, and the honeycomb is sweet to the taste. ¹⁴In the same way, wisdom is sweet to your soul. If you find it, you will have a bright future, and your hopes will not be cut short.

¹⁵Do not lie in wait like an outlaw at the home of the godly. And don't raid the house where the godly live. ¹⁶They may trip seven times, but each time they will rise again. But one calamity is enough to lay the wicked low.

¹⁷Do not rejoice when your enemies fall into trouble. Don't be happy when they stumble. ¹⁸For the LORD will be displeased with you and will turn his anger away from them.

¹⁹Do not fret because of evildoers; don't envy the wicked. ²⁰For the evil have no future; their light will be snuffed out.

23:24 Hebrew *a wise son.*   23:27 Hebrew *is a narrow well.*   24:5 As in Greek version; Hebrew reads *A wise man is strength.*   24:13 Hebrew *My son;* also in 24:21.

21My child, fear the LORD and the king, and don't associate with rebels. 22For you will go down with them to sudden disaster. Who knows where the punishment from the LORD and the king will end?

More Sayings of the Wise

23Here are some further sayings of the wise:

It is wrong to show favoritism when passing judgment. 24A judge who says to the wicked, "You are innocent," will be cursed by many people and denounced by the nations. 25But blessings are showered on those who convict the guilty.

26It is an honor to receive an honest reply.

27Develop your business first before building your house.

28Do not testify spitefully against innocent neighbors; don't lie about them. 29And don't say, "Now I can pay them back for all their meanness to me! I'll get even!"

30I walked by the field of a lazy person, the vineyard of one lacking sense. 31I saw that it was overgrown with thorns. It was covered with weeds, and its walls were broken down. 32Then, as I looked and thought about it, I learned this lesson: 33A little extra sleep, a little more slumber, a little folding of the hands to rest—34and poverty will pounce on you like a bandit; scarcity will attack you like an armed robber.

CHAPTER 25

More Proverbs of Solomon

These are more proverbs of Solomon, collected by the advisers of King Hezekiah of Judah.

2It is God's privilege to conceal things and the king's privilege to discover them.

3No one can discover the height of heaven, the depth of the earth, or all that goes on in the king's mind!

4Remove the dross from silver, and the sterling will be ready for the silversmith. 5Remove the wicked from the king's court, and his reign will be made secure by justice.

6Don't demand an audience with the king or push for a place among the great. 7It is better to wait for an invitation than to be sent to the end of the line, publicly disgraced!

Just because you see something, 8don't be in a hurry to go to court. You might go down before your neighbors in shameful defeat. 9So discuss the matter with them privately. Don't tell anyone else, 10or others may accuse you of gossip. Then you will never regain your good reputation.

11Timely advice is as lovely as golden apples in a silver basket.

12Valid criticism is as treasured by the one who heeds it as jewelry made from finest gold.

13Faithful messengers are as refreshing as snow in the heat of summer. They revive the spirit of their employer.

14A person who doesn't give a promised gift is like clouds and wind that don't bring rain.

15Patience can persuade a prince, and soft speech can crush strong opposition.

16Do you like honey? Don't eat too much of it, or it will make you sick!

¹⁷Don't visit your neighbors too often, or you will wear out your welcome.

¹⁸Telling lies about others is as harmful as hitting them with an ax, wounding them with a sword, or shooting them with a sharp arrow.

¹⁹Putting confidence in an unreliable person is like chewing with a toothache or walking on a broken foot.

²⁰Singing cheerful songs to a person whose heart is heavy is as bad as stealing someone's jacket in cold weather or rubbing salt in a wound.

²¹If your enemies are hungry, give them food to eat. If they are thirsty, give them water to drink. ²²You will heap burning coals on their heads, and the LORD will reward you.

²³As surely as a wind from the north brings rain, so a gossiping tongue causes anger!

²⁴It is better to live alone in the corner of an attic than with a contentious wife in a lovely home.

²⁵Good news from far away is like cold water to the thirsty.

²⁶If the godly compromise with the wicked, it is like polluting a fountain or muddying a spring.

²⁷Just as it is not good to eat too much honey, it is not good for people to think about all the honors they deserve.

²⁸A person without self-control is as defenseless as a city with broken-down walls.

CHAPTER 26

Honor doesn't go with fools any more than snow with summer or rain with harvest.

²Like a fluttering sparrow or a darting swallow, an unfair curse will not land on its intended victim.

³Guide a horse with a whip, a donkey with a bridle, and a fool with a rod to his back!

⁴When arguing with fools, don't answer their foolish arguments, or you will become as foolish as they are.

⁵When arguing with fools, be sure to answer their foolish arguments, or they will become wise in their own estimation.

⁶Trusting a fool to convey a message is as foolish as cutting off one's feet or drinking poison!

⁷In the mouth of a fool, a proverb becomes as limp as a paralyzed leg.

⁸Honoring a fool is as foolish as tying a stone to a slingshot.

⁹A proverb in a fool's mouth is as dangerous as a thornbush brandished by a drunkard.

¹⁰An employer who hires a fool or a bystander is like an archer who shoots recklessly.

¹¹As a dog returns to its vomit, so a fool repeats his folly.

¹²There is more hope for fools than for people who think they are wise.

¹³The lazy person is full of excuses, saying, "I can't go outside because there might be a lion on the road! Yes, I'm sure there's a lion out there!"

¹⁴As a door turns back and forth on its hinges, so the lazy person turns over in bed.

¹⁵Some people are so lazy that they won't lift a finger to feed themselves.

¹⁶Lazy people consider themselves smarter than seven wise counselors.

¹⁷Yanking a dog's ears is as foolish as interfering in someone else's argument.

¹⁸Just as damaging as a mad man shooting a lethal weapon ¹⁹is someone who lies to a friend and then says, "I was only joking."

²⁰Fire goes out for lack of fuel, and quarrels disappear when gossip stops.

²¹A quarrelsome person starts fights as easily as hot embers light charcoal or fire lights wood.

²²What dainty morsels rumors are—but they sink deep into one's heart.

²³Smooth* words may hide a wicked heart, just as a pretty glaze covers a common clay pot.

²⁴People with hate in their hearts may sound pleasant enough, but don't believe them. ²⁵Though they pretend to be kind, their hearts are full of all kinds of evil. ²⁶While their hatred may be concealed by trickery, it will finally come to light for all to see.

²⁷If you set a trap for others, you will get caught in it yourself. If you roll a boulder down on others, it will roll back and crush you.

²⁸A lying tongue hates its victims, and flattery causes ruin.

CHAPTER 27

Don't brag about tomorrow, since you don't know what the day will bring.

²Don't praise yourself; let others do it!

³A stone is heavy and sand is weighty, but the resentment caused by a fool is heavier than both.

⁴Anger is cruel, and wrath is like a flood, but who can survive the destructiveness of jealousy?

⁵An open rebuke is better than hidden love!

⁶Wounds from a friend are better than many kisses from an enemy.

⁷Honey seems tasteless to a person who is full, but even bitter food tastes sweet to the hungry.

⁸A person who strays from home is like a bird that strays from its nest.

⁹The heartfelt counsel of a friend is as sweet as perfume and incense.

¹⁰Never abandon a friend—either yours or your father's. Then in your time of need, you won't have to ask your relatives for assistance. It is better to go to a neighbor than to a relative who lives far away.

¹¹My child,* how happy I will be if you turn out to be wise! Then I will be able to answer my critics.

¹²A prudent person foresees the danger ahead and takes precautions. The simpleton goes blindly on and suffers the consequences.

¹³Be sure to get collateral from anyone who guarantees the debt of a stranger. Get a deposit if someone guarantees the debt of an adulterous woman.

26:23 As in Greek version; Hebrew reads *Burning*.   27:11 Hebrew *My son*.

¹⁴If you shout a pleasant greeting to your neighbor too early in the morning, it will be counted as a curse!

¹⁵A nagging wife is as annoying as the constant dripping on a rainy day. ¹⁶Trying to stop her complaints is like trying to stop the wind or hold something with greased hands.

¹⁷As iron sharpens iron, a friend sharpens a friend.

¹⁸Workers who tend a fig tree are allowed to eat its fruit. In the same way, workers who protect their employer's interests will be rewarded.

¹⁹As a face is reflected in water, so the heart reflects the person.

²⁰Just as Death and Destruction* are never satisfied, so human desire is never satisfied.

²¹Fire tests the purity of silver and gold, but a person is tested by being praised.

²²You cannot separate fools from their foolishness, even though you grind them like grain in mortar and pestle.

²³Know the state of your flocks, and put your heart into caring for your herds, ²⁴for riches don't last forever, and the crown might not be secure for the next generation. ²⁵After the hay is harvested, the new crop appears, and the mountain grasses are gathered in, ²⁶your sheep will provide wool for clothing, and your goats will be sold for the price of a field. ²⁷And you will have enough goats' milk for you, your family, and your servants.

CHAPTER 28
The wicked run away when no one is chasing them, but the godly are as bold as lions.

²When there is moral rot within a nation, its government topples easily. But with wise and knowledgeable leaders, there is stability.

³A poor person who oppresses the poor is like a pounding rain that destroys the crops.

⁴To reject the law is to praise the wicked; to obey the law is to fight them.

⁵Evil people don't understand justice, but those who follow the LORD understand completely.

⁶It is better to be poor and honest than rich and crooked.

⁷Young people who obey the law are wise; those who seek out worthless companions bring shame to their parents.

⁸A person who makes money by charging interest will lose it. It will end up in the hands of someone who is kind to the poor.

⁹The prayers of a person who ignores the law are despised.

¹⁰Those who lead the upright into sin will fall into their own trap, but the honest will inherit good things.

¹¹Rich people picture themselves as wise, but their real poverty is evident to the poor.

¹²When the godly succeed, everyone is glad. When the wicked take charge, people go into hiding.

¹³People who cover over their sins will not prosper. But if they confess and forsake them, they will receive mercy.

¹⁴Blessed are those who have a tender conscience,* but the stubborn are headed for serious trouble.

27:20 Hebrew *Sheol and Abaddon.*   28:14 Hebrew *those who fear.*

¹⁵A wicked ruler is as dangerous to the poor as a lion or bear attacking them.

¹⁶Only a stupid prince will oppress his people, but a king will have a long reign if he hates dishonesty and bribes.

¹⁷A murderer's tormented conscience will drive him into the grave. Don't protect him!

¹⁸The honest will be rescued from harm, but those who are crooked will be destroyed.

¹⁹Hard workers have plenty of food; playing around brings poverty.

²⁰The trustworthy will get a rich reward. But the person who wants to get rich quick will only get into trouble.

²¹Showing partiality is never good, yet some will do wrong for something as small as a piece of bread.

²²A greedy person tries to get rich quick, but it only leads to poverty.

²³In the end, people appreciate frankness more than flattery.

²⁴Robbing your parents and then saying, "What's wrong with that?" is as serious as committing murder.

²⁵Greed causes fighting; trusting the LORD leads to prosperity.

²⁶Trusting oneself is foolish, but those who walk in wisdom are safe.

²⁷Whoever gives to the poor will lack nothing. But a curse will come upon those who close their eyes to poverty.

²⁸When the wicked take charge, people hide. When the wicked meet disaster, the godly multiply.

CHAPTER 29

Whoever stubbornly refuses to accept criticism will suddenly be broken beyond repair.

²When the godly are in authority, the people rejoice. But when the wicked are in power, they groan.

³The man who loves wisdom brings joy to his father, but if he hangs around with prostitutes, his wealth is wasted.

⁴A just king gives stability to his nation, but one who demands bribes destroys it.

⁵To flatter people is to lay a trap for their feet.

⁶Evil people are trapped by sin, but the righteous escape, shouting for joy.

⁷The godly know the rights of the poor; the wicked don't care to know.

⁸Mockers can get a whole town agitated, but those who are wise will calm anger.

⁹If a wise person takes a fool to court, there will be ranting and ridicule but no satisfaction.

¹⁰The bloodthirsty hate the honest, but the upright seek out the honest.

¹¹A fool gives full vent to anger, but a wise person quietly holds it back.

¹²If a ruler honors liars, all his advisers will be wicked.

¹³The poor and the oppressor have this in common—the LORD gives light to the eyes of both.

¹⁴A king who is fair to the poor will have a long reign.

¹⁵To discipline and reprimand a child produces wisdom, but a mother is disgraced by an undisciplined child.

¹⁶When the wicked are in authority, sin increases. But the godly will live to see the tyrant's downfall.

¹⁷Discipline your children, and they will give you happiness and peace of mind.

¹⁸When people do not accept divine guidance, they run wild. But whoever obeys the law is happy.

¹⁹For a servant, mere words are not enough—discipline is needed. For the words may be understood, but they are not heeded.

²⁰There is more hope for a fool than for someone who speaks without thinking.

²¹A servant who is pampered from childhood will later become a rebel.

²²A hot-tempered person starts fights and gets into all kinds of sin.

²³Pride ends in humiliation, while humility brings honor.

²⁴If you assist a thief, you are only hurting yourself. You will be punished if you report the crime, but you will be cursed if you don't.

²⁵Fearing people is a dangerous trap, but to trust the LORD means safety.

²⁶Many seek the ruler's favor, but justice comes from the LORD.

²⁷The godly despise the wicked; the wicked despise the godly.

CHAPTER 30

The Sayings of Agur

The message of Agur son of Jakeh. An oracle.*

I am weary, O God; I am weary and worn out, O God.* ²I am too ignorant to be human, and I lack common sense. ³I have not mastered human wisdom, nor do I know the Holy One.

⁴Who but God goes up to heaven and comes back down? Who holds the wind in his fists? Who wraps up the oceans in his cloak? Who has created the whole wide world? What is his name—and his son's name? Tell me if you know!

⁵Every word of God proves true. He defends all who come to him for protection. ⁶Do not add to his words, or he may rebuke you, and you will be found a liar. ⁷O God, I beg two favors from you before I die. ⁸First, help me never to tell a lie. Second, give me neither poverty nor riches! Give me just enough to satisfy my needs. ⁹For if I grow rich, I may deny you and say, "Who is the LORD?" And if I am too poor, I may steal and thus insult God's holy name.

¹⁰Never slander a person to his employer. If you do, the person will curse you, and you will pay for it.

¹¹Some people curse their father and do not thank their mother. ¹²They feel pure, but they are filthy and unwashed. ¹³They are proud beyond description and disdainful. ¹⁴They devour the poor with teeth as sharp as swords or knives. They destroy the needy from the face of the earth.

30:1a Or *son of Jakeh from Massa.*   30:1b The Hebrew can also be translated *The man declares this to Ithiel, to Ithiel and to Ucal.*

15The leech has two suckers that cry out, "More, more!"* There are three other things—no, four!—that are never satisfied:
16 the grave,
   the barren womb,
   the thirsty desert,
   the blazing fire.

17The eye that mocks a father and despises a mother will be plucked out by ravens of the valley and eaten by vultures.

18There are three things that amaze me—no, four things I do not understand:
19 how an eagle glides through the sky,
   how a snake slithers on a rock,
   how a ship navigates the ocean,
   how a man loves a woman.
20Equally amazing is how an adulterous woman can satisfy her sexual appetite, shrug her shoulders, and then say, "What's wrong with that?"

21There are three things that make the earth tremble—no, four it cannot endure:
22 a slave who becomes a king,
   an overbearing fool who prospers,
23 a bitter woman who finally gets a husband,
   a servant girl who supplants her mistress.

24There are four things on earth that are small but unusually wise:
25 Ants—they aren't strong,
      but they store up food for the winter.
26 Rock badgers*—they aren't powerful,
      but they make their homes among the rocky cliffs.
27 Locusts—they have no king,
      but they march like an army in ranks.
28 Lizards—they are easy to catch,
      but they are found even in kings' palaces.

29There are three stately monarchs on the earth—no, four:
30 the lion, king of animals, who won't turn aside for anything,
31 the strutting rooster,
   the male goat,
   a king as he leads his army.

32If you have been a fool by being proud or plotting evil, don't brag about it—cover your mouth with your hand in shame.

33As the beating of cream yields butter, and a blow to the nose causes bleeding, so anger causes quarrels.

C H A P T E R   3 1
The Sayings of King Lemuel
These are the sayings of King Lemuel, an oracle* that his mother taught him.
   2O my son, O son of my womb, O son of my promises, 3do not spend your strength on women, on those who ruin kings.

30:15 Hebrew *two daughters who cry out, "Give, give!"*   30:26 Or *coneys,* or *hyraxes.*
31:1 Or *of Lemuel, king of Massa.*

⁴And it is not for kings, O Lemuel, to guzzle wine. Rulers should not crave liquor. ⁵For if they drink, they may forget their duties and be unable to give justice to those who are oppressed. ⁶Liquor is for the dying, and wine for those in deep depression. ⁷Let them drink to forget their poverty and remember their troubles no more.

⁸Speak up for those who cannot speak for themselves; ensure justice for those who are perishing. ⁹Yes, speak up for the poor and helpless, and see that they get justice.

A Wife of Noble Character

¹⁰Who can find a virtuous and capable wife? She is worth more than precious rubies. ¹¹Her husband can trust her, and she will greatly enrich his life. ¹²She will not hinder him but help him all her life.

¹³She finds wool and flax and busily spins it. ¹⁴She is like a merchant's ship; she brings her food from afar. ¹⁵She gets up before dawn to prepare breakfast for her household and plan the day's work for her servant girls. ¹⁶She goes out to inspect a field and buys it; with her earnings she plants a vineyard.

¹⁷She is energetic and strong, a hard worker. ¹⁸She watches for bargains; her lights burn late into the night. ¹⁹Her hands are busy spinning thread, her fingers twisting fiber.

²⁰She extends a helping hand to the poor and opens her arms to the needy.

²¹She has no fear of winter for her household because all of them have warm* clothes. ²²She quilts her own bedspreads. She dresses like royalty in gowns of finest cloth.

²³Her husband is well known, for he sits in the council meeting with the other civic leaders.

²⁴She makes belted linen garments and sashes to sell to the merchants.

²⁵She is clothed with strength and dignity, and she laughs with no fear of the future. ²⁶When she speaks, her words are wise, and kindness is the rule when she gives instructions. ²⁷She carefully watches all that goes on in her household and does not have to bear the consequences of laziness.

²⁸Her children stand and bless her. Her husband praises her: ²⁹"There are many virtuous and capable women in the world, but you surpass them all!"

³⁰Charm is deceptive, and beauty does not last; but a woman who fears the LORD will be greatly praised. ³¹Reward her for all she has done. Let her deeds publicly declare her praise.

31:21 As in Greek version; Hebrew *scarlet*.

TRANSLATION PHILOSOPHY OF THE NEW LIVING TRANSLATION

Translation Philosophy and Methodology

There are two general theories or methods of Bible translation. The first has been called "formal equivalence." According to this theory, the translator attempts to render each word of the original language into the receptor language and seeks to preserve the original word order and sentence structure as much as possible. The second has been called "dynamic equivalence" or "functional equivalence." The goal of this translation theory is to produce in the receptor language the closest natural equivalent of the message expressed by the original-language text—both in meaning and in style. Such a translation attempts to have the same impact on modern readers as the original had on its own audience.

A dynamic-equivalence translation can also be called a thought-for-thought translation, as contrasted with a formal-equivalence or word-for-word translation. Of course, to translate the thought of the original language requires that the text be interpreted accurately and then be rendered in understandable idiom. So the goal of any thought-for-thought translation is to be both reliable and eminently readable. Thus, as a thought-for-thought translation, the New Living Translation seeks to be both exegetically accurate and idiomatically powerful.

In making a thought-for-thought translation, the translators must do their best to enter into the thought patterns of the ancient authors and to present the same ideas, connotations, and effects in the receptor language. In order to guard against personal biases and to ensure the accuracy of the message, a thought-for-thought translation should be created by a group of scholars who employ the best exegetical tools and who also understand the receptor language very well. With these concerns in mind, the Bible Translation Committee assigned each book of the Bible to three different scholars. Each scholar made a thorough review of the assigned book and submitted suggested revisions to the appropriate general reviewer. The general reviewer reviewed and summarized these suggestions and then proposed a first-draft revision of the text. This draft served as the basis for several additional phases of exegetical and stylistic committee review. Then the Bible Translation Committee jointly reviewed and approved every verse in the final translation.

A thought-for-thought translation prepared by a group of capable scholars has the potential to represent the intended meaning of the original text even more accurately than a word-for-word translation. This is illustrated by the various renderings of the Greek word *dikaiosune*. This term cannot be adequately translated by any single English word because it can connote human righteousness, God's righteousness, doing what is right, justice, being made right in God's sight, goodness, etc. The context—not the lexicon—must determine which English term is selected for translation.

The value of a thought-for-thought translation can be illustrated by comparing 2 Corinthians 9:1 in the King James Version, the New International Version, and the New Living Translation. "For as touching the ministering to the saints, it is superfluous for me to write to you" (KJV). "There is no need for me to write to you about this service to the saints" (NIV). "I really don't need to write to you about this gift for the Christians in Jerusalem" (NLT). Only the New Living Translation clearly translates the real meaning of the Greek idiom "service to the saints" into contemporary English.

Written to Be Read Aloud
It is evident in Scripture that the biblical documents were written to be read aloud, often in public worship (see Luke 4:16-20; 1 Timothy 4:13; Revelation 1:3). It is still the case today that more people will hear the Bible read aloud in church than are likely to read it for themselves. Therefore, a new translation must communicate with clarity and power when it is read aloud. For this reason, the New Living Translation is recommended as a Bible to be used for public reading. Its living language is not only easy to understand, but it also has an emotive quality that will make an impact on the listener.

The Texts behind the New Living Translation
The translators of the Old Testament used the Masoretic Text of the Hebrew Bible as their standard text. They used the edition known as *Biblia Hebraica Stuttgartensia* (1977) with its up-to-date textual apparatus, a revision of Rudolf Kittel's *Biblia Hebraica* (Stuttgart, 1937). The translators also compared the Dead Sea Scrolls, the Septuagint and other Greek manuscripts, the Samaritan Pentateuch, the Syriac Peshitta, the Latin Vulgate, and any other versions or manuscripts that shed light on textual problems.

The translators of the New Testament used the two standard editions of the Greek New Testament: the *Greek New Testament*, published by the United Bible Societies (fourth revised edition, 1993), and *Novum Testamentum Graece*, edited by Nestle and Aland (twenty-seventh edition, 1993). These two editions, which have the same text but differ in punctuation and textual notes, represent the best in modern textual scholarship.

Translation Issues
The translators have made a conscious effort to provide a text that can be easily understood by the average reader of modern English. To this end, we have used the vocabulary and language structures

commonly used by the average person. The result is a translation of the Scriptures written generally at the reading level of a junior high school student. We have avoided using language that is likely to become quickly dated or that reflects a narrow subdialect of English, with the goal of making the New Living Translation as broadly useful as possible.

But our concern for readability goes beyond the concerns of vocabulary and sentence structure. We are also concerned about historical and cultural barriers to understanding the Bible, and we have sought to translate terms shrouded in history or culture in ways that can be immediately understood by the contemporary reader. Thus, our goal of easy readability expresses itself in a number of other ways:

- Rather than translating ancient weights and measures literally, which communicates little to the modern reader, we have expressed them by means of recognizable contemporary equivalents. We have converted ancient weights and measures to modern English (American) equivalents, and we have rendered the literal Hebrew or Greek measures, along with metric equivalents, in textual footnotes.

- Instead of translating ancient currency values literally, we have generally expressed them in terms of weights in precious metals. In some cases we have used other common terms to communicate the message effectively. For example, "three shekels of silver" might become "three silver coins" or "three pieces of silver" to convey the intended message. Again, a rendering of the literal Hebrew or Greek is given in textual footnotes.

- Since ancient references to the time of day differ from our modern methods of denoting time, we used renderings that are instantly understandable to the modern reader. Accordingly, we have rendered specific times of day by using approximate equivalents in terms of our common "o'clock" system. On occasion, translations such as "at dawn the next morning" or "as the sun began to set" have been used when the biblical reference is general.

- Many words in the original texts made sense to the original audience but communicate something quite different to the modern reader. In such cases, some liberty must be allowed in translation to communicate what was intended. Places identified by the term normally translated "city," for example, are often better identified as "towns" or "villages." Similarly, the term normally translated "mountain" is often better rendered "hill."

- Many words and phrases carry a great deal of cultural meaning that was obvious to the original readers but needs explanation in our own culture. For example, the phrase "they beat their breasts" (Luke 23:48) in ancient times meant that people were very upset. In our translation we chose to translate this phrase dynamically: "They went home *in deep sorrow.*" In some cases, however, we have simply illuminated the existing expression to make it immediately understandable. For example, we might have expanded the literal phrase to read "they beat their breasts *in sorrow.*"

• Metaphorical language is often difficult for contemporary readers to understand, so at times we have chosen to translate or illuminate the metaphor. For example, the ancient poet writes, "Their throat is an open grave" (Psalm 5:9, and quoted in Romans 3:13). To help the modern reader, who might be confused or distracted by a literal visualization of this image, we converted the metaphor to a simile to make the meaning immediately clear: "Their talk is foul, *like* the stench from an open grave." Here we also translated "throat" as "talk" to help the modern reader catch the significance of the metaphoric expression.

• One challenge we faced was in determining how to translate accurately the ancient biblical text that was originally written in a context where male-oriented terms were used to refer to humanity generally. We needed to respect the nature of the ancient context while also trying to make the translation clear to a modern audience that tends to read male-oriented language as applying only to males. Often the original text, though using masculine nouns and pronouns, clearly intends that the message be applied to both men and women. One example is found in the New Testament epistles, where the believers are called "brothers" *(adelphoi)*. Yet it is clear that these epistles were addressed to all the believers—male and female. Thus, we have usually translated this Greek word "brothers and sisters" in order to represent the historical situation more accurately.

We have also been sensitive to passages where the text applies generally to human beings or to the human condition. In many instances we have used plural pronouns (they, them) in place of the masculine singular (he, him). For example, a traditional rendering of Proverbs 22:6 is: "Train up a child in the way he should go, and when he is old he will not turn from it." We have rendered it: "Teach your children to choose the right path, and when they are older, they will remain upon it." At times, we have also replaced third person pronouns with the second person to ensure clarity. A traditional rendering of Proverbs 26:27 is: "He who digs a pit will fall into it, and he who rolls a stone, it will come back on him." We have rendered it: "If you set a trap for others, you will get caught in it yourself. If you roll a boulder down on others, it will roll back and crush you." All such decisions were driven by the concern to reflect accurately the intended meaning of the original texts of Scripture.

We should emphasize, however, that all masculine nouns and pronouns used to represent God (for example, "Father") have been maintained without exception. We believe that essential traits of God's revealed character can only be conveyed through the masculine language expressed in the original texts of Scripture.

Lexical Consistency in Terminology
For the sake of clarity, we have maintained lexical consistency in areas such as divine names, synoptic passages, rhetorical structures,

and nontheological technical terms (i.e., liturgical, cultic, zoological, botanical, cultural, and legal terms). For theological terms, we have allowed a greater semantic range of acceptable English words or phrases for a single Hebrew or Greek word. We avoided weighty theological terms that do not readily communicate to many modern readers. For example, we avoided using words such as "justification," "sanctification," and "regeneration." In place of these words (which are carryovers from Latin), we provided renderings such as "we are made right with God," "we are made holy," and "we are born anew."

The Rendering of Divine Names

All appearances of *'el*, *'elohim*, or *'eloah* have been translated "God," except where the context demands the translation "god(s)." We have rendered the tetragrammaton *(YHWH)* consistently as "the LORD," utilizing a form with small capitals that is common among English translations. This will distinguish it from the name *'adonai*, which we render "Lord." When *'adonai* and *YHWH* appear in conjunction, we have rendered it "Sovereign LORD." This also distinguishes *'adonai YHWH* from cases where *YHWH* appears with *'elohim*, which is rendered "LORD God." When *YH* (the short form of *YHWH*) and *YHWH* appear together, we have rendered it "LORD GOD." The Hebrew word *'adon* is rendered "lord," or "master," or sometimes "sir."

In the New Testament, the Greek word *Christos* has been translated as "Messiah" when the context assumes a Jewish audience. When a Gentile audience can be assumed, *Christos* has been translated as "Christ." The Greek word *kurios* is consistently translated "Lord," except in four quotations of Psalm 110:1, where it is translated "LORD."

Textual Footnotes

The New Living Translation provides several kinds of textual footnotes:

- All Old Testament passages that are clearly quoted in the New Testament are identified in a textual footnote in the New Testament.
- Some textual footnotes provide cultural and historical information on places, things, and people in the Bible that are probably obscure to modern readers. Such notes should aid the reader in understanding the message of the text. For example, in Acts 12:1, "King Herod" is named in this translation as "King Herod Agrippa" and is identified in a footnote as being "the nephew of Herod Antipas and a grandson of Herod the Great."
- When various ancient manuscripts contain different readings, these differences are often documented in footnotes. For instance, textual variants are footnoted when the variant reading is very familiar (usually through the King James Version). We have used footnotes when we have selected variant readings that differ from the Hebrew and Greek editions normally followed.
- Textual footnotes are also used to show alternative renderings. These are prefaced with the word "Or."

AS WE SUBMIT this translation of the Bible for publication, we recognize that any translation of the Scriptures is subject to limitations and imperfections. Anyone who has attempted to communicate the richness of God's Word into another language will realize it is impossible to make a perfect translation. Recognizing these limitations, we sought God's guidance and wisdom throughout this project. Now we pray that he will accept our efforts and use this translation for the benefit of the Church and of all people.

We pray that the New Living Translation will overcome some of the barriers of history, culture, and language that have kept people from reading and understanding God's Word. We hope that readers unfamiliar with the Bible will find the words clear and easy to understand, and that readers well versed in the Scriptures will gain a fresh perspective. We pray that readers will gain insight and wisdom for living, but most of all that they will meet the God of the Bible and be forever changed by knowing him.

The Bible Translation Committee
JULY 1996

HOLY BIBLE
NEW LIVING TRANSLATION
Bible Translation Team

POETRY
Tremper Longman III, General Reviewer
Westminster Theological Seminary

PSALMS 1–75
Mark D. Futato, *Westminster Theological Seminary in California*
Douglas Green, *Westminster Theological Seminary*
Richard Pratt, *Reformed Theological Seminary*

PSALMS 76–150
David M. Howard Jr., *Trinity Evangelical Divinity School*
Raymond C. Ortlund Jr., *Trinity Evangelical Divinity School*
Willem VanGemeren, *Trinity Evangelical Divinity School*

PROVERBS
Ted Hildebrandt, *Grace College*
Richard Schultz, *Wheaton College*
Raymond C. Van Leeuwen, *Eastern College*

GOSPELS AND ACTS
Grant R. Osborne, General Reviewer
Trinity Evangelical Divinity School

MATTHEW
Craig Blomberg, *Denver Conservative Baptist Seminary*
Donald A. Hagner, *Fuller Theological Seminary*
David Turner, *Grand Rapids Baptist Seminary*

MARK
Robert Guelich (deceased), *Fuller Theological Seminary*
Grant R. Osborne, *Trinity Evangelical Divinity School*

LUKE
Darrell Bock, *Dallas Theological Seminary*
Scot McKnight, *North Park College*
Robert Stein, *Bethel Theological Seminary*

JOHN
Gary M. Burge, *Wheaton College*
Philip W. Comfort, *Wheaton College*
Marianne Meye Thompson, *Fuller Theological Seminary*

ACTS
D. A. Carson, *Trinity Evangelical Divinity School*
William J. Larkin, *Columbia Biblical Seminary*
Roger Mohrlang, *Whitworth College*

LETTERS AND REVELATION

Norman R. Ericson, *General Reviewer*
Wheaton College

ROMANS/GALATIANS
Gerald Borchert, *The Southern Baptist Theological Seminary*
Douglas J. Moo, *Trinity Evangelical Divinity School*
Thomas R. Schreiner, *Bethel Theological Seminary*

1 & 2 CORINTHIANS
Joseph Alexanian, *Trinity International University*
Linda Belleville, *North Park Theological Seminary*
Douglas A. Oss, *Central Bible College*
Robert Sloan, *Baylor University*

EPHESIANS–PHILEMON
Harold W. Hoehner, *Dallas Theological Seminary*
Moises Silva, *Gordon-Conwell Theological Seminary*
Klyne Snodgrass, *North Park Theological Seminary*

HEBREWS/JAMES/1 & 2 PETER/JUDE
Peter Davids, *Canadian Theological Seminary*
Norman R. Ericson, *Wheaton College*
William Lane, *Seattle Pacific University*
J. Ramsey Michaels, *S.W. Missouri State University*

1–3 JOHN/REVELATION
Greg Beale, *Gordon-Conwell Theological Seminary*
Robert Mounce, *Whitworth College*
M. Robert Mulholland Jr., *Asbury Theological Seminary*

BIBLE TRANSLATION COMMITTEE SCHOLARS

Daniel I. Block, *The Southern Baptist Theological Seminary*
Barry J. Beitzel, *Trinity Evangelical Divinity School*
Tremper Longman III, *Westminster Theological Seminary*
John N. Oswalt, *Asbury Theological Seminary*
Grant R. Osborne, *Trinity Evangelical Divinity School*
Norman R. Ericson, *Wheaton College*

COORDINATING TEAM

Mark R. Norton, *Managing Editor*
Philip W. Comfort, *N.T. Coordinating Editor*
Ronald A. Beers, *Executive Director and Stylist*
Mark D. Taylor, *Director and Chief Stylist*
Daniel W. Taylor, *Consultant*

SPECIAL REVIEWERS

F. F. Bruce (deceased), *University of Manchester*
Kenneth N. Taylor, *Tyndale House Publishers*